ENVIRONMENTAL LAW
FOR ENGINEERS,
SCIENTISTS,
AND MANAGERS

**McGRAW-HILL SERIES IN WATER RESOURCES
AND ENVIRONMENTAL ENGINEERING**

Ven Te Chow, Rolf Eliassen, and Ray K. Linsley, *Consulting Editors*

Hells Canyon of the Snake River.   (*Courtesy of Carol Firs*

ENVIRONMENTAL LAW FOR ENGINEERS, SCIENTISTS, AND MANAGERS

JOSEPH T. BOCKRATH

Assistant Professor
School of Law
Louisiana State University
Baton Rouge, Louisiana

McGRAW-HILL BOOK COMPANY

New York   St. Louis   San Francisco   Auckland   Bogota   Düsseldorf   Johannesburg
London   Madrid   Mexico   Montreal   New Delhi   Panama   Paris
São Paulo   Singapore   Sydney   Tokyo   Toronto

ENVIRONMENTAL LAW FOR ENGINEERS, SCIENTISTS, AND MANAGERS

1 2 3 4 5 6 7 8 9 0   K P K P   7 8 3 2 1 0 9 8 7 6

This book was set in Times Roman by Rocappi, Inc. The editors were B. J. Clark and Susan Gamer; the cover was designed by Irving Freedman; the production supervisor was Charles Hess.

Library of Congress Cataloging in Publication Data

Bockrath, Joseph T.
    Environmental law for engineers, scientists, and managers.

    (McGraw-Hill series in water resources and environmental engineering)
      Bibliography: p.
      Includes index.
      1.   Environmental law—United States—Cases.   I.   Title.

KF3775.A7B6   344'.73'0460246   76-13472
ISBN   0-07-006327-3

For my father and mother,
and especially for my wife, Gloria,
whose indulgence made it possible.

Contents

Preface

This book is an attempt to present the evolution and basic concepts of environmental law to an audience of engineers, scientists, and managers possessed of reasonable sophistication but lacking any substantial legal background. Technical and esoteric topics are avoided but, like all law books, this one is meant to be studied rather than read.

The book should prove suitable for use by both undergraduate and graduate students and also by practitioners of engineering, science, or mangement who seek a conceptual and broadly based introduction to environmental law and possess the discipline to acquire it.

Experience in teaching concepts of environmental law to nonlawyers indicates that the case method is most satisfactory in imparting legal knowledge at the conceptual level. Mere statement of rules of law, assuming that they can be accurately ascertained, is inadequate to demonstrate the variety of situations which give rise to the need for their application. Decisions often turn, or purport to turn, on peculiarities of fact, and readers should be allowed to judge for themselves the substance of factual distinctions.

Case law proliferates at an astounding rate and selection of materials is necessarily a subjective process. I have tried to include:

1. Cases which give insights into the history and evolution of environmental law
2. Cases which state clearly the general rules of law
3. Cases which give insight into the structure of statutes
4. Cases which demonstrate the power and discretion of the judiciary
5. Cases which enunciate the role of administrative agencies
6. Cases which demonstrate the court's handling of technical or scientific
   material

Naturally, not all criteria could be met in every instance, but it is felt that those materials presented are the best available given this book's purpose—to impart a conceptual knowledge of the workings of environmental law.

The cases used in this book have been edited to eliminate materials not relevant to the issues under discussion. Likewise, footnotes to the cases have been abridged or omitted in some instances. To aid the ambitious reader who wishes to study the original cases, the numbers of the footnotes included in this book correspond to those in the original case reports. Ellipses and specific comments are used to indicate omissions.

The study of law at any level ordinarily produces more questions than answers. The "Questions for Discussion" provided throughout this text are general and policy-oriented, and probably have no clear-cut answers. The reader should, however, consider the political, economic, and technical issues they pose. Near the end of each chapter, problems are offered which may test the reader's grasp of the essence of the case material. Students will profit from attempting to answer the problems, but should be aware that the true resolution of such problems may depend on factors not reflected in the materials presented, and that five different lawyers would probably offer five different answers and approaches, each equally good.

Study of these materials by students of management, science, and engineering will, it is hoped, prepare them to operate effectively in a climate highly charged with legal responsibilities and opportunities. Such ability is critical because it is they, as much as politicians and lawyers, who will shape the environment and laws concerning it in the future.

ACKNOWLEDGMENTS

Much of the credit for any teacher's book is due to the students who annually force a reexamination of both substance and approach. Thanks to them is offered here. Credit is also due to those of my colleagues who have offered advice, on occasion without their knowledge; to my research assistant David Hume III; to the many reviewers who offered valuable criticism; and particularly to the administration and staff of the College of Marine Studies, University of Delaware, for their support and indulgence while this work was completed.

Joseph T. Bockrath

ENVIRONMENTAL LAW
FOR ENGINEERS,
SCIENTISTS,
AND MANAGERS

Chapter 1

Introduction

That a knowledge of the basics of the legal system is desirable and necessary for management personnel in every industry is axiomatic. Indeed, many high corporate officials are themselves lawyers. Dramatic increases in government regulation in the past few decades have made it imperative that managers be at least conversant with the basics of law. Concern over a deteriorating environment has resulted in a plethora of regulations by which business and government both must abide. A knowledge of how environmental law approaches the problems is desirable, however, not only for the manager in industry who must abide by it but also for the concerned scientist or engineer whose work may affect the environment.

This book then aims at two audiences.

It is for present and future managers who seek a nontechnical, conceptual introduction to environmental law which will enable them to function better in the highly regulated business atmosphere.

It is also for scientists and engineers who seek an understanding of environmental law sufficient to enable them to recognize where it might benefit from their ability. Such an understanding may also help the scientist or engineer to move into the world of administration.

Law is a learned profession, and even a modest mastery of it requires years of concentrated study. Of course, mastery is unnecessary for nonlawyers. What is necessary for managers and those scientists and engineers who want to expand their interests is an elemental understanding of how law works: that is, a knowledge of concepts. Therefore, in this book technicalities and esoteric fields such as aesthetics and wildlife management are deemphasized in favor of more general materials which impart the flavor of the law. Law is inconsistent and dynamic. Even lawyers have fewer answers than the public might believe. What they do have is the questions. If a manager, scientist, or engineer, after a study of this work, can recognize situations in his work which give rise to legal questions, the book will have succeeded. Learning to answer the questions would require years, and restructuring of the thought process; but it is unnecessary.

A scientist or engineer ordinarily uses a logical and controlled method to solve problems, trying generally to identify and control variables and eliminate from the final equation the consequences of feelings and guesswork. An objective thought process is sought. The result of the process generally has few subjective components or disregards them in the interests of maintaining the integrity of the scientific process.

In law, however, the logic of the process is secondary to the fact of the result. The life of the law, said Holmes, has not been logic; it has been experience.[a] Experience and analogy are most important in the process of legal thought. This ability to analogize, and to know when not to do so, is critical to the lawyer's training. While many lawyers' analogies may seem absurd to one to whom factual variables are items to be controlled or eliminated, the facts may be *legally* similar to the legal questions at issue. It is result rather than method with which the lawyer must be concerned. A number of reasons for this are proffered. The lawyer, rather like the engineer, must please a client rather than himself. It has been said, in this regard, that "the client cares little for a beautiful case."[b] A favorable outcome is what is sought.

Much of the difficulty in this area is inherent in the adversary process. Unlike the scientist, the lawyer is engaged not to find the truth but to present his or her client's position and counter, if possible, the arguments of the opponent. Although a lawyer should not subvert the truth, concern with the correct or "just" resolution of the issue is beyond the province of the individual lawyer. The legal process is one devoted to the resolution of the conflicts. Law which is either arbitrary or based on historical irrelevancy[c] or error may well serve a unitarian purpose if everyone (at least the lawyers) knows what it is and that it will be applied in like circumstances in the future.

To achieve a result in a reasonable time, with at least a semblance of right reason, the law regularly utilizes a device which science may find anathema and akin to putting up the correct solution of a mathematical problem to a vote: compromise. This method of resolving conflicts may be utilized in the law either for expediency or in recognition of the fact that rarely is the side of righteousness easily discernible or all with one party. A jury's finding of guilt based on marginal evidence may be balanced by a light sentence. Likewise, although negligence may in theory be, like pregnancy, a yes or no question,

[a] Oliver Wendell Holmes, *The Common Law,* Belknapp Press of Harvard University Press, Cambridge, Mass., 1963, p. 1.
[b] William Galbraith Miller, *Data of Jurisprudence,* Green, London, 1903, p. 1.
[c] See, for example, the Rivers and Harbors Act, page 178.

completely separate from damages, a jury unsure of the liability but sympathetic with the victim may compromise its unsureness with a finding of less damage, or the plaintiff's lawyer may settle for less than full compensation if the liability issue is unclear.

The idea of a balancing of interests in determining a result is deeply rooted in all areas of the law. Injunctions are issued after a balance of equities, custody litigation weighs the interests of the child, the parent, and the community. The "right" answer from the law's view is often fully satisfactory to neither party. The scientist's ability, or effort, to tolerate if not accept this aspect of legal methodology may determine his or her usefulness as a participant in the making and implementation of policy decisions with a scientific component, or at least measure the desire to do so. It is not rare for the scientist or engineer studying law to be appalled at the impotence of the judicial system with respect to unwise or foolish legislative or administrative action. In view of the average citizen's constantly eroding right to be foolish, it seems to many unconscionable that a legislature or administrative agency has its prerogatives in that area so well protected from the supposedly superior wisdom and political isolation of the judiciary. This view, however, is myopic in two respects.

The legislature, in theory if not in fact, does not have a license to be foolish other than that granted by the voters. The voters' recourse, should they choose to exercise it, is obvious, however slow-working it may be. To think that judges are not subject to political pressures and prejudices is to be naïve. Many judges are elected, and most of those appointed are politicians or party loyalists. Appointment to the bench, even for life, cannot displace one's political and social views acquired over a lifetime.

Most significant, however, is the single fact that judges and lawyers are human, subject to the same prejudices, lapses, and foibles as any citizen. Referring to oneself as "the court" rather than "Judge Smith" does not obscure the fact that a person is deciding questions within the confines of a system designed, or at least accumulated, by human beings.

As Cardozo phrased it, "It is often through these subconscious forces that judges are kept consistent with themselves, and inconsistent with one another. All their lives, forces which they do not recognize and cannot name, have been tugging at them—inherited instincts, traditional beliefs, acquired convictions; and the resultant is an outlook on life, a conception of social needs, a sense in James's phrase of 'the total push and pressure of the cosmos,' which, when reasons are nicely balanced, must determine where choice falls. Deep below consciousness are other forces, the likes and dislikes, the predilections and prejudices, the complex of instincts and emotions and habits and convictions, which make the man, whether he be litigant or judge."[d]

Speaking of the process of judicial decision making, it has been suggested, in fact, that "one wills at the beginning the result; one finds the principle afterwards; such is the genesis of all judicial construction."[e] While this is

[d] Benjamin Cardozo, *The Nature of the Judicial Process,* Yale University Press, New Haven, Conn., 1921, pp. 12, 167.
[e] Raymond Saleilles, *De la personnalité juridique,* Rosisseau, Paris, 1910, pp. 45–46.

probably an exaggeration when applied to persons schooled in the value of precedent and continuity, it is true in one degree or another to all persons who face choices. It would be less, or more, than human for persons not to tailor their logic or procedure in some manner to compel the desired result. The legal profession has labored under the weight of this accusation for some extensive time, but scientists might do well to examine their own work for signs of like rationalizations. They should not be unduly disturbed if they find such deviations from the scientific method, however, since they are part of human nature. The scientist should remember that he may try to conquer such rationalizations in himself and not expect to find them present in the organisms and objects with which he works. The lawyer, on the other hand, may strive to eliminate such feelings in himself but must *deal with other people possessed of other predilections* as well as a system of law which, owing to the nature of its creator, lacks the logic, symmetry, and impartiality of nature.

The judicial framework and process are both intricate and cumbersome, and a brief introduction to them may be helpful. Law may be classified first as either civil[f] or criminal. Civil law deals with private rights and wrongs; criminal law deals with those activities which government considers offenses against the society and worthy of punishment. Civil offenses may be halted or prevented by injunctions or recompensed by monetary damages. Environmental cases may be either criminal or civil depending on the conduct involved, and one incident may lead to both, such as where an oil spill might violate a criminal statute for which the polluter may be arrested and may also subject him to civil suits for damage or cleanup costs.

Laws may come from a variety of sources. Statutes are passed by legislatures, approved by executives, and construed and applied by the judiciary. But this simplistic organization is complicated by the realities of big government and complex problems. The majority of statutes passed by legislatures are initiated by the executive branch. Both the legislative and executive branches have delegated awesome powers to the administrative agencies which have become, in essence, the fourth branch. In few areas of law is the role of administrative agencies of more importance than in environmental law. Thus, the enforcement arm, the executive, through administrative agencies such as EPA, is involved in law making to a very real extent. Likewise, the judiciary, through its power to fashion common-law rights and to interpret and apply statutes, can be said to be engaged in law making. Taken together then, the law is the work product of all three branches and includes statutes, decided cases and the precedents they set, and the regulations, standards, and discretionary powers of administrative agencies.

Similarly, the federal system of government of the United States creates overlaps and potential for conflict and inconsistency.[9] All levels of government are involved in environmental law. However, the national scope of the problem at hand, and the reluctance or inability of the states to deal with it, have led to a situation where federal law is most important although many

---

[f] Civil law may also refer to the jurisprudential system of Rome and later continental Europe which was brought to Louisiana by the French and remains, with modification, the basis of that state's law today.
[9] See Chapter 5, page 99, for a fuller discussion of this most important topic.

federal plans encourage or require state enforcement or implementation. In some areas state governments have taken the initiative, and their role is dominant in land-use law.[h]

Federal courts have jurisdiction over violations of federal law and in cases where the citizenship of the parties is diverse. Thus, litigation involving federal environmental statutes or constitutional protections usually occurs in federal court. State courts, however, are the final arbiters of state law.

Courts of law are designed for the resolution of conflicts between interested parties.[i] When a person believes that he has been injured, he ordinarily seeks the advice of a lawyer with regard to whether the claim is one which, if proved, the law will remedy. If it appears to be so, a period of negotiation in hopes of a settlement is usually attempted and a trial may be thought of as the result of a failure of the settlement process. After resolving to go to trial, and often before as leverage in negotiation, the attorney and his client marshall their facts and arguments and produce a succinct document setting forth the facts upon which the claim is based. This document is the complaint, and the client thereafter is referred to as the plaintiff. Copies of the complaint and supporting technical documents are served on the opposition, referred to as the defendant, and the defendant files an answer which may be a general denial or an affirmative defense. Or the defendant may demur; that is, contend that even if the facts of the complaint are true, the law can provide no remedy. The complaint, answer, and often other preliminary documents are called the pleadings. If the pleadings show that no questions of fact are at issue, a trial is unnecessary and a summary proceeding may decide the law and render judgment. If, as is usually the case, facts are in dispute, a pretrial conference is convened where the attorneys and the judge endeavor to eliminate from the case questions not really at issue, specious claims, and the like, and frame the issues for trial.

The trial itself is designed for the orderly presentation of evidence and argument under rules of evidence which aim to eliminate testimony which is inherently unreliable, deprives a party of his right of confrontation, or is privileged. The judge rules on points of procedure and admissibility and, after the presentation of evidence is complete, instructs the jury. The jury is the sole arbiter of disputed *facts,* and the judge is the arbiter of the law. Thus, the judge will instruct the jury on the law of the case, and the jury must decide what the facts are and apply them to the law as stated by the judge. It should be here noted that many trials in environmental law seek injunctions. Owing to a historical quirk predating the independence of the United States by some centuries, actions for injunctions are decided by the judge alone.

After a verdict is reached, dissatisfied parties may appeal errors of law that they feel have been prejudicial to them. Because factual conclusions of a jury are not appealable, appeals often turn on alleged errors in the instructions, admission of evidence, or other rulings on points of law. The person prosecuting the appeal, referred to as the appellant, ordinarily has one level of appeal open to him as a matter of right. In the federal system a Court of Appeals, of which there are eleven, is the first avenue of appeal. Courts of

[h] See Chapter 4, page 62.
[i] See Chapter 2, page 7.

Appeal do not utilize juries or hear evidence, for their function is to decide only questions of law, presented by the parties by written briefs and oral argument.

The Supreme Court of the United States hears cases of its choosing, and there is no right to an appeal to it. In a few constitutionally mandated circumstances, such as suits between states, a case may originate in the Supreme Court. By and large, however, its jurisdiction is appellate. State court hierarchies are usually similar although the nomenclature may vary. A few of the smaller states have no intermediate appellate court, and a state supreme court hearing is a right.

Law should be thought of as a process rather than a set of rules: a process by which disputes are resolved. Oftentimes the dispute has no right or wrong but rather is a contest between competing interests, both of which are legitimate. Rules exist to be sure, but economic and political pressures and considerations are a part of the process, as are the personalities of the litigants, judges, and attorneys. To expect perfect justice from a process of human invention and administration is to court disappointment.

Chapter 2

Parties to Environmental Litigation

STANDING

An understanding of the rather amorphous concept of standing requires a brief review of the function of a court system. Unlike legislatures, courts do not ordinarily purport to solve problems besetting a community or a political subdivision as a whole, but rather seek to resolve the differences between specific individuals concerned with a specific claim of injury or wrongdoing. The question of standing in environmental litigation is most significant because it is often not the person who is harmed by the allegedly unlawful action who desires to bring the suit; rather it is a "public interest" group which may not itself have been injured by the wrongdoing. Since polluting industries and governments tend to be large and well-endowed, it has become of major significance whether or not a group, no member of which himself may have been injured, may band together to protect the public interest.[a]

While a Supreme Court decision may certainly have ramifications far beyond the parties to the suit, it is they, and lower courts in future cases, who are bound by the decision. A court, then, is a forum in which disputes between real parties to a controversy may be heard.

---

[a] On a larger scale, this issue may be basic to our political structure since the government is supposed to represent the public interest but is often on the defense in environmental litigation. Perhaps claiming to represent the public interest is easier than determining what that interest is.

Standing has been called by the Supreme Court a "complicated specialty of federal jurisdiction, the solution of whose problems is in any event more or less determined by the specific circumstances in individual situations." This foreboding pronouncement has been substantially tempered by recent Supreme Court cases, and standing questions in federal court are much clearer than they were over five years ago.[b]

Standing may be generally defined as an individual's right to a judicial determination of a controversy. In the absence of the required "right," the legal action may not be maintained. The presence of standing to sue does not give rise to any inferences regarding the ultimate outcome of a case. Without it, one may not present evidence or proceed to trial in any manner. The establishment of standing merely allows the trial to proceed to a decision on the merits. In ordinary practice, standing is usually self-evident, as where an injured pedestrian sues the driver of the car for damages or a buyer of goods sues the seller for breach of contract. An individual always has standing where he is instructed by the government to act or refrain from acting. Also, a party may have standing if he seeks relief under a statute designed to protect a class to which he belongs. In addition, a statute may grant a party standing as a matter of law.[c]

It is only where issues of a public nature are encountered, such as a judicial determination of the legality of some governmental action, that we find the question of standing susceptible of varied interpretations.

Some courts have granted standing to conservationist groups seeking to protect the interests of the general public even though the groups themselves have not sustained "injury" distinct from that of the public at large.[d] In contrast, other courts have denied standing to environmental organizations which merely alleged that one of their purposes was the "protection of the public interest."[e]

In *Cape May County Chapter, Inc., Izaak Walton League v. Macchia*, the plaintiffs, an environmental group expressing a deep interest in preserving the natural ecology of the area, sought to enjoin the defendants, land developers, from draining and filling an area of salt marsh. The plaintiffs alleged that the filling of the marshland would destroy the existing ecosystem and injure the present and future rights of the public and their members to enjoy the natural area. The League relied upon a section of the National Environmental Policy Act which they alleged granted them standing. The defendants challenged the plaintiffs' standing to sue. The court confronted this issue in *Cape May v. Macchia* and gave a detailed explanation of the history and legal philosophy behind the standing doctrine in environmental litigation.

---

[b] Standing has not been nearly as substantial a problem in the environmental context in state courts because states generally permit their citizens to test the legality of official conduct by a writ of mandamus. See K. C. Davis, *The Liberalized Law of Standing*, 37 U. Chi. L. Rev. 450 (1970). This is important since most environmental litigation is against the government.

[c] See, for example, the statute reproduced on page 25. The Clean Air Amendments of 1970 also provide for citizen suits (42 U.S.C. § 1857h-2).

[d] See *Environmental Defense Fund, Inc., v. Hardin*, 428 F.2d 1093 (D.C. 1970).

[e] See *National Audubon Society v. Johnson*, 317 F. Supp. 1330 (D.C. Tex. 1970), aff. 456 F.2d 68 (5th Cir. 1972), cert. den. 409 U.S. 887 (1972).

Cape May County Chapter, Inc., Izaak Walton League v. Macchia

329 F. Supp. 504 (1971)

. . . The threshold question, of course, in this domino-erection of issues, is that of standing. Absent such, all others are moot and must fall. It is the opinion of this Court that the plaintiff does have sufficient legal standing under NEPA to maintain this action, both in its own right and representatively on behalf of the class it purports to represent. The reasons dictating this conclusion will be advanced and the other issues treated appropriately.

Although not providing complete resolution, much light has been cast upon the ever controversial question of "standing to sue" by two recent cases in which guidelines have at least been indicated: *Association of Data Processing Service Organizations, Inc. v. Camp,* 397 U.S. 150, 90 S. Ct. 827, 25 L. Ed. 2d 184 (1970) and *Barlow v. Collins,* 397 U.S. 159, 90 S. Ct. 832, 25 L. Ed. 2d 192 (1970). As observed in *Data Processing,* generalizations are of little value, for we must be mindful of the more compelling Constitutional concept of "cases and controversies," in order to establish standing in the truly adversary sense. At least this is the jumping-off point in approaching each particular problem.

As stated by former Chief Justice Warren in *Flast v. Cohen,* 392 U.S. 83, 101, 88 S. Ct. 1942, 1953, 20 L. Ed. 2d 947 (1968):

> [I]n terms of Article III limitations on federal court jurisdiction, the question of standing is related only to whether the dispute sought to be adjudicated will be presented in an adversary context and in a form historically viewed as capable of judicial resolution.

Data Processing reaffirmed this beginning point. In that case, the petitioners challenged a ruling by the Comptroller of the Currency which permitted national banks to provide data processing services, similar to those of petitioners, to other banks and customers. Petitioners claimed that this ruling authorized unfair competition in violation of their rights. The Court held that the petitioners had standing to maintain their action, as they experienced economic injury and were "aggrieved" persons within the Administrative Procedure Act, 5 U.S.C. sec. 701 et seq. The Court then laid down two tests regarding the federal adversary requirement: (1) "* * * whether the plaintiff alleges that the challenged action has caused him injury in fact, economic or otherwise;" and (2) "* * * whether the interest sought to be protected by the complainant is arguably within the zone of interests to be protected or regulated by the statute or constitutional guarantee in question." (397 U.S. pp. 152-153, 90 S. Ct. p. 830.)

In *Barlow,* decided the same day as *Data Processing,* the petitioners, tenant farmers, challenged an amended federal agency regulation permitting the withholding by their landlords of moneys due these farmers for farming and produce, which funds were to be applied first toward rents due the landlords under the farm leases. Under these circumstances, the Supreme Court declared that the petitioners had "standing to sue" within the requirements of *Data Processing*. Apparently, the tenant farmers suffered economic "injury in fact" and were "arguably within the zone of interests" sought to be protected.

Gauged against the criteria set down by the United States Supreme Court in these recent cases, there seems no doubt that the plaintiff, a local chapter of the Izaak Walton League, a renowned environmentalist group, will resolutely press forward in this action well within the "constitutional adversary context," and that plaintiff meets the requirements of "injury of fact" and "zone of interests." We find support for this position in several recent federal decisions. As observed in *Izaak Walton League v. St. Clair*, 313 F. Supp. 1312 at page 136 (D.C. Minn. 1970):

> The League has a long history of activity in conservation matters and natural resource preservation. It has been active for many years in urging congressional and legislative action.

>   *   *   *   *   *   *   *   *   *   *   *   *   *   *   *

> The second *Association of Data Processing* requirement, a nonconstitutional one, is that plaintiff must allege "that the challenged action has caused him injury in fact, economic or otherwise." It is of course a fact that plaintiff does not own any of the land nor does it claim to own any mineral rights in the Boundary Waters Canoe Area, nor does it have any real economic interest in the outcome of the suit since it is a not-for-profit corporation.

However, the Court continues at page 1317:

> The Izaak Walton League is not a "johnny-come-lately" or an *ad hoc* organization and its interest in the wilderness movement is continuing, basic and deep. It therefore has an "aesthetic, conservational and recreational" interest to protect. This gives it standing and meets the second requirement of *Association of Data Processing*. . . .

We do not share the fear of some earlier decisions that liberalized concepts of "standing to sue" will flood the Courts with litigation. However, if that should be the price for the preservation and protection of our natural resources and environment against uncoordinated or irresponsible conduct, so be it. But such seems most improbable. Courts can always control the obviously frivolous suitor. . . . The better view, we think, in approaching the vexatious problems confronting the Court's endeavor to give effect to National and State environmental legislation, is the maintenance of a sensitive balance between the continuing march of technicological advance and preservation of our natural resources. This view is espoused and comprehensively discussed in an outstanding article entitled An Environmental Bill of Rights: The Citizen Suit and The National Environmental Policy Act of 1969, 24 Rutgers Law Review 230 (1970). The authors, Professor Eva H. Hanks of

Rutgers University and Professor John L. Hanks, Associate in Law at Columbia University, here make a distinct contribution in their review of the issue of "standing to sue." The following observations seem most pertinent:

> In the past, we have often accepted the non sequitur that where all are the intended beneficiaries of an interest, none has standing to protect it. The dangers inherent in this philosophy are now apparent: Both logic and experience support the emerging view that an interest so fundamental that all are within the protected class must be permitted its champion. The National Environmental Policy Act has created such an interest (at p. 248).
>
> In the past, economic considerations have carried the day. The Environmental Policy Act meant to throw a new value into the scales—an ethical one. More specifically, an "ecological ethic of understanding and respect for the bonds that unite the species man with the natural systems of the planet." "It is an ethic whose yardstick for progress should be: Is it good for people?" What is "good for people" is often difficult to say. But a consensus seems to be emerging which would have us: reject any notion that progress means destroying Everglades National Park with massive airport development * * * or that it is progress to fill hundreds of square miles of our bays and coastal wetlands, destroying natural habitat for thousands of species of fish and wildlife, polluting our waters, and in many other ways wreaking havoc with this fragile ecological system in the name of providing new space for industry, commerce, and subdivisions." [Footnote omitted.] (p. 268 and citing 116 Cong. Rec. S. 80, remarks of Senator Nelson, introducing S.J. Res. 169, 91st Cong. 2nd Sess. (1970) proposing an amendment to the U.S. Constitution declaring that every person has an inalienable right to a decent environment and that the United States and every State shall guarantee such right.)
>
> . . . Accordingly, it is the conclusion of this Court that the plaintiff has adequate legal standing to maintain this action.[f]

The standing thus accorded seems to be based on a concept of injury to the public's right to use and enjoy the natural areas of the land. The League, however, included an allegation of injury "in fact or otherwise" to some of its members as a basis for standing.

A major question exists after reading the preceding opinion: Would the courts allow a genuinely established environmental group to bring suit on the public's behalf without alleging injury to its members; to act as a private attorney general? The court in *Cape May v. Macchia* seemed to lean heavily toward the areas to be protected rather than the requirement of a legally cognizable injury.

The question left unanswered (because it was not asked) in *Cape May v. Macchia* was answered in the landmark case on the issue of standing in environmental litigation, *Sierra Club v. Morton*.

[f] See *Just v. Marinette County*, page 88.

Sierra Club v. Morton, Secretary of the Interior, et al.

405 U.S. 727 (1972)

Mr. Justice Stewart delivered the opinion of the Court.

I

The Mineral King Valley is an area of great natural beauty nestled in the Sierra Nevada Mountains in Tulare County, California, adjacent to Sequoia National Park. It has been part of the Sequoia National Forest since 1926, and is designated as a national game refuge by special Act of Congress.[1] Though once the site of extensive mining activity, Mineral King is now used almost exclusively for recreational purposes. Its relative inaccessibility and lack of development have limited the number of visitors each year, and at the same time have preserved the valley's quality as a quasi-wilderness area largely uncluttered by the products of civilization.

The United States Forest Service, which is entrusted with the maintenance and administration of national forests, began in the late 1940's to give consideration to Mineral King as a potential site for recreational development. Prodded by a rapidly increasing demand for skiing facilities, the Forest Service published a prospectus in 1965, inviting bids from private developers for the construction and operation of a ski resort that would also serve as a summer recreation area. The proposal of Walt Disney Enterprises, Inc., was chosen from those of six bidders, and Disney received a three-year permit to conduct surveys and explorations in the valley in connection with its preparation of a complete master plan for the resort.

The final Disney plan, approved by the Forest Service in January 1969, outlines a $35 million complex of motels, restaurants, swimming pools, parking lots, and other structures designed to accommodate 14,000 visitors daily. This complex is to be constructed on 80 acres of the valley floor under a 30-year use permit from the Forest Service. Other facilities, including ski lifts, ski trails, a cog-assisted railway, and utility installations, are to be constructed on the mountain slopes and in other parts of the valley under a revocable special-use permit. To provide access to the resort, the State of California proposes to construct a highway 20 miles in length. A section of this road would traverse Sequoia National Park, as would a proposed high-voltage power line needed to provide electricity for the resort. Both the highway and the power line require the approval of the Department of the Interior, which is entrusted with the preservation and maintenance of the national parks.

[1] Act of July 3, 1926, § 6, 44 Stat. 821, 16 U.S.C. § 688.

Representatives of the Sierra Club, who favor maintaining Mineral King largely in its present state, followed the progress of recreational planning for the valley with close attention and increasing dismay. They unsuccessfully sought a public hearing on the proposed development in 1965, and in subsequent correspondence with officials of the Forest Service and the Department of the Interior, they expressed the Club's objections to Disney's plan as a whole and to particular features included in it. In June 1969 the Club filed the present suit in the United States District Court for the Northern District of California, seeking a declaratory judgment that various aspects of the proposed development contravene federal laws and regulations governing the preservation of national parks, forests, and game refuges,[2] and also seeking preliminary and permanent injunctions restraining the federal officials involved from granting their approval or issuing permits in connection with the Mineral King project. The petitioner Sierra Club sued as a membership corporation with "a special interest in the conservation and the sound maintenance of the national parks, game refuges and forests of the country," and invoked the judicial-review provisions of the Administrative Procedure Act, 5 U.S.C. § 701 et seq.

After two days of hearings, the District Court granted the requested preliminary injunction. It rejected the respondents' challenge to the Sierra Club's standing to sue, and determined that the hearing had raised questions "concerning possible excess of statutory authority, sufficiently substantial and serious to justify a preliminary injunction. . . ." The respondents appealed, and the Court of Appeals for the Ninth Circuit reversed. 433 F.2d 24. With respect to the petitioner's standing, the court noted that there was "no allegation in the complaint that members of the Sierra Club would be affected by the actions of [the respondents] other than the fact that the actions are personally displeasing or distasteful to them," id., at 33, and concluded:

"We do not believe such club concern without a showing of more direct interest can constitute standing in the legal sense sufficient to challenge the exercise of responsibilities on behalf of all the citizens by two cabinet level officials of the government acting under Congressional and Constitutional authority," Id., at 30.

Alternatively, the Court of Appeals held that the Sierra Club had not made an adequate showing of irreparable injury and likelihood of success on the merits to

---

[2] As analyzed by the District Court, the complaint alleged violations of law falling into four categories. First, it claimed that the special-use permit for construction of the resort exceeded the maximum-acreage limitation placed upon such permits by 16 U.S.C. § 497, and that issuance of a "revocable" use permit was beyond the authority of the Forest Service. Second, it challenged the proposed permit for the highway through Sequoia National Park on the grounds that the highway would not serve any of the purposes of the park, in alleged violation of 16 U.S.C. § 1, and that it would destroy timber and other natural resources protected by 16 U.S.C. §§ 41 and 43. Third, it claimed that the Forest Service and the Department of the Interior had violated their own regulations by failing to hold adequate public hearings on the proposed project. Finally, the complaint asserted that 16 U.S.C. § 45c requires specific congressional authorization of a permit for construction of a power transmission line within the limits of a national park.

justify issuance of a preliminary injunction. The court thus vacated the injunction. The Sierra Club filed a petition for a writ of certiorari which we granted, 401 U.S. 907, to review the questions of federal law presented.

II

The first question presented is whether the Sierra Club has alleged facts that entitle it to obtain judicial review of the challenged action. Whether a party has a sufficient stake in an otherwise justiciable controversy to obtain judicial resolution of that controversy is what has traditionally been referred to as the question of standing to sue. Where the party does not rely on any specific statute authorizing invocation of the judicial process, the question of standing depends upon whether the party has alleged such a "personal stake in the outcome of the controversy," *Baker v. Carr,* 369 U.S. 186, 204, as to ensure that "the dispute sought to be adjudicated will be presented in an adversary context and in a form historically viewed as capable of judicial resolution." *Flast v. Cohen,* 392 U.S. 83, 101. Where, however, Congress has authorized public officials to perform certain functions according to law, and has provided by statute for judicial review of those actions under certain circumstances, the injury as to standing must begin with a determination of whether the statute in question authorizes review at the behest of the plaintiff.[3]

The Sierra Club relies upon § 10 of the Administrative Procedure Act (APA), 5 U.S.C. § 702, which provides:

> "A person suffering legal wrong because of agency action, or adversely affected or aggrieved by agency action within the meaning of a relevant statute, is entitled to judicial review thereof."

Early decisions under this statute interpreted the language as adopting the various formulations of "legal interest" and "legal wrong" then prevailing as constitutional requirements of standing.[4] But, in *Data Processing Service v. Camp,* 397 U.S. 150, and *Barlow v. Collins,* 397 U.S. 159, decided the same day, we held more broadly that persons had standing to obtain judicial review of federal agency

---

[3] Congress may not confer jurisdiction on Art. III federal courts to render advisory opinions, *Muskrat v. United States,* 219 U.S. 346, or to entertain "friendly" suits, *United States v. Johnson,* 319 U.S. 302, or to resolve "political questions," *Luther v. Borden,* 7 How. 1, because suits of this character are inconsistent with the judicial function under Art. III. But where a dispute is otherwise justiciable, the question whether the litigant is a "proper party to request an adjudication of a particular issue," *Flast v. Cohen,* 392 U.S. 83, 100, is one within the power of Congress to determine. Cf. *FCC v. Sanders Bros. Radio Station,* 309 U.S. 470, 477; *Flast v. Cohen, supra,* at 120 (Harlan, J., dissenting); *Associated Industries v. Ickes,* 134 F.2d 694, 704. See generally Berger, Standing to Sue in Public Actions: Is it a Constitutional Requirement?, 78 Yale L.J. 816, 837 et seq. (1969); Jaffe, The Citizen as Litigant in Public Actions: The Non-Hohfeldian or Ideological Plaintiff, 116 U. Pa. L. Rev. 1033 (1968).

[4] See, e.g., *Kansas City Power & Light Co. v. McKay,* 96 U.S. App. D.C. 273, 281, 225 F.2d 924, 932; *Ove Gustavsson Contracting Co. v. Floete,* 278 F.2d 912, 914; *Duba v. Schuetzle,* 303 F.2d 570, 574. The theory of a "legal interest" is expressed in its extreme form in *Alabama Power Co. v. Ickes,* 302 U.S. 464, 479–481. See also *Tennessee Electric Power Co. v. TVA,* 306 U.S. 118, 137–139.

action under § 10 of the APA where they had alleged that the challenged action had caused them "injury in fact," and where the alleged injury was to an interest "arguably within the zone of interests to be protected or regulated" by the statutes that the agencies were claimed to have violated.[5]

In *Data Processing,* the injury claimed by the petitioners consisted of harm to their competitive position in the computer-servicing market through a ruling by the Comptroller of the Currency that national banks might perform data-processing services for their customers. In *Barlow,* the petitioners were tenant farmers who claimed that certain regulations of the Secretary of Agriculture adversely affected their economic position vis-à-vis their landlords. These palpable economic injuries have long been recognized as sufficient to lay the basis for standing, with or without a specific statutory provision for judicial review.[6] Thus, neither *Data Processing* nor *Barlow* addressed itself to the question, which has arisen with increasing frequency in federal courts in recent years, as to what must be alleged by persons who claim injury of a noneconomic nature to interests that are widely shared.[7] That question is presented in this case.

III

The injury alleged by the Sierra Club will be incurred entirely by reason of the change in the uses to which Mineral King will be put, and the attendant change in the aesthetics and ecology of the area. Thus, in referring to the road to be built through Sequoia National Park, the complaint alleged that the development "would destroy or otherwise adversely affect the scenery, natural and historic objects and wildlife of the park and would impair the enjoyment of the park for future generations." We do not question that this type of harm may amount to an "injury in fact" sufficient to lay the basis for standing under § 10 of the APA. Aesthetic and environmental well-being, like economic well-being, are important ingredients of the quality of life in our society, and the fact that particular environmental interests are shared by the many rather than the few does not make them less deserving of legal protection through the judicial process. But the "injury in fact" test requires more than an injury to a cognizable interest. It requires that the party seeking review be himself among the injured.

The impact of the proposed changes in the environment of Mineral King will not fall indiscriminately upon every citizen. The alleged injury will be felt directly

---

[5] In deciding this case we do not reach any questions concerning the meaning of the "zone of interests" test or its possible application to the facts here presented.

[6] See, e.g., *Hardin v. Kentucky Utilities Co.,* 390 U.S. 1, 7; *Chicago v. Atchison, T. & S.F.R. Co.,* 357 U.S. 77, 83; *FCC v. Sanders Bros. Radio Station, supra,* at 477.

[7] No question of standing was raised in *Citizens to Preserve Overton Park v. Volpe,* 401 U.S. 402. The complaint in that case alleged that the organizational plaintiff represented members who were "residents of Memphis, Tennessee who use Overton Park as a park land and recreation area and who have been active since 1964 in efforts to preserve and protect Overton Park as a park land and recreation area."

only by those who use Mineral King and Sequoia National Park, and for whom the aesthetic and recreational values of the area will be lessened by the highway and ski resort. The Sierra Club failed to allege that it or its members would be affected in any of their activities or pastimes by the Disney development. Nowhere in the pleadings or affidavits did the Club state that its members use Mineral King for any purpose, much less that they use it in any way that would be significantly affected by the proposed actions of the respondents.[8]

The Club apparently regarded any allegations of individualized injury as superfluous, on the theory that this was a "public" action involving questions as to the use of natural resources, and that the Club's longstanding concern with and expertise in such matters were sufficient to give it standing as a "representative of the public."[9] This theory reflects a misunderstanding of our cases involving so-called "public actions" in the area of administrative law.

The origin of the theory advanced by the Sierra Club may be traced to a dictum in *Scripps-Howard Radio v. FCC,* 316 U.S. 4, in which the licensee of a radio station in Cincinnati, Ohio, sought a stay of an order of the FCC allowing another radio station in a nearby city to change its frequency and increase its range. In discussing its power to grant a stay, the Court noted that "these private litigants have standing only as representatives of the public interest." Id., at 14. But that observation did not describe the basis upon which the appellant was allowed to obtain judicial review as a "person aggrieved" within the meaning of the statute involved in that case,[10] since Scripps-Howard was clearly "aggrieved" by reason of the economic injury that it would suffer as a result of the Commis-

---

[8] The only reference in the pleadings to the Sierra Club's interest in the dispute is contained in paragraph 3 of the complaint, which reads in its entirety as follows:
"Plaintiff Sierra Club is a non-profit corporation organized and operating under the laws of the State of California, with its principal place of business in San Francisco, California since 1892. Membership of the club is approximately 78,000 nationally, with approximately 27,000 members residing in the San Francisco Bay Area. For many years the Sierra Club by its activities and conduct has exhibited a special interest in the conservation and the sound maintenance of the national parks, game refuges and forests of the country, regularly serving as a responsible representative of persons similarly interested. One of the principal purposes of the Sierra Club is to protect and conserve the national resources of the Sierra Nevada Mountains. Its interests would be vitally affected by the acts hereinafter described and would be aggrieved by those acts of the defendants as hereinafter more fully appears."
In an amici curiae brief filed in this Court by the Wilderness Society and others, it is asserted that the Sierra Club has conducted regular camping trips into the Mineral King area, and that various members of the Club have used and continue to use the area for recreational purposes. These allegations were not contained in the pleadings, nor were they brought to the attention of the Court of Appeals. Moreover, the Sierra Club in its reply brief specifically declines to rely on its individualized interest, as a basis for standing. See n. 15, infra. Our decision does not, of course, bar the Sierra Club from seeking in the District Court to amend its complaint by a motion under Rule 15, Federal Rules of Civil Procedure.
[9] This approach to the question of standing was adopted by the Court of Appeals for the Second Circuit in *Citizens Committee for the Hudson Valley v. Volpe,* 425 F.2d 97, 105:
"We hold, therefore, that the public interest in environmental resources—an interest created by statutes affecting the issuance of this permit—is a legally protected interest affording these plaintiffs, as responsible representatives of the public, standing to obtain judicial review of agency action alleged to be in contravention of that public interest."
[10] The statute involved was § 402(b)(2) of the Communications Act of 1934, 48 Stat. 1093.

sion's action.[11] The Court's statement was, rather, directed to the theory upon which Congress had authorized judicial review of the Commission's actions. That theory had been described earlier in *FCC v. Sanders Bros. Radio Station,* 309 U.S. 470, 477, as follows:

> "Congress had some purpose in enacting § 402(b)(2). It may have been of opinion that one likely to be financially injured by the issue of a license would be the only person having a sufficient interest to bring to the attention of the appellate court errors of law in the action of the Commission in granting the license. It is within the power of Congress to confer such standing to prosecute an appeal."

Taken together, *Sanders* and *Scripps-Howard* thus established a dual proposition: the fact of economic injury is what gives a person standing to seek judicial review under the statute, but once review is properly invoked, that person may argue the public interest in support of his claim that the agency has failed to comply with its statutory mandate.[12] It was in the latter sense that the "standing" of the appellant in *Scripps-Howard* existed only as a "representative of the public interest." It is in a similar sense that we have used the phrase "private attorney general" to describe the function performed by persons upon whom Congress has conferred the right to seek judicial review of agency action. See *Data Processing, supra,* at 154.

The trend of cases arising under the APA and other statutes authorizing judicial review of federal agency action has been toward recognizing that injuries other than economic harm are sufficient to bring a person within the meaning of the statutory language, and toward discarding the notion that an injury that is widely shared is *ipso facto* not an injury sufficient to provide the basis for judicial review.[13] We noted this development with approval in *Data Processing,* 397 U.S., at 154, in saying that the interest alleged to have been injured "may reflect 'aesthetic, conservational, and recreational' as well as economic values." But broadening the categories of injury that may be alleged in support of standing is a different matter from abandoning the requirement that the party seeking review must himself have suffered an injury.

---

[11] This much is clear from the *Scripps-Howard* Court's citation of *FCC v. Sanders Bros. Radio Station,* 309 U.S. 470, in which the basis for standing was the competitive injury that the appellee would have suffered by the licensing of another radio station in its listening area.

[12] The distinction between standing to initiate a review proceeding, and standing to assert the rights of the public or of third persons once the proceeding is properly initiated, is discussed in 3 K. Davis, Administrative Law Treatise §§ 22.05–22.07 (1958).

[13] See, e.g., *Environmental Defense Fund v. Hardin,* 138 U.S. App. D.C. 391, 395, 428 F.2d 1093, 1097 (interest in health affected by decision of Secretary of Agriculture refusing to suspend registration of certain pesticides containing DDT); *Office of Communication of the United Church of Christ v. FCC,* 123 U.S. App. D.C. 328, 339, 359 F.2d 994, 1005 (interest of television viewers in the programming of a local station licensed by the FCC); *Scenic Hudson Preservation Conf. v. FPC,* 354 F.2d 608, 615–616 (interests in aesthetics, recreation, and orderly community planning affected by FPC licensing of a hydroelectric project); *Reade v. Ewing,* 205 F.2d 630, 631–632 (interest of consumers of oleomargarine in fair labeling of product regulated by Federal Security Administration); *Crowther v. Seaborg,* 312 F. Supp. 1205, 1212 (interest in health and safety of persons residing near the site of a proposed atomic blast).

Some courts have indicated a willingness to take this latter step by conferring standing upon organizations that have demonstrated "an organizational interest in the problem" of environmental or consumer protection. *Environmental Defense Fund v. Hardin,* 138 U.S. App. D.C. 391, 395, 428 F.2d 1093, 1097.[14] It is clear that an organization whose members are injured may represent those members in a proceeding for judicial review. See, e.g., *NAACP v. Button,* 371 U.S. 415, 428. But a mere "interest in a problem," no matter how longstanding the interest and no matter how qualified the organization is in evaluating the problem, is not sufficient by itself to render the organization "adversely affected" or "aggrieved" within the meaning of the APA. The Sierra Club is a large and long-established organization, with a historic commitment to the cause of protecting our Nation's natural heritage from man's depredations. But if a "special interest" in this subject were enough to entitle the Sierra Club to commence this litigation, there would appear to be no objective basis upon which to disallow a suit by any other bona fide "special interest" organization, however small or short-lived. And if any group with a bona fide "special interest" could initiate such litigation, it is difficult to perceive why any individual citizen with the same bona fide special interest would not also be entitled to do so.

The requirement that a party seeking review must allege facts showing that he is himself adversely affected does not insulate executive action from judicial review, nor does it prevent any public interests from being protected through the judicial process.[15] It does serve as at least a rough attempt to put the decision as to whether review will be sought in the hands of those who have a direct stake in the outcome. That goal would be undermined were we to construe the APA to authorize judicial review at the behest of organizations or individuals who seek to do no more than vindicate their own value preferences through the judicial process.[16]

[14] See *Citizens Committee for the Hudson Valley v. Volpe,* n. 9, *supra; Environmental Defense Fund, Inc. v. Corps of Engineers,* 325 F. Supp. 728, 734–736; *Izaak Walton League v. St. Clair,* 313 F. Supp. 1312, 1317. See also *Scenic Hudson Preservation Conf. v. FPC, supra,* at 616:
"In order to insure that the Federal Power Commission will adequately protect the public interest in the aesthetic, conservational, and recreational aspects of power development, those who by their activities and conduct have exhibited a special interest in such areas, must be held to be included in the class of 'aggrieved' parties under § 313(b) [of the Federal Power Act]."
In most, if not all, of these cases, at least one party to the proceeding did assert an individualized injury either to himself or, in the case of an organization, to its members.
[15] In its reply brief, after noting the fact that it might have chosen to assert individualized injury to itself or to its members as a basis for standing, the Sierra Club states:
"The Government seeks to create a 'heads I win, tails you lose' situation in which either the courthouse door is barred for lack of assertion of a private, unique injury or a preliminary injunction is denied on the ground that the litigant has advanced private injury which does not warrant an injunction adverse to a competing public interest. Counsel have shaped their case to avoid this trap."
The short answer to this contention is that the "trap" does not exist. The test of injury in fact goes only to the question of standing to obtain judicial review. Once this standing is established, the party may assert the interests of the general public in support of his claims for equitable relief. See n. 12 and accompanying text, *supra.*
[16] Every schoolboy may be familiar with Alexis de Tocqueville's famous observation, written in the 1830's, that "[s]carcely any political question arises in the United States that is not resolved, sooner or later, into a judicial question." 1 Democracy in America 280 (1945). Less familiar, however, is de

The principle that the Sierra Club would have us establish in this case would do just that.

As we conclude that the Court of Appeals was correct in its holding that the Sierra Club lacked standing to maintain this action, we do not reach any other questions presented in the petition, and we intimate no view on the merits of the complaint. The judgment is *Affirmed.*

Mr. Justice Powell and Mr. Justice Rehnquist took no part in the consideration or decision of this case.

Mr. Justice Douglas, dissenting.

I share the view of my Brother BLACKMUN and would reverse the judgment below.

The critical question of "standing"[1] would be simplified and also put neatly in focus if we fashioned a federal rule that allowed environmental issues to be litigated before federal agencies or federal courts in the name of the inanimate object about to be despoiled, defaced, or invaded by roads and bulldozers and where injury is the subject of public outrage. Contemporary public concern for protecting nature's ecological equilibrium should lead to the conferral of standing upon environmental objects to sue for their own preservation. See Stone, Should Trees Have Standing?—Toward Legal Rights for Natural Objects, 45 S. Cal. L. Rev. 450 (1972). This suit would therefore be more properly labeled as *Mineral King v. Morton.*

Inanimate objects are sometimes parties in litigation. A ship has a legal personality, a fiction found useful for maritime purposes.[2] The corporation sole—a creature of ecclesiastical law—is an acceptable adversary and large fortunes ride

---

Tocqueville's further observation that judicial review is effective largely because it is not available simply at the behest of a partisan faction, but is exercised only to remedy a particular, concrete injury.

"It will be seen, also, that by leaving it to private interest to censure the law, and by intimately uniting the trial of the law with the trial of an individual, legislation is protected from wanton assaults and from the daily aggressions of party spirit. The errors of the legislator are exposed only to meet a real want; and it is always a positive and appreciable fact that must serve as the basis of a prosecution." Id., at 102.

[1] See generally *Data Processing Service v. Camp,* 397 U.S. 150 (1970); *Flast v. Cohan,* 392 U.S. 83 (1968). See also MR. JUSTICE BRENNAN'S separate opinion in *Barlow v. Collins, supra,* at 167. The issue of statutory standing aside, no doubt exists that "injury in fact" to "aesthetic" and "conservational" interests is here sufficiently threatened to satisfy the case-or-controversy clause. *Data Processing Service v. Camp, supra,* at 154.

[2] *In rem* actions brought to adjudicate libelants' interests in vessels are well known in admiralty. G. Gilmore & C. Black, The Law of Admiralty 31 (1957). But admiralty also permits a salvage action to be brought in the name of the rescuing vessel. *The Camanche,* 8 Wall. 448, 476 (1869). And, in collision litigation, the first-libeled ship may counterclaim in its own name. *The Gylfe v. The Trujillo,* 209 F.2d 386 (CA2 1954). Our case law has personified vessels:

"A ship is born when she is launched, and lives so long as her identity is preserved. Prior to her launching she is a mere congeries of wood and iron . . . In the baptism of launching she receives her name, and from the moment her keel touches the water she is transformed . . . She acquires a personality of her own." *Tucker v. Alexandroff,* 183 U.S. 424, 438.

on its cases.[3] The ordinary corporation is a "person for purposes of the adjudicatory processes, whether it represents proprietary, spiritual, aesthetic, or charitable causes.[4]

So it should be as respects valleys, alpine meadows, rivers, lakes, estuaries, beaches, ridges, groves of trees, swampland, or even air that feels the destructive pressures of modern technology and modern life. The river, for example, is the living symbol of all the life it sustains or nourishes—fish, aquatic insects, water ouzels, otter, fisher, deer, elk, bear, and all other animals, including man, who are dependent on it or who enjoy it for its sight, its sound, or its life. The river as plaintiff speaks for the ecological unit of life that is part of it. Those people who have a meaningful relation to that body of water—whether it be a fisherman, a canoeist, a zoologist, or a logger—must be able to speak for the values which the river represents and which are threatened with destruction.

I do not know Mineral King. I have never seen it nor traveled it, though I have seen articles describing its proposed "development"[5] notably Hano, Protectionists vs. Recreationists—The Battle of Mineral King, N.Y. Times Mag., Aug. 17, 1969, p. 25; and Browning, Mickey Mouse in the Mountains, Harper's, March 1972, p. 65. The Sierra Club in its complaint alleges that "[o]ne of the principal purposes of the Sierra Club is to protect and conserve the national resources of the Sierra Nevada Mountains." The District Court held that this uncontested allegation made the Sierra Club "sufficiently aggrieved" to have "standing" to sue on behalf of Mineral King.

---

[3] At common law, an officeholder, such as a priest or the king, and his successors constituted a corporation sole, a legal entity distinct from the personality which managed it. Rights and duties were deemed to adhere to this device rather than to the officeholder in order to provide continuity after the latter retired. The notion is occasionally revived by American courts. *E.g., Reid v. Barry,* 93 Fla. 849, 112 So. 846 (1927), discussed in Recent Cases, 12 Minn. L. Rev. 295 (1928), and in Note, 26 Mich. L. Rev. 545 (1928); see generally 1 W. Fletcher, Cyclopedia of the Law of Private Corporations §§ 50-53 (1963); 1 P. Potter, Law of Corporations 27 (1881).

[4] Early jurists considered the conventional corporation to be a highly artificial entity. Lord Coke opined that a corporation's creation "rests only in intendment and consideration of the law." *Case of Sutton's Hospital,* 77 Eng. Rep. 937, 973 (K. B. 1612). Mr. Chief Justice Marshall added that the device is "an artificial law." *Trustees of Dartmouth College v. Woodward,* 4 Wheat. 518, 636 (1819). Today, suits in the names of corporations are taken for granted.

[5] Although in the past Mineral King Valley has annually supplied about 70,000 visitor-days of simpler and more rustic forms of recreation—hiking, camping, and skiing (without lifts)—the Forest Service in 1949 and again in 1965 invited developers to submit proposals to "improve" the Valley for resort use. Walt Disney Productions won the competition and transformed the Service's idea into a mammoth project 10 times its originally proposed dimensions. For example, while the Forest Service prospectus called for an investment of at least $3 million and a sleeping capacity of at least 100, Disney will spend $35.3 million and will bed down 3,300 persons by 1978. Disney also plans a nine-level parking structure with two supplemental lots for automobiles, 10 restaurants and 20 ski lifts. The Service's annual license revenue is hitched to Disney's profits. Under Disney's projections, the Valley will be forced to accommodate a tourist population twice as dense as that in Yosemite Valley on a busy day. And, although Disney has bought up much of the private land near the project, another commercial firm plans to transform an adjoining 160-acre parcel into a "piggyback" resort complex, further adding to the volume of human activity the Valley must endure. See generally Note, Mineral King Valley: Who Shall Watch the Watchmen?, 25 Rutgers L. Rev. 103, 107 (1970); Thar's Gold in Those Hills, 206 The Nation 260 (1968). For a general critique of mass recreation enclaves in national forests see Christian Science Monitor, Nov. 22, 1965, p. 5, col. 1 (Western ed.). Michael Frome cautions that the national forests are "fragile" and "deteriorate rapidly with excessive recreation use" because "[t]he

Mineral King is doubtless like other wonders of the Sierra Nevada such as Tuolumne Meadows and the John Muir Trail. Those who hike it, fish it, hunt it, camp in it, frequent it, or visit it merely to sit in solitude and wonderment are legitimate spokesmen for it, whether they may be few or many. Those who have that intimate relation with the inanimate object about to be injured, polluted, or otherwise despoiled are its legitimate spokesmen.

The Solicitor General, whose views on this subject are in the Appendix to this opinion, takes a wholly different approach. He considers the problem in terms of "government by the Judiciary." With all respect, the problem is to make certain that the inanimate objects, which are the very core of America's beauty, have spokesmen before they are destroyed. It is, of course, true that most of them are under the control of a federal or state agency. The standards given those agencies are usually expressed in terms of the "public interest." Yet "public interest" has so many differing shades of meaning as to be quite meaningless on the environmental front. Congress accordingly has adopted ecological standards in the National Environmental Policy Act of 1969, Pub. L. 91-190, 83 Stat. 852, 42 U.S.C. § 4321 et seq., and guidelines for agency action have been provided by the Council on Environmental Quality of which Russell E. Train is Chairman. See 36 Fed. Reg. 7724.

Yet the pressures on agencies for favorable action one way or the other are enormous. The suggestion that Congress can stop action which is undesirable is true in theory; yet even Congress is too remote to give meaningful direction and its machinery is too ponderous to use very often. The federal agencies of which I speak are not venal or corrupt. But they are notoriously under the control of powerful interests who manipulate them through advisory committees, or friendly working relations, or who have that natural affinity with the agency which in time develops between the regulator and the regulated.[6] As early as 1894, Attorney

---

trampling effect alone eliminates vegetative growth, creating erosion and water runoff problems. The concentration of people, particularly in horse parties, on excessively steep slopes that follow old Indian or cattle routes, has torn up the landscape of the High Sierras in California and sent tons of wilderness soil washing downstream each year." M. Frome, The Forest Service 69 (1971).

[6] The federal budget annually includes about $75 million for underwriting about 1,500 advisory committees attached to various regulatory agencies. These groups are almost exclusively composed of industry representatives appointed by the President or by Cabinet members. Although public members may be on these committees, they are rarely asked to serve. Senator Lee Metcalf warns: "Industry advisory committees exist inside most important federal agencies, and even have offices in some. Legally, their function is purely as kibitzer, but in practice many have become internal lobbies— printing industry handouts in the Government Printing Office with taxpayers' money, and even influencing policies. Industry committees perform the dual function of stopping government from finding out about corporations while at the same time helping corporations get inside information about what government is doing. Sometimes, the same company that sits on an advisory council that obstructs or turns down a government questionnaire is precisely the company which is withholding information the government needs in order to enforce a law." Metcalf, The Vested Oracles: How Industry Regulates Government, 3 The Washington Monthly, July 1971, p. 45. For proceedings conducted by Senator Metcalf exposing these relationships, see Hearings on S. 3067 before the Subcommittee on Intergovernmental Relations of the Senate Committee on Government Operations, 91st Cong., 2d Sess. (1970); Hearings on S. 1637, S. 1964, and S. 2064 before the Subcommittee on Intergovernmental Relations of the Senate Committee on Government Operations, 92d Cong., 1st Sess. (1971).

General Olney predicted that regulatory agencies might become "industry-minded," as illustrated by his forecast concerning the Interstate Commerce Commission:

> "The Commission . . . is, or can be made, of great use to the railroads. It satisfies the popular clamor for a government supervision of railroads, at the same time that that supervision is almost entirely nominal. Further, the older such a commission gets to be, the more inclined it will be found to take the business and railroad view of things." M. Josephson, The Politicos 526 (1938).

Years later a court of appeals observed, "the recurring question which has plagued public regulation of industry [is] whether the regulatory agency is unduly oriented toward the interests of the industry it is designed to regulate, rather than the public interest it is designed to protect." *Moss v. CAB*, 139 U.S. App. D.C. 150, 152, 430 F.2d 891, 893. See also *Office of Communication of the United Church of Christ v. FCC*, 123 U.S. App. D.C. 328, 337-338, 359 F.2d 994, 1003-1004; *Udall v. FPC*, 387 U.S. 428; *Calvert Cliffs' Coordinating Committee, Inc. v. AEC*, 146 U.S. App. D.C. 33, 449 F.2d 1109; *Environmental Defense Fund, Inc. v. Ruckelshaus*, 142 U.S. App. D.C. 74, 439 F.2d 584; *Environmental Defense Fund, Inc. v. HEW*, 138 U.S. App. D.C. 381, 428 F.2d 1083; *Scenic Hudson Preservation Conf. v. FPC*, 354 F.2d 608, 620. But see Jaffe, The Federal Regulatory Agencies In Perspective: Administrative Limitations In A Political Setting, 11 B.C. Ind. & Com. L. Rev. 565 (1970) (labels "industry-mindedness" as "devil" theory).

The Forest Service—one of the federal agencies behind the scheme to despoil Mineral King—has been notorious for its alignment with lumber companies, although its mandate from Congress directs it to consider the various aspects of multiple use in its supervision of the national forests.[7]

The web spun about administrative agencies by industry representatives does not depend, of course, solely upon advisory committees for effectiveness. See Elman, Administrative Reform of the Federal Trade Commission, 59 Geo. L.J. 777, 788 (1971); Johnson, A New Fidelity to the Regulatory Ideal, 59 Geo. L.J. 869, 874, 906 (1971); R. Berkman & K. Viscusi, Damming The West, The Ralph Nader Study Group Report on The Bureau of Reclamation 155 (1971); R. Fellmeth, The Interstate Commerce Omission, The Ralph Nader Study Group Report on the Interstate Commerce Commission and Transportation 15-39 and passim (1970); J. Turner, The Chemical Feast, The Ralph Nader Study Group Report on Food Protection and the Food and Drug Administration passim (1970); Massel, The Regulatory Process, 26 Law & Contemp. Prob. 181, 189 (1961); J. Landis, Report on Regulatory Agencies to the President-Elect 13, 69 (1960).

[7] The Forest Reserve Act of 1897, 30 Stat. 35, 16 U.S.C. § 551, imposed upon the Secretary of the Interior the duty to "preserve the [national] forests . . . from destruction" by regulating their "occupancy and use." In 1905 these duties and powers were transferred to the Forest Service created within the Department of Agriculture by the Act of Feb. 1, 1905, 33 Stat. 628, 16 U.S.C. § 472. The phrase "occupancy and use" has been the cornerstone for the concept of "multiple use" of national forests, that is, the policy that uses other than logging were also to be taken into consideration in managing our 154 national forests. This policy was made more explicit by the Multiple-Use Sustained-Yield Act of 1960, 74 Stat. 215, 16 U.S.C. §§ 528-531, which provides that competing considerations should include outdoor recreation, range, timber, watershed, wildlife, and fish purposes. The Forest Service, influ-

The voice of the inanimate object, therefore, should not be stilled. That does not mean that the judiciary takes over the managerial functions from the federal agency. It merely means that before these priceless bits of Americana (such as a valley, an alpine meadow, a river, or a lake) are forever lost or are so transformed

---

enced by powerful logging interests, has, however, paid only lip service to its multiple-use mandate and has auctioned away millions of timberland acres without considering environmental or conservational interests. The importance of national forests to the construction and logging industries results from the type of lumber grown therein which is well suited to builders' needs. For example, Western acreage produces Douglas fir (structural support) and ponderosa pine (plywood lamination). In order to preserve the total acreage and so-called "maturity" of timber, the annual size of a Forest Service harvest is supposedly equated with expected yearly reforestation. Nonetheless, yearly cuts have increased from 5.6 billion board feet in 1950 to 13.74 billion in 1971. Forestry professionals challenge the Service's explanation that this harvest increase to 240% is not really overcutting but instead has resulted from its improved management of timberlands. "Improved management," answer the critics, is only a euphemism for exaggerated regrowth forecasts by the Service. N.Y. Times, Nov. 15, 1971, p. 48, col. 1. Recent rises in lumber prices have caused a new round of industry pressure to auction more federally owned timber. See Wagner, Resources Report/Lumbermen, conservationists head for new battle over government timber, 3 National J. 657 (1971).

Aside from the issue of how much timber should be cut annually, another crucial question is how lumber should be harvested. Despite much criticism, the Forest Service had adhered to a policy of permitting logging companies to "clearcut" tracts of auctioned acreage. "Clearcutting," somewhat analogous to strip mining, is the indiscriminate and complete shaving from the earth of all trees—regardless of size or age—often across hundreds of contiguous acres.

Of clearcutting, Senator Gale McGee, a leading antagonist of Forest Service policy, complains: "The Forest Service's management policies are wreaking havoc with the environment. Soil is eroding, reforestation is neglected if not ignored, streams are silting, and clearcutting remains a basic practice." N.Y. Times, Nov. 14, 1971, p. 60, col. 2. He adds: "In Wyoming . . . the Forest Service is very much . . . nursemaid . . . to the lumber industry. . . ." Hearings on Management Practices on the Public Lands before the Subcommittee on Public Lands of the Senate Committee on Interior and Insular Affairs, pt. 1, p. 7 (1971).

Senator Jennings Randolph offers a similar criticism of the leveling by lumber companies of large portions of the Monongahela National Forest in West Virginia. Id., at 9. See also 116 Cong. Rec. 36971 (reprinted speech of Sen. Jennings Randolph concerning Forest Service policy in Monongahela National Forest). To investigate similar controversy surrounding the Service's management of the Bitterroot National Forest in Montana, Senator Lee Metcalf recently asked forestry professionals at the University of Montana to study local harvesting practices. The faculty group concluded that public dissatisfaction had arisen from the Forest Service's "overriding concern for sawtimber production" and its "insensitivity to the related forest uses and to the . . . public's interest in environmental values." S. Doc. No. 91-115, p. 14 (1970). See also Behan, Timber Mining: Accusation or Prospect?, American Forests, Nov. 1971, p. 4 (additional comments of faculty participant); Reich, The Public and the Nation's Forests, 50 Calif. L. Rev. 381-400 (1962).

Former Secretary of the Interior Walter Hickel similarly faulted clearcutting as excusable only as a money-saving harvesting practice for large lumber corporations. W. Hickel, Who Owns America? 130 (1971). See also Risser, The U.S. Forest Service: Smokey's Strip Miners, 3 The Washington Monthly, Dec. 1971, p. 16. And at least one Forest Service study team shares some of these criticisms of clearcutting. U.S. Dept. of Agriculture, Forest Management in Wyoming 12 (1971). See also Public Land Law Review Comm'n, Report to the President and to the Congress 44 (1970); Chapman, Effects of Logging upon Fish Resources of the West Coast, 60 J. of Forestry 533 (1962).

A third category of criticism results from the Service's huge backlog of delayed reforestation projects. It is true that Congress has underfunded replanting programs of the Service but it is also true that the Service and lumber companies have regularly ensured that Congress fully funds budgets requested for the Forest Service's "timber sales and management." M. Frome, The Environment and Timber Resources, in What's Ahead for Our Public Lands? 23, 24 (H. Pyles ed. 1970).

as to be reduced to the eventual rubble of our urban environment, the voice of the existing beneficiaries of these environmental wonders should be heard.[8]

Perhaps they will not win. Perhaps the bulldozers of "progress" will plow under all the aesthetic wonders of this beautiful land. That is not the present question. The sole question is, who has standing to be heard?

Those who hike the Appalachian Trail into Sunfish Pond, New Jersey, and camp or sleep there, or run the Allagash in Maine, or climb the Guadalupes in West Texas, or who canoe and portage the Quetico Superior in Minnesota, certainly should have standing to defend those natural wonders before courts or agencies, though they live 3,000 miles away. Those who merely are caught up in environmental news or propaganda and flock to defend these waters or areas may be treated differently. That is why these environmental issues should be tendered by the inanimate object itself. Then there will be assurances that all of the forms of life[9] which it represents will stand before the court—the pileated woodpecker as

[8] Permitting a court to appoint a representative of an inanimate object would not be significantly different from customary judicial appointments of guardians ad litem, executors, conservators, receivers, or counsel for indigents.

The values that ride on decisions such as the present one are often not appreciated even by the so-called experts.

"A teaspoon of living earth contains 5 million bacteria, 20 million fungi, one million protozoa, and 200,000 algae. No living human can predict what vital miracles may be locked in this dab of life, this stupendous reservoir of genetic materials that have evolved continuously since the dawn of the earth. For example, molds have existed on earth for about 2 billion years. But only in this century did we unlock the secret of the penicillins, tetracyclines, and other antibiotics from the lowly molds, and thus fashion the most powerful and effective medicines ever discovered by man. Medical scientists still wince at the thought that we might have inadvertently wiped out the rhesus monkey, medically, the most important research animal on earth. And who knows what revelations might lie in the cells of the blackback gorilla nesting in his eyrie this moment in the Virunga Mountains of Rwanda? And what might we have learned from the European lion, the first species formally noted (in 80 A.D.) as extinct by the Romans?

"When a species is gone, it is gone forever. Nature's genetic chain, billions of years in the making, is broken for all time." Conserve—Water, Land and Life, Nov. 1971, p. 4.

Aldo Leopold wrote in Round River 147 (1953):

"In Germany there is a mountain called the Spessart. Its south slope bears the most magnificent oaks in the world. American cabinetmakers, when they want the last word in quality, use Spessart oak. The north slope, which should be the better, bears an indifferent stand of Scotch pine. Why? Both slopes are part of the same state forest; both have been managed with equally scrupulous care for two centuries. Why the difference?

"Kick up the litter under the oaks and you will see that the leaves rot almost as fast as they fall. Under the pines, though, the needles pile up as a thick duff; decay is much slower. Why? Because in the Middle Ages the south slope was preserved as a deer forest by a hunting bishop; the north slope was pastured, plowed, and cut by settlers, just as we do with our woodlots in Wisconsin and Iowa today. Only after this period of abuse was the north slope replanted to pines. During this period of abuse something happened to the microscopic flora and fauna of the soil. The number of species was greatly reduced, i.e., the digestive apparatus of the soil lost some of its parts. Two centuries of conservation have not sufficed to restore these losses. It required the modern microscope, and a century of research in soil science, to discover the existence of these 'small cogs and wheels' which determine harmony or disharmony between men and land in the Spessart."

[9] Senator Cranston has introduced a bill to establish a 35,000-acre Pupfish National Monument to honor the pupfish which are one inch long and useless to man. S. 2141, 92d Cong., 1st Sess. They are too small to eat and unfit for a home aquarium. But as Michael Frome has said: "Still, I agree with Senator Cranston that saving the pupfish would symbolize our appreciation of diversity in God's tired old biosphere, the qualities which hold it together and the interaction of life forms. When fishermen rise up united to save the pupfish they can save the world as well." Field & Stream, Dec. 1971, p. 74.

well as the coyote and bear, the lemmings as well as the trout in the streams. Those inarticulate members of the ecological group cannot speak. But those people who have so frequented the place as to know its values and wonders will be able to speak for the entire ecological community.

Ecology reflects the land ethic; and Aldo Leopold wrote in A Sand County Almanac 204 (1949), "The land ethic simply enlarges the boundaries of the community to include soils, waters, plants, and animals, or collectively: the land."

That, as I see it, is the issue of "standing" in the present case and controversy.

APPENDIX TO OPINION OF DOUGLAS, J., DISSENTING

*Extract From Oral Argument of the Solicitor General**

"As far as I know, no case has yet been decided which holds that a plaintiff which merely asserts that, to quote from the complaint here, its interest would be widely affected [a]nd that 'it would be aggrieved' by the acts of the defendant, has standing to raise legal questions in court.

"But why not? Do not the courts exist to decide legal questions? And are they not the most impartial and learned agencies that we have in our governmental system? Are there not many questions which must be decided by the courts? Why should not the courts decide any question which any citizen wants to raise?

"As the tenor of my argument indicates, this raises, I think, a true question, perhaps a somewhat novel question, in the separation of powers. . . .

"Ours is not a government by the Judiciary. It is a government of three branches, each of which was intended to have broad and effective powers subject to checks and balances. In litigable cases, the courts have great authority. But the Founders also intended that the Congress should have wide powers, and that the Executive Branch should have wide powers.

"All these officers have great responsibilities. They are not less sworn than are the members of this Court to uphold the Constitution of the United States.

"This, I submit, is what really lies behind the standing doctrine, embodied in those cryptic words 'case' and 'controversy' in Article III of the Constitution."

NOTE: ENVIRONMENTAL PROTECTION ACT OF 1970
(MICH. COMP. L. ANNO. § 691.1202)

"(1) The Attorney General, any political subdivision of the state, any instrumentality or agency of the state or of a political subdivision thereof, any person, partnership, corporation, association, organization or other legal entity may maintain an action in the circuit court having jurisdiction where the alleged violation occurred or is likely to occur for declaratory and equitable relief against the state, any political subdivision thereof, any instrumentality or agency of the state or of a political subdivision thereof, any person, partnership, corporation, association, organization or other legal entity for the protection of the air, water or other natural resources and the public trust therein from pollution, impairment or destruction."

* Tr. of Oral Arg. 31-35.

NOTE: SUBSEQUENT CASES

After *Sierra Club v. Morton* the Supreme Court twice decided standing cases in the environmental context. In *United States v. Students Challenging Regulatory Procedures* (*SCRAP*) et al., 412 U.S. 669 (1973), an unincorporated group of five law students was held to have standing to challenge a railroad rate increase they claimed would discourage recycling of wastes and promote use of raw materials. The contention of the opposition that the SCRAP claim was "vague, unsubstantial, and insufficient" was rejected, the court noting the allegation of SCRAP that they used the forest resources and "suffered economic, recreational, and aesthetic harm."

    Warth v. Sedlin, 422 U.S. 490 (1975), involved a challenge to local zoning restrictions which the plaintiffs, persons of low income, alleged excluded low-income people from town. Holding that the requisites for standing were not met, the court said that there must be alleged concrete facts that the challenged practices harm the plaintiff, or that he would benefit if the challenged law were otherwise. Specifically noted was the fact that the plaintiff had not tried to buy property in the town or sought a zoning variance.

QUESTIONS FOR DISCUSSION

1   Are any standing requirements desirable or necessary? What would be the consequences of the elimination of the requirement of standing?

2   Does *Sierra Club v. Morton* mark a major setback for the environmental movement or a dramatic change from past rulings?

3   Was the Sierra Club "arguably within the zone of interests"?

4   Is it not possible for one to suffer an "injury in fact" even though one is not a user of the area in question?

5   Could the pleading of the Sierra Club have been phrased in such a way as to meet the court's requirements? Is there any reason why the Sierra Club might have chosen not to do so?

6   Are administrative issues such as possible aggravation of already congested court calendars relevant to the legal issues at hand?

7   Can the decision in *Sierra Club v. Morton* be disputed in light of the traditional role of courts? Do you share the Solicitor General's fear of "government by the judiciary"?

8   Suppose an association of construction engineers felt that a new environmental law was going to slow construction and diminish their livelihood as a group. Would such a group have standing to challenge the law?

9   Standing is a "threshold question," one that is decided at the outset of a trial by the judge. Do you suppose that the judge's assessment of the plaintiff's chances to prevail on the merits enters into his decision? How about his personal view of environmental litigation?

10   Should a court take cognizance of claims of spiritual or aesthetic inquiries? Is it competent to do so?

11   Do you see any problems with the Michigan act quoted on page 25?

12   The rules of standing expounded in *Data Processing Service v. Camp* and *Sierra Club v. Morton* are generally considered rather vague and unhelpful. Can you formulate a rule or rules that would serve the interests of all the parties to litigation?

GOVERNMENTAL IMMUNITY

The origins of the doctrine of governmental immunity are found in the early common law. An ancient adage provided that "the King can do no wrong," thus insulating the sovereign from suit. This concept of governmental or sovereign immunity carried over from the English common law and was established as a viable principle of American law. The substance of the contemporary doctrine is based not so much on historical precepts as on practical, administrative foundations to the end that governments not be unduly burdened in carrying out their functions.

As a general rule, federal, state, and some local governmental bodies and their major officials, when acting in their official capacity, are immune from suit. There are five major exceptions: (1) where the acts complained of are beyond the scope of the statutory powers granted or the powers themselves are constitutionally void, (2) where the government is acting in a proprietary sense, (3) where there is a dispute over title to real property, (4) where the right to sue is granted by statute, and (5) by waiver or consent of the governmental body involved.

In *Elliot v. Volpe,* plaintiffs sought to enjoin certain federal and state officials from the constructing and funding of Interstate Highway 93 in Massachusetts. Defendants raised the defense of sovereign immunity.

Elliot v. Volpe

321 F. Supp. 831 (1971)

This case came on to be heard on cross-motions for summary judgment filed by plaintiffs and each defendant. Plaintiffs are two residents of Somerville, Massachusetts, and two organizations. One of the organizations is a community group of Somerville citizens (referred to in the complaint as SCAT); the other is a nonprofit Massachusetts corporation concerned with transportation issues and problems in the metropolitan area of Boston (referred to in the complaint as GBC).

The defendants herein sometimes referred to as "federal defendants" are: *John A. Volpe,* the Secretary of Transportation of the United States; *Francis C. Turner,* the Director of Public Roads of the Federal Highway Administration of the United States; *Edward J. DePina,* the Massachusetts District Division Engineer of the Bureau of Public Roads of the United States; and *Russell Train,* the Chairman of the Council for Environmental Quality in the Executive Department of the United States.

Other defendants herein sometimes referred to as "state defendants" are: *Edward W. Ribbs,* the Commissioner of the Department of Public Works of the Commonwealth of Massachusetts; *M. DeMatteo Construction Company* (DeMatteo), a Massachusetts corporation engaged in the construction of public highways; and *The Barletta Company* (Barletta), a Massachusetts corporation also engaged in the construction of public highways.

Plaintiffs seek to halt the further construction of Interstate Highway 93 (I-93). To accomplish that result they ask that the state defendants be enjoined from the actual construction work, and from approval of, and commitment of the resources of the Commonwealth to, construction of I-93 through the City of Somerville, and that the federal defendants be enjoined from further authorization and payment of federal funds, and that defendant Train be ordered to fulfill his responsibilities to protect the aesthetic and environmental values in Somerville from the effects threatened by the construction. Plaintiffs object to the actions of the defendants in furthering the construction, and seek the relief referred to, on the ground there has been no compliance with the requirements of law applicable to the design of I-93 through Somerville. At the hearing of the motions for summary judgment plaintiffs expressly disavowed any objection to the location and route of I-93 through Somerville.

The contentions of plaintiffs are that:

(a) the provisions of 23 U.S.C. § 128, as amended August 23, 1968, and the provisions of the Policy and Procedure Memorandum of 20-8 (PPM 20-8), promulgated January 14, 1969, apply to project I-93 in Somerville, and defendants have failed to comply with the requirements thereof applicable to the design of I-93; and

(b) the provisions of 42 U.S.C. § 4321, et seq., effective January 1, 1970, apply to project I-93 in Somerville, and defendants have failed to comply with the requirements thereof applicable to the design of I-93.

All defendants contend that none of the provisions of law relied upon by plaintiffs are applicable on the issues of the design of the highway, and further contend plaintiffs are guilty of laches. The state defendants contend in addition that the action is an action against the Commonwealth of Massachusetts in its governmental capacity, and that Massachusetts has not consented to be sued. This will be the first question considered. The City of Boston and City of Somerville were permitted to file a brief as amicus curiae which supports plaintiffs' claims.

A. DEFENSE OF SOVEREIGN IMMUNITY

1. The action against the defendant Ribbs is declared to be against him individually and as he is Commissioner of Public Works of the Commonwealth. The only relief sought is that he be enjoined "from further commitment of state resources and approval to construction of I-93 through Somerville." Such relief, if granted, would interfere directly with the administration of the public business of the Commonwealth and prevent it from carrying out its governmental obligations. *See Larson v. Domestic & Foreign Committee Corp.,* 337 U.S. 682 (1949); *Land v. Dollar,* 330 U.S. 731 (1947); *Ex parte New York,* 256 U.S. 490 (1921). There are no allegations that defendant Ribbs, apart from his capacity as Commissioner, can exercise any control or has any role in the further construction of I-93 in Somer-

ville. No relief is sought [other] than relief against him as Commissioner of Public Works. There is no evidence that the Commonwealth has given its consent to be sued in the context of this litigation. The court concludes that the defense of sovereign immunity of the Commonwealth can be raised by Ribbs as a defense against the complaint, for the action against him is in fact and in law one against the State. *See In re Avers,* 123 U.S. 443 (1887); *Citizens Comm. for the Hudson Valley v. Volpe,* 297 F. Supp. 809 [1 ERC 1096] (S.D.N.Y. 1969); *DeLong Corp. v. Oregon State Highway Comm'n,* 233 F. Supp. 7 (D. Ore. 1964), aff'd, 343 F.2d 911 (9th Cir.), cert. denied, 382 U.S. 877 (1965).

2. The plaintiffs argue, however, that in the circumstances of this case the defense is not available. They assert the Commonwealth impliedly waived its immunity to be sued in this action when it voluntarily undertook construction of its highway system subject to the regulation and control of the Federal Government. To support this contention they cite *Parden v. Terminal Ry. of the Ala. State Docks Dept.,* 377 U.S. 184 (1964), and *Chesapeake Bay Bridge & Tunnel Dist. v. Lauritzen,* 404 F.2d 1001 (4th Cir.). These cases, however, are not applicable to the case at bar. The question of waiver of governmental immunity is, as plaintiffs assert, one of federal and not state law. But the "conclusion that there has been a waiver of immunity will not be lightly inferred." *Petty v. Tennessee-Missouri Bridge Comm'n,* 359 U.S. 275, 276 (1959). Such determination must be made from clear and explicit language. *Kennecott Copper Corp. v. State Tax Comm'n,* 327 U.S. 573 (1946); *Ford Motor Co. v. Dept. of Treasury of Ind.,* 323 U.S. 459 (1945); *Hamilton Mfg. Co. v. Trustees of State Colleges in Colo.,* 356 F.2d 599 (10th Cir. 1966); *S. J. Groves & Sons Co. v. New Jersey Turnpike Authority,* 268 F. Supp. 568 (D.N.J. 1967). The mere entrance of a state into an area of federal control does not thereby bring about a waiver of governmental immunity. *Citizens Comm. for the Hudson Valley v. Volpe,* 297 F. Supp. 809, 812 (S.D.N.Y. 1969). The cases of *Parden v. Terminal Ry., supra,* and *Chesapeake Bay Bridge & Tunnel Dist. v. Lauritzen, supra,* are distinguishable, as the court in *Citizens Comm. for the Hudson Valley v. Volpe, supra,* pointed out, and are not apposite here. Waiver of governmental immunity could be inferred when a state "directly enter[s] a sphere of operation subject to causes of action specifically created by Congress in favor of a specific class. . . ." 297 F. Supp. at 812. But such is not the case here, for there is no showing that Congress has created any causes of action favoring plaintiffs, or others. The Administrative Procedure Act, 5 U.S.C. §§ 701, 702, creates no cause of action against the Commonwealth; neither do the requirements of 23 U.S.C. § 128(a). The plaintiffs have not shown any basis for an inference that the Commonwealth has waived the defense of immunity. Accordingly, the defendant Ribbs is entitled to avail himself of it as a complete defense against this action.

3. The relief sought against DeMatteo and Barletta is that they be enjoined from doing further construction work on I-93 in Somerville. DeMatteo entered into a contract with the Commonwealth on September 26, 1969 for construction of a segment of I-93 through Somerville, and commenced work under the contract on October 30, 1969. Barletta made a contract with the Commonwealth for construction of another Somerville segment in February 1970, and began work March

25, 1970. There are no allegations and no claims that these contractors are performing their work in any manner than in accord with their contracts. On the contrary, the complaint of plaintiffs is that the contractors are, indeed, following the highway design in their contracts. In the construction of the highway work under their contracts DeMatteo and Barletta are instrumentalities of the Commonwealth. *Pennsylvania Environmental Council v. Bartlett*, 315 F. Supp. 238 [1 ERC 1271] (M.D. Pa. 1970), appeals docketed, Nos. 19453 and 19437, 3d Cir., November 30, 1970. The relief sought against them, if granted, would interfere with the public business of the Commonwealth and prevent the carrying on of its governmental operations. *See generally, Larson v. Domestic & Foreign Commerce Corp., supra; Land v. Dollar, supra; Ex parte New York, supra; Pennsylvania Environmental Council v. Barlett, supra.* No other relief is sought against the contractors. As in the case against defendant Ribbs, the action here against each contractor must be realistically viewed as action against the Commonwealth, and each contractor as the State's "alter ego." *See generally, In re Avers, supra; Citizens Comm. for the Hudson Valley v. Volpe, supra; DeLong v. Oregon State Highway Comm'n, supra.* What has been said above rejecting plaintiffs' contention of waiver of the defense of immunity is applicable with equal force when the defense is raised by the contractors. *Pennsylvania Environmental Council v. Bartlett, supra.* Accordingly, each of them is entitled to raise it as a complete defense to the complaint against them.

From *Elliot v. Volpe,* we see that the court's constant reference to "interference with the administration of the public business of the Commonwealth" and the "prevention of carrying on its governmental obligations" belies the historical origins of the doctrine.

In contrast to *Elliot v. Volpe,* the court, in *Environmental Defense Fund v. Corps of Engineers,*[9] found a clear violation of statutory powers by governmental officials and disallowed the defense of sovereign immunity. Judge Parker states (page 879):

> The plaintiffs in this proceeding are the Environmental Defense Fund (EDF), the Florida Defenders of the Environment (FDE), and certain individual residents of Florida who have benefited and desire to continue to benefit from the hunting, fishing, and other recreational as well as aesthetic advantages of the Oklawaha River ecosystem. They seek preliminary injunctive relief against the Corps of Engineers of the United States Army, Secretary of the Army Stanley R. Resor, and General Frederick B. Clarke, Chief of Engineers, Corps of Engineers, claiming that the Cross-Florida Barge Canal, hereinafter the Canal, although duly authorized, is being constructed in violation of numerous statutes designed to preserve the natural resources of the nation and to salvage to the extent possible those resources already endangered particularly the National Environmental Policy Act, hereinafter NEPA, the Fish and Wildlife Coordination Act, and the Act of July 23,

[9] 324 F. Supp. 878 (D.C.D.C., 1971).

1942 which authorizes construction of the Canal. The plaintiffs assert that unless the requested relief is granted irreparable damage will result—notably extensive destruction of unique timber and aquatic life upstream from Eureka Dam as well as in Rodman Reservoir, and almost certain pollution of a considerable portion of the water supply for the State of Florida.

The defendants have filed a motion to dismiss . . . asserting that the Court lacks jurisdiction of the defendants and the subject matter because this action is allegedly barred by sovereign immunity. They further contend that there is a failure to state a claim upon which relief can be granted, again asserting sovereign immunity, and further arguing that the statutes upon which plaintiffs rely do not apply to the Canal which was authorized in 1942 and begun in 1964. The structures of the Canal are allegedly one-third completed and the overall project is allegedly one-sixth completed.

For the reasons set forth, the Court denies the defendants' motion to dismiss and grants the plaintiffs' motion for a preliminary injunction.

. . . Nor is the doctrine of sovereign immunity applicable. This suit seeks to challenge actions by officers on grounds that the actions are allegedly "beyond their statutory powers" or "even though within the scope of their authority, the powers themselves or the manner in which they are exercised are constitutionally void," *Dugan et al. v. Rank et al.*, 372 U.S. 609, 620–622, 83 S. Ct. 999, 1007, 10 L. Ed. 2d 15 (1963). This is a review of administrative compliance with statutory duties, and there is no clear and convincing evidence of Congressional intent to bar judicial review of such compliance in this instance. The situation is clearly distinguishable from those in *Dugan, supra,* and *Larson v. Domestic & Foreign Commerce Corp.*, 337 U.S. 682, 69 S. Ct. 1457, 93 L. Ed. 1628 (1949), cited by defendants. Those cases involved, respectively, an alleged tortious diversion of water rights and a breach of contract. In both instances government officers had concededly acted within the framework of the statutory grant of authority.

A suit against the government to settle title to real property represents another exception to the doctrine of sovereign immunity. In *O'Neill v. State Highway Department,*[h] plaintiff sued the state of New Jersey regarding a dispute of ownership of certain tidelands. The court, in discussing the previously mentioned exception, gave additional reasons for the required implementation of the doctrine:

We need not recount the uneven history of sovereign immunity. Suffice it to say that today courts are disposed to hear an action against the State unless good reason stands in the way. It is currently said the doctrine bars suits which seek to control State action or to subject it to liability. *Duke Power Co. v. Patten*, 20 N.J. 42, 50, 118 A.2d 529 (1955); *Gallena v. Scott*, 11 N.J. 231, 237, 94 A.2d 312 (1953); *Abelson's Inc. v. New Jersey State Board of Optometrists*, 5 N.J. 412, 417, 75 A.2d 867, 22 A.L.R.2d 929 (1950).

. . . A suit to settle title to property does not collide with considerations upon which the State's immunity from suit now rests. The private claimant does not ask the judiciary to compel the Legislature or the Chief Executive to do anything. Nor does the claimant seek a dollar judgment. He asks only that it be decided that he, and not the State, is the owner of some specific property. Cf. *Michalski v. United States,* 49 N.J. Super. 104, 110, 139 A.2d 324 (Ch. Div. 1958).

h 235 A.2d 1, 50 N.J. 307 (1967).

NOTES: WAIVER; ELEVENTH AMENDMENT

(1) Immunity may be waived either on a case-by-case basis or by legislation waiving immunity for particular types of claims.

See, for example, 28 U.S.C. §§ 2671–2680, the Federal Tort Claims Act, whereby the United States consents to be sued for "injury or loss of property or personal injury or death caused by the negligent or wrongful act or omission of any employee of the government while acting within the scope of his office or employment" (28 U.S.C. §§ 1346, 2672, 2674).

(2) Amendment XI: "The judicial power of the United States shall not be construed to extend to any suit in law or equity, commenced or prosecuted against one of the United States by Citizens of another State, or by Citizens or Subjects of any Foreign State."

QUESTIONS FOR DISCUSSION

1 How would the abolishment of the doctrine of sovereign immunity affect the carrying on of governmental operations?

2 Did the court in *Elliot v. Volpe* stretch the protection afforded governmental officials in protecting the contractors from suit? What would be the better argument (expansion or reduction of immunity) in the contractors' case? Why?

3 What reasonable alternatives are available to a party injured by a governmental action, where the defense of sovereign immunity presents an absolute bar to any judicial action?

4 If the government represents the taxpayers and acts in their behalf, should not the taxpayers, rather than the innocent injured party, bear the cost of the government's neglect?

5 In general, children and mental incompetents are responsible in damages for their torts. Should the government be held to a lesser responsibility?

6 Is sovereign immunity a doctrine which has been or should be abolished? One court has recently stated that the doctrine has been relegated "to the dust bin of history" (*Massengill v. Yuma County* (1969) 104 Ariz. 518, 456 P.2d 376, 41 A.L.R.3d 692.) while another has declined "to take one step further in the decimation of the doctrine . . ." (*Keane v. Chicago* (1968) 98 Ill. App. 2d 460, 240 N.E.2d 321).

7 Does a court have the power to overturn a doctrine such as sovereign immunity if the doctrine is incorporated in the state constitution? See, for example, *Shellhorn v. State,* 187 A.2d 71 (Del. 1962).

8 What might be the effect of the provision of the Administrative Procedure Act (5 U.S.C. § 702) which states, "A person suffering legal wrong because of agency action, or adversely affected or aggrieved by agency action within the meaning of a relevant statute, is entitled to judicial review thereof"?

9 What might be the financial consequences of the abolition of sovereign immunity?

PROBLEMS

1 Suppose a student organization, concerned with the water quality of the Atlantic coast in general, the landside impacts of offshore development, and possible deleterious ef-

fects on oceanographic research conducted by the university, decides to sue the polluters, and also the state and the United States for their failure to enforce the law. What problems might they encounter?

2 A military establishment, in apparent violation of water-quality regulations, releases its sewage untreated into a local river. Downstream landowners form an association and bring suit against the commanding officer personally and against the civilian architects of the base disposal system. Would either defendant be protected by sovereign immunity?

3 The plaintiff is arrested by the Coast Guard for illegally dumping oil. In the course of his arrest he is injured by allegedly unreasonable force and sues the United States and the guardsman. Would either defendant be protected by sovereign immunity?

4 Suppose a federal flood-control program will inundate an area which includes an ancient Indian burial ground. The project will enhance the economic value of the surrounding land but is opposed by the Indian tribe, which claims a sentimental and religious loss, and by an association of archaeologists who seek to study the area. Would either group have standing to contest the project in court? Would sovereign immunity bar the action?

SUGGESTIONS FOR FURTHER READING

Berger, R.: *Standing to Sue in Public Actions: Is It a Constitutional Requirement?* 78 YALE L.J. 816, 1969.

Davis, K. C.: *The Liberalized Law of Standing,* 37 U. CHI. L. REV. 450, 1970.

Hughes, H. O.: *Who's Standing? Problems with Inanimate Plaintiffs,* 4 ENVIRONMENTAL L. 315, 1974.

Inadequacies of Federal Sovereign Immunity: A New Perspective, 61 GEO. L.J. 1535, 1973.

Jaffe, L.: *Judicial Control of Administrative Action,* Little, Brown, Boston, 1965.

Standing and Sovereign Immunity: Hurdles for Environmental Litigants, 12 SANTA CLARA L. REV. 122, 1972.

Standing to Sue and Conservation Values, 38 U. COLO. L. REV. 391, 1966.

State Legislation to Grant Standing—Questions and Answers and Alternatives, 2 ENVIRONMENTAL L. 313, 1972.

State Sovereign Immunity: No More King's X? 52 TEXAS L. REV. 100, 1973.

Stone, C. D.: *Should Trees Have Standing?—Toward Legal Rights for Natural Objects,* 45 SO. CAL. L. REV. 450, 1972.

Tremaine, J. R.: *Standing in Federal Courts for Conservation Groups,* 6 URBAN L.J. 116, 1974.

Van Doren, J. W.: *Air Pollution—Expanding Citizens Remedies,* 32 OHIO ST. L.J. 16, 1971.

Federal-State Prerogatives

SOURCES OF FEDERAL AND STATE POWER

A variety of most important environmental issues concern the relationship of the federal government's authority under the commerce clause and state police power. The supremacy clause[a] states:

> This Constitution, and the laws of the United States which shall be made in pursuance thereof; . . . shall be the supreme law of the land; and the judges in every state shall be bound thereby, any thing in the Constitution or laws of any state to the contrary notwithstanding.

This language, however, does not dispose of the problem.

The major source of federal regulatory power in the field of pollution is found in the commerce clause[b] of the United States Constitution:

> The Congress shall have power . . . to regulate commerce with foreign nations, and among the several states, and with the Indian tribes.

[a] U.S. Constitution, Art. 6, par. 2.
[b] U.S. Constitution, Art. 1, sec. 8, par. 3 (1791).

The original purposes of this clause were to ensure uniformity of mercantile regulation throughout the nation, to provide free trade among the states, to protect the free flow of commerce against harmful regulations, and to eliminate the many commercial conflicts which existed among the states at the time of the adoption of the Constitution.[c]

The scope of the term "commerce" has been held to include every kind of traffic, trade, and transportation—whether for commercial purposes or not—by land, water, or air, and those individual incidences and interferences with interstate commerce.[d] The power of Congress to promote interstate commerce has included the power to regulate local activities which have a substantial and harmful effect on interstate commerce.[e] The Supreme Court has also held that the commerce power may be exercised to achieve socially desirable objectives, even in the absence of economic considerations.[f]

The powers of the federal government under the commerce clause may be divided into three major categories:

(1) That in which the authority is exclusive;
(2) That in which the power of the state is exclusive; and
(3) That in which the state may act in the absence of legislation by Congress.[g]

Thus, a question may arise as to whether federal domain is exclusive where Congress has not acted, or, if Congress has acted, whether there is any room left for state action. In *Cooley v. Board of Wardens,*[h] the question was said to be whether the subject of state legislation "is in nature national, or admits of only one uniform system or plan of regulation." If so, the subject is exclusively federal. Later decisions utilized tests involving whether the burden on commerce was direct or indirect, substantial, undue, and a variety of equally unhelpful synonyms.

In 1943 the case of *Parker v. Brown*[i] deprecated earlier tests as "mechanical" and approved state legislation under a test "accommodating . . . the competing demands of state and national interests involved." This balancing test may be summarized as follows:

> Although the criteria for determining the validity of State statutes affecting interstate commerce have been variously stated, the general rule that emerges can be phrased as follows: where the statute regulates evenhandedly to effectuate a legitimate local public interest, and its effects on interstate commerce are only incidental, it will be upheld unless the burden imposed on such commerce is clearly excessive in relation to the putative local benefits. If a legitimate local purpose is found, then the question becomes one of degree. And the extent of the burden

[c] See Gottfried Dietze, *The Federalist,* Johns Hopkins Press, Baltimore, 1966, pp. 50–51, 205, 214.
[d] See *United States v. Bishop* (D.C. Md. 1968) 287 F. Supp. 624. See also Robert Kimbrough, *Summary of American Law,* Lawyers Cooperative Publishing Company, Rochester, N.Y., 1974.
[e] For a historical discussion on this point see *Heart of Atlanta Motel, Inc. v. United States,* 379 U.S. 241 (1964); *United States v. Bishop,* page 37.
[f] *Brooks v. United States,* 267 U.S. 432 (1959).
[g] Kimbrough, op. cit., p. 45.
[h] 53 U.S. (12 How.) 299 (1851).
[i] 317 U.S. 341 (1943).

that will be tolerated will, of course, depend on the nature of the local interest involved, and on whether it could be promoted as well with a lesser impact on interstate activities.[j]

The states' power to regulate the area of environmental pollution is not derived from a specific constitutional grant, but is the inherent power of a government to take the necessary action to protect the safety, welfare, and health of the people.[k] Police power is frequently characterized as being flexible and adaptable to changing needs and as an inalienable power of the states which may not be modified or diluted by the legislature.[l] The police powers are not unlimited and are subject to a constitutionally "reasonable exercise"; however, the states in the exercise of these powers may, at times, act in the areas of interstate commerce and maritime activities concurrently with the federal government.[m]

Furthermore, the federal government has no general police power, as there is no delegation of police power to the United States by the Constitution. The police power rests solely with the legislatures of the individual states.[n]

Frequently, the exercise of the states' or federal government's powers in controlling pollution will be conflicting. Much of this problem can be traced to the somewhat general terms used to define the sources of the powers or the inability of a legislature to establish all-encompassing definitions for certain terminology. This "problem" is not new and perhaps may be characterized as the price to be paid for a flexible and viable Constitution. Justice Story, in the leading case of *Martin v. Hunter's Lessee,*[o] discussed the problem of general terms in regard to defining constitutional powers (pages 326–327):

> This constitution unavoidably deals in general language. It did not suit the purposes of the people, in framing this great charter of our liberties, to provide for minute specifications of its powers, or to declare the means by which those powers should be carried into execution. It was foreseen that this would be a perilous and difficult, if not an impracticable, task. The instrument was not intended to provide merely for the exigencies of a few years, but was to endure through a long lapse of ages, the events of which were locked up in the inscrutable purposes of Providence. It could not be foreseen what new changes and modifications of power might be indispensable to effectuate the general objects of the charter; and restrictions and specifications, which at the present, might seem salutary, might, in the end, prove the overthrow of the system itself. Hence its powers are expressed in general terms, leaving to the legislature, from time to time, to adopt its own means to effectuate legitimate objects, and to mould and model the exercise of its powers, as its own wisdom, and the public interests should require.

[j] *Pike v. Bruce Church, Inc.,* 397 U.S. 137 (1970).

[k] See page 62.

[l] See Kimbrough, op. cit., p. 46.

[m] See *Cooley v. Board of Wardens,* 12 How. 299; The Minnesota Rate Cases, 230 U.S. 352; *State v. Schuster's Express, Inc.,* 5 Conn. Cir. 472, 256 A.2d 792. See also *Huron v. Detroit,* page 42.

Note: It is not practical to attempt to define the exact limits of the police power since the courts favor a case-by-case examination of the validity of its exercise. See *Berman v. Parker,* 348 U.S. 26 (1954).

[n] See 16 C.J.S. 906 *Const. Law.* The federal government does have a power comparable to the police power of a state when appropriate to the exercise of any attribute of sovereignty specifically granted to the federal government by the states such as under the general welfare provisions of the Constitution.

[o] *Martin v. Hunter's Lessee,* 14 U.S. (1 Wheat.) 304 (1816).

EXTENT OF COMMERCE POWER

The case of *United States v. Bishop Processing Company,* the first air-pollution abatement case under the Clean Air Act, provides illustration of the extent to which the commerce clause can be and has been utilized as the rationale for federal action in the environmental context. Consider, as you read the opinion, the limits of commerce and whether there is any aspect of environmental protection which is not a possible subject of federal action.

United States v. Bishop Processing Company

287 F. Supp. 624 (D.C. Md. 1968), Cert. Den., 398 U.S. 904 (1970)

Action by United States against rendering company for abatement of alleged air pollution. On defendant's motion to dismiss, the District Court, Thomsen, Chief Judge, held that Congress had rational basis for finding that air pollution affected commerce. . . .

Motion denied.

Thomsen, Chief Judge.

This action has been brought by the United States under the Clean Air Act (the Act), 42 U.S.C. § 1857 et seq., particularly section 180(g)(1) of the Act, as amended November 21, 1967, 81 Stat. 496, 507, now codified as 42 U.S.C. § 1857d(g)(1). The government seeks to enjoin Bishop Processing Company (the defendant), the operator of a rendering and animal reduction plant near Bishop, Worcester County, Maryland, from discharging malodorous air pollutants, which it is alleged, move across the state line and pollute the air in and around Selbyville, Delaware. Defendant has filed a motion to dismiss the complaint on four grounds, namely: (I) that the Act is an unconstitutional attempt by Congress to control purely local intrastate activities over which Congress has no power to legislate . . .

The first ground stated in defendant's motion to dismiss is that the Clean Air Act is an unconstitutional attempt by Congress to control purely local intrastate activities over which Congress has no power to legislate. Defendant argues (a) that the movement of pollutants across state lines is not interstate commerce itself, and (b) has no substantial effect on interstate commerce.

(a) The movement of pollutants across a state line is a proper jurisdictional basis for the provisions of the Act relating to the abatement of interstate air pollution. Such movement of pollutants across state lines constitutes interstate commerce subject to the power granted to Congress by the Constitution to regulate such commerce.

Whether the originator of the pollution directs it across state borders intentionally is immaterial. In *Thornton v. United States,* 271 U.S. 414, 46 S. Ct. 585, 70 L. Ed. 1013 (1926), the owner of cattle which ranged on land near the Florida–Georgia border claimed that they were not within interstate commerce and, consequently, that he could not be required to comply with a federal requirement for the inspection and preventive treatment of cattle in an area under quarantine. The Supreme Court upheld the constitutionality of the applicable statute, stating:

"* * * [I]t is said that these cattle do not appear to have been intended to be transported by rail or boat from one state to another and this only is interstate commerce in cattle under the Constitution. They were on the line between the two states. To drive them across the line would be interstate commerce, and the act of 1905 expressly prohibits driving them on foot when carrying contagion. It is argued, however, that when the cattle only range across the line between the states and are not transported or driven, their passage is not interstate commerce. We do not think that such passage by ranging can be differentiated from interstate commerce. It is intercourse between states, made possible by the failure of owners to restrict their ranging and is due, therefore, to the will of their owners." 271 U.S. at 425, 46 S. Ct. at 588.

In *United States v. Darby,* 312 U.S. 100, 114, 61 S. Ct. 451, 457, 85 L. Ed. 609 (1941), the Court quoted from *Gibbons v. Ogden,* 22 U.S. (9 Wheat.) 1, 196, 6 L. Ed. 23 (1924) as follows:

"The power of Congress over interstate commerce 'is complete in itself, may be exercised to its utmost extent, and acknowledges no limitations other than are prescribed in the Constitution.' * * * It is no objection to the assertion of the power to regulate interstate commerce that its exercise is attended by the same incidents which attend the exercise of the police power of the states."

The commerce power may be exercised to achieve socially desirable objectives, even in the absence of economic considerations. *Brooks v. United States,* 267 U.S. 432, 436, 45 S. Ct. 345, 69 L. Ed. 699 (1959).*

(b) Defendant contends that pollution has no substantial and harmful effect on commerce, arguing that the congressional finding that air pollution has resulted in hazards to air and ground transportation is clearly erroneous, and that if pollution has any effect on air and ground transportation, such effect has been isolated and insubstantial.

Since the provisions of the Act relating to the abatement of interstate air pollution may properly be based on the interstate movement of the pollutants themselves, it is not necessary that such pollutants interfere with interstate com-

---

* The Supreme Court has upheld the application of the commerce power to the interstate transportation of lottery tickets, *Champion v. Ames,* 188 U.S. 321, 23 S. Ct. 321, 47 L. Ed. 492 (1903); stolen cars, *Brooks v. United States, supra;* kidnapped persons, *Gooch v. United States,* 297 U.S. 124, 56 S. Ct. 395, 80 L. Ed. 522 (1936); to prostitution, *Caminetti v. United States,* 242 U.S. 470, 37 S. Ct. 192, 61 L. Ed. 442 (1917); *Hoke v. United States,* 227 U.S. 308, 33 S. Ct. 281, 57 L. Ed. 523 (1913); and to racial discrimination, *Heart of Atlanta Motel, Inc. v. United States,* 379 U.S. 241, 85 S. Ct. 348, 13 L. Ed. 2d 258 (1964). [Other footnotes in this case have been omitted.]

merce in order to sustain this exercise of the commerce power. Congress, however, concluded that:

> "the growth in the amount and complexity of air pollution brought about by urbanization, industrial development, and the increasing use of motor vehicles, has resulted in mounting dangers to the public health and welfare, including injury to agricultural crops and livestock, damage to and the deterioration of property, and hazards to air and ground transportation." Section 1857(a)(2).

The finding in section 1857(a)(2), quoted above, is adequately supported by the legislative history.

A court's review of such a congressional finding is limited. The only questions are whether Congress had a rational basis for finding that air pollution affects commerce, and if it had such a basis, whether the means selected to eliminate the evil are reasonable and appropriate. *Heart of Atlanta Motel, Inc. v. United States,* 379 U.S. 241, 248, 259, 85 S. Ct. 348, 13 L. Ed. 2d 258 (1964); *Katzenbach v. McClung,* 379 U.S. 294, 303, 304, 85 S. Ct. 377, 13 L. Ed. 2d 290 (1964); *Maryland v. Wirtz,* 392 U.S. 183, 88 S. Ct. 2017, 20 L. Ed. 2d 1020 (1968).

Defendant argues that the congressional finding that air pollution has an effect on air and ground transportation is "clearly erroneous", since the legislative history provides only "isolated and insubstantial" interferences with transportation. The power of Congress to regulate activities affecting interstate commerce is to be determined not only by the quantitative effect of individual operations, but also by the total effect of many individual interferences with commerce, *United States v. Darby, supra,* 312 U.S. at 123, 61 S. Ct. 451, and their recurring nature, *Chicago Bd. of Trade v. Olsen,* 262 U.S. 1, 40, 43 S. Ct. 470, 67 L. Ed. 839 (1923).

Defendant next argues that non-visible pollution has no effect upon commerce and consequently Congress has no authority over "odorous pollution."

The complaint recites the following findings of fact made by the Hearing Board:

> "3. The malodorous pollution consists of sickening, nauseating and highly offensive odors which are pervasive in effect to the interstate Selbyville, Delaware–Bishop, Maryland area. Such noxious, malodorous air pollution endangers the health and welfare of persons in the town of Selbyville, Delaware and adjacent and contiguous areas. It causes nausea, sleeplessness, and revulsion, thereby imposing a physiological and psychological burden on persons subjected thereto; and it adversely affects business conditions and property values and impedes industrial development." (Complaint, paragraph II, p. 6).

Paragraph VII of the complaint alleges, inter alia, that "said air pollution is now continuing unabated".

Whether or not the findings of fact made by the Hearing Board will be treated as evidence of the facts so found when this case comes on for trial, the complaint alleges them as facts, and they must be considered to have been admitted by defendant for the purposes of its motion to dismiss.

Malodorous pollution which "adversely affects business conditions and property values and impedes industrial development" would clearly interfere with interstate commerce.

Defendant's argument that there is no economic relationship between the activity regulated and the commerce protected must also fail. As we have seen, Congress undertook to regulate the movement of pollutants across state borders, and it is alleged that those pollutants do interfere with interstate commerce. Hence, the "local activity" (the operation of the rendering plant) is subject to the power of Congress to regulate interstate commerce. In *Heart of Atlanta Motel, Inc. v. United States,* 379 U.S. 241, 258, 85 S. Ct. 348, 358, 13 L. Ed. 2d 258 (1964), the Court said:

> "It is said that the operation of the motel here is of a purely local character. But, assuming this to be true, '[i]f it is interstate commerce that feels the pinch, it does not matter how local the operation which applies the squeeze'. *United States v. Women's Sportswear Mfg. Association,* 336 U.S. 460, 464, 69 S. Ct. 714, 93 L. Ed. 805 (1949)."

The court added:

> " 'The power of Congress over interstate commerce is not confined to the regulation of commerce among the states. It extends to those activities intrastate which so affect interstate commerce or the exercise of the power of Congress over it as to make regulation of them appropriate means to the attainment of a legitimate end, the exercise of the granted power of Congress to regulate interstate commerce. See *McCulloch v. Maryland,* 4 Wheat. 316, 421, 4 L. Ed. 579.' 312 U.S. at 118, 61 S. Ct. at 459.
>
> "Thus the power of Congress to promote interstate commerce also includes the power to regulate the local incidents thereof, including local activities in both the States of origin and destination, which might have a substantial and harmful effect upon that commerce." 379 U.S. at 258, 85 S. Ct. at 358.

Congress had a rational basis for finding that air pollution affects commerce, and the means selected by Congress to eliminate the harmful effects of the interstate movement of air pollutants are reasonable and appropriate.

NOTE: OTHER SOURCES OF FEDERAL POWER

There are also other sources of authority for federal action to be found in the Constitution.

(1) *Admiralty power.* Article 3, Section 2, of the Constitution extends the judicial power of the federal government to "all Cases of admiralty and maritime Jurisdiction." Although this does not amount by its terms to a grant of legislative power to Congress, such a construction has been placed upon it. The admiralty power is distinct from the power over navigable water under the commerce clause, but may be sufficient to authorize federal action in such areas as oil-spill prevention or size of ships.

(2) *Tax.* The power of Congress under Article 1, Section 8, to "lay and collect Taxes" may be a basis on which to legislate so as to completely discourage environmentally offensive behavior, if such taxes do not violate other constitutional guarantees, or to authorize legislation for effluent charges or other methods of cost internalization.

(3) *Federal property.* Article 4, Section 3, of the Constitution provides that "the Congress shall have power to dispose of and make all needful Rules and Regulations respecting the Territory or other Property belonging to the United States . . . ." Congress thus is empowered to make laws enhancing or preserving the environment of federal lands.

(4) *Treaty power.* Article 2, Section 2, gives to the President the power to make treaties with the concurrence of the Senate, and Article 6 makes such treaties the supreme law of the land, along with laws passed to implement them. This power has been held to justify laws protecting migratory birds although an earlier statute on the same subject, not based on a treaty, was held unconstitutional. See *Missouri v. Holland,* 252 U.S. 416 (1920).

QUESTIONS FOR DISCUSSION

1 Is there any limit to the federal government's power to regulate in the environmental area?
2 Suggest a business which does not have an effect on interstate commerce sufficient to be within the scope of the commerce power.
3 Is a conclusion that Congress had a "rational basis" for finding an effect on interstate commerce an adequate basis for a court to make a constitutional ruling?
4 Is the movement of pollutants commerce?
5 Is the opinion more convincing on defendant's ground a or b?
6 Does a reasonable construction of the commerce clause allow the argument that the total effect of a number of separate incidents which individually have no effect on interstate commerce may be the subject of federal regulation under this power?
7 Is the decision centered on the argument that pollutants crossing state lines are in commerce or that they affect commerce?
8 Is a "substantial *and* harmful" effect required?

STATE POWERS AND PREEMPTION

One of the most politically intriguing questions in environmental law is the extent of state government authority in areas where the federal government has acted or could act. In *Huron Portland Cement Company v. City of Detroit* the issue of a state subdivision's authority to abate air pollution from ships in interstate commerce, operating under federal license, is squarely addressed.

Huron Portland Cement Company v. City of Detroit

362 U.S. 440 (1960)

Mr. Justice Stewart delivered the opinion of the Court.

This appeal from a judgment of the Supreme Court of Michigan draws in question the constitutional validity of certain provisions of Detroit's Smoke Abatement Code as applied to ships owned by the appellant and operated in interstate commerce.

The appellant is a Michigan corporation, engaged in the manufacture and sale of cement. It maintains a fleet of five vessels which it uses to transport cement from its mill in Alpena, Michigan, to distributing plants located in various states bordering the Great Lakes. Two of the ships, the S. S. *Crapo* and the S. S. *Boardman,* are equipped with hand-fired Scotch marine boilers. While these vessels are docked for loading and unloading it is necessary, in order to operate deck machinery, to keep the boilers fired and to clean the fires periodically. When the fires are cleaned, the ship's boiler stacks emit smoke which in density and duration exceeds the maximum standards allowable under the Detroit Smoke Abatement Code. Structural alterations would be required in order to insure compliance with the Code.

Criminal proceedings were instituted in the Detroit Recorder's Court against the appellant and its agents for violations of the city law during periods when the vessels were docked at the Port of Detroit. The appellant brought an action in the State Circuit Court to enjoin the city from further prosecuting the pending litigation in the Recorder's Court, and from otherwise enforcing the smoke ordinance against its vessels, "except where the emission of smoke is caused by the improper firing or the improper use of the equipment upon said vessels." The Circuit Court refused to grant relief, and the Supreme Court of Michigan affirmed, 355 Mich. 227, 93 N.W.2d 888. An appeal was lodged here, and we noted probable jurisdiction, 361 U.S. 806.

In support of the claim that the ordinance cannot constitutionally be applied to appellant's ships, two basic arguments are advanced. First, it is asserted that since the vessels and their equipment, including their boilers, have been inspected, approved and licensed to operate in interstate commerce in accordance with a comprehensive system of regulation enacted by Congress, the City of Detroit may not legislate in such a way as, in effect, to impose additional or inconsistent standards. Secondly, the argument is made that even if Congress has not expressly pre-empted the field, the municipal ordinance "materially affects interstate commerce in matters where uniformity is necessary." We have concluded that neither of these contentions can prevail, and that the Federal Constitution does not prohibit application to the appellant's vessels of the criminal provisions of the Detroit ordinance.[1]

The ordinance was enacted for the manifest purpose of promoting the health and welfare of the city's inhabitants. Legislation designed to free from pollution the very air that people breathe clearly falls within the exercise of even the most traditional concept of what is compendiously known as the police power. In the exercise of that power, the states and their instrumentalities may act, in many areas of interstate commerce and maritime activities, concurrently with the federal government. *Gibbons v. Ogden*, 9 Wheat. 1; *Cooley v. Board of Wardens of Port of Philadelphia*, 12 How. 299; *The Steamboat New York v. Rea*, 18 How. 223; *Morgan v. Louisiana*, 118 U.S. 455; The Minnesota Rate Cases, 230 U.S. 352; *Wilmington Transp. Co. v. California Railroad Comm.*, 236 U.S. 151; *Vandalia R. Co. v. Public Service Comm.*, 242 U.S. 255; *Stewart & Co. v. Rivara*, 274 U.S. 614; *Welch Co. v. New Hampshire*, 306 U.S. 79.

The basic limitations upon local legislative power in this area are clear enough. The controlling principles have been reiterated over the years in a host of this Court's decisions. Evenhanded local regulation to effectuate a legitimate local public interest is valid unless preempted by federal action, *Erie R. Co. v. New York*, 233 U.S. 671; *Oregon-Washington Co. v. Washington*, 270 U.S. 87; *Napier v. Atlantic Coast Line*, 272 U.S. 605; *Missouri Pacific Co. v. Porter*, 273 U.S. 341; *Service Transfer Co. v. Virginia*, 359 U.S. 171, or unduly burdensome on maritime activities or interstate commerce, *Minnesota v. Barber*, 136 U.S. 313; *Morgan v. Virginia*, 328 U.S. 373; *Bibb v. Navajo Freight Lines*, 359 U.S. 520.

In determining whether state regulation has been preempted by federal action, "the intent to supersede the exercise by the State of its police power as to matters not covered by the Federal legislation is not to be inferred from the mere fact that Congress has seen fit to circumscribe its regulation and to occupy a limited field. In other words, such intent is not to be implied unless the act of Congress fairly interpreted is in actual conflict with the law of the State." *Savage v. Jones*, 225 U.S. 501, 533. See also *Reid v. Colorado*, 187 U.S. 137; *Asbell v. Kansas*, 209 U.S. 251; *Welch Co. v. New Hampshire*, 306 U.S. 79; *Maurer v. Hamilton*, 309 U.S. 598.

In determining whether the state has imposed an undue burden on interstate commerce, it must be borne in mind that the Constitution when "conferring upon Congress the regulation of commerce, . . . never intended to cut the States off from legislating on all subjects relating to the health, life, and safety of their citizens, though the legislation might indirectly affect the commerce of the country. Legis-

---

[1] The Detroit legislation also contains provisions making it unlawful to operate any combustion equipment in the city without a certificate, § 2.16, providing for an annual inspection of all such equipment used in the city, § 2.17, and further providing for the sealing of equipment in the event that the inspection requirements are repeatedly ignored, § 2.20. There is nothing in the record to indicate that the city has at any time attempted to enforce these provisions with respect to the appellant's ships. Accordingly, we do not reach the question of the validity of the inspection sections as they might be applied to appellant, but limit our consideration solely to what is presented upon this record—the enforcement of the criminal provisions of the Code for violation of the smoke emission provisions.

lation, in a great variety of ways, may affect commerce and persons engaged in it without constituting a regulation of it, within the meaning of the Constitution." *Sherlock v. Alling,* 93 U.S. 99, 103; *Austin v. Tennessee,* 179 U.S. 343; *Louisville & Nashville R. Co. v. Kentucky,* 183 U.S. 503; The Minnesota Rate Cases, 230 U.S. 352; *Boston & Maine R. Co. v. Armburg,* 285 U.S. 234; *Collins v. American Buslines, Inc.,* 350 U.S. 528. But a state may not impose a burden which materially affects interstate commerce in an area where uniformity of regulation is necessary. *Hall v. DeCuir,* 95 U.S. 485; *Southern Pacific Co. v. Arizona,* 325 U.S. 761; *Bibb v. Navajo Freight Lines,* 359 U.S. 520.

Although verbal generalizations do not of their own motion decide concrete cases, it is nevertheless within the framework of these basic principles that the issues in the present case must be determined.

I

For many years Congress has maintained an extensive and comprehensive set of controls over ships and shipping. Federal inspection of steam vessels was first required in 1838, 5 Stat. 304, and the requirement has been continued ever since. 5 Stat. 626; 10 Stat. 61; 14 Stat. 227; 16 Stat. 440; 22 Stat. 346; 28 Stat. 699; 32 Stat. 34; 34 Stat. 68; 60 Stat. 1097; 73 Stat. 475. Steam vessels which carry passengers must pass inspection annually, 46 U.S.C. § 391(a), and those which do not, every two years. 46 U.S.C. § 391(b). Failure to meet the standards invoked by law results in revocation of the inspection certificate, or refusal to issue a new one, 46 U.S.C. § 391(d). It is unlawful for a vessel to operate without such a certificate. 46 U.S.C. § 390c(a).

These inspections are broad in nature, covering "the boilers, unfired pressure vessels, and appurtenances thereof, also the propelling and auxiliary machinery, electrical apparatus and equipment, of all vessels subject to inspection . . . ." 46 U.S.C. § 392(b). The law provides that "No boiler . . . shall be allowed to be used if constructed in whole or in part of defective material or which because of its form, design, workmanship, age, use, or for any other reason is unsafe." 46 U.S.C. § 392(c).

As is apparent on the face of the legislation, however, the purpose of the federal inspection statutes is to insure the seagoing safety of vessels subject to inspection. Thus 46 U.S.C. § 392(c) makes clear that inspection of boilers and related equipment is for the purpose of seeing to it that the equipment "may be safely employed in the service proposed." The safety of passengers, 46 U.S.C. § 391(a), and of the crew, 46 U.S.C. § 391(b), is the criterion. The thrust of the federal inspection laws is clearly limited to affording protection from the perils of maritime navigation. Cf. *Ace Waterways v. Fleming,* 98 F. Supp. 666. See also *Steamship Co. v. Joliffe,* 2 Wall. 450.

By contrast, the sole aim of the Detroit ordinance is the elimination of air pollution to protect the health and enhance the cleanliness of the local community. Congress recently recognized the importance and legitimacy of such a purpose, when in 1955 it provided:

"[I]n recognition of the dangers to the public health and welfare, injury to agricultural crops and livestock, damage to and deterioration of property, and hazards to air and ground transportation, from air pollution, it is hereby declared to be the policy of Congress to preserve and protect the primary responsibilities and rights of the States and local governments in controlling air pollution, to support and aid technical research to devise and develop methods of abating such pollution, and to provide Federal technical services and financial aid to State and local government air pollution control agencies and other public or private agencies and institutions in the formulation and execution of their air pollution abatement research programs." 69 Stat. 322; 42 U.S.C. § 1857.

Congressional recognition that the problem of air pollution is peculiarly a matter of state and local concern is manifest in this legislation. Such recognition is underlined in the Senate Committee Report:

"The committee recognizes that it is the primary responsibility of State and local governments to prevent air pollution. The bill does not propose any exercise of police power by the Federal Government and no provision in it invades the sovereignty of States, counties or cities." S. Rep. No. 389, 84th Cong., 1st Sess. 3.

We conclude that there is no overlap between the scope of the federal ship inspection laws and that of the municipal ordinance here involved.[2] For this reason we cannot find that the federal inspection legislation has pre-empted local action. To hold otherwise would be to ignore the teaching of this Court's decisions which enjoin seeking out conflicts between state and federal regulation where none clearly exists. *Savage v. Jones,* 225 U.S. 501; *Welch Co. v. New Hampshire,* 306 U.S. 79; *Maurer v. Hamilton,* 309 U.S. 598.

An additional argument is advanced, however, based not upon the mere existence of the federal inspection standards, but upon the fact that the appellant's vessels were actually licensed, 46 U.S.C. § 263, and enrolled, 46 U.S.C. §§ 259–260, by the national government. It is asserted that the vessels have thus been given a dominant federal right to the use of the navigable waters of the United States, free from the local impediment that would be imposed by the Detroit ordinance.

The scope of the privilege granted by the federal licensing scheme has been well delineated. A state may not exclude from its waters a ship operating under a federal license. *Gibbons v. Ogden,* 9 Wheat. 1. A state may not require a local occupation license, in addition to that federally granted, as a condition precedent to the use of its waters. *Moran v. New Orleans,* 112 U.S. 69. While an enrolled and licensed vessel may be required to share the costs of benefits it enjoys, *Huse v. Glover,* 119 U.S. 543, and to pay fair taxes imposed by its domicile, *Transportation Co. v. Wheeling,* 99 U.S. 273, it cannot be subjected to local license imposts exacted for the use of a navigable waterway, *Harman v. Chicago,* 147 U.S. 396. See also *Sinnot v. Davenport,* 22 How. 227.

---

[2] Compare, *Napier v. Atlantic Coast Line R. Co.,* where the Court concluded that "the [Locomotive] Boiler Inspection . . . was intended to occupy the field." 272 U.S. 605, 613.

The mere possession of a federal license, however, does not immunize a ship from the operation of the normal incidents of local police power, not constituting a direct regulation of commerce. Thus, a federally licensed vessel is not, as such, exempt from local pilotage laws, *Cooley v. Board of Wardens of Port of Philadelphia,* 12 How. 299, or local quarantine laws, *Morgan's Steamship Co. v. Louisiana Board of Health,* 118 U.S. 455, or local safety inspections, *Kelly v. Washington,* 302 U.S. 1, or the local regulation of wharves and docks, *Packet Co. v. Catlettsburg,* 105 U.S. 559. Indeed this Court has gone so far as to hold that a state, in the exercise of its police power, may actually seize and pronounce the forfeiture of a vessel "licensed for the coasting trade, under the laws of the United States, while engaged in that trade." *Smith v. Maryland,* 18 How. 71, 74. The present case obviously does not even approach such an extreme, for the Detroit ordinance requires no more than compliance with an orderly and reasonable scheme of community regulation. The ordinance does not exclude a licensed vessel from the Port of Detroit, nor does it destroy the right of free passage. We cannot hold that the local regulation so burdens the federal license as to be constitutionally invalid.

II

The claim that the Detroit ordinance, quite apart from the effect of federal legislation, imposes as to the appellant's ships an undue burden on interstate commerce needs no discussion. State regulation, based on the police power, which does not discriminate against interstate commerce or operate to disrupt its required uniformity, may constitutionally stand. *Hennington v. Georgia,* 163 U.S. 299; *Lake Shore & Mich. South. R. Co. v. Ohio,* 173 U.S. 285; *Pennsylvania Gas Co. v. Public Service Comm.,* 252 U.S. 23; *Milk Board v. Eisenberg Co.,* 306 U.S. 346; *Bob-Lo Excursion Co. v. Michigan,* 333 U.S. 28.

It has not been suggested that the local ordinance, applicable alike to "any person, firm or corporation" within the city, discriminates against interstate commerce as such. It is a regulation of general application, designed to better the health and welfare of the community. And while the appellant argues that other local governments might impose differing requirements as to air pollution, it has pointed to none. The record contains nothing to suggest the existence of any such competing or conflicting local regulations. Cf. *Bibb v. Navajo Freight Lines,* 359 U.S. 520. We conclude that no impermissible burden on commerce has been shown.

The judgment is affirmed.

DISSENT

Mr. Justice Douglas, with whom **Mr. Justice Frankfurter** concurs, dissenting.

The Court treats this controversy as if it were merely an inspection case with the City of Detroit supplementing a federal inspection system as the State of Washington did in *Kelly v. Washington,* 302 U.S. 1. There a state inspection system touched matters "which the federal laws and regulations" left "untouched." Id., at 13. This is not that type of case. Nor is this the rare case where state law adopts the standards and requirements of federal law and is allowed to exact a permit in addition to the one demanded by federal law. *California v. Zook,* 336 U.S. 725, 735. Here we have a criminal prosecution against a shipowner and officers of two of its vessels for using the very equipment on these vessels which the Federal Government says may be used. At stake are a possible fine of $100 on the owner and both a fine and a 30-day jail sentence on the officers.

Appellant has a federal certificate for each of its vessels—S. S. John W. Boardman, S. S. S. T. Crapo, and others. The one issued on March 21, 1956, by the United States Coast Guard for S. S. S. T. Crapo is typical. The certificate states "The said vessel is permitted to be navigated for one year on the Great Lakes." The certificate specifies the boilers which are and may be used—"Main Boilers Number 3, Year built 1927, Mfr. Manitowoc Boiler Wks." It also specifies the fuel which is used and is to be used in those boilers—"Fuel coal."

Appellant, operating the vessel in waters at the Detroit dock, is about to be fined criminally for using the precise equipment covered by the federal certificate because, it is said, the use of that equipment will violate a smoke ordinance of the City of Detroit.

The federal statutes give the Coast Guard the power to inspect "the boilers" of freight vessels every two years,[1] and provide that when the Coast Guard approves the vessel and her equipment throughout, a certificate to that effect shall be made.[2]

The requirements of the Detroit smoke ordinance are squarely in conflict with the federal statute. Section 2.2A of the ordinance prohibits the emission of the kind of smoke which cannot be at all times prevented by vessels equipped with hand-fired Scotch marine boilers such as appellant's vessels use. Section 2.16 of the ordinance makes it unlawful to use any furnace or other combustion equipment or device in the city without a certificate of operation which issues only after inspection. Section 2.17 provides for an annual inspection of every furnace or other combustion equipment used within the city. Section 2.20 provides that if an owner has been previously notified of three or more violations of the ordinance within any consecutive 12-month period he shall be notified to show cause before the Commissioner why the equipment should not be sealed. At the hearing, if the Commissioner finds that adequate corrective means have not been employed to remedy the situation, the equipment shall be sealed. Section 3.2 provides for a fine of not more than $100 or imprisonment for not more than 30 days or both upon conviction of any violation of any provision of the ordinance, and each day a violation is permitted to exist constitutes a separate offense.

Thus it is plain that the ordinance requires not only the inspection and approval of equipment which has been inspected and approved by the Coast Guard but also the sealing of equipment, even though it has been approved by the Coast

---

[1] Omitted.
[2] Omitted.

Guard. Under the Detroit ordinance a certificate of operation would not issue for a hand-fired Scotch marine boiler, even though it had been approved by the Coast Guard.[3] In other words, this equipment approved and licensed by the Federal Government for use on navigable waters cannot pass muster under local law.

If local law required federally licensed vessels to observe local speed laws, obey local traffic regulations, or dock at certain times or under prescribed conditions, we would have local laws not at war with the federal license, but complementary to it. In *Kelly v. Washington, supra,* at 14-15, the Court marked precisely that distinction. While it allowed state inspection of hull and machinery of tugs over and above that required by federal statutes, it noted that state rules which changed the federal standards "for the structure and equipment of vessels" would meet a different fate:

> "The state law is a comprehensive code. While it excepts vessels which are subject to inspection under the laws of the United States, it has provisions which may be deemed to fall within the class of regulations which Congress alone can provide. For example, Congress may establish standards and designs for the structure and equipment of vessels, and may prescribe rules for their operation, which could not properly be left to the diverse action of the States. The State of Washington might prescribe standards, designs, equipment and rules of one sort, Oregon another, California another, and so on. But it does not follow that in all respects the state Act must fail."

This case, like *Napier v. Atlantic Coast Line R. Co.,* 272 U.S. 605, involves the collision between a local law and a federal law which gives a federal agency the power to specify or approve the equipment to be used by a federal licensee. In that case one State required automatic fire doors on locomotives of interstate trains and another State required cab curtains during the winter months. The Interstate Commerce Commission, though it had the power to do so under the Boiler Inspection Act, had never required a particular kind of fire door or cab curtain. The Court, speaking through Mr. Justice Brandeis, said, at 612-613:

> "The federal and the state statutes are directed to the same subject—the equipment of locomotives. They operate upon the same object. It is suggested that the power delegated to the Commission has been exerted only in respect to minor changes or additions. But this, if true, is not of legal significance. It is also urged that, even if the

---

[3] The trial court in its opinion said: "It is agreed that it is impossible to prevent emission of the kind of smoke prohibited by the smoke ordinance if the vessel is equipped with hand-fired Scotch marine boilers. The Boardman has two boilers each with two doors and one steam air jet over each door. The Crapo has three boilers, each with two doors and one steam air jet over each door. The steam jets being installed at the suggestion of Benjamin Linsky, former Chief of the Bureau of Smoke Abatement for the City.

"Testimony showed also that the plaintiff used a chemical in an attempt to reduce the smoke. Plaintiff urges it has done everything that it could possibly do with the equipment it has to prevent the emission of smoke. It was shown on trial that the fleet is subject to periodic inspection by the coast guard, which issues a search [sic] of inspection. The Crapo in 1955, docked at Detroit twenty-two times for an average docking of 23.9 hours and the Boardman docked at Detroit 25 times that year with an average stay of 16.2 hours. Both vessels were constantly engaged in interstate and foreign commerce during this period."

Commission has power to prescribe an automatic firebox door and a cab curtain, it has not done so; and that it has made no other requirement inconsistent with the state legislation. This, also, if true, is without legal significance. The fact that the Commission has not seen fit to exercise its authority to the full extent conferred, has no bearing upon the construction of the Act delegating the power. We hold that state legislation is precluded, because the Boiler Inspection Act, as we construe it, was intended to occupy the field."

Here the Coast Guard would be entitled to insist on different equipment. But it has not done so. The boats of appellant, therefore, have credentials good for any port; and I would not allow this local smoke ordinance to work in derogation of them. The fact that the Federal Government in certifying equipment applies standards of safety for seagoing vessels, while Detroit applies standards of air pollution seems immaterial. Federal pre-emption occurs when the boilers and fuel to be used in the vessels are specified in the certificate. No state authority can, in my view, change those specifications. Yet that is in effect what is allowed here.

As we have seen, the Detroit ordinance contains provisions making it unlawful to operate appellant's equipment without a certificate from the city and providing for the sealing of the equipment in case of three or more violations within any 12-month period. The Court says that those sanctions are not presently in issue, that it reserves decision as to their validity, and that it concerns itself only with "the enforcement of the criminal provisions" of the ordinance. Yet by what authority can a local government fine people or send them to jail for using in interstate commerce the precise equipment which the federal regulatory agency has certified and approved? The burden of these criminal sanctions on the owners and officers, particularly as it involves the risk of imprisonment, may indeed be far more serious than a mere sealing of the equipment. Yet whether fine or imprisonment is considered, the effect on the federal certificate will be crippling. However the issue in the present case is stated it comes down to making criminal in the Port of Detroit the use of a certificate issued under paramount federal law. *Mintz v. Baldwin,* 289 U.S. 346, upheld the requirement of a state inspection certificate where a federal certificate might have been, but was not, issued. Cf. *California v. Thompson,* 313 U.S. 109, 112. Never before, I believe, have we recognized the right of local law to make the use of an unquestionably legal federal license a criminal offense.

What we do today is disregard of the doctrine long accepted and succinctly stated in the 1851 Term in *Pennsylvania v. Wheeling & Belmont Bridge Co.,* 13 How. 518, 566, "No State law can hinder or obstruct the free use of a license granted under an act of Congress."[4] The confusion and burden arising from the

[4] *Smith v. Maryland,* 18 How. 71, is not to the contrary. There a vessel enrolled under the laws of the United States was allowed to be forfeited by Maryland for dredging for oysters in violation of Maryland law. But the enrollment of vessels serves only a limited purpose. *Smith v. Maryland, supra,* was explained in *Stewart & Co. v. Rivara,* 274 U.S. 614. The Court said, "The purpose of the enrollment of vessels is to give to them the privileges of American vessels as well as the protection of our flag." Id., at 618. Enrollment without more did not give the enrolled vessel a license to disregard the variety of pilotage, health and other such local laws which the opinion of the Court in the famous case

imposition by one State of requirements for equipment which the Federal Government has approved was emphasized in *Kelly v. Washington, supra,* in the passage already quoted. The requirements of Detroit may be too lax for another port. Cf. *People v. Cunard White Star, Ltd.,* 280 N.Y. 413, 21 N.E.2d 489. The variety of requirements for equipment which the States may provide in order to meet their air pollution needs underlines the importance of letting the Coast Guard license serve as authority for the vessel to use, in all our ports, the equipment which it certifies.

QUESTIONS FOR DISCUSSION

1 Would the Court's decision have been different if the vessels were merely passing by in the harbor and not docked?
2 What constitutes federal preemption of an area?
3 To what extent may a police-power regulation affect interstate commerce?
4 Does prior federal action indicate an attempt to preempt the field?
5 Does the court here attempt to distinguish between a present and a potential conflict? Is such a distinction a valid ground for upholding the state law? Does it merely postpone the inevitable?

In *Askew v. American Waterways Operators* the preemption issue is examined in the context of water pollution and navigation, areas traditionally in the federal realm. Note that the problem arises in Florida, a state particularly susceptible to economic loss from oil spills.

Askew v. American Waterways Operators

411 U.S. 325 (1973)

Mr. Justice Douglas delivered the opinion of the court.

This action was brought by merchant shippers, world shipping associations, members of the Florida coastal barge and towing industry and owners and operators of oil terminal facilities and heavy industries located in Florida, to enjoin application of the Florida Oil Spill Prevention and Pollution Control Act, L. Fla. 1970, c. 70-244 (hereafter referred to as the Florida Act). Officials responsible for enforc-

---

of *Cooley v. Board of Port Wardens,* 12 How. 299 (written by Mr. Justice Curtis who also wrote for the Court in *Smith v. Maryland*), had left to the States to be obeyed by all vessels. The local regulations approved in the Cooley case never qualified the license to ply as a vessel nor penalized its movement on navigable waters. The federal license in the instant case, however, specifically describes the only equipment and fuel which these vessels are allowed to use, and Detroit is permitted to make their use criminal.

ing the Florida Act were named as defendants, but the State of Florida intervened as a party defendant, asserting that her interests were much broader than those of the named defendants. A three-judge court was convened pursuant to 28 U.S.C. § 2281.

The Florida Act imposes strict liability for any damage incurred by the State or private persons as a result of an oil spill in the State's territorial waters from any waterfront facility used for drilling oil or handling the transfer or storage of oil ("terminal facility") and from any ship destined for or leaving such facility. Each owner or operator of a terminal facility or ship subject to the Act must establish evidence of financial responsibility by insurance or a surety bond. In addition, the Florida Act provides for regulation by the State Department of Natural Resources with respect to containment gear and other equipment which must be maintained by ships and terminal facilities for the prevention of oil spills.

Several months prior to the enactment of the Florida Act, Congress enacted the Water Quality Improvement Act of 1970, 33 U.S.C. § 1161 et seq. (hereinafter referred to as the Federal Act). This Act subjects ship owners and terminal facilities to liability without fault up to $14,000,000 and $8,000,000, respectively, for cleanup costs incurred by the Federal Government as a result of oil spills. It also authorizes the President to promulgate regulations requiring ships and terminal facilities to maintain equipment for the prevention of oil spills. It is around that Act and the federally protected tenets of maritime law evidenced by *Southern Pacific Co. v. Jensen,* 244 U.S. 205, and its progeny that the controversy turns. The District Court held that the Florida Act is an unconstitutional intrusion into the federal maritime domain. It declared the Florida Act null and void and enjoined its enforcement. 335 F. Supp. 1241.

The case is here on direct appeal. We reverse. We find no constitutional or statutory impediment in permitting Florida, in the present setting of this case, to establish any "requirement or liability" concerning the impact of oil spillages on Florida's interests or concerns. To rule as the District Court has done is to allow federal admiralty jurisdiction to swallow most of the police power of the States over oil-spillage—an insidious form of pollution of vast concern to every coastal city or port and to all the estuaries on which the life of the ocean and the lives of the coastal people are greatly dependent.

I

It is clear at the outset that the Federal Act does not preclude but in fact allows state regulation. Section 1161(o) provides that:

> "(1) Nothing in this section shall affect or modify in any way the obligations of any owner or operator of any vessel, or of any owner or operator of any onshore facility or offshore facility to any person or agency under any provision of law for damages to any publicly-owned or privately-owned property resulting from a discharge of any oil or from the removal of any such oil.

"(2) Nothing in this section shall be construed as pre-empting any State or political subdivision thereof from imposing any requirement or liability with respect to the discharge of oil into any waters within such state.

"(3) Nothing in this section shall be construed . . . to affect any State or local law not in conflict with this section."

According to the Conference Report, "any State would be free to provide requirements and penalties similar to those imposed by this section or additional requirements and penalties. These, however, would be separate and independent from those imposed by this section and would be enforced by the States through its courts." The Florida Act covers a wide range of "pollutants," § 3(7), and a restricted definition of pollution. § 3(8). We have here, however, no question concerning any pollutant except oil.

The Federal Act, to be sure, contains a pervasive system of federal control over discharges of oil "into or upon the navigable waters of the United States adjoining shorelines, or into or upon the waters of the contiguous zone." § 1161(b)(1). So far as liability is concerned, an owner or operator of a vessel is liable to the United States for actual costs incurred for the removal of oil discharged in violation of § 1161(b)(2) in an amount "not to exceed $100 per gross ton of such vessel, or $14,000,000 whichever is lesser," § 1161(f)(1), except for discharges caused solely by an act of God, act of war, negligence of the United States or act or omission of another party. With like exceptions the owner or operator of an onshore or offshore facility is liable to the United States for the actual costs incurred by the United States in an amount not to exceed $8,000,000. § 1161(f)(2-3). But in each case the owner or operator is liable to the United States for the full amount of the costs where the United States can show that the discharge of oil was "the result of willful negligence or willful misconduct within the privity and knowledge of the owner." Comparable provisions of liability spell out the obligations of "a third party" to the United States for its actual costs incurred for the removal of the oil. § 1161(g).

So far as vessels are concerned the Federal Limitation of Liability Act, 46 U.S.C. §§ 181–189, extends to damages caused by oil spills even where the injury is to the shore. *Richardson v. Harmon*, 222 U.S. 96, 106. That Act limits the liabilities of the owners of vessels to the "value of such vessels and freight pending." 46 U.S.C. § 189.

Section 12 of the Florida Act makes all licensees of terminal facilities "liable to the state for all terminal facilities, liable to the state for all costs of cleanup or other damage incurred by the State and for damages resulting from injury to others," it not being necessary for the State to plead or prove negligence. There is no conflict between § 12 of the Florida Act and § 1161 of the Federal Act when it comes to damages, to property interests, for the Federal Act reaches only costs of cleaning up. As respects damages, § 14 of the Florida Act requires evidence of financial responsibility of a terminal facility or vessel—provisions which do not conflict with the Federal Act.

The Solicitor General says that while the Limitation of Liability Act, so far as vessels are concerned, would override § 12 of the Florida Act by reason of the Supremacy Clause, the Limitation of Liability Act has no bearing on "facilities" regulated by the Florida Act. Moreover, § 12 has not yet been construed by the Florida courts and it is susceptible of an interpretation so far as vessels are concerned which would be in harmony with the Federal Act. Section 12 does not in terms provide for unlimited liability.

Moreover, while the Federal Act determines damages measured by the cost to the United States for cleaning up oil pollution, the damages specified in the Florida Act relate in part to the cost to the State of Florida in cleaning up the spillage. Those two sections are harmonious parts of an integrated whole. Section 1161(c)(2) directs the President to prepare a National Contingency for the containment, dispersal and removal of oil. The plan must provide that federal agencies "shall" act "in coordination with State and local agencies." Cooperative action with the States is also contemplated by § 1161(e), which provides that "[i]n addition to any other action taken by a State or local government" the President may, when there is an imminent and substantial threat to the public health or welfare, direct the United States Attorney of the district in question to bring suit to abate the threat. The reason for the provision in § 1161(o)(2) stating that nothing in § 1161 pre-empts any State "from imposing any requirement or liability with respect to the discharge of oil into any waters within such State" is that the scheme of the Act is one which allows—though it does not require—cooperation of the federal regime with a state regime.

If Florida wants to take the lead in cleaning up oil spillage in her waters, she can use § 12 of the Florida Act and recoup her costs from those who did the damage. Whether the amount of costs she could recover from a wrongdoer are limited to those specified in the Federal Act and whether in turn this new Federal Act removes the pre-existing limitations of liability in the Limitation of Liability Act are questions we need not reach here. Any opinion on them is premature. It is sufficient for this day to hold that there is room for state action in cleaning up the waters of a State and recouping, at least within federal limits so far as vessels are concerned, her costs.

Beyond that is the potential claim under § 12 of the Florida Act for "other damage incurred by the state and for damage resulting from injury to others." The Federal Act in no way touches those areas. A State may have public beaches ruined by oil spills. Shrimp, clam, oyster, and scallop beds may be ruined and the livelihood of fishermen imperiled. The Federal Act takes no cognizance of those claims but only of costs to the Federal Government, if it does the cleaning-up.

We held in *Skiriotes v. Florida,* 313 U.S. 69, that while Congress had regulated the size of commercial sponges taken in Florida waters, it had not dealt with any diving apparatus that might be used. Florida had such a law and was allowed to enforce it against one of its citizens. Chief Justice Hughes, speaking for the Court, said: "It is also clear that Florida has an interest in the proper maintenance of the sponge fishing and that the statute so far as applied to conduct within the territorial waters of Florida, in the absence of conflicting federal legislation, is within the police power of the State." Id., at 75.

Similarly, in *Manchester v. Massachusetts,* 139 U.S. 240, 266, we stated that if Congress fails to assume control of fisheries in a bay, "the right to control such fisheries must remain with the State which contains such bays."

Florida in her brief accurately states that no remedy under the Federal Act exists for state or private property owners damaged by a massive oil slick such as hit England and France in 1967 in the Torrey Canyon disaster. The Torrey Canyon carried 880,000 barrels of crude oil. Today not only is more oil being moved by sea each year but the tankers are much larger.

"The average tanker used during World War II had a capacity of 16,000 tons, but by 1965 that average had risen to 27,000 tons, and new tankers delivered in 1966 averaged about 76,000 tons. A Japanese Company has launched a 276,000 ton tanker, and other Japanese yards have orders for tankers as large as 312,000 tons. More than 60 tankers of 150,000 tons or more are on order throughout the world, tankers of 500,000 to 800,000 tons are on the drawing boards, and those of more than one million tons are thought to be feasible. On the new 1,010 foot British tanker 'Esso Mercia' two officers have been issued bicycles to help patrol the decks of the 166,890 ton vessel.

"The size of the tanker fleet itself is growing at a rate that rivals the growth in average size of new tankers. In 1955 the world tanker fleet numbered about 2,500 vessels. By 1965 it had increased to 3,500, and in 1968 it had numbered some 4,300 ships. At the present time nearly one ship out of every five in the world merchant fleet is engaged in transporting oil, and nearly the entire fleet is powered by oil."

Our Coast Guard reports that while in 1970 there were 3,711 oil spills in our waters, in 1971 there were 8,736. The damage to state interests already caused by oil spills, the increase in the number of oil spills, and the risk of ever-increasing damage by reason of the size of modern tankers underlie the concern of coastal States.

While the Federal Act is concerned only with actual clean-up costs incurred by the Federal Government, the State of Florida is concerned with its own clean-up costs. Hence there need be no collison between the Federal Act and the Florida Act because, as noted, the Federal Act presupposes a coordinated effort with the States, and any federal limitation of liability runs to "vessels" not to shore "facilities." That is one of the reasons why the Congress decided that the Federal Act does not pre-empt the States from establishing either "any requirement or liability" respecting oil spills.

Moreover, since Congress dealt only with "clean-up costs," it left the States free to impose "liability" in damages for losses suffered both by the State and by private interests. The Florida Act imposes liability without fault. So far as liability without fault for damages to state and private interests is concerned, the police power has been held adequate for that purpose. State statutes imposing absolute liability on railroads for all property lost through fires caused by sparks emitted from locomotive engines have been sustained. *St. Louis & San Francisco R. Co. v.*

Mathews, 165 U.S. 1. The Federal Act, however, while restricted to clean-up costs incurred by the United States, imposes limited liability for those costs and provides certain exceptions, unless willfulness is established. Where liability is imposed by § 1161(f) to (g), previously summarized, the United States may recover the full amount of the costs where the oil spillage was the result of "willful negligence or willful misconduct." If the coordinated federal plan in actual operation leaves the State of Florida to do the clean-up work, there might be financial burdens imposed greater than would have been imposed had the Federal Government done the clean-up work. But it will be time to resolve any such conflict between federal and state regimes when it arises.

Nor can we say at this point that regulations of the Florida Department of Natural Resources requiring "containment gear" pursuant to § 7(2)(a) of the Florida Act would be per se invalid because the subject to be regulated requires uniform federal regulation. Cf. *Huron Cement Co. v. Detroit,* 362 U.S. 440. Resolution of this question, as well as the question whether such regulations will conflict with Coast Guard regulations promulgated on December 21, 1972, pursuant to § 1161(j)(1) of the Federal Act, 37 CFR § 28250, should await a concrete dispute under applicable Florida regulations. Finally, the provision of the Florida Act requiring the licensing of terminal facilities, a traditional state concern, creates no conflict per se with federal legislation. Section 1171(b)(1) of the Federal Act provides that federal permits will not be issued to terminal facility operators or owners unless the applicant first supplies a certificate from the State that his operation "will be conducted in a manner which will not violate applicable water quality standards." And Tit. I, § 102(b), of the recently enacted Ports and Waterways Safety Act of 1972, Pub. L. 92-340, 86 Stat. 424, provides that the Act does not prevent "a State or political subdivision thereof from prescribing for structures only higher safety equipment requirements or safety standards than those which may be prescribed pursuant to this title."

II

And so, in the absence of federal pre-emption and any fatal conflict between the statutory schemes, the issue comes down to whether a State constitutionally may exercise its police power respecting maritime activities concurrently with the Federal Government.

The main barrier found by the District Court to the Florida Act are *Southern Pacific Co. v. Jensen,* 244 U.S. 205, and its progeny. *Jensen* held a maritime worker on a vessel in navigable waters could not constitutionally receive an award under New York's workmen's compensation law, because the remedy in admiralty was exclusive. Later in *Knickerbocker Ice Co. v. Stewart,* 253 U.S. 149, after Congress expressly allowed the States in such cases to grant a remedy, the Court held that Congress had no such power.

But those decisions have been limited by subsequent holdings of this Court. As stated by Mr. Justice Frankfurter in *Romero v. International Terminal Co.,* 358 U.S. 354, 373, *Jensen* and its progeny mark isolated instances where "state law must yield to the needs of a uniform federal maritime law when the Court finds inroads on a harmonious system." Justice Frankfurter added, however: "But this limitation still leaves the State a wide scope. State-created liens are enforced in admiralty. State remedies for wrongful death and state statutes providing for the survival of actions, both historically absent from the relief offered by the admiralty, have been upheld when applied to maritime causes of action. Federal courts have enforced these statutes. State rules for the partition and sale of ships, state laws governing the specific performance of arbitration agreements, state laws regulating the effect of a breach of warranty under contracts of maritime insurance—all these laws and others have been accepted as rules of decision in admiralty cases, even, at times, when they conflicted with a rule of maritime law which did not require conformity." Id., at 373-374.

Moreover, in *Just v. Chambers,* 312 U.S. 383, we gave our approval to The City of Norwalk, 55 F. 98, written by Judge Addison Brown, holding that a State may modify or supplement maritime law even by creating a liability which a court of admiralty would recognize and enforce, provided the state action is not hostile "to the characteristic features of the maritime law or inconsistent with federal legislation," 312 U.S., at 388. Chief Justice Hughes after citing *Steamboat Co. v. Chase,* 16 Wall. 522, and *Sherlock v. Alling,* 93 U.S. 99, went on to hold that, while no suit for wrongful death would lie in the federal courts under general maritime law, state statutes giving damages in such cases were valid. He said, "The grounds of objection to the admiralty jurisdiction in enforcing liability for wrongful death were similar to those urged here; that is, that the Constitution presupposes a body of maritime law, that this law, as a matter of interstate and international concern, requires harmony in its administration and cannot be subject to defeat or impairment by the diverse legislation of the States, and hence that Congress alone can make any needed changes in the general rules of the maritime law. But these contentions proved unavailing and the principle was maintained that a State, in the exercise of its police power, may establish rules applicable on land and water within its limits, even though these rules incidentally affect maritime affairs, provided that the state action 'does not contravene any acts of Congress, nor work any prejudice to the characteristic features of the maritime law, nor interfere with its proper harmony and uniformity in its international and interstate relations. It was decided that the state legislation encountered none of these objections. The many instances in which state action had created new rights, recognized and enforced in admiralty, were set forth in The City of Norwalk and reference was also made to the numerous local regulations under state authority concerning the navigation of rivers and harbors. There was the further pertinent observation that the maritime law was not a complete and perfect system and that in all maritime countries there is a considerable body of municipal law that underlies the maritime law as the basis of its administration. These views find abundant support in the history of the maritime law and in the decisions of this Court." 312 U.S. 389-390.

Chief Justice Hughes added that our decisions as of 1941, the date of *Just v. Chambers,* gave broad "recognition of the authority of the States to create rights and liabilities with respect to conduct within their borders, when the state action does not run counter to federal laws or the essential features of an exclusive federal jurisdiction." Id., at 391.

Historically, damages to the shore or to shore facilities were not cognizable in admiralty. See, e.g., The Plymouth, 3 Wall. 20; *Martin v. West,* 222 U.S. 191. Justice Story wrote in 1834, "In regard to torts I have always understood that the jurisdiction of the Admiralty is exclusively dependent upon the locality of the act. The Admiralty has not, and never I believe deliberately claimed to have any jurisdiction over torts, except such as are maritime torts, that is, such as are committed on the high seas, or on waters within the ebb and flow of the tide." *Thomas v. Lane,* 2 Summ. 1, 9.

On June 19, 1948, Congress enacted the Admiralty Extension Act, 46 U.S.C. § 740.* The Court considered the Act in *Victory Carriers, Inc. v. Law,* 404 U.S. 202. In that case the Court held that the Admiralty Extension Act did not apply to a longshoreman performing loading and unloading services on the dock. The longshoreman was relegated to his remedy under the state workmen's compensation law. Id., at 215. The Court said, "At least in the absence of explicit congressional authorization, we shall not extend the historic boundaries of the maritime law." Id., at 214.

The Admiralty Extension Act has survived constitutional attack in the lower federal courts and was applied without question by this Court in *Gutierrez v. Waterman S. S. Corp.,* 373 U.S. 206 (1963). The Court recognized in *Victory Carriers,* however, that the Act may "intrude on an area that has heretofore been reserved for state law." Id., at 212. It cautioned that under these circumstances, "we should proceed with caution in construing constitutional and statutory provisions dealing with the jurisdiction of the federal courts." Ibid. While Congress has extended admiralty jurisdiction beyond the boundaries contemplated by the Framers, it hardly follows from the constitutionality of that extension that we must sanctify the federal courts with exclusive jurisdiction to the exclusion of powers traditionally within the competence of the States. One can read the history of the Admiralty Extension Act without finding any clear indication that Congress intended that sea-to-shore injuries could be exclusively triable in the federal courts.

Even though Congress has acted in the admiralty area, state regulation is permissible, absent a clear conflict with the federal law. Thus in *Kelly v. Washington,* 302 U.S. 1, it appeared that, while Congress had provided a comprehensive system of inspection of vessels on the navigable water, id., at 4, the State of Washington also had a comprehensive code of inspection. Some of those state standards conflicted with the federal requirements, id., at 14–15; but those provisions of the Washington law relating to safety and seaworthiness were not in conflict with the federal law. So the question was whether the absence of congres-

---

* It provides in relevant part: "The admiralty and maritime jurisdiction of the United States shall extend to and include all cases of damage or injury, to person or property, caused by a vessel on navigable water, notwithstanding that such damage or injury be done or consummated on land." [Other footnotes in this case have been omitted.]

sional action and the need for uniformity of regulation barred state action. Chief Justice Hughes, writing for the Court, ruled in the negative, saying:

> "A vessel which is actually unsafe and unseaworthy in the primary and commonly understood sense is not within the protection of that principle. The State may treat it as it may treat a diseased animal or unwholesome food. In such a matter, the State may protect its people without waiting for federal action providing the state action does not come into conflict with federal rules. If, however, the State goes farther and attempts to impose particular standards as to structure, design, equipment and operation which in the judgment of its authorities may be desirable but pass beyond what is plainly essential to safety and seaworthiness, the State will encounter the principle that such requirements, if imposed at all, must be through the Action of Congress which can establish a uniform rule. Whether the State in a particular matter goes too far must be left to be determined when the precise question arises." Id., at 15.

That decision was rendered before the Admiralty Extension Act was passed. *Huron Cement Co. v. Detroit, supra,* however, arose after that Act became effective. Ships cruising navigable waters and inspected and licensed under federal acts were charged with violating Detroit's Smoke Abatement Code. The company and its agents were indeed criminally charged with violating that Code. The Court in sustaining the state prosecution said:

> "The ordinance was enacted for the manifest purpose of promoting the health and welfare of the city's inhabitants. Legislation designed to free from pollution the very air that people breathe clearly falls within the exercise of even the most traditional concept of what is compendiously known as the police power. In the exercise of that power, the states and their instrumentalities may act, in many areas of interstate commerce and maritime activities, concurrently with the federal government." 362 U.S., at 442.

The Court reasoned that there was room for local control since federal inspection was "limited to affording protection from the perils of maritime navigation," while the Detroit ordinance was aimed at "the elimination of air pollution to protect the health and enhance the cleanliness of the local community." Id., at 445. The Court, in reviewing prior decisions, noted that a federally licensed vessel was not exempt (1) "from local pilotage laws"; (2) "local quarantine laws"; (3) "local safety inspections"; or (4) "local regulations of wharves and docks." Id., at 447.

It follows a fortiori that sea-to-shore pollution—historically within the reach of the police power of the State—is not silently taken away from the States by the Admiralty Extension Act, which does not purport to supply the exclusive remedy.

As discussed above, we cannot say with certainty at this stage that the Florida Act conflicts with any federal act. We have only the question whether the waiver of pre-emption by Congress in § 1161(o)(2) concerning the imposition by a State of "any requirement or liability" is valid.

It is valid unless the rule of Jensen and Knickerbocker Ice is to engulf everything that Congress chose to call "admiralty," pre-empting state action. Jensen and Knickerbocker Ice have been confined to their facts, viz. to suits relating to the relationship of vessels, plying the high seas and our navigable waters, to their crews. The fact that a whole system of liabilities was established on the basis of those two cases, led us years ago to establish the "twilight zone" where state regulation was permissible. See *Davis v. Department of Labor*, 317 U.S. 249, 252–253. Where there was a hearing by a federal agency that the case fell within the federal jurisdiction, we made its findings final. Ibid. Where there were no such findings, we presumed state law, in terms applicable, was constitutional. Id., at 257–258. That is the way the "twilight zone" has been defined.

Jensen thus has vitality left. But we decline to move the Jensen line of cases shoreward to oust state law from any situations involving shoreside injuries by ships on navigable waters. The Admiralty Extension Act does not pre-empt state law in those situations. See *Nacierema Operating Co. v. Johnson*, 396 U.S. 212.

The judgment below is Reversed.

NOTES

(1) Federal law, in this case the Noise Control Act of 1972, has been held preemptive where a city placed a curfew on jet aircraft, the federal scheme being termed "pervasive." *City of Burbank v. Lockheed Air Terminal, Inc.*, 411 U.S. 624.

(2) In *Northern States Power Company v. Minnesota*, 447 F.2d 1143, aff'd, 405 U.S. 1035 (1972), a state attempt to control radioactive emissions from a nuclear facility was upset, the court citing the potential for state interference with the federal purpose, the need for federal exclusivity, and the history and pervasiveness of the Atomic Energy Act.

(3) For another case dealing with the permissible scope of state activity—in the context of air pollution in this instance—see *Allway Taxi, Inc., v. City of New York*, Chapter 8.

QUESTIONS FOR DISCUSSION

1   Was *Askew v. American Waterways* decided on strictly legal-historical precedent, or did the Court extend the state's authority on practical grounds?
2   Is it possible, in light of the cases in this chapter, to predict the direction of future cases in the area of pollution regulation?
3   How much control should a state have over actions which affect its environment?
4   Would the decision have been the same if the case had involved a state whose coast, instead of being of high commercial importance, had had more subtle environmental value?
5   Would equipment requirements hinder state-to-state movement of ships? Suppose it had been shown that equipment required by Florida was illegal in another state.
6   What might be the public consequences of unlimited liability for oil spills? No-fault liability?
7   Does the court in *Askew v. American Waterways* postpone any critical decisions?
8   Both the commerce power and the admiralty power are involved in *Askew v. American*

Waterways. Did the state prevail on both? Does consistency require that both be decided the same way?

9 Is Justice Douglas's decision in *Askew v. American Waterways* consistent with his dissent in *Huron v. Detroit?*

PROBLEMS

1 Menhaden are a commercially valuable fish, the products of which are shipped in interstate commerce. Maryland enacted a statute making it a criminal offense for non-residents to fish for menhaden in Maryland waters, but a Delaware commercial fisherman who contends that 20 percent of his income comes from his catch of menhaden in Maryland waters seeks to enjoin the law's enforcement. What would the arguments of the litigants be?

2 Suppose the federal government set quality standards for oysters shipped in interstate commerce. State X, in an effort both to protect the health of its citizens and to protect local industry, sets its own higher standards and forbids importation of oysters which do not meet them. What arguments could be made by state X and by other states seeking to ship oysters to state X?

3 Owing to congested conditions, excessive costs, and pollution, a beach town in New Jersey imposes on people who are not New Jersey residents a fee of $1 per day to enter the beach area. Could such a fee be validly imposed?

4 California has border checkpoints to inspect vehicles for fruit and plants which may be diseased. Suppose that in an effort to improve air quality these checkpoints were empowered by state law to measure automobile emissions and refuse entry to vehicles which pollute excessively. Could a state validly enact such a law?

5 Suppose Congress decided that all land in the United States should be zoned as either residential, agricultural, commercial, or industrial, and proceeded to enact a federally administered program which would supersede all state and local zoning authority. Could such a program be validly enacted under the authority of the commerce clause? Under any other power?

SUGGESTIONS FOR FURTHER READING

Bronstein, D. A.: *State Regulation of Power Plant Siting,* 3 ENVIRONMENTAL L. 273, 1973.
Challenge to Oregon's Bottle Bill: American Can Co. v. OLCC, 4 ENVIRONMENTAL L. 419, 1974.
Currie, D. P.: *Motor Vehicle Air Pollution: State Authority and Federal Preemption,* 68 MICH. L. REV. 1083, 1970.
Environmental Law—Federal Regulation of Aircraft Noise under Federal Aviation Act Precludes Local Police Power Noise Restrictions, 15 BOSTON COLLEGE IND. & COMM. L. REV. 848, 1974.
Morgenstern, A.: *Relationship between Federal and State Laws to Control and Prevent Pollution,* 1 ENVIRONMENTAL L. 238, 1970.
State Environmental Protection Legislation and the Commerce Clauses, 87 HARV. L. REV. 1762, 1974.

State Protection from Oil Spills: Askew v. American Waterways Operators, Inc., 4 ENVIRON-
MENTAL L. 433, 1974.

Use of the Commerce Clause to Invalidate Anti-Phosphate Legislation: Will It Wash? 45 U.
COLO. L. REV. 487, 1974.

Wilkes, D.: *Constitutional Dilemmas Posed by State Policies against Marine Pollution—the
Maine Example,* 23 ME. L. REV. 143, 1971.

Regulation of the Use of Property

TAKING WITHOUT JUST COMPENSATION

The final phrase of the Fifth Amendment, "nor shall private property be taken for public use without just compensation," gives rise to perhaps the most difficult and pervasive constitutional problem which affects environmental law. This seemingly innocuous language has bred extensive litigation and, indeed, entire books have been written on it.[a]

The police power is that by which a government regulates in the interest of public health, welfare, or morals. Such regulation and ordering of a society may be the very reason for existence of the governmental entity.[b] Police-power regulation may take a variety of forms, including building codes, health regulations, fire regulations, and zoning. All the forms infringe to some extent the uses to which one may put his own property.

Restrictions on the degree to which the government may appropriate private property apparently have their genesis in the Magna Carta forced upon King John by English property owners seeking to resist levies and forfei-

[a] Fred Bosselman, David Callies, and John Banta, *The Taking Issue,* Council on Environmental Quality, Washington, D.C., 1973.
[b] See Richard Powell and Patrick Rohan, *Real Property,* Matthew Bender & Company, Inc., New York, 1968, sec. 859.

tures to pay for foreign wars.[c] Regulation of the use of property apparently did not offend medieval justice, but by the eighteenth century the opinion of legal scholars of the level of Blackstone was: "So great moreover is the regard of the law for private property, that it will not authorize the least violation of it; no, not even for the general good of the whole community."[d] Although this probably was an exaggeration and there is a dearth of information concerning the exact intentions of the framers of the Fifth Amendment, it is clear that the reverence for private property rights retains its vitality into the second half of the twentieth century.

The question of how much regulation on the use of property constitutes a "taking" within the meaning of the Fifth Amendment arises in a vast variety of contexts and has no answer. The Supreme Court has said, ". . . there is no set formula to determine where regulation ends and taking begins."[e] There are, however, a number of theories which surface with some regularity if with inconsistent result.

An examination of cases from each factual circumstance in which taking problems arise would be time-consuming and fruitless. Thus, *Pennsylvania Coal Company v. Mahon* is offered as a classic case on the subject, and *State of Maine v. Johnson, Candlestick v. San Francisco Bay,* and *Just v. Marinette County* are three cases on virtually identical facts which display the difficulties and foibles of this constitutional problem in the environmental setting.

DIMINUTION OF VALUE

Pennsylvania Coal Company v. Mahon is the decision on which virtually every land-use regulation case, no matter which way decided, seems to depend. The majority opinion by Oliver Wendell Holmes is much criticized but, in conjunction with the dissent of Louis Brandeis, offers a classic philosophical clash on the issue of private property rights.

Pennsylvania Coal Company v. Mahon

260 U.S. 393 (1922)

Mr. Justice Holmes delivered the opinion of the Court.

This is a bill in equity brought by the defendants in error to prevent the Pennsylvania Coal Company from mining under their property in such way as to remove the supports and cause a subsidence of the surface and of their house. The bill sets out a deed executed by the Coal Company in 1878, under which the plaintiffs claim. The deed conveys the surface, but in express terms reserves the right to

[c] For a complete history, see Bosselman et al., op. cit.
[d] William Blackstone, *Commentaries,* J. B. Lippincott Company, Philadelphia, 1888, pp. 138–139.
[e] *Goldblatt v. Town of Hempstead,* 369 U.S. 590, 594 (1962).

remove all the coal under the same, and the grantee takes the premises with the risk, and waives all claim for damages that may arise from mining out the coal. But the plaintiffs say that whatever may have been the Coal Company's rights, they were taken away by an Act of Pennsylvania, approved May 27, 1921, P. L. 1198, commonly known there as the Kohler Act. The Court of Common Pleas found that if not restrained the defendant would cause the damage to prevent which the bill was brought, but denied an injunction, holding that the statute if applied to this case would be unconstitutional. On appeal the Supreme Court of the State agreed that the defendant had contract and property rights protected by the Constitution of the United States, but held that the statute was a legitimate exercise of the police power and directed a decree for the plaintiffs. A writ of error was granted bringing the case to this Court.

The statute forbids the mining of anthracite coal in such way as to cause the subsidence of, among other things, any structure used as a human habitation, with certain exceptions, including among them land where the surface is owned by the owner of the underlying coal and is distant more than one hundred and fifty feet from any improved property belonging to any other person. As applied to this case the statute is admitted to destroy previously existing rights of property and contract. The question is whether the police power can be stretched so far.

Government hardly could go on if to some extent values incident to property could not be diminished without paying for every such change in the general law. As long recognized, some values are enjoyed under an implied limitation and must yield to the police power. But obviously the implied limitation must have its limits, or the contract and due process clauses are gone. One fact for consideration in determining such limits is the extent of the diminution. When it reaches a certain magnitude, in most if not in all cases there must be an exercise of eminent domain and compensation to sustain the act. So the question depends upon the particular facts. The greatest weight is given to the judgment of the legislature, but it always is open to interested parties to contend that the legislature has gone beyond its constitutional power.

This is the case of a single private house. No doubt there is a public interest even in this, as there is in every purchase and sale and in all that happens within the commonwealth. Some existing rights may be modified even in such a case. *Rideout v. Knox,* 148 Mass. 368. But usually in ordinary private affairs the public interest does not warrant much of this kind of interference. A source of damage to such a house is not a public nuisance even if similar damage is inflicted on others in different places. The damage is not common or public. *Wesson v. Washburn Iron Co.,* 13 Allen 95, 103. The extent of the public interest is shown by the statute to be limited, since the statute ordinarily does not apply to land when the surface is owned by the owner of the coal. Furthermore, it is not justified as a protection of personal safety. That could be provided for by notice. Indeed the very foundation of this bill is that the defendant gave timely notice of its intent to mine under the house. On the other hand the extent of the taking is great. It purports to abolish what is recognized in Pennsylvania as an estate in land—a very valuable estate—and what is declared by the Court below to be a contract hitherto binding the plaintiffs. If we were called upon to deal with the plaintiffs' position alone, we should think it clear that the statute does not disclose a public interest sufficient to warrant so extensive a destruction of the defendant's constitutionally protected rights.

But the case has been treated as one in which the general validity of the act should be discussed. The Attorney General of the State, the City of Scranton, and the representatives of other extensive interests were allowed to take part in the argument below and have submitted their contentions here. It seems, therefore, to be our duty to go farther in the statement of our opinion, in order that it may be known at once, and that further suits should not be brought in vain.

It is our opinion that the act cannot be sustained as an exercise of the police power, so far as it affects the mining of coal under streets or cities in places where the right to mine such coal has been reserved. As said in a Pennsylvania case, "For practical purposes, the right to coal consists in the right to mine it." *Commonwealth v. Clearview Coal Co.,* 256 Pa. St. 328, 331. What makes the right to mine coal valuable is that it can be exercised with profit. To make it commercially impracticable to mine certain coal has very nearly the same effect for constitutional purposes as appropriating or destroying it. This we think that we are warranted in assuming that the statute does.

It is true that in *Plymouth Coal Co. v. Pennsylvania,* 232 U.S. 531, it was held competent for the legislature to require a pillar of coal to be left along the line of adjoining property, that, with the pillar on the other side of the line, would be a barrier sufficient for the safety of the employees of either mine in case the other should be abandoned and allowed to fill with water. But that was a requirement for the safety of employees invited into the mine, and secured an average reciprocity of advantage that has been recognized as a justification of various laws.

The rights of the public in a street purchased or laid out by eminent domain are those that it has paid for. If in any case its representatives have been so short sighted as to acquire only surface rights without the right of support, we see no more authority for supplying the latter without compensation than there was for taking the right of way in the first place and refusing to pay for it because the public wanted it very much. The protection of private property in the Fifth Amendment presupposes that it is wanted for public use, but provides that it shall not be taken for such use without compensation. A similar assumption is made in the decisions upon the Fourteenth Amendment. *Hairston v. Danville & Western Ry. Co.,* 208 U.S. 598, 605. When this seemingly absolute protection is found to be qualified by the police power, the natural tendency of human nature is to extend the qualification more and more until at last private property disappears. But that cannot be accomplished in this way under the Constitution of the United States.

The general rule at least is, that while property may be regulated to a certain extent, if regulation goes too far it will be recognized as a taking. It may be doubted how far exceptional cases, like the blowing up of a house to stop a conflagration, go—and if they go beyond the general rule, whether they do not stand as much upon tradition as upon principle. *Bowditch v. Boston,* 101 U.S. 16. In general it is not plain that a man's misfortunes or necessities will justify his shifting the damages to his neighbor's shoulders. *Spade v. Lynn & Boston R. R. Co.,* 172 Mass. 488, 489. We are in danger of forgetting that a strong public desire to improve the public condition is not enough to warrant achieving the desire by a shorter cut than the constitutional way of paying for the change. As we already have said, this is a question of degree—and therefore cannot be disposed of by general propositions. But we regard this as going beyond any of the cases decided by this Court. The late decisions upon laws dealing with the congestion of Washington and New York, caused by the war, dealt with laws intended to meet a temporary emergency and providing for compensation determined to be reasonable by an impartial board. They went to the verge of the law but fell far short of the present act. *Block v. Hirsh,* 256 U.S. 135. *Marcus Brown Holding Co. v. Feldman,* 256 U.S. 170. *Levy Leasing Co. v. Siegel,* 258 U.S. 242.

We assume, of course, that the statute was passed upon the conviction that an exigency existed that would warrant it, and we assume that an exigency exists that would warrant the exercise of eminent domain. But the question at bottom is upon whom the loss of the changes desired should fall. So far as private persons or communities have seen fit to take the risk of acquiring only surface rights, we cannot see that the fact that their risk has become a danger warrants the giving to them greater rights than they bought.

Decree reversed.

Mr. Justice Brandeis, dissenting.

The Kohler Act prohibits, under certain conditions, the mining of anthracite coal within the limits of a city in such a manner or to such an extent "as to cause the . . . subsidence of any dwelling or other structure used as a human habitation, or any factory, store, or other industrial mercantile establishment in which human labor is employed." Coal in place is land; and the right of the owner to use his land is not absolute. He may not so use it as to create a public nuisance; and uses, once harmless, may, owing to changed conditions, seriously threaten the public welfare. Whenever they do, the legislature has power to prohibit such uses without paying compensation; and the power to prohibit extends alike to the manner, the character and the purpose of the use. Are we justified in declaring that the Legislature of Pennsylvania has, in restricting the right to mine anthracite, exercised this power so arbitrarily as to violate the Fourteenth Amendment?

Every restriction upon the use of property imposed in the exercise of the police power deprives the owner of some right theretofore enjoyed, and is, in that sense, an abridgment by the State of rights in property without making compensation. But restriction imposed to protect the public health, safety or morals from dangers threatened is not a taking. The restriction here in question is merely the prohibition of a noxious use. The property so restricted remains in the possession of its owner. The State does not appropriate it or make any use of it. The State merely prevents the owner from making a use which interferes with paramount rights of the public. Whenever the use prohibited ceases to be noxious,—as it may because of further change in local or social conditions,—the restriction will have to be removed and the owner will again be free to enjoy his property as heretofore.

The restriction upon the use of this property can not, of course, be lawfully imposed, unless its purpose is to protect the public. But the purpose of a restriction does not cease to be public, because incidentally some private persons may thereby receive gratuitously valuable special benefits. Thus, owners of low buildings may obtain, through statutory restrictions upon the height of neighboring structures, benefits equivalent to an easement of light and air. *Welch v. Swasey,* 214 U.S. 91. Compare *Lindsley v. Natural Carbonic Gas Co.,* 220 U.S. 61; *Walls v. Midland Carbon Co.,* 254 U.S. 300. Furthermore, a restriction, though imposed for a public purpose, will not be lawful, unless the restriction is an appropriate means to the public end. But to keep coal in place is surely an appropriate means of preventing subsidence of the surface; and ordinarily it is the only available means. Restriction upon use does not become inappropriate as a means, merely because it deprives the owner of the only use to which the property can be profitably put. The liquor and the oleomargarine cases settled that. *Mugler v. Kansas,* 123 U.S. 623, 668, 669; *Powell v. Pennsylvania,* 127 U.S. 678, 682. See also *Hadacheck v. Los Angeles,* 239 U.S. 394; *Pierce Oil Corporation v. City of Hope,* 248 U.S. 498. Nor is a restriction imposed through exercise of the police power inappropriate as a means, merely because the same end might be effected through exercise of the power of eminent domain, or otherwise at public expense. Every restriction upon the height of buildings might be secured through acquiring by eminent domain the right of each owner to build above the limiting height; but it is settled that the State need not resort to that power. Compare *Laurel Hill Cemetery v. San Francisco,* 216 U.S. 358; *Missouri Pacific Ry. Co. v. Omaha,* 235 U.S. 121. If by mining anthracite coal the owner would necessarily unloose poisonous gasses, I suppose no one would doubt the power of the State to prevent the mining, without buying his coal fields. And why may not the State, likewise, without paying compensation, prohibit one from digging so deep or excavating so near the surface, as to expose the community to like dangers? In the latter case, as in the former, carrying on the business would be a public nuisance.

It is said that one fact for consideration in determining whether the limits of the police power have been exceeded is the extent of the resulting diminution in value; and that here the restriction destroys existing rights of property and contract. But values are relative. If we are to consider the value of the coal kept in place by the restriction, we should compare it with the value of all other parts of the land. That is, with the value not of the coal alone, but with the value of the whole property. The rights of an owner as against the public are not increased by dividing the interests in his property into surface and subsoil. The sum of the rights in the parts can not be greater than the rights in the whole. The estate of an owner in land is grandiloquently described as extending *ab orco usque ad coelum.* But I suppose no one would contend that by selling his interest above one hundred feet from the surface he could prevent the State from limiting, by the police power, the height of structures in a city. And why should a sale of underground rights bar the State's power? For aught that appears the value of the coal kept in place by the restriction may be negligible as compared with the value of the whole property, or even as compared with that part of it which is represented by the coal remaining in place and which may be extracted despite the statute. Ordinarily a police regulation, general in operation will not be held void as to a particular property, although proof is offered that owing to conditions peculiar to it the restriction could not reasonably be applied. See *Powell v. Pennsylvania,* 127 U.S. 678, 681, 684; *Murphy v. California,* 225 U.S. 623, 629. But even if the particular facts are to govern, the statute should, in my opinion, be upheld in this case. For the defendant has failed to adduce any evidence from which it appears that to restrict its mining operations was an unreasonable exercise of the police power. Compare *Reinman v. Little Rock,* 237 U.S. 171, 177, 180; *Pierce Oil Corporation v. City of Hope,* 248 U.S. 498, 500. Where the surface and the coal belong to the same person, self-interest would ordinarily prevent mining to such an extent as to cause a subsidence. It was, doubtless, for this reason that the legislature, estimating the degrees of danger, deemed statutory restriction unnecessary for the public safety under such conditions.

It is said that this is a case of a single dwelling house; that the restriction upon mining abolishes a valuable estate hitherto secured by a contract with the plaintiffs; and that the restriction upon mining cannot be justified as a protection of personal safety, since that could be provided for by notice. The propriety of deferring a good deal to tribunals on the spot has been repeatedly recognized. *Welch v. Swasey,* 214 U.S. 91, 106; *Laurel Hill Cemetery v. San Francisco,* 216 U.S. 358, 365; *Patsone v. Pennsylvania,* 232 U.S. 138, 144. May we say that notice would afford adequate protection of the public safety where the legislature and the highest court of the State, with greater knowledge of local conditions, have declared, in effect, that it would not? If public safety is imperiled, surely neither grant, nor contract, can prevail against the exercise of the police power. *Fertilizing Co. v. Hyde Park,* 97 U.S. 659; *Atlantic Coast Line R. R. Co. v. Goldsboro,* 232 U.S. 548; *Union Dry Goods Co. v. Georgia Public Service Corporation,* 248 U.S. 372; *St. Louis Poster Advertising Co. v. St. Louis,* 249 U.S. 269. The rule that the State's power to take appropriate measures to guard the safety of all who may be within its jurisdiction may not be bargained away was applied to compel carriers to establish grade crossings at their own expense, despite contracts to the contrary; *Chicago, Burlington & Quincy R. R. Co. v. Nebraska,* 170 U.S. 57; and, likewise, to supersede, by an employers' liability act, the provision of a charter exempting a railroad from liability for death of employees, since the civil liability was deemed a matter of public concern, and not a mere private right. *Texas & New Orleans R. R. Co. v. Miller,* 221 U.S. 408. Compare *Boyd v. Alabama,* 94 U.S. 645; *Stone v. Mississippi,* 101 U.S. 814; *Butchers' Union Co. v. Crescent City Co.,* 111 U.S. 746; *Douglas v. Kentucky,* 168 U.S. 488; *Pennsylvania Hospital v. Philadelphia,* 245 U.S. 20, 23. Nor can existing contracts between private individuals preclude exercise of the police power. "One whose rights, such as they are, are subject to state restriction, cannot remove them from the power of the State by making a contract about them." *Hudson County Water Co. v. McCarter,* 209 U.S. 349, 357; *Knoxville Water Co. v. Knoxville,* 189 U.S. 434, 438; *Rast v. Van Deman & Lewis Co.,* 240 U.S. 342. The fact that this suit is brought by a private person is, of course, immaterial; to protect the community through invoking the aid, as litigant, of interested private citizens is not a novelty in our law. That it may be done in Pennsylvania was decided by its Supreme Court in this case. And it is for a State to say how its public policy shall be enforced.

This case involves only mining which causes subsidence of a dwelling house. But the Kohler Act contains provisions in addition to that quoted above; and as to these, also, an opinion is expressed. These provisions deal with mining under cities to such an extent as to cause subsidence of—

(a) Any public building or any structure customarily used by the public as a place of resort, assemblage, or amusement, including, but not being limited to, churches, schools, hospitals, theatres, hotels, and railroad stations.

(b) Any street, road, bridge, or other public passageway, dedicated to public use or habitually used by the public.

(c) Any track, roadbed, right of way, pipe, conduit, wire, or other facility, used in the service of the public by any municipal corporation or public service company as defined by the Public Service Company Law.

A prohibition of mining which causes subsidence of such structures and facilities is obviously enacted for a public purpose; and it seems, likewise, clear that mere notice of intention to mine would not in this connection secure the public safety. Yet it is said that these provisions of the act cannot be sustained as an exercise of the police power where the right to mine such coal has been reserved. The conclusion seems to rest upon the assumption that in order to justify such exercise of the police power there must be "an average reciprocity of advantage" as between the owner of the property restricted and the rest of the community; and that here such reciprocity is absent. Reciprocity of advantage is an important consideration, and may even be an essential, where the State's power is exercised for the purpose of conferring benefits upon the property of a neighborhood, as in drainage projects, *Wurts v. Hoagland,* 114 U.S. 606; *Fallbrook Irrigation District v. Bradley,* 164 U.S. 112; or upon adjoining owners, as by party wall provisions, *Jackman v. Rosenbaum Co., ante,* 22. But where the police power is exercised, not to confer benefits upon property owners, but to protect the public from detriment and danger, there is, in my opinion, no room for considering reciprocity of advantage. There was no reciprocal advantage to the owner prohibited from using his oil tanks in 248 U.S. 498; his brickyard, in 239 U.S. 394; his livery stable, in 237 U.S. 171; his billiard hall, in 225 U.S. 623; his oleomargarine factory, in 127 U.S. 678; his brewery, in 123 U.S. 623; unless it be the advantage of living and doing business in a civilized community. That reciprocal advantage is given by the act to the coal operators.

Thirty years after *Pennsylvania Coal Company v. Mahon,* in *Pittsburgh Coal Co., etc. v. Sanitary Water Board,* 286 A.2d 459 (Com. Ct. Pa. 1972), it was held that where a Clean Streams law required mine operators to treat drainage waters, such a requirement would be unconstitutional where the waters had become polluted while in an adjacent abandoned mine and had then seeped into the active mine. Citing *Pennsylvania Coal Company v. Mahon,* the court said:

The application of the Board's interpretation of the statutory law to appellant, to the extent that it denies to appellant the use and enjoyment of its property unless it assumed responsibility for the treatment of fugitive water entering its mine through no fault of appellant, constitutes an unreasonable, arbitrary and oppressive exercise of the police power. The Board would hold that the legislature, in exercise of its police power, not only imposes new and stringent conditions upon appellant's use and enjoyment of its property but would also charge appellant with responsibility for fugitive water under penalty of denying appellant any use and enjoyment of its property as a mine. While appellant in the use and enjoyment of its property is subject to reasonable exercise of the police power, *Bortz Coal Company v. Air Pollution Commission,* 2 Pa. Cmlwth. 441, 279 A.2d 388 (1971), the exercise of the police power becomes unreasonable and constitutionally violative of appellant's property rights when it imposes upon appellant a burden unrelated to its otherwise lawful operation over the years and not of its making. No matter how meritorious the desired results may be, the use and enjoyment of property by its owner should not be burdened or impaired in the name of public health, safety or welfare absent a rational relationship between the evil sought to be cured and the use of property as contributing to the evil. It is at this point that curing the evil should be assumed as a direct responsibility of government and not placed upon the property owner in the guise of an exercise of the police power.

The requirement of the Clean Streams Act that mine operators treat their own waste was upheld. It was the application of the act to the particular facts which was held unconstitutional.

NOTE

The framers of the constitution said little regarding the purpose of the taking clause. See J. Sax, *Taking and the Police Power,* 74 YALE L.J. 36, 58 (1964).

Blackstone, writing in 1803, suggested that the clause "was probably intended to restrain the arbitrary and oppressive mode of obtaining supplies for the Army and other public uses, by impressment, as was frequently practiced during the Revolutionary War, without any compensation whatever."[f]

QUESTIONS FOR DISCUSSION

1 Does a restriction on any commercial use of property constitute a taking of that property?
2 At the time of the adoption of the Fifth Amendment, regulation on the use of property was already common. What was the intent of the drafters as regards the taking clause?
3 Would ownership of property prior to the enactment of a regulation exempt the property from its coverage?
4 Does property have any value apart from the right to use or develop it?
5 Is the balance test enunciated by Holmes adequate in light of the irreversible nature of many environmentally hazardous projects? Is irreversibility merely one more factor to be balanced?
6 Holmes states the general rule to be: "While property may be regulated to a certain extent, if regulation goes too far it will be recognized as a taking." Does such a rule give legislatures adequate guidance in the construction of regulatory schemes? Does such a rule breed litigation?
7 Holmes's reputation is generally that of a "strict constructionist." Does the decision in *Pennsylvania Coal Company v. Mahon* conform to that image?

[f] Blackstone, op. cit., pp. 305–306.

8 *Pennsylvania Coal Company v. Mahon* involved the coal industry in Pennsylvania. What is the impact of the size or value of an industry on a court's willingness to impair or terminate it? What impact should such factors have where environmental protection is at issue? Suppose a decision contrary to an industry would result in a cleaner environment but substantial or concentrated unemployment. Should a court consider such factors? Note that the Pennsylvania court ruled against the coal company and was reversed by the Supreme Court of the United States.

9 Would a regulation which decreases a property's value by 10 percent be constitutional? 30 percent? 90 percent?

10 Is the problem solved by a constitutional provision that "private property shall not be taken *or damaged* for public use without just compensation"? See CALIF. CONST. art. I, § 14.

WETLANDS SETTING

Wetlands and tidal marshes are unique in that they are at once of high ecological value and little economic value. After dredging and filling, however, their value increases dramatically as building sites or new waterfront property useful for residential, recreational, and commercial purposes. Unlike conventional zoning where the diminution of value is relatively modest in most instances, the wetlands cases provide the all-or-nothing alternative which demands that a position be taken. *State of Maine v. Johnson* illustrates the traditional or conservative approach.

State of Maine v. Johnson

265 A.2d 711 (Me. 1970)

Marden, Justice.

On appeal from an injunction granted under the provisions of 12 M.R.S.A. §§ 4701–4790, inclusive, the Wetlands Act (Act),[1] originating in Chapter 348 P. L. 1967, which places restrictions upon the alteration and use of wetlands, as therein defined, without permission from the municipal officers concerned and the State Wetlands Control Board (Board). The Act is a conservation measure under the

---

[1] Pertinent portions are quoted.

"§ 4701.   *Procedure; hearing*

"No person, agency or municipality shall remove, fill, dredge or drain sanitary sewage into, or otherwise alter any coastal wetland, as defined herein, without filing written notice of his intention to do so, including such plans as may be necessary to describe the proposed activity, with the municipal officers in the municipality affected and with the Wetlands Control Board. Such notice shall be sent to each body by registered mail at least 60 days before such alteration is proposed to commence. The municipal officers shall hold a public hearing on the proposal within 30 days of receipt of the notice and shall notify by mail the person proposing the alteration and the public by publication in a newspaper published in the county where the wetlands are located, the Wetlands Control Board and all abutting owners of the hearing.

"For purposes of this chapter, coastal wetland is defined as any swamp, marsh, bog, beach, flat or other contiguous lowland above extreme low water which is subject to tidal action or normal storm flowage at any time excepting periods of maximum storm activity."

police power of the State to protect the ecology of areas bordering coastal waters. The 1967 Act has been amended in no way pertinent to the present issue except by Section 8 of Chapter 379 of the Public Laws of 1969, which authorized alternatively a mandatory injunction for the restoration of any wetlands previously altered in violation of the Act.

The appellants own a tract of land about 220 feet wide and 700 feet long extending across salt water marshes between Atlantic Avenue on the east and the Webhannet River on the west in the Town of Wells. Westerly of the lots fronting on Atlantic Avenue the strip has been subdivided into lots for sale. The easterly 260 feet approximately of the strip has been filled and bears seasonal dwellings. Westerly of this 260 foot development is marsh-land flooded at high tide and drained, upon receding tide, into the River by a network of what our Maine historical novelist Kenneth E. Roberts called "eel runs," but referred to in the record as creeks. Similar marsh-land, undeveloped, lies to the north and south of appellants' strip, and westerly of the River, all of which makes up a substantial acreage (the extent not given in testimony, but of which we take judicial notice) of marsh-land known as the Wells Marshes. Appellants' land, by raising the grade above high water by the addition of fill, is adaptable to development for building purposes.

Following the effective date of the Act, an application to the municipal officers, with notice to the Wetlands Control Board, for permission to fill a portion of this land was denied by the Board, an administrative appeal was taken and the case reported to this Court, which appears sub nom. *Johnson v. Maine Wetlands Control Board,* Me., 250 A.2d 825 (Case No. 1) and in which the constitutionality of the Act was challenged. We held, by decision filed March 11, 1969 that absent

---

* * * * * * * * * * * * * * *

"§ 4702. *Permits*

"Permit to undertake the proposed alteration shall be issued by the municipal officers within 7 days of such hearing providing the Wetlands Control Board approves. Such permit may be conditioned upon the applicant amending his proposal to take whatever measures are deemed necessary by either the municipality or the Wetlands Control Board to protect the public interest. Approval may be withheld by either the municipal officers or the board when in the opinion of either body the proposal would threaten the public safety, health or welfare, would adversely affect the value or enjoyment of the property of abutting owners, or would be damaging to the conservation of public or private water supplies or of wildlife or freshwater, estuarine or marine fisheries."

* * * * * * * * * * * * * * *

"§ 4704. *Appeal*

"Appeal may be taken to the Superior Court within 30 days after the denial of a permit or the issuance of a conditional permit for the purpose of determining whether the action appealed from so restricts the use of the property as to deprive the owner of the reasonable use thereof, and is therefore an unreasonable exercise of police power, or which constitutes the equivalent of a taking without compensation. The court upon such a finding may set aside the action appealed from."

* * * * * * * * * * * * * * *

"§ 4705. *Wetlands Control Board*

"The Wetlands Control Board shall be composed of the Commissioners of Sea and Shore Fisheries and of Inland Fisheries and Game, the Chairman of the Water and Air Environmental Improvement Commission, the Chairman of the State Highway Commission, the Forest Commissioner and the Commissioner of Health and Welfare or their delegates."

§ 4709. Violators are subject to fine or injunctive process.

a record of evidence as to the nature of the land involved and the benefits or harm to be expected from the denial of the permit, the case would have to be remanded.

Subsequent to March 11, 1969 fill was deposited on the land in question, as the result of which the State sought an injunction, the granting of which brings this case before us on appeal (Case No. 2). It is stipulated that the evidence in this case should be accepted as the evidence lacking in (Case No. 1) and that the two cases be consolidated for final determination of both.

The record establishes that the land which the appellants propose to build up by fill and build upon for sale, or to be offered for sale to be built upon, are coastal wetlands within the definition of the Act and that the refusal by the Board to permit the deposit of such fill prevents the development as proposed. The single Justice found that the property is a portion of a salt marsh area, a valuable natural resource of the State, that the highest and best use for the land, so filled, is for housing, and that unfilled it has no commercial value.

The issue is the same in both, namely, whether the denial of permit (Case No. 1) and the injunction (Case No. 2) so limit the use of plaintiffs of their land that such deprivation of use amounts to a taking of their property without constitutional due process and just compensation.[2]

DUE PROCESS

Due process of law has a dual aspect, procedural and substantive. 16 Am. Jur. 2d, Constitutional Law § 548.

Procedurally, "notice and opportunity for hearing are of the essence" *Randall v. Patch,* 118 Me. 303, 305, 108 A. 97, 98, and as attributed to Daniel Webster in the Dartmouth College case it is "a law which hears before it condemns, which proceeds upon inquiry; and renders judgment only after trial." *Trustees of Dartmouth College v. Woodward,* 4 Wheat. (U.S.) 518, 4 L. Ed. 629, and see *New York Harbor Village Corporation v. Libby,* 126 Me. 537, 539, 140 A. 382.

The guaranty of procedural due process requires no particular form of procedure. 16 Am. Jur. 2d, Constitutional Law § 549, and *Green v. State,* Me., 247 A.2d 117, [9] 121. The Act meets all requirements of procedural due process.

Substantively, "the terms 'law of the land' and 'due process of law' * * * are identical in meaning." *Michaud v. City of Bangor,* 159 Me. 491, 493, 196 A.2d 106, 108.

It is "the constitutional guaranty that no person shall be deprived of * * * property for arbitrary reasons, such as deprivation being constitutionally supportable only if the conduct from which the deprivation flows is proscribed by reasonable legislation (that is, legislation the enactment of which is within the scope of legislative authority) reasonably applied (that is, for a purpose consonant with the purpose of the legislation itself)." 16 Am. Jur. 2d, Constitutional Law § 550.

It is this substantive due process which is challenged in the Act. In this

---

[2] Maine Constitution Article I § 6. "He shall not be * * * deprived of his * * * property * * * but by * * * the law of the land." "Section 21. Private property shall not be taken for public uses without just compensation, * * *."

connection it must be noted that § 4704 (Footnote 1) by its terms equates a deprivation "of the reasonable use" of an owner's property with "an unreasonable exercise of police power."

The constitutional aspect of the current problem is to be determined by consideration of the extent to which appellants are deprived of their usual incidents of ownership,—for the conduct of the public authorities with relation to appellants' land is not a "taking" in the traditional sense. Our State has applied a strict construction of the constitutional provisions as to land. See Opinion of the Justices, 103 Me. 506, 511, 69 A. 627, and *State v. McKinnon,* 153 Me. 15, 20, 133 A.2d 885.

We find no constitutional definition of the word "deprive," *Munn v. Illinois,* 94 U.S. 113, 123, 24 L. Ed. 77, since the constitutionally protected right of property is not unlimited. It is subject to reasonable restraints and regulations in the public interest by means of the legitimate exercise of police power. 16 Am. Jur. 2d, Constitutional Law § 363. The exercise of this police power may properly regulate the use of property and if the owner suffers injury "it is either damnum absque injuria, or, in the theory of the law, he is compensated for it by sharing in the general benefits which the regulations are intended * * * to secure." *State v. Robb,* 100 Me. 180, 186, 60 A. 874, 876. The determination of unconstitutional deprivation is difficult and judicial decisions are diverse. Broadly speaking, deprivation of property contrary to constitutional guaranty occurs "if it deprives an owner of one of its essential attributes, destroys its value, restricts or interrupts its common necessary, or profitable use, hampers the owner in the application of it to the purpose of trade, or imposes conditions upon the right to hold or use it and thereby seriously impairs its value." 16 Am. Jur. 2d, Constitutional Law § 367. See also *State v. Union Oil Company,* 151 Me. 438, 446, 120 A.2d 708.

Conditions so burdensome may be imposed that they are equivalent to an outright taking, although the title to the property and some vestiges of its uses remain in the owner. *East Coast Lumber Terminal, Inc. v. Town of Babylon,* 174 F.2d 106, [5–7] 110 (2 CCA, 1949).

A guiding principle appears in the frequently cited case of *Pennsylvania Coal Company v. Mahon et al.,* 260 U.S. 393, 413, 43 S. Ct. 158, 159–160, 67 L. Ed. 322 (1922) where Mr. Justice Holmes declared:

> "Government hardly could go on if to some extent values incident to property could not be diminished without paying for every such change in the general law. As long recognized some values are enjoyed under an implied limitation and must yield to the police power. But obviously the implied limitation must have its limits or the contract and due process clauses are gone. One fact for consideration in determining such limits is the extent of the diminution. When it reaches a certain magnitude, in most if not in all cases there must be an exercise of eminent domain and compensation to sustain the act. So the question depends upon the particular facts."
>
>   *   *   *   *   *   *   *   *   *   *   *   *   *   *
>
> "We are in danger of forgetting that a strong public desire to improve the public condition is not enough to warrant achieving the desire by a shorter cut than the constitutional way of paying for the change. As we already have said this is a question of degree—and therefore cannot be disposed of by general propositions." At page 416.

See also *Pumpelly v. Green Bay Company,* 13 Wall. (U.S.) 166, 177–178, 20 L. Ed. 557 (1871).

Confrontation between public interests and private interests is common in the application of zoning laws, with which the Wetlands Act may be analogized, and the great majority of which, upon their facts, are held to be reasonable exercise of the police power. There are, however, zoning restrictions which have been recognized as equivalent to a taking of the property restricted. See *Frankel v. City of Baltimore,* 223 Md. 97, 162 A.2d 447, [2] 451 (1960); *City of Plainfield v. Borough of Middlesex,* 69 N.J. Super. 136, 173 A.2d 785, 788 (1961); and *Arverne Bay Const. Co. v. Thatcher,* 278 N.Y. 222, 15 N.E.2d 587, [10–13] 591 (N.Y. 1938).

The same result has been reached as to zoning laws which identify their purposes as ones of conservation. See *Dooley v. Town Plan. and Zoning Commission of Town of Fairfield,* 151 Conn. 304, 197 A.2d 770, [5, 6] 773 (1964, flood control); and *Morris County Land Improvement Company v. Township of Parsippany-Troy Hills et al.,* 40 N.J. 539, 193 A.2d 232, [6, 7] 241 (1963, swampland preservation), and the rationale expressed in *Commissioner of Natural Resources et al. v. S. Volpe & Co., Inc.,* 349 Mass. 104, 206 N.E.2d 666 (1965, involving "dredge and fill" Act); and *MacGibbon et al. v. Board of Appeals of Duxbury,* 347 Mass. 690, 200 N.E.2d 254 (1964) and 255 N.E. 2d 347 (Mass. 1970).

There has, as well, been restrictive conservation legislation which has been held not equivalent to taking. See *Patterson v. Stanolind Oil & Gas Co.,* 182 Okla. 155, 77 P.2d 83, [1–3] 89 (1938, oil and gas "well spacing" Act); *Iowa Natural Resources Council v. Van Zee,* 158 N.W.2d 111, [10], [11] 117 (Iowa 1968, flood control Act), and *Swisher v. Brown,* 157 Colo. 378, 402 P.2d 621 (1965, marketing control Act). See also *Greenleaf-Johnson Lumber Company v. Garrison,* 237 U.S. 251, 260, 35 S. Ct. 551, 59 L. Ed. 939 (1914, directing removal of docks in navigable waters, with dissent), and *Miami Beach Jockey Club, Inc. v. Dern,* 66 App. D.C. 254, 86 F.2d 135 (1936, legislative prohibition of filling submerged land).

Of the above, the Massachusetts cases are of particular significance inasmuch as the "dredge and fill" Act discussed in *Volpe* is expressed in terms closely parallel to our Wetlands Act and the zoning ordinance in *MacGibbon* deals with facts closely akin to those before us.

Between the public interest in braking and eventually stopping the insidious despoliation of our natural resources which have for so long been taken for granted, on the one hand, and the protection of appellants' property on the other, the issue is cast.

Here the single Justice has found that the area of which appellants' land is a part "is a valuable natural resource of the State of Maine and plays an important role in the conservation and development of aquatic and marine life, game birds and waterfowl," which bespeaks the public interest involved and the protection of which is sought by Section 4702 of the Act. With relation to appellants' interest the single Justice found that appellants' land absent the addition of fill "has no commercial value whatever." These findings are supported by the evidence and are conclusive. *Danby v. Hanscom,* 157 Me. 189, 191, 163 A.2d 372.

As distinguished from conventional zoning for town protection, the area of Wetlands representing a "valuable natural resource of the State," of which appellants' holdings are but a minute part, is of state-wide concern. The benefits from its preservation extend beyond town limits and are state-wide. The cost of its preservation should be publicly borne. To leave appellants with commercially valueless land in upholding the restriction presently imposed, is to charge them with more than their just share of the cost of this state-wide conservation program, granting fully its commendable purpose. In the phrasing of *Robb, supra,* their compensation by sharing in the benefits which this restriction is intended to secure is so disproportionate to their deprivation of reasonable use that such exercise of the State's police power is unreasonable.

The application of the Wetlands restriction in the terms of the denial of appellants' proposal to fill, and enjoining them from so doing deprives them of the reasonable use of their property and within Section 4704 is both an unreasonable exercise of police power and equivalent to taking within constitutional consider-ations.

While we have turned the case upon the uncompensated "taking" issue, ap-pellants have urged also that the standards by which the land owner's proposal must be measured are unconstitutionally vague. We do not agree. The Constitu-tion requires no more than "an adequate warning as to what conduct falls under its ban," and demarcation of "boundaries sufficiently distinct" for the Courts to administer the law in accordance with the legislative will. *United States v. Petrillo,* 332 U.S. 1, 67 S. Ct. 1538, [4-7] 1542, 91 L. Ed. 1877. See also 50 Am. Jur., Statutes § 473; *Swed et al. v. Inhabitants of Town of Bar Harbor,* 158 Me. 220, 226, 182 A.2d 664, and *State v. Fantastic Fair et al.,* 158 Me. 450, 468, 186 A.2d 352. The standards herein fixed are markedly more explicit than those found wanting in *Waterville Hotel Corp. v. Board of Zoning Appeals,* Me., 241 A.2d 50, and those found adequate in *MacGibbon, supra,* 255 N.E.2d [3-6] at page 350. Constitutional standards are met.

Holding, as we do, that the prohibition against the filling of appellants' land, upon the facts peculiar to the case, is an unreasonable exercise of police power, it does not follow that the restriction as to draining sanitary sewage into coastal wetland is subject to the same infirmity. Additional considerations of health and pollution which are "separable from and independent of" the "fill" restriction may well support validity of the Act in those areas of concern. See *Hamilton et als. v. Portland Pier Site District et als.,* 120 Me. 15, 24, 112 A. 836, and La Fleur ex rel. *Anderson v. Frost et als.,* 146 Me. 270, 289, 80 A.2d 407.

Within the provisions of Section 4704, the denial of the permit to fill (Case No. 1) and the injunction (Case No. 2) are "set aside."

Appeal sustained in both cases.

NOTE

Are the limits of police power constant?

In short, the police power, as such, is not confined within the narrow circumspec-tion of precedents, resting upon past conditions which do not cover and control present day conditions . . . that is to say, as a commonwealth develops politically, economically, and socially, the police power likewise develops, within reason, to meet the changed and changing conditions.[9]

Does a changing scope of police power adequately protect property investments?

Can a property owner rely on past judicial decisions?

Would a static police power be able to meet the pressures of increased population and advancing technology?

QUESTIONS FOR DISCUSSION

1 Does a denial of a permit to dredge or fill marsh deprive the owner of all reasonable use of his property?

2 If it is the public which benefits from the Wetlands Act, should the public rather than the individual property owner bear the expense?

3 Is the "strict construction" of the constitutional provisions as to land favored by the Maine court in *State of Maine v. Johnson* a viable philosophy in view of possible environmental catastrophes?

4 Would the court have reached a different conclusion if there had been additional considerations of health and pollution? Is it reasonable to allow the filling of ecologically priceless marsh while prohibiting "pollution" of it?

The California case of *Candlestick Properties, Inc. v. San Francisco Bay Conservation and Development Commission* is factually similar to *State of Maine v. Johnson* although the filling in the latter was preparatory to use rather than the use itself. The case demonstrates the procedural problems of permit schemes and is illustrative of the more liberal view of the regulation of private property.

[9] *Candlestick Properties, Inc. v. San Francisco Bay Conservation and Development Commission*, 89 Cal. Rptr. 897, 905 (1970), citing *Miller v. Board of Public Works*, 234 P.2d 381 at 383.

Candlestick Properties, Inc., v. San Francisco Bay Conservation and Development Commission

11 Cal. App. 3d 557, 89 Cal. Rptr. 897 (1970)

Caldecott, J.

Appellant, Candlestick Properties, Inc. (Candlestick) filed an application with the San Francisco Bay Conservation and Development Commission of the State of California (BCDC or Commission) for a permit to fill a parcel of land. After hearings the permit was denied. Candlestick then filed an action with the San Francisco Superior Court seeking a review of BCDC's action by way of a petition for writ of mandate pursuant to Code of Civil Procedure section 1094.5 and, in the alternative, damages for an alleged taking of its property without just compensation. The petition for writ of mandate was denied and a demurrer without leave to amend was sustained to the cause of action for damages. Candlestick has appealed from the judgment.

Appellant is the owner of a parcel of land submerged at high tide by the waters of San Francisco Bay. The parcel cost $40,000 and was acquired in 1964 as a place to deposit fill from construction projects. The parcel is located within the boundaries of the Hunters Point Reclamation District, which was created by the Legislature in 1955. (Stats. 1955, ch. 1573, p. 2855; Water Code Appendix § 78-1 to 18.) The parcel is adjoined by other parcels which have either been filled or are in the process of being filled. Appellant's parcel is not navigable at high tide and contains the remnants of ship hulls. According to appellant the record establishes that the property has no value except as a place to deposit fill and as filled land. Respondents dispute the accuracy of this contention and indicate that there is no information in the record relative to alternative uses of the property, such as dredging for some water-related use or partial filling of the parcel for some water-related use instead of Candlestick's proposal to totally fill the property with demolition debris.

Appellant applied for the fill permit required by the City and County of San Francisco on August 20, 1965, and it was granted on September 7, 1965. Appellant then applied to the BCDC for a permit to fill the property. There is a question as to the date the application was filed. The material to be used was to be debris from demolition projects in the City and County of San Francisco.

The Commission heard the application of Candlestick at its meetings on January 5, 1967, and January 20, 1967. The application was denied by the Commission on January 20, 1967. Following this decision appellant commenced these proceedings.

Appellant contends, and respondents agree, that the legislation creating the BCDC did not repeal the Hunters Point Reclamation District Act by implication. Appellant maintains that the two legislative declarations should be reconciled so that the Hunters Point Reclamation District Act "constitutes a specific declaration that fill within the Hunters Point Reclamation District will not adversely affect the comprehensive plan" being prepared by the BCDC. Under appellant's approach the BCDC would be required to grant permits for fill projects within the district established by the Hunters Point Reclamation District Act. As stated by appellant: "a specific legislative declaration that certain bay land should be filled is a legislative statement that filling that particular land could not affect the comprehensive plan being prepared by the Commission for the entire Bay. . . . Under that analysis the Commission would have jurisdiction to pass upon fill permits within the District but could not deny them unless, for example, the composition of the proposed fill (not involved in this case) was such that it might adversely affect the water quality of the Bay or the fish and wildlife therein."

Respondents, however, contend that the powers of the Hunters Point Reclamation District are not involved in this case. As indicated by respondents, the Hunters Point Reclamation District Act gives the district the power to reclaim and protect the lands within the district and to fill the lands within the district in private ownership. (Water Code Appendix § 78-9.) The Act states "The district may fill the lands of the district in private ownership . . . and, to that end, may, if necessary, obtain the right to do so by purchase, by agreement with the owners thereof, by condemnation or other legal means." (Id.) The application to the BCDC in this case came from a private entity, Candlestick. There is nothing in the record of this case which indicates that the Hunters Point Reclamation District has determined to fill Candlestick's parcel by agreement or condemnation. Thus, the situation presented is one in which the owner of private land, which happens to be located within the Hunters Point Reclamation District, has applied to the BCDC for a permit to fill that land. Clearly, this situation does not raise an issue concerning the powers of the Reclamation District as opposed to those of the BCDC. Therefore, it is not necessary to attempt to reconcile the effects of the two acts.

However, if construction of the two acts is required, it is clear the McAteer-Petris Act controls. The Supreme Court in *People ex rel. S. F. Bay etc. Com. v. Town of Emeryville,* 69 Cal. 2d 533 at 544-45 stated: "The 'objective sought to be achieved' by the McAteer-Petris Act is depicted with remarkable clarity. In the preamble the Legislature describes the public interest in the San Francisco Bay: 'The Legislature hereby finds and declares that the public interest in the San Francisco Bay is in its beneficial use for a variety of purposes; that the public has an interest in the bay as the most valuable single body of water that can be used for many purposes, from conservation to planned development; and that the bay operates as a delicate physical mechanism in which changes that affect one part of the bay may also affect all other parts. It is therefore declared to be in the public interest to create a politically-responsible, democratic process by which the San Francisco Bay and its shoreline can be analyzed, planned, and regulated as a unit.' (Gov. Code § 66600.)

"In the next section the Legislature stresses the dangers inherent in self-generated and unrelegated fill activities: 'The Legislature further [finds and declares that the present uncoordinated, haphazard manner in which the San Francisco Bay is being filled threatens the bay] itself and is therefore inimical to the welfare of both present and future residents of the area surrounding the bay; that while some individual fill projects may be necessary and desirable for the needs of the entire bay region, and while some cities and counties may have prepared detailed master plans for their own bay lands, the fact remains that no governmental mechanism exists for evaluating individual projects as to their effect on the entire bay; and that further piecemeal filling of the bay may place serious restrictions on navigation in the bay, may destroy the irreplaceable feeding and breeding grounds of fish and wildlife in the bay, may adversely affect the quality of bay waters and even the quality of air in the bay area, and would therefore be harmful to the needs of the present and future population of the bay region.' (Gov. Code, § 66601.)

"The Legislature then finds that a new, regional approach is necessary, and charges the BCDC with the task of preparing 'a comprehensive and enforceable plan for the conservation of the water of the bay and the development of its shoreline.' The BCDC is specifically obligated to consider the master plans of cities and counties surrounding the bay in formulating its own plan. (Gov. Code, § 66603.) In the next section the Legislature empowers the BCDC 'to issue or deny permits, after public hearings, for any proposed project that involves placing fill in the bay or extracting submerged materials from the bay.' This power is deemed 'essential' in order 'to protect the present shoreline and body of the San Francisco Bay to the maximum extent possible.' (Gov. Code, § 66604.)"

In creating the Hunters Point Reclamation District in 1955, the Legislature found "that a compelling economic necessity exists for the reclaiming, drainage, and development of tidelands and submerged lands now lying in the district . . . which area now serves no useful purpose for industry, commerce, or navigation. . . ." (Water Code Appendix § 78-1.) Yet, when the BCDC was created in 1965, it was stated to be the policy of the State "to protect the present shoreline and body of the San Francisco Bay to the maximum extent possible. . . ." (Gov. Code, § 66604.) As contended by respondents, to the extent that these expressions of policy are in conflict, the act creating the BCDC, being more recent in time, should control. (See *Coker v. Supreme Court,* 70 Cal. App. 2d 199, 201.)

The strong public purpose behind the McAteer-Petris Act is readily apparent from a reading of the act and the above quoted language from the California Supreme Court. In view of this purpose, and the power given the BCDC "to issue or deny permits, after public hearings, for any proposed project that involves placing fill in the bay," (Gov. Code § 66604) it would be clearly inconsistent to construe the two acts in the manner urged by appellant.

Furthermore, the filling of the bay lands located within the Hunters Point Reclamation District is definitely an "individual project" which may have an effect upon the entire bay. One of the purposes for which the BCDC was created was to study the effect of such projects upon the entire bay. (Gov. Code § 66601.) To exempt lands located within the Hunters Point Reclamation District from the control of the BCDC could impede the BCDC in carrying out its functions.

Appellant also argues that the Hunters Point Reclamation District Act is a specific act and that the McAteer-Petris Act is a general act, and therefore the former controls the latter because of the principle that where two legislative acts are in conflict the specific must control over the general. (*People v. Pacific Im. Co.,* 130 Cal. 442, 446; *Bixby v. Volk,* 273 A.C.A. 826, 838.) However, the specific controls the general only in absence of a clear intention of the legislature to the contrary. (See *Warne v. Harkness,* 60 Cal. 2d 579, 588; *Bixby v. Volk, supra.*) In the instant case, the language of the McAteer-Petris Act is so strong as to make it abundantly clear that the Legislature intended the BCDC to have authority to grant or deny any request for permission to fill the bay lands. It necessarily follows that the BCDC has authority to deny a request to fill bay land located within the Hunters Point Reclamation District if that land would otherwise be within the jurisdiction of the BCDC.

Appellant contends that on April 9, 1966 it submitted a permit application on the printed application form provided by the Commission; that the application contained all the information requested by the printed form and since no action was taken on the application within 60 days, the permit must be deemed granted pursuant to Government Code section 66632(d). Government Code section 66632(d) provided, at the time the application was filed, that the permit shall be automatically granted if the Commission fails to take specific action on the permit within 60 days after it is received.

The trial court found that on April 9, 1966, Candlestick submitted to the Commission a draft application for a permit to fill its land; that additional information requested by the deputy director of the Commission relative to the draft application was supplied by Candlestick without objection; that the application of Candlestick for a permit was filed with the Commission on December 6, 1966, and the application for a permit was denied on January 20, 1967. It was therefore found that Candlestick did not obtain an automatic permit pursuant to the provisions of Government Code section 66632(d) because the Commission took specific action denying the permit application within 60 days of receipt of said application.

By letter of January 5, 1966 the Commission staff requested that the enclosed application form be submitted first in a single draft copy which would be reviewed and commented upon by the Commission if necessary. The applicant would then be requested to submit 100 copies of the completed application. On April 8, 1966, Candlestick sent a draft application to the Commission with a covering letter stating: "Please notify us if any further information or material is required." By letter dated May 6, 1966, the BCDC staff requested additional information in the form of a map of the area prepared to a certain scale and certain factual information. On November 12, 1965, the BCDC adopted a motion providing that the Commission should not consider an application unless the applicant provided answers on the application for all of the applicable questions. Alvin Baum, Jr., deputy director of the BCDC, testified in his deposition that the question on the application form relating to placement of fill was not adequately answered in the April 9, 1966 draft application. By letter dated June 7, 1966, the BCDC staff requested further information which was provided under cover of a letter dated November 20, 1966. On December 1, 1966, Mr. Baum, of the BCDC staff, sent a letter to Candlestick which indicated that the map provided was not adequate for their needs but that he was having another prepared. Mr. Baum requested Candlestick to stipulate that for purposes of the 60-day automatic approval provision of Government Code section 66632(d) the application shall be treated as if it were filed on December 6, 1966, which would be the approximate date that the extra five copies of the application and the map exhibit would be received. The stipulation was apparently executed by Candlestick on December 6, 1966.

Appellant, citing *Napa Savings Bank v. County of Napa,* 17 Cal. App. 545, 548–549, contends that the stipulation is not binding because the April 9, 1966 submission was an application which must be deemed automatically granted after 60 days, and any further action by the Commission would be null and void because it loses jurisdiction after that time. However, appellant's argument assumes that the April 9, 1966 submission was an application. The correspondence between appellant and the Commission and the testimony of Mr. Baum in his deposition were sufficient to justify the court's finding that the document submitted on April 9, 1966 was a draft application rather than a completed application. In view of the finding that this document was only a draft application for a permit, it cannot be said that the Commission lost jurisdiction over the matter 60 days after it was filed.

Therefore, the stipulation was a valid agreement. "Of course, a finding made contrary to a deliberate stipulation cannot stand in the trial court or upon appeal" (*Grand v. Griesinger,* 160 Cal. App. 2d 397, 408, and cases cited therein.) Further, as contended by respondents, the April 9, 1966 draft can have no significance since mere receipt by the BCDC of the incomplete draft application cannot be considered in law to start the 60-day time period. (Cf. *Rakow v. Swain,* 178 Cal. App. 2d 895, 899.) Consequently, appellant's application was not automatically granted by the failure of the Commission to act upon it within 60 days after the draft application of April 9, 1966 was received.

Appellant contends that the provisions of section 66622 of the Government Code, which allowed commission members to designate proxies to act and vote in their place, constitute an unconstitutional delegation of legislative power because no standards were provided for the selection of proxies.

Although there are no standards governing the qualifications of members of the Commission or their proxies set forth in the McAteer-Petris Act itself, the provisions of Government Code sections 1202 *et seq.,* relating to the disqualifications from office of public officers and employees, must be read in conjunction with the McAteer-Petris Act. The basic qualifications for office are that the person holding the office be at least 21 years of age, a citizen of this State and cannot have been convicted of a felony. (Gov. Code §§ 1020, 1021.)

Furthermore, the selection of a proxy is not a legislative act, any more than the selection of the commissioners by the respective appointing powers listed in Government Code section 66620 would be considered a legislative act. Appellant does not contend that there has been an unconstitutional delegation of legislative power to the BCDC when it is acting through the regular members of the Commission. Clearly, there has been no attempt to vest in the commissioners an arbitrary power, or an uncontrolled and unguided discretion in matters concerning the functioning of the Commission in studying the development of the San Francisco Bay and in determining whether to grant a request for a permit to fill bay lands because adequate standards have been set forth in the act. (See Gov. Code § 66632(d); *Tarpey v. McClure,* 190 Cal. 593, 600.) Likewise, proxies acting in the place of the commission members are guided by the same standards.

Appellant argues that discretionary powers committed to an administrative tribunal cannot be delegated to others, citing *Chamber of Commerce v. Stephens,* 212 Cal. 607, 610. While this is true as a general proposition of law, it is not applicable in the present situation. Here the Legislature has created an administrative tribunal and committed discretionary powers to the commission members and their proxies. This situation is manifestly different from a situation in which the Legislature commits discretionary powers to an administrative tribunal and the members of that tribunal delegate their power to others without any prior authorization from the Legislature. In this latter situation the attempted delegation would clearly be contrary to law and void. But that situation is not present here, because the Legislature specifically authorized proxies to act in the place of the commissioners.

Appellant also contends that the Commission was powerless to act on its application because only 12 members of the Commission were present who were entitled to vote when the application was denied. Appellant's position is that Government Code section 66632(d) requires 13 affirmative votes of members of the Commission before a permit will be granted and that the section does not provide that such votes may be by proxies. This contention is without merit. The cardinal rule of statutory construction is that a statute must be read and considered as a whole in order that the true legislative intention may be determined. The various parts of a statute must be constructed together, and harmonized, so far as it is possible to do without doing violence to the language or to the spirit and purpose of the act, so that the statute may stand in its entirety. (In re Bandmann, 51 Cal. 2d 388, 393; *People v. Moroney,* 24 Cal. 2d 638, 642–643.) " 'The numbering of sections of a statute is an artificial practice resorted to purely for convenience, and does not prevent the construction of the statute as a whole.' " (*Renken v. Compton City School Dist.,* 207 Cal. App. 2d 106, 117.) The sections are to be considered together. In the instant case, Government Code section 66622 authorized members of the Commission to appoint proxies to attend meetings and to vote. When section 66632 is considered along with section 66622 it is obvious that the Legislature intended proxies to have authority to vote upon an application for a permit. *Bandini Estate Co. v. Los Angeles,* 28 Cal. App. 2d 224, 229, relied upon by appellant, is not in point because it involved a situation in which one member of the board of supervisors constituted himself a board of equalization when the statutes involved required the whole "Board" to act.

Appellant also claims that some of the proxies who voted to deny its application were not designated at the time of the appointment of the designating member of the Commission and thus section 66622 was violated. This contention is also without merit. A statute must be given a reasonable construction, and its words " 'must be given such interpretation as will promote rather than defeat the general purpose of the law.' " (*Western States Newspapers, Inc. v. Gehringer,* 203 Cal. App. 2d 793, 798, quoting from *In re Lyndood Herald American,* 152 Cal. App. 2d 901, 909.) If appellant's construction of the statute were adopted it would prevent the replacement of a proxy if it became necessary to do so because the replacement would not be appointed at the time of the appointment of the commission member.

Appellant contends that it was denied due process of law because it was not permitted to cross-examine adverse witnesses or to rebut evidence received by the Commission dehors the record. An examination of the transcript of the hearing shows that this contention is without merit. Candlestick was at all times represented by counsel who did not once request to question any person. The right to cross-examination may be waived. (*People v. Dessauer,* 38 Cal. 2d 547, 552.)

Appellant's second point is that it was not given an opportunity to rebut evidence received by the Commission dehors the record. The record shows that the Commission received letters from various organizations and individuals which disagreed with Candlestick's reply to certain questions or which expressed a personal protest against the granting of a permit to fill bay lands. The receipt of these letters was disclosed at the hearing. There was also a discussion concerning the location of a new freeway in the area of appellant's land. Appellant's counsel was present and could have challenged any statement made during the discussion of the location of the freeway.

Perhaps Candlestick's contention goes to the fact that the staff of the Commission, in answering questions and making its recommendation, brought out information in its own without relying solely on statements by persons at the hearings. However, there was nothing wrong with this procedure. Government Code section 66632(c) provides that the Commission shall hold a public hearing as to the proposed project and "conduct such further investigation as it deems necessary." The statute contemplates that the BCDC may seek facts through its staff to aid it in determining whether or not a permit should be granted. Such a practice is sanctioned so long as the information obtained is not concealed. Here, as in the case of *Flagstad v. City of San Mateo,* 156 Cal. App. 2d 138, there was no concealment.

English v. City of Long Beach, 35 Cal. 2d 155, 158, relied upon by appellant, is not controlling in this case because in *English* the evidence received by the civil service board was not disclosed.

Appellant's final contention is that the lower court erred in sustaining without leave to amend, respondents' demurrer to the cause of action seeking damages for the taking of its property without just compensation.

Respondents argue that the legislation creating the BCDC is a valid exercise of the police power and thus the Commission's actions do not constitute a "taking" of private property. As stated by the California Supreme Court in *Miller v. Board of Public Works,* 195 Cal. 477 at 484: "The police power of a state is an indispensable prerogative of sovereignty and one that is not to be lightly limited. Indeed, even though at times its operation may seem harsh, the imperative necessity for its existence precludes any limitation upon its exercise save that it be not unreasonably and arbitrarily invoked and applied. (Citations)

"In short, the police power, as such, is not confined within the narrow circumspection of precedents, resting upon past conditions which do not cover and control present-day conditions obviously calling for revised regulations to promote the health, safety, morals, or general welfare of the public. That is to say, as a commonwealth develops politically, economically, and socially, the police power likewise develops, within reason, to meet the changed and changing conditions. . . ."

It is a well settled rule that determination of the necessity and form of regulations enacted pursuant to the police power "is primarily a legislative and not a judicial function, and is to be tested in the courts not by what the judges individually or collectively may think of the wisdom or necessity of a particular regulation, but solely by the answer to the question is there any reasonable basis in fact to support the legislative determination of the regulation's wisdom and necessity?" (*Consolidated Rock Products Co. v. City of Los Angeles,* 57 Cal. 2d 515, 522.) Furthermore, even if the reasonableness of the regulation is fairly debatable, the legislative determination will not be disturbed. (*Hamer v. Town of Ross,* 59 Cal. 2d 776, 783, and cases cited therein.) Under the power of eminent domain property cannot be taken for public use without just compensation. However, under the police power property is not taken for use by the public; its use by private persons is regulated or prohibited where necessary for the public welfare. (3 Witkin, Summary of Cal. Law, Constitutional Law, § 159, p. 1970; see *Pac. Telephone etc. Co. v. Eshleman,* 166 Cal. 640.)

As contended by respondents, the legislative statements in Government Code section 66600, 66601 and 66603 clearly define the public interest in San Francisco Bay and establish a rational basis for the legislation creating the Commission and for preventing an owner of bay lands from filling those lands. In those sections the Legislature has determined that the bay is the most valuable single natural resource of the entire region and changes in one part of the bay may also affect all other parts; that the present uncoordinated, haphazard manner in which the bay is being filled threatens the bay itself and is therefore inimical, to the welfare of both present and future residents of the bay area; and that a regional approach is necessary to protect the public interest in the bay. In order to protect the bay during the formulation of the conservation and development plan for the bay the Commission must have the power to regulate any proposed project that involves placing fill in the bay. (Gov. Code § 66604.)

Appellant, however, contends that the police power invades the areas of eminent domain when the result of that power is to deprive the private property in question of any value it may have had.

Without question, an undue restriction on the use of private property is as much a taking for constitutional purposes as appropriating or destroying it. (*Pennsylvania Coal Co. v. Mahon,* 260 U.S. 393, 415–416; *People v. Associated Oil Co.,*

211 Cal. 93, 100.) However, it cannot be said that refusing to allow appellant to fill its bay amounts to an undue restriction on its use. In view of the necessity for controlling the filling of the bay, as expressed by the Legislature in the provisions discussed above, it is clear that the restriction imposed does not go beyond proper regulation such that the restriction would be referable to the power of eminent domain rather than the police power. (See *Pacific Telephone etc. Co. v. Eshleman, supra*, 166 Cal. 640, 662.)

The remaining cases cited by appellant are distinguishable on their facts. In *Dooley v. Town Plan. & Zoning Commission*, 151 Conn. 304, 197 A.2d 770, the restrictions placed upon the use of the plaintiff's land were so extensive that the land could be used for no other purpose than for a flood control district, with the result that the land was depreciated in value by 75%. In *Morris County Land, etc. v. Parsippany-Troy Hills Tp.*, 40 N.J. 539, 139 A.2d 233, the practical effect of the regulation was to appropriate private property for a flood water detention basin and open space. The purpose of the regulations and restrictions imposed in the instant case is not merely to provide open spaces. Rather, they are designed to preserve the existing character of the bay while it is determined how the bay should be developed in the future. *Peacock v. County of Sacramento*, 271 Cal. App. 2d 845, is also not in point because in that case it was found that the restrictions imposed by the county were done with the intent to prevent any increase in the cost of acquisition of the lands between the time of the enactment of the ordinance and such time as the county would be ready to acquire or purchase the subject property. (Id. at 853.) Restrictions for this purpose are clearly unreasonable.

Therefore, the restrictions placed upon appellant's use of its land are a valid exercise of the police power. Consequently, appellant was not entitled to damages for confiscation of its property without compensation. In this situation appellant could not allege facts sufficient to constitute a cause of action, and the demurrer was properly sustained without leave to amend. (2 Witkin, Cal. Proc., pleading, § 506, p. 1498.)

The judgment is affirmed.

Draper, P.J., and **H. C. Brown, J.,** concur.

QUESTIONS FOR DISCUSSION

1 Is a finding of fact by a legislature as to the value of an area to the public relevant to the solution of a constitutional question regarding the use of the area? May a court properly disregard a legislative statement as to the purpose of a statute?

2 Note the difference between the 1955 and 1965 legislative findings. What caused the change in attitude?

3 What should a court's attitude be toward claims or defenses based upon procedural requirements such as those involved in *Candlestick v. San Francisco Bay*?

4 The court, after citing *Pennsylvania Coal Company v. Mahon* with apparent approval, concludes that ". . . it cannot be said that refusing to allow appellant to fill its bay amounts to an undue restriction on its use." Is such a response adequate and convincing on a question of such importance?

5   Given the tendency of ecosystems to ignore jurisdictional boundaries, what is the
    appropriate level of government in which to vest regulatory powers? Does the subject
    matter of the regulation make a difference? What political realities might aid or thwart
    proposals for change? Constitutional barriers?
6   Is the difference between a taking and a regulation one of kind or degree?
7   Is the fact that a restriction is temporary relevant? If a property's value is the right one
    has to use it indefinitely, can a temporary restriction be considered only a modest
    diminution of value? What factors might influence such a decision? Market fluctu-
    ations? Age of owner?
8   Would the fact that a property was owned before the regulation was promulgated be
    of significance?
9   Would a statute with a substantial flood-control basis fare better than one obviously
    designed for conservation purposes?
10 How much weight should be accorded the presumption of validity in the case of
    environmental statutes?

ABSOLUTE BANS

Delaware Coastal Zone Act

TITLE 7 DEL. CODE §§ 7001–7014 (1971)

§ 7003.   *Uses absolutely prohibited in the Coastal Zone*

Heavy industry uses of any kind not in operation on the date of enactment of this
chapter are prohibited in the Coastal Zone and no permits may be issued therefor.
In addition, offshore gas, liquid, or solid bulk product transfer facilities which are
not in operation on the date of enactment of this chapter are prohibited in the
Coastal Zone, and no permit may be issued therefor. Provided, that this section
shall not apply to public sewage treatment or recycling plants.

§ 7004.   *Uses allowed by permit only. Non-conforming uses.*

(a) Except for heavy industry uses, as defined in section 7002 of this chapter
manufacturing uses not in existence and in active use [on] the date of enactment of
this chapter are allowed in the Coastal Zone by permit only, as provided for under
this section. Any non-conforming use in existence and in active use on the effective date of this chapter shall not be prohibited by this chapter. All expansion or
extension of non-conforming manufacturing uses, as defined herein, and all expansion or extension of uses for which a permit is issued pursuant to this chapter,
are likewise allowed only by permit. Provided, that no permit may be granted
under this chapter unless the county or municipality having jurisdiction has first
approved the use in question by zoning procedures provided by law.

NATURAL USE

Also adopting a liberal viewpoint on the constitutional issues involved in land-use regulation is the Wisconsin case of *Just v. Marinette County*. This imaginative opinion is significant for its introduction of the "natural use" approach to private rights in property.

Just v. Marinette County

201 N.W.2d 761 (Wis. 1972)

Hallows, Chief Justice

Marinette county's Shoreland Zoning Ordinance Number 24 was adopted September 19, 1967, became effective October 9, 1967, and follows a model ordinance published by the Wisconsin Department of Resource Development in July of 1967. See Kusler, Water Quality Protection For Inland Lakes in Wisconsin: A Comprehensive Approach to Water Pollution, 1970 Wis. L. Rev. 35, 62-63. The ordinance was designed to meet standards and criteria for shoreland regulation which the legislature required to be promulgated by the department of natural resources under sec. 144.26, Stats. These standards are found in 6 Wis. Adm. Code, sec. NR 115.03, May, 1971, Register No. 185. The legislation, secs. 59.971 and 114.26, Stats., authorizing the ordinance was enacted as a part of the Water Quality Act of 1965 by ch. 614, Laws of 1965.

Shorelands for the purpose of ordinances are defined in sec. 59.971(1), Stats., as lands within 1,000 feet of the normal high-water elevation of navigable lakes, ponds, or flowages and 300 feet from a navigable river or stream or to the landward side of the flood plain, whichever distance is greater. The state shoreland program is unique. All county shoreland zoning ordinances must be approved by the department of natural resources prior to their becoming effective. 6 Wis. Adm. Code, sec. NR 115.04, May, 1971, Register No. 185. If a county does not enact a shoreland zoning ordinance which complies with the state's standards, the department of natural resources may enact such an ordinance for the county. Sec. 59.971(6), Stats.

There can be no disagreement over the public purpose sought to be obtained by the ordinance. Its basic purpose is to protect navigable waters and the public rights therein from the degradation and deterioration which results from uncontrolled use and development of shorelands. In the Navigable Waters Protection Act, sec. 144.26, the purpose of the state's shoreland regulation program is stated as being to "aid in the fulfillment of the state's role as trustee of its navigable waters and to promote public health, safety, convenience and general welfare".[1]

---

[1] "144.26 Navigable waters protection law (1) To aid in the fulfillment of the state's role as trustee of its navigable waters and to promote public health, safety, convenience and general welfare, it is declared to be in the public interest to make studies, establish policies, make plans and authorize

In sec. 59.971(1), which grants authority for shoreland zoning to counties, the same purposes are reaffirmed.[2] The Marinette county shoreland zoning ordinance in sec. 1.2 and 1.3 states the uncontrolled use of shorelands and pollution of navigable waters of Marinette county adversely affect public health, safety, convenience, and general welfare and impair the tax base.

The shoreland zoning ordinance divides the shorelands of Marinette county into general purpose districts, general recreation districts, and conservancy districts. A "conservancy" district is required by the statutory minimum standards and is defined in sec. 3.4 of the ordinance to include "all shorelands designated as swamps or marshes on the United States Geological Survey maps which have been designated as the Shoreland Zoning Map of Marinette County, Wisconsin or on the detailed Insert Shoreland Zoning Maps." The ordinance provides for permitted uses[3] and conditional uses.[4] One of the conditional uses requiring a permit under sec. 3.42(4) is the filling, drainage or dredging of wetlands according to the provisions of sec. 5 of the ordinance. "Wetlands" are defined in sec. 2.29 as "(a)reas where ground water is at or near the surface much of the year or where

---

municipal shoreland zoning regulations for the efficient use, conservation, development and protection of this state's water resources. The regulation shall relate to lands under, abutting or lying close to navigable waters. The purposes of the regulations shall be to further the maintenance of safe and healthful conditions; prevent and control water pollution; protect spawning grounds, fish and aquatic life; control building sites, placement of structure and land uses and reserve shore cover and natural beauty . . . ."

[2] "59.971 Zoning of shorelands on navigable waters   (1) To effect the purposes of s. 144.26 and to promote the public health, safety and general welfare, counties may, by ordinance enacted separately from ordinances pursuant to s. 59.97, zone all lands (referred to herein as shorelands) in their unincorporated areas within the following distances from the normal high-water elevation of navigable waters as defined in s. 144.26(2)(d): 1,000 feet from a lake, pond or flowage; 300 feet from a river or stream or to the landward side of the flood plain, whichever distance is greater. If the navigable water is a glacial pothole lake, the distance shall be measured from the high water-mark thereof."

[3] "3.41   Permitted Uses.

(1) Harvesting of any wild crop such as marsh hay, ferns, moss, wild rice, berries, tree fruits and tree seeds.

(2) Sustained yield forestry subject to the provisions of Section 5.0 relating to removal of shore cover.

(3) Utilities such as, but not restricted to, telephone, telegraph and power transmission lines.

(4) Hunting, fishing, preservation of scenic, historic and scientific areas and wildlife preserves.

(5) Non-resident buildings used solely in conjunction with raising water fowl, minnows, and other similar lowland animals, fowl or fish.

(6) Hiking trails and bridle paths.

(7) Accessory uses.

(8) Signs, subject to the restriction of Section 2.0."

[4] "3.42   Conditional Uses. The following uses are permitted upon issuance of a Conditional Use Permit as provided in Section 9.0 and issuance of a Department of Resource Development permit where required by Section 30.11, 30.12, 30.19, 30.195 and 31.05 of the Wisconsin Statutes.

(1) General farming provided farm animals shall be kept one hundred feet from any non-farm residence.

(2) Dams, power plants, flowages and ponds.

(3) Relocation of any water course.

(4) Filling, drainage or dredging of wetlands according to the provisions of Section 5.0 of this ordinance.

(5) Removal of topsoil or peat.

(6) Cranberry bogs.

(7) Piers, docks, boathouses."

any segment of plant cover is deemed an aquatic according to N. C. Fassett's "Manual of Aquatic Plants." Section 5.42(2) of the ordinance requires a conditional-use permit for any filling or grading "Of any area which is within three hundred feet horizontal distance of a navigable water and which has surface drainage toward the water and on which there is: (a) Filling of more than five hundred square feet of any wetland which is contiguous to the water . . . (d) Filling or grading of more than 2,000 square feet on slopes of twelve per cent or less."

In April of 1961, several years prior to the passage of this ordinance, the Justs purchased 36.4 acres of land in the town of Lake along the south shore of Lake Noquebay, a navigable lake in Marinette county. This land had a frontage of 1,266.7 feet on the lake and was purchased partially for personal use and partially for resale. During the years 1964, 1966, and 1967, the Justs made five sales of parcels having frontage and extending back from the lake some 600 feet, leaving the property involved in these suits. This property has a frontage of 366.7 feet and the south one half contains a stand of cedar, pine, various hard woods, birch and red maple. The north one half, closer to the lake, is barren of trees except immediately along the shore. The south three fourths of this north one half is populated with various plant grasses and vegetation including some plants which N. C. Fassett in his manual of aquatic plants has classified as "aquatic." There are also non-aquatic plants which grow upon the land. Along the shoreline there is a belt of trees. The shoreline is from one foot to 3.2 feet higher than the lake level and there is a narrow belt of higher land along the shore known as a "pressure ridge" or "ice heave," varying in width from one to three feet. South of this point, the natural level of the land ranges one to two feet above lake level. The land slopes generally toward the lake but has a slope less than twelve per cent. No water flows onto the land from the lake, but there is some surface water which collects on land and stands in pools.

The land owned by the Justs is designated as swamps or marshes on the United States Geological Survey Map and is located within 1,000 feet of the normal high-water elevation of the lake. Thus, the property is included in a conservancy district, and by sec. 2.29 of the ordinance, classified as "wetlands." Consequently, in order to place more than 500 square feet of fill on this property, the Justs were required to obtain a conditional-use permit from the zoning administrator of the county and pay a fee of $20 or incur a forfeiture of $10 to $200 for each day of violation.

In February and March of 1968, six months after the ordinance became effective, Ronald Just, without securing a conditional-use permit, hauled 1,040 square yards of sand onto his property and filled an area approximately 20-feet wide commencing at the southwest corner and extending almost 600 feet north to the northwest corner near the shoreline, then easterly along the shoreline almost to the lot line. He stayed back from the pressure ridge about 20 feet. More than 500 square feet of this fill was upon wetlands located contiguous to the water and which had surface drainage toward the lake. The fill within 300 feet of the lake also was more than 2,000 square feet on a slope less than 12 per cent. It is not seriously contended that the Justs did not violate the ordinance and the trial court correctly found a violation.

The real issue is whether the conservancy district provisions and the wetlands-filling restrictions are unconstitutional because they amount to a constructive taking of the Justs' land without compensation. Marinette county and the state of Wisconsin argue the restrictions of the conservancy district and wetlands provisions constitute a proper exercise of the police power of the state and do not so severely limit the use or depreciate the value of the land as to constitute a taking without compensation.

To state the issue in more meaningful terms, it is a conflict between the public interest in stopping the despoliation of natural resources, which our citizens until recently have taken as inevitable and for granted, and an owner's asserted right to use his property as he wishes. The protection of public rights may be accomplished by the exercise of the police power unless the damage to the property owner is too great and amounts to a confiscation. The securing or taking of a benefit not presently enjoyed by the public for its use is obtained by the government through its power of eminent domain. The distinction between the exercise of the police power and condemnation has been said to be a matter of degree of damage to the property owner. In the valid exercise of the police power reasonably restricting the use of property, the damage suffered by the owner is said to be incidental. However, where the restriction is so great the landowner ought not to bear such a burden for the public good, the restriction has been held to be a constructive taking even though the actual use or forbidden use has not been transferred to the government so as to be a taking in the traditional sense. *Stefan Auto Body v. State Highway Comm.*, (1963), 21 Wis. 2d 363, 124 N.W.2d 319; *Buhler v. Racine County*, (1966), 33 Wis. 2d 137, 146 N.W.2d 403; *Nick v. State Highway Comm.*, (1961), 13 Wis. 2d 511, 109 N.W.2d 71, 111 N.W.2d 95; *State v. Becker*, (1934), 215 Wis. 564, 255 N.W. 144. Whether a taking has occurred depends upon whether "the restriction practically or substantially renders the land useless for all reasonable purposes." *Buhler v. Racine County, supra.* The loss caused the individual must be weighed to determine if it is more than he should bear. As this court stated in *Stefan,* at pp. 369–370, 124 N.W.2d 319, p. 323, ". . . if the damage is such as to be suffered by many similarly situated and is in the nature of a restriction on the use to which land may be put and ought to be borne by the individual as a member of society for the good of the public safety, health or general welfare, it is said to be a reasonable exercise of the police power, but if the damage is so great to the individual that he ought not to bear it under contemporary standards, then courts are inclined to treat it as a 'taking' of the property or an unreasonable exercise of the police power."

Many years ago, Professor Freund stated in his work on The Police Power, sec. 511, at 546–547, "It may be said that the state takes property by eminent domain because it is useful to the public, and under the police power because it is harmful . . . From this results the difference between the power of eminent domain and the police power, that the former recognizes a right to compensation, while the latter on principle does not." Thus the necessity for monetary compensation for loss suffered to an owner by police power restriction arises when restrictions are placed on property in order to create a public benefit rather than to prevent a public harm. Rathkopf, The Law of Zoning and Planning, Vol. 1, ch. 6, pp. 6-7.

This case causes us to reexamine the concepts of public benefit in contrast to public harm and the scope of an owner's right to use his property. In the instant case we have a restriction on the use of a citizen's property, not to secure a benefit for the public, but to prevent a harm from the change in the natural character of the citizen's property. We start with the premise that lakes and rivers in their natural state are unpolluted and the pollution which now exists is man made. The state of Wisconsin under the public trust doctrine has a duty to eradicate the present pollution and to prevent further pollution in its navigable waters. This is not, in a legal sense, a gain or a securing of a benefit by the maintaining of the natural *status quo* of the environment. What makes this case different from most condemnation or police power zoning cases is the interrelationship of the wetlands, the swamps and the natural environment of shorelands to the purity of the water and to such natural resources as navigation, fishing, and scenic beauty. Swamps and wetlands were once considered wasteland, undesirable, and not picturesque. But as the people became more sophisticated, an appreciation was acquired that swamps and wetlands serve a vital role in nature, are part of the balance of nature and are essential to the purity of the water in our lakes and streams. Swamps and wetlands are a necessary part of the ecological creation and now, even to the uninitiated, possess their own beauty in nature.

Is the ownership of a parcel of land so absolute that man can change its nature to suit any of his purposes? The great forests of our state were stripped on the theory man's ownership was unlimited. But in forestry, the land at least was used naturally, only the natural fruit of the land (the trees) were taken. The despoilage was in the failure to look to the future and provide for the reforestation of the land. An owner of land has no absolute and unlimited right to change the essential natural character of his land so as to use it for a purpose for which it was unsuited in its natural state and which injures the rights of others. The exercise of the police power in zoning must be reasonable and we think it is not an unreasonable exercise of that power to prevent harm to public rights by limiting the use of private property to its natural uses.

This is not a case where an owner is prevented from using his land for natural and indigenous uses. The uses consistent with the nature of the land are allowed and other uses recognized and still others permitted by special permit. The shoreland zoning ordinance prevents to some extent the changing of the natural character of the land within 1,000 feet of a navigable lake and 300 feet of a navigable river because of such land's interrelation to the contiguous water. The changing of wetlands and swamps to the damage of the general public by upsetting the natural environment and the natural relationship is not a reasonable use of that land which is protected from police power regulation. Changes and filling to some extent are permitted because the extent of such changes and fillings does not cause harm. We realize no case in Wisconsin has yet dealt with shoreland regulations and there are several cases in other states which seem to hold such regulations unconstitutional; but nothing this court has said or held in prior cases indicate that destroying the natural character of a swamp or a wetland so as to make that location available for human habitation is a reasonable use of that land when the new use, although of a more economical value to the owner, causes a harm to the general public.

Wisconsin has long held that laws and regulations to prevent pollution and to protect the waters of this state from degradation are valid police-power enactments. State ex rel. *Martin v. Juneau* (1941), 238 Wis. 564, 300 N.W. 187; State ex rel. *LaFollette v. Reuter* (1967), 33 Wis. 2d 384, 147 N.W.2d 304; *Reuter v. Department of Natural Resources* (1969), 43 Wis. 2d 272, 168 N.W.2d 860. The active public trust duty of the state of Wisconsin in respect to navigable waters requires the state not only to promote navigation but also to protect and preserve those waters for fishing, recreation, and scenic beauty. *Muench v. Public Service Comm.* (1952), 261 Wis. 492, 53 N.W.2d 514, 55 N.W.2d 40. To further this duty, the legislature may delegate authority to local units of the government, which the state did by requiring counties to pass shoreland zoning ordinances. *Menzer v. Elkhart Lake* (1971), 51 Wis. 2d 70, 186 N.W.2d 290.

This is not a case of an isolated swamp unrelated to a navigable lake or stream, the change of which would cause no harm to public rights. Lands adjacent to or near navigable waters exist in a special relationship to the state. They have been held subject to special taxation, *Soens v. City of Racine* (1860), 10 Wis. 271, and are subject to the state public trust powers, *Wisconsin P. & L. Co. v. Public Service Comm.* (1958), 5 Wis. 2d 167, 92 N.W.2d 241; and since the Laws of 1935, ch. 303, counties have been authorized to create special zoning districts along waterways and zone them for restrictive conservancy purposes.[5] The restrictions in the Marinette county ordinance upon wetlands within 1,000 feet of Lake Noquebay which prevent the placing of excess fill upon such land without a permit is not confiscatory or unreasonable.

Cases wherein a confiscation was found cannot be relied upon by the Justs. In *State v. Herwig* (1962), 17 Wis. 2d 442, 117 N.W.2d 335, a "taking" was found where a regulation which prohibited hunting on farmland had the effect of establishing a game refuge and resulted in an unnatural, concentrated foraging of the owner's land by waterfowl. In *State v. Becker, supra,* the court held void a law which established a wildlife refuge (and prohibited hunting) on private property. In *Benka v. Consolidated Water Power Co.* (1929), 198 Wis. 472, 224 N.W. 718, the court held if damages to plaintiff's property were in fact caused by flooding from a dam constructed by a public utility, those damages constituted a "taking" within the meaning of the condemnation statutes. In *Bino v. Hurley* (1955), 273 Wis. 10, 76 N.W.2d 571, the court held unconstitutional as a "taking" without compensation an ordinance which, in attempting to prevent pollution, prohibited the own-

---

[5] In *Jefferson County v. Timmel* (1952), 261 Wis. 39, 51 N.W.2d 518, the constitutionality of a conservancy district use restriction was upheld as being based on a valid exercise of police power. The purpose of this conservancy district, however, was for highway safety and not for the prevention of pollution and the protection of the police trust in navigable waters.

ers of land surrounding a lake from bathing, boating, or swimming in the lake. In *Piper v. Ekern* (1923), 180 Wis. 586, 593, 194 N.W. 159, 162, the court held a statute which limited the height of buildings surrounding the state capitol to be unnecessary for the public health, safety, or welfare and, thus, to constitute an unreasonable exercise of the police power. In all these cases the unreasonableness of the exercise of the police power lay in excessive restriction of the natural use of the land or rights in relation thereto.

Cases holding the exercise of police power to be reasonable likewise provide no assistance to Marinette county in their argument. In *More-Way North Corp. v. State Highway Comm.* (1969), 44 Wis. 2d 165, 175 N.W.2d 749, the court held that no "taking" occurred as a result of the state's lowering the grade of a highway, which necessitated plaintiff's reconstruction of its parking lot and loss of 42 parking spaces. In *Wisconsin Power & Light Co. v. Columbia County* (1958), 3 Wis. 2d 1, 87 N.W.2d 279, no "taking" was found where the county, in relocating a highway, deposited gravel close to plaintiff's tower causing it to tilt. In *Nick v. State Highway Comm., supra,* the court held that where property itself is not physically taken by the state, a restriction of access to a highway, while it may decrease the value of the land, does not entitle the owner to compensation. In *Buhler* the court held the mere depreciation of value was not sufficient ground to enjoin the county from enforcing the ordinance. In *Hasslinger v. Hartland* (1940), 234 Wis. 201, 290 N.W. 647, the court noted that "(a)ssuming an actionable nuisance by the creation of odors which make occupation of plaintiffs' farm inconvenient . . . and impair its value, it cannot be said that defendant has dispossessed plaintiffs or taken their property."

The Justs rely on several cases from other jurisdictions which have held zoning regulations involving flood plain districts, flood basins and wetlands to be so confiscatory as to amount to a taking because the owners of the land were prevented from improving such property for residential or commercial purposes. While some of these cases may be distinguished on their facts, it is doubtful whether these differences go to the basic rationale which permeates the decision that an owner has a right to use his property in any way and for any purpose he sees fit. In *Dooley v. Town Plan. & Zon. Comm. of Town of Fairfield* (1964), 151 Conn. 304, 197 A.2d 770, the court held the restriction on land located in a flood plain district prevented its being used for residential or business purposes and thus the restriction destroyed the economic value to the owner. The court recognized the land was needed for a public purpose as it was part of the area in which the tidal stream overflowed when abnormally high tides existed, but the property was half a mile from the ocean and therefore could not be used for marina or boathouse purposes. In *Morris County Land I. Co. v. Parsippany-Troy Hills Tp.* (1963), 40 N.J. 539, 193 A.2d 232, a flood basin zoning ordinance was involved which required the controversial land to be retained in its natural state. The plaintiff owned 66 acres of a 1,500-acre swamp which was part of a river basin and acted as a natural detention basin for flood waters in times of very heavy rainfall. There was an extraneous issue that the freezing regulations were intended as a stop-gap until such time as the government would buy the property under a flood-control project. However, the court took the view the zoning had an effect of preserving the land as an open space as a water-detention basin and only the government or the public would be benefited, to the complete damage of the owner.

In *State v. Johnson* (1970), Me., 265 A.2d 711, the Wetlands Act restricted the alteration and use of certain wetlands without permission. The act was a conservation measure enacted under the police power to protect the ecology of areas bordering the coastal waters. The plaintiff owned a small tract of a saltwater marsh which was flooded at high tide. By filling, the land would be adapted for building purposes. The court held the restrictions against filling constituted a deprivation of a reasonable use of the owner's property and, thus, an unreasonable exercise of the police power. In *MacGibbon v. Board of Appeals of Duxbury* (1970), 356 Mass. 635, 255 N.E.2d 347, the plaintiff owned seven acres of land which were under water about twice a month in a shoreland area. He was denied a permit to excavate and fill part of his property. The purpose of the ordinance was to preserve from despoilage natural features and resources such as salt marshes, wetlands, and ponds. The court took the view the preservation of privately owned land in its natural, unspoiled state for the enjoyment and benefit of the public by preventing the owner from using it for any practical purpose was not within the limit and scope of the police power and the ordinance was not saved by the use of special permits.

It seems to us that filling a swamp not otherwise commercially usable is not in and of itself an existing use, which is prevented, but rather is the preparation for some future use which is not indigenous to a swamp. Too much stress is laid on the right of an owner to change commercially valueless land when that change does damage to the rights of the public. It is observed that a use of special permits is a means of control and accomplishing the purpose of the zoning ordinance as distinguished from the old concept of providing for variances. The special permit technique is not common practice and has met with judicial approval, and we think it is of some significance in considering whether or not a particular zoning ordinance is reasonable.

A recent case sustaining the validity of a zoning ordinance establishing a flood plain district is *Turnpike Realty Company v. Town of Dedham* (June, 1972), 72 Mass. 1303, 284 N.E.2d 891. The court held the validity of the ordinance was not supported by valid considerations of public welfare, the conservation of "natural conditions, wildlife and open spaces." The ordinance provided that lands which were subject to seasonal or periodic flooding could not be used for residences or other purposes in such a manner as to endanger the health, safety or occupancy thereof and prohibited the erection of structures or buildings which required land to be filled. This case is analogous to the instant facts. The ordinance had a public purpose to preserve the natural condition of the area. No change was allowed which would injure the purposes sought to be preserved and through the special-permit technique, particular land within the zoning district could be excepted from the restrictions.

The Justs argue their property has been severely depreciated in value. But this depreciation of value is not based on the use of the land in its natural state but on what the land would be worth if it could be filled and used for the location of a dwelling. While loss of value is to be considered in determining whether a restriction is a constructive taking, value based upon changing the character of the land at the expense of harm to public rights is not an essential factor or controlling.

We are not unmindful of the warning in *Pennsylvania Coal Co. v. Mahon* (1922), 260 U.S. 393, 416, 43 S. Ct. 158, 160, 67 L. Ed. 322:

> ". . . We are in danger of forgetting that a strong public desire to improve the public condition is not enough to warrant achieving the desire by a shorter cut than the constitutional way of paying for the change."

This observation refers to the improvement of the public condition, the securing of a benefit not presently enjoyed and to which the public is not entitled. The shoreland zoning ordinance preserves nature, the environment, and natural resources as they were created and to which the people have a present right.[6] The ordinance does not create or improve the public condition but only preserves nature from the despoilage and harm resulting from the unrestricted activities of humans.

NOTE: BALANCING OF INTERESTS

Another taking-issue theory which appears, sometimes discretely and sometimes in combination with another, and which is probably present if unacknowledged in many cases, is termed the balancing-of-interests test. Under this theory the harm to the individual whose property is regulated is balanced against the good to the public resulting from the regulation. (See *Pennsylvania Coal Company v. Mahon*, page 63.)

The balancing test is suspect on a number of grounds and has been severely criticized. See, for example, Michelman, *Property, Utility, and Fairness: Comments on the Ethical Foundations of Just Compensation Law*, 80 HARV. L. REV. 1165 (1967); and E.L.I. Federal Environmental Law, p. 55.

QUESTIONS FOR DISCUSSION

1 The restriction of the use of property to its natural uses was specifically disapproved in *Morris County Land, etc., v. Parsippany-Troy Hills Township*. What dangers exist in the application of such a doctrine? What would be the natural uses of desert or forest land?

2 Is the decision in *Just v. Marinette County* consistent with the rule that taking occurs when a restriction renders land useless for all reasonable purposes?

3 Do you find *Pennsylvania Coal Company v. Mahon* adequately distinguished?

4 Do you note any similarity between *Just v. Marinette County* and the dissenting opinion of Brandeis in *Pennsylvania Coal Company v. Mahon*?

5 What problems are inherent in permit schemes?

6 Given a finite amount of property within the jurisdiction of the permit scheme, are the criteria to be applied the same for the tenth permit application as they were for the first if a number of permits have been granted and ecologically sensitive areas destroyed?

---

[6] On the letterhead of the Jackson County Zoning and Sanitation Department, the following appears: "The land belongs to the people . . . a little of it to those dead . . . some to those living . . . but most of it belongs to those yet to be born . . ."

7   How might the Fifth Amendment be modified so as to better facilitate environmental and land-use plans? Should it be?
8   Is the "public trust doctrine" capable of specific definition? What problems may arise in attempting a precise definition?
9   How far may the state go in regulating land not in its "natural state"?
10 How might *Pennsylvania Coal Company v. Mahon* be decided if it were to be litigated today? What attitudinal changes might affect the outcome?
11 Is zoning an adequate substitute for environmental impact assessment?

NUISANCE

The abatement of public nuisances is within the scope of the police power. Nuisance, a concept of law which has been said to be an "impenetrable jungle" "incapable of any exact or comprehensive definition"[f] may be generally considered to be the use of property which is injurious to the health of others, is indecent or offensive to the senses, or works hurt, inconvenience, or damage.[g] The scope of nuisance actions is nearly unlimited; it may include, for example, the drilling of an oil well in the city,[h] burying dead animals,[i] or unreasonable noise, dust, or pollution.[j]

Public nuisances, those which obstruct or cause inconvenience or damage to the public in the exercise of common rights, rather than those peculiar to one individual, or several,[k] may be abated by government action without compensation although the loss to the property owner may be substantial. The line between nuisance and taking-issue cases is often obscure, however, since the facts and claims may well fall into both categories. Thus, many sources of pollution may be abated as nuisances instead of being made the subject of a regulatory scheme. Such individual action is, of course, substantially more cumbersome than a blanket ban or permit scheme covering a class of actions.[l] Nuisance is also covered in Chapter 5.

PROBLEMS

1   Suppose an owner of open-space property purchased it in the expectation of subdividing into fifty ½-acre lots and the price he paid was based upon that expectation. Thereafter, a zoning ordinance is passed restricting lot size in the area to a 2-acre minimum and thereby reducing the property's value by one-half. Could such an ordi-

---

[f] William Prosser, *Torts,* 3d ed., West Publishing Company, St. Paul, Minn., 1964, sec. 87.
[g] *Black's Law Dictionary,* 4th ed., West Publishing Company, St. Paul, Minn., 1951.
[h] *Green v. General Petroleum Corporation,* 270 P. 952 (Cal., 1928).
[i] *Waters v. McNeary,* 185 N.Y.S.2d 29, *aff'd* 202 N.Y.S.2d 24 (1955).
[j] For a detailed examination of the types of pollution which have been held to constitute nuisances, see AM. JUR. 2d ed., *Pollution Control.*
[k] The pollution of a stream which damages only riparian owners might be a private nuisance whereas pollution causing a fish kill would be a public nuisance. *State ex rel. Wear v. Springfield Gas and Electric Company,* Mo. App. 1918, 204 S.W. 542.
[l] For a modern application of nuisance law in the environmental field, see *United States v. Reserve Mining* Chapter 9, where a mining company's discharge of taconite tailings containing fibers similar to amosite asbestos, a human carcinogen, was held to constitute a common-law nuisance. See also *Illinois v. City of Milwaukee,* 406 U.S. 91.

nance be validly applied to this property, which was previously owned and designated for small-lot residential use?

2   Given the facts above, would the result be different if the 2-acre restriction was in force at the time of the purchase?

3   A local zoning board, relying on *Just v. Marinette County,* restricts the use of forest property to its "natural" use and forbids the cutting of trees. Owners of wooded property contend that their property is reduced in value by 95 percent and that the regulation is unconstitutional. Does the decision in *Just v. Marinette County* validate the board's action?

4   A factory has been located in one place for thirty years. The surrounding area has built up over that time so that the area is now primarily residential. In the interests of health and safety the zoning board rezones the factory property from industrial to residential. What might be the factory's argument in its defense?

5   Suppose Mr. X owned 5 acres of marshland and Mr. Y 5,000 acres and both were subject to regulation which essentially prevented use other than in its natural state. Would the same decision be made on the taking issue for each? Would the result be different if Mr. X owned only marsh while Mr. Y owned marsh and adjoining upland? Suppose Y's upland property is not adjoining.

SUGGESTIONS FOR FURTHER READING

Berger, L.: *Policy Analysis of the Taking Problem,* 49 N.Y.U. L. REV. 165, 1974.

Just Compensation and the Assassin's Bequest: A Utilization Approach, 122 U. PA. L. REV. 1012, 1974.

Kurland, P. B.: *Magna Carta and Constitutionalism in the United States: "The Noble Lie" in the Great Charter, Four Essays on Magna Carta and The History of Our Liberty,* University of Chicago Press, Chicago, 1965.

Peabody, J. B., ed.: *The Holmes-Einstein Letters,* St. Martin's Press, New York, 1964.

Plater, Z. J. B.: *Taking Issue in a National Setting: Floodlines and the Police Power,* 52 TEXAS L. REV. 201, 1974.

Sax, J.: *Taking and the Police Power,* 74 YALE L.J. 36, 1964.

State and Local Wetlands Regulation: The Problem of Taking without Just Compensation, 58 VA. L. REV. 876, 1972.

State Land Use Regulation: A Survey of Recent Legislative Approaches, 56 MINN. L. REV. 869, 1972.

Stever, D. W.: *Land Use Controls, Takings and the Police Power—a Discussion of the Myth,* 15 N.H.B.J. 149, 1974.

Taking, Private Property and Public Rights, 81 YALE L.J. 149, 1971.

Chapter 5

Common-Law
Pollution Control

ORIGINS

The common law recognized in the United States was formulated and developed in ancient England. Its origins may be traced to the early Anglo-Saxon peoples who derived a complex body of unwritten laws based mainly on custom and usage. This body of law was transported to this country with early colonists, and as a general rule, American common law is basically composed of that common law which was in use on July 4, 1776, and not repugnant to the Constitution. This is not to say, however, that the development of common law stopped in 1776. It has adapted with rather good grace to modern conditions and has been refined and interpreted substantially in the modern era. The Supreme Court, in speaking of American common law, has stated:

> As distinguished from law created by the enactment of legislatures, the common law comprises the body of those principles and rules of action, relating to the government and security of persons and property, which derive their authority solely from usages and customs of immemorial antiquity, or from the judgments and decrees of the courts recognizing, affirming and enforcing such usages and customs; and, in this sense, particularly the ancient unwritten law of England.[a]

[a] *Western Union Company v. Call Pub. Company.*, 181 U.S. 92 (1900).

In many state jurisdictions, the basic principles of common law have been somewhat modified and enacted into statutory form and codified. There also exists a field of federal common law which is often referred to where no applicable federal statute exists. The Supreme Court has stated, "It is not uncommon for federal courts to fashion federal law where federal rights are concerned."[b] In defining federal common law, one prominent scholar states that in using federal common law, ". . . the Court draws on federal law, state law, and international law, as the exigencies of the particular case may demand."[c] Therefore, it may be stated that common law, both state and federal, is made up of case law as opposed to legislative enactments.

As a general rule, in pollution cases common-law doctrines are used in the absence of a specific statutory cause of action or as an alternative method of abating such pollution.

There are four basic common-law doctrines which may be used in anti-pollution litigation: (1) nuisance (both public and private), (2) negligence, (3) strict liability, and (4) trespass.

Nuisance may be defined as "a substantial invasion of interests in the use or enjoyment of land" (private) or "any form of material annoyance or inconvenience interfering with the common public rights" (public).[d] A private nuisance is a civil wrong which may be prosecuted by the individual whose interest in land has been disturbed. However, a public nuisance is considered a criminal offense because it is an interference with the rights of the public at large and the remedy for it is generally in the hands of the state.[e]

Additionally, a nuisance may result from act or omission which is negligent or which may be defined as an abnormally dangerous activity.[f]

A nuisance may also be considered both public and private where an existing noxious condition such as a rendering plant would substantially interfere with a property owner's use and enjoyment of his own land and at the same time cause considerable discomfort to the community at large.

STATE LAW—PRIVATE NUISANCE

Nuisance as a pollution-control remedy is of primary value in state law where statutory schemes are less well developed. In *Urie v. Franconia Paper Corporation* the use of nuisance was upheld where the goal was to abate an existing unpleasantness.

---

[b] *Textile Workers v. Lincoln Mills,* 353 U.S. 448 at 457.
[c] Charles Wright, *Federal Courts,* 2d ed., West Publishing Company, St. Paul, Minn., 1970, p. 504.
[d] See William Prosser, *Torts,* 3d ed., West Publishing Company, St. Paul, Minn., 1964.
[e] At common law, a public nuisance was always a crime, and punishable as such.
[f] See *Restatement of Torts,* 2d ed., American Law Institute at Washington, D.C., 1964, p. 520.

Urie v. Franconia Paper Corporation

218 A.2d 360 (1966)

Wheeler, Justice.

This action is a bill in equity brought by H. Thomas Urie and fifteen others seeking to enjoin and restrain the defendant from further pollution of the waters of the Pemigewasset River and that defendant be ordered to take such reasonable measures as may be required to abate the private nuisance resulting to the plaintiffs.

It is alleged in the petition that the plaintiffs are owners of real estate situated in the Bristol-New Hampton area in the valley of the Pemigewasset River. Certain of the plaintiffs are riparian owners of real estate bordering said Pemigewasset River. The defendant, Franconia Paper Corporation is engaged in the manufacture of pulp and paper products at Lincoln on or near the Pemigewasset River upstream from the lands of the plaintiffs.

It is further alleged that the defendant in the course of its manufacturing processes is and for several years has been discharging sulfite waste liquors, wood and pulp waste material and other pollution into the waters of said river, that the intensity and volume of such discharge has been increasing in the last three or four years and that the waste and pollution is and has been flowing downstream in said river through and past the land of the plaintiffs during this period.

Further, the petition alleges that in times of warm weather or low water conditions in the river the said wastes, solids and pollution by the time they have made their way downstream to a point near the lands of the plaintiffs, have worked, fermented or decayed to the point that they have become foul and offensive to human beings and there has thereby resulted the deposit of foul and offensive sludge and decayed matter in substantial quantities on the lands of those plaintiffs who are riparian owners. It is further alleged that during such warm weather periods the pollution of the waters by the defendant has caused the discharge of vile, obnoxious and offensive odors which have permeated the atmosphere on and near the lands and premises of the plaintiffs causing substantial appreciable injury to the plaintiffs in their use and enjoyment of their property and rendering their enjoyment of their property uncomfortable and inconvenient.

The plaintiffs assert that the action of the defendant in the circumstances alleged is an unreasonable use of its premises and of the waters of the said Pemigewasset River and constitutes a private nuisance as to these plaintiffs and that such pollution by the defendant in the circumstances alleged is a constantly recurring grievance, day by day.

In their brief the plaintiffs advise that since the instant action was instituted there has been determined and they will offer to prove that the odors discharged from the polluted river are hydrogen sulfide gas which is not only highly offensive to human beings but also attacks the lead-based paint on dwellings and other buildings in the vicinity causing them to turn black, and that the existence of this condition has also caused a substantial depreciation in property values of the plaintiffs which plaintiffs stand ready to prove.

The defendant in its answer makes a general denial of the allegation that its operations are polluting the Pemigewasset River and by way of affirmative defense alleges that the East Branch of the Pemigewasset River, in the towns of Lincoln and Woodstock, from the dam of the Franconia Paper Corporation to the confluence with the Pemigewasset River has been classified by the Legislature as Class D water and that the Pemigewasset River from its confluence with the East Branch of the Pemigewasset River in the town of Woodstock to the crest of the Eastman Falls Dam in Franklin has been classified by the Legislature as Class D water. Laws of 1959, 243:1, VII, VIII. See note following RSA 149:6.

The defendant further alleges that no order for abatement of pollution of the waters of the East Branch of the Pemigewasset River from the dam of the Franconia Paper Corporation to the confluence with the Pemigewasset River and of the Pemigewasset River from its confluence with the East Branch of the Pemigewasset River to the crest of the Eastman Falls Dam in Franklin may be entered prior to September 1, 1969. Laws of 1959, 243:2. Defendant's answer further alleges that if the waters of the Pemigewasset River are polluted as alleged by the plaintiffs such pollution has been caused by persons and municipalities other than by the defendant.

The plaintiffs demurred to the affirmative defense pleaded in the defendant's answer on the grounds that said defense as pleaded is not sufficient in law.

All questions of law raised by the plaintiffs' demurrer was reserved and transferred in advance of trial by Griffith, J.

The plaintiffs seek relief from a private nuisance, as landowners, and not as members of the public, specially damaged by a public nuisance. Cf. *St. Regis Paper Co. v. New Hampshire Water Resources Board,* 92 N.H. 164, 26 A.2d 832. A nuisance may simultaneously be a public and private nuisance. *McKinney v. Riley,* 105 N.H. 249, 254, 197 A.2d 218; *White v. Suncook Mills,* 91 N.H. 92, 97, 13 A.2d 729. See also discussion in Restatement, Torts, pp. 217, 218.

It has been held by the weight of authority that what is authorized by law cannot be a public nuisance, but such authorization does not affect any claim of a private citizen for damages for injury "caused by the authorized act not experienced by the public at large, or for an injunction." 39 Am. Jur., Nuisances, p. 481, ss. 204, 205. See also *Commerce Oil Refining Corp. v. Miner,* 281 F.2d 465 (1st Cir.).

As the plaintiffs point out, there is nothing in RSA ch. 149 to indicate a legislative intent to take away any private rights of individual landowners to seek redress in equity to prevent pollution of the river. It seems doubtful if the Legislature has constitutional power to permit the defendant to continue to commit private nuisances until September 1, 1969, since such legislation would constitute taking private property for a non-public purpose. *Eaton v. Boston, C. & M. R. Railroad,* 51 N.H. 504, 510; *Thompson v. Androscoggin River Imp. Company,* 58 N.H. 108.

RSA ch. 149 is essentially an act to prohibit the pollution of public waters in the interest of protecting the public health and welfare. *State v. Town of Goffstown,* 100 N.H. 131, 134, 121 A.2d 317; *Shirley v. New Hampshire Water Pollution Commission,* 100 N.H. 294, 299, 300, 124 A.2d 189. It has not intended to abrogate or suspend protection of the rights of individual landowners to be free from private nuisance.

The Class D classification is the "lowest classification" established by the statute, but even it is intended to permit "transportation of sewage or industrial wastes, or both without nuisance." RSA 149:3 IV, *supra.* The provisions of Laws 1959, 243:2 allow a period of ten years within which to abate pollution which lowers the quality of the water below the Class D requirements. However, the language defining the classification as one which shall permit use "without nuisance" was not intended to sanction the continuance of a private nuisance in the meantime, or to suspend injunctive relief calculated to cause abatement of such a nuisance.

If, as the plaintiffs assert, the nuisance can be abated by appropriate measures short of the complete prohibition of pollution which the first prayer of their bill seems to seek, no reason appears why the employment of such measures may not be required by appropriate order prohibiting further pollution unless such measures are employed within a reasonable time. See Annot. 46 A.L.R. 8, 35, par. V. On the other hand, an unconditional order which would require immediate cessation of all pollution of the waters in question may be entered if the private nuisance can be abated in no other way.

The allegations in the plaintiffs' petition state a cause of action for equitable relief.

The order is

Plaintiffs' demurrer sustained; remanded.

All concurred.

QUESTIONS FOR DISCUSSION

1 How are a private citizen's rights under the common law affected by the passage of pollution-control legislation?
2 Could a legislature legalize by legislation an act which is a common-law nuisance?
3 If the mill in *Urie v. Franconia* would have had to close down to control its pollution, would the decision have been the same?

STATE LAW—PREVENTIVE ACTIONS

In appropriate circumstances the law of nuisance may be the basis of an injunction aimed at preventing the creation of a nuisance. *City of Bowie v. Board of County Commissioners* illustrates the problems that are encountered in preventing a prospective nuisance.

City of Bowie v. Board of County Commissioners

271 A.2d 657 (Md. 1970)

Argued before Hammond, C.J., and Barnes, McWilliams, Singley and Smith, JJ.
McWilliams, Judge.

We shall be concerned here with another skirmish, perhaps the last, in the revolt of the appellants (Bowie) against the proposed Prince George's County airport. In the court below Bowie sought to enjoin the appellees (County) from "offering for sale or selling [the airport] bonds" and from "acquiring * * * [and] clearing land * * * or taking any other action to develop or construct an airport" in the southwest quadrant of the intersection of U.S. Route 301 and State Route 214 (Central Avenue). . . .[1]

The County proposes the construction of a runway 5,400 feet long on a course running N by W and, reciprocally, S by E. Plans for the future contemplate a 1,600 foot extension (to 7,000 feet) and the construction of a parallel runway 4,500 feet long.[2] The airport will be what the Federal Aviation Administration (FAA) calls a "larger than general utility airport," designed to accommodate "large business-type jets," weighing 60,000 pounds and capable of carrying 24 passengers. In the beginning only operations[3] subject to Visual Flight Rules (VFR) will be allowed. It is expected, however, that in about three years operations subject to Instrument Flight Rules (IFR) will be possible. In 1975, it is said, there will be about 150,000 operations, 30,000 of which, give or take a few thousand, will be accounted for by heavy aircraft. If these hopes are realized there is no doubt that the airport will be a very busy place.

The north end of the runway will be 5,000 feet south of the city limits of Bowie which now has a population of about 36,000; by 1980, they say, the figure will be about 68,000. It is alleged that aircraft taking off from and landing at the airport "will emit unusual, unreasonable, and unnecessary noise, vibration, dust, stench and filth * * * creat[ing] danger, fear, hurt, [and] inconvenience" and that they will "make life unbearable" for the citizens of Bowie and deprive them "of the use of their properties." . . .[4]

Bowie's next and apparently principal contention is that the proposed airport is a prospective nuisance which equity can and ought to enjoin. Judge Powers put the issue in this fashion:

> "The allegations of the bill focusing on the prospective nuisances of vibration, dust, stench, filth, or contamination of the atmosphere were not supported by any evidence

---

[1] Omitted.
[2] The length, in feet, of other runways provides informative comparisons: Dulles, 11,500; Andrews 9,755; Friendship 9,450; Washington National 6,870.
[3] An "operation" is one takeoff or one landing.
[4] Omitted.

that would form the basis of a conclusion that there was a prospective nuisance. Thus, we are left with the two contentions urged strongly by the plaintiffs; that is as to danger and as to noise."

Bowie's chief witness in respect of danger was Lt. Col. Paul E. Skinner, USAF, a flyer with more than ten years' experience and possessed of considerable expertise in the field of airport operations. In March 1970 his job (Chief, Flight Operations Division) entailed control of military air traffic in the Washington area and coordination "with the Federal Aviation Agency on matters pertaining to the Air Force." Andrews Air Force Base, he said, was his "primary responsibility." Col. Skinner's testimony is both interesting and instructive but, in the end, it comes to this: that there is a relatively small area where "those airplanes [patrons of the proposed airport] will * * * be using for a variety of reasons the same air space through which we [Air Force pilots] will be trying to fly. There will be conflict, * * * midair collisions." He conceded, however, that the tower at Andrews is under the control of FAA and that the Andrews pattern of operations must be approved by FAA. He thought it was true that FAA "believes it can provide a compatible environment between aircraft utilizing Andrews and aircraft utilizing this proposed airport," but he said he did not share that belief.

By way of rebuttal the County produced Martin Warskow, a vice president of R. Dixon Speas Associates, aviation consultants, whose forte is "air traffic systems analysis." We shall not attempt a synopsis of his comprehensive testimony. It suffices to state the conclusion he announced and which his testimony seems to support. He said:

> "So in looking at the air space situation, all of these things of the future must be taken into account, and it was our conclusion that with the proper location of the airports and their runway directions, which we feel are proper, the two airports can be operated at their capacities, safely and efficiently."

There was also the testimony of Robert Nickelsberg, the Assistant (Washington) Area Manager of FAA, that his "air traffic people" had determined that the proposed airport "would be compatible, and that includes [the] Andrews operation or Freeway[5] or anybody else in the area, and the routes out of Washington and into Washington."

Judge Powers "presumed that the authorities will conduct the operation of the [proposed] airport properly and utilize proper safeguards to protect the public." On the issue of danger he said he could not find "that there was evidence of such sufficient probative force as to support injunctive relief." We agree.

Many pages of the record deal with noise in terms of nuisance. Each side produced an expert with impeccable qualifications. Each one based his opinion on other testimony in respect of the number of operations expected to occur in the years 1975 and 1980. It seems that nearly all of the citizens (present and future) of

[5] A relatively small airport in the southeast quadrant of Hanson Highway and Church Road, about five miles northwest of the proposed airport.

Bowie reside (or will reside) within an area classified by FAA as "Zone 1" and from which "essentially no complaints would be expected * * * [but where] noise may, however, interfere with certain activities of the residents." Bowie's expert thought more people would be affected than did the County's expert. Otherwise their opinions did not differ in significant degree. Indeed, the testimony of Dr. John O. Powers, the acting director of the Office of Noise Abatement of FAA, suggests the opinions of the noise experts in respect of conditions in 1975 or 1980 may be based on premises now shifting or about to shift. He spoke of the continuing development of "retrofit"[6] regulations. He said he could "imagine the reduction [of noise] on some aircraft would be possibly as much as 15 decibels." He expressed the hope that the regulations, to be issued "within the next * * * two months," could be implemented "in early 1971." It would be well to observe, at this point, that there is very little in the record concerning operations prior to 1975. It has been assumed that operations would begin in 1970 but it is common knowledge, at this writing, that actual construction has not yet commenced.[7] If operations actually begin in 1971 it seems fair to say that they would gradually increase during the years 1972, 1973 and 1974. But just when during that period the noise generated by aircraft would reach the "nuisance" level, if indeed it ever rises that high, it seems impossible to say. Judge Powers noted the possibility that "they may have the sound question licked by 1975."

While we have not heretofore been called upon to consider the enjoining of a proposed airport we think our predecessors have laid down both firmly and clearly the principles of law controlling the restraint of prospective nuisances. In *Adams v. Michael,* 38 Md. 123 (1873), the plaintiffs sought to restrain the defendant from erecting a factory for the manufacture of felt roofing alleging that "owing to the dirt, odor, smoke, and appurtenances of such a factory" there would ensue "irreparable and continuing injury" to their property. The chancellor's dismissal of the bill of complaint was affirmed. Judge Alvey (later Chief Judge) said, for the Court:

> "There is no question or difficulty in regard to the principles invoked by the complainants in this case. The power to interfere by injunction to restrain a party from so using his own property as to destroy or materially prejudice the rights of his neighbor, and thus to enforce the maxim, 'sic utere tuo ut alienum non laedas,' is not only a well established jurisdiction of the Court of Chancery, but is one of great utility, and which is constantly exercised. Indeed, without such jurisdiction, parties would, in many cases, suffer the greatest wrongs, for which actions at law would afford them no adequate redress. It is not every inconvenience, however, in the nature of a nuisance to a party's dwelling, especially in a large commercial manufacturing city, that will call forth the restraining power of a Court of Chancery by injunction. To justify an injunction to restrain an existing or threatened nuisance to a dwelling-house, the injury must be shown to be of such a character as to diminish materially the value of

---

[6] "Retrofit" appears to be Federalese for a project requiring the modification of existing aircraft, including all jets, so as "to reduce their noise levels."

[7] But see Editorial, Bowie Airpark—and a Board in Flight, The Washington Post, Nov. 19, 1970, at A19.

the property as a dwelling, and seriously interfere with the ordinary comfort and enjoyment of it. Unless such a case is presented a Court of Chancery does not interfere. It must appear to be a case of real injury, and where a court of law would award substantial damages. * * * ." Id. at 125-126.

*   *   *

"The granting of injunctions on applications of this character involves the exercise of a most delicate power, and the Court is always reluctant to act except in cases where the right is clear and unquestioned, and the facts show an urgent necessity. The general rule is, that an injunction will only be granted to restrain an actual existing nuisance; but where it can be plainly seen that acts which, when completed, will certainly constitute or result in a grievous nuisance, or where a party threatens, or begins to do, or insists upon his right to do certain acts, the Court will interfere, though no nuisance may have been actually committed, if the circumstances of the case enable the Court to form an opinion as to the illegality of the acts complained of, and the irreparable injury which will ensue." Id. at 129.

To the same effect see *Sullivan v. Northwest Garage & Storage Co.,* 223 Md. 544, 551-553, 165 A.2d 881 (1960); *Mayor and City Council of Baltimore v. Board of Health for Baltimore County,* 139 Md. 210, 218-219, 115 A. 43 (1921); *Mayor and City Council of Baltimore v. Sackett,* 135 Md. 56, 62-63, 107 A. 557 (1919); *Hamilton Corp. v. Julian,* 130 Md. 597, 600-601, 101 A. 558 (1917); *King v. Hamill,* 97 Md. 103, 111, 54 A. 625 (1903).

No case has been cited, nor have we found one, in which the construction of an airport has been enjoined as a prospective nuisance. But there are cases in which applications for such injunctions have been refused. *Oechsle v. Ruhl,* 140 N.J. Eq. 355, 54 A.2d 462 (Ch. 1947), is such a case. There the plaintiffs who lived near a proposed airport sought to enjoin its construction on the ground that they would suffer from noise, dust and falling aircraft. The court said:

"In order for the complainants to succeed in their prayer for an injunction against the construction of the airport it must be clear that the airport cannot be so conducted as to not be a nuisance. Only very infrequently does the Court of Chancery enjoin the construction of a building or a facility upon the anticipation that there will be a threatened prospective nuisance by the conduct of the business in such building or facility. Normally, if the business is a lawful one the defendant is permitted to complete the structure and the question of nuisance is left to await the operation of the conduct of the business therein. Equity will not normally interfere in advance of the creation of a nuisance where the apprehended injury is doubtful or contingent * * * and especially where the anticipated or threatened injury arises from the use to which a proposed structure is to be put and not from the structure itself. In the present case it cannot be said that the structure itself, i.e., the airport, is a nuisance and is of such a nature that it cannot be put to a lawful use." 54 A.2d at 468.

To the same effect see *Elder v. City of Winder,* 201 Ga. 511, 40 S.E.2d 659 (1946); *Warren Township School Dist. No. 7, Macomb County v. City of Detroit,* 308 Mich. 460, 14 N.W.2d 134 (1944); *Antonik v. Chamberlain,* 81 Ohio App. 465, 78 N.E.2d 752 (1947).

Bowie seems to have encountered a great dearth of authorities in its effort to sustain its position. Indeed it has had to resort to equating the proposed airport with a bawdy-house. In *Hamilton v. Whitridge*, 11 Md. 128 (1857), the plaintiffs sought to enjoin Margaret Hamilton from occupying and using a recently purchased house as a bordello. She had been thrice convicted of keeping a bawdy-house in the years 1854 and 1855 and Judge Tuck, who wrote for the Court, noted that "between the last of these convictions and * * * [the filing of the bill of complaint] not one circumstance is shown from which we can infer that she had changed her course of life." He went on to observe that the evidence clearly indicated her firm intention to pursue her "profession" in the new house. The distinctions between Hamilton and the case at bar are at once apparent. Madame Hamilton's proposed use of her house would, without question, have been a nuisance on the very day she opened up for business; the operations at the proposed airport admittedly will not be a nuisance in the beginning and may never rise to that level. Madame Hamilton was denied only the use of her house as a bordello; Bowie seeks to prevent not the use but the construction of the airport.

We think Judge Powers has applied correctly the controlling law and we cannot say that his findings of fact are clearly erroneous. . . .

QUESTIONS FOR DISCUSSION

1 Can a noise level be below the federal maximum and still be a common-law nuisance?
2 Is it reasonable to wait until an "actual existing nuisance" exists before bringing an action where the development which precipitates the nuisance may involve a substantial investment?
3 Besides water and noise pollution what other applications does the nuisance doctrine have in environmental protection?
4 In litigation to enjoin a prospective nuisance, should a court assume that public authorities will conduct themselves so as to protect the public?
5 If large sums are invested in facilities such as those in *Bowie v. County Commissioners* after a preventive injunction is denied, can the facility defend another suit after completion by arguing that the "balance" is tilted in their favor by the large capital investment?
6 Should requirements for preventive injunctions be eased?

FEDERAL INTERSTATE NUISANCE

The law of nuisance may be used to fill the gaps in statutory schemes. *Illinois v. City of Milwaukee* turned on the jurisdictional question of whether a common-law pollution remedy was within the scope of the power of the federal courts. Although the action was unsuccessful procedurally, the case does establish the existence of federal interstate nuisance as a basis for pollution control.

Illinois v. City of Milwaukee

406 U.S. 91 (1972)

Mr. Justice Douglas delivered the opinion of the Court.

This is a motion by Illinois to file a complaint under our original jurisdiction against four cities of Wisconsin, the Sewerage Commission of the City of Milwaukee, and the Metropolitan Sewerage Commission of the County of Milwaukee. The cause of action alleged is pollution by the defendants of Lake Michigan, a body of interstate water. According to plaintiff, some 200 million gallons of raw or inadequately treated sewage and other waste materials are discharged daily into the lake in the Milwaukee area alone. Plaintiff alleges that it and its subdivisions prohibit and prevent such discharges, but that the defendants do not take such actions. Plaintiff asks that we abate this public nuisance. . . .[1]

II

28 U.S.C. § 1331(a) provides that "The district courts shall have original jurisdiction of all civil actions wherein the matter in controversy exceeds the sum or value of $10,000, exclusive of interest and costs, and arising under the Constitution, laws, or treaties of the United States."

The considerable interests involved in the purity of interstate waters would seem to put beyond question the jurisdictional amount provided in § 1331(a). See *Glenwood Light & Water Co. v. Mutual Light, Heat & Power Co.,* 239 U.S. 121; *Mississippi & Missouri R. v. Ward,* 2 Black 485, 492; *Rozio v. Denver & R. G. W. R.,* 116 F.2d 604, 606; C. Wright, The Law of Federal Courts 117–119 (2d ed. 1970); Note, 73 Harv. L. Rev. 1369. The question is whether pollution of interstate or navigable waters creates actions arising under the "laws" of the United States within the meaning of § 1331(a). We hold that it does; and we also hold that § 1331(a) includes suits brought by a State.

MR. JUSTICE BRENNAN, speaking for the four members of this Court in *Romero v. International Terminal Operating Co.,* 358 U.S. 354, 393, who reached the issue, concluded that "laws," within the meaning of § 1331(a), embraced claims founded on federal common law:

> "The contention cannot be accepted that since petitioner's rights are judicially defined, they are not created by 'the laws . . . of the United States' within the meaning of § 1331. . . . In another context, that of state law, this Court has recognized that the statutory word 'laws' includes court decisions. The converse situation is presented here in that federal courts have an extensive responsibility of fashioning rules of substantive law. . . . These rules are as fully 'laws' of the United States as if they had been enacted by Congress." (Citations omitted.)

[1] Section I and footnote 1 omitted.

Lower courts have reached the same conclusion. See, e.g., *Murphy v. Colonial Federal Savings & Loan Assn.,* 388 F.2d 609, 611–612 (CA2 1967); *Stokes v. Adair,* 265 F.2d 662 (CA4 1959); *Mater v. Holley,* 200 F.2d 123 (CA5 1952); ALI, Study of the Division of Jurisdiction Between State and Federal Courts 180–182 (1969).

Judge Harvey M. Hohnsen in *Texas v. Pankey,* 441 F.2d 236, 240 [2 ERC 1200], stated the controlling principle:

> "As the field of federal common law has been given necessary expansion into matters of federal concern and relationship (where no applicable federal statute exists, as there does not here), the ecological rights of a State in the improper impairment of them from sources outside the State's own territory, now would and should, we think, be held to be a matter having basis and standard in federal common law and so directly constituting a question arising under the laws of the United States."

Chief Judge Lumbard, speaking for the panel in *Ivy Broadcasting Co. v. American Tel. & Tel. Co.,* 391 F.2d 486, 492, expressed the same view as follows:

> "We believe that a cause of action similarly 'arises under' federal law if the dispositive issues stated in the complaint require the application of federal common law. . . . The word 'laws' in § 1331 should be construed to include laws created by federal judicial decisions as well as by congressional legislation. The rationale of the 1875 grant of federal question jurisdiction—to insure the availability of a forum designed to minimize the danger of hostility toward, and specially suited to the vindication of, federally created rights—is as applicable to judicially created rights as to rights created by statute." (Citations omitted.)

We see no reason not to give "laws" its natural meaning, see *Romero v. International Terminal Operating Co., supra,* at 393 n. 5 (BRENNAN, J., dissenting), and therefore conclude that § 1331 jurisdiction will support claims founded upon federal common law as well as those of a statutory origin.

As respects the power of a State to bring an action under § 1331(a), *Ames v. Kansas,* 111 U.S. 449, 470–472, is controlling. There Kansas had sued a number of corporations in its own courts and, since federal rights were involved, the defendants had the cases removed to the federal court. Kansas resisted saying that the federal court lacked jurisdiction because of Art. III, § 2, cl. 2 of the Constitution which gives this Court "original jurisdiction" in "all cases . . . in which a State shall be a party." The Court held that, where a State is suing parties who are not other States, the original jurisdiction of this Court is not exclusive (Id., at 470) and that those suits "may now be brought in or removed to the Circuit Courts [now the District Courts] without regard to the character of the parties."[2] Ibid. We adhere to that ruling.

[2] See also H.R. Rep. No. 308, 80th Cong., 1st Sess., A 104 (1947): "The original jurisdiction conferred on the Supreme Court by Article 3, section 2, of the Constitution is not exclusive by virtue of that provision alone. Congress may provide for or deny exclusiveness."

III

Congress had enacted numerous laws touching interstate waters. In 1899 it established some surveillance by the Corps of Engineers over industrial pollution, not including sewage, Rivers and Harbors Act of March 3, 1899, c. 425, 30 Stat. 1121, a grant of power which we construed in *United States v. Republic Steel Corp.*, 362 U.S. 482 [1 ERC 1022], and in *United States v. Standard Oil Co.*, 384 U.S. 224 [1 ERC 1033].

The 1899 Act has been reinforced and broadened by a complex of laws recently enacted. The Federal Water Pollution Control Act, 33 U.S.C. § 1151, tightens control over discharges into navigable waters so as not to lower applicable water quality standards. By the National Environmental Policy Act of 1969, 42 U.S.C. § 4321, Congress "authorizes and directs" that "the policies, regulations, and public laws of the United States shall be interpreted and administered in accordance with the policies set forth in this Act" and that "all agencies of the Federal Government shall . . . identify and develop methods and procedures . . . which will insure that presently unquantified environmental amenities and values may be given appropriate consideration in decision-making along with economic and technical considerations." Congress has evinced increasing concern with the quality of the aquatic environment as it affects the conservation and safeguarding of fish and wildlife resources. See, e.g., Fish and Wild Life Act of 1956, 16 U.S.C. § 742a; the Migratory Marine Game Fish Act, 16 U.S.C. § 760c; and the Fish and Wildlife Coordination Act, 16 U.S.C. § 661.

Buttressed by these new and expanding policies, the Corps of Engineers has issued new Rules and Regulations governing permits for discharges or deposits into navigable waters. 36 Fed. Reg. 6564 et seq.

The Federal Water Pollution Control Act in § 1(b) declares that it is federal policy "to recognize, preserve, and protect the primary responsibilities and rights of the States in preventing and controlling water pollution." But the Act makes clear that it is federal, not state, law that in the end controls the pollution of interstate or navigable waters.[3] While the States are given time to establish water quality standards, § 10(c)(1), if a State fails to do so the federal administrator[4] promulgates one. § 10(c)(2). Section 10(a) makes pollution of interstate or navigable waters subject "to abatement" when it "endangers the health or welfare of any persons." The abatement that is authorized follows a long, drawn-out procedure unnecessary to relate here. It uses the conference procedure, hoping for amicable settlements. But if none is reached, the federal administrator may request the

---

[3] The contrary indication in *Ohio v. Wyandotte Chemicals Corp.*, 401 U.S. 493, 498, n. 3, [2 ERC 1331] was based on the preoccupation of that litigation with public nuisance under Ohio law, not the federal common law which we now hold is ample basis for federal jurisdiction under 28 U.S.C. § 1331(a).

[4] The powers granted the Secretary of the Interior under the Federal Water Quality Act were assigned by the President to the Administrator of the Environmental Protection Agency pursuant to Reorganization Plan No. 3 of 1970. See 35 Fed. Reg. 15623.

Attorney General to bring suit on behalf of the United States for abatement of the pollution. § 10(g).

The remedy sought by Illinois is not within the precise scope of remedies prescribed by Congress. Yet the remedies which Congress provides are not necessarily the only federal remedies available. "It is not uncommon for federal courts to fashion federal law where federal rights are concerned." *Textile Workers v. Lincoln Mills,* 353 U.S. 448, 457. When we deal with air or water in their ambient or interstate aspects, there is a federal common law,[5] as *Texas v. Pankey,* 441 F.2d 236, [2 ERC 1200], recently held.

The application of federal common law to abate a public nuisance in interstate or navigable waters is not inconsistent with the Water Pollution Control Act. Congress provided in § 10(b) of that Act that, save as a court may decree otherwise in an enforcement action, "State and interstate action to abate pollution of interstate and navigable waters shall be encouraged and shall not . . . be displaced by federal enforcement action."

The leading air case is *Georgia v. Tennessee Copper Co.,* 206 U.S. 230, where Georgia filed an original suit in this Court against a Tennessee company whose noxious gases were causing a wholesale destruction of forests, orchards, and crops in Georgia. The Court said:

> "The caution with which demands of this sort, on the part of a State, for relief from injuries analogous to torts, must be examined, is dwelt upon in *Missouri v. Illinois,* 200 U.S. 496, 520, 521. But it is plain that some such demands must be recognized, if the grounds alleged are proved. When the States by their union made the forcible abatement of outside nuisances impossible to each, they did not thereby agree to submit to whatever might be done. They did not renounce the possibility of making reasonable demands on the ground of their still remaining quasi-sovereign interests; and the alternative to force is a suit in this court. *Missouri v. Illinois,* 180 U.S. 208, 241." 206 U.S., at 237.

---

[5] While the various federal environmental protection statutes will not necessarily mark the outer bounds of the federal common law, they may provide useful guidelines in fashioning such rules of decision. What we said in another connection in *Textile Workers v. Lincoln Mills,* 353 U.S. 448, 456-457, is relevant here:

"The question then is, what is the substantive law to be applied in suits brought under § 301(a)? We conclude that the substantive law to apply in suits under § 301(a) is federal law, which the courts must fashion from the policy of our national labor laws. The Labor Management Relations Act expressly furnishes some substantive law. It points out what the parties may or may not do in certain situations. Other problems will lie in the penumbra of express statutory mandates. Some will lack express statutory sanction but will be solved by looking at the policy of the legislation and fashioning a remedy that will effectuate that policy. The range of judicial inventiveness will be determined by the nature of the problem. Federal interpretation of the federal law will govern, not state law. But state law, if compatible with the purpose of § 301, may be resorted to in order to find the rule that will best effectuate the federal policy. Any state law applied, however, will be absorbed as federal law and will not be an independent source of private rights." (Citations omitted.) See also Woods & Reed, The Supreme Court and Interstate Environmental Quality: Some Notes on the Wyandotte Case, 12 Ariz. L. Rev. 691, 713-714; Note, 56 Va. L. Rev. 458.

The nature of the nuisance was described as follows:

"It is a fair and reasonable demand on the part of a sovereign that the air over its territory should not be polluted on a great scale by sulphurous acid gas, that the forests on its mountains, be they better or worse, and whatever domestic destruction they have suffered, should not be further destroyed or threatened by the act of persons beyond its control, that the crops and orchards on its hills should not be endangered from the same source. If any such demand is to be enforced this must be, notwithstanding the hesitation that we might feel if the suit were between private parties, and the doubt whether for the injuries which they might be suffering to their property they should not be left to an action at law." Id., at 238.

Our decisions concerning interstate waters contain the same theme. Rights in interstate streams, like questions of boundaries, "have been recognized as presenting federal questions."[6] *Hinderlider v. LaPlata Co.,* 304 U.S. 92, 110. The question of apportionment of interstate waters is a question of "federal common law" upon which state statutes or decisions are not conclusive.[7] Ibid.

In speaking of the problem of apportioning the waters of an interstate stream, the Court said in *Kansas v. Colorado,* 206 U.S. 46, 98, that "through these successive disputes and decisions this Court is practically building up what may not improperly be called interstate common law." And see *Texas v. New Jersey,* 379 U.S. 674 (escheat of intangible personal property), *Texas v. Florida,* 306 U.S. 398, 405 (suit by bill in the nature of interpleader to determine the true domicile of a decedent as the basis of death taxes).

Equitable apportionment of the waters of an interstate stream has often been made under the head of our original jurisdiction. *Nebraska v. Wyoming,* 325 U.S. 589; *Kansas v. Colorado,* 206 U.S. 469; cf. *Arizona v. California,* 373 U.S. 546, 562. The applicable federal common law depends on the facts peculiar to the particular case.

"Priority of appropriation is the guiding principle. But physical and climatic conditions, the consumptive use of water in the several sections of the river, the character, and rate of return flows, the extent of established uses, the availability of storage

---

[6] Thus, it is not only the character of the parties which requires us to apply federal law. See *Georgia v. Tennessee Copper Co.,* 206 U.S. 230, 237; cf. *Wisconsin v. Pelican Ins. Co.,* 127 U.S. 265, 269; The Federalist No. 80 (A. Hamilton). As Mr. Justice Harlan indicated for the Court in *Banco Nacional de Cuba v. Sabbatino,* 376 U.S. 398, 421–427, where there is an overriding federal interest in the need for a uniform rule of decision or where the controversy touches basic interests of federalism, we have fashioned federal common law. See also *Clearfield Trust Co. v. United States,* 318 U.S. 363; *D'Oench, Duhme & Co. v. Federal Deposit Ins. Corp.,* 315 U.S. 447; C. Wright, The Law of Federal Courts 249 (2d ed. 1970); Woods & Reed, The Supreme Court and Interstate Environmental Quality: Some Notes on the Wyandotte Case, 12 Ariz. L. Rev. 691, 703–713; Note, 50 Texas L. Rev. 183. Certainly these same demands for applying federal law are present in the pollution of a body of water such as Lake Michigan bounded, as it is, by four States.

[7] Those who maintain that state law governs overlook the fact that the *Hinderlider* case was authorized by Mr. Justice Brandeis who also wrote for the Court in *Erie R. Co. v. Tompkins,* 304 U.S. 64, the two cases being decided the same day.

water, the practical effect of wasteful uses on downstream areas, the damage to upstream areas as compared to the benefits to downstream areas if a limitation is imposed on the former—these are all relevant factors. They are merely an illustrative,
not an exhaustive catalogue. They indicate the nature of the problem of apportionment and the delicate adjustment of interests which must be made." 325 U.S.,
at 618.

When it comes to water pollution this Court has spoken in terms of "a public
nuisance,"[8] *New York v. New Jersey,* 256 U.S. 296, 313; *New Jersey v. New York
City,* 283 U.S. 473, 481, 482. In *Missiouri v. Illinois,* 200 U.S. 496, 520-521, the
Court said, "It may be imagined that a nuisance might be created by a State upon
a navigable river like the Danube, which would amount to a casus belli for a State
lower down, unless removed. If such a nuisance were created by a State upon the
Mississippi the controversy would be resolved by the more peaceful means of a
suit in this Court."

It may happen that new federal laws and new federal regulations may in time
pre-empt the field of federal common law of nuisance. But until that comes to
pass, federal courts will be empowered to appraise the equities of the suits alleging
creation of a public nuisance by water pollution. While federal law governs,[9]
consideration of state standards may be relevant. Cf. *Connecticut v. Massachusetts,*
282 U.S. 660, 670; *Kansas v. Colorado,* 185 U.S. 125, 146-147. Thus a State with
high water quality standards may well ask that its strict standards be honored and
that it not be compelled to lower itself to the more degrading standards of a
neighbor. There are no fixed rules that govern; these will be equity suits in which
the informed judgment of the chancellor will largely govern.

We deny, without prejudice, the motion for leave to file. While this original
suit normally might be the appropriate vehicle for resolving this controversy, we
exercise our discretion to remit the parties to an appropriate district court[10] whose
powers are adequate to resolve the issues.

---

[8] In *North Dakota v. Minnesota,* 263 U.S. 365, 374, the Court said: ". . . where one State, by a
change in its method of draining water from lands within its border, increases the flow into an
interstate stream, so that its natural capacity is greatly exceeded and the water is thrown upon the
farms of another State, the latter State has such an interest as quasi-sovereign in the comfort, health
and prosperity of its farm owners that resort may be had to this Court for relief. It is the creation of a
public nuisance of simple type for which a State may properly ask an injunction."

[9] "Federal common law and not the varying common law of the individual States is, we think,
entitled and necessary to be recognized as a basis for dealing in uniform standard with the environmental rights of a State against improper impairment by sources outside its domain. The more would
this seem to be imperative in the present era of growing concern on the part of a State about its
ecological conditions and impairments of them. In the outside sources of such impairment, more
conflicting disputes, increasing assertions and proliferating contentions would seem to be inevitable.
Until the field has been made the subject of comprehensive legislation or authorized administrative
standards, only a federal common law basis can provide an adequate means for dealing with claims as
alleged federal rights. And the logic and practicality of regarding such claims as being entitled to be
asserted within the federal-question jurisdiction of § 1331(a) would seem to be self-evident." *Texas v.
Pankey, supra,* 241-242 [2 ERC 1200].

[10] Omitted.

QUESTIONS FOR DISCUSSION

1   Is common law necessary to fill gaps in statutes?
2   Does the existence of common-law rights give the courts too free a hand?
3   Can courts modify common law at will?
4   Can a legislature supersede a common-law right?
5   Would the federal courts have jurisdiction over a nuisance that was not interstate in character?
6   What weaknesses do you see in a case-by-case or balancing approach to pollution control?
7   A nuisance must cause or threaten harm to be enjoined. What problems of proof does this requirement create? Compare the Federal Water Pollution Control Act, page 204.
8   *Illinois v. City of Milwaukee* concerns primarily the question of jurisdiction. What may be inferred from the opinion regarding the substance of federal law of interstate nuisance?
9   Do you agree that the "natural meaning" of laws, when that term is used in a statute written by legislators, includes court decisions?
10 If Congress has acted legislatively on a particular problem such as water pollution, could it be inferred that no further federal action or law was intended? Or could it be inferred that Congress knew that common-law remedies existed and did not attempt to duplicate their effect in legislation?
11 Does the court invite Congress to preempt the field?
12 What did the court do in the final paragraph of the decision?

OTHER COMMON-LAW ACTIONS: NEGLIGENCE, TRESPASS, STRICT LIABILITY

The doctrine of negligence, before the nineteenth century, was not recognized as a separate tort (civil wrong) and in fact was used in a general sense to describe the breach of any legal obligation. Even during the early 1800s, the law of negligence was concerned with positive acts (misfeasance), rather than with failure to act (nonfeasance). Not until the rise of the industrial revolution and the concurrent rise in the number of serious accidents was negligence recognized as a separate and independent basis of tort liability.[9]

Today, it is readily accepted in the law that a cause of action based on negligence requires four basic elements:

1   A duty, or obligation, recognized by the law, requiring the actor to conform to a certain standard of conduct, for the protection of others against unreasonable risks.
2   A failure on his part to conform to the standard required. These two elements go to make up what the courts usually have called negligence; but the term quite frequently is applied to the second alone. Thus it may be said that the defendant was negligent, but is not liable because he was under no duty to the plaintiff not to be.
3   A reasonably close causal connection between the conduct and the resulting injury. This is commonly known as "legal cause," or "proximate cause."

[9] See Prosser, op. cit., pp. 142–143.

4 Actual loss or damage resulting to the interests of another. Since the action for negligence developed chiefly out of the old form of action on the case, it retained the rule of that action, that proof of damage was an essential part of the plaintiff's case.[h]

The standard of care imposed by the law in determining whether or not an act is negligent is generally held to be the care which a reasonable and prudent person would exercise under similar conditions. The degree of care depends upon all the circumstances of a particular situation; thus it follows that the greater the danger, the greater the degree of care required.

Negligence has been used as the basis of actions involving pollution of springs, wells, and water supplies;[i] and also noise from aircraft.[j]

Trespass, as used in environmental litigation, may be defined as any intrusion or invasion of the protected interest in exclusive possession of one who is in possession of land, by visible or invisible matter or energy.[k] Trespass may be distinguished from nuisance in that nuisance is an interference with the use or enjoyment of land, whereas trespass is an invasion of a possessory interest in the land. For example, the mere existence of a neighboring factory which emits heavy smoke and particulate matter may be a nuisance, while the falling of smoke or microscopic particles upon the land may be a trespass. The major departure, however, from historical trespass actions has been the courts' decisions in contemporary suits relying on modern scientific evidence and finding a trespass in the entry of invisible gases and microscopic particles which are harmful. The reason for the old requirement of the entry of something tangible is said to have been due to the ancient courts' failure to accept what they could not see.[l]

A modern use of trespass in the environmental context may be found in *Martin v. Reynolds Metals Company,* 342 P.2d 790, where it was alleged that an aluminum reduction plant caused fluoride compounds in the form of gases and particulates to become airborne and settle on the plaintiff's land, rendering it unfit for raising livestock. The court, equating mass with energy and concluding that our concept of "things" must be reframed, held that the invading object's energy or force is more significant than its size. Thus, the court said that "we may define trespass as any intrusion which invades the possessor's protected interest in exclusive possession, whether that intrusion is by visible or invisible pieces of matter or by energy which can be measured only by the mathematical language of the physicist."

The doctrine of strict liability for abnormally dangerous conditions and activities was developed from the leading case of *Rylands v. Fletcher,*[m] decided in England in 1868. The defendants in that case constructed a reservoir upon their land which eventually broke through an abandoned coal mine

[h] Prosser, p. 146.

[i] See *Long v. Louisville & N. R. Company,* 128 Ky. 26. *Collins v. Charter's Valley Gas Company,* 131 Pa. 143. *United Fuels Gas Company v. Sawyers,* (Ky.) 259 S.W.2d 466.

[j] See *Weisburg v. United States* (D.C. Md.) 193 F. Supp. 815; *Leisy v. United States,* (D.C. Minn.) 102 F. Supp. 789.

[k] *Martin v. Reynolds Metals Company,* 221 Or. 86, 342 P.2d 790 (1959). See also *Fairview Farms v. Reynolds Metals* (1959) 176 F. Supp. 178. *Hall v. DeWeld Mica Corporation,* 244 N.C. 182, 935 S.E.2d (1956). *Gregg v. Delhi–Taylor Oil Corporation,* 162 Tex. 26, 344 S.W.2d 411 (1961).

[l] Prosser, op. cit., p. 66.

[m] *Fletcher v. Rylands,* 3 H. & C. 774, 159 Eng. Rep. 737 (1865), reversed in *Fletcher v. Rylands,* L.R. 1 Ex. 265 (1866), affirmed in *Rylands v. Fletcher,* L.R. 3 H.L. 330 (1868).

shaft, flooding the adjoining mine owned by the plaintiff. The court found no trespass because the flooding was not "direct or immediate"; nor did they find any nuisance—as nuisance was then understood—since there was nothing which was offensive to the senses. However, the court found that the plaintiff might recover, analogizing to the strict liability for dangerous animals and trespassing cattle:

> We think that the true rule of law is that the person who for his own purposes brings on his land and collects and keeps there anything likely to do mischief if it escapes, must keep it at his peril, and if he does not do so it is prima facie answerable for all the damage which is the natural consequence of its escape.[n]

After a somewhat stormy period of rejection, the majority of American courts today have accepted the doctrine. As a further qualification, Prosser states that the American decisions have applied the principle of *Rylands v. Fletcher* "only to the thing out of place, the abnormally dangerous condition or activity which is not a 'natural' one where it is."[o] The main thrust of the doctrine involves the finding of liability without fault or negligence. It is sufficient that the activity which causes the harm is ultrahazardous—involving the risk of serious harm to others—and that it is not a matter of common usage or customarily carried on:[p]

QUESTIONS FOR DISCUSSION

1 Should one be responsible for consequences which were not his fault?
2 Should one always be responsible for the consequences of his acts?
3 Should the doctrine of strict liability be applied to situations not involving dangerous objects?
4 Should one be held liable under the doctrine of strict liability if he has done everything possible to avoid injury?
5 Need an activity be "extravagant" or "bizarre" to invoke the doctrine?
6 Does strict liability make the actor an insurer?
7 Should the very existence of such objects as nuclear power plants be sufficient to invoke strict liability?
8 Does or should the utility of the polluting project influence whether or not strict liability is imposed?
9 Do common-law rights still have vitality in light of extensive pollution-control legislation?

PROBLEMS

1 A factory which emits unpleasant odors is located in an area which is primarily residential and commercial. At the time of the factory's construction, however, the surrounding area was undeveloped. The local citizenry seek to close the factory as a public nuisance. What impact would or should the prior existence of the factory have on the decision?

[n] *Rylands v. Fletcher, supra* at 338.
[o] See Prosser, op. cit., p. 527.
[p] See *Lutheridge v. Moore,* 31 Cal. 2d 489, 190 P.2d (1948).

2 Suppose a factory emits an effluent which is shown to cause cancer in human beings. The factory contends that it has exercised reasonable care in the control of its effluents and in warning workers and citizens who may be affected. If reasonable care under the circumstances has indeed been exercised, could a common-law remedy be fashioned to allow the recovery to an affected plaintiff?

3 The air quality in a city has reached the point of hazard. Ten factories are identified as equal contributors, but if eight of the factories were in operation the air quality would be usually acceptable. If a nuisance action was brought against two factories, what might their defense be and who might prevail?

4 Workers in a chemical plant are shown to die from lung cancer at a rate four times the national average. An employee of long standing contracts the disease and files a suit against his employer. Assuming that a basis of liability (negligence, strict liability, etc.) can be established, what problems will be encountered in proving proximate cause? Suppose the worker was also a heavy smoker.

5 It is proposed that an automobile assembly plant be built on the outskirts of a small town which, fearing increased traffic congestion and related problems, seeks to enjoin the construction as a prospective nuisance. How might they frame their argument, and what must they prove in order to prevail? If they are unsuccessful and the plant is built, and it does result in the problems which the town feared, could the operation of the plant be halted as a nuisance? What defenses might be raised?

SUGGESTIONS FOR FURTHER READING

Campbell, N. T.: *Illinois v. City of Milwaukee: Federal Question Jurisdiction through Federal Common Law,* 3 ENVIRONMENTAL L. 267, 1973.

Federal Common Law and Interstate Pollution, 85 HARV. L. REV. 1439, 1972.

Federal Common Law in Interstate Water Pollution Disputes, 1973 U. ILL. L.F. 141, 1973.

Hollman, K. F.: *Doctrine of Primary Jurisdiction Misconceived: End to Common Law Environmental Protection?* 2 FLA. STATE U.L. REV. 491, 1974.

Private Nuisance Law: Protection of the Individual's Environmental Rights, 8 SUFFOLK U.L. REV. 1162, 1974.

Rice, D. A.: *Pollution as a Nuisance: Problems, Prospects and Proposals,* 34 AM. TRIAL LAW. L.J. 202, 1972.

Viability of Common Law Actions for Pollution Caused Injuries and Proof of Facts, 18 N.Y.L.F. 935, 1973.

Virginia Supreme Court: Authority versus Power to Abolish the Common Law, 8 U. RICHMOND L. REV. 276, 1974.

National Environmental Policy Act

Perhaps the single most significant example of federal environmental legislation has been the National Environmental Policy Act (NEPA) of 1969.[a] The act has three major thrusts:

1 It establishes the encouragement of a productive harmony between man and his environment as a national policy.[b]

[a] Pub. L. 91–190.

[b] Purpose

Sec. 2.   The purposes of this Act are: To declare a national policy which will encourage productive and enjoyable harmony between man and his environment; to promote efforts which will prevent or eliminate damage to the environment and biosphere and stimulate the health and welfare of man; to enrich the understanding of the ecological systems and natural resources important to the Nation; and to establish a Council on Environmental Quality.

Title 1

Declaration of National Environmental Policy

Sec. 101.   (1) The Congress, recognizing the profound impact of man's activity on the interrelations of all components of the natural environment, particularly the profound influences of population growth, high-density urbanization, industrial expansion, resource exploitation, and new and expanding technological advances and recognizing further the critical importance of restoring and maintaining environmental quality to overall welfare and development of man, declares that it is the continuing policy of the Federal Government, in cooperation with State and local governments, and other concerned public and private organizations, to use all practicable means and measures, including financial and technical assistance, in a manner calculated to foster and promote the general welfare, to create and maintain conditions under which man and nature can exist in productive harmony, and fulfill the social, economic, and other requirements of present and future generations of Americans.

2 It requires federal agencies to include in every recommendation or report on proposals for legislation and other major federal actions significantly affecting the quality of the human environment, an environmental impact statement.[c]

3 It established the Council on Environmental Quality.[d]

[c] Sec. 102. The Congress authorizes and directs that, to the fullest extent possible: (1) the policies, regulations, and public laws of the United States shall be interpreted and administered in accordance with the policies set forth in this Act, and (2) all agencies of the Federal Government shall—

(A) utilize a systematic, interdisciplinary approach which will insure the integrated use of the natural and social sciences and the environmental design arts in planning and in decisionmaking which may have an impact on man's environment;

(B) identify and develop methods and procedures, in consultation with the Council on Environmental Quality established by Title II of this Act, which will insure that presently unquantified environment amenities and values may be given appropriate consideration in decisionmaking along with economic and technical considerations;

(C) include in every recommendation or report on proposals for legislation and other Federal actions significantly affecting the quality of the human environment, a detailed statement by the responsible official on—

(i)   the environmental impact of the proposed action,

(ii)   any adverse environmental effects which cannot be avoided should the proposal be implemented,

(iii) alternatives to the proposed action,

(iv) the relationship between local short-term uses of man's environment and the maintenance and enhancement of long-term productivity, and

(v)   any irreversible and irretrievable commitments of resources which would be involved in the proposed action should it be implemented.

Prior to making any detailed statement, the responsible Federal official shall consult with and obtain the comments of any Federal agency which has jurisdiction by law or special expertise with respect to any environmental impact involved. Copies of such statement and the comments and views of the appropriate Federal, State, and local agencies, which are authorized to develop and enforce environmental standards, shall be made available to the President, the Council on Environmental Quality and to the public as provided by Section 552 of Title 5, United States Code, and shall accompany the proposal through the existing agency review processes;

(D) study, develop, and describe appropriate alternatives to recommended courses of action in any proposal which involves unresolved conflicts concerning alternative uses of available resources;

(E) recognize the worldwide and long-range character of environmental problems and, where consistent with the foreign policy of the United States, lend appropriate support to initiatives, resolutions, and programs designed to maximize international cooperation in anticipating and preventing a decline in the quality of mankind's world environment;

(F) make available to States, counties, municipalities, institutions, and individuals, advice and information useful in restoring, maintaining, and enhancing the quality of the environment.

[d] Sec. 202. There is created in the Executive Office of the President a Council on Environmental Quality (hereinafter referred to as the "Council"). The Council shall be composed of three members who shall be appointed by the President to serve at his pleasure, by and with the advice and consent of the Senate. The President shall designate one of the members of the Council to serve as Chairman. Each member shall be a person who, as a result of his training, experience, and attainments, is exceptionally well qualified to analyze and interpret environmental trends and information of all kinds; to appraise programs and activities of the Federal Government in the light of the policy set forth in Title I of this Act; to be conscious of and responsive to the scientific, economic, social, esthetic, and cultural needs and interests of the Nation; and to formulate and recommend national policies to promote the improvement of the quality of the environment.

*   *   *   *

Sec. 204. It shall be the duty and function of the Council—

(1) to assist and advise the President in the preparation of the Environmental Quality Report required by Section 201;

(2) to gather timely and authoritative information concerning the conditions and trends in the quality of the environment both current and prospective, to analyze and interpret such information for the purpose of determining whether such conditions and trends are interfering, or are likely to interfere, with the achievement of the policy set forth in Title I of this Act, and to compile and submit to the President studies relating to such conditions and trends;

(3) to review and appraise the various programs and activities of the Federal Government in the light of the policy set forth in Title I of this Act for the purpose of determining the extent to which such programs and activities are contributing to the achievement of such policy, and to make recommendations to the President with respect thereto;

NEPA is composed of extremely general phraseology, and hardly a word or phrase has escaped judicial scrutiny. As well, the Act is silent with regard to the propriety and scope of judicial review, and its skeletal frame has been given flesh by numerous court decisions.

Litigation under the National Environment Policy Act has been profuse and has been concerned with a variety of aspects of environmental impact statement preparation. The cases which follow illustrate the working of NEPA and the problems which have been encountered in the implementation.

PHILOSOPHY AND BACKGROUND

Calvert Cliffs Coordinating Committee v. United States Atomic Energy Commission sets the tone and establishes the judicial philosophy of construction and interpretation adopted in most subsequent NEPA litigation.

Calvert Cliffs Coordinating Committee v. United States Atomic Energy Commission

449 F.2d 1109, 2 ERC 1779 (D.C. Cir. 1971)

Before Wright, Tamm and Robinson, Circuit Judges.
Wright, Circuit Judge:

These cases are only the beginning of what promises to become a flood of new litigation—litigation seeking judicial assistance in protecting our natural environment. Several recently enacted statutes attest to the commitment of the Government to control, at long last, the destructive engine of material "progress."[1] But it remains to be seen whether the promise of this legislation will become a reality.

---

(4) to develop and recommend to the President national policies to foster and promote the improvement of environmental quality to meet the conservation, social, economic, health, and other requirements and goals of the Nation;

(5) to conduct investigations, studies, surveys, research, and analyses relating to ecological systems and environmental quality;

(6) to document and define changes in the natural environment, including the plant and animal systems and to accumulate necessary data and other information for a continuing analysis of these changes or trends and an interpretation of their underlying causes;

(7) to report at least once each year to the President on the state and condition of the environment; and

(8) to make and furnish such studies, reports thereon, and recommendations with respect to matters of policy and legislation as the President may request.

[1] See, e.g., Environmental Education Act, 20 U.S.C.A. § 1531 (1971 Pocket Part); Air Quality Act of 1967, 42 U.S.C. § 1857 (Supp. V 1965-1969); Environmental Quality Improvement Act of 1970, 42 U.S.C.A. §§ 4372-4374 (1971 Pocket Part); Water and Environmental Quality Improvement Act of 1970, Pub. L. 91-224, 91st Cong., 2d Sess. (1970).

Therein lies the judicial role. In these cases, we must for the first time interpret the broadest and perhaps most important of the recent statutes: the National Environmental Policy Act of 1969 (NEPA).[2] We must assess claims that one of the agencies charged with its administration has failed to live up to the congressional mandate. Our duty, in short, is to see that important legislative purposes, heralded in the halls of Congress, are not lost or misdirected in the vast hallways of the federal bureaucracy.

NEPA, like so much other reform legislation of the last 40 years, is cast in terms of a general mandate and broad delegation of authority to new and old administrative agencies. It takes the major step of requiring all federal agencies to consider values of environmental preservation in their spheres of activity, and it prescribes certain procedural measures to ensure that those values are in fact fully respected. Petitioners argue that rules recently adopted by the Atomic Energy Commission to govern consideration of environmental matters fail to satisfy the rigor demanded by NEPA. The Commission, on the other hand, contends that the vagueness of the NEPA mandate and delegation leaves much room for discretion and that the rules challenged by petitioners fall well within the broad scope of the Act. We find the policies embodied in NEPA to be a good deal clearer and more demanding than does the Commission. We conclude that the Commission's procedural rules do not comply with the congressional policy. Hence we remand these cases for further rule making.

I

We begin our analysis with an examination of NEPA's structure and approach and of the Atomic Energy Commission rules which are said to conflict with the requirements of the Act. The relevant portion of NEPA is Title I, consisting of five sections.[3] Section 101 sets forth the Act's basic substantive policy: that the federal government "use all practicable means and measures" to protect environmental values. Congress did not establish environmental protection as an exclusive goal; rather, it desired a reordering of priorities, so that environmental costs and benefits will assume their proper place along with other considerations. In Section 101(b), imposing an explicit duty on federal officials, the Act provides that "it is the continuing responsibility of the Federal Government to use all practicable means, consistent with other essential considerations of national policy," to avoid environmental degradation, preserve "historic, cultural, and natural" resources, and promote "the widest range of beneficial uses of the environment without * * * undesirable and unintended consequences."

Thus the general substantive policy of the Act is a flexible one. It leaves room for a responsible exercise of discretion and may not require particular substantive results in particular problematic instances. However, the Act also contains very important "procedural" provisions—provisions which are designed to see that all federal agencies do in fact exercise the substantive discretion given them. These

---

[2] 42 U.S.C.A. § 4321 et seq. (1971 Pocket Part).
[3] Omitted.

provisions are not highly flexible. Indeed, they establish a strict standard of compliance.

NEPA, first of all, makes environmental protection a part of every federal agency and department. The Atomic Energy Commission, for example, had continually asserted, prior to NEPA, that it had no statutory authority to concern itself with the adverse environmental effects of its actions.[4] Now, however, its hands are no longer tied. It is not only permitted, but compelled, to take environmental values into account. Perhaps the greatest importance of NEPA is to require the Atomic Energy Commission and other agencies to consider environmental issues just as they consider other matters within their mandates. This compulsion is most plainly stated in Section 102. There, "Congress authorizes and directs that, to the fullest extent possible: (1) the policies, regulations, and public laws of the United States shall be interpreted and administered in accordance with the policies set forth in this Act * * *." Congress also "authorizes and directs" that "(2) all agencies of the Federal Government shall" follow certain rigorous procedures in considering environmental values.[5] Senator Jackson, NEPA's principal sponsor, stated that "[n]o agency will [now] be able to maintain that it has no mandate or no requirement to consider the environmental consequences of its actions."[6] He characterized the requirements of Section 102 as "action-forcing" and stated that "[o]therwise, these lofty declarations [in Section 101] are nothing more than that."[7]

[4] Before the enactment of NEPA, the Commission did recognize its separate statutory mandate to consider the specific radiological hazards caused by its actions; but it argued that it could not consider broader environmental impacts. Its position was upheld in *State of New Hampshire v. Atomic Energy Commission*, 1 Cir., 406 F.2d 170, [1 ERC 1053] cert. denied, 395 U.S. 962 (1969).

[5] Only once—in § 102(2)(B)—does the Act state, in terms, that federal agencies must give full "consideration" to environmental impact as part of their decision making processes. However, a requirement of consideration is clearly implicit in the substantive mandate of § 101, in the requirement of § 102(1) that all laws and regulations be "interpreted and administered" in accord with that mandate, and in the other specific procedural measures compelled by § 102(2). The only circuit to interpret NEPA to date has said that "[t]his Act essentially states that every federal agency shall consider ecological factors when dealing with activities which may have an impact on man's environment." *Zabel v. Tabb*, 5 Cir., 430 F.2d 199, 211 [1 ERC 1449] (1970). Thus a purely mechanical compliance with the particular measures required in § 102(2)(C) & (D) will not satisfy the Act if they do not amount to full good faith consideration of the environment. . . . The requirements of § 102(2) must not be read so narrowly as to erase the general import of §§ 101, 102(1) and 102(2)(A) & (B).

On April 23, 1971, the Council on Environmental Quality—established by NEPA—issued guidelines for federal agencies on compliance with the Act. 36 FED. REG. 7723 (April 23, 1971). The Council stated that "[t]he objective of section 102(2)(C) of the Act and of these guidelines is to build into the agency decision making process an appropriate and careful consideration of the environmental aspects of proposed action * * *." Id. at 7724.

[6] Hearings on S. 1075, S. 237 and S. 1752 Before Senate Committee on Interior and Insular Affairs, 91st Cong., 1st Sess. 206 (1969). Just before the Senate finally approved NEPA, Senator Jackson said on the floor that the Act "directs all agencies to assure consideration of the environmental impact of their actions in decisionmaking." 115 CONG. REC. (Part 30) 40416 (1969).

[7] Hearings on S. 1075, *supra* Note 6, at 116. Again, the Senator reemphasized his point on the floor of the Senate, saying: "To insure that the policies and goals defined in this act are infused into the ongoing programs and actions of the Federal Government, the act also established some important 'action-forcing' procedures." 115 CONG. REC. (Part 30) at 40416. The Senate Committee Report on NEPA also stressed the importance of the "action-forcing" provisions which require full and rigorous consideration of environmental values as an integral part of agency decision making. S. Rep. No. 91-296, 91st Cong., 1st Sess. (1969).

The sort of consideration of environmental values which NEPA compels is clarified in Section 102(2)(A) and (B). In general, all agencies must use a "systematic, interdisiplinary approach" to environmental planning and evaluation "in decisionmaking which may have an impact on man's environment." In order to include all possible environmental factors in the decisional equation, agencies must "identify and develop methods and procedures * * * which will insure that presently unquantified environmental amenities and values may be given appropriate consideration in decisionmaking along with economic and technical considerations."[8] "Environmental amenities" will often be in conflict with "economic and technical considerations." To "consider" the former "along with" the latter must involve a balancing process. In some instances environmental costs may outweigh economic and technical benefits and in other instances they may not. But NEPA mandates a rather finely tuned and "systematic" balancing analysis in each instance.[9]

To ensure that the balancing analysis is carried out and given full effect, Section 102(2)(C) requires that responsible officials of all agencies prepare a "detailed statement" covering the impact of particular actions on the environment, the environmental costs which might be avoided, and alternative measures which might alter the cost-benefit equation. The apparent purpose of the "detailed statement" is to aid in the agencies' own decision making process and to advise other interested agencies and the public of the environmental consequences of planned federal action. Beyond the "detailed statement," Section 102(2)(D) requires all agencies specifically to "study, develop, and describe appropriate alternatives to recommended courses of action in any proposal which involves unresolved conflicts concerning alternative uses of available resources." This requirement, like the "detailed statement" requirement, seeks to ensure that each agency decision maker has before him and takes into proper account all possible approaches to a particular project (including total abandonment of the project) which would alter the environmental impact and the cost-benefit balance. Only in that fashion is it likely that the most intelligent, optimally beneficial decision will ultimately be made. Moreover, by compelling a formal "detailed statement" and a description of alternatives, NEPA provides evidence that the mandated decision making process has in fact taken place and, most importantly, allows those removed from the initial process to evaluate and balance the factors on their own.

---

[8] The word "appropriate" in § 102(2)(B) cannot be interpreted to blunt the thrust of the whole Act or to give agencies broad discretion to downplay environmental factors in their decision making process. The Act requires consideration "appropriate" to the problem of protecting our threatened environment, not consideration "appropriate" to the whims, habits or other particular concerns of federal agencies. See Note 5 *supra*.

[9] Senator Jackson specifically recognized the requirement of a balancing judgment. He said on the floor of the Senate: "Subsection 102(b) requires the development of procedures designed to insure that all relevant environmental values and amenities are considered in the calculus of project development and decisionmaking; Subsection 102(c) establishes a procedure designed to insure that in instances where a proposed major Federal action would have a significant impact on the environment that the impact has in fact been considered, that any adverse effects which cannot be avoided are justified by some other stated consideration of national policy, that short-term uses are consistent with long-term productivity, and that any irreversible and irretrievable commitments of resources are warranted." 115 CONG. REC. (Part 21) 29055 (1969).

Of course, all of these Section 102 duties are qualified by the phrase "to the fullest extent possible." We must stress as forcefully as possible that this language does not provide an escape hatch for footdragging agencies; it does not make NEPA's procedural requirements somehow "discretionary." Congress did not intend the Act to be such a paper tiger. Indeed, the requirement of environmental consideration "to the fullest extent possible" sets a high standard for the agencies, a standard which must be rigorously enforced by the reviewing courts.

Unlike the substantive duties of Section 101(b), which require agencies to "use all practicable means consistent with other essential considerations," the procedural duties of Section 102 must be fulfilled to the "fullest extent possible." [10] This contrast, in itself, is revealing. But the dispositive factor in our interpretation is the expressed views of the Senate and House conferees who wrote the "fullest extent possible" language into NEPA. They stated: [11]

"* * * The purpose of the new language is to make it clear that each agency of the Federal Government shall comply with the directives set out in * * * [Section 102(2)] unless the existing law applicable to such agency's operations expressly prohibits or makes full compliance with one of the directives impossible. * * * Thus, it is the intent of the conferees that the provision 'to the fullest extent possible' shall not be used by any Federal agency as a means of avoiding compliance with the directives set out in section 102. Rather, the language in section 102 is intended to assure that all agencies of the Federal Government shall comply with the directives set out in said section 'to the fullest extent possible' under their statutory authorizations and that no agency shall utilize an excessively narrow construction of its existing statutory authorizations to avoid compliance."

Thus the Section 102 duties are not inherently flexible. They must be complied with to the fullest extent, unless there is a clear conflict of statutory authority. [12]

---

[10] The Commission, arguing before this court, has mistakenly confused the two standards, using the § 101(b) language to suggest that it has broad discretion in performance of § 102 procedural duties. We stress the necessity to separate the two, substantive and procedural, standards. See text at [pages 139-140] *infra*.

[11] The Senators' views are contained in "Major Changes in S. 1075 as Passed by the Senate," 115 CONG. REC. (Part 30) at 40417-40418. The Representatives' views are contained in a separate statement filed with the Conference Report, 115 CONG. REC. (Part 29) 39702-39703 (1969).

[12] Section 104 of NEPA provides that the Act does not eliminate any duties already imposed by other "specific statutory obligations." Only when such specific obligations conflict with NEPA do agencies have a right under § 104 and the "fullest extent possible" language to dilute their compliance with the full letter and spirit of the Act. . . . Sections 103 and 105 also support the general interpretation that the "fullest extent possible" language exempts agencies from full compliance only when there is a conflict of statutory obligations. Section 103 provides for agency review of existing obligations in order to discover and, if possible, correct any conflicts. . . . And § 105 provides that "[t]he policies and goals set forth in this Act are supplementary to those set forth in existing authorizations of Federal agencies." The report of the House conferees states that § 105 "does not * * * obviate the requirement that the Federal agencies conduct their activities in accordance with the provisions of this bill unless to do so would clearly violate their existing statutory obligations." 115 CONG. REC. (Part 29) at 39703. The section-by-section analysis by the Senate makes exactly the same point in slightly different language. 115 CONG. REC. (Part 30) at 40418. The guidelines published by the Council on Environmental Quality state that "[t]he phrase 'to the fullest extent possible' * * * is meant to make clear that each agency of the Federal Government shall comply with the requirement unless existing law applicable to the agency's operations expressly prohibits or makes compliance impossible." 36 FED. REG. at 7724.

Considerations of administrative difficulty, delay or economic cost will not suffice to strip the section of its fundamental importance.

We conclude, then, that Section 102 of NEPA mandates a particular sort of careful and informed decisionmaking process and creates judicially enforceable duties. The reviewing courts probably cannot reverse a substantive decision on its merits, under Section 101, unless it be shown that the actual balance of costs and benefits that was struck was arbitrary or clearly gave insufficient weight to environmental values. But if the decision was reached procedurally without individualized consideration and balancing of environmental factors—conducted fully and in good faith—it is the responsibility of the courts to reverse. As one District Court has said of Section 102 requirements: "It is hard to imagine a clearer or stronger mandate to the Courts."[13]

In the cases before us now, we do not have to review a particular decision by the Atomic Energy Commission granting a construction permit or an operating license. Rather, we must review the Commission's recently promulgated rules which govern consideration of environmental values in such individual decisions.[14] The rules were devised strictly in order to comply with the NEPA procedural requirements—but petitioners argue that they fall far short of the congressional mandate.

The period of the rules' gestation does not indicate overenthusiasm on the Commission's part. NEPA went into effect on January 1, 1970. On April 2, 1970—three months later—the Commission issued its first, short policy statement on implementation of the Act's procedural provisions.[15] After another span of two months, the Commission published a notice of proposed rule making in the Fed-

[13] *Texas Committee on Natural Resources v. United States,* W.D. Tex., 1 Envir. Rpts—Cas. 1303, 1304 (1970). A few of the courts which have considered NEPA to date have made statements stressing the discretionary aspects of the Act. See, e.g., *Pennsylvania Environmental Council v. Bartlett,* M.D. Pa., 315 F. Supp. 238 (1970); *Bucklein v. Volpe,* N.D. Cal., 2 Envir. Rpts—Cas. 1082, 1083 (1970). The Commission and intervenors rely upon these statements quite heavily. However, their reliance is misplaced, since the courts in question were not referring to the procedural duties created by NEPA. Rather, they were concerned with the Act's substantive goals or with such peripheral matters as retroactive application of the Act.

The general interpretation of NEPA which we outline in text at [page 122] *supra* is fully supported by the scholarly commentary. See, e.g., Donovan, The Federal Government and Environmental Control: Administrative Reform on the Executive Level, 12 B.C. IND. & COM. L. REV. 541 (1971); Hanks & Hanks, An Environmental Bill of Rights: The Citizen Suit and the National Environmental Policy Act of 1969, 24 RUTG. L. REV. 231 (1970); Sive, Some Thoughts of an Environmental Lawyer in the Wilderness of Administrative Law, 70 COLUM. L. REV. 612, 643-650 (1970); Peterson, An Analysis of Title I of the National Environmental Policy Act of 1969, 1 ENVIR. L. RPTR. 50035 (1971); Yannacone, National Environmental Policy Act of 1969, 1 ENVIR. LAW 8 (1970); Note, The National Environmental Policy Act: A Sheep in Wolf's Clothing?, 37 BROOKLYN L. REV. 139 (1970).

[14] In Case No. 24,871, petitioners attack four aspects of the Commission's rules, which are outlined in text. In Case No. 24,839, they challenge a particular application of the rules in the granting of a particular construction permit—that for the Calvert Cliffs Nuclear Power Plant. However, their challenge consists largely of an attack on the substance of one aspect of the rules also attacked in Case No. 24,871. Thus we are able to resolve both cases together, and our remand to the Commission for further rule making includes a remand for further consideration relating to the Calvert Cliffs Plant in Case No. 24,839. See Part V of this opinion, *infra.*

[15] 35 FED. REG. 5463 (April 2, 1970).

eral Register.[16] Petitioners submitted substantial comments critical of the proposed rules. Finally, on December 3, 1970, the Commission terminated its long rule making proceeding by issuing a formal amendment, labelled Appendix D, to its governing regulations.[17] Appendix D is a somewhat revised version of the earlier proposal and, at last, commits the Commission to consider environmental impact in its decision making process.

The procedure for environmental study and consideration set up by the Appendix D rules is as follows: Each applicant for an initial construction permit must submit to the Commission his own "environmental report," presenting his assessment of the environmental impact of the planned facility and possible alternatives which would alter the impact. When construction is completed and the applicant applies for a license to operate the new facility, he must again submit an "environmental report" noting any factors which have changed since the original report. At each stage, the Commission's regulatory staff must take the applicant's report and prepare its own "detailed statement" of environmental costs, benefits and alternatives. The statement will then be circulated to other interested and responsible agencies and made available to the public. After comments are received from those sources, the staff must prepare a final "detailed statement" and make a final recommendation on the application for a construction permit or operating license.

Up to this point in the Appendix D rules petitioners have raised no challenge. However, they do attack four other, specific parts of the rules which, they say, violate the requirements of Section 102 of NEPA. Each of these parts in some way limits full consideration and individualized balancing of environmental values in the Commission's decision making process. (1) Although environmental factors must be considered by the agency's regulatory staff under the rules, such factors need not be considered by the hearing board conducting an independent review of staff recommendations, unless affirmatively raised by outside parties or staff members. (2) Another part of the procedural rules prohibits any such party from raising non-radiological environmental issues at any hearing if the notice for that hearing appeared in the Federal Register before March 4, 1971. (3) Moreover, the hearing board is prohibited from conducting an independent evaluation and balancing of certain environmental factors if other responsible agencies have already certified that their own environmental standards are satisfied by the proposed federal action. (4) Finally, the Commission's rules provide that when a construction permit for a facility has been issued before NEPA compliance was required and when an operating license has yet to be issued, the agency will not formally consider environmental factors or require modifications in the proposed facility until the time of the issuance of the operating license. Each of these parts of the Commission's rules will be described at greater length and evaluated under NEPA in the following sections of this opinion.

[16] 35 FED. REG. 8594 (June 3, 1970).
[17] 35 FED. REG. 18469 (December 4, 1970). The version of the rules finally adopted is now printed in 10 C.F.R. § 50, App. D, pp. 246-250 (1971).

II

NEPA makes only one specific reference to consideration of environmental values in agency review processes. Section 102(2)(C) provides that copies of the staff's "detailed statement" and comments thereon "shall accompany the proposal through the existing agency review processes." The Atomic Energy Commission's rules may seem in technical compliance with the letter of that provision. They state:

> "12.   If any party to a proceeding * * * raises any [environmental] issue * * * the Applicant's Environmental Report and the Detailed Statement will be offered in evidence. The atomic safety and licensing board will make findings of fact on, and resolve, the matters in controversy among the parties with regard to those issues. Depending on the resolution of those issues, the permit or license may be granted, denied, or appropriately conditioned to protect environmental values.

> "13.   When no party to a proceeding * * * raises any [environmental] issue * * * such issues will not be considered by the atomic safety and licensing board. Under such circumstances, although the Applicant's Environmental Report, comments thereon, and the Detailed Statement will accompany the application through the Commission's review processes, they will not be received in evidence, and the Commission's responsibilities under the National Environmental Policy Act of 1969 will be carried out in toto outside the hearing process."[18]

The question here is whether the Commission is correct in thinking that its NEPA responsibilities may "be carried out in toto outside the hearing process"—whether it is enough that environmental data and evaluations merely "accompany" an application through the review process, but receive no consideration whatever from the hearing board.

We believe that the Commission's crabbed interpretation of NEPA makes a mockery of the Act. What possible purpose could there be in the Section 102(2)(C) requirement (that the "detailed statement" accompany proposals through agency review processes) if "accompany" means no more than physical proximity—mandating no more than the physical act of passing certain folders and papers, unopened, to reviewing officials along with other folders and papers? What possible purpose could there be in requiring the "detailed statement" to be before hearing boards, if the boards are free to ignore entirely the contents of the statement? NEPA was meant to do more than regulate the flow of papers in the federal bureaucracy. The word "accompany" in Section 102(2)(C) must not be read so narrowly as to make the Act ludicrous. It must, rather, be read to indicate a congressional intent that environmental factors, as compiled in the "detailed statement," be considered through agency review processes.[19]

[18] C.F.R. § 50, App. D, at 249.

[19] The guidelines issued by the Council on Environmental Quality emphasize the importance of consideration of alternatives to staff recommendations during the agency review process: "A rigorous exploration and objective evaluation of alternative actions that might avoid some or all of the adverse environmental effects is essential. Sufficient analysis of such alternatives and their costs and impact on the environment should accompany the proposed action through the agency review process in order not to foreclose prematurely options which might have less detrimental effects." 36 FED. REG. at 7725. The Council also states that an objective of its guidelines is "to assist agencies in implementing not only the letter, but the spirit, of the Act." Id. at 7724.

Beyond Section 102(2)(C), NEPA requires that agencies consider the environmental impact of their actions "to the fullest extent possible." The Act is addressed to agencies as a whole, not only to their professional staffs. Compliance to the "fullest" possible extent would seem to demand that environmental issues be considered at every important stage in the decision making process concerning a particular action—at every stage where an overall balancing of environmental and non-environmental factors is appropriate and where alterations might be made in the proposed action to minimize environmental costs. Of course, consideration which is entirely duplicative is not necessarily required. But independent review of staff proposals by hearing boards is hardly a duplicative function. A truly independent review provides a crucial check on the staff's recommendations. The Commission's hearing boards automatically consider nonenvironmental factors, even though they have been previously studied by the staff. Clearly, the review process is an appropriate stage at which to balance conflicting factors against one another. And, just as clearly, it provides an important opportunity to reject or significantly modify the staff's recommended action. Environmental factors, therefore, should not be singled out and excluded, at this stage, from the proper balance of values envisioned by NEPA.

The Commission's regulations provide that in an uncontested proceeding the hearing board shall on its own "determine whether the application and the record of the proceeding contain sufficient information, and the review of the application by the Commission's regulatory staff has been adequate, to support affirmative findings on" various nonenvironmental factors.[20] NEPA requires at least as much automatic consideration of environmental factors. In uncontested hearings, the board need not necessarily go over the same ground covered in the "detailed statement." But it must at least examine the statement carefully to determine whether "the review * * * by the Commission's regulatory staff has been adequate." And it must independently consider the final balance among conflicting factors that is struck in the staff's recommendation.

The rationale of the Commission's limitation of environmental issues to hearings in which parties affirmatively raise those issues may have been one of economy. It may have been supposed that, whenever there are serious environmental costs overlooked or uncorrected by the staff, some party will intervene to bring those costs to the hearing board's attention. Of course, independent review of the "detailed statement" and independent balancing of factors in an uncontested hearing will take some time. If it is done properly, it will take a significant amount of time. But all of the NEPA procedures take time. Such administrative costs are not enough to undercut the Act's requirement that environmental protection be considered "to the fullest extent possible." . . . It is, moreover, unrealistic to assume that there will always be an intervenor with the information, energy and money required to challenge a staff recommendation which ignores environmental costs. NEPA establishes environmental protection as an integral part of the Atomic Energy Commission's basic mandate. The primary responsibility for fulfilling that mandate lies with the Commission. Its responsibility is not simply to sit

[20] 10 C.F.R. § 2.104(b)(2) (1971).

back, like an umpire, and resolve adversary contentions at the hearing stage. Rather, it must itself take the initiative of considering environmental values at every distinctive and comprehensive stage of the process beyond the staff's evaluation and recommendation.[21]

III

Congress passed the final version of NEPA in late 1969, and the Act went into full effect on January 1, 1970. Yet the Atomic Energy Commission's rules prohibit any consideration of environmental issues by its hearing boards at proceedings officially noticed before March 4, 1971.[22] This is 14 months after the effective date of NEPA. And the hearings affected may go on for as much as a year longer until final action is taken. The result is that major federal actions having a significant environmental impact may be taken by the Commission, without full NEPA compliance, more than two years after the Act's effective date. In view of the importance of environmental consideration during the agency review process, see Part II *supra*, such a time lag is shocking.

The Commission explained that its very long time lag was intended "to provide an orderly period of transition in the conduct of the Commission's regulatory proceedings and to avoid unreasonable delays in the construction and operation of nuclear power plants urgently needed to meet the national requirements for electric power."[23] Before this court, it has claimed authority for its action, arguing that "the statute did not lay down detailed guidelines and inflexible timetables for its implementation; and we find in it no bar to agency provisions which are designed to accommodate transitional implementation problems."[24]

Again, the Commission's approach to statutory interpretation is strange indeed—so strange that it seems to reveal a rather thoroughgoing reluctance to meet the NEPA procedural obligations in the agency review process, the stage at which deliberation is most open to public examination and subject to the participation of public intervenors. The Act, it is true, lacks an "inflexible timetable" for its imple-

---

[21] In recent years, the courts have become increasingly strict in requiring that federal agencies live up to their mandates to consider the public interest. They have become increasingly impatient with agencies which attempt to avoid or dilute their statutorily imposed role as protectors of public interest values beyond the narrow concerns of industries being regulated. See, e.g., *Udall v. FPC,* 387 U.S. 428 (1967); *Environmental Defense Fund, Inc. v. Ruckelshaus,* 142 U.S. App. D.C. 74, 439 F.2d 584 (1971); *Moss v. C.A.B.,* 139 U.S. App. D.C. 150, 430 F.2d 891 (1970); *Environmental Defense Fund, Inc. v. U.S. Dept. of H.E. & W.,* 138 U.S. App. D.C. 381, 428 F.2d 1083 (1970). In commenting on the Atomic Energy Commission's pre-NEPA duty to consider health and safety matters, the Supreme Court said "the responsibility for safeguarding that health and safety belongs under the statute to the Commission." *Power Reactor Development Co. v. I.U.E.R.M.W.,* 367 U.S. 396, 404 (1961). The Second Circuit has made the same point regarding the Federal Power Commission: "In this case, as in many others, the Commission has claimed to be the representative of the public interest. This role does not permit it to act as an umpire blandly calling balls and strikes for adversaries appearing before it; the right of the public must receive active and affirmative protection at the hands of the Commission." *Scenic Hudson Preservation Conference v. FPC,* 2 Cir., 354 F.2d 608, 620 (1965).

[22] 10 C.F.R. § 50, App. D, at 249.

[23] 35 FED. REG. 18470 (December 4, 1970).

[24] Brief for respondents in No. 24,871 at 49.

mentation. But it does have a clear effective date, consistently enforced by reviewing courts up to now. Every federal court having faced the issues has held that the procedural requirements of NEPA must be met in order to uphold federal action taken after January 1, 1970.[25] The absence of a "timetable" for compliance has never been held sufficient, in itself, to put off the date on which a congressional mandate takes effect. The absence of a "timetable" rather, indicates that compliance is required forthwith.

The only part of the Act which even implies that implementation may be subject, in some cases, to some significant delay is Section 103. There, Congress provided that all agencies must review "their present statutory authority, administrative regulations, and current policies and procedures for the purpose of determining whether there are any deficiencies or inconsistencies therein which prohibit full compliance" with NEPA. Agencies finding some such insuperable difficulty are obliged to "propose to the President not later than July 1, 1971, such measures as may be necessary to bring their authority and policies into conformity with the intent, purposes, and procedures set forth in this Act."

The Commission, however, cannot justify its time lag under these Section 103 provisions. Indeed, it has not attempted to do so; only intervenors have raised the argument. Section 103 could support a substantial delay only by an agency which in fact discovered an insuperable barrier to compliance with the Act and required time to formulate and propose the needed reformative measures. The actual review of existing statutory authority and regulations cannot be a particularly lengthy process for experienced counsel of a federal agency. Of course, the Atomic Energy Commission discovered no obstacle to NEPA implementation. Although it did not report its conclusion to the President until October 2, 1970, that nine-month delay (January to October) cannot justify so long a period of noncompliance with the Act. It certainly cannot justify a further delay of compliance until March 4, 1971.

No doubt the process of formulating procedural rules to implement NEPA takes some time. Congress cannot have expected that federal agencies would immediately begin considering environmental issues on January 1, 1970. But the effective date of the Act does set a time for agencies to begin adopting rules and it demands that they strive, "to the fullest extent possible," to be prompt in the process. The Atomic Energy Commission has failed in this regard.[26] Consideration of environmental issues in the agency review process, for example, is quite clearly compelled by the Act.[27] The Commission cannot justify its 11-month delay in

---

[25] In some cases, the courts have had a difficult time determining whether particular federal actions were "taken" before or after January 1, 1970. But they have all started from the basic rule that any action taken after that date must comply with NEPA's procedural requirements. See Note, Retroactive Application of the National Environmental Policy Act of 1969, 69 MICH. L. REV. 732 (1971), and cases cited therein. Clearly, any hearing held between January 1, 1970 and March 4, 1971 which culminates in the grant of a permit or license is a federal action taken after the Act's effective date.

[26] Omitted.

[27] As early as March 5, 1970, President Nixon stated in an executive order that NEPA requires consideration of environmental factors at public hearings. Executive Order 11514, 35 FED. REG. 4247 (March 5, 1970). See also Part II of this opinion.

adopting rules on this point as part of a difficult, discretionary effort to decide whether or not its hearing boards should deal with environmental questions at all.

Even if the long delay had been necessary, however, the Commission would not be relieved of all NEPA responsibility to hold public hearings on the environmental consequences of actions taken between January 1, 1970 and final adoption of the rules. Although the Act's effective date may not require instant compliance, it must at least require that NEPA procedures, once established, be applied to consider prompt alterations in the plans or operations of facilities approved without compliance.[28] Yet the Commission's rules contain no such provision. Indeed, they do not even apply to the hearings still being conducted at the time of their adoption on December 3, 1970—or, for that matter, to hearings initiated in the following three months. The delayed compliance date of March 4, 1971, then, cannot be justified by the Commission's long drawn out rule making process.

Strangely, the Commission has principally relied on more pragmatic arguments. It seems an unfortunate affliction of large organizations to resist new procedures and to envision massive roadblocks to their adoption. Hence the Commission's talk of the need for an "orderly transition" to the NEPA procedures. It is difficult to credit the Commission's argument that several months were needed to work the consideration of environmental values into its review process. Before the enactment of NEPA, the Commission already had regulations requiring that hear-

---

[28] In Part V of this opinion, we hold that the Commission must promptly consider the environmental impact of projects initially approved before January 1, 1970 but not yet granted an operating license. We hold that the Commission may not wait until construction is entirely completed and consider environmental factors only at the operating license hearings; rather, before environmental damage has been irreparably done by full construction of a facility, the Commission must consider alterations in the plans. Much the same principle—of making alterations while they still may be made at relatively small expense—applies to projects approved without NEPA compliance after the Act's effective date. A total reversal of the basic decision to construct a particular facility or take a particular action may then be difficult, since substantial resources may already have been committed to the project. Since NEPA must apply to the project in some fashion, however, it is essential that it apply as effectively as possible—requiring alterations in parts of the project to which resources have not yet been inalterably committed at great expense.

One District Court has dealt with the problem of instant compliance with NEPA. It suggested another measure which agencies should take while in the process of developing rules. It said: "The NEPA does not require the impossible. Nor would it require, in effect, a moratorium on all projects which had an environmental impact while awaiting compliance with § 102(2)(B). It would suffice if the statement pointed out this deficiency. The decisionmakers could then determine whether any purpose would be served in delaying the project while awaiting the development of such criteria." *Environmental Defense Fund, Inc. v. Corps of Engineers,* E.D. Ark., 325 F. Supp. 749, 758 [2 ERC 1260] (1971). Apparently, the Atomic Energy Commission did not even go this far toward considering the lack of a NEPA public hearing as a basis for delaying projects between the Act's effective date and adoption of the rules.

Of course, on the facts of these cases, we need not express any final view on the legal effect of the Commission's failure to comply with NEPA after the Act's effective date. Mere post hoc alterations in plans may not be enough, especially in view of the Commission's long delay in promulgating rules. Less than a year ago, this court was asked to review a refusal by the Atomic Energy Commission to consider environmental factors in granting a license. We held that the case was not yet ripe for review. But we stated: "If the Commission persists in excluding such evidence, it is courting the possibility that if error is found a court will reverse its final order, condemn its proceeding as so much waste motion, and order that the proceeding be conducted over again in a way that realistically permits de novo consideration of the tendered evidence." *Thermal Ecology Must be Preserved v. AEC,* 139 U.S. App. D.C. 366, 368, 433 F.2d 524, 526 [2 ERC 1379] (1970).

ings include health, safety and radiological matters.[29] The introduction of environmental matters cannot have presented a radically unsettling problem. And, in any
event, the obvious sense of urgency on the part of Congress should make clear that
a transition, however "orderly," must proceed at a pace faster than a funeral
procession.

In the end, the Commission's long delay seems based upon what it believes to
be a pressing national power crisis. Inclusion of environmental issues in pre-
March 4, 1971 hearings might have held up the licensing of some power plants for
a time. But the very purpose of NEPA was to tell federal agencies that environmental protection is as much a part of their responsibility as is protection and
promotion of the industries they regulate. Whether or not the spectre of a national
power crisis is as real as the Commission apparently believes, it must not be used
to create a blackout review process. NEPA compels a case-by-case examination
and balancing of discrete factors. Perhaps there may be cases in which the need
for rapid licensing of a particular facility would justify a strict time limit on a
hearing board's review of environmental issues; but a blanket banning of such
issues until March 4, 1971 is impermissible under NEPA.

IV

The sweep of NEPA is extraordinarily broad, compelling consideration of any
and all types of environmental impact of federal action. However, the Atomic
Energy Commission's rules specifically exclude from full consideration a wide
variety of environmental issues. First, they provide that no party may raise and
the Commission may not independently examine any problem of water quality—
perhaps the most significant impact of nuclear power plants. Rather, the Commission indicates that it will defer totally to water quality standards devised and
administered by state agencies and approved by the federal government under the
Federal Water Pollution Control Act.[30] Secondly, the rules provide for similar
abdication of NEPA authority to the standards of other agencies:

> "With respect to those aspects of environmental quality for which environmental
> quality standards and requirements have been established by authorized Federal,
> State, and regional agencies, proof that the applicant is equipped to observe such
> standards and requirements will be considered a satisfactory showing that there will
> not be a significant, adverse effect on the environment. Certification by the appropri-

[29] See 10 C.F.R. § 20 (1971) for the standards which the Commission had developed to deal with
radioactive emissions which might pose health or safety problems.

[30] 10 C.F.R. § 50, App. D, at 249. Appendix D does require that applicants' environmental
reports and the Commission's "detailed statements" include "a discussion of the water quality aspects
of the proposed action." Id. at 248. But, as is stated in text, it bars independent consideration of those
matters by the Commission's reviewing boards at public hearings. It also bars the Commission from
requiring—or even considering—any water protection measures not already required by the approving
state agencies. See Note 31 *infra.*

[The section of the Federal Water Pollution Control Act establishing a system of state agency
certification is § 21, as amended in the Water Quality Improvement Act of 1970. 33 U.S.C.A. § 1171
(1970). In the text below, this section is discussed as part of the Water Quality Improvement Act.]

ate agency that there is reasonable assurance that the applicant for the permit or license will observe such standards and requirements will be considered dispositive for this purpose."[31]

The most the Commission will do is include a condition in all construction permits and operating licenses requiring compliance with the water quality or other standards set by such agencies.[32] The upshot is that the NEPA procedures, viewed by the Commission as superfluous, will wither away in disuse, applied only to those environmental issues wholly unregulated by any other federal, state or regional body.

We believe the Commission's rule is in fundamental conflict with the basic purpose of the Act. NEPA mandates a case-by-case balancing judgment on the part of federal agencies. In each individual case, the particular economic and technical benefits of planned action must be assessed and then weighed against the environmental costs; alternatives must be considered which would effect the balance of values. . . . The magnitude of possible benefits and possible costs may lie anywhere on a broad spectrum. Much will depend on the particular magnitudes involved in particular cases. In some cases, the benefits will be great enough to justify a certain quantum of environmental costs; in other cases, they will not be so great and the proposed action may have to be abandoned or significantly altered so as to bring the benefits and costs into a proper balance. The point of the individualized balancing analysis is to ensure that, with possible alterations, the optimally beneficial action is finally taken.

Certification by another agency that its own environmental standards are satisfied involves an entirely different kind of judgment. Such agencies, without overall responsibility for the particular federal action in question, attend only to one aspect of the problem: the magnitude of certain environmental costs. They simply determine whether those costs exceed an allowable amount. Their certification does not mean that they found no environmental damage whatever. In fact, there may be significant environmental damage (e.g., water pollution), but not quite enough to violate applicable (e.g., water quality) standards. Certifying agencies do not attempt to weigh that damage against the opposing benefits. Thus the balancing analysis remains to be done. It may be that the environmental costs, though passing prescribed standards, are nonetheless great enough to outweigh the particular economic and technical benefits involved in the planned action. The only agency in a position to make such a judgment is the agency with overall responsibility for the proposed federal action—the agency to which NEPA is specifically directed.

The Atomic Energy Commission, abdicating entirely to other agencies' certifications, neglects the mandated balancing analysis. Concerned members of the public are thereby precluded from raising a wide range of environmental issues in order to affect particular Commission decisions. And the special purpose of NEPA is subverted.

[31] 10 C.F.R. § 50, App. D, at 249.
[32] Ibid.

Arguing before this court, the Commission has made much of the special environmental expertise of the agencies which set environmental standards. NEPA did not overlook this consideration. Indeed, the Act is quite explicit in describing the attention which is to be given to the views and standards of other agencies. Section 102(2)(C) provides:

> "Prior to making any detailed statement, the responsible Federal official shall consult with and obtain the comments of any Federal agency which has jurisdiction by law or special expertise with respect to any environmental impact involved. Copies of such statement and the comments and views of the appropriate Federal, State, and local agencies, which are authorized to develop and enforce environmental standards, shall be made available to the President, the Council on Environmental Quality and to the public * * *."

Thus the Congress was surely cognizant of federal, state and local agencies "authorized to develop and enforce environmental standards." But it provided, in Section 102(2)(C), only for full consultation. It most certainly did not authorize a total abdication to those agencies. Nor did it grant a license to disregard the main body of NEPA obligations.

Of course, federal agencies such as the Atomic Energy Commission may have specific duties, under acts other than NEPA, to obey particular environmental standards. Section 104 of NEPA makes clear that such duties are not to be ignored:

> "Nothing in Section 102 or 103 shall in any way affect the specific statutory obligations of any Federal agency (1) to comply with criteria or standards of environmental quality, (2) to coordinate or consult with any other Federal or State agency, or (3) to act, or refrain from acting contingent upon the recommendations or certification of any other Federal or State agency."

On its face, Section 104 seems quite unextraordinary, intended only to see that the general procedural reforms achieved in NEPA do not wipe out the more specific environmental controls imposed by other statutes. Ironically, however, the Commission argues that Section 104 in fact allows other statutes to wipe out NEPA.

Since the Commission places great reliance on Section 104 to support its abdication to standard setting agencies, we should first note the section's obvious limitation. It deals only with deference to such agencies which is compelled by "specific statutory obligations." The Commission has brought to our attention one "specific statutory obligation": the Water Quality Improvement Act of 1970 (WQIA).[33] That Act prohibits federal licensing bodies, such as the Atomic Energy Commission, from issuing licenses for facilities which pollute "the navigable waters of the United States" unless they receive a certification from the appropriate agency that compliance with applicable water quality standards is reasonably assured. Thus Section 104 applies in some fashion to consideration of water qual-

---

[33] The relevant portion is 33 U.S.C.A. § 1171. See Note 30 *supra*.

ity matters. But it definitely cannot support—indeed, it is not even relevant to— the Commission's wholesale abdication to the standards and certifications of any and all federal, state and local agencies dealing with matters other than water quality.

As to water quality, Section 104 and WQIA clearly require obedience to standards set by other agencies. But obedience does not imply total abdication. Certainly, the language of Section 104 does not authorize an abdication. It does not suggest that other "specific statutory obligations" will entirely replace NEPA. Rather, it ensures that three sorts of "obligations" will not be undermined by NEPA: (1) the obligation to "comply" with certain standards, (2) the obligation to "coordinate" or "consult" with certain agencies, and (3) the obligation to "act, or refrain from acting contingent upon" a certification from certain agencies. WQIA imposes the third sort of obligation. It makes the granting of a license by the Commission "contingent upon" a water quality certification. But it does not re- quire the Commission to grant a license once a certification has been issued. It does not preclude the Commission from demanding water pollution controls from its licensees which are more strict than those demanded by the applicable water quality standards of the certifying agency.[34] It is very important to understand these facts about WQIA. For all that Section 104 of NEPA does is to reaffirm other "specific statutory obligations." Unless those obligations are plainly mutu- ally exclusive with the requirements of NEPA, the specific mandate of NEPA must remain in force. In other words, Section 104 can operate to relieve an agency of its NEPA duties only if other "specific statutory obligations" clearly preclude performance of those duties.

Obedience to water quality certifications under WQIA is not mutually exclu- sive with the NEPA procedures. It does not preclude performance of the NEPA duties. Water quality certifications essentially establish a minimum condition for the granting of a license. But they need not end the matter. The Commission can then go on to perform the very different operation of balancing the overall benefits and costs of a particular proposed project, and consider alterations (above and beyond the applicable water quality standards) which would further reduce envi- ronmental damage. Because the Commission can still conduct the NEPA balanc- ing analysis, consistent with WQIA, Section 104 does not exempt it from doing so. And it, therefore, must conduct the obligatory analysis under the prescribed pro- cedures.

We believe the above result follows from the plain language of Section 104 of NEPA and WQIA. However, the Commission argues that we should delve be-

---

[34] The relevant language in WQIA seems carefully to avoid any such restrictive implication. It provides that "[e]ach Federal agency * * * shall * * * insure compliance with applicable water quality standards * * *." 33 U.S.C.A. § 1171(a). It also provides that "[n]o license or permit shall be granted until the certification required by this section has been obtained or has been waived * * *. No license or permit shall be granted if certification has been denied * * *." 33 U.S.C.A. § 1171(b)(1). Nowhere does it indicate that certification must be the final and only protection against unjustified water pollution—a fully sufficient as well as a necessary condition for issuance of a federal license or permit.

We also take note of § 21(c) of WQIA, which states: "Nothing in this section shall be construed to limit the authority of any department or agency pursuant to any other provision of law to require compliance with applicable water quality standards. * * *" 33 U.S.C.A. § 1171(c).

neath the plain language and adopt a significantly different interpretation. It relies entirely upon certain statements made by Senator Jackson and Senator Muskie, the sponsors of NEPA and WQIA respectively.[35] Those statements indicate that Section 104 was the product of a compromise intended to eliminate any conflict between the two bills then in the Senate. The overriding purpose was to prevent NEPA from eclipsing obedience to more specific standards under WQIA. Senator Muskie, distrustful of "self-policing by Federal agencies which pollute or license pollution," was particularly concerned that NEPA not undercut the independent role of standard setting agencies.[36] Most of his and Senator Jackson's comments stop short of suggesting that NEPA would have no application in water quality matters; their goal was to protect WQIA, not to undercut NEPA. Our interpretation of Section 104 is perfectly consistent with that purpose.

Yet the statements of the two Senators occasionally indicate they were willing to go further, to permit agencies such as the Atomic Energy Commission to forego at least some NEPA procedures in consideration of water quality. Senator Jackson, for example, said, "The compromise worked out between the bills provides that the licensing agency will not have to make a detailed statement on water quality if the State or other appropriate agency has made a certification pursuant to [WQIA]."[37] Perhaps Senator Jackson would have required some consideration and balancing of environmental costs—despite the lack of a formal detailed statement—but he did not spell out his views. No Senator, other than Senators Jackson and Muskie, addressed himself specifically to the problem during floor discussion. Nor did any member of the House of Representatives.[38] The section-by-section analysis of NEPA submitted to the Senate clearly stated the overriding purpose of Section 104: that "no agency may substitute the procedures outlined in this Act for more restrictive and specific procedures established by law governing its activities."[39] The report does not suggest there that NEPA procedures should be entirely abandoned, but rather that they should not be "substituted" for more spe-

---

[35] The statements by Senators Jackson and Muskie were made, first, at the time the Senate originally considered WQIA. 115 CONG. REC. (Part 21) at 29052–29056. Another relevant colloquy between the two Senators occurred when the Senate considered the Conference Report on NEPA. 115 CONG. REC. (Part 30) at 40415–40425. Senator Muskie made a further statement at the time of final Senate approval of the Conference Report on WQIA. 116 CONG. REC. (daily ed.) S4401 (March 24, 1970).

[36] 115 CONG. REC. (Part 21) at 29053.

[37] Ibid. See also id. at 29056. Senator Jackson appears not to have ascribed major importance to the compromise. He said, "It is my understanding that there was never any conflict between this section [of WQIA] and the provisions of [NEPA]. If both bills were enacted in their present form, there would be a requirement for State certification, as well as a requirement that the licensing agency make environmental findings." Id. at 29053. He added, "The agreed-upon changes mentioned previously would change the language of some of these requirements, but their substance would remain relatively unchanged." Id. at 29055. Senator Muskie seemed to give greater emphasis to the supposed conflict between the two bills. See id. at 29053; 115 CONG. REC. (Part 30) at 40425; 116 CONG. REC. (daily ed.) at S4401.

[38] The Commission has called to our attention remarks made by Congressman Harsha. The Congressman did refer to a statement by Senator Muskie regarding NEPA, but it was a statement regarding application of the Act to established environmental control agencies, not regarding the relationship between NEPA and WQIA. 115 CONG. REC. (Part 30) at 40927–40928.

[39] Id. at 40420.

cific standards. In one rather cryptic sentence, the analysis does muddy the waters somewhat, stating that "[i]t is the intention that where there is no more effective procedure already established, the procedure of this act will be followed."[40] Notably, however, the sentence does not state that in the presence of "more effective procedures" the NEPA procedure will be abandoned entirely. It seems purposefully vague, quite possibly meaning that obedience to the certifications of standard setting agencies must alter, by supplementing, the normal "procedure of this act."

This rather meager legislative history, in our view, cannot radically transform the purport of the plain words of Section 104. Had the Senate sponsors fully intended to allow a total abdication of NEPA responsibilities in water quality matters—rather than a supplementing of them by strict obedience to the specific standards of WQIA—the language of Section 104 could easily have been changed. As the Supreme Court often has said, the legislative history of a statute (particularly such relatively meager and vague history as we have here) cannot radically affect its interpretation if the language of the statute is clear. See, e.g., *Packard Motor Car Co. v. NLRB*, 330 U.S. 485 (1947); *Kuehner v. Irving Trust Co.*, 299 U.S. 445 (1937); *Fairport, Painesville & Eastern R. Co. v. Meredith*, 292 U.S. 589 (1934); *Wilbur v. United States ex rel. Vindicator Consolidated Gold Mining Co.*, 284 U.S. 231 (1931). In a recent case interpreting a veterans' act, the Court set down the principle which must govern our approach to the case before us:

> "Having concluded that the provisions of § 1 are clear and unequivocal on their face, we find no need to resort to the legislative history of the Act. Since the State has placed such heavy reliance upon that history, however, we do deem it appropriate to point out that this history is at best inconclusive. It is true, as the State points out, that Representative Rankin, as Chairman of the Committee handling the bill on the floor of the House, expressed his view during the course of discussion of the bill on the floor that the 1941 Act would not apply to [the sort of case in question] * * *. But such statements, even when they stand alone, have never been regarded as sufficiently compelling to justify deviation from the plain language of a statute. * * *"

United States v. Oregon, 366 U.S. 643, 648 (1961). (Footnotes omitted.) It is, after all, the plain language of the statute which all the members of both houses of Congress must approve or disapprove. The courts should not allow that language to be significantly undercut. In cases such as this one, the most we should do to interpret clear statutory wording is to see that the overriding purpose behind the wording supports its plain meaning. We have done that here. And we conclude that Section 104 of NEPA does not permit the sort of total abdication of responsibility practiced by the Atomic Energy Commission.

V

Petitioners' final attack is on the Commission's rules governing a particular set of nuclear facilities: those for which construction permits were granted without consideration of environmental issues, but for which operating licenses have yet to be

_____
[40] Ibid.

issued. These facilities, still in varying stages of construction, include the one of most immediate concern to one of the petitioners: the Calvert Cliffs nuclear power plant on Chesapeake Bay in Maryland.

The Commission's rules recognize that the granting of a construction permit before NEPA's effective date does not justify bland inattention to environmental consequences until the operating license proceedings, perhaps far in the future. The rules require that measures be taken now for environmental protection. Specifically, the Commission has provided for three such measures during the pre-operating license stage. First, it has required that a condition be added to all construction permits, "whenever issued," which would oblige the holders of the permits to observe all applicable environmental standards imposed by federal or state law. Second, it has required permit holders to submit their own environmental report on the facility under construction. And third, it has initiated procedures for the drafting of its staff's "detailed environmental statement" in advance of operating license proceedings.[41]

The one thing the Commission has refused to do is take any independent action based upon the material in the environmental reports and "detailed statements." Whatever environmental damage the reports and statements may reveal, the Commission will allow construction to proceed on the original plans. It will not even consider requiring alterations in those plans (beyond compliance with external standards which would be binding in any event), though the "detailed statements" must contain an analysis of possible alternatives and may suggest relatively inexpensive but highly beneficial changes. Moreover, the Commission has, as a blanket policy, refused to consider the possibility of temporarily halting construction in particular cases pending a full study of a facility's environmental impact. It has also refused to weigh the pros and cons of "backfitting" for particular facilities (alteration of already constructed portions of the facilities in order to incorporate new technological developments designed to protect the environment). Thus reports and statements will be produced, but nothing will be done with them. Once again, the Commission seems to believe that the mere drafting and filing of papers is enough to satisfy NEPA.

The Commission appears to recognize the severe limitation which its rules impose on environmental protection. Yet it argues that full NEPA consideration of alternatives and independent action would cause too much delay at the pre-operating license stage. It justifies its rules as the most that is "practicable, in the light of environmental needs and 'other essential considerations of national policy'."[42] It cites, in particular, the "national power crisis" as a consideration of national policy militating against delay in construction of nuclear power facilities.

The Commission relies upon the flexible NEPA mandate to "use all practicable means consistent with other essential considerations of national policy." As we have previously pointed out, however, that mandate applies only to the substantive guidelines set forth in Section 101 of the Act. . . . The procedural duties, the duties to give full consideration to environmental protection, are subject to a

[41] 10 C.F.R. § 50, App. D. ¶¶ 1, 14.
[42] Brief for respondents in No. 24,871 at 59.

much more strict standard of compliance. By now, the applicable principle should be absolutely clear. NEPA requires that an agency must—to the fullest extent possible under its other statutory obligations—consider alternatives to its actions which would reduce environmental damage. That principle establishes that consideration of environmental matters must be more than a pro forma ritual. Clearly, it is pointless to "consider" environmental costs without also seriously considering action to avoid them. Such a full exercise of substantive discretion is required at every important, appropriate and nonduplicative stage of an agency's proceedings. . . .

The special importance of the pre-operating license stage is not difficult to fathom. In cases where environmental costs were not considered in granting a construction permit, it is very likely that the planned facility will include some features which do significant damage to the environment and which could not have survived a rigorous balancing of costs and benefits. At the later operating license proceedings, this environmental damage will have to be fully considered. But by that time the situation will have changed radically. Once a facility has been completely constructed, the economic cost of any alteration may be very great. In the language of NEPA, there is likely to be an "irreversible and irretrievable commitment of resources," which will inevitably restrict the Commission's options. Either the licensee will have to undergo a major expense in making alterations in a completed facility or the environmental harm will have to be tolerated. It is all too probable that the latter result would come to pass.

By refusing to consider requirement of alterations until construction is completed, the Commission may effectively foreclose the environmental protection desired by Congress. It may also foreclose rigorous consideration of environmental factors at the eventual operating license proceedings. If "irreversible and irretrievable commitment[s] of resources" have already been made, the license hearing (and any public intervention therein) may become a hollow exercise. This hardly amounts to consideration of environmental values "to the fullest extent possible."

A full NEPA consideration of alterations in the original plans of a facility, then, is both important and appropriate well before the operating license proceedings. It is not duplicative if environmental issues were not considered in granting the construction permit. And it need not be duplicated, absent new information or new developments, at the operating license stage. In order that the pre-operating license review be as effective as possible, the Commission should consider very seriously the requirement of a temporary halt in construction pending its review and the "backfitting" of technological innovations. For no action which might minimize environmental damage may be dismissed out of hand. Of course, final operation of the facility may be delayed thereby. But some delay is inherent whenever the NEPA consideration is conducted—whether before or at the license proceedings. It is far more consistent with the purposes of the Act to delay operation at a stage where real environmental protection may come about than at a stage where corrective action may be so costly as to be impossible.

Thus we conclude that the Commission must go farther than it has in its present rules. It must consider action, as well as file reports and papers, at the pre-operating license stage. As the Commission candidly admits, such consideration does not amount to a retroactive application of NEPA. Although the projects in question may have been commenced and initially approved before January 1, 1970, the Act clearly applies to them since they must still pass muster before going into full operation.[43] All we demand is that the environmental review be as full and fruitful as possible.

VI

We hold that, in the four respects detailed above, the Commission must revise its rules governing consideration of environmental issues. We do not impose a harsh burden on the Commission. For we require only an exercise of substantive discretion which will protect the environment "to the fullest extent possible." No less is required if the grand congressional purposes underlying NEPA are to become a reality.

NOTE: FEDERAL ACTIONS

NEPA applies only to "federal" actions. Often, the federal government is involved in a project only to a limited extent, as in licensing or permits, but NEPA compliance is required. A lease by an Indian tribe of their land (*Davis v. Morton,* 335 F. Supp. 1258, *rev'd,* 469 F.2d 593) has been held to require an EIS. Federal block grants seem to be the outer reach of NEPA at present. *Ely v. Velde,* 451 F.2d 1130.

The timing of federal involvement is also a factor. See, for example, *La Roya Unida v. Volpe,* 337 F. Supp. 221 (1971).

QUESTIONS FOR DISCUSSION

1 Does vagueness in legislation indicate a congressional wish for wide applicability, administrative discretion, or general inaction?
2 What do you suppose Congress meant when it said "to the fullest extent possible"?

[43] The courts which have held NEPA to be nonretroactive have not faced situations like the one before us here—situations where there are two, distinct stages of federal approval, one occurring before the Act's effective date and one after that date. See Note, *supra* Note 25.

The guidelines issued by the Council on Environmental Quality urge agencies to employ NEPA procedures to minimize environmental damage, even when approval of particular projects was given before January 1, 1970: "To the maximum extent practicable the section 102(2)(C) procedure should be applied to further major Federal actions having a significant effect on the environment even though they arise from projects or programs initiated prior to enactment of [NEPA] on January 1, 1970. Where it is not practicable to reassess the basic course of action, it is still important that further incremental major actions be shaped so as to minimize adverse environmental consequences. It is also important in further action that account be taken of environmental consequences not fully evaluated at the outset of the project or program." 36 FED. REG. at 7724.

3 Who must prepare an environmental impact statement? Who actually does the preparation?

4 Do you agree that the AEC gave NEPA a "crabbed interpretation"?

5 Why do you suppose the AEC took the position it did?

6 What features of AEC procedure did the court find failed to meet the NEPA mandate?

7 Are government agencies all capable of assessing the environmental impacts of their activities?

8 The court seemed to doubt the argument that a national power crisis was coming. Had *Calvert Cliffs v. AEC* arisen in the summer of 1974, might the decision have been different?

9 NEPA, like so many other environmental laws, "compels a case-by-case examination and balancing of discrete factors." Is this a sensible way to approach a problem of such magnitude? What advantages does it offer? Are there any alternatives?

10 Do you find the legislative history argument made by the court in Part IV of its opinion convincing? Can it be argued that the AEC position with regard to water pollution is environmentally preferable?

11 Would the court have been more receptive to the AEC argument regarding plants under construction had the AEC not delayed the commencement of NEPA obligations?

12 Could NEPA be extended to state or private construction?

13 Does the fact that NEPA precipitated a flood of litigation indicate poor drafting? Agency recalcitrance?

14 Should unelected judges construe statutes broadly or narrowly? Of what importance is the congressional statement of policy? The act's history? The climate of the country? The economic conditions?

15 Does the broadness of the act leave wide room for agency discretion? Was this intentional? What were the alternatives?

16 Is environmental protection possible if it might be "consistent with other essential considerations of national policy"?

17 What are the barriers to a "systematic, interdisciplinary approach" to environmental planning?

18 Have we succeeded in developing procedures to assure that "unquantified environmental amenities" are included in decision making?

19 Does NEPA really require a "rather finely tuned" balancing process? Is such a thing possible, given the numerous and diverse nature of the factors?

20 How does one assess all possible approaches to a problem?

21 Is the language "to the fullest extent possible" a limitation on agency responsibility or a high standard to be rigorously enforced? Would "to the fullest extent reasonable" be better?

22 Is the "major federal action" question one of law or fact?

23 Why was NEPA necessary?

24 Does the opinion in *Calvert Cliffs v. AEC* require a formal cost-benefit study or consideration of a wider range of factors?

PROJECTS REQUIRING ENVIRONMENTAL IMPACT STATEMENT (EIS)

Environmental impact statements are required by the National Environmental Policy Act only for major federal actions significantly affecting the quality of the human environment. The case of *Save Our Ten Acres v. Kreger* fails to reach a definite conclusion (the proposed action was the construction of an office building) but exemplifies the issue and directly attacks the question of the standard by which the courts will judge an agency's action in failing to file an environmental impact statement.

Save Our Ten Acres v. Kreger

472 F.2d 463, 4 ERC 1941 (5th Cir. 1973)

Before Morgan, Clark and Ingraham, Circuit Judges
Clark, Circuit Judge:

What is the proper standard for judicial review of an agency's threshold determination not to file an environmental impact statement under the National Environmental Policy Act of 1969 (NEPA)?[1]

This is an action to enjoin the construction of a federal office building on a downtown site in Mobile, Alabama, brought by an organization known as Save Our Ten Acres (alphabetically shorthanded: "SOTA"). SOTA is a voluntary unincorporated association comprised of approximately 572 employees of the Corps of Engineers, formed to resist the selection of the urban site. The Corps of Engineers is to occupy the greater part of the new building on completion. The site selection decision was made by the General Services Administration (GSA). The basis of SOTA's attack on that decision in the court below and in the instant appeal is limited to an alleged failure of the GSA to comply with the NEPA requirement that all federal agencies file a detailed statement of the environmental impact of all major federal actions which may significantly affect the quality of the human environment.[2]

It is undisputed that the defendants have proceeded with this site selection and construction without preparing an NEPA statement. However, they argue that no such environmental impact statement was required in this case because the building, even if it be a major federal action within the meaning of the statute,[3] will not significantly affect the quality of the human environment. The court

---

[1] 42 U.S.C.A. § 4331 et seq. (Supp. 1972).

[2] Omitted.

[3] The agency, although stopping short of actually conceding that the project constitutes a major federal action, has pitched its argument in this court as well as the court below in terms of whether or not the building will significantly affect the environment, and the trial court based its opinion on that ground.

below refused any relief, reasoning that the foregate determination by GSA that this project did not significantly affect the quality of the human environment could not be disturbed unless the court found it to be arbitrary, capricious or an abuse of discretion. To best effectuate the Act this decision should have been court-measured under a more relaxed rule of reasonableness, rather than by the narrower standard of arbitrariness or capriciousness. We therefore vacate and remand.

The question presented in this case has not yet been addressed by this circuit, though the question has arisen in a number of reported cases.[4] In support of its argument that the arbitrary or capricious standard should govern, the agency relies on the well-settled proposition that, in the absence of fraud, administrative findings of fact are conclusive if supported by any substantial record evidence. However, this usual fact determination review rule ought not be applied to test the basic jurisdiction-type conclusion involved here. NEPA was intended not only to insure that the appropriate responsible official considered the environmental effects of the project, but also to provide Congress (and others receiving such recommendation or proposal) with a sound basis for evaluating the environmental aspects of the particular project or program. The spirit of the Act would die aborning if a facile, ex parte decision that the project was minor or did not significantly affect the environment were too well shielded from impartial review. Every such decision pretermits all consideration of that which Congress has directed be considered "to the fullest extent possible." The primary decision to give or bypass the consideration required by the Act must be subject to inspection under a more searching standard.

We find solid support for this position in the recent Supreme Court decision in *Citizens to Preserve Overton Park, Inc. v. Volpe*, 401 U.S. 402, 91 S. Ct. 814, 28 L. Ed. 2d 136 [2 ERC 1250] (1971). There the Court narrowly construed the

---

[4] In *Ely v. Velde*, 451 F.2d 1130, 1138 (4th Cir. 1971), the court, relying on *Calvert Cliffs' Coordinating Comm. v. United States A.E.C.*, 449 F.2d 1109 (D.C. Cir. 1971), held that the statutory scheme placed a heavy burden on the agency to show its compliance with the procedural requirements of the NEPA, and apparently required the filing of an impact statement. In *Calvert Cliffs' supra*, the District of Columbia Circuit enunciated a stricter standard than arbitrariness to determine whether an agency had complied with the procedural requirements of the NEPA, and in *Natural Resources Defense Council, Inc. v. Morton*, 458 F.2d 827, 834 (D.C. Cir. 1972), it announced the application of "[a] rule of reason" to test the agency's decision to omit from the impact statement a discussion of the possible alternatives to the project; neither of these cases, however, dealt with the precise question involved in this case. See also *Environmental Defense Fund, Inc. v. United States Army Corps of Engineers*, 41 L.W. 2299 (8th Cir., Nov. 25, 1972). The question was raised but left unanswered in *Scherr v. Volpe*, 466 F.2d 1027, 1034 (7th Cir. 1972); and in *Hanly v. Mitchell*, 460 F.2d 640, 647 (2d Cir. 1972). At least two district courts have gone so far as to say that the agency has no discretion to exercise relative to whether the impact statement is required, but that a court will determine as a matter of law whether the project is a major program significantly affecting the environment. *Scherr v. Volpe*, 336 F. Supp. 886, 888 [3 ERC 1588] (W.D. Wisc. 1971), aff'd on alternate holding, 466 F.2d 1027, 1034 (7th Cir. 1974); *National Resources Defense Council, Inc. v. Grant*, 341 F. Supp. 356, 366 (E.D.N.C. 1972). Another district court has held that the impact statement is required if the action would arguably have an adverse environmental impact, at least where the agency has not provided a detailed explanation of its decision. *Students Challenging Regulatory Agency Procedures v. United States*, 346 F. Supp. 189, 201 & n. 17 (D.D.C. 1972). But see *Goose Hollow Foothills League v. Romney*, 334 F. Supp. 877, 879 (D. Ore. 1971), which appears to have applied the standard of arbitrariness. See also *Citizens for Reid State Park v. Laird*, 336 F. Supp. 783, 788-89 (D. Me. 1972).

discretion of the Secretary of Transportation to approve highway routes under a "no prudent and feasible alternative" standard. Conceding the statutory language at issue in Overton Park differs from that of the NEPA, nevertheless, both statutes (at a minimum) require the acting agency or the administrator to consider particular environmental factors before making certain determinations. While the Court made it clear that the ultimate merit decision based upon a weighing of these environmental considerations should be reviewed under the arbitrary, capricious, or abuse of discretion standard, a thorough study of Overton Park teaches that a more penetrating inquiry is appropriate for court-testing the entry-way determination of whether all relevant factors should ever be considered by the agency.[5] We reject as overly formalistic the argument that Overton Park's stricter standard of reasonableness is applicable only if the wording of the statute expressly conditions the exercise of authority upon a determination that certain prerequisites are met.

Under the review standard we hold is required, the court must determine whether the plaintiff has alleged facts which, if true, show that the recommended project would materially degrade any aspect of environmental quality. In this case SOTA charges, inter alia, that the construction of the building will create severe urban parking and traffic congestion problems, will aggravate an already substantial air pollution problem, and is to be improperly located on the flood plain of the Mobile River. Though we express no opinion on the merits of SOTA's claim, we note that SOTA's allegations on their face may well satisfy the criteria of GSA's own statement of policy for implementation of the NEPA.[6]

Since SOTA has raised substantial environmental issues concerning the proposed recommended project here, the court should proceed to examine and weigh the evidence of both the plaintiff and the agency to determine whether the agency reasonably concluded that the particular project would have no effects which would significantly degrade our environmental quality. This inquiry must not necessarily be limited to consideration of the administrative record, but supplemental affidavits, depositions, and other proof concerning the environmental impact of the project may be considered if an inadequate evidentiary development before the agency can be shown. See *Citizens to Preserve Overton Park, Inc. v. Volpe*, 335 F. Supp. 873, 876–77 [3 ERC 1510] (W.D. Tenn. 1972) (on remand). If the court concludes that no environmental factor would be significantly degraded

---

[5] *Environmental Defense Fund, Inc. v. United States Army Corps of Engineers*, 41 L.W. 2299 (8th Cir. Nov. 28, 1972), presented the question of the proper standard of review of the completeness and accuracy of the NEPA statement. In that case the court applied the bifurcated test of *Overton Park*, indicating that the more searching scope of authority test would apply to a review of the impact statement to "determine if the agency reached its decision after a full, good faith consideration and balancing of environmental factors."

[6] c. Environmental subject areas include, but are not limited to:

* * *

(2) Human population distribution changes and its effect upon urban congestion (including vehicular traffic), water supply, sewage treatment facilities, other public services, and threats to health;

(3) Actions which directly and indirectly affect human beings through water, air, and noise pollution, and undesirable land use patterns . . .

PBS 1095.1A, Attachment B.

See also *Hanly v. Mitchell, supra* n. 4, at 647.

by the project, GSA's determination not to file the impact statement should be upheld. On the other hand, if the court finds that the project may cause a significant degradation of some human environmental factor (even though other environmental factors are affected beneficially or not at all),[7] the court should require the filing of an impact statement or grant SOTA such other equitable relief as it deems appropriate.

Not only do we iterate that this decision has not the slightest intent of indicating what ruling should eventuate from the retest we require, but we also would emphasize that it is not the province of the courts to review any actual decision on the merits (if one be required) as to the desirability vel non of the project. We merely hold that it is the courts' function to insure that the mandate of the statute has been carried out and that all relevant environmental effects of the project be given appropriate consideration by the responsible official whenever it is unreasonable to conclude that the project is without the purview of the Act. . . .

NOTE

A complex composed of two 9-story buildings in New York to be built by GSA was the subject of *Hanly v. Mitchell*, 560 F.2d 640, *cert. denied*, 409 U.S. 990. There a preliminary injunction was granted stopping construction because GSA had failed to provide an impact statement on the grounds that there was no "major Federal action significantly affecting the quality of the human environment."

Does "major" refer to the project's cost? Amount of planning? Effect on environment?

Suppose the building had been a private enterprise?

See also *Hanly v. Kleindiest*, 471 F.2d 823, *cert. denied*, 412 U.S. 908.

Would a raise in municipal transit fares during a price freeze require an EIS? See *Cohen v. Price Comm.*, 337 F. Supp. 1236 (1972).

QUESTIONS FOR DISCUSSION

1   For what projects must an environmental impact statement be filed?
2   Who determines what constitutes a major federal action?
3   Is the question of whether or not a project may substantially affect the human environment answerable before the impact statement research is conducted?

---

[7] 1. Determination of what is a "major Federal action significantly affecting the quality of the human environment." This is in large part a judgment based on the circumstances of the proposed action, and the determination shall be included as a normal part of the decision-making process.
* * *
  b. Actions significantly affecting the human environment can be construed to be those that:
  (1) Degrade environmental quality even if beneficial effects outweigh the detrimental ones;
  (2) Curtail range of possible beneficial uses of the environment including irreversible and irretrievable commitments of resources;
  (3) Serve short-term rather than long-term environmental goals;
  (4) May be localized in their effect, but nevertheless, have a harmful environmental impact; and
  (5) Are attributable to many small actions; possibly taken over a period of time, that collectively have an adverse impact on the environment.
  PBS 1095.1A, Attachment B.

4   Is NEPA an "environmental" statute or merely a "notice" statute?
5   Who should make the decision to file or not to file an environmental impact statement? Do you agree with the standard of judicial review adopted in *Save Our Ten Acres v. Kreger?*

TIMING OF EIS

The decision-making process in projects of large scale may be the product of many smaller decisions made at different times. The question of when in the process an environmental assessment must be made and an environmental impact statement prepared is examined in *Upper Pecos Association v. Stans.*

Upper Pecos Association v. Stans

452 F.2d 1233, 3 ERC 1418 (10th Cir. 1971), Aff'd, 500 F.2d 17 (1974)

Before Phillips, Murrah and Hill, United States Circuit Judges.
Hill, Circuit Judge:

. . . On November 27, 1968, the Board of County Commissioners of San Miguel County, New Mexico, acting through the North Central New Mexico Economic Development District, applied for a grant of funds from the E.D.A. equal to 80% of the total estimated cost of constructing a proposed road in the Elk Mountain area of San Miguel County. Pursuant to its authority under the Public Works and Economic Development Act of 1965[1] to grant funds for meritorious projects in economically depressed areas, the E.D.A. made an offer to grant to the county the sum of $3,795,200 on October 21, 1970. The county accepted that offer on October 30, 1970. The project will include 26 miles of new road and the surfacing of 7.5 miles of existing road which now terminates at Johnson Mesa, and will traverse an area of the Santa Fe National Forest near the summit of Elk Mountain. . . .[2,3]

Appellant asserts that the granting of funds by the E.D.A. to San Miguel County was "a major federal action" within the meaning of § 102(2)(C) of the National Environmental Policy Act,[4] and § 5 of the Interim Guidelines of the Council on Environmental Quality.[5] As an environmental impact statement was not prepared prior to the E.D.A.'s offer of grant, the grant is illegal and disbursement of the funds authorized thereunder should be enjoined. Appellee argues that the provisions of the National Environmental Policy Act, as implemented by the Guidelines of the Council on Environmental Quality,[6] have been complied with

[1] 42 U.S.C. §§ 3121 et seq.
[2,3] Omitted.
[4] 42 U.S.C. §§ 4321 et seq.
[5] 35 Fed. Reg. 7390 (1970).
[6] 35 Fed. Reg. 7390 (1970) and 36 Fed. Reg. 7724 (1971).

by the Forest Service, which is the lead agency. The issues thus presented are which is the proper agency to prepare the environmental impact statement, and at what point in time must such statement be available.

A reading of the record reveals that the parties are in agreement that the proposed road is "a major federal action" within the meaning of § 102(2)(C) of the N.E.P.A. Furthermore, both parties agree that the environmental impact statement is to be prepared by the agency with overall responsibility for the project.[7] There is no dispute that the Forest Service has the continuing commitment to the course of action to build the road and the expertise to prepare the statement, whereas a requirement that the E.D.A. do so would be unduly burdensome to that agency. The trial court found that the Forest Service was the lead agency, and thereby had the responsibility of preparing the environmental impact statement. The findings of the trial court will not be disturbed on review unless unsupported by substantial evidence or clearly erroneous. *Northern Natural Gas Co. v. Grounds,* 441 F.2d 704 (10 Cir. 1971). We hold the trial court's finding that the Forest Service is the lead agency with responsibility for preparation of the environmental impact statement to be supported by substantial evidence; this finding is affirmed.

The second question presented for solution is at what point in time must the environmental impact statement be available. Appellant argues that preparation of the environmental impact statement after the offer of grant has been made is a meaningless gesture. Appellee contends that preparation and submission by the Forest Service of its preliminary environmental impact statement on February 9, 1971, fully meets the requirements of the N.E.P.A. This Court has recently dealt with the requirements of the N.E.P.A. The mandates of the N.E.P.A. pertain to procedure and not to substance, that is, decision-making in a given agency is required to meet certain procedural standards, yet the agency is left in control of the substantive aspects of the decision.[8] The N.E.P.A. creates no substantive rights in citizens to safe, healthful, productive and culturally pleasing surroundings.[9] Instead, the responsible agency is required to take these factors into account at some point before commencement of the project.

Case law on the question of the point in time at which the environmental impact statement must be available is understandably sparse. The N.E.P.A. became effective only on January 1, 1970. The Act was applied to projects then existent. In such situations, the requirements of the N.E.P.A. were satisfied if the environmental impact statement was prepared before the contract in question was executed; the project could be evaluated openmindedly if work had not commenced.[10] A recent decision in the United States District Court for the District of Alaska presents an analogous fact situation to the instant case. Pursuant to a

---

[7] Final Guidelines of the Council on Environmental Quality, 36 Fed. Reg. 7724 (1971); *Calvert Cliff's Coordinating Comm., Inc. v. A.E.C.,* 441 F.2d 1109, (D.C. Cir. 1971).

[8] *Nat'l Helium Corp. v. Morton,* . . . [3 ERC 1129] (10th Cir. 1971).

[9] *Environmental Defense Fund, Inc. v. Corps of Eng. of U.S. Army,* 325 F. Supp. 749 (E.D. Ark. 1971).

[10] *Environmental Defense Fund, Inc. v. Corps of Eng. of U.S. Army,* 325 F. Supp. 728, 325 F. Supp. 749 (E.D. Ark. 1970, 1971).

contract for harvesting of certain timber in the North Tongass National Forest, a mill site was to be granted the successful bidder. A blue-ribbon panel of conservationists selected from universities in the United States and Canada had supervised the selection of the mill site to insure minimization of environmental impact by comprehensive site planning; the paper company involved had spent substantial sums to this end. An environmental impact statement had been submitted the day before the Forest Service issued its "Conditions of Use" pending the patent of the site to the paper company. The court found compliance with the N.E.P.A. *Sierra Club v. Hardin,* 325 F. Supp. 99 [2 ERC 1385] (D. Alas. 1971). The point at which the project had become more than a mere proposition—here the letting of the contract for the harvesting of timber and the selection of the mill site, in the instant case the offer of grant by the E.D.A.—had been passed before the environmental impact statement was prepared. Certainly the project must be of sufficient definiteness before an evaluation of its environmental impact can be made and alternatives proposed.

Preparation and submission of the environmental impact statement at the point in time selected by the Forest Service is not a meaningless gesture, as appellant argues. The Forest Service must still approve the location and construction plans and specifications of the proposed road before a grant of right-of-way easement necessary to permit the use of National Forest Lands for highway purposes is possible. The final environmental impact statement will provide the basis on which the Forest Service will decide on the issuance of the right-of-way easement. The trial court thus has found that the directives of the N.E.P.A. and the recommendations issued pursuant thereto have been satisfied to date. This Court is bound to uphold such finding unless unsupported by substantial evidence or clearly erroneous. *Northern Natural Gas Co. v. Grounds, supra.* The finding of compliance with the N.E.P.A. today is supported by substantial evidence, and is not clearly erroneous.

Affirmed.

Murrah, Circuit Judge (dissenting):

It is agreed that both the E.D.A. action in making the grant of funds and the Forest Service action in granting the right-of-way easement were "major Federal actions" as that term is used in the N.E.P.A. We also agree that the Forest Service was the "lead agency" with the duty of preparing the environmental impact statement.

However, after a close reading of the statute and its implementing regulations, it is my opinion that they clearly express the intention that "compliance to the 'fullest' possible extent would seem to demand that environmental issues be considered at every important stage in the decision making process concerning a particular action. . . ." *Calvert Cliffs' Coordinating Comm., Inc. v. A.E.C.,* 449 F.2d 1109, 2 ERC 1779 (D.C. Cir. July 23, 1971). On this record it does not appear that E.D.A. has ever considered the environmental consequences of its action. I do not believe that the impact statement prepared by the Forest Service after the grant of funds has been made satisfied the statutorily imposed duty of E.D.A. to consider the environmental consequences of its action to the "fullest possible extent."

I would reverse and remand with directions to vacate the E.D.A. offer of grant in order to permit E.D.A. to comply with the procedural safeguards set out in the statute before taking the major Federal action of granting funds for this project.

QUESTIONS FOR DISCUSSION

1 When must an environmental impact statement be made available?
2 Can any general rule be formulated on the question?
3 Is anything beyond a "meaningless gesture" adequate?
4 Are environmental factors so dependent on site location that a preliminary decision must be made before the environmental impact analysis?

CONTENTS OF EIS

The most important and most litigated issue in National Environmental Policy Act controversy has been the contents of the environmental impact statement. Whether or not statements must include discussion of alternatives to the proposed project, and their environmental consequences, is a key issue and is illustrated by *Natural Resources Defense Council v. Morton.*

Natural Resources Defense Council v. Morton

458 F.2d 827, 3 ERC 1558 (D.C. Cir. 1972), dismissed as moot, 337 F. Supp. 170 (D.D.C. 1972)

Before Tamm, Leventhal and Mackinnon, Circuit Judges.
Opinion for the Court filed by Leventhal, Circuit Judge. . . .
Leventhal, Circuit Judge:

This appeal raises a question as to the scope of the requirement of the National Environmental Policy Act (NEPA)[1] that environmental impact statements contain a discussion of alternatives. Before us is the Environmental Impact Statement filed October 28, 1971, by the Department of Interior with respect to its proposal, under § 8 of the Outer Continental Shelf Lands Act,[2] for the oil and gas general

---

[1] See, e.g., *Calvert Cliffs' Coordinating Committee, Inc. v. Atomic Energy Commission,* 449 F.2d 1109, [2 ERC 1779] (D.C. Cir. 1971); *Committee for Nuclear Responsibility, Inc. v. Seaborg,* No. 71-1732, October 5, 1971 [3 ERC 1126].
[2] 43 U.S.C. § 1337 (1970). This Act, P.L. 83-212, appears at 43 U.S.C. § 1331 et seq.

lease sale, of leases to some 80 tracts of submerged lands, primarily off eastern Louisiana. The proposal was finally structured so as to embrace almost 380,000 acres, about 10% of the offshore acreage presently under Federal lease. . . .[3]

I. BACKGROUND

A. Chronology and Impact Statements

On June 15, 1971, Secretary of Interior Rogers Morton, a defendant in this litigation, announced that a general oil and gas lease sale of tracts on the Outer Continental Shelf (OCS) off eastern Louisiana would take place in December, 1971. This was responsive to the directive in President Nixon's June 4, 1971, Message on Supply of Energy and Clean Air.[4] On July 31, 1971, Mr. Burton W. Silcock, Director of the Bureau of Land Management, also a defendant, promulgated and circulated for comment a "Draft Environmental Impact Statement" pursuant to § 102(2)(C) of NEPA and § 10(b) of the Guidelines of the Council on Environmental Quality.[5] Plaintiffs submitted comments on this draft statement. Hearings were held in September 1971 in New Orleans, at which oral testimony was presented. On October 28, 1971, Mr. Silcock promulgated the "Final Environmental Impact Statement," (hereafter Statement), 36 Fed. Reg. 20707 (1971). On November 20, 1971, the Interior Department announced that the proposed lease sale would take place, that 80 tracts would be offered for leasing, and that sealed bids would be received until December 21.

B. Statement—Adverse Environmental Impact Disclosed

While the Statement presents questions, subsequently delineated, this document—67 pages in length, exclusive of appendices—is not challenged on the ground of failure to disclose the problems of environmental impact of the proposed sale. On the contrary, these problems are set forth in considerable range and detail. Indeed, the complaint voiced by the Audubon Society's witness in testimony was that the draft Statement gives a green light for the sale while its contents seem to cry out for the opposite conclusion. Without purporting to summarize, we identify some of the Statement's highlights:

Adjacent to the proposed lease area is the greatest estuarine coastal marsh complex in the United States, some 7.9 million acres, providing food, nursery habitat and spawning ground vital to fish, shellfish and wildlife, as well as food and shelter for migratory waterfowl, wading birds and fur-bearing animals. This complex provides rich nutrient systems which make the Gulf of Mexico, blessed also with warm waters and shallow depths, the most productive fishing region in the country. It yielded $71 million [worth of] fish and shellfish to Louisiana and

---

[3] Omitted.

[4] The text of this Message appears at 112 CONG. REC. S8313-17 (June 4, 1971).

[5] See 36 F.R. 7724 (1971) for the Council's Guidelines for the preparation of Statements on Proposed Federal Actions Affecting the Environment.

Mississippi commercial fishermen in 1970, and some 9 million man-days of sport fishing.

The coastal regions of Louisiana and Mississippi contain millions of acres suitable for outdoor recreation, with a number of state and federal recreation areas, and extensive beach shorelines (397 miles for Louisiana, and 100 miles for Mississippi). These serve millions—not only the residents of the seven-state region (23 million in all; 10 million within 250 miles of the coast), but visitors attracted to the beaches in increasing numbers (estimated at 3.5 millions within five years and ultimately 10 millions).

As to probable impact of issuance of leases on the environment the Statement did not anticipate continuation of debris from drilling operations, in view of recent regulations prohibiting dumping of debris on the OCS. The Statement acknowledged some impact from construction of platforms, pipelines and other structures. A concluding section (III D) on "Unavoidable Adverse Environmental Effects" particularly noted the destruction of marsh and of marine species and plants from dredging incident to pipeline installation, and the effect of pipeline canals in e.g., increasing ratio of water to wetlands and increasing salt water intrusion.

Oil pollution is the problem most extensively discussed in the Statement and its exposition of unavoidable adverse environmental effects. The Statement acknowledges that both short and long term effects on the environment can be expected from spillage, including in that term major spills (like that in the Santa Barbara Channel in 1969); minor spills from operations and unidentified sources; and discharge of waste water contaminated with oil.

These adverse effects relate both to the damage to the coastal region—beaches, water areas and historic sites; and the forecast that oil pollution "may seriously damage the marine biological community"—both direct damage to the larger organisms, visible more easily and sooner, and to smaller life stages which would lead one step removed to damage later in the food chain.

The Statement noted the diverse conclusions and comments in existing reports on oil spills, some minimizing damage done, others stressing that oil spillage has effects beyond the period of visible evidence; that oil may mix with water, especially in a turbulent sea, and disperse downward into the sea; that emulsifiers used to remove surface oil may have toxic consequences, etc.

The Statement asserted that while past major spills in the Gulf resulted in minimal damage, this was due to a fortunate combination of offshore winds and surface currents. The Statement rates blocks in the sale on an estimated probability of impact basis, calculated principally on proximity to high value/critically vulnerable area.

C. Statement—Discussion of Alternatives

Section IV of the Statement, containing its discussion of Alternatives, is attached as an Appendix. Subsection A deals with possible modifications to delete tracts with higher environmental risks. Government counsel advises that, in order to lessen environmental risk, the acreage covered by the proposed sale was reduced from that originally contemplated, with the withdrawal of eight of the tracts most nearly located to the Delta Migratory Waterfowl Refuge.

Subsection IV B ("Withdraw Sale"), containing the material principally involved in this case, will be discussed subsequently in this opinion.

D. Ruling of District Court

The District Court recognized both that there is a profound national energy crisis and that the Outer Continental Shelf has been a prolific source of oil and gas. But it further noted that the Shelf, in President Nixon's words, "has been the source of troublesome oil spills in recent years." The Court found that the Statement failed to provide the "detailed statement" required by NEPA of environmental impact and alternatives. The Court stated:

> The Court finds that the defendants failed to comply with NEPA by failing to discuss some alternatives at all, such as meeting energy demands by federal legislation or administrative action freeing current onshore and state-controlled offshore production from state market demand prorationing or a change in the Federal Power Commission's natural gas pricing policies. In addition the defendants only superficially discussed the alternatives listed in their Final Impact Statement, and they failed to discuss in detail the environmental impacts of the alternatives they listed in the statement. The Court does not wish to give the impression that it believes the alternatives are better than the proposed lease sale, but it believes that these alternatives must be explored and discussed thoroughly in order to comport with the intent and requirements of Section 4332(2)(C) of NEPA.

E. Scope of Appellate Consideration

We pause before our discussion of the meaning of NEPA to take note of plaintiffs' contention that the Government's motion should be denied because the granting or denial of a preliminary injunction calls for the exercise of judicial discretion, and is not to be disturbed on appeal except on a finding of abuse or improvident exercise of judicial discretion.[6] And a party moving in an appellate court for a summary reversal—i.e., on motion papers, without usual briefs and full argument—has a "heavy burden of demonstrating both that his remedy is proper and that the merits of his claim so clearly warrant relief as to justify expeditious action."[7]

However, a greater amplitude of judicial review is called for when the appeal presents a substantial issue that the action of the trial judge was based on a premise as to the pertinent rule of law that was erroneous. Not only the avowed forecast as to probability of success on the merits, but also the analysis of injury to either or both parties, the public interest, and the balancing of interests, may well come to depend on an assumption of underlying legal premise. When this can be identified, the appellate court furthers the interest of justice by providing a ruling

---

[6] See *Meccano, Ltd. v. Wanamaker,* 253 U.S. 136, 141 (1920); *A Quaker Action Group v. Hickel,* 137 U.S. App. D.C. 176, 180, 421 F.2d 1111, 1115 (1969).

[7] *United States v. Allen,* 133 U.S. App. D.C. 84, 85, 408 F.2d 1287, 1288 (1969).

on the merits to the extent that the matter is ripe, though technically the case is only at the stage of application for preliminary injunction.[8] And a reversal based on a disagreement with the underlying legal premise of the trial court is not based on, or to be construed as, a determination of arbitrary abuse of judicial discretion.[9]

Similarly this court's function extends to disposition on motion for summary reversal—when the critical issue in cases of public moment, and the appraisal of the possibility of irreparable harm to the public interest, depend on the applicable legal premise. This conception of the motion for summary reversal does not require that the case be free of troublesome issues, but is rather based on the approach that there is a public interest in expedition in extraordinary cases, whether the appeal is brought by the Government or others, and that the case is ripe for decision, e.g., is unlikely to turn significantly on fact findings or further legal researches, as in legislative history.

Although the case is not presented on customary printed briefs the court has the benefit of the legal researchers and positions of the parties. While it is typical for oral argument on such motions to be scheduled initially at 15 minutes per side, it is also typical for time to be extended in accordance with the needs of counsel and the court and the complexity of the issues.

The present case is one of public moment, where expedition should be provided if possible. While the application was for a preliminary injunction, the District Court properly made its determination on the basis of underlying legal assumptions. We think it appropriate to give full consideration to the Government's motion for summary reversal, and to the issue, insofar as ripe for determination, of the rightful scope of NEPA's requirement as to alternatives.

II. DISCUSSION OF REQUIREMENT OF NEPA AS TO ALTERNATIVES

The pertinent instruction of Congress appears in § 102 of NEPA, 42 U.S.C. § 4332:

. . .

Paragraph (iii) of § 102(2)(C) is a terse notation for: "The alternative ways of accomplishing the objectives of the proposed action and the results of not accomplishing the proposed action."[10]

Congress contemplated that the Impact Statement would constitute the environmental source material for the information of the Congress as well as the Executive, in connection with the making of relevant decisions, and would be available to enhance enlightenment of—and by—the public.[11] The impact state-

---

[8] See *Youngstown Sheet & Tube Co. v. Sawyer,* 343 U.S. 579, 584-85 (1952).

[9] See *Delaware and Hudson Ry. Co. v. United Transportation Union,* 450 F.2d 603 (1971).

[10] Thus is the language of the Section-by-Section Analysis presented by Senator Jackson, in charge of the legislation and chairman of the Senate Interior Committee, in explaining and recommending approval of the bill as agreed in conference. 115 CONG. REC. 40420 (Dec. 20, 1969).

[11] See *Committee for Nuclear Responsibility, Inc. v. Seaborg,* No. 71-1732, October 5, 1971, slip opin., p. 7; No. 71-1854, October 28, 1971, slip opin., pp. 2, 12.

ment provides a basis for (a) evaluation of the benefits of the proposed project in light of its environmental risk, and (b) comparison of the net balance for the proposed project with the environmental risks presented by alternative courses of action.[12]

Need to Discuss Environmental Consequences of Alternatives

We reject the implication of one of the Government's submissions which began by stating that while the Act requires a detailed statement of alternatives, it "does not require a discussion of the environmental consequences of the suggested alternative."[13] A sound construction of NEPA, which takes into account both the legislative history and contemporaneous executive construction (see notes 10 and 12), requires a presentation of the environmental risks incident to reasonable alternative courses of action. The agency may limit its discussion of environmental impact to a brief statement, when that is the case, that the alternative course involves no effect on the environment, or that their effect, briefly described, is simply not significant. A rule of reason is implicit in this aspect of the law, as it is in the requirement that the agency provide a statement concerning those opposing views that are responsible.[14]

Alternatives as to Oil Import Quotas

We think the Secretary's Statement erred in stating that the alternative of elimination of oil import quotas was entirely outside its cognizance. Assuming as the Statement puts it, that this alternative "involves complex factors and concepts, including national security, which are beyond the scope of this statement," it does not follow that the Statement should not present the environmental effects of that alternative. While the consideration of pertinent alternatives requires a weighing of numerous matters, such as economics, foreign relations, national security, the fact remains that, as to the ingredient of possible adverse environmental impact, it is the essence and thrust of NEPA that the pertinent Statement serve to gather in one place a discussion of the relative environmental impact of alternatives.

The Government also contends that the only "alternatives" required for discussion under NEPA are those which can be adopted and put into effect by the official or agency issuing the statement. The Government seeks to distinguish the kind of impact statement required for a major Federal action from that required

---

[12] The legislative history indicates the importance of this source of environmental input into the decision making process. See S. Rep. No. 91–296, 91st Cong., 1st Sess., 21:

> ... the agency shall develop information and provide descriptions of the alternatives in adequate detail for subsequent reviewers and decision makers, both within the executive branch and the Congress, to consider the alternatives along with the principle recommendations.

That the impact statement is the proper instrument to provide this focus is recognized by the guidelines promulgated by the Council on Environmental Quality: A rigorous exploration and objective evaluation of alternative actions that might avoid some or all of the adverse effects is essential. Sufficient analysis of such alternatives and their costs and impact on the environment should accompany the proposed action through the agency review process in order not to foreclose prematurely options which might have less detrimental effects. 36 F.R. 7724, 7725 (1971).

[13] Defendants' Memorandum of Points and Authorities, Dec. 8, 1971, p. 7.

[14] *Committee for Nuclear Responsibility, Inc. v. Seaborg,* October 5, 1971, slip opin., p. 7.

with a legislative proposal.[15] And it stresses that the objective of the Secretary's action was to carry out the directive in the President's clean energy message of June 4, 1971.

While we agree with so much of the Government's presentation as rests on the assumption that the alternatives required for discussion are those reasonably available, we do not agree that this requires a limitation to measures the agency or official can adopt. This approach would be particularly inapposite for the lease sale of offshore oil lands hastened by Secretary Morton in response to the directive which President Nixon set forth in his message to Congress on the Supply of Energy and Clean Air, as part of an overall program of development to provide an accommodation of the energy requirements of our country with the growing recognition of the necessity to protect the environment. The scope of this project is far broader than that of other proposed Federal actions discussed in impact statements, such as a single canal or dam.[16] The Executive's proposed solution to a national problem, or a set of inter-related problems, may call for each of several departments or agencies to take a specific action; this cannot mean that the only discussion of alternatives required in the ensuing environmental impact statements would be the discussion by each department of the particular actions it could take as an alternative to the proposal underlying its impact statement.

When the proposed action is an integral part of a coordinated plan to deal with a broad problem,[17] the range of alternatives that must be evaluated is broadened. While the Department of the Interior does not have the authority to eliminate or reduce oil import quotas such action is within the purview of both Congress and the President, to whom the impact statement goes. The impact statement is not only for the exposition of the thinking of the agency, but also for the guidance of these ultimate decision-makers, and must provide them with the environmental effects of both the proposal and the alternatives, for their consideration along with the various other elements of the public interest.

An evaluation of the environmental effects of all the alternatives in the area of the energy crisis might have been provided by an impact statement issued by an officer or agency with broad responsibility. This could have been done in June 1971 when the President abstained from exercising his authority to invoke a change in import quota administration and issued the Message that included the directive as to offshore leasing. This course would have been in furtherance of the

---

[15] See Defendants' Memorandum, Dec. 8, 1971, at 11:

When proposing legislation the responsible official may properly be expected to consider alternative methods of achieving the same goal which require legislation, because his impact statement is to assist the Congress in determining how it should act and the Congress is able to enact any legislation within the scope of the Constitution. When the responsible official is considering a major Federal action which he is to take himself, he is properly concerned only with those alternatives which he himself has discretion to adopt.

[16] See e.g., *Environmental Defense Fund, Inc. v. Corps of Engineers,* 325 F. Supp. 749 (E.D. Ark. 1971) (dam), *Environmental Defense Fund v. Corps of Engineers,* 2 ERC 1173 (D.D.C. 1971) (canal).

[17] The President's message set out eleven areas of research and development toward the goal of clean energy; three areas of making available the energy resources of federal lands, including the leasing of offshore oil lands; and further discussed six other aspects of the overall problem.

NEPA objective of securing impact statements in case of a "major Federal action significantly affecting the quality of the human environment," though we do not suggest it was improper to defer the impact statement from the time of programmatic directive to the time of the implementing specific actions. The impact statement function could have been assigned to the group designated by the President to coordinate and analyze overall energy questions for the executive branch—the Energy Subcommittee of the Domestic Council.[18] In the absence of assignment of the impact statement function to an agency with broader responsibility, the implementation of the statutory requirement of the environmental review mandated by NEPA fell on the Interior Department when it took the first step in carrying out the broader energy program.

In defense of the Statement as written Government counsel suggest that nothing else was required because it was apparently assumed that there would be no adverse environmental impact from increased imports. This was not stated— and, for all we know, a contrary implication may have been intended by the Statement (at p. 37) when it referred to the problem of spillage from drilling as not even approaching the pollution from routine discharges of tankers and other vessels. As to this contention—like another statement of counsel, unsupported in the record, that offshore drilling has less adverse environmental impact than onshore drilling because the oil produced has lower sulfur content—our comment is simply this: The subject of environmental impact is too important to relegate either to implication or to subsequent justification by counsel.[19] The Statement must set forth the material contemplated by Congress in form suitable for the enlightenment of the others concerned.

The need for continuing review of environmental impact of alternatives under NEPA cannot be put to one side on the ground of past determinations by Congress or the President. We are aware that the 1953 Outer Continental Shelf Lands Act contains a finding of an urgent need for OCS development and authorization of leasing. Similarly we are aware that the oil import quota program was instituted by the President on a mandatory basis in 1959, following earlier voluntary programs, and that the President's authority, based on national security considerations, is contained in legislation derived from a 1955 enactment and subsequent amendments, 19 U.S.C. § 1862. But these enactments are not dispositive. As to both programs Congress contemplated continuing review. The OCS leasing was specifically made subject to executive authority to withdraw unleased lands from disposition from time to time, 43 U.S.C. § 1341(a). Import controls were from the outset dependent on continuing Presidential findings as to the nature and duration of controls deemed necessary. A Cabinet Task Force on Oil Import Control was

---

[18] In his message to Congress, the President designated the Energy Subcommittee as the body with the power to make overall policy in the field until his proposed Department of Natural Resources comes into being. 112 CONG. REC. 8317.

[19] Cf., *Burlington Truck Lines, Inc. v. United States,* 371 U.S. 156, 168–169 (1962); *Braniff Airways, Inc. v. CAB,* 126 U.S. App. D.C. 399, 411, 379 F.2d 453, 465 (1967); *National Air Carrier Assn. v. CAB,* 141 U.S. App. D.C. 31, 41, 436 F.2d 185, 195 (1970). While these cases relate to fact findings, this aspect—the need for agency statement, as opposed to counsel's rationalization—is a requirement that applies to environmental impact statements.

created in March 1961 to conduct a review of mandatory oil import restriction and its report, in February 1970, recommended a substantial change in the method and direction of import controls.

What NEPA infused into the decision-making process in 1969 was a directive as to environmental impact statements that was meant to implement the Congressional objectives of Government coordination, a comprehensive approach to environmental management, and a determination to face problems of pollution "while they are still of manageable proportions and while alternative solutions are still available" rather than persist in environmental decision-making wherein "policy is established by default and inaction" and environmental decisions "continue to be made in small but steady increments" that perpetuate the mistakes of the past without being dealt with until "they reach crisis proportions." S. Rep. No. 91-296, 91st Cong., 1st Sess. (1969) p. 5.

We reiterate that the discussion of environmental effects of alternatives need not be exhaustive. What is required is information sufficient to permit a reasoned choice of alternatives so far as environmental aspects are concerned. As to alternatives not within the scope of authority of the responsible official, reference may of course be made to studies of other agencies—including other impact statements. Nor is it appropriate, as Government counsel argues, to disregard alternatives merely because they do not offer a complete solution to the problem. If an alternative would result in supplying only part of the energy that the lease sale would yield, then its use might possibly reduce the scope of the lease sale program and thus alleviate a significant portion of the environmental harm attendant on offshore drilling.

Other "Alternatives"

The foregoing establishes that we cannot grant the Government's motion for summary reversal. We discuss other aspects of the case in anticipation that the Secretary may choose to supplement or modify the Statement—perhaps even, assuming approval by the District Court, in an effort to open the sealed bids without a new offering.

We think there is merit to the Government's position insofar as it contends that no additional discussion was requisite for such "alternatives" as the development of oil shale, desulfurization of coal, coal liquefaction and gasification, tar sands and geothermal resources.

The Statement sets forth (see Appendix) that while these possibilities hold great promise for the future, their impact on the energy supply will not likely be felt until after 1980, and will be dependent on environmental safeguards and technological developments. Since the Statement also sets forth that the agency's proposal was put forward to meet a near-term requirement, imposed by an energy short-fall projected for the mid-1970's, the possibility of the environmental impact of long-term solutions requires no additional discussion at this juncture. We say "at this juncture" for the problem requires continuing review, in the nature of things, and these alternatives and their environmental consequences may be more germane to subsequent proposals for OCS leases, in the light of changes in technology or in the variables or energy requirements and supply.

Furthermore, the requirement in NEPA of discussion as to reasonable alternatives does not require "crystal ball" inquiry. Mere administrative difficulty does not interpose such flexibility into the requirements of NEPA as to undercut the duty of compliance "to the fullest extent possible."[20] But if this requirement is not rubber, neither is it iron. The statute must be construed in the light of reason if it is not to demand what is, fairly speaking, not meaningfully possible, given the obvious, that the resources of energy and research—and time—available to meet the Nation's needs are not infinite.

Still different considerations are presented by the "alternatives" of increasing nuclear energy development, listed in the Statement, and the possibilities, identified by the District Court as a critical omission, of federal legislation or administrative action freeing current offshore and state-controlled offshore production from state market demand prorationing, or changing the Federal Power Commission's natural gas pricing policies.

The mere fact that an alternative requires legislative implementation does not automatically establish it as beyond the domain of what is required for discussion, particularly since NEPA was intended to provide a basis for consideration and choice by the decision-makers in the legislative as well as the executive branch. But the need for an overhaul of basic legislation certainly bears on the requirements of the Act. We do not suppose Congress intended an agency to devote itself to extended discussion of the environmental impact of alternatives so remote from reality as to depend on, say, the repeal of the antitrust laws.

In the last analysis, the requirement as to alternatives is subject to a construction of reasonableness, and we say this with full awareness that this approach necessarily has both strengths and weaknesses. Where the environmental aspects of alternatives are readily identifiable by the agency, it is by those concerned with the consequences of the decision and its alternatives. As already noted, the agency may make references to studies already made by other agencies (including impact statements) or appearing in responsible journals.

There is reason for concluding that NEPA was not meant to require detailed discussion of the environmental effects of "alternatives" put forward in comments when these effects cannot be readily ascertained and the alternatives are deemed only remote and speculative possibilities, in view of basic changes required in statutes and policies of other agencies—making them available, if at all, only after protracted debate and litigation not meaningfully compatible with the time-frame of the needs to which the underlying proposal is addressed.

A final word. In this as in other areas, the functions of courts and agencies, rightly understood, are not in opposition but in collaboration, toward achievement of the end prescribed by Congress.[21] So long as the officials and agencies

---

[20] Omitted.

[21] Cf. *United States v. Morgan,* 307 U.S. 183, 191 (1939); *Niagara Mohawk Power Corp. v. FPC,* 126 U.S. App. D.C. 376, 383, 379 F.2d 153, 160 (1967); *Greater Boston TV Corp. v. FCC,* 444 F.2d 841, 851 (D.C. Cir. 1970), cert. denied 35 U.S.L.W. 3549, June 14, 1971.

have taken the "hard look"[22] at environmental consequences mandated by Congress, the court does not seek to impose unreasonable extremes or to interject itself within the area of discretion of the executive as to the choice of the action to be taken.[23]

Informed by our judgment that discussion of alternatives may be required even though the action required lies outside the Interior Department, the Secretary will, we have no doubt, be able without undue delay to provide the kind of reasonable discussion of alternatives and their environmental consequences that Congress contemplated.

Motion denied.

APPENDIX

Excerpt from Final Environmental Impact Statement on Proposed 1971 Outer Continental Shelf Oil and Gas General Lease Sale Offshore Eastern Louisiana Prepared by the Department of the Interior

IV. Alternatives to the Proposed Action

A. Hold the Sale in Modified Form The proposed sale could be held by offering only those tracts determined to have a lower potential for environmental risks. Those tracts believed to have high environmental risks could be deleted from the sale and considered for offering at a later date, should improved technology or other circumstances warrant.

This alternative could also allow for special stipulations on any proposed tract where additional requirements might be necessary to protect the environment or to minimize or eliminate possible conflicts with or potential damage to other resource values or commercial uses of the Gulf of Mexico and the adjacent land areas.

B. Withdraw Sale The proposed sale could be withdrawn from consideration for leasing on the basis of possible environmental impacts. If such a decision were made, new domestic sources of clean energy would need to be developed. In the long run, new technology must be made available to produce clean energy at a cost to help offset the critical need for oil and gas; in the short run, few alternatives exist and the ones that do exist are of questionable practicability. The following possible sources of energy for short-run needs are "alternatives"[1] to offshore oil and gas.

Many of these alternatives have their individual environmental effects which must be considered: however, analysis of these impacts is beyond the scope of this statement.

[22] Cf., *WAIT Radio v. FCC*, 136 U.S. App. D.C. 317, 418 F.2d 1153 (1969); *Greater Boston TV Corp. v. FCC, supra*, 444 F.2d at 851.
[23] See *Calvert Cliffs' Coordinating Committee, Inc., supra* note 1, 449 F.2d at 1115.

[1] In many cases, they are not necessarily alternatives, but are supplemental to other sources. The national energy requirement exceeds the potential of any one "alternative."

1   Eliminations of import quotas.
2   Increase onshore exploration and development.
3   Development of oil shale.
4   Increase nuclear energy development.
5   Increase use of low sulfur coal and/or desulfurization of coal.
6   Development of coal liquification [*sic*] and gasification.
7   Development of geothermal resources.
8   Development of tar sands.

While the elimination of oil import quotas could be an alternative to continued development of offshore oil and gas, such a determination involves complex
factors and concepts, including national security, which are beyond the scope of
this statement. The remaining alternative energy sources should best be considered as supplements, not true alternatives, in the short run (e.g. 5 to 15 years).
While the development of oil shale, nuclear energy, desulfurization of coal, coal
liquification [*sic*], coal gasification, tar sands and geothermal resources hold great
promise for the future, their impact on the energy supply will not likely be felt
until after 1980, and will be dependent on environmental safeguards and technological developments. Until recently, the petroleum industry has been able to
satisfy domestic demand for oil and gas from the onshore areas. With the exception of Alaska, however, current seismic exploration techniques have not been
able to identify sufficient numbers of new prospective oil and gas bearing geologic
structures onshore that are suitable for further exploration or development investments. This has been reflected by a significant decline in both onshore drilling and
proved reserves. In contrast, however, the geologic structures in the relatively
unexplored or virgin areas are more easily identifiable using current seismic technology.

**C.   Delay Sale Until New Technology is Available to Provide Increased Envi-
ronmental Protection**   Since basically safe technology is available provided its
application and use are properly regulated and controlled, there appears to be no
advantage in the postponement of the proposed sale for this specific reason.
As new technology relating to safety and environmental protection is developed, it can be incorporated with the existing requirements and applied to all OCS
leases so that bringing on additional production now will not generally preclude
adaptation of new advances to the prospective leases.
Delay of the proposed sale could result in retarded development of energy
resources.

NOTE: PROPOSALS FOR LEGISLATION

NEPA requires that environmental impact statements be prepared on proposals for legislation. This requirement has not met with great enthusiasm, and
most statements have been filed by agencies already operating in the environmental area. For a discussion of the curious role of OMB in this process, see
Dolgin and Guilbert (eds.), *Federal Environmental Law,* pages 331–335.

For an example of an impact statement on a proposal for legislation, see the Final Environmental Impact Statement by the AEC on legislation to amend the Price-Anderson Act.

See also *International Harvester Company v. Ruckelshaus,* page 247, for a consideration of the EPA's duty with regard to NEPA and legislation.

QUESTIONS FOR DISCUSSION

1 Is the fact that an environmental impact statement "seems to cry out for the opposite conclusion" sufficient reason for a court to stop a project?
2 What alternatives need to be discussed? War with Saudi Arabia? Elimination of the automobile?
3 Does the court's position that "the requirement as to alternatives is subject to a construction of reasonableness" define a workable standard?
4 Would a detailed evaluation of the environmental effects of all alternatives be a desirable or feasible requirement?
5 Did the Bureau of Land Management meet its obligation under the act?
6 Should an EIS discuss the probabilities that other pollution-control acts, such as that prohibiting dumping of debris on the shelf, will be violated?
7 Is it feasible to discuss the environmental impacts of all the alternatives?
8 Do you think that the authors of NEPA intended that agencies evaluate alternatives which they are powerless to inaugurate?
9 If the "fullest extent possible" requirement is "not rubber, neither is it iron," how is an agency to judge its compliance? Is a court better qualified to say what those words mean? Is agency bias or inertia an adequate justification for turning to the judiciary?

EIS CONTENTS, AGENCY BIAS, JUDICIAL REVIEW

Environmental Defense Fund v. Corps of Engineers examines the contents of an environmental impact statement in light of the fact that the agency seeking to construct the project is also the agency which prepared the statement, thus raising a specter of agency bias. Also considered is the proper judicial role with respect to NEPA, a most important question where statutory language is general and agency bias a possibility.

Environmental Defense Fund
v. Corps of Engineers

470 F.2d 289, 4 ERC 1721 (8th Cir. 1972), cert. den., 412 U.S. 931 (1973)

Before Matthes, Chief Judge, Lay and Heaney, Circuit Judges.
Matthes, Chief Judge:

This is another of the rapidly increasing number of cases which are focused in large part upon, and result from the adoption of, the National Environmental Policy Act (NEPA), 42 U.S.C. §§ 4321–4347, which was passed by the Congress of the United States in December, 1969, and became effective January 1, 1970.

This litigation was triggered by the construction of a project known as Gillham Dam in the Cossatot River in Arkansas. The case is here on appeal by plaintiffs from the final order of the United States District Court, Eastern District of Arkansas, dissolving an injunction entered by that court on February 19, 1971, and dismissing the case.

I. HISTORY OF THE PROJECT

Judge Eisele has recorded a clear and graphic description of the Cossatot River and its environs, and we are not inclined to attempt to improve on what has been written. See 325 F. Supp. at 744–745. We are content to pinpoint the subject by making a few observations which lie at the heart of the controversy over the Gillham project.

During normal water stage the Cossatot, like many mountainous streams, is a valuable asset to man. The splendor of the scenery is magnificent. The clean water attracts many species of game fish, and wildlife abounds in the area. Fishermen, hunters and outdoor enthusiasts frequent the region; the rapids and pools challenge canoeists. But there is another side to the coin. When heavy rains descend in the Ouichita Mountain Range, as they have from time immemorial, the normal flow of water in the Cossatot becomes a raging torrent and the floods become an enemy of man. Thus, competing forces have aligned themselves for and against the dam. In part, the proponents are interested in controlling the floods, creating the recreational facilities and commercial development which accompany man-made lakes, and supplying pure water to the City of DeQueen, Arkansas. The opponents advance, among other arguments, the value of conserving one of the few remaining free-flowing rivers in southwest Arkansas, the sports of stream fishing and hunting, and the diversity of canoeing experiences.

Gillham Dam is a part of a massive flood control plan authorized by Congress in the Flood Control Act of 1958.[1] The subject dam is one of seven autho-

---

[1] Act of July 3, 1958, Pub. L. No. 85-500, § 201, 72 Stat. 305, 309.

rized to be constructed in the Little River Basin. Of these, three have been completed, and three, including Gillham, are under construction. The Gillham project is designed to provide flood control, water supply and water quality control. Funds for construction were initially made available by the Public Works Appropriation Act of 1963.[2] Work began in 1963, and Congress has since regularly funded the project including appropriations of 1.5 million dollars for fiscal year 1973.[3] As of September 1, 1970, the project was approximately two-thirds complete at a cost of 9.8 million dollars. Total project cost is estimated at 15.3 million dollars. While the spillway and outlet works have been substantially constructed, the dam itself remains to be built. At full flood control pool, which will occur on the average of once in twenty-five years, the reservoir created by the dam would inundate 13.5 miles of the Cossatot River and 4,680 acres of surrounding countryside. At top of conservation pool, sometimes referred to as "normal pool," the reservoir would inundate 7.7 miles of river and 1,370 acres of land. . . .[4]

II. HISTORY OF THE LITIGATION

The district court dealt with the case in a series of six memorandum opinions filed over a period of one and one-half years. The first opinion held venue was proper. 325 F. Supp. 728 (Nov. 16, 1970). The second considered jurisdiction over the defendants and the subject matter, standing and failure of the complaint to state a claim upon which relief could be granted. 325 F. Supp. 732 (Dec. 22, 1970). The third denied a preliminary injunction since defendants had failed to demonstrate danger of imminent harm. 325 F. Supp. 737 (Dec. 22, 1970). In its fourth memorandum opinion, the court found that NEPA was intended to be applied not only to contemplated agency action, but also to ongoing projects.[5] 325 F. Supp. 741 (Jan. 21, 1971). The case was tried to the court on the merits on February 8, 9 and 10, 1971. In the fifth memorandum opinion, 325 F. Supp. 749 [2 ERC 1261] (Feb. 19, 1971), the court found that of the eleven claims for relief set forth in the complaint, only the two premised upon NEPA, claims one and eleven, were sufficient to grant relief. Accordingly, claims two through ten were dismissed.[6] The

---

[2] Act of October 24, 1962, Pub. L. No. 87-880, 76 Stat. 1216.

[3] Public Works for Water and Power Development and Atomic Energy Commission Appropriation Act of 1973, Pub. L. No. 92-405, 86 Stat. 621.

[4] Omitted.

[5] Other courts have held that NEPA is applicable to projects under construction. See *Arlington Coalition on Transportation v. Volpe*, 458 F.2d 1323 (4th Cir. 1972); *Environmental Law Fund v. Volpe*, 340 F. Supp. 1328 (N.D. Cal. 1972); *Morningside-Lenox Park Assn. v. Volpe*, 334 F. Supp. 132 [3 ERC 1327] (N.D. Ga. 1971); *Nolop v. Volpe*, 333 F. Supp. 1364 (D.S.D. 1971). See also Guidelines for Federal Agencies under the National Environmental Policy Act, 36 Fed. Reg. 7724, 7727 (1971).

[6] Aside from the two claims arising under NEPA, plaintiffs sought relief in the district court under the fifth, ninth and fourteenth amendments; the Civil Rights Act of 1871, 42 U.S.C. § 1983; § 2(b) of the Fish and Wildlife Coordination Act of 1934, 16 U.S.C. § 662(b); § 301(b) of the Water Supply Act of 1958 as amended by § 10 of the Water Pollution Control Act Amendments of 1961, 43 U.S.C. § 3906(b), and the Clean Water Restoration Act of 1966, 33 U.S.C. § 466a(b)(1). Plaintiffs also argued that the benefits of the project were less than the estimated costs, in violation of 33 U.S.C. § 701(a), and that defendants were proceeding without due regard for wildlife conservation, in violation of 33 U.S.C. § 540, and in excess of legislative authorization.

court went on to find that defendants had not complied with the provisions of NEPA which require a detailed statement of the environmental impact of the project and a development of appropriate alternatives to the proposed course of action. Therefore, the court enjoined defendants from proceeding further with the Gillham Dam project unless and until they fully complied with the Act. Both parties appealed to this court, but the appeals were dismissed by agreement on July 22, 1971.

On January 13, 1972, defendants filed with the district court the new environmental impact statement (EIS) and simultaneously filed a motion for summary judgment in which they requested the court to dissolve and set aside the injunction theretofore granted. After an evidentiary hearing on April 27 and 28, 1972, the court approved the new impact statement, granted summary judgment for defendants and dissolved the injunction. The court's supporting opinion, the sixth one filed, is reported at 342 F. Supp. 1211 (May 5, 1972). It is from this final order that plaintiffs bring the present appeal.

Appellants contend that, contrary to the conclusion of the district court, appellees have not sufficiently complied with NEPA for the following reasons: (1) the objectivity of the final EIS was tainted by the alleged bias of its draftor; (2) the final EIS makes a less-than-full disclosure and contains important errors of fact; (3) the defendants have failed to study, develop and describe appropriate alternatives; and (4) the administrative determination by defendants that the dam should be constructed was reviewable by the court on the merits. . . .[7,8]

IV. ADEQUACY OF THE FINAL ENVIRONMENTAL IMPACT STATEMENT

Appellants argue that the final EIS filed by the Corps falls short of the "detailed statement" required by § 102(2)(C) of NEPA for two reasons: (1) the statement contains an inadequate and inaccurate disclosure of fact; and (2) the statement lacks objectivity either on its face or because of the alleged bias of the District Director responsible for its preparation. We disagree.

The final EIS submitted by the Corps of Engineers in this case was prepared at an alleged cost of approximately $250,000, and is 200 pages in length. Attached to the statement are six appendices containing an additional 1500 pages.[9]

The main text is divided into eight divisions which describe, respectively, the project, the environmental setting without the project, environmental impact of the proposed action, adverse environmental effects which cannot be avoided should the proposal be implemented, alternatives to the proposed action, the rela-

---

[7,8] Section III and footnotes 7 and 8 omitted.

[9] Appendix I contains copies of all correspondence between the Corps and concerned public and private agencies and individuals, and the transcripts of several public hearings. Appendix II contains photographs of the project area. Appendix III discusses the local archeology, geology, botany, zoology, economic conditions, social relationships and human well-being, hydrology and water quality. Appendix IV contains a bibliography of all literature cited in the statement. Appendix V contains a transcript of the district court proceedings, and Appendix VI sets forth the qualifications of the personnel utilized by the Corps in preparing the statement.

tionship between short term uses of man's environment and the maintenance and enhancement of long term productivity, irrevocable or irretrievable commitment of resources which would be involved in the proposed action should it be implemented, and coordination by the Corps with interested agencies, groups and individuals in the preparation of the statement.[10]

We have read the statement and found it to contain a full and accurate disclosure of the information required by § 102(2)(C).

Nevertheless, appellants contend that the EIS is partial and biased, either on its face or as the work product of a biased agency official. The latter claim is based upon statements allegedly made by Colonel Vernon W. Pinkey, District Engineer in charge of preparing the EIS until his retirement, before a local Chamber of Commerce meeting, assuring his listeners that the Gillham Dam would definitely be built.

We agree with appellants, as did the district court, that NEPA "requires the agencies of the United States Government to objectively evaluate their projects." 342 F. Supp. at 1222. However, we do not agree with the view implicit in the contentions of appellants that NEPA requires agency officials to be subjectively impartial. The purpose of the procedural requirements of § 102 is

> "to ensure that each agency decision maker has before him and takes into proper account all possible approaches to a particular project (including total abandonment of the project) which would alter the environmental impact and the cost-benefit balance. Only in that fashion is it likely that the most intelligent, optimally beneficial decision will ultimately be made. Moreover, by compelling a formal 'detailed statement' and a description of alternatives, NEPA provides evidence that the mandated decision making process has in fact taken place and, importantly, allows those removed from the initial process to evaluate and balance the factors on their own."

Calvert Cliffs' Coordinating Committee v. U.S. Atomic Energy Commission, 449 F.2d 1109, 1114 [2 ERC 1779] (D.C. Cir. 1971). Thus NEPA assumes as inevitable an institutional bias within an agency proposing a project and erects the procedural requirements of § 102 to insure that "there is no way [the decision-maker]

---

[10] Coordination on the new EIS began on July 2, 1971, with a letter to all known interested agencies, groups and individuals enclosing portions of a preliminary draft statement and requesting recipients to furnish any environmental data which should be used in its preparation. Subsequent letters enclosed new or revised sections of the preliminary draft. Responses received in reply to the request are summarized in this division, together with a response by the agency to each comment received. Public meetings were held on two occasions, and the comments and suggestions arising therein were also incorporated into the division. According to the EIS, comments were received for the following federal agencies: National Oceanic and Atmospheric Administration, Environmental Protection Agency, Department of Health, Education and Welfare, Department of Recreation, Soil Conservation Service, Forest Service, Bureau of Sport Fisheries and Wildlife, Department of State, Federal Power Commission, Federal Highway Administration. State agencies: Archeological Survey, Soil and Water Conservation Commission, Department of Health, Department of Pollution Control and Ecology, Department of Planning, and Game and Fish Commission. Also heard from were over thirty conservation groups or other organizations, and ninety-one individuals.

can fail to note the facts and understand the very serious arguments advanced by plaintiffs if he carefully reviews the entire environmental impact statement." 342 F. Supp. at 1218. An institutional bias will most often be found when the project has been partially completed. Several courts have held that an agency involved in an ongoing federal project may approach the required compliance with § 102 differently from what might be required with respect to new projects. *Arlington Coalition on Transportation v. Volpe,* 458 F.2d 1323 [3 ERC 1995] (4th Cir. 1972); *Environmental Law Fund v. Volpe,* 340 F. Supp. 1328 [3 ERC 1941] (N.D. Cal. 1972); *Morningside-Lenox Park Assn. v. Volpe,* 334 F. Supp. 132, 145 [3 ERC 1327] (N.D. Ga. 1971). Here, the Gillham Dam project was almost two-thirds complete when the procedural requirements of NEPA went into effect on January 1, 1970. The federal funds expended, nearly ten million dollars, could not, in large part, be recouped if the project were abandoned. The Council on Environmental Quality (CEQ) has recognized that it may become impracticable to reassess the basic course of action where the project was initiated prior to the effective date of NEPA.[11] Accordingly, in the words of Judge Eisele,

> "it is possible for federal officials and federal employees to comply in good faith with [NEPA] even though they personally oppose its philosophy, are 'anti-environmentalists,' and have unshakable, preconceived attitudes and opinions as to the 'rightness" of the project under consideration."

342 F. Supp. at 1233.

The test of compliance with § 102, then, is one of good faith objectivity rather than subjective impartiality. *Committee for Nuclear Responsibility v. Schlesinger,* 404 U.S. 917, 918 [3 ERC 1276] (1971) (Douglas, J., dissenting from denial of injunction); *Committee for Nuclear Responsibility v. Seaborg,* 463 F.2d 783 [3 ERC 1126] (D.C. Cir. 1971); *Calvert Cliffs' Coordinating Committee v. U.S. Atomic Energy Commission, supra* at 1115 n.5; *Citizens for Reid State Park v. Laird,* 336 F. Supp, 783, 789 [3 ERC 1580] (D. Maine 1972); *Environmental Defense Fund v. Hardin,* 325 F. Supp. 1401, 1403 [2 ERC 1425] (D.D.C. 1971).

Employing this standard, we are satisfied that the district court's findings and conclusion as to the objectivity of the EIS are supported by substantial evidence. Therefore we decline to hold that appellees have not complied in good faith with the procedural requirements of § 102(2)(C).

---

[11] Guidelines for Federal Agencies under the National Environmental Policy Act, 36 Fed. Reg. 7724, 7727 (1971):

"11. Application of Section 102(2)(C) procedures to existing projects and programs. To the maximum extent practicable the Section 102(2)(C) procedure should be applied to further major federal actions having a significant effect on the environment even though they arise from projects or programs initiated prior to enactment of the Act on January 1, 1970. Where it is not practicable to reassess the basic course of action, it is still important that further incremental major actions be shaped so as to minimize adverse environmental consequences. It is also important in further action that account be taken of environmental consequences not fully evaluated at the outset of the project or program."

V. DEVELOPMENT OF ALTERNATIVES

Appellants also contend that appellees have failed to develop important and reasonable alternatives to the proposed dam project, in violation of § 102(2)(D) of NEPA. Section 102(2)(D) requires that the agency "study, develop, and describe appropriate alternatives to recommended courses of action on any proposal which involves unresolved conflicts concerning alternative uses of available resources." This provision follows and is in addition to the § 102(2)(C) requirement of a detailed statement discussing, inter alia, alternatives to the proposed action. This is not to suggest, however, that the more extensive treatment of alternatives required by § 102(2)(D) cannot be incorporated in the EIS. Indeed, "it is the essence and thrust of NEPA that the pertinent statement serve to gather in one place a discussion of the relative environmental impact alternatives." *Natural Resources Defense Council v. Morton,* 458 F.2d 827, 834 [3 ERC 1558] (D.C. Cir. 1972). So too, the guidelines to the federal agencies issued by the CEQ explain the import of § 102(2)(D) under the general heading "Content of Environmental Statement." 36 Fed. Reg. 7724, 7725 (1971). The guidelines suggest:

> "A rigorous exploration and objective evaluation of alternative actions that might avoid some or all of the adverse environmental effects is essential. Sufficient analysis of such alternatives and their costs and impact on the environment should accompany the proposed action through the agency review process in order not to foreclose prematurely options which might have less detrimental effects."

Defendants have devoted thirty-seven pages of the 200-page impact statement to the discussion of alternatives, among them, total abandonment of the project. Particular attention is given to the suggestion that the Cossatot be preserved as a scenic river under the National Wild and Scenic Rivers Act, 16 U.S.C. § 1271 et seq. The economic benefits and environmental impact of each alternative are developed in great detail.

The most recent case to fully discuss § 102(2)(D) decided that the statute was subject to a construction of reasonableness. "The statute must be construed in the light of reason if it is not to demand what is, fairly speaking, not meaningfully possible, given the obvious, that the resources of energy and research—and time— available to meet the Nation's needs are not infinite." *Natural Resources Defense Council v. Morton, supra* at 837.

We are reminded of the suggestion of the district court in this case that "[i]t is doubtful that any agency, however objective, however sincere, however well-staffed, and however well-financed, could come up with a perfect environmental impact statement in connection with any major project. Further studies, evaluations and analyses by experts are almost certain to reveal inadequacies or deficiencies. But even such deficiencies and inadequacies, discovered after the fact, can be brought to the attention of the decision-makers, including ultimately, the President and the Congress itself." 342 F. Supp. at 1217.

Again, we concur in the finding of the district court, implicit in its opinion, that the EIS contains the study, development and description of reasonable alternatives required by § 102(2)(D).

VI. JUDICIAL REVIEW OF SUBSTANTIVE MERITS

Finally, appellants contend that appellees' administrative determination that the dam should be constructed was arbitrary and capricious, contrary to the requirements of § 101 of NEPA, and reviewable by the courts under the Administrative Procedure Act 5 U.S.C. § 706.

The district court found that NEPA "falls short of creating the type of 'substantive rights' claimed by the plaintiffs," and therefore "plaintiffs are relegated to the procedural requirements of the Act." 325 F. Supp. at 755.

We disagree. The language of NEPA, as well as its legislative history, make it clear that the Act is more than an environmental full-disclosure law. NEPA was intended to effect substantive changes in decision making. Section 101(b) of the Act states that agencies have an obligation "to use all practical means, consistent with other essential considerations of national policy, to improve and coordinate Federal plans, functions, programs and resources" to preserve and enhance the environment. To this end, § 101 sets out specific environmental goals to serve as a set of policies to guide agency action affecting the environment.

Section 102(1) directs that the policies, regulations and public laws of the United States be interpreted in accordance with these policies to the fullest extent possible. [12] Section 102(2), of course, sets forth the procedural requirements of the Act, discussed previously in this opinion. The purpose is to "insure that the policies enunciated in section 101 are implemented." S. Rep. 91–296, 91st Cong., 1st Sess. 19 (1969). The procedures included in § 102 of NEPA are not ends in themselves. They are intended to be "action forcing." Id. at 9. [13]

[12] The court in *Calvert Cliffs' Coordinating Committee v. U.S. Atomic Energy Commission*, 449 F.2d 1109, 1114 [2 ERC 1779] (D.C. Cir. 1971), pointed out that "the requirement of environmental consideration 'to the fullest extent possible' sets a high standard for the agencies, a standard which must be rigorously enforced by the reviewing courts."

[13] Senate Report 91–296, 91st Cong., 1st Session (1969), states in part:

"1. Management of the environment is a matter of critical concern to all Americans. Virtually every agency of the Federal Government plays some role in determining how well the environment is managed. Yet, many of these agencies do not have a mandate, a body of law, or a set of policies to guide their actions which have an impact on the environment. * * *

"Section 101 of S. 1075 rectifies this by providing a congressional declaration that it is the continuing policy and responsibility of the Federal Government to use all practicable means, consistent with other essential considerations of national policy, to improve and coordinate Federal planning and activities to the end that certain broad national goals in the management of the environment may be attained.

"2. A statement of national policy for the environment—like other major policy declarations— is in large measure concerned with principle rather than detail; with an expression of broad national goals rather than narrow and specific procedures for implementation. But, if goals and principles are

The unequivocal intent of NEPA is to require agencies to consider and give effect to the environmental goals set forth in the Act, not just to file detailed impact studies which will fill governmental archives.

The application of the substantive principles of NEPA is to be made by the agency through "a careful and informed decisionmaking process." *Calvert Cliffs' Coordinating Committee v. U.S. Atomic Energy Commission, supra* at 1115. The agency must give environmental factors consideration along with economic and technical factors. "To 'consider' the former 'along with' the latter must involve a balancing process." Id. at 1113.

Given an agency obligation to carry out the substantive requirements of the Act, we believe that courts have an obligation to review substantive agency decisions on the merits. Whether we look to common law or the Administrative Procedure Act, absent "legislative guidance as to reviewability, an administrative determination affecting legal rights is reviewable unless some special reason appears for not reviewing." K. DAVIS, 4 ADMINISTRATIVE LAW TREATISE 18, 25 (1958).[14] Here, important legal rights are affected. NEPA is silent as to judicial review, and no special reasons appear for not reviewing the decision of the agency. To the contrary, the prospect of substantive review should improve the quality of agency decisions and should make it more likely that the broad purposes of NEPA will be realized.

---

to be effective, they must be capable of being applied in action. S. 1075 thus incorporates certain 'action-forcing' provisions and procedures which are designed to assure that all Federal agencies plan and work toward meeting the challenge of a better environment."

Mr. Henry M. Jackson, the principal Senate sponsor of NEPA, stated:

"If an environmental policy is to become more than rhetoric, and if the studies and advice of any high-level, advisory group are to be translated into action, each of these agencies must be enabled and directed to participate in active and objective-oriented environmental management. Concern for environmental quality must be made part of every phase of Federal action." 115 Cong. Rec. 29087 (1969).

In its Interim Guidelines of April 30, 1970, the CEQ stated that

"[i]n essence the Section 102(2)(C) process is designed to insure that environmental considerations are given careful attention and appropriate weight in all Federal Government decision making." In its most recent guidelines, 36 Fed. Reg. 7724, April 23, 1971, the Council stated that the objective of § 102(2)(C) is "to build into the agency decision making process an appropriate and careful consideration of the environmental aspects of proposed action." The agencies must "assess in detail the potential environmental impact in order that adverse effects are avoided, and environmental quality is restored or enhanced, to the fullest extent practicable."

In view of the foregoing matter, we conclude that a purely mechanical compliance with the procedures of § 102 is not sufficient to satisfy the provisions of NEPA.

[14] Agency action is subject to review on the merits under the Administrative Procedure Act, 5 U.S.C. §§ 701 and 706, except where there is a statutory prohibition on review or where "agency action is committed to agency discretion by law." 5 U.S.C. § 701(a)(1) and (2). In *Citizens to Preserve Overton Park v. Volpe*, 401 U.S. 402, 410 (1971), the Supreme Court construed the latter exception very narrowly.

"The legislative history of the Administrative Procedure Act indicates that it is applicable in those rare instances where 'statutes are drawn in such broad terms that in a given case there is no law to apply.' "

Here, the substantive requirements of NEPA, which we have discussed above, provide law for the courts to apply in reviewing agency decisions. See generally Recent Developments, 60 Georgetown L.J. 1101 (1972); The Supreme Court, 1970 Term, 85 Harv. L. Rev. 315-326 (1971).

The conclusion we reach with respect to substantive review of agency decisions is supported by the District of Columbia Circuit, the Second Circuit and the Fourth Circuit, [15] and by the analogous decision of the Supreme Court in *Citizens to Preserve Overton Park v. Volpe,* 401 U.S. 402 [2 ERC 1250] (1971). The CEQ, surveying the state of the law in its third annual report, concluded "that, after an agency has considered environmental effects, its decision to act is subject to * * * limited judicial review." ENVIRONMENTAL QUALITY (August, 1972). [16] Our conclusion is supported by scholarly opinion as well. [17]

[15] The District of Columbia Circuit in *Calvert Cliffs' Coordinating Committee v. U.S. Atomic Energy Commission, supra* note 12, at 1115, stated:
"The reviewing courts probably cannot reverse a substantive decision on its merits, under Section 101, unless it be shown that the actual balance of costs and benefits that was struck was arbitrary or clearly gave insufficient weight to environmental values."
This position was reiterated in *Natural Resources Council, Inc. v. Morton,* 458 F.2d 827, 838 (D.C. Cir. 1972). Nothing in *Committee for Nuclear Responsibility v. Seaborg,* 463 F.2d 783 (D.C. Cir. 1971), indicates a departure from the principles enunciated in *Calvert Cliffs.* While the question of judicial review on the merits was not at issue in Seaborg, the court's opinion at 787 indicated reliance on *Calvert Cliffs* for the proposition that limited review was appropriate. In light of these cases, the contrary decision of the District of Columbia District Court in *Environmental Defense Fund v. Hardin,* 325 F. Supp. 1401 (D.D.C. 1971), carries little weight.
The Second Circuit in *Scenic Hudson Preserv. Conf. v. Federal Power Com'n,* 453 F.2d 463, 468-469 (2d Cir. 1971), cert. denied, 407 U.S. 926 (1972) (Douglas, J., dissenting), reviewed the merits of a Federal Power Commission decision to determine if it was in compliance with NEPA. A reading of Judge Oakes' dissent, 453 F.2d at 482, as well as the dissent of Mr. Justice Douglas from the order denying certiorari, reveals that the only point in controversy was whether a standard of review stricter than the arbitrary or capricious test should have been used. Similarly, a three-judge court in *City of New York v. United States,* 344 F. Supp. 929 (E.D.N.Y. 1972), made a limited review on the merits of an agency decision. The question as to whether or not a stricter standard of review should be used was left open. See also *Hanly v. Mitchell,* 460 F.2d 640 (2d Cir. 1972). However, in the instant case, the appellants have argued only for the arbitrary and capricious test rather than any stricter standard of review.
The Fourth Circuit in *Ely v. Velde,* 451 F.2d 1130, 1138-1139 (1971), indicated that the purpose of impact studies is to create a record which can be reviewed to determine if the agency's actions were arbitrary. But subsequently, a district court of the Fourth Circuit indicated that no review on the merits is available, *North Carolina Conservation Council v. Froehlke,* 340 F. Supp. 222 (M.D.N.C. 1972), and that decision as affirmed by the Fourth Circuit in a brief per curiam opinion. *North Carolina Conservation Council v. Froehlke,* No. 72-1276 (4th Cir., May 2, 1972). Thus, the position of the Fourth Circuit on this issue is not completely clear.
The Tenth Circuit, however, has held that no review on the merits is available. *National Helium Corporation v. Morton,* 455 F.2d 650 (1971). See *Bradford Township v. Illinois State Toll Highway Authority,* 4 E.R.C. 1301 (7th Cir., June 22, 1972) (dictum).
District court decisions supporting a limited review on the merits are *Lathan v. Volpe,* 4 E.R.C. 1487 (W.D. Wash., August 4, 1972); *Brooks v. Volpe,* 4 E.R.C. 1492 (W.D. Wash., August 4, 1972); *Citizens for Reid State Park v. Laird,* 336 F. Supp. 783, 789 (D. Maine 1972); *Morningside-Lenox Park Assn. v. Volpe, supra* note 5 at 145. While the court in *Environmental Defense Fund, Inc. v. Corps of Engineers,* 4 E.R.C. 1408 (N.D. Miss., August 4, 1972), indicated its belief that review on the merits was inappropriate, it actually reviewed the conclusions of the Corps of Engineers in a careful and systematic manner.
[16] The Council on Environmental Quality stated in its third annual report:
"NEPA commands firmly that an agency must, to the fullest extent possible, take environmental values into account. It must also prepare environmental impact statements for major actions significantly affecting the quality of the human environment. If an agency fails to do either, it can be ordered to comply by a court. But neither NEPA's substantive duty nor its 102 process purports to dictate the agency's choice of a course of action in particular situations. The courts have uniformly said that, after

The standard of review to be applied here and in other similar cases is set forth in *Citizens to Preserve Overton Park v. Volpe, supra* at 416. The reviewing court must first determine whether the agency acted within the scope of its authority, and next whether the decision reached was arbitrary, capricious, an abuse of discretion, or otherwise not in accordance with law. In making the latter determination, the court must decide if the agency failed to consider all relevant factors in reaching its decision, or if the decision itself represented a clear error in judgment.

Where NEPA is involved, the reviewing court must first determine if the agency reached its decision after a full, good faith consideration and balancing of environmental factors. The court must then determine, according to the standards set forth in §§ 101(b) and 102(1) of the Act, whether "the actual balance of costs and benefits that was struck was arbitrary or clearly gave insufficient weight to environmental values." *Calvert Cliffs' Coordinating Committee v. U.S. Atomic Energy Commission, supra* at 1115.

> "Although this inquiry into the facts is to be searching and careful, the ultimate standard of review is a narrow one. The court is not empowered to substitute its judgment for that of the agency."

Citizens to Preserve Overton Park v. Volpe, supra at 416.

The trial court's opinion is in error insofar as it holds that courts are precluded from reviewing agencies' decisions to determine if they are in accord with the substantive requirements of NEPA. In light of our holding, there is no alternative but to subject the decision of the Corps to build Gillham Dam to review under the arbitrary and capricious standard. Ordinarily, we would remand the matter to the trial court for such review, but it is not necessary to do so in this case. The complete record, including the environmental impact statement and the transcript of the proceeding below, is before us. We have reviewed the record thoroughly and are convinced that even if all factual disputes are resolved in favor of the plaintiffs, the decision of the Corps to complete the dam cannot be set aside as arbitrary and capricious. See 28 U.S.C. § 2106. We have reached this conclusion after a serious consideration of the arguments in favor of and against comple-

---

an agency has considered environmental effects, its decision to act is subject to the limited judicial review afforded by the traditional arbitrary-or-capricious and substantial evidence tests." ENVIRONMENTAL QUALITY 253-54 (August, 1972).

For the reasons stated by the Supreme Court in *Citizens to Preserve Overton Park v. Volpe, supra* note 14, at 414-415, we do not believe that the substantial evidence test is applicable here.

[17] See Cohen and Warren, Judicial Recognition of the Substantive Requirements of the National Environmental Policy Act of 1969, 13 B.C. Ind. & Com. L. Rev. 685 (1972); Rheingold, A Primer on Environmental Litigation, 38 Brook. L. Rev. 113, 119-120 (1971); Sandler, The National Environmental Policy Act; A Sheep in Wolf's Clothing, 37 Brook. L. Rev. 139, 155 (1970); Sive, Some Thoughts on an Environmental Lawyer in the Wilderness of Administrative Law, 70 Colum. L. Rev. 612 (1970); Comment, Judicial Review of Factual Issues under the National Environmental Policy Act, 51 Ore. L. Rev. 408, 415-416 (1972); 25 Vand. L. Rev. 258, 270 (1972); 40 Geo. Wash. L. Rev. 558, 568-569 (1972); Jaffe, Book Review, 84 Harv. L. Rev. 1562 (1971).

tion of the project. In large part this has necessitated a balancing, on the one hand, of the benefits to be derived from flood control, and, on the other, of the importance of a diversified environment. We have also taken into account, as we must, that the overall project was authorized by Congress eleven years prior to the passage of NEPA, and was sixty-three percent completed at the date this action was instituted. Almost ten million dollars has been expended and would be lost if the project were completely abandoned now.

We therefore, affirm the judgment of the trial court for the reasons set forth in the opinion. Costs will be taxed equally to the parties.

QUESTIONS FOR DISCUSSION

1   What portions of NEPA are constructed to reduce "institutional" bias? Is "institutional" bias really inevitable?
2   What standards, if any, are required for objectivity in an EIS?
3   How far must an agency go in proposing alternative uses for resources? Can you define the limits of "agency consideration"?
4   Should NEPA be amended to include a limitation of judicial review?
5   If $10 million had not been expended, might the court's decision have been different?
6   Should independent consultants write the environmental impact statements? A government agency created for that purpose?
7   Do you find the court's handling of the institutional bias issue convincing?
8   Do you agree that NEPA was intended to be more than a full-disclosure statute?
9   What may be inferred from NEPA's silence on the issue of judicial review?
10   Can it be assumed that members of Congress who voted for the act knew of or agreed with the statements of its sponsors in committees when the sponsors' sentiments are not included in the Act's language?
11   Is the "arbitrary and capricious" standard of review adequate? What might be substituted?

LEGISLATIVE MODIFICATIONS

Litigation under NEPA, such as that illustrated in the previous cases, may delay projects for long periods. Such was the case in the proposed construction of the trans-Alaska pipeline, which was delayed for several years by protracted litigation. These delays, combined with energy shortages and the petroleum embargo of 1973, resulted in the passage of the Trans-Alaska Pipeline Authorization Act. Note particularly Section 203(d).

Trans-Alaska Pipeline Authorization Act

Public Law 93–153, approved November 16, 1973

TITLE I

Section 101.   Section 28 of the Mineral Leasing Act of 1920 (41 Stat. 449), as amended (30 U.S.C. 185), is further amended to read as follows: . . .

CONGRESSIONAL FINDINGS

Sec. 202.   The Congress finds and declares that:

(a) The early development and delivery of oil and gas from Alaska's North Slope to domestic markets is in the national interest because of growing domestic shortages and increasing dependence upon insecure foreign sources.

(b) The Department of the Interior and other Federal agencies, have, over a long period of time, conducted extensive studies of the technical aspects and of the environmental, social, and economic impacts of the proposed trans-Alaska oil pipeline, including consideration of a trans-Canada pipeline.

(c) The earliest possible construction of a trans-Alaska oil pipeline from the North Slope of Alaska to Port Valdez in that State will make the extensive proven and potential reserves of low-sulfur oil available for domestic use and will best serve the national interest.

(d) A supplemental pipeline to connect the North Slope with a trans-Canada pipeline may be needed later and it should be studied now, but it should not be regarded as an alternative for a trans-Alaska pipeline that does not traverse a foreign country.

CONGRESSIONAL AUTHORIZATION

Sec. 203.   (a) The purpose of this title is to insure that, because of the extensive governmental studies already made of this project and the national interest in early delivery of North Slope oil to domestic markets, the trans-Alaska oil pipeline be constructed promptly without further administrative or judicial delay or impediment. To accomplish this purpose it is the intent of the Congress to exercise its constitutional powers to the fullest extent in the authorizations and directions herein made and in limiting judicial review of the actions taken pursuant thereto.

(b) The Congress hereby authorizes and directs the Secretary of the Interior and other appropriate Federal officers and agencies to issue and take all necessary action to administer and enforce rights-of-way, permits, leases, and other authorizations that are necessary for or related to the construction, operation, and maintenance of the trans-Alaska oil pipeline system, including roads and airstrips, as that system is generally described in the Final Environmental Impact Statement issued by the Department of the Interior on March 20, 1972. The route of the pipeline may be modified by the Secretary to provide during construction greater environmental protection.

(c) Rights-of-way, permits, leases, and other authorizations issued pursuant to this title by the Secretary shall be subject to the provisions of section 28 of the Mineral Leasing Act of 1920, as amended by title I of this Act (except the provisions of subsections (h)(1), (k), (q), (w)(2), and (x)); all authorizations issued by the Secretary and other Federal officers and agencies pursuant to this title shall include the terms and conditions required, and may include the terms and conditions permitted, by the provisions of law that would otherwise be applicable if this title had not been enacted, and they may waive any procedural requirements of law or regulation which they deem desirable to waive in order to accomplish the purposes of this title. The direction contained in section 203(b) shall supersede the provisions of any law or regulation relating to an administrative determination as to whether the authorizations for construction of the trans-Alaska oil pipeline shall be issued.

(d) The actions taken pursuant to this title which relate to the construction and completion of the pipeline system, and to the applications filed in connection therewith necessary to the pipeline's operation at full capacity, as described in the Final Environmental Impact Statement of the Department of the Interior, shall be taken without further action under the National Environmental Policy Act of 1969; and the actions of the Federal officers concerning the issuance of the necessary rights-of-way, permits, leases, and other authorizations for construction and initial operation at full capacity of said pipeline system shall not be subject to judicial review under any law except that claims alleging the invalidity of this section may be brought within sixty days following its enactment, and claims alleging that an action will deny rights under the Constitution of the United States, or that the action is beyond the scope of authority conferred by this title, may be brought within sixty days following the date of such action. A claim shall be barred unless a complaint is filed within the time specified. Any such complaint shall be filed in a United States district court, and such court shall have exclusive jurisdiction to determine such proceeding in accordance with the procedures hereinafter provided, and no other court of the United States, of any State, territory, or possession of the United States, or of the District of Columbia, shall have jurisdiction of any such claim whether in a proceeding instituted prior to or on or after the date of the enactment of this Act. Any such proceeding shall be assigned for hearing at the earliest possible date, shall take precedence over all other matters pending on the docket of the district court at that time, and shall be expedited in every way by such court. Such court shall not have jurisdiction to grant any injunctive relief against the issuance of any rights-of-way, permit, lease, or other authorization pursuant to this section except in conjunction with a final judgment entered in a case involving a claim filed pursuant to this section. Any review of an interlocutory or final judgment, decree, or order of such district court may be had only upon direct appeal to the Supreme Court of the United States.

PROBLEMS

1   A private aircraft company, operating under a federal loan guarantee, proposes to construct an airplane the environmental consequences of which are unclear. Would the federal agency administering the loan guarantee have to file an environmental impact statement? If the plane is built, would the agency that certifies it for flight have to prepare an EIS?

2   Suppose an environmental impact statement prepared by a federal agency for a major construction project indicates that the costs equal or exceed the benefits, but the agency concludes that the project should proceed. If challenged on the basis that the project simply doesn't make sense given the results of the impact assessment, would a court have the authority to enjoin construction?

3   Suppose an environmental impact statement is filed for offshore oil drilling which considers all reasonable alternatives, energy sources, and effects on biota and flora in the vicinity. The statement is challenged on the basis that it did not address the impacts on the socioeconomic and cultural patterns of the affected land bordering the ocean. Must such issues be addressed in environmental impact statements?

4   A government agency required to prepare an environmental impact statement before construction of a nuclear facility is staffed primarily by former employees of companies in the energy field. Further, the agency is charged with the promotion as well as regulation of nuclear power. If you were to challenge the environmental impact statement on the ground of agency bias, what would you be required to show in order to prevail? What would happen if you won?

5   State environmental policy acts requiring environmental impact statements are proliferating. If the federal statement concludes that the benefits outweigh the costs, and the state assessment is to the contrary, how might the state version be utilized in an attack on the sufficiency of the federal statement?

SUGGESTIONS FOR FURTHER READING

Bronstein, D. A.: *The AEC Decision Making Process and the Environment: A Case Study of the Calvert Cliffs Nuclear Plant,* 1 ECOLOGY L.Q. 689, 1971.

Brown, E.: *Applying NEPA to Joint Federal and Non-Federal Projects,* 4 ENVIRONMENTAL AFF. 135, 1975.

Cramton, R. L., and R. K. Berg: *On Leading a Horse to Water: NEPA and the Federal Bureaucracy,* 71 MICH. L. REV. 511, 1973.

Enk, G. A.: *Beyond NEPA: Criteria for Environmental Impact Review,* The Institute of Man and Science, Rensselaerville, N.Y., 1973.

Hanks, J. L., and E. H. Hanks: *An Environmental Bill of Rights: The Citizens Suit and the National Environmental Policy Act of 1969,* 24 RUTGERS L. REV. 230, 1970.

Humphreys, D. L.: *NEPA and Multi-Agency Actions—Is the "Lead Agency" Concept Valid?* 6 NATURAL RESOURCES LAW. 257, 1973.

Jordan, R. E.: *Alternatives under NEPA: Toward an Accommodation,* 3 ECOLOGY L.Q. 705, 1973.

Judicial Review of Cost-Benefit Analysis under NEPA, 53 NEB. L. REV. 540, 1974.

Kroos, B. C.: *Preparation of an Environmental Impact Statement,* 44 U. COLO. L. REV. 81, 1972.

NEPA's Impact Statement in the Federal Courts: A Case Study of NRDC v. Morton, 2 ENVIRONMENTAL AFF. 807, 1973.

Robie, R. B.: *Recognition of Substantive Rights under NEPA,* 7 NATURAL RESOURCES LAW. 387, 1974.

Sax, J. L.: *(Unhappy) Truth about NEPA,* 26 OKLA. L. REV. 239, 1973.

Yannacone, V. J.: *National Environmental Policy Act of 1969,* 1 ENVIRONMENTAL L. 8, 1970.

Yost, N. C.: *NEPA's Progeny: State Environmental Policy Acts,* 3 ENVIRONMENTAL L. REP. 50090, 1973.

Federal Statutory Control of Water Pollution

Federal statutory law concerned with the control of water pollution does not lend itself naturally to a conceptual discussion, because it is composed of a number of statutes with detailed technical requirements, it is dynamic and rapidly changing, and it is largely intertwined with the administrative process. For the purposes of this book, detailed analysis is unnecessary, however, and the materials following illustrate the basic workings of the statutory scheme.

RIVERS AND HARBORS ACT OF 1899

Congressional power to regulate commerce, which is derived from the commerce clause, includes jurisdiction over navigable waters.[a] However, the power to regulate commerce is not restricted solely to navigation, but includes virtually all matters relating to navigable waters.[b]

[a] *Gibbons v. Ogden,* 9 Wheat. 1, 197 (1824). See The Daniel Ball, 77 U.S. (10 Wall.) 557 (1870). Waters are defined as navigable, by the Supreme Court, "when they are used . . . in their ordinary condition, as highways for commerce, over which trade and travel are or may be conducted in the customary modes of trade and travel on water." Id. at 563.

[b] See *United States v. Standard Oil Company,* 384 U.S. 224 (1966) 4; *Zabel v. Tabb,* 430 F.2d 199 (1970).

Congress enacted the Rivers and Harbors Act of 1899[c] primarily to prevent impediments to navigation.[d] This congressional action was taken in response to the Supreme Court's 1888 decision in *Willamette Iron Bridge Company v. Hatch,*[e] where the court held that there was no federal common law prohibiting obstructions and nuisances in navigable waters. After that case Congress enacted a series of laws, beginning with the Rivers and Harbors Act of 1890, which were later reenacted as the Rivers and Harbors Act of 1899.[f]

Two sections of the act are of primary importance.

SECTION 10

Section 10 of the act[g] prohibits the creation of an "obstruction" which affects "navigable capacity."

> The creation of any obstruction not affirmatively authorized by Congress, to the navigable capacity of any of the waters of the United States is prohibited; and it shall not be lawful to build or commence the building of any wharf, pier, dolphin, boom, weir, breakwater, bulkhead, jetty, or other structures in any port, roadstead, haven, harbor, canal, navigable river, or other water of the United States, outside established harbor lines, or where no harbor lines have been established, except on plans recommended by the Chief of Engineers and authorized by the Secretary of the Army; and it shall not be lawful to excavate or fill, or in any manner to alter or modify the course, location, condition, or capacity of, any port, roadstead, haven, harbor, canal, lake, harbor of refuge, or inclosure within the limits of any breakwater, or of the channel of any navigable water of the United States, unless the work has been recommended by the Chief of Engineers and authorized by the Secretary of the Army prior to beginning the same.

This language, clearly intended at the time of its drafting to remedy problems of navigation, and authorizing a permit system for both obstructions to navigation and dredge and fill projects, has been judicially expanded to apply to other situations.

Zabel v. Tabb is the best-known Rivers and Harbors Act case in recent years because in it the Corps's right to consider factors other than navigation in the issuance of Section 10 permits is established with clarity, thus greatly altering and expanding the role of Section 10 in environmental litigation.

[c] 33 U.S.C. § 401 et seq.
[d] See S. Rep. No. 224, 50th Cong., 1st Sess., 1 (1888).
[e] 125 U.S. 1 (1888).
[f] See *United States v. Pennsylvania Industrial Chemical Corporation*, 411 U.S. 655 (1973).
[g] 33 U.S.C. § 403.

Zabel v. Tabb

430 F.2d 199 (1970)

John R. Brown, Chief Judge:

It is the destiny of the Fifth Circuit to be in the middle of great, oftentimes explosive issues of spectacular public importance. So it is here as we enter in depth the contemporary interest in the preservation of our environment. By an injunction requiring the issuance of a permit to fill in eleven acres of tidelands in the beautiful Boca Ciega Bay in the St. Petersburg-Tampa, Florida area for use as a commercial mobile trailer park, the District Judge held that the Secretary of the Army and his functionary, the Chief of Engineers, had no power to consider anything except interference with navigation. There being no such obstruction to navigation, they were ordered to issue a permit even though the permittees acknowledge that "there was evidence before the Corps of Engineers sufficient to justify an administrative agency finding that [the] fill would do damage to the ecology or marine life on the bottom." We hold that nothing in the statutory structure compels the Secretary to close his eyes to all that others see or think they see. The establishment was entitled, if not required, to consider ecological factors and, being persuaded by them, to deny that which might have been granted routinely five, ten, or fifteen years ago before man's explosive increase made all, including Congress, aware of civilization's potential destruction from breathing its own polluted air and drinking its own infected water and the immeasurable loss from a silent-spring-like disturbance of nature's economy. We reverse.

I GENESIS: THE BEGINNING

In setting the stage we draw freely on the Government's brief. This suit was instituted by Landholders, Zabel and Russell, on May 10, 1967, to compel the Secretary of the Army to issue a permit to dredge and fill in the navigable waters of Boca Ciega Bay, in Pinellas County near St. Petersburg, Florida. On August 15, 1967, the United States and its officers, Defendants-Appellants, filed a motion to dismiss the suit for lack of jurisdiction which was denied. The United States and other defendants then answered the complaint alleging lack of jurisdiction and that the Court lacks power to compel a discretionary act by the Secretary of the Army. The United States and other defendants moved for summary judgment. Landholders, Zabel and Russell, also moved for summary judgment. After a hearing, the District Court, on February 17, 1969, granted summary judgment for Landholders and directed the Secretary of the Army to issue the permit. It granted a stay of execution of the judgment until this appeal could be heard and decided. We invert the summary judgments, reversing Appellees and rendering judgment for the United States.

Landholders own land riparian to Boca Ciega Bay, and adjacent land underlying the Bay. It is navigable water of the United States on the Gulf side of

Pinellas Peninsula, its length being traversed by the Intracoastal Waterway, which enters Tampa Bay from Boca Ciega Bay and is thus an arm of the Gulf of Mexico. The Zabel and Russell property is located about one mile from the Intracoastal Waterway.

Landholders desire to dredge and fill on their property in the Bay for a trailer park, with a bridge or culvert to their adjoining upland. To this purpose they first applied to the state and local authorities for permission to perform the work and obtained the consent or approval of all such agencies having jurisdiction to prohibit the work, namely Pinellas County Water and Navigation Control Authority (which originally rejected permission, but ultimately issued a permit pursuant to state Court order),[1] Trustees of the Internal Improvement Fund of the State of Florida, Central and South Florida Flood Control District, and Board of Pilot Commissioners for the Port of St. Petersburg.

Landholders then applied to the Corps of Engineers for a federal permit to perform the dredging and filling. The Pinellas County Water and Navigation Control Authority (which originally rejected permission, but ultimately issued a permit pursuant to state Court order) continued to oppose the work as did the Board of County Commissioners of Pinellas County, who also comprise the Pinellas County Water and Navigation Control Authority, the County Health Board of Pinellas County, the Florida Board of Conservation, and about 700 individuals who filed protests. The United States Fish and Wildlife Service, Department of the Interior, also opposed the dredging and filling because it "would have a distinctly harmful effect on the fish and wildlife resources of Boca Ciega Bay."

A public hearing was held in St. Petersburg in November, 1966, and on December 30, 1966, the District Engineer at Jacksonville, Florida, Colonel Tabb, recommended to his superiors that the application be denied. He said that "The proposed work would have no material adverse effect on navigation"[2] but that:

> "Careful consideration has been given to the general public interest in this case. The virtually unanimous opposition to the proposed work as expressed in the protests which were received and as exhaustively presented at the public hearing have convinced me that approval of the application would not be in the public interest. The continued opposition of the U.S. Fish & Wildlife Service despite efforts on the part of the applicants to reduce the extent of damage leads me to the conclusion that ap-

[1] The Authority's denial of a permit was affirmed by the Florida District Court of Appeal in *Zabel v. Pinellas County Water & Navigation Control Authority,* Fla. Ct. App., 1963, 154 So. 2d 181. The Supreme Court of Florida reversed that decision because Zabel had been required by the Authority to show that there would be no adverse effect on the public interest, rather than the burden of adverse effect being placed on the Authority. It held that on this record there was insufficient showing of adverse effect, so that denial of a permit would be a taking of property without compensation: It said (p. 381): "In view of the foregoing, the decision appealed from is quashed and the cause remanded for disposition consistent herewith." *Zabel v. Pinellas County Water & Nav. Con. Auth.,* Fla., 1965, 171 So. 2d 376. Against the Authority's contention that this ruling intended further proceedings on the application, to accord it a chance to establish adverse effect, the District Court of Appeal directed issuance of a permit. *Pinellas County Water & Nav. Con. Auth. v. Zabel,* Fla. Ct. App., 1965, 179 So. 2d 370.
[2] There was evidence both that it would aid navigation and that it would obstruct navigation. There was similar evidence on pollution.

proval of the work would not be consistent with the intent of Congress as expressed in the Fish & Wildlife Coordination Act, as amended, 12 August 1958. Further, the opposition of the State of Florida and of county authorities as described in paragraph 5 above gives additional support to my conclusion that the work should not be authorized."

The Division Engineer, South Atlantic Division, Atlanta, Georgia, concurred in that recommendation stating: "In view of the wide spread opposition to the proposed work, it is apparent that approval of the application would not be in the public interest." The Chief of Engineers concurred for the same reasons. Finally, the Secretary of the Army denied the application on February 28, 1967, because issuance of the requested permit:

    1 Would result in a distinctly harmful effect on the fish and wildlife resources in Boca Ciega Bay,
    2 Would be inconsistent with the purposes of the Fish and Wildlife Coordination Act of 1958, as amended (16 U.S.C. 662),
    3 Is opposed by the Florida Board of Conservation on behalf of the State of Florida, and by the County Health Board of Pinellas County and the Board of County Commissioners of Pinellas County, and
    4 Would be contrary to the public interest.

    Landholders then instituted this suit to review the Secretary's determination and for an order compelling him to issue a permit. They urged that the proposed work would not hinder navigation and that the Secretary had no authority to refuse the permit on other grounds. They acknowledged that "there was evidence before the Corps of Engineers sufficient to justify an administrative agency finding that our fill would do damage to the ecology or marine life on the bottom." The Government urged lack of jurisdiction and supported the denial of the permit on authority of § 10 of the Rivers and Harbors Act of March 3, 1899, 30 Stat. 1121, 1151, 33 U.S.C.A. § 403, giving the Secretary discretion to issue permits and on the Fish and Wildlife Coordination Act of March 10, 1934, 48 Stat. 401, as amended, 16 U.S.C.A. §§ 661 and 662(a), requiring the Secretary to consult with the Fish and Wildlife Service and state conservation agencies before issuing a permit to dredge and fill.
    The District Court held that it had jurisdiction, that the Fish and Wildlife Coordination Act was not authority for denying the permit, and that:

"The taking, control or limitation in the use of private property interests by an exercise of the police power of the government or the public interest or general welfare should be authorized by legislation which clearly outlines procedure which comports to all constitutional standards. This is not the case here.

"As this opinion is being prepared the Congress is in session. Advocates of conservation are both able and effective. The way is open to obtain a remedy for future situations like this one if one is needed and can be legally granted by the Congress."

The Court granted summary judgment for Landholders and directed the Secretary of the Army to issue the permit. This appeal followed.

The question presented to us is whether the Secretary of the Army can refuse to authorize a dredge and fill project in navigable waters for factually substantial ecological reasons even though the project would not interfere with navigation, flood control, or the production of power. To answer this question in the affirmative, we must answer two intermediate questions affirmatively. (1) Does Congress for ecological reasons have the power to prohibit a project on private riparian submerged land in navigable waters? (2) If it does, has Congress committed the power to prohibit to the Secretary of the Army?

II CONSTITUTIONAL POWER

The starting point here is the Commerce Clause[3] and its expansive reach. The test for determining whether Congress has the power to protect wildlife in navigable waters and thereby to regulate the use of private property for this reason is whether there is a basis for the Congressional judgment that the activity regulated has a substantial effect on interstate commerce. *Wickard v. Filburn,* 1942, 317 U.S. 111, 125, 63 S. Ct. 82, 89, 87 L. Ed. 122, 135. That this activity meets this test is hardly questioned.[4] In this time of awakening to the reality that we cannot continue to despoil our environment and yet exist,[5] the nation knows, if Courts do not, that the destruction of fish and wildlife in our estuarine waters does have a substantial, and in some areas a devastating, effect on interstate commerce. Landholders do not contend otherwise. Nor is it challenged that dredge and fill projects are activities which may tend to destroy the ecological balance and thereby affect commerce substantially. Because of these potential effects Congress has the power to regulate such projects.

[3] "The Congress shall have power to regulate Commerce with foreign nations, and among the several states, and with the Indian Tribes." U.S. Const. Art. I, § 8, Cl. 3.

[4] Landholders cite *Weber v. State Harbor Comm'rs,* 1873, 85 U.S. (18 Wall.) 65, 21 L. Ed. 798 and *United States v. River Rouge Improvement Co.,* 1926, 269 U.S. 411, 46 S. Ct. 144, 70 L. Ed. 339 as limiting the power of the Federal Government over navigable waters to control for navigational purposes. Not surprisingly, the narrow view these cases take of the Commerce Clause is pre-*United States v. Darby,* 1941, 312 U.S. 100, 61 S. Ct. 451, 85 L. Ed. 609.

[5] Complete documentation of the concern over environmental problems would surely be voluminous, but it is indirectly evidenced by the amount of very recent legal activity. See National Environmental Policy Act of 1969. Pub. Law 91-190 (Jan. 1, 1970) . . . ; Our Waters and Wetlands: How the Corps of Engineers Can Help Prevent Their Destruction and Pollution, H. Rep. 91-917, 91st Cong., 2d Sess., March 18, 1970, *infra* text at note 26; Executive Order 11507, Feb. 4, 1970, 38 L.W. 2436; *United States v. Ray,* 5 Cir., 1970, 423 F.2d 16 [Jan. 22, 1970]; *E. B. Elliott Advertising Co. v. Hill,* 5 Cir., 1970, 425 F.2d 1141 [April 3, 1970]; *Citizens Committee for the Hudson Valley v. Volpe,* S.D.N.Y., 1969, 302 F. Supp. 1083, aff'd, 2 Cir., 1970, 425 F.2d 97 [No. 428-33, April 16, 1970]; *National Advertising Co. v. Monterey, Calif.,* 1970, 1 Cal. 3d 875, 83 Cal. Rptr. 577, 464 P.2d 33 [Jan. 30, 1970]; *MacGibbon v. Duxbury Board of Appeals, Mass.,* 1970, 255 N.E.2d 347 [Jan. 29, 1970]; *California v. SS Bournemouth,* C.D. Cal., 1969, 307 F. Supp. 922; Creation of ABA Special Committee on Environmental Quality, 15 Am. Bar News No. 3, March 1970.

III RELINQUISHMENT OF THE POWER

Landholders do not challenge the existence of power. They argue that Congress in the historic compromise over the oil rich tidelands controversy abandoned its power over other natural resources by the relinquishment to the states in the Submerged Lands Act.[6] By it they urge the Government stripped itself of the power to regulate tidelands property except for purposes relating to (i) navigation, (ii) flood control, and (iii) hydroelectric power. This rests on the expressed Congressional reservation of control for these three purposes over the submerged lands, title to and power over which Congress relinquished to the states.[7]

The argument assumes that when Congress relinquished title to the land and the right and power to manage and use the land, it relinquished its power under the Commerce Clause except in particulars (i), (ii), and (iii). It also assumes that reservation of these three enumerated aspects of the commerce power implied that Congress gave up its plenary power over the myriad other aspects of commerce. See, e.g., *Heart of Atlanta Motel, Inc. v. United States,* 1964, 379 U.S. 241, 85 S. Ct. 348, 13 L. Ed. 2d 258; *Katzenbach v. McClung,* 1964, 379 U.S. 294, 85 S. Ct. 377, 13 L. Ed. 2d 290.

A nice argument can be contrived that the net effect of these provisions was to vest in the adjacent states [1] title in these tidelands and their natural resources and [2] [a] the exclusive power to use, exploit and manage these lands [b] only subject to the reserved power of the Federal Government regarding (i) navigation, (ii) flood control, and (iii) production of power. Certainly, this brief synopsis of (1) and (2)(a) is the literal import of § 1311(a)(1)(2). Likewise, the reservation summa-

---

[6] 43 U.S.C.A. § 1301 et seq. See *Continental Oil Co. v. London Steamship Owners' Mut. Ins. Ass'n.,* 5 Cir., 1969, 417 F.2d 1030, A.M.C., cert. denied, 1970, 397 U.S. 911, 90 S. Ct. 911, 25 L. Ed. 2d 92, A.M.C.; *Atlantis Development Corp. v. United States,* 5 Cir., 1967, 379 F.2d 818.

[7] The relinquishing provision states, 43 U.S.C.A. § 1311(a) and (b):

"(a) It is determined and declared to be in the public interest that (1) title to and ownership of the lands beneath navigable waters within the boundaries of the respective States, and the natural resources within such lands and waters, and (2) the right and power to manage, administer, lease, develop, and use the said lands and natural resources all in accordance with applicable State law be, and they are, subject to the provisions hereof, recognized, confirmed, established, and vested in and assigned to the respective States or the persons who were on June 5, 1950, entitled thereto under the law of the respective States in which the land is located, and the respective grantees, lessees, or successors in interest thereof;

"(b) (1) The United States releases and relinquishes unto said States and persons aforesaid, except as otherwise reserved herein, all right, title, and interest of the United States, if any it has, in and to all said lands, improvements, and natural resources * * *."

The reservation provision referred to states, 43 U.S.C.A. § 1311(d):

"(d) Nothing in this chapter shall affect the use, development, improvement, or control by or under the constitutional authority of the United States of said lands and waters for the purposes of navigation or flood control or the production of power, or be construed as the release or relinquishment of any rights of the United States arising under the constitutional authority of Congress to regulate or improve navigation, or to provide for flood control, or the production of power * * *."

The term "natural resources" is broadly defined to include both the animate and inanimate:

"The term 'natural resources' includes, without limiting the generality thereof, oil, gas, and all other minerals, and fish, shrimp, oysters, clams, crabs, lobsters, sponges, kelp, and other marine animal and plant life but does not include water power, or the use of water for the production of power;" 43 U.S.C.A. § 1301(e).

rized as (2)(b) is literally specified in § 1311(d). On this approach, the Federal Government turned over to adjacent states the full management and use of the tidelands reserving only those limited powers over commerce comprehended within the three particulars.

But this argument ignores both language found elsewhere and the legislative purpose of the Act. The controversy, often pressed with emotional overtones, was over oil and gas and whether the states were to reap the economic benefits of development royalties and to regulate the exploration and development or whether these benefits and these controls were to be exercised by the Federal Government as an adjunct of the newly declared "paramount rights." *United States v. California,* 1947, 332 U.S. 804, 805, 68 S. Ct. 20, 21, 92 L. Ed. 382, 383. The Act and this relinquishment reflect the legislative compromise found in the combination of the Submerged Lands Act and the Outer Continental Shelf Act.[8] The adjacent states were to be the "owner" of the resources and reap exclusively the economic benefits of resources in the tidelands and have full control over management and exploitation. The Federal Government, on the other hand, was given exclusive ownership and control vis-à-vis the states in the Outer Continental Shelf.

Although it was easy to make this division, the nature of the physical area of the controversy presented immediate operational problems growing out of the water. The Federal Government's traditional concern with navigation, especially on the high seas, its later but then quite extensive concern in flood control, hydro-electric power production, and the frequent combination of both under grandiose projects of a Corps of Engineers, raised specific problems calling for accommodation of the (i) sweeping Federal divesture and (ii) the continued fulfillment of the Federal government's role in these activities. Thus, for example, the states' exclusive right to grant exploration privileges, determine the location and spacing of development wells or drilling platforms posed prospects of maritime hazards. Without imposing its own notions of how development ought to be conducted, restricted, expanded, or controlled, the Federal Government had to have, and reserved expressly this power even to prohibit a drilling rig platform at a particular location. These specific reservations eliminated these frequent and extensive activities as a source of further state versus national controversy.

Whatever remaining doubt there might be on this reading was expressly eliminated by language in § 1314(a) which specifically retains in the Federal Government "all of its * * * rights in and powers of regulation and control of said lands and * * * waters for the constitutional purposes of commerce * * *" 43 U.S.C.A. § 1314(a).[9] This section, which encompasses and pervades the entire

---

[8] 43 U.S.C.A. § 1331 et seq.

[9] "The United States retains all its navigational servitude and rights in and powers of regulation and control of said lands and navigable waters for the constitutional purposes of commerce, navigation, national defense, and international affairs, all of which shall be paramount to, but shall not be deemed to include, proprietary rights of ownership, or the rights of management, administration, leasing, use, and development of the lands and natural resources which are specifically recognized, confirmed, established, and vested in and assigned to the respective States and others by section 1311 of this title." 43 U.S.C.A. § 1314(a).

Act, makes it clear that Congress intended to and did retain all its constitutional powers over commerce and did not relinquish certain portions of the power by specifically reserving others.[10]

All of this is additionally borne out by the legislative history[11] and *United States v. Rands,* 1967, 389 U.S. 121, 127, 88 S. Ct. 265, 269, 19 L. Ed. 2d 329, 335:

> "Finally, respondents urge that the Government's position subverts the policy of the Submerged Lands Act, which confirmed and vested in the States title to the lands beneath navigable waters within their boundaries and to natural resources within such lands and waters, together with the right and power to manage, develop, and use such lands and natural resources. However, reliance on that Act is misplaced, for it expressly recognized that the United States retained all its navigational servitude and rights in and power of regulation and control of said lands and navigable waters for the constitutional purposes of commerce, navigation, national defense, and international affairs, all of which shall be paramount to, but shall not be deemed to include, proprietary rights of ownership * * *. Nothing in the Act was to be construed as the release or relinquishment of any rights of the United States arising under the constitutional authority of Congress to regulate or improve navigation, or to provide for flood control, or the production of power. The Act left congressional power over commerce and the dominant navigational servitude of the United States precisely where it found them."

Congress clearly has the power under the Commerce Clause to regulate the use of Landholders' submerged riparian property for conservation purposes and has not given up this power in the Submerged Lands Act.

IV PROHIBITING OBSTRUCTIONS TO NAVIGATION

The action of the Chief of Engineers and the Secretary of the Army under attack rests immediately on the Rivers and Harbors Act, 33 U.S.C.A. § 403, which declares that "the creation of any obstruction * * * to the navigable capacity of

---

[10] It is argued that the retention in § 1314(a) is limited to the three aspects enumerated in § 1311(d) by the words "[the commerce power] shall be paramount to, but shall not be deemed to include [relinquished rights]." But we have already shown that the enumeration of these three, which are explicitly stated because they are particularly relevant to the regulation of land lying under navigable waters, does not imply that Congressional power over other types of commerce was among the rights relinquished. Because Congress did not give up any of its power over all of interstate commerce in § 1311 (see note 7, supra), they are not "[relinquished rights]" and the limitation portion of § 1314(a) is inapplicable.

To hold otherwise would render the reservation of constitutional commerce power in § 1314(a) a useless reiteration of the impliedly retained powers in § 1311(d). But to hold that it is an explicit reservation of all commerce powers gives the section meaning. The section may be unneeded and overly cautious in that it reserves a constitutional power that has been relinquished, but it should not be read in such a way as to render it otherwise useless.

[11] "This title does not affect any of the Federal constitutional powers of regulation and control over these areas within State boundaries. Such powers, as those over navigation, commerce, national defense, international affairs, flood control, and power production where the United States owns or acquires the water power."

H.R. Rep. No. 215, 83d Cong., 1st Sess. (March 27, 1953), 1953 U.S. Code Cong. & Admin. News, pp. 1385, 1389.

any of the waters of the United States is prohibited."[12] The Act covers both building of structures and the excavating and filling in of navigable waters. It is structured as a flat prohibition unless—the unless being the issuance of approval by the Secretary after recommendation of the Chief of Engineers.[13] The Act itself does not put any restrictions on denial of a permit or the reasons why the Secretary may refuse to grant a permit to one seeking to build structures on or dredge and fill his own property. Although the Act has always been read as tempering the outright prohibition by the rule of reason against arbitrary action, the Act does flatly forbid the obstruction. The administrator may grant permission on conditions and conversely deny permission when the situation does not allow for those conditions.

But the statute does not prescribe either generally or specifically what those conditions may be. The question for us is whether under the Act the Secretary may include conservation considerations as conditions to be met to make the proposed project acceptable. Until now there has been no absolute answer to this question. In fact, in most cases under the Rivers and Harbors Act the Courts have been faced only with navigation problems."[14] See, e.g., *Sanitary Dist. v. United States*, 1925, 266 U.S. 405, 45 S. Ct. 176, 69 L. Ed. 352; *Wisconsin v. Illinois*, 1929, 278 U.S. 367, 49 S. Ct. 163, 73 L. Ed. 426; *United States v. Republic Steel Corp.*, 1960, 362 U.S. 482, 80 S. Ct. 884, 4 L. Ed. 2d 903.

[12] "The creation of any obstruction not affirmatively authorized by Congress, to the navigable capacity of any of the waters of the United States is prohibited; and it shall not be lawful to build or commence the building of any wharf, pier, dolphin, boom, weir, breakwater, bulkhead, jetty, or other structures in any port, roadstead, haven, harbor, canal, navigable river, or other water of the United States, outside established harbor lines, or where no harbor lines have been established, except on plans recommended by the Chief of Engineers and authorized by the Secretary of the Army; and it shall not be lawful to excavate or fill, or in any manner to alter or modify the course, location, condition, or capacity of, any port, roadstead, haven, harbor, canal, lake, harbor of refuge, or inclosure within the limits of any breakwater, or of the channel of any navigable water of the United States, unless the work has been recommended by the Chief of Engineers and authorized by the Secretary of the Army prior to beginning the same." 33 U.S.C.A. § 403.

[13] This Court recently held that under this same section together with the Outer Continental Shelf Lands Act, 43 U.S.C.A. § 1333(f), a permit must be obtained before a project can be begun on the Outer Continental Shelf. *United States v. Ray, supra*, note 5, which followed the remand and trial on the merits in *Atlantis Development Corp. v. United States*, 5 Cir., 1967, 379 F.2d 818.

[14] Landholders cite authority holding that the Secretary is empowered to deny a permit only for navigational reasons, United States Attorney General's opinion of February 13, 1925, 30 U.S. Atty. Gen. Ops. 410 at 412, 415, 416; *Miami Beach Jockey Club, Inc. v. Dern*, 1936, 66 App. D.C. 254, 86 F.2d 135, 136 (on petition for rehearing). These determinations, by no means inexorable under the wording of the statute, see *Greathouse v. Dern, infra*, predate the changes wrought by the Fish and Wildlife Coordination Act, *infra*.

And they are out of step with the sweeping declaration of power over commerce in *United States v. Appalachian Electric Power Co.*, 1940, 311 U.S. 377, 423–427, 61 S. Ct. 291, 307, 85 L. Ed. 243, 261–263:

"The state and respondent, alike, however, hold the waters and the lands under them subject to the power of Congress to control the waters for the purpose of commerce. The power flows from the grant to regulate, i.e., to 'prescribe the rule by which commerce is to be governed.' This includes the protection of navigable waters in capacity as well as use. This power of Congress to regulate commerce is so unfettered that its judgment as to whether a structure is or is not a hindrance is conclusive. Its determination is legislative in character. The Federal Government has domination over the water

One very big exception is United States ex rel. *Greathouse v. Dern,* 1933, 289 U.S. 352, 53 S. Ct. 614, 77 L. Ed. 1250. There petitioners sought a writ of mandamus to compel the Secretary of War and the Chief of Engineers to issue a permit to build a wharf in navigable waters. The Secretary, specifically finding that it would not interfere with navigation, denied the permit. The Supreme Court held that mandamus would not issue because the allowance of mandamus "is controlled by equitable principles * * * and it may be refused for reasons comparable to those which would lead a court of equity, in the exercise of a sound discretion, to withhold its protection of an undoubted legal right." The reason was that the United States had plans to condemn petitioners' land for use as a means of access to a proposed parkway. Allowing a wharf to be built would increase the expense to the government since it would increase the market value of the land and would require the government to pay for tearing down the wharf. The importance of Greathouse is that it recognized that the Corps of Engineers does not have to wear navigational binders when it considers a permit request. That there must be a reason does not mean that the reason has to be navigability.

Another case holds that the Corps has a duty to consider factors other than navigational. *Citizens Committee for the Hudson Valley v. Volpe,* S.D.N.Y., 1969, 302 F. Supp. 1083, aff'd., 2 Cir., 1970, 425 F.2d 97 [No. 428–33, April 16, 1970]. There the District Court held that the Corps must consider a fill project in the context of the entire expressway project of which it was a part rather than just considering the fill and its effect on navigation. The reasoning was that the approval of the Secretary of Transportation was necessary before a proposed causeway could be constructed. The causeway, along with the fill, was an integral part of the expressway project. However, if the Corps and Secretary of the Army approved the fill and the State completed it, the Secretary of Transportation, considering the enormous expense of the fill, would have no choice, other than approving the causeway. The Army thus had exceeded its authority in approving

---

power inherent in the flowing stream. It is liable to no one for its use or nonuse. The flow of a navigable stream is in no sense private property; 'that the running water in a great navigable stream is capable of private ownership is inconceivable.' Exclusion of riparian owners from its benefits without compensation is entirely within the Government's discretion."

*   *   *   *   *   *

"In our view, it cannot properly be said that the constitutional power of the United States over its waters is limited to control for navigation. By navigation respondent means no more than operation of boats and improvement of the waterway itself. In truth the authority of the United States is the regulation of commerce on its waters. Navigability, in the sense just stated, is but a part of this whole. Flood protection, watershed development, recovery of the cost of improvements through utilization of power are likewise parts of commerce control. * * * That authority is as broad as the needs of commerce. * * * The point is that navigable waters are subject to national planning and control in the broad regulation of commerce granted the Federal Government. The license conditions to which objection is made have an obvious relationship to the exercise of the commerce power. Even if there were no such relationship the plenary power of Congress over navigable waters would empower it to deny the privilege of constructing an obstruction in those waters."

the fill on only navigational considerations since approval of the fill was effectually approval of the causeway.[15]

But such circuity is not necessary. Governmental agencies in executing a particular statutory responsibility ordinarily are required to take heed of, sometimes effectuate and other times not thwart other valid statutory governmental policies. And here the governmentwide policy of environmental conservation is spectacularly revealed in at least two statutes, The Fish and Wildlife Coordination Act[16] and the National Environmental Policy Act of 1969.[17]

The Fish and Wildlife Coordination Act[18] clearly requires the dredging and filling agency (under a governmental permit), whether public or private, to consult with the Fish and Wildlife Service,[19] with a view of conservation of wildlife resources. If there be any question as to whether the statute directs the licensing agency (the Corps) to so consult it can quickly be dispelled. Common sense and reason dictate that it would be incongruous for Congress, in light of the fact that it intends conservation to be considered in private dredge and fill operations (as evidenced by the clear wording of the statute), not to direct the only federal agency concerned with licensing such projects both to consult and to take such factors into account.

The second proof that the Secretary is directed and authorized by the Fish and Wildlife Coordination Act to consider conservation is found in the legislative history. The Senate Report on the Fish and Wildlife Coordination Act states:

"Finally, the nursery and feeding grounds of valuable crustaceans, such as shrimp, as well as the young of valuable marine fishes, may be affected by dredging, filling, and

---

[15] The Court essentially held that the Corps, where approval of Transportation is also required, cannot be oblivious to the effect of fill projects on the beauty and conservation of natural resources. This inference arises from the fact that the Secretary of Transportation is statutorily required to consider conservation before granting a permit. But if the fill on which the causeway was to be built were completed at the time the permit for the causeway was requested, there would be no conservation factors for Transportation to consider. The Court held that the Corps could not blind itself to this fact and thereby cut off considerations of conservation by granting a fill permit without Transportation's approval of the causeway.

[16] 16 U.S.C.A. §§ 661–666.

[17] Public Law 91–190, 42 U.S.C.A. §§ 4331–4347.

[18] The Fish and Wildlife Coordination Act states:

"Except as hereafter stated in subsection (h) of this section [not applicable], whenever the waters of any stream or other body of water are proposed or authorized to be impounded, diverted, the channel deepened, or the stream or other body of water otherwise controlled or modified for any purpose whatever, including navigation and drainage, by any department or agency of the United States, or by any public or private agency under Federal permit or license, such department or agency first shall consult with the United States Fish and Wildlife Service, Department of the Interior, and with the head of the agency exercising administration over the wildlife resources of the particular State wherein the impoundment, diversion, or other control facility is to be constructed, with a view to the conservation of wildlife resources by preventing loss of and damage to such resources as well as providing for the development and improvement thereof in connection with such water-resource development." 16 U.S.C.A. § 662(a).

[19] Presumably Landholders must first obtain the Corps of Engineers' permit before becoming a "private agency under Federal permit or license."

diking operations often carried out to improve navigation and provide new industrial or residential land.

   *   *   *   *   *   *   *   *   *   *   *   *   *   *

Existing law has questionable application to projects of the Corps of Engineers for the dredging of bays and estuaries for navigation and filling purposes. More seriously, existing law has no application whatsoever to the dredging and filling of bays and estuaries by private interests or other non-Federal entities in navigable waters under permit from the Corps of Engineers. This is a particularly serious deficiency from the standpoint of commercial fishing interests. The dredging of these bays and estuaries along the coastlines to aid navigation and also to provide land fills for real estate and similar developments, both by Federal agencies or other agencies under permit from the Corps of Engineers, has increased tremendously in the last 5 years. Obviously, dredging activity of this sort has a profound disturbing effect on aquatic life, including shrimp and other species of tremendous significance to the commercial fishing industry. The bays, estuaries, and related marsh areas are highly important as spawning and nursery grounds for many commercial species of fish and shellfish."[20]

S. Rep. No. 1981, 85th Cong., 2d Sess. (July 28, 1958). 1958 U.S. Code Cong. & Admin. News, pp. 3446, 3448, 3450. This Report clearly shows that Congress intended the Chief of Engineers and Secretary of the Army to consult with the Fish and Wildlife Service before issuing a permit for a private dredge and fill operation.

This interpretation was judicially accepted in *Udall v. FPC:*

"Section 2(a), 16 USC § 662(a) provides that an agency evaluating a license under which 'the waters of any stream or other body of water are proposed * * * to be impounded first shall consult with the United States Fish and Wildlife Service, Department of the Interior * * * with a view to the conservation of wildlife resources by preventing loss of and damage to such resources * * *.' Certainly the wildlife conservation aspect of the project must be explored and evaluated."

1967, 387 U.S. 428, 443-444, 87 S. Ct. 1712, 1720, 18 L. Ed. 2d 869, 879. The meaning and application of the Act are also reflected by the actions of the Executive that show the statute authorizes and directs the Secretary to consult with the Fish and Wildlife Service in deciding whether to grant a dredge and fill permit.

---

[20] The Senate Report also shows how the exercise of the commerce power in the conservation arena ties in with its exercise in other areas:

"The amendments proposed by this bill would remedy these deficiencies and have several other important advantages. The amendments, would provide that wildlife conservation shall receive equal consideration with other features in the planning of Federal water resource development programs. This would have the effect of putting fish and wildlife on the basis of equality with flood control, irrigation, navigation, and hydroelectric power in our water resource programs, which is highly desirable and proper, and represents an objective long sought by conservationists of the Nation." 1958 U.S. Code Cong. & Admin. News, at 3450.

In a Memorandum of Understanding[21] between the Secretary of the Army and the Secretary of the Interior, it is provided that, upon receipt of an application for a permit to dredge or fill in navigable waters, the District Engineer of the Corps of Engineers concerned is required to send notices to all interested parties, including the appropriate Regional Directors of the Federal Water Pollution Control Administration, the Fish and Wildlife Service, the National Park Service and the appropriate state conservation, resources, and water pollution agencies. The District Engineer is given the initial responsibility of evaluating all relevant factors in reaching a decision as to whether the particular permit involved should be granted or denied. The Memorandum also provides that in case of conflicting views the ultimate decision shall be made by the Secretary of the Army after consultation with the Secretary of the Interior.

This Executive action has almost a virtual legislative imprimatur from the November 1967 Report of the House Committee on Merchant Marine and Fisheries, in reporting favorably on a bill[22] to protect estuarine areas which was later enacted into law.[23] As a result of the effective operation of the Interdepartmental Memorandum of Understanding, the Interior Department and the Committee

---

[21]   "POLICIES

1. It is the policy of the two Secretaries that there shall be full coordination and cooperation between their respective Departments on the above responsibilities at all organizational levels, and it is their view that maximum efforts in the discharge of those responsibilities, including the resolution of differing views, must be undertaken at the earliest practicable time and at the field organizational unit most directly concerned. Accordingly, District Engineers of the U.S. Army Corps of Engineers shall coordinate with the Regional Directors of the Secretary of the Interior on fish and wildlife, recreation, and pollution problems associated with dredging, filling, and excavation operations to be conducted under permits issued under the 1899 Act in the navigable waters of the United States, and they shall avail themselves of the technical advice and assistance which such Directors may provide.

2. The Secretary of the Army will seek the advice and counsel of the Secretary of the Interior on difficult cases. If the Secretary of the Interior advises that proposed operations will unreasonably impair natural resources or the related environment, including the fish and wildlife and recreational values thereof, or will reduce the quality of such waters in violation of applicable water quality standards, the Secretary of the Army in acting on the request for a permit will carefully evaluate the advantages and benefits of the operations in relation to the resultant loss or damage, including all data presented by the Secretary of the Interior, and will either deny the permit or include such conditions in the permit as he determines to be in the public interest, including provisions that will assure compliance with water quality standards established in accordance with law. * * *."

[22] H. Rept. 989, 90th Cong., 1st sess., to accompany H.R. 25, pp. 4-5. See also S. Rept. No. 1419, July 17, 1968, 90th Cong., 2d sess., Senate Committee on Commerce, reporting on S. 695 and H.R. 25, pp. 13-14. H.R. 25 with revisions became the Act of August 3, 1968, 82 Stat. 625 (Pub. L. 90-454).

[23] "As a result of the hearings and the discussions which ensued from the circularized draft proposal—particularly with respect to the permit provision for dredging, filling, and excavation—a memorandum of understanding was entered into between the Secretary of the Interior and the Secretary of the Army. This agreement set forth the policies and procedures to be followed regarding the control of dredging, filling, and excavation in the navigable waters of the United States, which would include many of our Nation's estuarine areas.

On August 2, the Department of the Interior filed a supplemental report on the bill. In its report to the committee, the Department stated that we believe that this memorandum of understanding provides an effective administrative solution to the problem of preventing unreasonable impairment of the natural resources of the Nation's waterways and related environment, and preventing the pollution of the waters. In our opinion, the agreement makes the legislative approach set forth in H.R. 25 * * * for control for dredging, et cetera, unnecessary * * * (Omissions by the Committee.)."

concluded that it was not necessary to provide for dual permits from Interior and Army.

The intent of the three branches has been unequivocally expressed: The Secretary must weigh the effect a dredge and fill project will have on conservation before he issues a permit lifting the Congressional ban.

The parallel of momentum as the three branches shape a national policy gets added impetus from the National Environmental Policy Act of 1969, Public Law 91-190, 42 U.S.C.A. §§ 4331-4347. This Act essentially states that every federal agency shall consider ecological factors when dealing with activities which may have an impact on man's environment.[24]

Although this Congressional command was not in existence at the time the permit in question was denied, the correctness of that decision must be determined by the applicable standards of today. The national policy is set forth in plain terms in § 101 and the disclaimer of § 104(3) neither affects it nor the duty of all departments to consider, consult, collaborate and conclude. For we hold that while it is still the action of the Secretary of the Army on the recommendation of the Chief of Engineers, the Army must consult with, consider and receive, and then evaluate the recommendations of all these other agencies articulately on all these environmental factors. In rejecting a permit on non-navigational grounds, the Secretary of the Army does not abdicate his sole ultimate responsibility and authority. Rather in weighing the application, the Secretary of the Army is acting under a Congressional mandate to collaborate and consider all of these factors.[25]

To judge the ebb and flow of the national tide, he can look to the Report of the House Committee on Governmental Operations. Although this perhaps lacks traditional standing of legislative history, it certainly has relevance somewhat comparable to an Executive Commission Report. On March 17, 1970, it approved and adopted a Report,[26] based on a study made by its Conservation and Natural Resources Subcommittee, entitled Our Waters and Wetlands: How the Corps of Engineers Can Help Prevent Their Destruction and Pollution. (H. Rep. No. 91-917, 91st Cong. 2d Sess. (1970)) The first section stifles any doubt as to how

---

[24] Omitted.

[25] For like reasons the following disclaimer in the Fish and Wildlife Act of 1956, 70 Stat. 1119, 16 U.S.C.A. §§ 742a-742j, specifically 70 Stat. 1124, 16 U.S.C.A. § 742i is not decisive:

"THE RIGHTS OF STATES.—Nothing in this Act (subsection 742a and note-742d, 742e-742j of this title; 15 subsection 713c-3 and note) shall be construed (1) to interfere in any manner with the rights of any State under the Submerged Lands Act (Public Law 31, Eighty-third Congress) (43 subsection 1301 and notes-1303, 1311-1315) or otherwise provided by law, or to supersede any regulatory authority over fisheries exercised by the States either individually or under interstate compacts."

[26] The heading of the Report reads:

"The Corps of Engineers, which is charged by Congress with the duty to protect the nation's navigable waters, should, when considering whether to approve applications for landfills, dredging and other work in navigable waters, increase its consideration of the effects which the proposed work will have, not only on navigation, but also on conservation of natural resources, fish and wildlife, air and water quality, esthetics, scenic view, historic sites, ecology, and other public interest aspects of the waterway."

this part of Congress construes the Corps' duty under the Rivers and Harbors Act. The section traces the historical interpretation of the Corps' power under the Rivers and Harbors Act. It commends the Corps for recognizing ecological considerations under the Act to protect against unnecessary fills and cites the instant case.[27] But following the temper of the times, the report by bold face black type cautions against any easy overconfidence and charges the Corps with ever-increasing vigilance.[28]

When the House Report and the National Environmental Policy Act of 1969 are considered together with the Fish and Wildlife Coordination Act and its interpretations, there is no doubt that the Secretary can refuse on conservation grounds to grant a permit under the Rivers and Harbors Act.

V DUE PROCESS

Landholders next contend that the denial of a permit without a hearing before the Fish and Wildlife Service is a deprivation of property without due process of law. Administrative law requires that before an agency can regulate a party, it must allow that party to be heard. Here, Landholders were given such a hearing before the Corps of Engineers, the body empowered to grant or deny a permit. They were not entitled to a hearing before the Fish and Wildlife Service because it is not "the one who decides." *Morgan v. United States,* 1935, 289 U.S. 468, 481, 56 S. Ct. 906, 912, 80 L. Ed. 1288, 1295. They were allowed to rebut the findings and conclusions of the Fish and Wildlife Service before the deciding body and thus were not denied due process for lack of a hearing.

[27] "In 1968, the Corps revised its regulations to state that the Corps, in considering an application for a permit to fill, dredge, discharge or deposit materials, or conduct other activities affecting navigable waters, will evaluate "all relevant factors, including the effect of the proposed work on navigation, fish and wildlife, conservation, pollution, esthetics, ecology, and the general public interest." 33 CFR 209.120(d)(1). The Corps applied this policy when it recently rejected the efforts of land developers to fill in a major part of Boca Ciega Bay, near St. Petersburg, Fla. See *Zabel v. Tabb,* 296 F. Supp. 764 (D.C.M.D. Fla., Tampa Div., Feb. 17, 1969), now on appeal to the U.S. Court of Appeals, Fifth Circuit, 430 F.2d 199.

The committee commends the Corps for recognizing its broader responsibilities to protect against unnecessary fills and other alteration of water bodies * * *" H. Rep. No. 91-917, p. 5.

[28] "The Corps of Engineers should instruct its district engineers and other personnel involved in considering applications for fills, dredging, or other work in estuaries, rivers, and other bodies of navigable water to increase their emphasis on how the work will affect all aspects of the public interest, including not only navigation but also conservation of natural resources, fish and wildlife, air and water quality, esthetics, scenic view, historical sites, ecology, and other public interest aspects of the waterway." H. Rep. No. 91-917.

As the Committee views it, not only should the Corps consider conservation, but it should consider conservation to be endangered by every dredge and fill project and place the burden of proving otherwise on the applicant. See, e.g., the conclusion of the first section of the Report and its bold face type recommendation:

"The Corps of Engineers should permit no further landfills or other work in the Nation's estuaries, rivers and other waterways except in those cases where the applicant affirmatively proves that the proposed work is in accord with the public interest, including the need to avoid the piecemeal destruction of these water areas." H. Rep. No. 91-917, p. 6.

VI   TAKING WITHOUT COMPENSATION

Landholders' last contention is that their private submerged property was taken for public use without just compensation. They proceed this way: (i) the denial of a permit constitutes a taking since this is the only use to which the property could be put; (ii) the public use is as a breeding ground for wildlife; and (iii) for that use just compensation is due.

Our discussion of this contention begins and ends with the idea that there is no taking. The waters and underlying land are subject to the paramount servitude in the Federal government which the Submerged Lands Act expressly reserved as an incident of power incident to the Commerce Clause. (See Part II supra.)

VII   CONCLUSION

Landholders' contentions fail on all grounds. The case is reversed and since there are no questions remaining to be resolved by the District Court, judgment is rendered for the Government and the associated agent-defendants.

Reversed and rendered.

QUESTIONS FOR DISCUSSION

1   By what authority does a court apply an act designed to remedy one evil to another without legislative approval?
2   Does the Corps of Engineers have the abilities necessary to judge factors other than navigation? Who does?
3   How does the Rivers and Harbors Act interrelate with the Fish and Wildlife Coordination Act? With NEPA?
4   It is an axiom that legislative history is not to be considered if the statute is not ambiguous. Does the court's reliance on legislative history and other legislation convince you?
5   Do you find the court's reliance on NEPA convincing?
6   Do you see any danger in a court, the judges of which are not elected and serve for life, reaching conclusions such as that in *Zabel v. Tabb?*
7   Is it significant that in *Zabel v. Tabb* the Corps of Engineers *wanted* to consider factors other than navigation?
8   Might the result have been different had this been a question as to the ecological damage the project would cause?
9   Apart from any legal claim, what effect might the opposition of agencies such as Fish and Wildlife have on the court's decision?
10 Should the division engineer have taken notice of the "widespread opposition to the proposed work"?
11 Reread Section 10 and the four reasons given by the Army for denying the permit. Are the reasons offered valid in light of the language of Section 10?
12 Is the trial court's conclusion that Congress rather than the court should remedy the problem convincing? Practical?
13 What should be inferred from the fact that Section 10 does not list reasons for denial of permits?

14   Do you agree that "although the Congressional command [NEPA] was not in existence at the time the permit in question was denied, the correctness of that decision must be determined by the applicable standards of today"? Suppose NEPA had been in existence at the time of the denial and repealed at the time of the litigation?

SECTION 13

Section 13 of the Rivers and Harbors Act is known as the Refuse Act. The Refuse Act, on its face, prohibits the deposit or discharge of "refuse matter of any kind" into navigable waters or their tributaries, providing in part

> that it shall not be lawful to throw, discharge, or deposit, or cause, suffer, or procure to be thrown, discharged, or deposited either from or out of any ship, barge, or other floating craft of any kind, or from the shore, wharf, manufacturing establishment, or mill of any kind, any refuse matter of any kind or description whatever other than that flowing from streets and sewers and passing therefrom in a liquid state, into any navigable water of the United States, or into any tributary of any navigable water. . . .

The term "refuse matter" has been interpreted to mean almost every conceivable type of foreign substance, both commercially valuable and value-less, including gasoline, iron tailings, wood, oil, and, more recently, heat.[h] Refuse "flowing from streets and sewers and passing therefrom in a liquid state"[i] is specifically excepted from the provisions of the act.[j]

Criminal penalties are provided by Section 16 for violation of Section 13:

> Every person and every corporation that shall violate, or that shall knowingly aid, abet, authorize, or instigate a violation of the provisions of Sections 407, 408, and 409 of this title shall be guilty of a misdemeanor, and on conviction thereof shall be punished by a fine not exceeding $2,500 nor less than $500, or by imprisonment (in the case of a natural person) for not less than thirty days nor more than one year, or by both such fine and imprisonment, in the discretion of the court, one-half of said fine to be paid to the person or persons giving information which shall lead to conviction.[k]

For the first sixty years of its existence, Section 13 was applied only to discharges affecting navigation. Beginning in 1960, however, the section was construed to encompass discharges which had no effect on navigation.

The Refuse Act is analyzed from two perspectives in *United States v. Standard Oil Company*. The case is framed by the majority in terms of the

[h] See, for gas, *United States v. Standard Oil*, 384 U.S. 224 (1966); for iron tailings, *United States v. Republic Steel*, 362 U.S. 482 (1960); for wood, *Pile Driver No. 2*, 239 F. 489 (2d Cir. 1916); for oil, *United States v. Ballard Oil Company*, 195 F.2d 369 (2d Cir. 1952); for heat, see Permits for Discharges or Deposits into Navigable Waters, 33 C.F.R. § 209.131(d)(1) (1971).

[i] 33 U.S.C. § 407.

[j] Section 13 of the Rivers and Harbors Act provides two separate actions. The first clause prohibits all discharges into navigable waters and their tributaries while the second clause prohibits discharges or deposits on the banks of navigable waters or their tributaries "whereby navigation shall or may be impeded or obstructed." Therefore, direct discharges into navigable waters alone result in a violation of the first clause of Section 13, whereas discharges *resulting in an obstruction of navigation* are required by the wording of the second clause.

[k] 33 U.S.C. § 411 (1964).

definition of refuse, but the issue of note is the demise of the obstruction-to-navigation requirement. Note that the case is a criminal prosecution, and consider with care the dissenters' arguments regarding strict construction of penal statutes and their views of the judicial role vis-à-vis that of Congress.

United States v. Standard Oil Company

384 U.S. 224 (1966)

Mr. Justice Douglas delivered the opinion of the Court.

The question presented for decision is whether the statutory ban on depositing "any refuse matter of any kind or description"[1] in a navigable water covers the discharge of commercially valuable aviation gasoline.

Section 13 of the Rivers and Harbors Act provides:

> "It shall not be lawful to throw, discharge, or deposit . . . any refuse matter of any kind or description whatever other than that flowing from streets and sewers and passing therefrom in a liquid state, into any navigable water of the United States. . . ." 33 U.S.C. § 407 (1964 ed.).

The indictment charged appellee, Standard Oil (Kentucky), with violating § 13 by allowing to be discharged in the St. Johns River "refuse matter" consisting of 100-octane aviation gasoline. Appellee moved to dismiss the indictment, and, for the purposes of the motion, the parties entered into a stipulation of fact. It states that the gasoline was commercially valuable and that it was discharged into the St. Johns only because a shut-off valve at dockside had been "accidentally" left open.

The District Court dismissed the indictment because it was of the view that the statutory phrase "refuse matter" does not include commercially valuable oil. The United States appealed directly to this Court under the Criminal Appeals Act (18 U.S.C. § 3731 (1964 ed.)). We noted probable jurisdiction. 382 U.S. 807.

This case comes to us at a time in the Nation's history when there is greater concern than ever over pollution—one of the main threats to our free-flowing rivers and to our lakes as well. The crisis that we face in this respect would not, of course, warrant us in manufacturing offenses where Congress has not acted nor in stretching statutory language in a criminal field to meet strange conditions. But whatever may be said of the rule of strict construction, it cannot provide a substitute for common sense, precedent, and legislative history. We cannot construe § 13 of the Rivers and Harbors Act in a vacuum. Nor can we read it as Baron Parke[2] would read a pleading.

---

[1] 30 Stat. 1152, 33 U.S.C. § 407 (1964 ed.).
[2] A man whose "fault was an almost superstitious reverence for the dark technicalities of special pleading." XV Dictionary of National Biography, p. 226 (Stephen and Lee ed. 1937–1938).

The statutory words are "any refuse matter of any kind or description." We said in United States v. Republic Steel Corp., 362 U.S. 482, 491, that the history of this provision and of related legislation dealing with our free-flowing rivers "forbids a narrow, cramped reading" of § 13. The District Court recognized that if this were waste oil it would be "refuse matter" within the meaning of § 13 but concluded that it was not within the statute because it was "valuable" oil.[3] That is "a narrow cramped reading" of § 13 in partial defeat of its purpose.

Oil is oil and whether useable or not by industrial standards it has the same deleterious effect on waterways. In either case, its presence in our rivers and harbors is both a menace to navigation and a pollutant. This seems to be the administrative construction of § 13, the Solicitor General advising us that it is the basis of prosecution in approximately one-third of the oil pollution cases reported to the Department of Justice by the Office of the Chief of Engineers.

Section 13 codified pre-existing statutes:

An 1886 Act (24 Stat. 329) made it unlawful to empty "any ballast, stone, slate, gravel, earth, slack, rubbish, wreck, filth, slabs, edgings, sawdust, slag, or cinders, or other refuse or mill-waste of any kind into New York Harbor"—which plainly includes valuable pre-discharge material.

An 1888 Act (25 Stat. 209) "to prevent obstruction and injurious deposits" within the Harbor of New York and adjacent waters banned the discharge of "refuse, dirt, ashes, cinders, mud, sand, dredgings, sludge, acid, *or any other matter of any kind,* other than that flowing from streets, sewers, and passing therefrom in a liquid state"—which also plainly includes valuable pre-discharge material (Emphasis added.)

The 1890 Act (26 Stat. 453) made unlawful emptying into navigable waters "any ballast, stone, slate, gravel, earth, rubbish, wreck, filth, slabs, edgings, sawdust, slag, cinders, ashes, refuse, or other waste of any kind . . . which shall tend to impede or obstruct navigation." Here also valuable pre-discharge materials were included.

The 1894 Act (28 Stat. 363) prohibited deposits in harbors and rivers for which Congress had appropriated money for improvements, of "ballast, refuse, dirt, ashes, cinders, mud, sand, dredgings, sludge, acid, *or any other matter of any kind* other than that flowing from streets, sewers, and passing therefrom in a liquid state." (Emphasis added.) This Act also included valuable pre-discharge material.

The Acts of 1886 and 1888, then, dealt specifically with the New York Harbor; the scope of the latter was considerably broader, covering as it did the deposit of "any other matter of any kind." The Acts of 1890 and 1894 paralleled the earlier enactments pertaining to New York, applying their terms to waterways throughout the Nation.

The 1899 Act now before us was no more than an attempt to consolidate these prior Acts into one. It was indeed stated by the sponsor in the Senate to be "in accord with the statutes now in existence, only scattered . . . from the begin-

---

[3] The District Court followed the decision of the United States District Court in United States v. The Delvalle, 45 F. Supp. 746, 748, where it was said: "The accidental discharge of *valuable, usable oil* . . . does not constitute . . . a violation of the statute." (Emphasis added.)

ning of the statutes down through to the end" (32 Cong. Rec. 2296), and reflecting merely "[v]ery slight changes to remove ambiguities." Id., p. 2297.

From an examination of these statutes, several points are clear. First, the 1894 Act and its antecedent, the 1888 Act applicable to the New York Harbor,[4] drew on their face no distinction between valuable and valueless substances. Second, of the enumerated substances, some may well have had commercial or industrial value prior to discharge into the covered waterways. To be more specific, ashes and acids were banned whether or not they had any remaining commercial or industrial value. Third, these Acts applied not only to the enumerated substances but also to the discharge of "any other matter of any kind." Since the enumerated substances included those with a pre-discharge value, the rule of *ejusdem generis* does not require limiting this latter category to substances lacking a pre-discharge value. Fourth, the coverage of these Acts was not diminished by the codification of 1899. The use of the term "refuse" in the codification serves in the place of the lengthy list of enumerated substances found in the earlier Acts and the catch-all provision found in the Act of 1890. The legislative history demonstrates without contradiction that Congress intended to codify without substantive change the earlier Acts.

The philosophy of those antecedent laws seems to us to be clearly embodied in the present law. It is plain from its legislative history that the "serious injury" to our watercourses (S. Rep. No. 224, 50th Cong., 1st Sess., p. 2) sought to be remedied was caused in part by obstacles that impeded navigation and in part by pollution—"the discharge of sawmill waste into streams" (ibid.) and the injury of channels by "deposits of ballast, steam-boat ashes, oysters, and rubbish from passing vessels." Ibid. The list is obviously not an exhaustive list of pollutants. The words of the Act are broad and inclusive: "any refuse matter of any kind or description whatever." Only one exception is stated: "other than that flowing from streets and sewers and passing therefrom in a liquid state, into any navigable water of the United States." More comprehensive language would be difficult to select. The word "refuse" does not stand alone; the "refuse" banned is "of any kind or description whatever," apart from the one exception noted. And, for the reasons already stated, the meaning we must give the term "refuse" must reflect the present codification's statutory antecedents.

The Court of Appeals for the Second Circuit in United States v. Ballard Oil Co., 195 F.2d 369 (L. Hand, Augustus Hand, and Harrie Chase, JJ.) held that causing good oil to spill into a watercourse violated § 13. The word "refuse" in that setting, said the court, "is satisfied by anything which has become waste,

---

[4] The codification did not include the Acts of 1886 and 1888 which pertained only to New York. These remain in effect and are found at 33 U.S.C. §§ 441–451 (1964 ed.). The New York Harbor statute has been held to apply not only to waste oil which was unintentionally discharged (The Albania, 30 F.2d 727) but also to valuable oil negligently discharged. The Columbo, 42 F.2d 211.

however useful it may earlier have been."[5] Id., p. 371. There is nothing more deserving of the label "refuse" than oil spilled into a river.

That seems to us to be the common sense of the matter. The word "refuse" includes all foreign substances and pollutants apart from those "flowing from streets and sewers and passing therefrom in a liquid state" into the watercourse.

That reading of § 13 is in keeping with the teaching of Mr. Justice Holmes that a "river is more than an amenity, it is a treasure." New Jersey v. New York, 283 U.S. 336, 342. It reads § 13 charitably as United States v. Republic Steel Corp., supra, admonished.

We pass only on the quality of the pollutant, not on the quantity of proof necessary to support a conviction nor on the question as to what *scienter* requirement of the Act imposes, as those questions are not before us in this restricted appeal.[6]

Reversed.

Mr. Justice Harlan, whom **Mr. Justice Black** and **Mr. Justice Stewart** join, dissenting.

Had the majority in judging this case been content to confine itself to applying relevant rules of law and to leave policies affecting the proper conservation of the Nation's rivers to be dealt with by the Congress, I think that today's decision in this criminal case would have eventuated differently. The best that can be said for the Government's case is that the reach of the provision of § 13 of the Rivers and Harbors Act of 1899, 30 Stat. 1152, 33 U.S.C. § 407 (1964 ed.), under which this indictment is laid, is uncertain. This calls into play the traditional rule that penal statutes are to be strictly construed. In my opinion application of that rule requires a dismissal of the indictment.

I

Section 13 forbids the deposit of all kinds of "refuse matter" into navigable rivers "other than that flowing from streets and sewers and passing therefrom in a liquid state." As the Court notes, this 1899 Act was part of a codification of prior

---

[5] The decisions in the instant case below and in United States v. The Delvalle, supra, n. 3, are against the stream of authority. An unreported decision of the United States District Court in 1922 (United States v. Crouch), holding § 13 inapplicable to polluting but nonobstructing deposits, caused the Oil Pollution Act, 1924, 43 Stat. 604, 33 U.S.C. § 431 et seq. (1964 ed.), to be passed. See S. Rep. No. 66, 68th Cong., 1st Sess.; H.R. Rep. No. 794, 68th Cong., 1st Sess. It is applicable to the discharge of oil by vessels into coastal waters but not to deposits into inland navigable waters; and it explicitly provides that it does not repeal or modify or in any manner affect other existing laws. 33 U.S.C. § 437 (1964 ed.).

[6] Having dealt with the construction placed by the court below upon the Sherman Act, our jurisdiction on this appeal is exhausted. We are not at liberty to consider other objections to the indictment or questions which may arise upon the trial with respect to the merits of the charge. For it is well settled that where the District Court has based its decision on a particular construction of the underlying statute, the review here under the Criminal Appeals Act is confined to the question of the propriety of that construction." United States v. Borden Co., 308 U.S. 188, 206-207.

statutes. This revamping was not discussed at any length on the floor of either House of Congress; the Senate was informed only that the provisions were merely a codification of existing law, without changes in substance. 32 Cong. Rec. 2296–2297 (1899). Section 13 was in fact based on two very similar prior statutes. The rivers and harbors appropriation act of 1890 provided the first national anti-obstruction provision, 26 Stat. 453:

> "Sec. 6.   That it shall not be lawful to cast, throw, empty, or unlade, or cause, suffer, or procure to be cast, thrown, emptied, or unladen either from or out of any ship, vessel, lighter, barge, boat, or other craft, or from the shore, pier, wharf, furnace, manufacturing establishments, or mills of any kind whatever, any ballast, stone, slate, gravel, earth, rubbish, wreck, filth, slabs, edgings, sawdust, slag, cinders, ashes, refuse, or other waste of any kind, into any port, road, roadstead, harbor, haven, navigable river, or navigable waters of the United States which shall tend to impede or obstruct navigation. . . ."

A later statute, § 6 of the Rivers and Harbors Act of 1894, 28 Stat. 363, provided somewhat similarly:

> "That it shall not be lawful to place, discharge, or deposit, by any process or in any manner, ballast, refuse, dirt, ashes, cinders, mud, sand, dredgings, sludge, acid, or any other matter of any kind other than that flowing from streets, sewers, and passing therefrom in a liquid state, in the waters of any harbor or river of the United States, for the improvement of which money has been appropriated by Congress. . . ."

The Court relies primarily on the latter Act, contending that its applicability to "any other matter of any kind" would surely encompass oil, even though commercially valuable. Further, the Court notes (ante, p. 198) that the 1894 statute was modeled after a federal statute of 1888 dealing with New York Harbor, 25 Stat. 209. Under this New York Harbor Act, which still remains on the books, 33 U.S.C. § 441 et seq. (1964 ed.), prosecutions for accidental deposits of commercially useful oil have been sustained. *The Colombo*, 42 F.2d 211. This background is thought to reinforce the view that oil of any type would fall within the 1894 statute's purview. Since the present enactment was intended to be merely a codification, the majority concludes that the construction of the broader 1894 predecessor should govern.

Whatever might be said about how properly to interpret the 1890 and, more especially, the 1894 statutes, it is the 1899 Act that has been on the books for the last 67 years, and its purpose and language must guide the determination of this case. To the extent that there were some differences in scope between the 1890 and 1894 Acts, these were necessarily resolved in the 1899 codification, which while embodying the essential thrust of both prior statutes, appears from its plain language to have favored the more restrictive coverage of the 1890 Act. Moreover, it is questionable to what extent the Court's speculation as to the meaning of a phrase in one of the prior statutes is relevant at all when the language of the present statute, which is penal in nature, is in itself explicit and unambiguous.

The purpose of § 13 was essentially to eliminate obstructions to navigation and interference with public works projects. This 1899 enactment, like the two preexisting statutes which it was intended to codify, was a minor section attached to a major appropriation act together with other measures dealing with sunken wrecks,[1] trespassing at public works sites,[2] and obstructions caused by improperly constructed bridges, piers, and other structures.[3] These statutes were rendered necessary primarily because navigable rivers, which the Congress was appropriating funds to improve, were being obstructed by depositing of waste materials by factories and ships.[4] It is of course true, as the Court observes, that "oil is oil," ante, p. 197, and that the accidental spillage of valuable oil may have substantially the same "deleterious effect on waterways" as the wholesale deposition of waste oil. But the relevant inquiry is not the admittedly important concerns of pollution control, but Congress' purpose in enacting this anti-obstruction act, and that appears quite plainly to be a desire to halt through the imposition of criminal penalties the depositing of obstructing refuse matter in rivers and harbors.

The Court's construction eschews the everyday meaning of "refuse matter"— waste, rubbish, trash, debris, garbage, see Webster's New International Dictionary, 3d ed.—and adopts instead an approach that either reads "refuse" out of the Act altogether, or gives to it a tortured meaning. The Court declares, at one point, that "The word 'refuse' includes all foreign substances and pollutants apart from those 'flowing from streets and sewers and passing therefrom in a liquid state' into the watercourse." Ante, p. 199. Thus, dropping anything but pure water into a river would appear to be a federal misdemeanor. At the same time, the Court also appears to endorse the Second Circuit's somewhat narrower view that "refuse matter" refers to any material, however valuable, which becomes unsalvageable when introduced into the water. Ante, p. 198-199. On this latter approach, the imposition of criminal penalties would in effect depend in each instance on a prospective estimate of salvage costs. Such strained definitions of a phrase that is clear as a matter of ordinary English hardly commend themselves, and at the very least raise serious doubts as to the intended reach of § 13.

II

Given these doubts as to the proper construction of "refuse matter" in § 13, we must reckon with a traditional canon that a penal statute will be narrowly construed. See II Hale, Historia Placitorum Coronae 335 (1736); United States v.

---

[1] Rivers and Harbors Act of 1899, § 15, 30 Stat. 1152, 33 U.S.C. § 409 (1964 ed.).
[2] Rivers and Harbors Act of 1899, § 14, 30 Stat. 1152, 33 U.S.C. § 408 (1964 ed.).
[3] Rivers and Harbors Act of 1899, § 12, 30 Stat. 1151, 33 U.S.C. § 406 (1964 ed.).
[4] Congress was presented, when considering one of the predecessors of the 1899 Act, with the representations of the Office of the Chief of Army Engineers that there has been "serious injury to navigable waters by the discharge of sawmill waste into streams. . . . In fair-ways of harbors, channels are injured from deposits of ballast, steam-boat ashes, oysters, and rubbish from passing vessels." S. Rep. No. 224, 50th Cong., 1st Sess., 2 (1888). See also H.R. Rep. No. 1826, 55th Cong., 3rd Sess., 3-4 (1899). There is no support for the proposition that these statutes were directed at "pollution" independently of "obstruction."

Wiltberger, 5 Wheat. 76, 95. The reasons underlying this maxim are various. It appears likely that the rule was originally adopted in order to spare people from the effects of exceedingly harsh penalties. See Hall, Strict or Liberal Construction of Penal Statutes, 48 Harv. L. Rev. 748, 750 (1935). Even though this rationale might be thought to have force were the defendant a natural person,[5] I cannot say that it is particularly compelling in this instance where the maximum penalty to which Standard Oil might be subject is a fine of $2,500. 33 U.S.C. § 411 (1964 ed.).

A more important contemporary purpose of the notion of strict construction is to give notice of what the law is, in order to guide people in their everyday activities. Again, however, it is difficult to justify a narrow reading of § 13 on this basis. The spilling of oil of any type into rivers is not something one would be likely to do whether or not it is legally proscribed by a federal statute. A broad construction would hardly raise dangers of penalizing people who have been inno-cently pouring valuable oil into navigable waters, for such conduct in Florida is unlawful whatever the effect of § 13. A Florida statute penalizing as a misde-meanor the depositing into waters within the State of "any rubbish, filth, or poi-sonous or deleterious substance or substances, liable to affect the health of per-sons, fish, or live stock . . .," Fla. Stat. Ann., § 387.08 (1960 ed.), quite evidently reaches the dumping of commercial oil. And Florida's nuisance law would like-wise seem to make this conduct actionable in equity. See, e.g., The Ferry Pass Inspectors' & Shippers' Assn. v. The Whites River Inspectors' & Shippers' Assn., 57 Fla. 399, 48 So. 643. Finally, as noted earlier, ante, p. 199, n. 5, prior decisions by some lower courts have held § 13 applicable to spillage of oil. For these reasons this justification for the canon of strict construction is not persuasive in this in-stance.

There is, however, a further reason for applying a seemingly straightforward statute in a straightforward way. In McBoyle v. United States, 283 U.S. 25, this Court held that a statute making it a federal crime to move a stolen "motor vehicle" in interstate commerce did not apply to a stolen airplane. That too was a case in which precise clarity was not required in order to give due warning of the line between permissible and wrongful conduct, for there could not have been any question but that stealing aircraft was unlawful. Nevertheless, Mr. Justice Holmes declared that "Although it is not likely that a criminal will carefully consider the text of the law before he murders or steals, it is reasonable that a fair warning should be given to the world in language that the common world will understand, of what the law intends to do if a certain line is passed." 283 U.S., at 27. The policy thus expressed is based primarily on a notion of fair play: in a civilized state the least that can be expected of government is that it express its rules in language all can reasonably be expected to understand. Moreover, this require-ment of clear expression is essential in a practical sense to confine the discretion of

---

[5] The *minimum* sentence for an individual convicted of violating § 13 is a fine or 30 days' imprisonment, not an insignificant penalty for accidentally dropping foreign matter into a river. 33 U.S.C. § 411 (1964 ed.).

prosecuting authorities, particularly important under a statute such as § 13 which imposes criminal penalties with a minimal, if any, *scienter* requirement.[6]

In an area in which state or local law has traditionally regulated primary activity,[7] there is good reason to restrict federal penal legislation within the confines of its language. If the Federal Government finds that there is sufficient obstruction or pollution of navigable waters caused by the introduction of commercial oil or other nonrefuse material, it is an easy matter to enact appropriate regulatory or penal legislation.[8] Such legislation can be directed at specific types of pollution, and the remedies devised carefully to ensure compliance. Indeed, such a statute was enacted in 1924 to deal with oil pollution in coastal waters caused by vessels, 43 Stat. 605, 33 U.S.C. §§ 433, 434 (1964 ed.).

To conclude that this attempted prosecution cannot stand is not to be oblivious to the importance of preserving the beauties and utility of the country's rivers. It is simply to take the statute as we find it. I would affirm the judgment of the District Court.

QUESTIONS FOR DISCUSSION

1 Is the decision of the majority supported by a fair reading of the language of the act? Its legislative history?

2 Is such a construction of criminal statutes sound?

3 Is it within the proper judicial role for a court to construe a statute designed to protect navigation as a pollution-control measure? Should this be a legislative function? Should a court act if the legislature fails to do so? Suppose Congress has looked at the question and has been unwilling or unable to act?

4 Does the court's construction of "refuse" give it a "tortured meaning"? Would the majority argument be stronger had the oil been intentionally dumped?

5 Should criminal responsibility be imposed for accidental occurrences? Was this the purpose of the act?

6 Can you agree with the dissenters' comment that "it would be an easy matter to enact appropriate regulatory or panel legislation" to remedy this problem?

---

[6] The parties were not in agreement as to what *scienter* requirement the statute imposes. This question is not before us under the restricted jurisdiction granted to this Court under 18 U.S.C. § 3731 (1964 ed.), see United States v. Petrillo, 332 U.S. 1; United States v. Borden Co., 308 U.S. 188, and the Court today intimates no views on the question.

[7] Besides the Florida pollution adverted to earlier, Fla. Stat. Ann., § 387.08 (1960 ed.), the city of Jacksonville has enacted ordinances dealing generally with fire prevention, Jacksonville Ordinance Code §§ 19-4.1 to 19-4.24 (1958 Supp.), and pollution of the city water supply, § 27-52 (1953 Code).

[8] See, e.g., special message of the President dealing with new anti-pollution legislation, Preservation of Our Natural Heritage—Message from the President of the United States, H. Doc. No. 387, 89th Cong., 2d Sess., Cong. Rec., Feb. 23, 1966, pp. 3519-3522.

SECTION 13 AND NEPA

In 1971 the case of *Kalur v. Resor*[l] precipitated major changes in Section 13 procedures. In that case, the Corps of Engineers was held responsible for meeting the NEPA requirement of an environmental impact statement when issuing Section 13 permits. The Corps's argument that it was an agency dedicated to guarding the environment and that therefore the provisions and purposes of NEPA do not rationally apply to it was rejected, the court noting that NEPA applies to "all agencies," and that there were no specific statutory obligations preventing the Corps from complying with the letter of the statute. Further, the court said that water-quality certifications under the Water Quality Improvement Act establish a minimum condition for granting a license and that the Corps could then go on to perform the very different operation of balancing the overall costs and benefits of a particular proposed project, and consider alterations above and beyond the applicable water-quality standards that would further reduce environmental damage.

Thus, the court enjoined the joint Corps-EPA permit program which gave EPA the final authority on questions of water quality while limiting the Corps's concern to impacts on navigation.

The response of the Corps of Engineers to the decision in *Kalur v. Resor* was to refuse to issue any further Refuse Act permits. In 1972 Congress responded by amending the Federal Water Pollution Control Act to shift the permit function to EPA and to exempt the issuance of permits to existing industrial sources from NEPA impact statement requirements.

The Refuse Act may, however, still be of significance in the case of nonpoint sources.[m]

FEDERAL WATER POLLUTION CONTROL ACT (FWPCA): EVOLUTION AND SUBSTANCE

Before the enactment of the Federal Water Pollution Control Act of 1948 (FWPCA), the involvement of Congress in the field of water-pollution control was centered in the substance of three acts: the Refuse Act of 1899, which prohibited the discharge of refuse into navigable waters; the Public Health Service Act of 1912, which provided for investigations of water pollutants which caused disease in human beings; and the Oil Pollution Act of 1924, which prohibited the discharge of oil in coastal waters.[n]

The FWPCA, as passed in 1948, authorized the Surgeon General of the U.S. Public Health Service to make studies of waterborne pollution sources, the setting of standards for water quality and desired uses, and established programs for state and federal cooperation in water-basin pollution problems. However, Congress made it clear that primary responsibility for pollution con-

[l] 335 F. Supp. 1 (1971).

[m] See *NRDC v. Grant*, 355 F. Supp. 280 (1973).

[n] See P. Micklin, "Water Quality: A Question of Standards," in Richard A. Cooley and Geoffrey Wandesforde-Smith (eds.), *Congress and the Environment,* University of Washington Press, Seattle, 1970, p. 131.

trol rested with the states, with the federal government placed in the role of adviser. The original legislation was limited to a five-year period and was extended for an additional three years until 1956. In 1956, Congress passed the Federal Water Pollution Control Act Amendments, which strengthened and made permanent the original act of 1948. Although the amendments contained explicit federal-state enforcement procedures, the procedures themselves were bureaucratically intricate and time-consuming, containing provisions for hearings and delayed rehearings without providing for positive action. The preexisting program of loans was revised to provide outright grants for the construction of much-needed municipal waste-treatment facilities. Nevertheless, the impact of federal water-pollution control upon the states was minimal:

> Only a few states developed comprehensive pollution control programs, and those that had water quality standards failed to enforce them. The states seldom asked the Federal Government's help in establishing such standards, and, in light of the extent of the pollution problem, they requested surprisingly little Federal aid in enforcing pollution abatement (ten suits between 1948 and 1963). A parade of witnesses at the field hearings of the Senate Select Committee on National Water Resources held from October, 1959, through May, 1960, in twenty-two states convincingly pointed out numerous failures of the water pollution control program.[o]

Congress subsequently passed the Federal Water Pollution Control Act Amendments of 1961, which expanded the act's application from interstate waters to include all navigable waters. Previously, federal authority had been limited to water pollution which endangered lives in a state other than the state in which the pollution originated.

In 1965, Congress amended the FWPCA by enacting the Water Quality Act of 1965. Although the lengthy conference and hearing procedures were not substantially altered, an alternative method of pollution abatement was established. The amendment, while reinforcing the states' primary responsibility for implementation and enforcement of water-quality standards, provided for federal action if the states failed to act. The states were required to set water-quality standards for interstate waters within their boundaries, taking into consideration the value and use of such waters. If the states failed to set adequate water standards, the Secretary of Health, Education, and Welfare was authorized to establish such standards. Discharge of matter into interstate waters or their tributaries which reduced the quality below set standards was made subject to federal abatement procedures.

In passing the Clean Water Restoration Act of 1966, which further amended the FWPCA, Congress made two important changes concerning conference and hearing procedures. The Secretary of State and Administrator of the FWPCA—now the Administrator of the Environmental Protection Agency (EPA)—was authorized to invoke conference and hearing procedures of the FWPCA when pollution originating in the United States may endanger the health and welfare of persons in a foreign country. The second important aspect of the Water Restoration Act was that it authorized the Administrator of the EPA to require reports from alleged polluters, based on existing informa-

[o] Micklin. op. cit., p. 132.

tion concerning the "character, kind and quantity" of discharges and the means being used to prevent them.

The Water Quality Improvement Act of 1970 (WQIA) repealed the Oil Pollution Act of 1924 and added several new sections to the FWPCA dealing specifically with mine water pollution, pollution by hazardous substances other than oil, sewage discharge from vessels, and pollution control in Alaska and the Great Lakes. Subsequent sections require federal interagency cooperation concerning water-pollution control and provide for federal-state cooperation in controlling water pollution originating from federally owned and operated installations.

The present stage of the evolution of the federal water-pollution control program is embodied in the Federal Water Pollution Control Act (FWPCA) as amended in 1972.[p] The FWPCA has three principal foci: the regulation of point-source[q] discharges of pollutants, the control of spills of oil and hazardous substances, and financial assistance for the construction of municipal sewage-treatment facilities. These, along with regulation of vessel sewage and the disposal of dredge spoil, are the elements of the program designed to meet the "national goal that the discharge of pollutants into the navigable waters be eliminated by 1985."[r]

The FWPCA imposes two sets of requirements on direct discharges of pollutants.

Effluent standards regulate the amount of a pollutant that can be discharged per unit of time. These limitations are on discharges of particular types of pollutants and are based largely on the availability of technology. Thus, existing dischargers, except publicly owned sewage-treatment plants, must utilize the "best practicable control technology currently available" by July 1, 1977. By July 1, 1983, the "best available technology economically achievable" must be used. Existing publicly owned treatment facilities are required to adopt secondary treatment and the "best practicable waste treatment technology" by July 1, 1983.

The FWPCA also requires the Administrator of the EPA to set effluent standards for toxic pollutants,[s] based on their environmental effects. Standards for toxic pollutants must be set "at that level which the Administrator determines provides an ample margin of safety." The statute also provides that the standard for toxics may be a "prohibition" in line with the "national policy that the discharge of toxic pollutants in toxic amounts be prohibited."

Regulation of thermal pollution represents a reversal of the general FWPCA theme of uniform standards and instead utilizes a case-by-case approach. Thus, effluent standards for thermal wastes may be eased on a showing by the facility operator that a lesser degree of environmental protection is adequate.

---

[p] 33 U.S.C. §§ 1251 et seq.; see *United States v. Holland*, page 207, for a discussion of what waters are included within the scope of the act.

[q] The line between a point and a nonpoint source may not be easy to distinguish. Section 208 of the act (33 U.S.C. § 1288) attempts to deal with nonpoint sources and requires that the states establish regulatory programs to deal with the problem. There are no substantive requirements governing how the states are to do so. The weakness of the FWPCA in this regard may reflect the feelings that federal regulation of nonpoint sources is impossible.

[r] 33 U.S.C. § 1251(a)(1); FWPCA § 101(a)(1).

[s] 33 U.S.C. § 1317(a); FWPCA § 307(a).

All statutory phrases are defined by guidelines issued by the Environmental Protection Agency.

Water-quality standards mandated by the FWPCA define required water quality for ambient water. The standards are based upon data as to the minimum requirements to sustain the various uses to which particular bodies of water are put. The standards for ambient water quality are promulgated by the states for approval by EPA, and if they are disapproved, federal standards are drafted.

Direct dischargers of pollutants are required to comply with the stricter of the water-quality or effluent regulations.

Oil and hazardous substances are subject to a separate regulatory program. The EPA maintains a listing of hazardous substances and has promulgated a definition of "harmful discharge." The act requires that, in the event of a spill, the offender notify the EPA or Coast Guard and imposes cleanup costs on the discharger within limits.

The provisions of the FWPCA regarding vessel sewage require the drafting of standards for "marine sanitation devices," and the dredge spoil provisions establish a separate permit system for spoil disposal sites to be administered by the Army Corps of Engineers subject to EPA guidelines.

The basic enforcement mechanism of the FWPCA is a permit system which serves to define the discharger's obligations under the act. The Environmental Protection Agency is charged with the administration of the permit system although a state "desiring to administer its own permit program" may do so subject to EPA approval of its program. The FWPCA also requires that applicants for federal permits obtain a certification from the state, thus allowing the states to set water-quality standards more stringent than those of the federal program.

In *United States v. Holland* the expansive scope and reach of the FWPCA is illustrated, and the power and desire to attack water pollution at its source are verified. Examine with care the court's interpretation of the legislative history with respect to the "navigability" requirement.

United States v. Holland

373 F. Supp. 665 (1974)

MEMORANDUM OPINION

Krentzman, District Judge.

This is an action brought by the United States to enjoin allegedly unlawful landfilling operations in an area known as Harbor Isle, adjoining Papy's Bayou, St. Petersburg, Florida. The government contends that the defendants have begun filling the waters of the bayou with sand, dirt, dredged spoil and biological materials without the permits required by 33 U.S.C. §§ 403, 407 and 1311(a). For relief the government requests a stoppage of further filling and a restoration of some mangrove wetland.

A hearing was held on December 21, 1973, to consider the government's motion for a temporary restraining order. After considering the evidence and argument of both parties the motion was granted. On December 26th the temporary restraining order was extended in full force pending further hearings.

On January 9, 1974, plaintiff's motion for preliminary injunction was heard. At that proceeding the following were established to the Court's satisfaction:

1 Defendants are engaged in developing a 281 acre tract of land known as Harbor Isle.

2 For the purposes of the preliminary injunction hearing the Court accepted defendant's determination that the mean high water line is one foot above sea level.

3 Tide data, visual observation and classification of vegetation established that a substantial number of tides exceed two feet above sea level.

(a)   The United States Geological Survey tide gauge data indicated that 50–100 tides exceed two feet in the subject waters each year.

4 The parties stipulated to the accuracy of a land survey introduced by defendants. The survey and other evidence established that:

(a)   Most of the property is interlaced with artificial mosquito canals containing water.

(b)   The water in the mosquito canals is connected to Papy's Bayou.

(c)   The elevation of much of the property is less than two feet.

5 Without a permit issued under authority of Title 33, United States Code, Sections 407 and 1344, defendants have discharged sand, dirt, dredged spoil and biological materials into the man-made canals and into mangrove wetlands which are periodically inundated by tides exceeding two feet above sea level.

6 Defendants would continue to discharge sand, dirt, dredged spoil and biological materials until the fill created has effectively displaced tidal waters, thereby eliminating the normal ebb and flow of tides over the subject property.

7 Continued discharge would result in irreparable injury, loss and damage to the aquatic ecosystem of Papy's Bayou and to the commercial and sport fisheries which are dependent upon the estuaries of the Gulf of Mexico.

The Court felt these facts established acts of sufficient scope to warrant federal jurisdiction under the Federal Water Pollution Control Act, and of sufficient magnitude to justify a preliminary injunction. The motion for such an injunction was granted at the hearing. A brief order of injunction and findings was signed January 11, 1974.

Since the courts have not yet been faced with the question of whether federal jurisdiction over water pollution encompasses intertidal wetlands by virtue of the relatively new Federal Water Pollution Control Act Amendments of 1972, 33 U.S.C. § 1251 et seq., this opinion will offer the rationale for the grant of jurisdiction.

The Federal Water Pollution Control Act Amendments of 1972

The government charged the defendants with past and continuing violations of Section 301(a) of the Federal Water Pollution Control Act Amendments of 1972 (FWPCA).[1] To sustain this allegation two showings had to be made. First it had to be established that the defendants' acts were such as to be prohibited if done in waters within federal jurisdiction, and second, that the waters receiving the impact of the prohibited conduct were indeed within that jurisdictional ambit.

Prohibited Activities

The FWPCA is an admirably comprehensive piece of legislation. It was designed to deal with all facets of recapturing and preserving the biological integrity of the nation's water by creating a web of complex interrelated regulatory programs. Section 301(a), the enforcement hub of the statute, however, is stated very simply. It provides that except as otherwise permitted within the Act "the discharge of any pollutant by any person shall be unlawful."[2] The plainness of the prohibition is matched by the breadth given the definition of a "discharge of a pollutant."

> (A) Any addition of any pollutant to navigable waters from any point source,
> (B) Any addition of any pollutant to the waters of the contiguous zone or the ocean from any point source . . . other than a vessel or other floating craft. 33 U.S.C. § 1362(12).

"Pollutant" is in turn defined as

> . . . *Dredged spoil,* solid waste, incinerator residue, sewage, garbage, sewer sludge, munitions, chemical wastes, *biological materials,* radio-active materials, heat, wrecked or discarded equipment, rock, *sand,* cellar dirt and *industrial,* municipal, and agricultural waste discharged into water. . . . Id. § 1362(6) (emphasis added)

and "point source" is

> . . . any discernible, confined and discrete conveyance, *including* but not limited to any *pipe, ditch,* channel, tunnel, conduit, well, discrete fissure, container, *rolling stock,* concentrated animal feeding operation, or vessel or other floating craft, from which pollutants are or may be discharged. Id. § 1362(14) (emphasis added)

The evidence substantiates the defendant's admission that without a permit they have discharged and would continue to discharge from point sources, including dump trucks, drag lines, and bulldozers, materials defined as pollutants. Whether these pollutants were discharged into waters within federal jurisdiction was the key issue.

Jurisdiction Under the FWPCA

Throughout the course of this litigation there has been considerable discussion about whether the mosquito ditches that connect with Papy's Bayou are "naviga-

---

[1] 33 U.S.C. §§ 1151–1160.
[2] Id. § 1311(a).

ble" and much testimony about whether certain discharges of pollutants were above or below the "mean high water line." Argument was heard on the issue of whether federal jurisdiction under the FWPCA was limited to activities taking place in navigable waters below the mean high water line. Because the terms "navigability" and "mean high water line" have played such important parts in determining federal jurisdiction over water pollution in the past, the contention that these terms should be used in arguing jurisdiction under the FWPCA was not surprising.

For years the mainstays of the federal water pollution effort were Sections 10 and 13 of Rivers and Harbors Act of 1899.[3] Section 10 makes it illegal to fill, excavate, alter or modify the course, condition or capacity of waters within the boundaries of a navigable waterway without authorization from the Corps of Engineers. Section 13 prohibits the deposit of refuse in, or on the bank of, a navigable waterway without a Corps of Engineers' permit. Both of these laws are deemed navigable. Because of this limitation past discussion of federal jurisdiction over water pollution was largely a question of the navigability of the waterway being affected.

Why the Congress limited the Rivers and Harbors Act to navigable waters is no insoluble mystery. Although the Constitution does not mention navigable waters, it vests in Congress the power to "regulate commerce with foreign nations and among the several states."[4] Since much of the interstate commerce of the 19th century was water borne, it was early held that the commerce power necessarily included the power to regulate navigation. Gibbons v. Ogden, 9 Wheat. 1, 22 U.S. 1, 6 L. Ed. 23 (1824). See also Hall v. DeCuir, 95 U.S. 485, 24 L. Ed. 547 (1877); Veazie v. Moor, 14 How. 568, 55 U.S. 568, 14 L. Ed. 545 (1852); Norris v. City of Boston, 48 U.S. (7 How.) 282 (1849). To make this control effective Congress was deemed empowered to keep navigable waters open and free and to provide sanctions for interference. See, e.g., Gilman v. Philadelphia, 3 Wall., 713, 70 U.S. 713, 18 L. Ed. 96 (1865). The Rivers and Harbors Act of 1899 was an exercise of that power.

Whether Congressional power in 1899 was limited by judicial interpretation to navigable waters is now only of historical significance. At the time of the Act's passage, "commerce" was still nearly synonymous with "transportation"[5] and the term "interstate" was largely used in a geographical sense.[6] The extant case law

---

[3] 33 U.S.C. §§ 403, 407.

[4] U.S. Const. art. I, § 3.

[5] See United States v. E. C. Knight, 156 U.S. 1, 15 S. Ct. 249, 39 L. Ed. 325 (1895). See also Schechter Corp. v. United States, 295 U.S. 495, 55 S. Ct. 837, 79 L. Ed. 1570 (1935); Brooks v. United States, 267 U.S. 432, 45 S. Ct. 345, 69 L. Ed. 699 (1925); James Clark Dist. Co. v. Western Md. Co., 242 U.S. 311, 37 S. Ct. 180, 61 L. Ed. 326 (1915); Internat'l Textbook v. Pigg, 217 U.S. 91, 30 S. Ct. 481, 54 L. Ed. 678 (1910).

[6] See, e.g., Carter v. Carter Coal Co., 298 U.S. 238, 56 S. Ct. 855, 80 L. Ed. 1160 (1936); United States v. Butler, 297 U.S. 1, 56 S. Ct. 312, 80 L. Ed. 477 (1936); Oliver Iron v. Lord, 262 U.S. 172, 45 S. Ct. 526, 67 L. Ed. 929 (1923); Hanley v. Kansas City Ry., 187 U.S. 617, 23 S. Ct. 214, 47 L. Ed. 333 (1903).

relied upon the tenth amendment as a restraint upon the federal commerce power. The effects intrastate activity might have on commerce outside the state was of little concern. See Oliver Iron v. Lord, 262 U.S. 172, 43 S. Ct. 526, 67 L. Ed. 929 (1923); Hammer v. Dagenhart, 247 U.S. 251, 38 S. Ct. 529, 62 L. Ed. 1101 (1918).

Although the reach of federal power under the commerce clause widened dramatically in the twentieth century, the nineteenth century legacy of "navigation" lingered to limit federal control over water pollution. Since Congress had clearly limited the Rivers and Harbors Act to navigation, any subsequent judicial broadening of jurisdiction under the statute of necessity had to be in the form of expanding the definition of "navigability."

Starting with the basic definition of waters that

> . . . form in their ordinary condition by themselves, or by uniting with other waters, a continued highway over which commerce is or may be carried on with other States or foreign countries in the customary modes in which such commerce is conducted by water. (The Daniel Ball, 10 Wall. 557, 77 U.S. 557, 19 L. Ed. 999 (1870).

the test of navigability was enlarged in 1874 to embrace waters that had the capability of commercial use, not merely those in actual use.[7] The definition was again expanded in 1921 to bring in waterbodies whose past history of commercial use made it navigable despite subsequent physical or economic changes preventing present use for commerce.[8] In 1940 it was held that a waterway would be deemed navigable-in-fact if by "reasonable improvements" it could be made navigable.[9] Thus the jurisdictional basis broadened until only the most insignificant body of water could escape one of the tests of navigability.

But the limitation of navigability still worked to impede efforts to forestall the degradation of the aquatic environment. Not only did small feeder streams and tributaries remain exempt from federal jurisdiction but, more importantly, the wetland areas adjoining the waterways did also.[10]

Just as it was not surprising that Congress limited the Rivers and Harbors Act to navigable waters, it was not surprising to have limited enforcement under the statute to navigation-impeding activities taking place in the water. Those charged with enforcing the Act needed an easily discernible boundary for their jurisdictional power—i.e. the lateral extent of the waterbody. In tidal areas that boundary became the mean high water line.

The Mean High Water Line

Since the Rivers and Harbors Act was passed at a time when interstate commerce was thought of in a geographical sense, and since the Act was designed primarily to keep the navigable waters free of physical impediments, it was natural to draw

[7] The Montello, 20 Wall. 430, 441–442, 87 U.S. 430, 22 L. Ed. 391 (1974).

[8] Economy Light & Power Co. v. United States, 256 U.S. 113, 41 S. Ct. 409, 65 L. Ed. 847 (1921).

[9] United States v. Appalachian Electric Power Co., 311 U.S. 377, 61 S. Ct. 291, 85 L. Ed. 243 (1940); See, e.g., Puente de Reynosa, S.A. v. City of McAllen, 357 F.2d 43 (5 Cir. 1966); United States v. Underwood, 344 F. Supp. 486 (M.D. Fla. 1972).

[10] See, e.g., United States v. Cannon, 363 F. Supp. 1045 (D. Del. 1973); Hoyer, Corps of Engineers Dredge and Fill Jurisdiction: Buttressing a Citadel Under Siege, 26 U. Fla. L. Rev. 19 (1973).

on the property-law concept of the mean high water line to limit the scope of jurisdiction in tidal water areas. If an agency is responsible only for keeping a water body free of obstructions, there is little need to focus attention on activities beyond the ordinary reach of the water.

But because the mean high water line was, and is, used to demarcate authority in tidal zones does not necessarily mean that the line is an inviolate barrier to federal assumption of authority over activities landward of the line. Examining the history and use of the line underscores the point.

At common law the ordinary high tide marked the boundary between private and sovereign lands.[11] In Attorney General v. Chambers, 4 De G.M. & G. 206 (1854), Lord Chancellor Cranworth, citing Lord Hale's treatise De Jure Maris, rejected the ordinary high water line in favor of the line formed by the medium high tide between the spring and neap tides. The court decided that the upland owner should be entitled to so much of the land as is "for the most part of the year dry and maniorable." Id. at 214–15.

The United States Supreme Court in Borax Consolidated, Ltd. v. Los Angeles, 296 U.S. 10, 56 S. Ct. 23, 80 L. Ed. 9 (1935), cited Chambers when it adopted the similar "mean high water" line as the limit of a federal land grant. Borax became a landmark case in the law of tidal boundaries. And even though the test used by the Supreme Court was enunciated to settle a land dispute, and notwithstanding the fact that the test derived from an English court's desire to preserve to property owners so much of the land as is "dry and maniorable", the test of the mean high water mark became the inveterate standard to be applied in limiting federal authority over navigable waters. Courts were justified in relying on a rule of common law which did no harm to the purposes of the statutes in question. The need to protect the navigable capacity of a waterway above the mean high water line was obviously minimal.

If the instant case involved only the question of federal jurisdiction over non-navigable streams and wetland areas under the Rivers and Harbors Act the Court might be compelled to deny jurisdiction by the sheer weight of precedent. But such is not the case. Here the Court is presented with a dispute brought pursuant to a new federal law not limited to the traditional tests of navigability.

On October 18, 1972, the Congress exercised its power under the commerce clause by enacting the FWPCA, establishing regulatory programs to combat pollution of the nation's waters. Even though it seems certain that Congress sought to broaden federal jurisdiction under the Act, it did so in a manner that appears calculated to force courts to engage in verbal acrobatics. Although using the term "navigable waters" in the prohibitory phase of the statute, the definition of "navigable waters" is stated to be "waters of the United States, including the territorial seas." 33 U.S.C. § 1362(7). The definition stands with no limiting language.

If indeed the Congress saw fit to define away the navigability restriction, the sole limitation on the reach of federal power remaining would be the commerce

---

[11] See generally F. Maloney, S. Player & F. Baldwin, Water Law and Administration: The Florida Experience 67 (1968); Gay, The High Water Mark: Boundary Between Public and Private Lands, 18 U. Fla. L. Rev. 553 (1966).

clause. Thus two questions emerge. Did Congress intend to define away the old "navigability" restriction? And does the Congress have such power?

The answer to the first question is in the affirmative. The Court is of the opinion that the clear meaning of the statutory definition may be ascertained on its face without having to rely on the well established judicial philosophy that "forbids a narrow, cramped reading" of water pollution legislation. United States v. Ashland Oil and Transportation Co., 364 F. Supp. 349, 350 (W.D. Ky. 1973). See United States v. Standard Oil Co., 384 U.S. 224, 226 (1966); United States v. Republic Steel Corp., 362 U.S. 482, 491 (1960). The legislative history of the FWPCA supports this clear meaning.

The bill submitted to the Senate as S. 2770 defined "navigable waters" to mean "navigable waters of the United States, portions thereof, and the tributaries thereof, including the territorial seas and the Great Lakes." Legislative History of the Water Pollution Control Act Amendments of 1972, Vol. 2, p. 1698 (hereinafter cited as "Legislative History"). The report of the Senate Committee on Public Works submitted with S. 2770 explained the definition:

> The control strategy of the Act extends to navigable waters. The definition of this term means the navigable waters of the United States, portions thereof, tributaries thereof, and includes the territorial seas and the Great Lakes. Through narrow interpretation of the definition of interstate waters the implementation (of the) 1965 Act was severely limited. Water moves in hydrologic cycles and *it is essential that discharge of pollutants be controlled at the source.* Therefore, reference to the control requirements must be made to the navigable waters, portions thereof, and their tributaries. Legislative History, Vol. 2, p. 1495. (emphasis added)

The House of Representatives bill, H.R. 11896, contained a more restrictive definition: "The navigable waters of the United States, including the territorial seas." Legislative History, Vol. 1, p. 1069. Significantly, when the two bills went to the Committee of Conference, the word "navigable" was deleted from the House definition in creating the final standard. The reason for this change was stated in the Joint Explanatory Statement of the Committee of Conference:

> "The conferees fully intend that the term 'navigable waters' be given the broadest possible constitutional interpretation unencumbered by agency determinations which have been made or may be made for administrative purposes." Conference Report, Senate Report No. 92-1236, Sept. 28, 1972, page 144, U.S. Code Cong. & Admin. News 1972, p. 3822; Reprinted in Legislative History, Vol. 1, p. 327.

In presenting the Conference version to the House, Representative Dingell, a member of the Conference Committee, explained the Committee's intention on jurisdiction:

> "The Conference bill defined the term 'navigable waters' broadly for water quality purposes. (502(7)). It means 'all the waters of the United States' in a geographic sense. It does not mean 'navigable waters of the United States' in the technical sense as we sometimes see in some laws." Legislative History, Vol. 1, p. 250.

After a brief discussion of Court cases in which the judiciary has forced some expansion of the old navigability test for water quality purposes, Representative Dingell concluded:

> "Thus, this new definition clearly encompasses all water bodies, including main streams and their tributaries, for water quality purposes. No longer are the old, narrow definitions of navigability, as determined by the Corps of Engineers, going to govern matters covered by this bill. Id."

The foregoing compels the Court to conclude that the former test of navigability was indeed defined away in the FWPCA. The Court in United States v. Ashland Oil and Transportation Co., 364 F. Supp. 349 (W.D. Ky. 1973) reached the same conclusion when faced with a criminal prosecution brought under the Act. In Ashland the Government charged the defendant under Section 311(b)(5) for failing to notify the appropriate federal agency after gaining knowledge that it had discharged oil into a non-navigable stream. The defendant argued that the FWPCA applies only to classical navigable waters of the United States and that therefore the notification requirements of the FWPCA did not apply to the discharge. Chief Judge Gordon disagreed with defendant's interpretation, stating:

> "To determine the clear meaning of the questioned criminal provision, one need go no further than the definitions provided in the Act. Congress defined 'navigable waters' as 'waters of the United States.' [33 U.S.C. § 1362(7)]. To determine whether an oil discharge has entered waters regulated by Section 311 of the Act, a citizen simply inserts the statutory definition in place of the term 'navigable waters.' That navigable waters is sometimes followed by a prepositional phrase does not alter this obvious result except perhaps to emphasize the inclusion of the waters of all the geographic areas listed in the definition of 'United States.' [Section 311(b)(5) of the Act; 33 U.S.C. Section 1321(b)(5)." Id. 364 F. Supp. at 350.]

> *   *   *   *   *   *   *   *   *   *   *   *   *   *   *

> "Navigability is not an element of this offense as it is excluded from the Act by definition. 33 U.S.C. § 1362(7)" Id. 364 F. Supp. at 351.

This Court agrees.

Clearly Congress has the power to eliminate the "navigability" limitation from the reach of federal control under the Commerce Clause. The "geographic" and "transportation" conception of the Commerce Clause which may have placed the navigation restriction in the Rivers and Harbors Act of 1899 has long since been abandoned in defining federal power. Now when courts are forced with a challenge to congressional power under the Commerce Clause a statute's validity is upheld by determining first if the general activity sought to be regulated is reasonably related to, or has an effect on, interstate commerce and, second, whether the specific activities in the case before the court are those intended to be reached by Congress through the statute. Perez v. United States, 402 U.S. 146, 91 S. Ct. 1357, 28 L. Ed. 2d 686 (1970); Katzenbach v. McClung, 379 U.S. 294, 85 S. Ct. 377, 13 L. Ed. 2d 290 (1964); Heart of Atlanta Motel, Inc. v. United States,

379 U.S. 241, 85 S. Ct. 348, 13 L. Ed. 2d 258 (1964); United States v. Darby, 312 U.S. 100, 61 S. Ct. 451, 85 L. Ed. 609 (1941).

It is beyond question that water pollution has a serious effect on interstate commerce and that the Congress has the power to regulate activities such as dredging and filling which cause such pollution. As stated by the Court in Zabel v. Tabb, 430 F.2d 199, 203 (5 Cir. 1970):

> "[T]he nation knows, if the Courts do not, that the destruction of fish and wildlife in our estuarine waters does have a substantial effect on interstate commerce . . . Nor is it challenged that dredge and fill projects are activities which may tend to destroy the ecological balance and thereby affect commerce substantially."

Congress and the courts have become aware of the lethal effect pollution has on all organisms. Weakening any of the life support systems bodes disaster for the rest of the interrelated life forms.[12] To recognize this and yet hold that pollution does not affect interstate commerce unless committed in navigable waters below the mean high water line would be contrary to reason. Congress is not limited by the "navigable waters" test in its authority to control pollution under the Commerce Clause.

Having thus ascertained that Congress had the power to go beyond the "navigability" limitation in its control over water pollution and that it intended to do so in the FWPCA, the question remains whether the Congress intended to reach the type of activities involved in the instant case—the pollution of non-navigable mosquito canals and mangrove wetland areas.

As previously noted the defendants without a permit have filled and otherwise polluted various mosquito canals which connected with the waters of Papy's Bayou. The manmade canals were found to be non-navigable for the purposes of this action.

The conclusion that Congress intended to reach water-bodies such as these canals with the FWPCA is inescapable. The legislative history quoted supra manifests a clear intent to break from the limitations of the Rivers and Harbors Act to get at the sources of pollution. Polluting canals that empty into a bayou arm of Tampa Bay is clearly an activity Congress sought to regulate.[13] The fact that these canals were manmade makes no difference. They were constructed long before the development scheme was conceived. That the defendants used them to convey the pollutants without a permit is the matter of importance.

The Court is of the opinion that the waters of the mosquito canals were within definition of "waters of the United States" and that the filling of them without a permit was a violation of the FWPCA.

Whether the FWPCA was meant to reach activities such as those committed here in mangrove wetlands above the mean high water line is slightly less apparent. An examination of Congressional intent, however, leads this Court to the conclusion that such intertidal wetlands were indeed meant to be covered.

---

[12] See Little, New Attitudes about Legal Protection for Remains of Florida's Natural Environment, 23 U. Fla. L. Rev. 459, 462 (1971).

[13] United States v. Ashland Oil and Transportation Co., supra.

The first glimpse of Congressional intent comes from the FWPCA itself. Section 101(a) puts forth the purpose of the Act:

"The objective of this Act is to restore and maintain the chemical, physical, and biological integrity of the Nation's waters. In order to achieve this objective it is hereby declared that, consistent with the provisions of this Act—

(1) It is the national goal that the discharge of pollutants into the navigable waters be eliminated by 1985;

(2) It is the national goal that wherever attainable, an interim goal of water quality which provides for the protection and propagation of fish, shellfish, and wildlife and provides for recreation in and on the water be achieved by July 1, 1983." 33 U.S.C. § 1251(a).

In Section 102(c) the Administrator of the Environmental Protection Agency is authorized to make grants for basin studies to provide comprehensive water quality control plans for a basin. "Basin" in that section is defined to include "rivers and their tributaries, streams, coastal waters, sounds, estuaries, bays, lakes, and portions thereof, as well as the lands drained thereby." 33 U.S.C. § 1252(c).

Section 404 of the Act establishes a program for permitting the discharge of dredge or fill materials into waters of the United States. Subsection (c) provides for careful consideration of whether or not such discharges will have "unacceptable adverse effect on municipal water supplies, shellfish beds, and fishery areas (including spawning and breeding areas), wildlife, or recreational areas." 33 U.S.C. § 1344(c).

These three sections do not by themselves prove conclusively that Congress sought to assume jurisdiction over activities taking place in wetlands above the mean high water line. What these sections do reveal is a sensitivity to the value of a coastal breeding ground.[14] Composed of various interdependent ecological systems (i.e. marshes, mudflats, shallow open water, mud and sand bottoms, beach and dunes) the delicately balanced coastal environment is highly sensitive to human activities within its confines. See Cooper, Ecological Considerations, Coastal Zone Management 129 (J. Hite & J. Stepp ed. 1971).

---

[14] An ancillary statement of intent is found in the Coastal Zone Management Act of 1972, 16 U.S.C. § 1451 which articulated the intent of Congress to preserve and protect the resources of the Coastal Zone.

The term "coastal zone" is defined as:

". . . the coastal waters (including the lands therein and thereunder) and the adjacent shorelines (including the waters therein and thereunder), strongly influenced by each other and in proximity to the shorelines of the several coastal states, and includes *transitional and intertidal areas, salt marshes, and wetlands* and beaches. . . . The zone extends inland from the shorelines only to the extent necessary to control shorelines, the use of which have a direct and significant impact on the coastal waters. . . ." 16 U.S.C. 1453(a). (emphasis added).

In Section 302 of the Act, Congress made the following findings:

"(a) There is a *national interest* in the effective management, beneficial use, *protection,* and *development* of the coastal zone.

"(b) The coastal zone is rich in a variety of . . . resources of immediate and potential value to the present and future *well-being of the Nation;*

"(c) The *increasing* and competing *demands* upon the lands and *waters* of our coastal zone occasioned by . . . economic development, including requirements for . . . *residential developments* . . .

Congress realizes the coastal ecology is endangered by poorly planned development. It cannot be gainsaid that the discharge of pollutants into coastal, estuarine and adjacent waters have caused considerable damage to the marine environment. Estuaries, partially enclosed bodies of water within which there is a measurable dilution of sea water by fresh-water run off, and other breeding zones have suffered the most damage. Salt water marshes and other wetlands constitute a major component of the estuarine system.

Estuaries are not only highly productive in organic matter, but also are valuable in replenishing oxygen for the atmosphere. See Teclaff, The Coastal Zone—Control over Encroachments into the Tidewaters, 2 Environ. L. Rev. 618 (1971). Moreover, estuaries are vital to fish and shellfish. About two-thirds of all ocean animals either spend a part of their life there or feed upon a species that has lived there. The First Annual Report of the Council on Environmental Quality, 176 (1970). The FWPCA embodies the realization that pollution of these areas may be ecologically fatal.

In an attempt to combat these threats to the coastal environment, the Congress broadened its jurisdiction to encompass "all waters of the United States." In doing so Congress deemed it "essential that the discharge of pollutants be controlled *at the source.*" Legislative History Vol. 2, p. 1495. Getting at the source of pollution is going beyond the confines of a high water line. It cannot be doubted that most of the damage to marine life results from land-based and not sea-based activities.

One of the sources of pollution in the instant case was the discharge of sand, dirt and dredged spoil on land which although above the mean high water line, was periodically inundated with the waters of Papy's Bayou. Defendants argue that such activities are beyond the reach of the FWPCA. This Court does not agree. Even the occasional lapping of the bayou waters has conveyed these pollu-

---

have resulted in the loss of living, marine resources, wildlife, *nutrient-rich areas, permanent and adverse changes to ecological systems. . . .;*

(d) *The coastal zone . . . [is] ecologically fragile* and *extremely vulnerable to destruction* by *man's alteration;*

(e) Important *ecological . . . values* in the coastal zone which are *essential* to the well-being of all citizens are being *irretrievably damaged or lost;*

*   *   *   *   *   *

(h) The key to more effective protection and use of . . . water resources . . . is to encourage the states . . . by assisting the states, in cooperation with Federal and local governments . . . in developing . . . water use programs for the coastal zone. . . ." 16 U.S.C. § 1451 (emphasis added)

Based on those findings Congress declared in Section 303 it is the national policy . . .

"(a) to preserve, protect, develop, and where possible, to restore or enhance, the resources of the Nation's coastal zone for this and succeeding generations. . . ." 16 U.S.C. § 1452

The Coastal Zone Act establishes Federal grant programs to aid the States in developing and administering management agencies which would have the authority to ensure the wise use of land and water resources in the coastal zone. That this Act is in support and concert with the FWPCA is shown by Section 307(f) of the Coastal Zone Act which provides that the requirements established in the FWPCA or established pursuant to FWPCA will be incorporated as the water pollution control requirements in the water use programs to be developed by the States:

"Notwithstanding any other provision of this title, nothing in this title shall in any-way affect any requirement (1) established by the Federal Water Pollution Control Act, as amended. . . . or (2) established by the Federal Government . . . pursuant to such Acts. Such requirements shall be incorporated in any program developed pursuant to this title and shall be the water pollution control . . . requirements applicable to such program." 16 U.S.C. § 1456(f).

tants into the waters of the United States. That the pollutants are not so conveyed every day is of no consequence. Pollutants have been introduced into the waters of the United States without a permit and the mean high water mark cannot be used to create a barrier behind which such activities can be excused. The environment cannot afford such safety zones.

The Court is of the opinion that the mean high water line is no limit to federal authority under the FWPCA. While the line remains a valid demarcation for other purposes, it has no rational connection to the aquatic ecosystems which the FWPCA is intended to protect. Congress has wisely determined that federal authority over water pollution properly rests on the Commerce Clause and not on past interpretations of an act designed to protect navigation. And the Commerce Clause gives Congress ample authority to reach activities above the mean high water line that pollute the waters of the United States.

The defendants' filling activities on land periodically inundated by tidal waters constituted discharges entering "waters of the United States" and, since done without a permit, were thus in violation of 33 U.S.C. § 1311(a).

The Rivers and Harbors Act of 1899

Plaintiff has alleged violations of Sections 10 and 13 of the Rivers and Harbors Act of 1899 (33 U.S.C. §§ 403, 407). The evidence indicated that refuse or fill material has been deposited into navigable waters below the mean high water line. The area below the line is a small percentage of the total area for which an injunction is sought.

The government argued that any activity above mean high water which affects the quality of classical navigable-in-law waters may be properly enjoined as a violation of the 1899 Act. Plaintiff also contended that artificial mosquito canals are navigable-in-law when connected to navigable-in-fact water-bodies since the canals contain water at mean high tide.

Although these arguments are not unpersuasive, the Court's foregoing determination that the FWPCA encompasses the area included in the government's allegation under the Act makes it unnecessary to decide whether the theories based on the older statute are meritorious.

By determining that the defendants have violated the provisions of the FWPCA and by enjoining further unlawful activities, the Court has not permanently prohibited defendants from going forward with their plans. All the Court has said is that the activities cannot be continued without a federal permit.

The Court realizes that the thought of preserving huge stretches of coastline in a natural state and forbidding all commercial development in coastal areas is unrealistic. This is a societal choice which the government must observe. But the government can and should insure that the public interest in protecting all life forms is at least considered in the development plans. Any expense that might be incurred by this evaluative process will be dwarfed by the cost of neglecting the ecological interests.

FINAL DECREE

This cause having come before this Court for final disposition pursuant to a stipulation and joint motion by the Government and all Defendants herein for Consent Decree, and this Court being fully advised in the premises, it is hereby, ordered and adjudged as follows:

    1   Jurisdiction is founded upon Section 1319(b), Title 33, United States Code.

    2   Defendants reside and conduct business within the Middle District of Florida.

    3   The activities upon which the action is based were conducted on property known as Harbor Island Development on Papy's Bayou, St. Petersburg, Pinellas County, Florida, the boundary lines of which are shown on the attached Survey Plat No. 14021A by George F. Young, Inc. Revision dated February 1, 1974. (Omitted from published opinion.)

    4   On the property described hereinabove, defendants have discharged pollutants into waters of the United States in violation of Section 1311(a), Title 33, United States Code.

    5   Defendants shall perform all work necessary to allow establishment of 78.6 acres as mangrove preserve areas consistent with proper environmental planning, preservation, restoration, and ecological considerations. The mangrove preserve areas referred to are colored green and striped with dark parallel lines on the survey plat attached hereto. Defendants shall commence to create said preserve acres within 31 days from the date of this Decree, and shall complete all necessary contouring and debris removal in those areas within three months from the date of this Decree. The dikes withholding tide waters from the preserve areas shall then be removed after consultation with and the approval of the United States Environmental Protection Agency and the United States Army Corps of Engineers.

    6   A twenty-five-foot buffer zone having a gentle slope no greater than one foot vertical rise to four feet horizontal shall fringe all mangrove preserve areas, except those areas which are separated from retention ponds by an earthen berm or dike.

    7   The mangrove preserve areas shall remain as natural environmental areas in perpetuity. Defendant shall take the necessary legal precautions to insure that the mangrove preserve areas are properly protected from lawful destruction by present and future owners of this property.

    8   Should construction activities necessitate the discharge of water from any retention pond, defendants shall insure that total suspended solids shall not exceed concentrations of 30 parts per million as a "daily average," nor shall total suspended solids exceed concentrations of 50 parts per million as a "daily maximum."

Defendants shall measure total suspended solids concentrations at the point of discharge on at least one day in every two week period. Sample analysis shall be in compliance with methods of analysis specified in 40 CFR § 136.3, 38 Fed. Register 28759. Any violation of the effluent limitations provided in this paragraph shall be reported immediately to the Director of Enforcement Division,

United States Environmental Protection Agency, 1421 Peachtree Street, N.E., Atlanta, Georgia 30309.

The "daily average" concentration means the arithmetic average (weighed by flow) of all the daily determinations of concentrations made during a calendar month. Daily determinations of concentration made using a composite sample shall be the concentration of the composite sample. When grab samples are used, the daily determination of concentration shall be the arithmetic average (weighed by flow value) of all the samples collected during that calendar day.

The "daily maximum" concentration means the daily determination of concentration for any calendar day.

9 Within 30 days from the date of this Decree defendants shall apply to the appropriate Federal agency or agencies for any necessary permits for contemplated discharge during construction activities and shall meet the conditions outlined in paragraph 8, until such permits are issued or denied.

10 The temporary restraining order heretofore entered by this Court on December 21, 1973, and the preliminary injunction heretofore entered by this Court on January 11, 1974, are hereby dissolved.

11 Defendants are hereby authorized and permitted, from this date forward, to proceed with development activities on the property described hereinabove in any manner not inconsistent with the terms of this Final Decree. This Decree shall not be interpreted to affect, excuse, relieve, or modify any legal obligation of the defendants to comply with any requirements validly imposed by any applicable Federal or State laws or any local ordinances.

12 The provisions of this Decree shall apply to and be binding upon the parties to this action, their officers, agents, servants, employees, successors, and assigns, and upon all those in active concert or participation with those who receive actual notice of this Decree by personal service or otherwise.

13 Jurisdiction is retained for the purpose of enabling any party to this Decree to apply to this Court at any time for such further orders and directions as may be necessary for the construction or carrying out of this Decree, or for the modification or termination of any of the provisions herein, or for the enforcement of compliance herewith.

QUESTIONS FOR DISCUSSION

1 Could you improve on the FWPCA definition of "pollutant"? "Point source"?
2 Is all water in the United States now subject to the FWPCA?
3 Would an FWPCA permit be needed if a Section 10 permit under Rivers and Harbors had been issued?
4 Are there any negative consequences attending the demise, for FWPCA purposes, of the navigability standard?
5 Is the FWPCA clearly within the scope of the commerce power?
6 Can you conceive of a feasible system for the regulation of pollutants other than point-source pollutants?
7 Would industrywide effluent standards be more workable than individual permits?
8 Do you find the court's analysis of the legislative history convincing in light of the language finally included in the statute?

ECONOMIC AND POLITICAL INFLUENCES

Economic and political factors weigh heavily in the process of making environmental law. These factors are illustrated in the following veto message of President Nixon of the Federal Water Pollution Control Act Amendments of 1972. On October 18, 1972, one day after the veto, both the Senate and the House of Representatives overrode the veto by the necessary two-thirds majority.

Veto Message from the President of the United States

October 17, 1972

To the Senate of the United States:

The pollution of our rivers, lakes and streams degrades the quality of American life. Cleaning up the Nation's waterways is a matter of urgent concern to me, as evidenced by the nearly tenfold increase in my budget for this purpose during the past four years.

I am also concerned, however, that we attack pollution in a way that does not ignore other very real threats to the quality of life, such as spiraling prices and increasingly onerous taxes. Legislation which would continue our efforts to raise water quality, but which would do so through extreme and needless overspending, does not serve the public interest. There is a much better way to get this job done.

For this reason, I am compelled to withhold my approval from S. 2770, the Federal Water Pollution Control Act Amendments of 1972—a bill whose laudable intent is outweighed by its unconscionable $24 billion price tag. My proposed legislation, as reflected in my budget, provided sufficient funds to fulfill that same intent in a fiscally responsible manner. Unfortunately the Congress ignored our other vital national concerns and broke the budget with this legislation.

Environmental protection has been one of my highest priorities as President. The record speaks for itself. With the Council on Environmental Quality and the Environmental Protection Agency, we have established a strong new framework for developing and administering forceful programs in this problem area. I have proposed more than 25 far-reaching laws to deal with threats to the environment; most still await final action in the Congress. Pending enactment of new legislation, our enforcement agencies have cracked down on polluters under old laws seldom enforced by previous administrations.

The budget authority which I have requested for pollution control and abatement in fiscal year 1973 is more than four times the amount requested in 1969. Federal grants for local sewage treatment plant construction have increased almost tenfold, from an annual rate of $214 million appropriated up to the time I took office, to $2 billion in my budget for 1973. This dramatic growth in the share of Federal Government resources being devoted to the environment exceeds, many times over, the rate of increase for funds in most other major government programs.

Every environmental spending increase that I have proposed, however, has been within the strict discipline of a responsible fiscal policy—a policy which recognizes as the highest national priority the need to protect the working men and women of America against tax increases and renewed inflation. Specifically, the water pollution control bill which I originally sent to the Congress last year was fully consistent with the concept of a balanced, full-employment budget. It would have committed $6 billion in Federal funds over a three-year period, enough to continue and accelerate the momentum toward that high standard of cleanliness which all of us want in America's waters.

By contrast, the bill which has now come to my desk would provide for the commitment of a staggering, budget-wrecking $24 billion. Every extra dollar which S. 2770 contemplates spending beyond the level of my budget proposals would exact a price from the consumer in the form of inflated living costs, or from the taxpayer in the form of a new Federal tax bite, or both.

Ironically, however, only a portion of the $18 billion by which my bill was fattened on Capitol Hill would actually go to buy more pollution control than the Administration bill would have done. One backward-looking provision, for example, would provide $750 million to reimburse State and local governments for work already completed on sewage treatment plants between 1956 and 1966. The precedent this would set for retroactive reimbursement in other matching grant programs is an invitation to fiscal chaos. Another provision would raise the Federal share of the cost of future facilities from 55 percent to 75 percent. Neither of these costly actions would, in any real sense, make our waters any cleaner: they would simply increase the burden on the Federal taxpayer.

There is a well-worn political axiom which says that any election year spending bill, no matter how ill-advised, defies veto by the President. But I say that any spending bill this year which would lead to higher prices and higher taxes defies signature by this President. I have nailed my colors to the mast on this issue; the political winds can blow where they may.

I am prepared for the possibility that my action on this bill will be overridden. The defeat of my proposal for a spending ceiling showed that many Senators and Congressmen are simply AWOL in our fight against higher taxes. And some have been lured to the wrong side of the fight by the false glitter of public works money for their districts or states. They seem to forget that it is their constituents' pockets from which the higher taxes must come as a result of their votes this week. Others to their great credit, voted for the spending limit to try to hold taxes down. Taxpayers must be sad to learn that a majority are charge account Congressmen.

If this veto is not sustained, however, let the issue be clearly drawn. As with the spending ceiling, so with this bill, a vote to sustain the veto is a vote against a tax increase. A vote to override the veto is a vote to increase the likelihood of higher taxes.

Even if this bill is rammed into law over the better judgment of the Executive—even if the Congress defaults its obligation to the taxpayers—I shall not default mine. Certain provisions of S. 2770 confer a measure of spending discretion and flexibility upon the President, and if forced to administer this legislation I mean to use those provisions to put the brakes on budget-wrecking expenditures as much as possible.

But the law would still exact an unfair and unnecessary price from the public. For I am convinced, on the basis of 26 years' experience with the political realities here in Washington, that the pressure for full funding under this bill would be so intense that funds approaching the maximum authorized amount could ultimately be claimed and paid out, no matter what technical controls the bill appears to grant the Executive.

I still hope, with millions of taxpayers, that at least one third plus one of the members in one House will be responsible enough to vote for the public interest and sustain this veto. It should be noted that doing so would by no means terminate the existing Federal water quality programs, because the Environmental Protection Agency will continue to operate those programs until the merits of a new water bill can be dealt with as a first order of business in the new Congress.

I look forward to cooperating with the next Congress on a prudent bill, to achieve ends on which we are mutually agreed, and by means which I trust will take better account than S. 2770 did of the working men and women who must ultimately pay the bill for environmental quality.

Richard Nixon

OCEAN DUMPING

The Marine Protection, Research, and Sanctuaries Act of 1972 (33 U.S.C. § 1401 et seq.), also known as the Ocean Dumping Act, established a permit system under the Environmental Protection Agency for the disposal of wastes at sea. Specifically, a permit is required for the transportation from the United States of virtually all materials for dumping in ocean waters, the actual dumping of materials transported from outside the United States into the territorial sea or contiguous zone, and the transportation of materials by a United States agency or official from outside the United States for the purpose of dumping in any ocean waters. No permits may be issued for radioactive, chemical, or biological warfare agents or any highly radioactive substance. The act applies to all ocean waters seaward of the land or internal waters, and the states are preempted from adopting or enforcing any regulations relating to activities covered by the act.

PROBLEMS

1   An owner of coastal property wishes to construct a dock extending across wetlands owned by him to allow access to navigable water. To what federal agency, if any, must he address a permit application?

2   A farmer applies pesticides to his land which eventually run off into rivers and the sea. Must the farmer seek a federal effluent permit? If so, from whom? If there is no technology adequate to control the runoff, could a permit application be denied?

3   Suppose the Corps of Engineers receives an application for a Section 10 permit to build a trailer park on fill in a wetlands area. Its investigation discloses no major impediments to navigation and concludes that the area to be filled is neither unique nor of any particular ecological value. The Corps does find, however, that additional high-density housing will burden both the school and waste-treatment systems of the locality. Could the Corps validly deny a permit on either or both of those bases?

4   Suppose a factory with toxic by-products is located on a river which is so polluted that nothing lives in it. Thus, the river itself is already at a toxic level. In such a situation could the plant be denied an effluent permit?

5   A factory discharging pollutants into a river is in financial difficulty but is faced with the requirement that it utilize the "best available technology economically achievable" by 1983. Is the fact that the factory is in financial difficulty a factor which could be considered in the determination of what is economically achievable?

6   A farmer on his own property digs a ditch for the purpose of moving waste from one part of his land to another. No portion of the flow finds its way into streams or natural watercourses. Would the FWPCA apply to his discharge into the ditch? What about discharges of waste onto the land which find their way to groundwater?

7   A chemical plant produces a waste product which it wants to dump at sea. The EPA denies a permit to transport the material on the ground that the consequences of such dumping in the area requested are unknown. Could a court reverse the EPA denial on the argument that the alternative is to dump on land, where the waste would eventually enter estuarine waters through the groundwater?

8   Suppose a nuclear facility produces radioactive wastes for which a disposal site must be found. The facility can make a reasonable argument that the safest method of disposal, given the current state of knowledge, is deep-sea dumping. Since the Ocean Dumping Act specifically forbids such disposal, can you think of any basis on which the act might be challenged in court?

SUGGESTIONS FOR FURTHER READING

Ackerman, B. A., S. R. Ackerman, and D. W. Henderson: *Uncertain Search for Environmental Policy: The Costs and Benefits of Controlling Pollution along the Delaware River*, 121 U. PA. L. REV. 1225, 1973.

Bergman, S.: *No Fault Liability for Oil Pollution Damage*, 5 J. MAR. L. & COM. 1, 1973.

Bradley, P. G.: *Marine Oil Spills: A Problem in Environmental Management*, 14 NATURAL RESOURCES J. 337, 1974.

Environmental Law—Admiralty Law—Validity of States' Oil Pollution Sanctions, 15 BOSTON COLLEGE IND. & COM. L. REV. 829, 1974.

Hoyer, C.: *Corps of Engineers Dredge and Fill Jurisdiction: Buttressing a Citadel under Siege,* 26 FLA. L. REV. 19, 1973.

Judicial Review and the 1972 Amendments to the Federal Water Pollution Control Act: And Who Shall Guard the Guards? 68 NW. U.L. REV. 770, 1973.

Kramon, J. M.: *Section 10 of the Rivers and Harbors Act: The Emergence of a New Protection for Tidal Marshes,* 33 MD. L. REV. 229, 1973.

Miller, H. C.: *Ocean Dumping—Prelude and Fugue,* 9 J. MAR. L. & COM. 51, 1973.

Raisch, J. W.: *Enforcement under the Federal Water Pollution Control Act Amendments of 1972,* 9 LAND & WATER L. REV. 369, 1974.

Smith, C. W.: *Highlights of the Federal Water Pollution Control Act of 1972,* 1973 DICK. L. REV. 459, 1973.

Wenner, L. M.: *Federal Water Pollution Control Statutes in Theory and Practice,* 4 ENVIRONMENTAL L. 251, 1974.

Wulf, N. A.: *Contiguous Zones for Pollution Control,* 3 J. MAR. L. & COM. 537, 1972.

Air-Pollution Control

The rapid progress of industrial and technological development in the United States has increased the level of material benefits available to its people. However, these positive features have been accompanied by the negative externalities of environmental pollution. A readily identifiable form of this problem is the contamination of the air by visible and invisible gases and particulate matter of all types. The sources of these pollutants are varied—automobile exhaust, domestic and industrial heating plants, waste inciner-ation, the conversion of fossil fuels for power supply, and other chemical-releasing industrial processes.

Concern with the problem of air pollution is not a recently acquired vir-tue. Congress enacted the Air Pollution Control Act in 1955; and this prelimi-nary legislation gave authority to the Secretary of Health, Education, and Wel-fare and the Surgeon General of the Public Health Service to conduct programs of research, give technical assistance, and develop methods of controlling and abating air pollution. In so doing, Congress said:

That in recognition of the dangers to the public health and welfare, injury to agri-cultural crops and livestock, damage to and deterioration of property, and hazards to air and ground transportation, from air pollution, it is hereby declared to be the policy of Congress to preserve and protect the primary responsibilities and rights of the States and local governments in controlling air pollution, to support and aid technical research, to devise and develop methods of abating such pollution, and to provide Federal technical services and financial aid to State and local government air pollution control agencies and other public or private agencies and institutions in the formulation and execution of their air pollution abatement research programs. To this end, the Secretary of Health, Education, and Welfare and the Surgeon General of the Public Health Service (under the supervision and direction of the Secretary of Health, Education, and Welfare) shall have the authority relating to air pollution control vested in them respectively by this Act.

The primary responsibility of the state and local governments in controlling air pollution was also explicitly set out.

Following the enactment of the Air Pollution Control Act, the Special Subcommittee on Traffic Safety, in 1956, and the Subcommittee on Health and Safety, in 1958, 1959, and 1960, held hearings on the harmful and toxic effects of motor-vehicle exhaust, resulting in the enactment of a bill requiring an increased emphasis on research into the problem of motor-vehicle emissions.

In 1963, the Air Pollution Control Act of 1955 was largely replaced by the Clean Air Act. For the first time, explicit authority provided for federal regulatory action to abate interstate air-pollution problems. Further, federal funds were to be awarded to encourage the development of state and local regulatory control programs. Additionally, study of the specific motor-vehicle emissions of hydrocarbons, sulfur dioxide, and oxides of nitrogen was intensified.

The Clean Air Act was amended in 1965, providing for greater control of automotive emissions regulations by empowering the Secretary of Health, Education, and Welfare to establish national standards relating to exhaust emissions. Provisions were also made for reciprocal international conferences on air pollution problems.

The Air Quality Act of 1967 established a regional framework for the enactment and enforcement of federal-state air-quality standards. The Secretary of Health, Education, and Welfare was required within a one-year period to designate atmospheric areas based on climate, meteorology and topography, "which affect the interchange and diffusion of pollutants in the atmosphere." Air-quality control regions were also to be designated by the Secretary, "based on jurisdictional boundaries, urban-industrial concentrations," and additional factors which would be necessary to implement air-quality standards adequately.

Responsibility for the setting up of standards limiting levels of pollution was given to the states. The state standards were based on criteria issued by the Secretary relating to the harmful effects of certain pollutants. However, if the states failed to act, the Secretary was empowered to set the standards.

The procedures available under the act for adopting standards and implementation plans were cumbersome and lengthy, at times requiring almost two years for the mere implementation of a plan. This process had to be repeated for every set of criteria issued on a new pollutant.

The act was severely criticized as being too general in its three major sections—(1) air-pollution prevention and control; (2) motor-vehicle emission standards; (3) general provisions; as having implementation procedures

which encouraged rather than discouraged pollution because of lengthy procedures; and as being critically deficient in encompassing the entire field of
offending pollution.[a]

STATUTORY EVOLUTION OF THE CLEAN AIR ACT AMENDMENTS OF 1970

The legislative history of the amendments of 1970 contained the specific criticisms of the enactments of 1967:

> Air pollution continues to be a threat to the health and well-being of the American
> people. While a start has been made in controlling air pollution since the enact-
> ment of the Air Quality Act of 1967, progress has been regrettably slow. This has
> been due to a number of factors: (1) cumbersome and time-consuming proce-
> dures called for under the 1967 act; (2) inadequate funding on Federal, State, and
> local levels; (3) scarcity of skilled personnel to enforce control measures; (4) inad-
> equacy of available test and control technologies; (5) organizational problems on
> the Federal level where air pollution control has not been accorded a sufficiently
> high priority, and (6) last, but not least, failure on the part of the National Air
> Pollution Control Administration to demonstrate sufficient aggressiveness in im-
> plementing present law.[b]

In reaction to the severe criticism of the 1967 act and its basic procedural
impracticality, Congress enacted sweeping changes which resulted in the
Clean Air Act Amendments of 1970.[c] The act is divided into four major sections: Subchapter I, Air Pollution Prevention and Control, which deals primarily with air pollution from stationary sources; Subchapter II, Emission Standards for Moving Sources; Subchapter III, General Provisions, which includes
provisions for citizen suits and emergency powers; and Subchapter IV, Noise
Pollution.[d]

The administrative authority in the field of air pollution, heretofore the
province of HEW, is shifted by the 1970 Clean Air Act to the Administrator of
the Environmental Protection Agency. The Clean Air Act program regulates
virtually all sources of emissions and contributing factors which, in the judg-

---

[a] See M. Greco, *The Clean Air Amendments of 1970,* 12 Boston College Ind. & Com. L. Rev. 571 (1970).
[b] See 3 U.S. Code Cong. & Ad. News (1970) at 5360: Legislative History of Pub. L. 91–604.
[c] 42 U.S.C. §§ 1857 et seq., as amended by Pub. L. 91–604.
[d] In 1970, Congress established the Office of Noise Abatement and Control within the EPA. The
Administrator was required to submit an extensive report to Congress within one year detailing the sources,
causes, and effects of aircraft, surface transportation, and product noise. The report, released in early 1972,
concluded that existing noise levels were generally detrimental to the quality of American life and interfered
with hearing, sleep, and recreation, including possible lasting physiological effects in people exposed to
high levels over a long period of time.

Subsequently, Congress enacted the Noise Control Act of 1972. The act directs the EPA to propose
to the Federal Aviation Agency regulations necessary to make aircraft and their use quieter, especially in
certain noise-sensitive lands. Additionally, the EPA is required to regulate noise emissions from motor
carriers and railroads engaged in interstate commerce.

The EPA is also required to set noise emission standards for products distributed in interstate commerce that are considered major noise sources and to conduct studies on the impact of noise on public
health and welfare.

See also *Bowie v. County Commissioners,* page 104.

ment of the Administrator, have an adverse effect on public health and welfare and "result from numerous or diverse mobile or stationary sources."

The Clean Air Act of 1970 enumerates three goals:

1 The maintenance of existing ambient air which is not polluted.
2 Primary standards—the achievement of air quality necessary to protect public health by 1975.
3 Secondary standards—the achievement in a reasonable time of a level of air quality which will avoid any adverse effects on any environmental, man-made, or aesthetic factor or process.

To achieve these goals, the act mandates the designation of air-quality regions and serious air-pollution areas. Ambient standards are translated into actual numbers in the National Primary and Secondary Ambient Air Quality Standards. The states are then required to submit air-quality plans which will achieve the mandated goals. Should the state-promulgated implementation plan be disapproved by the EPA, the Administrator must prepare a suitable one, or revise the state plan. Acceptable implementation plans must include the expeditious attainment of primary and secondary ambient standards, emission limitations, schedules and timetables for compliance, and measures to ensure attainment and maintenance of standards including, but not limited to, land use and transportation control. The implementation plan must also include provision of monitoring systems, provisions for intergovernmental co-operation, and motor-vehicle testing.

The Clean Air Act Amendments of 1970 empower the Administrator of the Environmental Protection Agency to establish directly emission standards for pollutants which he determines are hazardous to health. The Administrator may also establish "standards of performance" for new sources of air pollution included within major categories of stationary sources.

Title II of the Act attacks the highly visible problem of motor-vehicle pollution. The Administrator of the EPA is authorized to set emission standards for all new vehicles on engines for use on the streets and highways and for aircraft. The dual mandate calls for the establishment of standards for vehicles likely to cause or contribute to air pollution endangering public health or welfare within the constraints of available technology, and also for standards for light-duty vehicles including cars which, on 1975 models, will produce a 90 percent reduction in the emissions of carbon monoxide and hydrocarbons from the 1970 levels. Further reduction of 90 percent from the average of emissions of oxides of nitrogen from 1971 models was required of 1976 models.[e]

The Clean Air Act of 1970 also made provision for vehicle testing procedures, maintenance requirements, and vehicle recalls. Also, the Administrator is empowered to regulate the composition of motor-vehicle fuels.

Enforcement of Clean Air Act mandates is primarily through civil penalties imposed by the EPA concurrently with state and local governments. Both fines and imprisonment are possible, and the abatement conference mechanism of earlier statutes is continued. The act also provides for record keeping,

[e] See, however, the Energy Supply and Environmental Coordination Act, page 231.

inspections, monitoring, and right of entry, and the Administrator may require the installation of monitoring equipment.

Federal agencies and enterprises must comply with Clean Air Act requirements and sovereign immunity is waived. In the case of a "paramount interest" the President may exempt specific installations for one year.

Suits by citizens on their own behalf are specifically authorized to enforce key regulatory requirements.[f] Most suits to date have been against the Administrator of EPA alleging a failure to perform nondiscretionary duties.

NOTE: EMERGENCY POWERS AND TIME EXTENSIONS

(1) Emergency powers. If the Administrator determines that there is "an imminent and substantial endangerment to the health of persons and that appropriate state or local authorities have not acted to abate such sources," he is granted by the Clean Air Act almost unlimited powers of abatement. 42 U.S.C. § 1857h-1; Clean Air Act § 303.

(2) Time extensions. A two-year extension of primary standards was made possible if a governor indicates and the Administrator finds that one or more emission sources or classes are unable to comply because the technology is unavailable and the alternatives are inadequate. Owners of particular stationary sources or a class of owners of moving sources were authorized to seek, upon application of the governor on their behalf, a postponement of one year if a good-faith effort to comply had been made, the technology was unavailable, and the delay was essential to national security or public walfare. See 42 U.S.C. §§ 1857C-5(e)(1) and 1857C-5(f)(1). See also the Energy Supply and Environmental Coordination Act of 1974, below, and *International Harvester Company v. Ruckelshaus,* page 247.

EFFECTS OF ECONOMICS

Clean-air legislation is subject to the same economic pressures as other topics of environmental law. The energy crisis of 1973 precipitated major changes in both environmental law and policy. The following excerpt from the Energy Supply and Environmental Coordination Act of 1974 illustrates the impacts that economic and energy developments may have on environmental law.

[f] 42 U.S.C. § 1857H-2, Clean Air Act § 304.
"Citizen suits—Establishment of right to bring suit (a) Except as provided in subsection (b) of this section, any person may commence a civil action on his own behalf—
(1) against any person (including (i) the United States, and (ii) any other governmental instrumentality or agency to the extent permitted by the Eleventh Amendment to the Constitution) who is alleged to be in violation of (A) an emission standard or limitation under this chapter or (B) an order issued by the Administrator or a State with respect to such a standard or limitation, or (2) against the Administrator where there is alleged a failure of the Administrator to perform any act or duty under this chapter which is not discretionary with the Administrator."

Energy Supply and Environmental Coordination Act of 1974

Public Law 93–319, 88 Stat. 246, June 22, 1974

SEC. 3. SUSPENSION AUTHORITY

Title I of the Clean Air Act is amended by adding at the end thereof the following new section:

"(b)(1)(A) The [EPA] Administrator may, for any period beginning on or after the date of enactment of this section and ending on or before June 30, 1975, temporarily suspend any stationary source fuel or emission limitation as it applies to any person—

"(i) if the Administrator finds that such person will be unable to comply with any such limitation during such period solely because of unavailability of types or amounts of fuels (unless such unavailability results from an order under section 2(a) of the Energy Supply and Environmental Coordination Act of 1974), or

"(ii) if such person is a source which is described in subsection (c)(1)(A) or (B) of this section and which has converted to coal, and the Administrator finds that the source will be able to comply during the period of the suspension with all primary standard conditions which will be applicable to such source.

Any suspension under this paragraph, the imposition of any interim requirement on which such suspension is conditioned under paragraph (3) of this subsection, and the imposition of any primary standard condition which relates to such suspension, shall be exempted from any procedural requirements set forth in this Act or in any other provision of Federal, State, or local law; except as provided in subparagraph (B) of this paragraph.

"(B) The Administrator shall give notice to the public and afford interested persons an opportunity for written and oral presentations of data, views, and arguments prior to issuing a suspension under subparagraph (A), or denying an application for such a suspension, unless otherwise provided by the Administrator for good cause found and published in the Federal Register. In any case, before issuing such a suspension, he shall give actual notice to the Governor of the State in which the affected source or sources are located, and to appropriate local governmental officials (as determined by the Administrator). The issuing or denial of such a suspension, the imposition of an interim requirement, and the imposition of any primary standard condition shall be subject to judicial review only on the grounds specified in paragraph (2)(B), (2)(C), or (2)(D), of section 706 of title 5, United States Code, and shall not be subject to any proceeding under section 304(a)(2) or 307(b) and (c) of this Act.

"(2) In issuing any suspension under paragraph (1), the Administrator is authorized to act on his own motion or upon application by any person (including a public officer or public agency).

"(3) Any suspension under paragraph (1) shall be conditioned upon compliance with such interim requirements as the Administrator determines are reasonable and practicable. Such interim requirements shall include, but need not be limited to, (A) a requirement that the persons receiving the suspension comply with such reporting requirements as the Administrator determines may be necessary, (B) such measures as the Administrator determines are necessary to avoid an imminent and substantial endangerment to health of persons, and (C) in the case of a suspension under paragraph (1)(A)(i), requirements that the suspension shall be inapplicable during any period during which fuels which would enable compliance with the suspended stationary source fuel or emission limitations are in fact reasonably available (as determined by the Administrator) to such person.

"(c)(1) Except as provided in paragraph (2) of this subsection, the Administrator shall issue a compliance date extension to any fuel-burning stationary source—

"(A) which is prohibited from using petroleum products or natural gas by reason of an order which is in effect under section 2(a) and (b) of the Energy Supply and Environmental Coordination Act of 1974, or

"(B) which the Administrator determines began conversion to the use of coal as its primary energy source during the period beginning on September 15, 1973, and ending on March 15, 1974,

and which, on or after September 15, 1973, converts to the use of coal as its primary energy source. If a compliance date extension is issued to a source, such source shall not, until January 1, 1979, be prohibited, by reason of the application of any air pollution requirement, from burning coal which is available to such source, except as provided in subsection (d)(3). For purposes of this paragraph, the term 'began conversion' means action by the source during the period beginning on September 15, 1973, and ending on March 15, 1974 (such as entering into a contract binding on such source for obtaining coal, or equipment or facilities to burn coal; expending substantial sums to permit such source to burn coal; or applying for an air pollution variance to enable such source to burn coal) which the Administrator finds evidences a decision (made prior to March 15, 1974) to convert to burning coal as a result of the unavailability of an adequate supply of fuels required for compliance with the applicable implementation plan, and a good faith effort to expeditiously carry out such decision.

"(2)(A) A compliance date extension under paragraph (1) of this subsection may be issued to a source only if—

"(i) the Administrator finds that such source will not be able to burn coal which is available to such source in compliance with all applicable air pollution requirements without a compliance date extension,

"(ii) the Administrator finds that the source will be able during the period of the compliance date extension to comply with all the primary standard conditions which are required under subsection (d)(2) to be applicable to such source, and with the regional limitation if applicable to such source, and

(iii) the source has submitted to the Administrator a plan for compliance for such source which the Administrator has approved.

A plan submitted under clause (iii) of the preceding sentence shall be approved only if it meets the requirements of regulations prescribed under subparagraph (B). The Administrator shall approve or disapprove any such plan within 60 days after such plan is submitted.

"(B) Not later than 90 days after the date of enactment of this section, the Administrator shall prescribe regulations requiring that any source to which a compliance date extension applies submit and obtain approval of its means for and schedule of compliance with the requirements of subparagraph (C) of this paragraph. Such regulations shall include requirements that such schedules shall include dates by which any such source must—

"(i) enter into contracts (or other obligations enforceable against such source) which the Administrator has approved as being adequate to provide for obtaining a long-term supply of coal which enables such source to achieve the emission reduction required by subparagraph (C), or

"(ii) if coal which enables such source to achieve such emission reduction is not available to such source, enter into contracts (or other obligations enforceable against such source) which the Administrator has approved as being adequate to provide for obtaining (I) a long-term supply of other coal, and (II) continuous emission reduction systems necessary to permit such source to burn such coal, and to achieve the degree of emission reduction required by subparagraph (C).

Regulations under this subparagraph shall provide that contracts or other obligations required to be approved under this subparagraph must be approved before they are entered into (except that a contract or obligation which was entered into before the date of enactment of this section may be approved after such date).

"(C) Regulations under subparagraph (B) shall require that the source achieve the most stringent degree of emission reduction that such source would have been required to achieve under the applicable implementation plan which was in effect on the date of submittal (under subparagraph (B) of this paragraph) of the means for and schedule of compliance (or if no applicable implementation plan was in effect on such date, under the first applicable implementation plan which takes effect after such date). Such degree of emission reduction shall be achieved as soon as practicable, but not later than December 31, 1978; except that, in the case of a source for which a continuous emission reduction system is required for sulfur-related emissions, reduction of such emissions shall be achieved on a date designated by the Administrator (but not later than January 1, 1979). Such regulations shall also include such interim requirements as the Administrator determines are reasonable and practicable, including requirements described in subparagraphs (A) and (B) of subsection (b)(3) and requirements to file progress reports.

"(D) A source which is issued a compliance date extension under this subsection, and which is located in an air quality control region in which a national primary ambient air quality standard for an air pollutant is not being met, may not emit such pollutant in amounts which exceed any emission limitation (and may not violate any other requirement) which applies to such source, under the applicable implementation plan for such pollutant. For purposes of this subparagraph, applicability of any such limitation or requirement to a source shall be determined without regard to this subsection or subsection (b).

"(3) A source to which this subsection applies may, upon the expiration of a compliance date extension, receive a one-year postponement of the application of any requirement of an applicable implementation plan under the conditions and in the manner provided in section 110(f).

"(4) The Administrator shall give notice to the public and afford an opportunity for oral and written presentations of data, views, and arguments before issuing any compliance date extension, prescribing any regulation under paragraph (2) of this subsection, making any finding under paragraph (2)(A) of this subsection, imposing any requirement on a source pursuant to paragraph (2) or any regulation thereunder, prescribing a primary standard condition under subsection (d)(2) which applies to a source to which an extension is issued under this subsection, or acting on any petition under subsection (d)(2)(C).

"(d)(1)(A) Whenever the Federal Energy Administrator issues an order under section 2(a) of the Energy Supply and Environmental Coordination Act of 1974 which will not apply after June 30, 1975, the Administrator of the Environmental Protection Agency shall certify to him—

> "(i) in the case of a source to which no suspension will be issued under subsection (b), the earliest date on which such source will be able to burn coal and to comply with all applicable air pollution requirements, or
> "(ii) in the case of a source to which a suspension will be issued under subsection (b) of this section, the date determined under paragraph (2)(B) of this subsection.

"(B) Whenever the Federal Energy Administrator issues an order under section 2(a) of such Act which will apply after June 30, 1975, the Administrator of the Environmental Protection Agency shall notify him if such source will be able, on and after July 1, 1975, to burn coal and to comply with all applicable air pollution requirements without a compliance date extension under subsection (c). If such notification is not given—

> "(i) in the case of a source which is eligible for a compliance date extension under subsection (c), the Administrator of the Environmental Protection Agency shall certify to the Federal Energy Administrator the date determined under paragraph (2)(B) of this subsection, and
> "(ii) in the case of a source which is not eligible for such an extension the Administrator of the Environmental Protection Agency shall certify to the Federal Energy Administrator the earliest date on which the source will be able to burn coal and to comply with all applicable air pollution requirements.

"(2)(A) The Administrator of the Environmental Protection Agency, after consultation with appropriate States, shall prescribe (and may from time to time, after such consultation, modify) emission limitations, requirements respecting pollution characteristics of coal, or other enforceable measures for control of emissions, for each source to which a suspension under subsection (b)(1)(A)(ii) will apply, and for each source to which a compliance date extension under subsection (c)(1) will apply. Such limitations, requirements, and measures shall be those which he determines must be complied with by the source in order to assure (throughout the period that the suspension or extension will be in effect) that the burning of coal by such source will not result in emissions which cause or contribute to concentrations of any air pollutant in excess of any national primary ambient air quality standard for such pollutant.

"(B) Whenever the Administrator prescribes a limitation, requirement, or measure under subparagraph (A) of this paragraph with respect to a source, he shall determine the earliest date on which such source will be able to comply with such limitation, requirement, or measure, and with any regional limitation applicable to such source.

"(C) An air pollution control agency may petition the Administrator (A) to modify any limitation, requirement, or other measure under this paragraph so as to assure compliance with the requirements of this paragraph or (B) to issue to the Federal Energy Administration the certification described in paragraph (3)(B) on the grounds described in clause (iii) thereof. The Administrator shall take the action requested in the petition, or deny the petition, within 90 days after the date of receipt of the petition.

"(3)(A) If the Administrator determines that a source to which a suspension under subsection (b)(1)(A)(ii) or to which a compliance date extension under subsection (c)(1) applies is not in compliance with any primary standard condition, or that a source to which a compliance date extension applies is not in compliance with a regional limitation applicable to it, he shall (except as provided in subparagraph (B)) either—

"(i) enforce compliance with such condition or limitation under section 113, or

"(ii) (after notice to the public and affording an opportunity for interested persons to present data, views, and arguments, including oral presentations, to the extent practicable) revoke such suspension or compliance date extension.

"(B) If the Administrator finds that for any period—

"(i) a source, to which an order under section 2(a) of the Energy Supply and Environmental Coordination Act of 1974 applies, will be unable to comply with a primary standard condition or regional limitation,

"(ii) such a source will not be in compliance with such a condition or limitation, but such condition or limitation cannot be enforced because of a court order restraining its enforcement, or "(iii) the burning of coal by such a source will result in an increase in emissions of any air pollutant for which national ambient air quality standards have not been promulgated (or an air pollutant which is transformed in the atmosphere into an air pollutant for which such a standard has not been promulgated), and that such increase may cause (or materially contribute to) a significant risk to public health,

he shall notify the Federal Energy Administrator of his finding and certify the period for which such order under section 2(a) shall not be in effect with respect to such source. Subject to the conditions of the preceding sentence, such certification may be modified from time to time. For purposes of this subsection, subsection (c), and section 2(a) or (b) of the Energy Supply and Environmental Coordination Act of 1974, a source shall be considered unable to comply with an air pollution requirement (including a primary standard condition or regional limitation) only if necessary technology or other alternative methods of control are not available or have not been available for a sufficient period of time.

"(4) Nothing in this Act shall prohibit a State, political subdivision of a State, or agency or instrumentality of either, from enforcing any primary standard condition or regional limitation.

"(5) A conversion to coal (A) to which a suspension under subsection (b) or a compliance date extension under subsection (c) applies or (B) by reason of an order under section 2(a) of the Energy Supply and Environmental Coordination Act of 1974 shall not be deemed to be a modification for purposes of section 111(a)(2) and (4) of this Act.

"(e) The Administrator may, by rule, establish priorities under which manufacturers of continuous emission reduction systems necessary to carry out subsection (c) shall provide such systems to users thereof, if he finds that priorities must be imposed in order to assure that such systems are first provided to sources in air quality control regions in which national primary ambient air quality standards have not been achieved. No rule under this subsection may impair the obligation of any contract entered into before the date of enactment of this section. To the extent necessary to carry out this section, the Administrator may prohibit any State or political subdivision of a State, or an agency or instrumentality of either, from requiring any person to use a continuous emission reduction system for which priorities have been established under this subsection, except in accordance with such priorities.

"(f) No State, political subdivision of a State, or agency or instrumentality of either, may require any person to whom a suspension has been issued under subsection (b)(1) to use any fuel the unavailability of which is the basis of such person's suspension (except that this subsection shall not apply to requirements identical to Federal requirements under subsection (b)(3) or subsection (d)(2)).

"(g)(1) It shall be unlawful for any person to whom a suspension has been issued under subsection (b)(1) to violate any requirement on which the suspension is conditioned pursuant to subsection (b)(3) or any primary standard condition applicable to him.

"(2) It shall be unlawful for any person to fail to comply with any requirement under subsection (c), or any regulation, plan, or schedule thereunder (including a primary standard condition or regional limitation), which is applicable to such person.

"(3) It shall be unlawful for any person to violate any rule under subsection (e).

"(4) It shall be unlawful for any person to fail to comply with an interim requirement under subsection (i)(3).

"(h) Nothing in this section shall affect the power of the Administrator to deal with air pollution presenting an imminent and substantial endangerment to the health of persons under section 303 of this Act.

"(i)(1) In order to reduce the likelihood of early phaseout of existing electric generating powerplants, any electric generating powerplant (A) which, because of the age and condition of the plant, is to be taken out of service permanently no later than January 1, 1980, according to the power supply plan (in existence on January 1, 1974) of the owner or operator of such plant, (B) for which a certification to that effect has been filed by the owner or operator of the plant with the Environmental Protection Agency and the Federal Power Commission, and (C) for which such Commission has determined that the certification has been made in good faith and that the plan to cease operations no later than January 1, 1980, will be carried out as planned in light of existing and prospective power supply requirements, shall be eligible for a single one-year postponement as provided in paragraph (2).

"(2) Prior to the date on which any powerplant eligible under paragraph (1) is required to comply with any requirement of an applicable implementation plan, such plant may apply (with the concurrence of the Governor of the State in which such plant is located) to the Administrator to postpone the applicability of such requirement to such plant for not more than one year. If the Administrator determines, after considering the risk to public health and welfare which may be associated with a postponement, that compliance with any such requirement is not reasonable in light of the projected useful life of the plant, the availability of rate base increases to pay for the costs of such compliance, and other appropriate factors, then the Administrator shall grant a postponement of any such requirement.

"(3) The Administrator shall, as a condition of any postponement under paragraph (2), prescribe such interim requirements as are practicable and reasonable in light of the criteria in paragraph (2).

"(j)(1) The Administrator may, after public notice and opportunity for presentation of data, views, and arguments in accordance with section 553 of title 5, United States Code, and after consultation with the Federal Energy Administrator, designate persons with respect to whom fuel exchange requirements should be imposed under paragraph (2) of this subsection. The purpose of such designation shall be to avoid or minimize the adverse impact on public health and welfare of any suspension under subsection (b) of this section or conversion to coal to which subsection (c) applies or of any allocation under section 2(d) of the Energy Supply and Environmental Coordination Act of 1974 or under the Emergency Petroleum Allocation Act of 1973.

"(2) The Federal Energy Administrator shall exercise his authority under section 2(d) of the Energy Supply and Environmental Coordination Act of 1974 and under the Energy Petroleum Allocation Act of 1973 with respect to persons designated by the Administrator of the Environmental Protection Agency under paragraph (1) in order to require the exchange of any fuel subject to allocation under such Acts effective no later than forty-five days after the date of such designation, unless the Federal Energy Administrator determines, after consultation with the Administrator of the Environmental Protection Agency, that the costs or consumption of fuel, resulting from requiring such exchange, will be excessive.

"(k)(1) The Administrator shall study, and report to Congress not later than six months after the date of enactment of this section with respect to—

"(A) the present and projected impact of fuel shortages and fuel allocation programs on the program under this Act;

"(B) availability of continuous emission reduction technology (including projections respecting the time, cost, and number of units available) and the effects that continuous emission reduction systems would have on the total environment and on supplies of fuel electricity;

"(C) the number of sources and locations which must use such technology based on projected fuel availability data;

"(D) a priority schedule for installation of continuous emission reduction technology, based on public health or air quality;

"(E) evaluation of availability of technology to burn municipal solid waste in electric powerplants or other major fuel burning installations, including time schedules, priorities, analysis of pollutants which may be emitted (including those for which national ambient air quality standards have not been promulgated), and a comparison of health benefits and detriments from burning solid waste and of economic costs;

"(F) evaluation of alternative control strategies for the attainment and maintenance of national ambient air quality standards for sulfur oxides within the time for attainment prescribed in this Act, including associated considerations of cost, time for attainment, feasibility, and effectiveness of such alternative control strategies as compared to stationary source fuel and emission regulations;

"(G) proposed priorities, for continuous emission reduction systems which do not produce solid waste, for sources which are least able to handle solid waste by-products of such systems;

"(H) plans for monitoring or requiring sources to which this section applies to monitor the impact of actions under this section on concentrations of sulfur dioxide in the ambient air; and

"(I) steps taken pursuant to authority of section 110(a)(3)(B) of this Act.

"(2) Beginning January 1, 1975, the Administrator shall publish in the Federal Register, at no less than one-hundred-and-eighty-day intervals, the following:

"(A) A concise summary of progress reports which are required to be filed by any person or source owner or operator to which subsection (c) applies. Such progress reports shall report on the status of compliance with all requirements which have been imposed by the Administrator under such subsection.

"(B) Up-to-date findings on the impact of this section upon—

"(i) applicable implementation plans, and

"(ii) ambient air quality."

SEC. 4. IMPLEMENTATION PLAN REVISIONS

(a) Section 110(a) of the Clean Air Act is amended in paragraph (3) by inserting "(A)" after "(3)" and by adding at the end thereof the following new subparagraph:

"(B) As soon as practicable, the Administrator shall, consistent with the purposes of this Act and the Energy Supply and Environmental Coordination Act of 1974, review each State's applicable implementation plans and report to the State on whether such plans can be revised in relation to fuel burning stationary sources (or persons supplying fuel to such sources) without interfering with the attainment maintenance of any national ambient air quality standard within the period permitted in this section. If the Administrator determines that any such plan can be revised, he shall notify the State that a plan revision may be submitted by the State. Any plan revision which is submitted by the State shall, after public notice and opportunity for public hearing, be approved by the Administrator if the revision relates only to fuel burning stationary sources (or persons supplying fuel to such sources), and the plan as revised complies with paragraph (2) of this subsection. The Administrator shall approve or disapprove any revision no later than three months after its submission."

(b) Subsection (c) of section 110 of the Clean Air Act is amended by inserting "(1)" after "(c)"; by redesignating paragraphs (1), (2), and (3) as subparagraphs (A), (B), and (C), respectively, and by adding at the end thereof the following new paragraph:

"(2)(A) The Administrator shall conduct a study and shall submit a report to the Committee on Interstate and Foreign Commerce of the United States House of Representatives and the Committee on Public Works of the United States Senate not later than three months after date of enactment of this paragraph on the necessity of parking surcharge, management of parking supply, and preferential bus/carpool lane regulations as part of the applicable implementation plans required under this section to achieve and maintain national primary ambient air quality standards. The study shall include an assessment of the economic impact of such regulations, consideration of alternative means of reducing total vehicle miles traveled, and an assessment of the impact of such regulations on other Federal and State programs dealing with energy or transportation. In the course of such study, the Administrator shall consult with other Federal officials including, but not limited to, the Secretary of Transportation, the Federal Energy Administrator, and the Chairman of the Council on Environmental Quality.

"(B) No parking surcharge regulation may be required by the Administrator under paragraph (1) of this subsection as a part of an applicable implementation plan. All parking surcharge regulations previously required by the Administrator shall be void upon the date of enactment of this subparagraph. This subparagraph shall not prevent the Administrator from approving parking surcharges if they are adopted and submitted by a State as part of an applicable implementation plan. The Administrator may not condition approval of any implementation plan submitted by a State on such plan's including a parking surcharge regulation.

"(C) The Administrator is authorized to suspend until January 1, 1975, the effective date or applicability of any regulations for the management of parking supply or any requirement that such regulations be a part of an applicable implementation plan approved or promulgated under this section. The exercise of the authority under this subparagraph shall not prevent the Administrator from approving such regulations if they are adopted and submitted by a State as part of an applicable implementation plan. If the Administrator exercises the authority under this subparagraph, regulations requiring a review or analysis of the impact of proposed facilities before construction which take effect on or after January 1, 1975, shall not apply to parking facilities on which construction has been initiated before January 1, 1975.

"(D) For purposes of this paragraph—

"(i) The term 'parking surcharge regulation' means a regulation imposing or requiring the imposition of any tax, surcharge, fee, or other charge on parking spaces, or any other area used for the temporary storage of motor vehicles.

"(ii) The term 'management of parking supply' shall include any requirement providing that any new facility containing a given number of parking spaces shall receive a permit or other prior approval, issuance of which is to be conditioned on air quality considerations.

"(iii) The term 'preferential bus/carpool lane' shall include any requirement for the setting aside of one or more lanes of a street or highway on a permanent or temporary basis for the exclusive use of buses or carpools, or both.

"(E) No standard, plan, or requirement, relating to management of parking supply or preferential bus/carpool lanes shall be promulgated after the date of enactment of this paragraph by the Administrator pursuant to this section, unless such promulgation has been subjected to at least one public hearing which has been held in the area affected and for which reasonable notice has been given in such area. If substantial changes are made following public hearings, one or more additional hearings shall be held in such area after such notice."

SEC. 5.   MOTOR VEHICLE EMISSIONS

(a) Section 202(b)(1)(A) of the Clean Air Act is amended by striking out "1975" and inserting in lieu thereof "1977"; and by inserting after "(A)" the following: "The regulations under subsection (a) applicable to emissions of carbon monoxide and hydrocarbons from light-duty vehicles and engines manufactured during model years 1975 and 1976 shall contain standards which are identical to the interim standards which were prescribed (as of December 1, 1973) under paragraph (5)(A) of this subsection for light-duty vehicles and engines manufactured during model year 1975."

(b) Section 202(b)(1)(B) of such Act is amended by striking out "1976" and inserting in lieu thereof "1978"; and inserting after "(B)" the following: "The regulations under subsection (a) applicable to emissions of oxides of nitrogen from light-duty vehicles and engines manufactured during model years 1975 and 1976 shall contain standards which are identical to the standards which were prescribed (as of December 1, 1973) under subsection (a) for light-duty vehicles and engines manufactured during model year 1975. The regulations under subsection (a) applicable to emissions of oxides of nitrogen from light-duty vehicles and engines manufactured during model year 1977 shall contain standards which provide that such emissions from such vehicles and engines may not exceed 2.0 grams per vehicle mile."

(c) Section 202(b)(5)(A) of such Act is amended to read as follows:

"(5)(A) At any time after January 1, 1975, any manufacturer may file with the Administrator an application requesting the suspension for one year only of the effective date of any emission standard required by paragraph (1)(A) with respect to such manufacturer for light-duty vehicles and engines manufactured in model year 1977. The Administrator shall make his determination with respect to any such application within sixty days. If he determines, in accordance with the provisions of this subsection, that such suspension should be granted, he shall simultaneously with such determination prescribe by regulation interim emission standards which shall apply (in lieu of the standards required to be prescribed by paragraph (1)(A) of this subsection) to emissions of carbon monoxide or hydrocarbons (or both) from such vehicles and engines manufactured during model year 1977."

(d) Section 202(b)(5)(B) of the Clean Air Act is repealed and the following subparagraphs redesignated accordingly.

NONDEGRADATION

At the time of the enactment of the Clean Air Act of 1970 not all regions of the United States had air quality poorer than that required in secondary standards. *Sierra Club v. Ruckelshaus* confronted the contention of the EPA that the agency lacked the power to require state implementation plans to prohibit degradation of areas with clean air.

Sierra Club v. Ruckelshaus

344 F. Supp. 253, 4 ERC 1205 (D.D.C. 1972), aff'd, 412 U.S. 541 (1973)

Pratt, District Judge:

Initially, this matter came before the Court on plaintiffs' motion for temporary restraining order wherein they sought to enjoin the Administrator of the Environmental Protection Agency from approving certain portions of state air pollution control plans—implementing the national primary and secondary standards—which had been submitted to the Administrator pursuant to Section 110 of the Clean Air Act of 1970. 42 U.S.C. § 1857c-5 (1970). Having been informed that the Administrator would not be approving the plans until May 31, 1972, we denied the motion for temporary restraining order and scheduled a hearing on the preliminary injunction for May 30. At the conclusion of the May 30 hearing, having considered the pleadings and memoranda and the arguments of counsel, we announced our findings and conclusions and granted plaintiffs' motion for preliminary injunction. We now set down those findings and conclusions in memorandum form. . . .

JURISDICTION

The Administrator challenges the jurisdiction of this Court to hear this case on the theory that the plaintiffs should wait until the Administrator approves the plans and then appeal the approval under 42 U.S.C. § 1857h-5. We disagree. It is our judgment that plaintiffs have the right to bring the action in this Court at this juncture under 42 U.S.C. § 1857h-2(a) which provides in pertinent part that

> "any person may commence a civil action on his own behalf—
>
> *   *   *
>
> (2) against the Administrator where there is alleged a failure of the Administrator to perform any act or duty under this chapter which is not discretionary with the Administrator.
>
> The district courts shall have jurisdiction without regard to the amount in controversy or the citizenship of the parties, . . . to order the Administrator to perform such act or duty, as the case may be."

The Administrator, in recent testimony before Congress, indicated that he had declined to require state implementation plans to provide against significant deterioration of the existing clean air areas—i.e., areas with levels of pollution lower than the secondary standard—because he believed that he lacked the power to act otherwise. Unpublished transcript of Hearings Before the Subcomm. on Public Health and the Environment of the House Comm. on Interstate and Foreign Commerce, 92d Cong., 2d Sess., at 351-52 (remarks delivered on Jan. 27-28, 1972).

Previously, the Administrator had promulgated a regulation permitting states to submit plans which would allow clean air areas to be degraded, so long as the plans were merely "adequate to prevent such ambient pollution levels from exceeding such secondary standard." 40 C.F.R. § 51.12(b) (1972).

Plaintiffs claim that the Administrator's interpretation of the extent of his authority is clearly erroneous and that his declination to assert his authority, evidenced in his remarks before Congress and his promulgation of a regulation that is contrary to the Clean Air Act, amounts to a failure to perform a nondiscretionary act or duty.

It would appear that such an allegation is precisely the type of claim which Congress, through 42 U.S.C. § 1857h-2(a), intended interested citizens to raise in the district courts. In view of this clear jurisdictional grant, the Administrator's assertion that plaintiffs should await his approval of the state plans (formulated, in part, pursuant to his allegedly illegal regulation) and then proceed to appeal his approval under 42 U.S.C. § 1857h-5 is, in our opinion, untenable.

In discussing the merits of the present action—i.e., the extent of the Administrator's authority and the validity of the questioned regulation—we turn to the stated purpose of the Clean Air Act of 1970, the available legislative history of the Act and its predecessor, and the administrative interpretation of the Act.

PURPOSE OF THE ACT

In Section 101(b) of the Clean Air Act, Congress states four basic purposes of the Act, the first of which is

> "to protect and enhance the quality of the Nation's air resources so as to promote the public health and welfare and the productive capacity of its population." 42 U.S.C. § 1857(b)(1).

On its face, this language would appear to declare Congress' intent to improve the quality of the nation's air and to prevent deterioration of that air quality, no matter how presently pure that quality in some sections of the country happens to be.

LEGISLATIVE HISTORY

The "protect and enhance" language of the Clean Air Act of 1970 stems directly from the predecessor Air Quality Act of 1967, 81 Stat. 485. The Senate Report underlying the 1967 Act makes it clear that all areas of the country were to come under the protection of the Act. S. Rep. No. 403, 90th Cong., 1st Sess. 203 (1967).

The administrative guidelines promulgated by the National Air Pollution Control Administration (NAPCA) of the Department of Health, Education and Welfare (HEW), which at that time had the responsibility of carrying out the directives of the Air Quality Act of 1967, point up the significance of the "protect and enhance" language as follows:

"[A]n explicit purpose of the Act is 'to protect and enhance the quality of the Nation's air resources.' Air quality standards which, even if fully implemented, would result in significant deterioration of air quality in any substantial portion of an air quality region clearly would conflict with this expressed purpose of the law." National Air Pollution Control Administration, U.S. Dept. of HEW, Guidelines for the Development of Air Quality Standards and Implementation Plans, Part I § 1.51, p. 7 (1969).

Turning now to the legislative history of the 1970 Act, we note at the outset that both Secretary Finch and Under Secretary Veneman of HEW testified before Congress that neither the 1967 Act nor the proposed Act would permit the quality of air to be degraded. Hearings on Air Pollution Before the Subcomm. on Air and Water Pollution of the Senate Public Works Comm., 91st Cong., 2d Sess., at 132–33, 143 (1970); Hearings on Air Pollution and Solid Waste Recycling Before the Subcomm. on Public Health and Welfare of the House Interstate and Foreign Commerce Comm., 91st Cong., 2d Sess., at 280, 287 (1970).

More important, of course, is the language of the Senate Report accompanying the bill which became the Clean Air Act of 1970. The Senate Report, in pertinent part, states:

"In areas where current air pollution levels are already equal to or better than the air quality goals, the Secretary shall not approve any implementation plan which does not provide, to the maximum extent practicable, for the continued maintenance of such ambient air quality." S. Rep. No. 1196, 91st Cong., 2d Sess., at 2 (1970).

The House Report, although not as clear, does not appear to contradict the Senate Report. See H. Rep. No. 1146, 91st Cong., 2d Sess., at 1, 2 and 5 (1970).

ADMINISTRATIVE INTERPRETATION

As we noted under our discussion of the legislative history of the 1967 Act, the 1969 guidelines promulgated by HEW's NAPCA emphasized that significant deterioration of air quality in any region would subvert the "protect and enhance" language of the 1967 Act. We also pointed out that Secretary Finch and Under Secretary Veneman applied this same administrative interpretation to the very same language found in the proposed 1970 Act.

On the other hand, the present Administrator, in remarks made in January and February of 1972 before certain House and Senate Subcommittees, has taken the position that the 1970 Act allows degradation of clean air areas. Several Congressional leaders voiced their strong disagreement with the Administrator's interpretation. Unpublished transcript of Hearings Before the Subcomm. on Public Health and the Environment of the House Comm. on Interstate and Foreign Commerce, 92d Cong., 2d Sess., at 352 (remarks of Congressman Paul Rogers, Chairman of the Subcommittee); Unpublished transcript of Hearings Before the Subcomm. on Air and Water Pollution of the Senate Comm. on Public Works,

92d Cong., 2d Sess. at 33–34, 260 et seq. (remarks of Senator Thomas Eagleton, Vice-Chairman of the Subcommittee, presiding over the hearings at the time.)

The Administrator's interpretation of the 1970 Act, as disclosed in his current regulations, appears to be self-contradictory. On the other hand, 40 C.F.R. § 50.2(c) (1970) provides:

> "The promulgation of national primary and secondary air quality standards shall not be considered in any matter to allow significant deterioration of existing air quality in any portion of any State."

Yet, in 40 C.F.C. § 51.12(b), he states:

> "In any region where measured or estimated ambient levels of a pollutant are below the levels specified by an applicable secondary standard, the State implementation plan shall set forth a control strategy which shall be adequate to prevent such ambient pollution levels from exceeding such secondary standard."

The former regulation appears to reflect a policy of nondegradation of clean air but the latter mirrors the Administrator's doubts as to his authority to impose such a policy upon the states in their implementation plans. In our view, these regulations are irreconcilable and they demonstrate the weakness of the Administrator's position in this case.

INITIAL CONCLUSIONS

Having considered the stated purpose of the Clean Air Act of 1970, the legislative history of the Act and its predecessor, and the past and present administrative interpretation of the Acts, it is our judgement that the Clean Air Act of 1970 is based in important part on a policy of non-degradation of existing clean air and that 40 C.R.F. § 51.12(b), in permitting the states to submit plans which allow pollution levels of clean air to rise to the secondary standard level of pollution, is contrary to the legislative policy of the Act and is, therefore, invalid. Accordingly, we hold that plaintiffs have made out a claim for relief.

INJUNCTIVE RELIEF

Whether this Court may properly grant injunctive relief depends on whether the plaintiffs have met the four criteria set forth in *Virginia Petroleum Jobbers Ass'n v. Federal Power Commission*, 104 U.S. App. D.C. 106, 259 F.2d 921 (1958) and such later authorities as *A Quaker Action Group v. Hickel*, 137 U.S. App. D.C. 176, 421 F.2d 111 (1969).

First, have the plaintiffs made a strong showing that they are likely to prevail on the merits? It appears to us, from our foregoing discussion, that the plaintiffs have made such a showing in this case.

Second, have the plaintiffs shown that without such relief they would suffer irreparable injury? In view of the nature and extent of the air pollution problem, once degradation is permitted the range of resulting damages could well have irreversible effects. Thus, we hold that plaintiffs have made the requisite showing of irreparable injury.

Third, will the issuance of a stay cause any significant harm or inconvenience to the Administrator or other parties interested in the proceedings? We are persuaded that no substantial harm or inconvenience will result from our order granting the preliminary injunction. The order is a very limited one. It was submitted by plaintiffs' counsel after consultation with counsel for the Administrator and, in our view, it provides the Administrator with sufficient time and flexibility so that he may exercise his expertise and carry out his duties under the Act with as little inconvenience as possible.

Fourth, and finally, where lies the public interest? It seems to us that the public interest in this case strongly supports the legislative policy of clean air and the non-degradation of areas in which clean air exists.

CONCLUSION

Having separately considered the four criteria for injunctive relief, and having found that plaintiffs have met each of these criteria, we conclude that we can and should grant the requested relief. The order effecting such relief is attached hereto.

QUESTIONS FOR DISCUSSION

1 Do you agree with the court's interpretation of the purpose of the Clean Air Act?
2 Is an absolute prohibition of any degradation of air quality a good idea? How else might the problem of air quality be approached?
3 Why would the Administrator take the position that he did? Does he not thereby reduce his own authority?
4 Would the injury alleged necessarily be "irreparable"?
5 Do you find the court's consideration of the "public interest" adequate?

DELAY; ECONOMICS; TECHNOLOGY

Law, economics, technology, and administrative power and discretion are intertwined in the environmental context. *International Harvester Company v. Ruckelshaus*, in which the automobile makers sought suspension of automobile emission standards, graphically demonstrates the interplay of factors which are the essence of environmental law.

International Harvester Company v. Ruckelshaus

478 F.2d 615, 4 ERC 2041 (D.C. Cir. 1973)

Leventhal, Circuit Judge:

These consolidated petitions of International Harvester and the three major auto companies, Ford, General Motors and Chrysler, seek review[1] of a decision by the Administrator of the Environmental Protection Agency denying petitioners' applications, filed pursuant to Section 202 of the Clean Air Act,[2] for one year suspensions of the 1975 emission standards prescribed under the statute for light duty vehicles in the absence of suspension.

I. STATEMENT OF THE CASE

The tension of forces presented by the controversy over automobile emission standards may be focused by two central observations:

(1) The automobile is an essential pillar of the American economy. Some 28 per cent of the nonfarm workforce draws its livelihood from the automobile industry and its products.[3]

(2) The automobile has had a devastating impact on the American environment. As of 1970, authoritative voices stated that "[a]utomotive pollution constitutes in excess of 60% of our national air pollution problem" and more than 80 per cent of the air pollutants in concentrated urban areas.[4]

A. Statutory Framework

Congressional concern over the problem of automotive emissions dates back to the 1950's,[5] but it was not until the passage of the Clean Air Act in 1965 that Congress established the principle of Federal standards for automobile emissions. Under the 1965 Act and its successor, the Air Quality Act of 1967, the Department of Health, Education and Welfare was authorized to promulgate emission limitations commensurate with existing technological feasibility.[6]

---

[1] Under Section 307 of the Clean Air Act, 42 U.S.C. § 1857h-5(b)(1), which provides for direct review of the Administrator's decision by the United States Court of Appeals for the District of Columbia Circuit (all citations are to the 1970 edition of the U.S. Code).

[2] 42 U.S.C. § 1857f-1(b)(5)(B).

[3] Statement of Sen. Robert Griffin, 116 Cong. Rec. 33,081 (1970).

[4] For the 60% figure, see H.R. Rep. No. 91-1146, 91st Cong., 2d Sess., 6 (1970); for 64% national figure and the 80% urban figure, see statement of Nat'l Assoc. of Professional Engineers in Hearings on S. 3229, S. 3466, and S. 3546, before Subcomm. on Air and Water Pollution, Senate Comm. on Public Works, 91st Cong., 2d Sess., 114 (1970).

[5] The Act of July 14, 1955, Ch. 360, 1-7, 69 Stat. 322, authorized the Department of Health, Education and Welfare to provide research and assistance to local and state governments attempting to deal with air pollution. The Act of June 8, 1960, 74 Stat. 162, called for a federal study on the specific problem of automotive emissions.

[6] Motor Vehicle Air Pollution Control Act § 202(a), P.L. 89-272, Oct. 20, 1965, 79 Stat. 992 (Amendments to Clean Air Act); National Emission Standards Act § 202(a), P.L. 90-148, Nov. 21, 1967, 81 Stat. 499 (part of Air Quality Act of 1967).

The development of emission control technology proceeded haltingly. The Secretary of HEW testified in 1967 that "the state of the art has tended to meander along until some sort of regulation took it by the hand and gave it a good pull. . . . There has been a long period of waiting for it, and it hasn't worked very well."[7]

The legislative background must also take into account the fact that in 1969 the Department of Justice brought suit against the four largest automobile manufacturers on grounds that they had conspired to delay the development of emission control devices.[8]

On December 31, 1970, Congress grasped the nettle and amended the Clean Air Act to set a statutory standard for required reductions in levels of hydrocarbons (HC) and carbon monoxide (CO) which must be achieved for 1975 models of light duty vehicles. Section 202(b) of the Act added by the Clean Air Amendments of 1970, provides that, beginning with the 1975 model year, exhaust emission of hydrocarbons and carbon monoxide from "light duty vehicles" must be reduced at least 90 per cent from the permissible emission levels in the 1970 model year.[9] In accordance with the Congressional directives, the Administrator on June 23, 1971, promulgated regulations limiting HC and CO emissions from 1975 model light duty vehicles to .41 and 3.4 grams per vehicle mile respectively. 36 Fed. Reg. 12,657 (1971).[10] At the same time, as required by section 202(b)(2) of the Act, he prescribed the test procedures by which compliance with these standards is measured.[11]

Congress was aware that these 1975 standards were "drastic medicine,"[12] designed to "force the state of the art."[13] There was, naturally, concern whether the manufacturers would be able to achieve this goal. Therefore, Congress provided, in Senator Baker's phrase, a "realistic escape hatch": The manufacturers could petition the Administrator of the EPA for a one-year suspension of the 1975 requirements, and Congress took the precaution of directing the National Academy of Sciences to undertake an ongoing study of the feasibility of compliance with the emission standards. The "escape hatch" provision addressed itself to the

[7] Hearings on Air Pollution—1967, Hearings before the Subcomm. on Air and Water Pollution, Sen. Comm. on Public Works, 90th Cong., 1st Sess., pt. 3, 1155-6 (1967).

[8] The suit was settled by consent decree *United States v. Automobile Manufacturers Ass'n.*, 307 F. Supp. 617 (C.D. Cal. 1969), aff'd sub nom. *City of New York v. United States, et al.*, 397 U.S. 248 (1970).

[9] 42 U.S.C. § 1857f-1(b)(A)(1) provides that "engines manufactured during or after model year 1975 shall contain standards which require a reduction of at least 90 per centum from emissions of carbon monoxide and hydrocarbons allowable under the standards . . . applicable to light duty vehicles and engines manufactured in model year 1970."

[10] Section 1201.21 of this regulation also prescribes an oxides of nitrogen standard of 3.0 grams per vehicle mile for 1975. That standard has apparently not been challenged. In any event, it is not before us in the present case.

[11] "Emission standards under paragraph (1), and measurement techniques on which such standards are based (if not promulgated prior to December 31, 1970), shall be prescribed by regulation within 180 days after such date." 42 U.S.C. § 1857f-1(b)(2).

[12] Sen. Muskie, 116 Cong. Rec. 32,904 (1970).

[13] 116 Cong. Rec. 33,120 (1970) (newspaper report of statement of Senator Eagleton introduced into the record by Senator Muskie).

possibility that the NAS study or other evidence might indicate that the standards would be unachievable despite all good faith efforts at compliance. This provision was limited to a one-year suspension, which would defer compliance with the 90% reduction requirement until 1976. Under section 202(b)(5)(D) of the Act, 42 U.S.C. § 1857f-1(b)(5)(D), the Administrator is authorized to grant a one-year suspension

> only if he determines that (i) such suspension is essential to the public interest or the public health and welfare of the United States, (ii) all good faith efforts have been made to meet the standards established by this subsection, (iii) the applicant has established that effective control technology, processes, operating methods, or other alternatives are not available or have not been available for a sufficient period of time to achieve compliance prior to the effective date of such standards, and (iv) the study and investigation of the National Academy of Sciences conducted pursuant to subsection (c) of this section and other information available to him has not indicated that such technology, processes, or other alternatives are available to meet such standards.

The statute provides that an application for suspension may be filed any time after January 1, 1972, and that the Administrator must issue a decision thereon within 60 days. On March 13, 1972, Volvo, Inc., filed an application for suspension and thereby triggered the running of the 60 day period for a decision. 37 Fed. Reg. 5766 (March 21, 1972).[14] Additional suspension requests were filed by International Harvester on March 31, 1972, and by Ford Motor Company, Chrysler Corporation, and General Motors Corporation on April 5, 1972. Public hearings were held from April 10-27, 1972. Representatives of most of the major vehicle manufacturers (in addition to the applicants), a number of suppliers of emission control devices and materials, and spokesmen from various public bodies and groups, testified at the hearings and submitted written data for the public record. The decision to deny suspension to all applicants was issued on May 12, 1972.

The Decision began with the statement of the grounds for denial: ". . . I am unable, on the basis of the information submitted by the applicants or otherwise available to me, to make the determinations required by section 202(b)(5)(D)(i), (iii), or (iv) of the Act."[15] The EPA Decision specifically focused on requirement (iii) that:

> the applicant has established that effective control technology, processes, operating methods, or other alternatives are not available or have not been available for a sufficient period of time to achieve compliance prior to the effective date of such standards . . . .

[14] Evidently the Administrator decided to avoid separate suspension hearings for different applicants and awaited further filings which he anticipated. Volvo's application triggered the time period on the assumption that all applications were to be considered together. For the subsequent filings, see 37 Fed. Reg. 7039 (April 7, 1972).

[15] In re: Applications for Suspension of 1975 Motor Vehicle Exhaust Emission Standards, Decision of the Administrator, May 12, 1972 [hereinafter Decision], at 1.

A Technical Appendix, containing the analysis and methodology used by the Administrator in arriving at his decision, was subsequently issued on July 27, 1972.

B. Initial Decision of the Administrator

The data available from the concerned parties related to 384 test vehicles run by the five applicants and the eight other vehicle manufacturers subpoenaed by the Administrator. In addition, 116 test vehicles were run by catalyst and reactor manufacturers subpoenaed by the Administrator. These 500 vehicles were used to test five principal types of control systems: noble metal monolithic catalysts, base metal pellet catalysts, noble metal pellet catalysts, reactor systems, and various reactor/catalyst combinations.

At the outset of his Decision, the Administrator determined that the most effective system so far developed was the noble metal oxidizing catalyst.[16] Additionally, he stated that the "most effective systems typically include: improved carburetion; a fast-release choke; a device for promoting fuel vaporization during warm-up; more consistent and durable ignition systems; exhaust gas recirculation; and a system for injecting air into the engine exhaust manifold to cause further combustion of unburned gases and to create an oxidizing atmosphere for the catalyst."[17] It was this system to which the data base was initially narrowed: only cars using this kind of system were to be considered in making the "available technology" determination.

The problem the Administrator faced in making a determination that technology was available, on the basis of these data, was that actual tests showed only one car with actual emissions which conformed to the standard prescribing a maximum of .41 grams, per mile, of HC and 3.4 grams per mile of CO.[18] No car had actually been driven 50,000 miles, the statutory "useful life" of a vehicle and the time period for which conformity to the emission standards is required.[19] In the view of the EPA Administrator, however, the reasons for the high test readings were uncertain or ambivalent.

Instead, certain data of the auto companies were used as a starting point for making a prediction, but remolded into a more useable form for this purpose. As the Administrator put it:[20]

[16] Id. at 14.

[17] Id.

[18] This was Chrysler car #333, but even this car had not been run 50,000 miles; and conformity with the 1975 standard depended on not taking into account certain emissions over the standards, claimed by the Administrator to be due to engine malfunction. See Appendix C to the Decision of the Administrator, Analysis of Vehicle Test Data [hereinafter Technical Appendix], at 17.

[19] U.S.C. § 1857f-1(d) provides that "The Administrator shall prescribe regulations under which the useful life of vehicles and engines shall be determined . . ." for purposes of the 1975 standards. "Such regulations shall provide that useful life shall—(1) in the case of light duty vehicles and light duty vehicle engines, be a period of use of five years or fifty thousand miles (or the equivalent), whichever first occurs. . . ."

[20] Decision at 16–17.

Much of the data reports emissions measured by test procedures different from the 1975 Federal test procedure and requires conversion to the 1975 procedure by calculations which cannot be regarded as precise. Emission data was frequently submitted without an adequate description of the vehicle being tested, the emission control system employed, or the purpose of the test. The fuel and oil used in tests were not always specified. Adjustments made to components of the engine or emission control system were frequently made and seldom fully explained. In most cases, tests were not repeated, even where results departed significantly from established trends, and little or no information was submitted to explain the diagnosis of failure, where test results showed poor results. Most important, only a few test cars were driven to 20,000 miles or more, and no vehicle employing all components of any applicant's proposed 1975 control systems has yet been driven to 50,000 miles. In the face of these difficulties, analysis and interpretation of the data required assumptions and analytical approaches which will necessarily be controversial to some degree.

In light of these difficulties, the Administrator "adjusted" the data of the auto companies by use of several critical assumptions.

First, he made an adjustment to reflect the assumption that fuel used in 1975 model year cars would either contain an average of .03 grams per gallon or .05 grams per gallon of lead.[21] This usually resulted in an increase of emissions predicted, since many companies had tested their vehicles on lead free gasoline.

Second, the Administrator found that the attempt of some companies to reduce emissions of nitrogen oxides below the 1975 Federal standard of 3.0 grams per vehicle mile[22] resulted in increased emissions of hydrocarbons and carbon monoxide. This adjustment resulted in a downward adjustment of observed HC and CO data, by a specified factor.[23]

Third, the Administrator took into account the effect the "durability" of the preferred systems would have on the emission control obtainable. This required that observed readings at one point of usage be increased by a deterioration factor (DF) to project emissions at a later moment of use. The critical methodological choice was to make this adjustment from a base of emissions observed at 4000 miles. Thus, even if a car had actually been tested over 4000 miles, predicted emissions at 50,000 miles would be determined by multiplying 4000 mile emissions by the DF factor.[24]

Fourth, the Administrator adjusted for "prototype-to-production slippage." This was an upward adjustment made necessary by the possibility that prototype cars might have features which reduced HC and CO emissions, but were not capable of being used in actual production vehicles.[25]

Finally, in accord with a regulation assumed, as to substance, in the test of the Decision, but proposed after the suspension hearing,[26] a downward adjust-

[21] Id. at 18.

[22] See note 10 *supra.*

[23] Decision at 18.

[24] Id. The choice of 4000 mile emissions as a base point corresponds to certification testing procedures. 37 Fed. Reg. 24,263 (1972), § 85.073-28.

[25] Decision at 20.

[26] 37 Fed. Reg. 23,778 (November 8, 1972).

ment in the data readings was made on the basis of the manufacturers' ability, in conformance with certification procedures, to replace the catalytic converter "once during 50,000 miles of vehicle operation," a change they had not used in their testing.[27]

With the data submitted and the above assumptions, the Administrator concluded that no showing had been made that requisite technology was not available. The EPA noted that this did not mean that the variety of vehicles produced in 1975 would be as extensive as before. According to EPA, "Congress clearly intended to require major changes in the kinds of automobiles produced for sale in the United States after 1974" and there "is no basis, therefore, for construing the Act to authorizing suspension of the standards simply because the range of performance of cars with effective emission control may be restricted as compared to present cars." As long as "basic demand" for new light duty motor vehicles was satisfied, the applicants could not establish that technology was not available.[28]

For purposes of judicial review, the initial EPA decision rests on the technology determination. The Administrator did state:[29]

> On the record before me, I do not believe that it is in the public interest to grant these applications, where compliance with 1975 standards by application of present technology can probably be achieved, and where ample additional time is available to manufacturers to apply existing technology to 1975 vehicles.

The statute apparently contemplates the possibility of an EPA denial of suspension for failure to meet criterion (i) of § 202(b)(5)(D) ("essential to the public interest") even though criterion (iii) has been satisfied ("applicant has established that effective control technology . . . [is] not available").[30] It suffices here to say that the EPA's 1972 "public interest" finding was obviously only a restatement of, and dependent on the validity of, the conclusion of a failure to satisfy standard (iii) by showing that effective control technology is not available.

The Administrator also offered some "comments" on issues pertinent to the required "good faith" determination under standard (ii), as guidance to applications who might seek a one year suspension next year of the 1976 oxides of nitrogen standard. But he explicitly disclaimed reaching that question in this proceeding. The thrust of his comment was to call into question the rigid "arms length" relationship structure which vehicle manufacturers imposed on their suppliers, as a source of a halter on progress in developing the required technology.[31]

---

[27] Decision at 20.

[28] Id. at 9.

[29] Id. at 30.

[30] See Part III of the opinion where factors which might properly enter into such a determination are discussed.

[31] The Administrator noted, however, that the "closest working relationship between a vehicle manufacturer and a catalyst company that has been brought to my attention has been the Ford technical interchange arrangement with Englehard." Decision at 26.

C. This Court's December 1972 Remand

After oral argument to this court on December 18, 1972, in a per curiam order issued December 19, 1972, we remanded the record to the Administrator, directing him to supplement his May 12, 1972 decision by setting forth:

> (a) the consideration given by the Administrator to the January 1, 1972 Semiannual Report on Technological Feasibility of the National Academy of Sciences; and (b) the basis for his disagreement, if any, with the findings and conclusion in that study concerning the availability of effective technology to achieve compliance with the 1975 model year standards set forth in the Act.

Our remand order was not intended to indicate that we had concluded that an EPA conclusion was required as to clause (iv)—concerning the evaluation based on the NAS study and other information (from sources other than applicants)—when the Administrator had determined under (iii) that the auto companies had not shown technology was not available. We were nevertheless troubled by arguments advanced by petitioners that the methodology used by the Administrator in reaching his conclusion, and indeed the conclusion itself, was inconsistent with that of the Academy. It was our view that if and to the extent such differences existed they should be explained by EPA, in order to aid us in determining whether the Administrator's conclusion under (iii) rested on a reasoned basis.

D. Supplement to the Decision of the Administrator

Our remand of the record resulted in a "Supplement to Decision of the Administrator" issued December 30, 1972. The Administrator in his Supplement stated that "In General I consider the factual findings and technical conclusions set forth in the NAS report and in the subsequent Interim Standards Report dated April 26, 1972 . . . to be consistent with my decision of May 12, 1972."[32]

The Report made by the NAS, pursuant to its obligation under 202(b)(5)(D) of the Clean Air Act, had concluded: "The Committee finds that the technology necessary to meet the requirements of the Clean Air Act Amendments for 1975 model year light-duty motor vehicles is not available at this time."[33]

The Administrator apparently relied, however, on the NAS Report to bolster his conclusion that the applicants had not established that technology was unavailable. The same NAS Report had stated:[34]

> . . . the status of development and rate of progress made it possible that the larger manufacturers will be able to produce vehicles that will qualify, provided that provi-

---

[32] In re: Applications For Suspension of 1975 Motor Vehicle Exhaust Emission Standards, Supplement to Decision of the Administrator, December 30, 1972 [hereinafter Supplement to Decision] at 1.

[33] Committee on Motor Vehicle Emissions, National Academy of Sciences, Semiannual Report to the Environmental Protection Agency, January 1, 1972 [hereinafter NAS Report] at 49.

[34] Id.

sions are made for catalyst replacement and other maintenance, for averaging emissions of production vehicles, and for the general availability of fuel containing suitably low levels of catalyst poisons.

The Administrator pointed out that two of NAS's provisos—catalytic converter replacement and low lead levels—had been accounted for in his analysis of the auto company data, and provision therefor had been insured through regulation.[35] As to the third, "averaging emissions of production vehicles,"[36] the Administrator offered two reasons for declining to make a judgment about this matter: (1) The significance of averaging related to possible assembly-line tests, as distinct from certification test procedure, and such tests had not yet been worked out. (2) If there were an appropriate assembly-line test it would be expected that each car's emissions could be in conformity, without a need for averaging, since the assembly-line vehicles "equipped with fresh catalysts can be expected to have substantially lower emissions at zero miles than at 4000 miles."[37]

The Administrator also claimed that he had employed the same methodology as the NAS used in its Interim Standards Report, evidently referring to the use of 4000 mile emissions as a base point, and correction for a deterioration factor and a prototype-production slippage factor.[38] The identity of methodology was also indicated, in his view, by the fact the EPA and NAS both agreed on the component parts of the most effective emission control system.

The Administrator did refer to the "severe driveability problems" underscored by the NAS Report, which in the judgment of NAS "could have significant safety implications,"[39] stating that he had not been presented with any evidence of "specific safety hazard" nor knew of any presented to the NAS. He did not address himself to issue of performance problems falling short of specific safety hazards.

II. REJECTION OF MANUFACTURERS' GENERAL CONTENTIONS

We begin with consideration, and rejection, of the broad objections leveled by petitioners against EPA's overall approach.

A. Future Technological Developments

We cannot accept petitioners' arguments that the Administrator's determination whether technology was "available," within the meaning of section 202(b)(5)(D) of the Act, must be based solely on technology in being as of the time of the

[35] Supplement to Decision at 2-3.
[36] Id. at 3-4.
[37] Id. at 4, quoting from Decision at 11.
[38] See Committee on Motor Vehicle Emissions, National Academy of Sciences, Interim Standards Report, April 26, 1972 [hereinafter Interim Standards Report].
[39] NAS Report at 30.

application, and that the requirement that this be "available" precludes any consideration by the Administrator of what he determines to be the "probable" or
likely sequence of the technology already experienced. Congress recognized that
approximately two years' time was required before the start of production for a
given model year, for the preparation of tooling and manufacturing processes.[40]
But Congress did not decide—and there is no reason for us to do so—that all
development had to be completed before the tooling-up period began. The manufacturers' engineers have admitted that technological improvements can continue
during the two years prior to production.[41] Thus there was a sound basis for the
Administrator's conclusion that the manufacturers could "improve, test, and apply" technology during the lead time period.[42]

The petitioners' references to the legislative history are unconvincing. None
of the statements quoted in their briefs specifically states that "available" as used
in the statute means "available in 1972." There is even comment that points to a
contrary interpretation.[43] In any event, we think the legislative history is consistent with the EPA's basic approach and evidences no ascertainable legislative
intent to the contrary.

While we reject the contention as broadly stated, principally by General
Motors, we hasten to add that the Administrator's latitude for projection is subject to the restraints of reasonableness, and does not open the door to " 'crystal
ball' inquiry."[44] The Administrator's latitude for projection is unquestionably limited by relevant considerations of lead time needed for production.[45] Implicit also
is a requirement of reason in the EPA projection. In the present case, the Administrator's prediction of available technology was based on known elements of
existing catalytic converter systems. This was a permissible approach subject, of
course, to the requirement that any technological developments or refinements of
existing systems, used as part of the EPA methodology, would have to rest on a
reasoned basis.

B. Claimed Right of Cross-Examination

Chrysler has advanced a due process claim based upon two principal features of
the proceeding, the inability to engage in cross-examination and the inability to

---

[40] Although various estimates were made during the debate, the consensus seemed to be that two
years is the most reasonable estimate. This was apparently the understanding of the Conference
Committee. See 116 Cong. Rec. 42,522 (1970) (Rep. Staggers, Manager on the part of the House).

[41] In testimony before the Administrator, Ford's Vice President for Engineering and Manufacturing identified as the "last date for incorporation of proven new technology" November 1, 1973—16
months after the start of the tooling-up period. He testified that the companies could be "developing
engineering solutions" until that date. Hearing Tr. at 1916; cf. id. at 203304. Cf. Statement of Lee A.
Iacocca in Hearings on S. 3229, S. 3446, S. 3546, before Subcomm. on Public Works, 91st Cong., 2d
Sess. pt. 5, 1620-21 (1970).

[42] Decision at 29.

[43] See 116 Cong. Rec. 33,086-87 (1970) (Statement of Senator Gurney).

[44] *National Resources Defense Council, Inc. v. Morton,* 148 U.S. App. D.C. 5, 15, 458 F.2d 827
(1972).

[45] Remarks of Senator Gurney, 116 Cong. Rec. 33,086 (1970).

present arguments against the methodology used in the Technical Appendix of the Administrator, which served as a basis for his decision.

The suspension provision of Section 202(b)(5)(D) does not require a trial type hearing. It provides:

> Within 60 days after receipt of the application for any such suspension, and after public hearing, the Administrator shall issue a decision granting or refusing such suspension.

First, this provision for a "public hearing" contrasts significantly with other provisions that specifically require an adjudicatory hearing.[46] More importantly, the non-adjudicatory nature of the "public hearing" contemplated is understood by the 60 day limit for a decision to be made. The procedure contemplated by Congress in its 1970 legislation must be appraised in light of its concern with "avoidance of previous cumbersome and time consuming procedures," see *Kennecott Copper Corp. v. EPA,* 149 U.S. App. D.C. 231, 234, 462 F.2d 846, 849 (1972).

As to legislative history of this provision, the starting point is the provision in Senate Bill 4358:[47]

> Upon receipt of such application, the Secretary shall promptly hold a public hearing to enable such manufacturer or manufacturers to present information relevant to the implementation of such standard. The Secretary, in his discretion, may permit any interested person to intervene to present information relevant to the implementation of such standard.

This was dropped in conference, along with a provision permitting six months for a suspension decision. The resulting legislation both expedited the decision-making, and contemplated EPA solicitation of a wide range of views, from sources other than the auto companies, though the companies' applications and presentation would surely be the focus of consideration. Underlying this approach of both shortening time for decision and enlarging input lies, we think, an assumption of an informative but efficient procedure without mandate for oral cross-examination.

In context, the "public hearing" provision amounts to an assurance by Congress that the issues would not be disposed of merely on written comments, the minimum protection assured by the Administrative Procedure Act for rule-making when "controversial regulations governing competitive practices" are involved. *American Airlines, Inc. v. CAB,* 123 U.S. App. D.C. 310, 317, 359 F.2d 624, 631 (en banc 1966), cert. denied, 385 U.S. 843 (1966); *Walter Holm & Co. v. Hardin,* 145 U.S. App. D.C. 347, 449 F.2d 1009 (1971). Even assuming oral sub-

---

[46] For instances in the Act where adjudicatory hearings are called for, see § 1857c-5(f)(2) (hearing on one-year postponement of a plan requirement on application of State Governor); § 206(b)(2)(B), 42 U.S.C. § 1857f-5(b)(2)(B) (hearing on suspension or revocation of motor vehicle certifications). Both determinations must be made "on the record."

[47] See S. 4358, 91st Cong., 2d Sess., printed in S. Rep. No. 91-1196, 91st Cong., 2d Sess., 103 (1970).

mission, in a situation where "general policy" is the focal question, a legislative-type hearing is appropriate.[48]

A complication is presented by the case before us in that the general policy questions became interfused with relatively specific technical issues. Yet within the context of a quasi-legislative hearing and the time constraints of the statute, we do not think the absence of a general right of cross-examination on the part of the companies was a departure from "basic considerations of fairness." *Walter Holm & Co. v. Hardin, supra,* 145 U.S. App. D.C. at 354, 449 F.2d at 1016. Hearings ran for two weeks and a wide range of participants was included within the proceeding: manufacturers, vendors of the control devices and public interest groups. The auto companies were allowed to submit written questions to the Hearing Panel to be asked to various witnesses. Opportunity to prepare written questions is not as satisfactory to counsel as the opportunity to proceed on oral cross-examination, with questions that develop from previous answers. But examination on interrogatories has long been used in the law when necessary, albeit second best. And interrogatories to a live witness—often arranged in private lawsuits by use of a commission—avoid the peril of "canned" affidavits and counsel-assisted, or even counsel-drafted responses to interrogatories. Their availability was a reasonable attempt by EPA to elicit the facts and at the same time cope with the time constraints. We do not think more was required. There was a meaningful opportunity to be heard. The specific nature of a "hearing" varies with circumstances. The heft of the hearing problem including the time constraints on decisions, convinces us that the assertion of a broad right of cross-examination cannot be successfully maintained.

We distinguish between the assertion of a broad right of cross-examination, such as that argued to this court, and a claim of a need for cross-examination of live witnesses on a subject of critical importance which could not be adequately ventilated under the general procedures. This is the kind of distinction that this court made in its en banc opinion in *American Airlines v. CAB, supra,* 123 U.S. App. D.C. at 318–19, 359 F.2d at 632–33. We see no principled manner in which firm time limits can be scheduled for cross-examination consistent with its unique potential as an "engine of truth"—the capacity given a diligent and resourceful counsel to expose subdued premises, to pursue evasive witnesses, to "explore" the whole witness, often traveling unexpected avenues.

Given the variances in counsel, the reality that seasoning and experience are required even for trial judges who seek to avoid repetitive and undue cross-examination, the enhancement of difficulties encountered with the breadth of issues involved in a "public interest" proceeding, the fairly-anticipated problem of provi-

---

[48] See *United States v. Florida East Coast R. Co.,* 410 U.S. 224 (1973) where the Court held that rule-making hearings, under 5 U.S.C. § 553, are sufficient where the agency's statute provides for a "hearing." The provision of 5 U.S.C. § 556(d) which gives the opportunity for cross-examination as a matter of right, would only be automatically applicable if "rules are required by statute to be made on the record after opportunity for an agency hearing. . . ." Without the precise words "on the record," § 556 does not automatically apply.

The words "on the record" are not incorporated into Section 202(b)(5)(D). Only a "public hearing" is required. Moreover, subsection (iv) of that provision allows consideration by the Administrator of "other information available to him" in reaching a conclusion on "available technology."

sion for redirect (and re-cross) and the interplay of different cross-examinations, there is not insignificant potential for havoc. What is most significant is that these complications are likely to be disproportionate to the values achieved, in a proceeding focusing on technical matters where other techniques generally are sufficient to adduce the pertinent information as to both what is known and unknown.

In context, we consider that the technique, adopted by EPA, of pre-screening written questions submitted in advance is reasonable and comports with basic fairness as the general procedure. This approach permits screening by the hearing officer so as to avoid irrelevance and repetition, permits a reasonable estimate of the time required for the questioning, and aids scheduling and allocation of available time among various participants and interests.[49] The record reveals that the hearing officers did not propound the pre-submitted questions like robots; they were charged with conducting a hearing for the purpose of focusing information needed for decision, and they quite appropriately "followed up" on questions.

We revert to our observation that a right of cross-examination, consistent with time limitations, might well extend to particular cases of need, on critical points where the general procedure proved inadequate to probe "soft" and sensitive subjects and witnesses. No such circumscribed and justified requests were made in this proceeding.

C. Right to Comment on EPA Methodology

A more serious problem, at least from the point of an informed decision-making process, is posed by the inability of petitioners to challenge the methodology of EPA at the hearing. In other contexts, it is commonplace for administrative proceedings to focus in detail on agency methodology,[50] and such elucidation is salutary, of particular aid to a reviewing court. Again, however, we cannot ignore the problem of time. In part, EPA developed its methodology on the basis of submissions made by the companies at the hearings, as to the parameters of its various data. The requirement of submission of a proposed rule for comment does not automatically generate a new opportunity for comment merely because the rule promulgated by the agency differs from the rule it proposed, partly at least in response to submissions.[51] Given the circumstances, we cannot hold the absence of the right to comment on the methodology a violation of the statute or due process, though such opportunity would certainly have been salutary.

---

[49] The procedure adopted may be justified, in part, on grounds like those supporting voir dire by the trial judge, using questions submitted by counsel. See *United States v. Bryant*, 471 F.2d 1040 (1972).

[50] E.g., Permian Basin Area Rate Cases, 390 U.S. 747 (1968).

[51] A contrary rule would lead to the absurdity that in rule-making under the APA the agency can learn from the comments on its proposals only at the peril of starting a new procedural round of commentary.

As we have stated in an analogous context of rule-making proceedings before the Federal Communications Commission, where petitioners have argued that the Commission was "changing the rules in the middle of the game" when it took into consideration factors not specifically indicated in its Section 4(a) notice under the Administrative Procedure Act, 5 U.S.C. § 1001(a), "[s]urely every time the Commission decided to take account of some additional factor it was not required to start the proceedings all over again. If such were the rule the proceedings might never be terminated." *Owensboro On the Air v. U.S.*, 104 U.S. App. D.C. 391, 397; 262 F.2d 702, 708 (1958); *Logansport Broadcasting Corp. v. United States*, 93 U.S. App. D.C. 342, 346, 210 F.2d 24, 28 (1954).

While the statute makes no express provision therefor, we assume that Congress contemplated a flexibility in the administrative process permitting the manufacturers to present to EPA any comments as to its methodology, in a petition for reconsideration or modification. However, this opportunity does not permit invocation of the doctrine of failure to exhaust administrative remedies as a bar to these appeals, for those petitions could not have affected or deferred the finality of the EPA decision or the time for seeking judicial review. The opportunity is noted to obviate any possibility that the law, or our comments, may be misunderstood to require a rigid procedure of prompt and unshakeable decision-making. Our own December remand requesting clarification of the Decision illustrates that while this statute imposes some unusual time restraints it does not jettison the flexibility and capacity of reexamination that is rooted in the administrative process. *American Airlines v. CAB, supra,* 123 U.S. App. D.C. at 319, 359 F.2d at 633.

As matters have shaped up, the central technical issue on this appeal concerns the reliability of EPA's methodology. While we do not say that the failure to provide reasonable opportunity to comment on EPA methodology invalidates the EPA Decision for lack of procedural due process, or similar contention, we must in all candor accompany that ruling with the comment that the lack of such opportunity has had serious implications for the court given the role of judicial review.

We shall subsequently develop the legal questions, primarily questions of EPA's burden of proof, that arise with respect to EPA methodology. We preface these with admission of our doubts and diffidence. We are beset with contentions of petitioners that bear indicia of substantiality. Yet we have no EPA comment on the specific questions raised, apart from some discussion by counsel which is not an adequate or appropriate substitute.[52] Our December 1972 remand opened the door to a candid discussion of these matters, but EPA fashioned a carefully limited response.

The EPA might have indicated that it desired to take a fresh look at its methodology on the basis of petitioners' criticisms, in which case, on an adaptation of the *Smith v. Pollin*[53] procedure, this court might have remanded the case to the agency. This remand would come during the course of our judicial review and would not conflict with the 60 day statutory time limit for the hearing and decision on the applications for suspension.

Indeed, the fact that the Administrator issued the Technical Appendix almost three months after his decision, at a time when judicial review had already begun to run its course, indicates that the agency did not believe that agency consideration was frozen from the moment that the suspension decision was rendered, a view we approve. The EPA had latitude to continue further consideration even without requesting a court remand (under *Smith v. Pollin*) that would suspend judicial consideration.

---

[52] *Burlington Truck Lines v. United States,* 371 U.S. 156, 168–9 (1962); *Braniff Airways, Inc. v. CAB,* 126 U.S. App. D.C. 399, 411, 379 F.2d 453, 465 (1967).

[53] 90 U.S. App. D.C. 178, 194 F.2d 349 (1952). See also *Greater Boston Television Corp. v. FCC,* 149 U.S. App. D.C. 322, 463 F.2d 268 (1971).

III. OVERALL PERSPECTIVE OF SUSPENSION ISSUE

This case ultimately involves difficult issues of statutory interpretation, as to the showing required for applicants to sustain their burden that technology is not available. It also taxes our ability to understand and evaluate technical issues upon which that showing, however it is to be defined, must rest. At the same time, however, larger questions are at stake. As Senator Baker put it, "This may be the biggest industrial judgment that has been made in the United States in this century." 116 Cong. Rec. 33,085 (1970). This task of reviewing the suspension decision was not assigned to us lightly. It was the judgment of Congress that this court, isolated as it is from political pressures, and able to partake of calm and judicious reflection would be a more suitable forum for review than even the Congress.[54]

Two principal considerations compete for our attention. On the one hand, if suspension is not granted, and the prediction of the EPA Administrator that effective technology will be available is proven incorrect, grave economic consequences could ensue. This is the problem Senator Griffin described as the "dangerous game of economic roulette." 116 Cong. Rec. 33,081 (1970). On the other hand, if suspension is granted and it later be shown that the Administrator's prediction of feasibility was achievable in 1975 there may be irretrievable ecological costs. It is to this second possibility to which we first turn.

A.   Potential Environmental Costs

The most authoritative estimate in the record of the ecological costs of a one-year suspension is that of the NAS Report. Taking into account such "factors as the vehicle-age distribution among all automobiles, the decrease in vehicle miles driven per year, per car as vehicle age increases, the predicted nation-wide growth in vehicle miles driven each year" and the effect of emission standards on exhaust control, NAS concluded that:[55]

> . . . the effect on total emissions of a one-year suspension with no additional interim standards appears to be small. The effect is not more significant because the emission reduction now required of model year 1974 vehicles, as compared with uncontrolled vehicles (80 percent for HC and 69 percent for CO), is already so substantial.

Other considerations may diminish the costs even further. There seems to be agreement that there are performance costs for automobiles in employing pollution control devices, even if the effects on performance cannot fairly be characterized as constituting safety hazards. The NAS Report summarized the problem, as follows:[56]

---

[54] An amendment to Senate Bill 4358 proposed by Senator Dole of Kansas, which would have made the suspension decision reviewable by Congress instead of the court, as proposed by the Committee, 116 Cong. Rec. 33,078 (1970), was rejected by the Senate, 116 Cong. Rec. 33,089 (1970).

[55] NAS Report at 45–48.

[56] Id. at 29.

Three areas of vehicle performance are likely to be adversely affected by the 1975 emission control systems. These are fuel economy, vehicle-acceleration capability, and vehicle driveability (or ability to perform adequately in all normal operating modes and ambient conditions).

The question in this context is not whether these are costs the consumer should rightly bear if ecological damage is to be minimized, but rather the general effect on consumer purchasing of 1975 model year cars in anticipation of lower performance. A drop-off in purchase of 1975 cars will result in a prolonged usage of older cars with less efficient pollution control devices. If the adverse performance effect deterred purchasing significantly enough, resulting in greater retention of "older" cars in the "mix" of cars in use, it might even come to pass that total actual emissions (of all cars in use) would be greater under the 1975 than the 1974 standards.

Many of the anticipated performance problems are traceable to the systems introduced to conform cars to control of nitrogen oxides to achieve prescribed 1975 standards, by use of exhaust-gas recycle (EGR). Such systems affect vehicle-acceleration capability because the power output for a given engine displacement, engine speed, and throttle setting is reduced.[57] The NAS Report indicates that such systems could result in direct fuel-economy penalties of up to 12 percent compared with 1973 prototype vehicles.[58]

The NAS Report states that the effects of emission controls on vehicle drive-ability are difficult to quantify, but nevertheless makes the following qualitative evaluation:[59]

Driveability after a cold-engine start, and especially with cold ambient conditions, is likely to be impaired. To reduce HC and CO emissions during engine warmup, the choke is set to release quickly, and the fuel-air mixture is leaned out as early as possible after engine startup. Under these conditions, problems of engine stall, and vehicle stumble and hesitation on rapid acceleration, have been prevalent.

The willingness of the consumer to buy 1975 model year cars may also be affected, to some degree, by the anticipated significant costs of pollution control devices. The problem is further bedeviled by the possibility that consumers, albeit rightly assigned the cost burden of pollution devices, may seek to avoid that burden, however modest,[60] and to exercise, at least in some measure, an option to use older cars. Again, this would have the thrust of increasing actual total emissions of cars in use.

[57] Id.
[58] Id.
[59] Id. at 30.
[60] The NAS estimated an increase in initial cost of about $214, Id. at 42 over the 1973–74 model year system, and $288 over the 1970 system. To this must be added the EPA assumption of at least one catalytic converter replacement during 50,000 miles of vehicle operation, see text at note 35, *supra*, and the possibility that considerable maintenance may be needed to keep converters at required level of efficient operation.

We may also note that it is the belief of many experts—both in and out of the automobile industry—that air pollution cannot be effectively checked until the industry finds a substitute for the conventional automotive power plant—the reciprocating internal combustion (i.e., "piston") engine.[61] According to this view, the conventional unit is a "dirty" engine. While emissions from such a motor can be "cleaned" by various thermal and catalytic converter devices, these devices do nothing to decrease the production of emissions in the engine's combustion chambers. The automobile industry has a multibillion-dollar investment in the conventional engine, and it has been reluctant to introduce new power plants or undertake major modifications of the conventional one.[62] Thus the bulk of the industry's work on emission control has focused narrowly on converter devices. It is clear from the legislative history that Congress expected the Clean Air Amendments to force the industry to broaden the scope of its research—to study new types of engines and new control systems.[63] Perhaps even a one-year suspension does not give the industry sufficient time to develop a new approach to emission control and still meet the absolute deadline of 1976. If so, there will be ample time for the EPA and Congress, between now and 1976, to reflect on changing the statutory approach. This kind of cooperation, a unique three-way partnership between the legislature, executive and judiciary, was contemplated by the Congress[64] and is apparent in the provisions of the Act.[65]

The NAS estimated that there would be a small environmental cost to suspension of 1975 standards even if the 1974 standards were retained, but further recommended intermediate standards that would dilute even such modest environmental cost.[66] The following table shows the various standards, and one put forward by Ford for 1975:

---

[61] See, e.g., U.S. General Accounting Office, Report to the Congress: Cleaner Engines for Cleaner Air, at 45–47 (May 15, 1972) (hereinafter "G.A.O. Report"); statement of Fred C. Hart, New York City Environmental Protection Agency, in Implementation of the Clean Air Act Amendments of 1970, Hearing before the Subcomm. on Air and Water Pollution, Senate Comm. on Public Works, 92d Cong., 2d Sess., pt. 3, 1597 (1972).

[62] The General Accounting Office reported in 1972 that the industry was "entrenched" in efforts to retain the conventional engine. G.A.O. Report at 45.

[63] 116 Cong. Rec. 32,906 (1970) (Sen. Muskie); H.R. Rep. No. 91-1146, 91st Cong., 2d Sess. 6 (1970).

[64] Congress made clear that it would be ready to exercise its right to intervene if it did not agree with the results its statutory "shock treatment" produced. See 116 Cong. Rec. 32,905 (1970) (Senator Muskie). Congress, through Oversight Hearings conducted by the Subcommittee on Air and Water Pollution of the United States Senate, continues to keep a watchful eye on the implementation of the Act. See Implementation of the Clean Air Act Amendments of 1970, Hearings before the Subcomm. on Air and Water Pollution, Senate Comm. on Public Works, 92d Cong., 2d Sess., pts. 103 (1970).

[65] The Act provides for various progress reports to be made by the Administrator to the Congress, 42 U.S.C. § 1857j-1 and 2. Additional information is supplied by the Semiannual Reports of the National Academy of Sciences. 42 U.S.C. § 1857f-1(c). More particularly, the Act provides, 42 U.S.C. § 1857f-1(b)(4), for the EPA to make "recommendations for additional congressional action" which he deems advisable.

[66] Interim Standards Report at 8.

Maximum emissions (grams per mile)

	HC	CO
1974 standards	3.4	39.0
Ford Proposal	1.6	19.0
NAS recommendation for Intermediate standards:		
No catalyst change	1.1	8.2
One catalyst change	0.8	6.3
1975 Standards	.41	3.4

Our concern that the 1975 standards may possibly be counter-productive, due to decreased driveability and increased cost, is not to be extrapolated into a caution against any improvement, and concomitant reduction in permitted emissions. In such matters, as the NAS recommendation for interim standards implicitly suggests, a difference in degree may be critical, and the insistence on absolute 1975 standards, without suspension or intermediate level, may stretch for the increment that is essentially counter-productive.

We also observe that Ford Motor Company is on record as to capability of greater emission controls, i.e., lower level of emissions, than those permitted for 1974 model year cars,[67] and Ford proposed that, given certain regulatory assumption,[68] the Administrator adopt an interim standard of 1.6 gm/mi HC and 19.0 gm/mi CO levels, about one half those permitted for the 1974 model year cars.

On balance the record indicates the environmental costs of a one-year suspension are likely to be relatively modest. This must be balanced against the potential economic costs—and ecological costs if the Administrator's prediction on the availability of effective technology is incorrect.

B. Potential Economic Costs

Theoretical Possibility of Industry Shutdown   If in 1974, when model year 1975 cars start to come off the production line, the automobiles of Ford, General Motors and Chrysler cannot meet the 1975 standards and do not qualify for certification, the Administrator of EPA has the theoretical authority, under the Clean Air Act, to shut down the auto industry, as was clearly recognized in Congressional debate.[69] We cannot put blinders on the facts before us so as to omit awareness of the reality that this authority would undoubtedly never be

---

[67] JA at 954–59; Doc. No. 135, Vol. II at 5-18 to 5-23.

[68] Ford's proposals were qualified by the following regulatory assumptions: (1) maximum lead grams per gallon of gasoline .03; (2) averaging of emissions for certification test procedures; (3) a methane allowance in interpreting hydrocarbon data; and (4) reasonable maintenance on durability test cars used in determining certification. Only the reasonable maintenance assumption corresponds to actual EPA regulations now in effect or proposed. Doc. No. 135, Vol. II, at 5-28 to 5-33.

[69] 116 Cong. Rec. 32,905 (1970).

exercised, in light of the fact that approximately 1 out of every 7 jobs in this country is dependent on the production of the automobile.[70] Senator Muskie, the principal sponsor of the bill, stated quite clearly in the debate on the Act that he envisioned the Congress acting if an auto industry shutdown were in sight.[71]

The Economic Consequence of an Approach Geared to Stringency, Relying on Relaxation as a Safety Valve   A more likely forecast, and one which enlightens what influenced the EPA decision to deny the suspension, was articulated by George Allen, Deputy Assistant Administrator for General Enforcement and a member of EPA's Hearing Panel:[72]

> The problem really comes down to this: A decision has to be made next month, early next month. If the decision is to suspend the standards and adopt an interim standard . . . and in 1975 it turns out that technology exists to meet the statutory standard, today's decision turns out to be wrong.
>
> *   *   *
>
> If, on the other hand, a decision is made today that the standards cannot lawfully be suspended, and we go down to 1975 and nobody can meet the standard, today's decision was wrong.
>
> In [the first] case, there is not much to do about the wrong decision; it was made, many people relied on it; it turns out the standard could have been met, but I doubt if we could change it.
>
> In the second case, if a wrong decision is made, there is probably a remedy, a reapplication and a recognition by the agency that it is not technically feasible to meet the standards. You can correct the one; you probably can't correct the other.

Grave problems are presented by the assumption that if technical feasibility proves to be a "wrong decision" it can be remedied by a relaxation.

Certain techniques available to the Administrator, through changes in the certification procedure, can be used in an even handed manner for all three auto companies to facilitate compliance with the 1975 standards. Already lower lead levels in fuel available for 1975 model year cars have been prescribed to increase the efficiency of the catalytic converter. Similarly certain changes in the regulatory system, through allowable maintenance and permitted change in the catalytic converter, have been made by EPA. These techniques work with reasonable impartiality as to the various auto companies.

However, a relaxation of standards, and promulgation of an interim standard, at a later hour—after the base hour for "lead time" has been passed, and the production sequence set in motion—forebodes quite different consequences. The record before us suggests that there already exists a technological gap between Ford and General Motors,[73] in Ford's favor. General Motors did not make the

---

[70] Estimate provided by Senator Griffin, 116 Cong. Rec. 32,906 (1970).

[71] 116 Cong. Rec. 32,905 (1970).

[72] Transcript at 2034–35.

[73] For purposes of a comparison, Chrysler is omitted from this comparison, although on the basis of the performance of car #333 and its testing of noble metal catalysts, Chrysler seems closer in technological advancement to Ford than to General Motors. See Technical Appendix at 17.

decision to concentrate on what EPA found to be the most effective system at the time of its decision—the noble metal monolithic catalyst. Instead it relied principally on testing the base metal catalyst as its first choice system.[74] In predicting that General Motors could meet the 1975 standards, EPA employed a unique methodological approach. Instead of taking emissions at 4000 miles of cars with preferred systems—with which none of the General Motors cars was equipped—and applying against this, adjustments for lead levels and deterioration, as had been done in the case of Ford and Chrysler, EPA took emissions at 4000 miles of GM cars which had no converters of any kind, and predicted how they would function with an Engelhard monolithic catalytic converter, based on auto manufacturers' use of this device in a number of cars—principally Ford's—when testing it for durability.[75] In his Supplemental Decision the Administrator recognized that this was a departure from NAS methodology, stating:[76]

> In its Interim Standards Report the National Academy recommended a methodology for predicting the emission levels achievable by manufacturers. This recommended methodology is the same methodology that was employed in the technical appendix to my decision in evaluating the test results of all manufacturers except General Motors.

The case is haunted by the irony that what seems to be Ford's technological lead[77] may operate to its grievous detriment, assuming the relaxation-if-necessary approach voiced by Mr. Allen.[78] If in 1974, when certification of production vehicles begins, any one of the three major companies cannot meet the 1975 standards,

---

[74] Id. at 44.

[75] The data on the efficiency of the Engelhard converter was from converters tested principally on Ford vehicles. Id. at 53.

[76] Supplement to Decision at 1.

[77] See also discussion of good faith in Administrator's Initial Decision at 26, where Ford was singled out as the only auto company which has developed a close relationship with a vendor of emission control devices, in its case Engelhard.

[78] We are not unaware of 42 U.S.C. § 1857h-6 which provides under certain specified procedures for the mandatory licensing of patents on pollution control devices to obviate competitive advantages. It provides:
Whenever the Attorney General determines, upon application of the Administrator—
(1) that—
(A) in the implementation of the requirements of section 1857c-6, 1857c-7, or 1857f-1 of this title, a right under any United States letters patent, which is being used or intended for public or commercial use and not otherwise reasonably available, is necessary to enable any person required to comply with such limitation to so comply, and
(B) there are no reasonable alternative methods to accomplish such purpose, and
(2) that the unavailability of such right may result in a substantial lessening of competition or tendency to create a monopoly in any line of commerce in any section of the country,
the Attorney General may so certify to a district court of the United States, which may issue an order requiring the person who owns such patent to license it on such reasonable terms and conditions as the court, after hearing, may determine. Such certification may be made to the district court for the district in which the person owning the patent resides, does business, or is found. No application has, however, been made by the Administrator, presumably because his methodology predicts all three manufacturers can meet the 1975 standards. Moreover, there is no evidence on the record to show that converters will perform equally well on different vehicles. This option may be effectively foreclosed as the lead time for production is approached, at which point the companies will be committed to their own individually developed systems.

it is a likelihood that standards will be set to permit the higher level of emission control achievable by the laggard. This will be the case whether or not the leader has or has not achieved compliance with the 1975 standards. Even if the relaxation is later made industry-wide, the Government's action, in first imposing a standard not generally achievable and then relaxing it, is likely to be detrimental to the leader who has tooled up to meet a higher standard than will ultimately be required.

In some contexts high achievement bestows the advantage that rightly belongs to the leader, of high quality. In this context before us, however, the high achievement in emission control results, under systems presently available, in lessened car performance—an inverse correlation. The competitive disadvantage to the ecological leader presents a forbidding outcome—if the initial assumption of feasibility is not validated, and there is subsequent relaxation—for which we see no remedy.[79]

C. Light Weight Trucks

We now take up the serious contention of International Harvester (IH) that the EPA decision effectively rules out the production of 1975 model year IH light weight trucks and multi-purpose passenger vehicles (MPVs). This requires us to focus on the Administrator's conception that the 1970 Clean Air Act envisioned restricting production of vehicles to that necessary to fill "basic demand."[80]

The Administrator does not dispute International Harvester's claim that it will not be able to produce the vehicles in question, and indeed the limited testing of one of its MPVs showed, even as evaluated by EPA methodology, that such standards could not be achieved.[81] Yet a suspension was not granted, presumably for the reasons advanced by EPA to this court, that International Harvester was "required to alter the performance characteristics of its vehicles in the interest of meeting the 1975 emission standards."[82] The inability of IH vehicles to meet the standards seems accountable by the uses to which they are put, hauling large loads or towing heavy trailers. To serve this purpose vehicles must be designed with higher than normal axle ratios, thus requiring greater power from the engine and producing higher exhaust gas temperatures in order to attain any given speed.[83] Therefore, for all practical purposes a redesign of performance characteristics will preclude the present uses to which IH vehicles are put.

---

[79] One could imagine some form of regulation through interim standards, whereby the laggard could be deprived of an expected windfall, through requiring some percentage of his vehicles to meet a standard which can only be met by the leader; but this form of economic regulation does not seem contemplated by Congress and would be subject to innumerable regulatory problems. Congressional indemnities might present a possibility. Obviously neither possibility could reasonably be taken into account as a basis for decision.

[80] Decision at 9–10.

[81] See Technical Appendix at 58–60.

[82] (1) Brief of Respondent at 37. (Respondents submitted two briefs to this court, one responsive only to the petition of International Harvester in case No. 72-1517, the other responsive to all four petitioners. For reference the former is denoted as (1), the latter as (2).

[83] Brief of IH at 24–25. Also see Transcript at 1167 et seq.

The Administrator, nonetheless, takes the position that International Harvester can be denied a suspension because he has found that "new car demand" will be satisfied by the production of the major auto companies, and thus apparently posits that the absence from the 1975 market of all light weight trucks and MPVs is fully consistent with the Act. We cannot agree.

Section 202(b)(1) of the Act applies its drastic standards to 1975 models of "light duty vehicles." It is our view that the legislative history reveals this term to mean "passenger cars." In the Report of the Senate Committee on Public Works on S. 4358,[84] the Committee clearly distinguished between the automobile, which must "meet a rigid timetable and a high degree of emission control compliance," and other vehicles, such as "trucks and buses and other commercial vehicles," which are governed by a different authority to promulgate standards. At another point of the Senate Report, the legislative use of the term light duty vehicles, as interchangeable with passenger cars, is made even more clear:[85]

> The authority provided in section 202(a) would continue to be available to the [Administrator] to establish standards for light duty motor vehicles (passenger cars) during the period prior to and following the effective date of the standards established by subsection (b).

References abound in Congressional debate to the same effect.[86] This kind of legislative intent must be given priority, in interpreting this law, over any presumption of continuance of prior administrative definitions of this term[87] or to the policy of upholding reasonable interpretations of statutes by administrative agencies[88] in the absence of other discernible legislative intent. *Volkswagenwerk v. FMC*, 390 U.S. 261, 272 (1967); *Greater Boston Television Corp. v. FCC* (I), 143 U.S. App. D.C. 383, 392, 444 F.2d 841, 850, cert. denied, 403 U.S. 923 (1971).

For the above reasons we cannot sustain the definition of "Light duty vehicle" as:[89]

> any motor vehicle either designed primarily for transportation of property and rated at 6,000 pounds GVW or less or designed primarily for transportation of persons and having a capacity of 12 persons or less

to the extent that it includes light weight trucks in the category that must meet the drastic emission reduction standards set for 1975 models. These light weight

---

[84] S. Rep. No. 91-1196, 91st Cong., 2d Sess. 23 (1970).

[85] Id. at 24.

[86] See e.g., 116 Cong. Rec. 42,383 (Senator Muskie): 116 Cong. Rec. 32,921-22 (Senator Baker) (standards envisioned to be for automobiles).

[87] EPA points out that prior regulation under the Clean Air Act in June 1968 had defined light duty vehicles as motor vehicles "designed for transportation of persons or property on a street or highway and weighing 6,000 pounds GVW or less" 33 Fed. Reg. 8305 (1968), but this cannot be conclusive, given the legislative intent to the contrary. Moreover, the prior regulation did not have the effect of eliminating IH vehicles from the market because the emission standards were within the reach of heavier vehicles at that time.

[88] The policies behind the decision of *Udall v. Tallman*, 380 U.S. 1 (1965) are thus inapplicable.

[89] 36 Fed. Reg. 22,448 (1971).

trucks will be governed by the standards duly promulgated by EPA for "trucks and buses and other commercial vehicles."

This is not to say that the modification of the "light duty vehicles" definition must exclude MPVs, which largely overlap in their usage with passenger cars. We merely hold the present regulation contrary to legislative intent. We have jurisdiction to decide this issue, even though the reasonableness of the regulation could be challenged in a separate proceeding in the District Court,[90] because the validity of the regulation is a premise of the refusal to grant suspension. "It would be an empty and useless thing to review an order . . . based on a regulation the validity of which might be subsequently nullified." *Doe v. Civil Aeronautics Board,* 356 F.2d 699, 701 (10th Cir. 1966).

We decline the proposal of International Harvester, therefore, that only its vehicles be granted a suspension. Light weight trucks of other manufacturers, such as Ford, equally demonstrated an inability to comply with the 1975 standards.[91] Under the view taken here, the light weight trucks of all manufacturers are properly exempted from the scope of "light duty vehicles." This comports with competitive as well as statutory considerations, as the Administrator's own brief delineates:[92]

> If International Harvester is granted a suspension, it should be able to sell its vehicles at a lower cost than competitors who met the standards. This is so because International Harvester's 1975 models would not include expensive catalytic devices to control emissions. Also the Company's vehicles would probably perform better for the same reason. Thus, if suspension is granted, it is likely that International Harvester will gain a substantial competitive advantage over manufacturers who sacrificed the performance of their vehicles, and perhaps profits, in order to comply with the 1975 standards.

Assuming light duty vehicles are defined by EPA to include MPVs a question may arise whether they are entitled to a one-year suspension, for lack of feasibility, even though passenger vehicles generally should be denied a suspension. We shall not consider this question unless and until EPA has had an opportunity to address itself to the problems in the light of our opinion herein.

D. The Issue of Feasibility Sufficient for Basic Auto Demand

The foregoing conclusion is not to be misunderstood as amounting to an acceptance of another "basic demand" contention raised by the auto manufacturers. We are inclined to agree with the Administrator that as long as feasible technology permits the demand for new passenger automobiles to be generally met, the basic requirements of the Act would be satisfied, even though this might occasion fewer models and a more limited choice of engine types. The driving preferences of hot rodders are not to outweigh the goal of a clean environment.

[90] See 42 U.S.C. § 1857h-5(b)(1).
[91] See e.g., Technical Appendix at 33-43 where no predictions as to conformity were made for any Ford trucks.
[92] (1) Brief of Respondent at 44.

A difficult problem is posed by the companies' contention that the production and major retooling capacity does not exist to shift production from a large number of previous models and engine types to those capable of complying with the 1975 standards and meeting the demand for new cars. The Administrator made no finding as to this problem. We believe the statute requires such a finding, explaining how the Administrator estimates "basic demand" and how his definition conforms to the statutory objective. The emission standards set for 1976 cannot be breached, since they represent an absolute judgment of Congress. But as to the decision on a one-year suspension, and the underlying issue of technological feasibility, Congress intended, we think, that the Administrator should take into account such "demand" considerations.

A significant decrease in auto production will have a major economic impact on labor and suppliers to the companies. We have no reason to believe that effective technology did not comport within its meaning sufficient technology to meet a basic level of consumer demand.

E. Balancing of Risks

This case inevitably presents, to the court as to the Administrator, the need for a perspective on the suspension that is informed by an analysis which balances the costs of a "wrong decision" on feasibility against the gains of a correct one. These costs include the risks of grave maladjustments for the technological leader from the eleventh-hour grant of a suspension, and the impact on jobs and the economy from a decision which is only partially accurate, allowing companies to produce cars but at a significantly reduced level of output. Against this must be weighed the environmental savings from denial of suspension. The record indicates that these will be relatively modest. There is also the possibility that failure to grant a suspension may be counterproductive to the environment, if there is significant decline in performance characteristics.

Another consideration is present, that the real cost to granting a suspension arises from the symbolic compromise with the goal of a clean environment. We emphasize that our view of a one year suspension, and the intent of Congress as to a one year suspension, is in no sense to be taken as any support for further suspensions. This would plainly be contrary to the intent of Congress to set an absolute standard in 1976. On the contrary, we view the imperative of the Congressional requirement as to the significant improvement that must be wrought no later than 1976, as interrelated with the provision for one-year suspension. The flexibility in the statute provided by the availability of a one-year suspension only strengthens the impact of the absolute standard. Considerations of fairness will support comprehensive and firm, even drastic, regulations, provided a "safety valve" is also provided—ordinarily a provision for waiver, exception or adjustment, in this case a provision for suspension.[93] "The limited safety valve permits a more rigorous adherence to an effective regulation." *WAIT Radio v. FCC, supra,*

---

[93] Permian Basin Area Rate Cases, 390 U.S. 747, 781 (1968); *WAIT Radio v. FCC,* 135 U.S. App. D.C. 317, 321, 418 F.2d 1153, 1157 (1969) and cases cited.

135 U.S. App. D.C. at 323, 418 F.2d at 1159. To hold the safety valve too rigidly is to interfere with the relief that was contemplated as an integral part of the firmness of the overall, enduring program.

We approach the question of the burden of proof on the auto companies with the previous considerations before us.

IV. THE REQUIRED SHOWING ON "AVAILABLE TECHNOLOGY"

It is with utmost diffidence that we approach our assignment to review the Administrator's decision on "available technology." The legal issues are intermeshed with technical matters, and as yet judges have no scientific aides. Our diffidence is rooted in the underlying technical complexities, and remains even when we take into account that ours is a judicial review, and not a technical or policy redetermination, our view is channeled by a salutary restraint, and deference to the expertise of an agency that provides reasoned analysis. Nevertheless we must proceed to the task of judicial review assigned by Congress.

The Act makes suspension dependent on the Administrator's determination that:

> the applicant has established that effective control technology, processes, operating methods, or other alternatives are not available or have not been available for a sufficient period of time to achieve compliance prior to the effective data of such standards . . .

A. Requirement of Observed Data From Manufacturers

Clearly this requires that the applicants come forward with data which showed that they could not comply with the contemplated standards. The normal rules place such a burden on the party in control of the relevant information.[94] It was the auto companies who were in possession of the data about emission performance of their cars.

The submission of the auto companies unquestionably showed that no car had actually been driven 50,000 miles and achieved conformity of emissions to the 1975 standards. The Administrator's position is that on the basis of the methodology outlined, he can predict that the auto companies can meet the standards, and that the ability to make a prediction saying the companies can comply means that the petitioners have failed to sustain their burden of proof that they cannot comply.

B. Requisite Reliability of Methodology Relied on by EPA to Predict Feasibility Notwithstanding Lack of Actual Experience

We agree with the Administrator's proposition in general. Its validity as applied to this case rests on the reliability of his prediction, and the nature of his assumptions. One must distinguish between prediction and prophecy. See *EDF v. Ruckel-*

---

[94] IX Wigmore, On Evidence § 2486 (3d ed. 1940).

shaus, 142 U.S. App. D.C. 74, 89, 439 F.2d 584, 597 (1971). In a matter of this importance, the predictor must make a showing of reliability of the methodology of prediction, when that is being relied on to overcome this "adverse" actual test data of the auto companies. The statute does not contemplate use of a "crystal ball." See *National Resources Defense Council, Inc. v. Morton,* 148 U.S. App. D.C. 5, 15, 458 F.2d 827, 837 (1972).

The Administrator, however, raises a different issue by contending that the companies, wholly aside from his methodology, did not submit sufficient evidence to enable him to make the required determination as to "available technology." This goes to the standard rather than the burden of proof, and comes close to adoption of "beyond a reasonable doubt" as the required showing. Aside from a possible finding of bad faith, which the Administrator specifically eschews making, this position cannot stand. The companies came forward with all the data that there was to be had, and the Administrator did not specifically ask for more. Additionally, our perspective on the interests furthered by a sound EPA decision, and jeopardized by a "wrong decision," are material to the issue of standard of proof. This is a situation where, as we have stated, the risks of an erroneous denial of suspension outweigh the risks of an erroneous grant. On the issue of burden of proof, the standard adopted must take into account the nature and consequences of risk of error. See In re Winship, 397 U.S. 358, 371-72 (1970) (Mr. Justice Harlan, concurring); *U.S. v. Brown,* 478 F.2d 606 (1973). This view of the standard of proof dictates the standard normally adopted in civil matters, a preponderance of the evidence.[95]

Our approach relates considerations of ecological and economic costs, dealt with above, to the legal issue of burden and standard of proof. Nominally the statute, in § 202(b)(5)(D), sets forth separate criteria as to "public interest," in clause (i), and "available technology," in clause (iii). But the assignment of the burden and standard of proof on "available technology" inescapably involves many of the same considerations as those involved in a "public interest" determination, and it would have been helpful to this court if the Administrator had expressly commented on the public interest in this connection.

The underlying issue is the reasonableness and reliability of the Administrator's methodology, for it alone offsets the data adduced by petitioners in support of suspension. It is the Administrator who must bear the burden on this matter, because the development and use of the methodology are attributable to his knowledge and expertise. When certain material "lies particularly within the knowledge" of a party he is ordinarily assigned the burden of adducing the pertinent information.[96] This assignment of burden to a party is fully appropriate when

---

[95] The fact that a preponderance of evidence standard was originally in Senate Bill 4358, but deleted in Conference, offers no basis for an opposite conclusion. No affirmative indication exists that Congress wanted a higher standard and the Conference delegation may simply have been intended to eliminate a requirement which is mere surplusage in the civil litigation context. See S. 4358, 91st Cong., 2d Sess., printed in S. Rep. No. 91-1196, 91st Cong., 2d Sess. 103 (1970), § 202(b)(4)(C)(iii). See also Conference Report, H.R. Rep. No. 91-1783, 91st Cong., 2d Sess. 48-49 (1970).

[96] Compare *Commonwealth of Puerto Rico v. FMC,* 152 U.S. App. D.C. 28, 468 F.2d 872 (1972).

the other party is confronted with the often-formidable task of establishing a "negative averment." *United States v. Denver & R.G.R. Co.*, 191 U.S. 84, 92 (1903). In the context of this proceeding, this requires that EPA bear a burden of adducing a reasoned presentation supporting the reliability of its methodology.

C. Analysis of EPA Assumptions

The multiple assumptions used by the Administrator in making his prediction are subject to serious doubts.

The basic formula used to make the prediction that each of the manufacturers could meet the 1975 standards was based on 1975 certification requirements, so that in part it paralleled testing procedures which would be used in 1975 to certify automobiles for sale. The formula is:[97]

50,000 mile emissions = 4000 mile emissions $\times$ deterioration factor

Four kinds of assumptions were used in making the 50,000 mile emission prediction: (1) regulatory, (2) engineering or scientific, (3) techniques of application of basic formula to particular companies, and (4) statistical reliability of the final prediction.

1. Regulatory Assumptions   First, EPA assumed that certain types of maintenance would have to be performed on 1975 model year cars, if its 50,000 miles emission predictions were to be meaningful. Subsequent to the issue of its Technical Appendix, a Proposed Rule Making formulated these requirements as part of 1975 certification procedure.[98] This assumption was necessary because much of the data supplied by the companies was obtained from cars that were under rigid controls during testing.[99] The problem with such maintenance assumptions is whether the ordinary driver will actually pay for this kind of maintenance just to reduce the emission levels of his automobile. It is one thing to build maintenance into the 1975 certification procedure, when fleet samples are durability tested. It is another to posit that such standards will be maintained, or are reasonably likely to be maintained, by consumers. A hard question is raised by the use of a methodological assumption without evidence that it will correspond to reality, or a reasonable and forthright prediction based on expertise.

Secondly, the prediction emission level assumes that there will be one total replacement of the catalytic converter at some time after 25,000 miles. This entered into the formula as an adjustment to the predicted deterioration factor.[100] The critical question is how much will the one replacement reduce emissions otherwise obtainable by use of a single catalyst. This relationship had to be assumed because manufacturers had not used catalytic converter replacements in

[97] Technical Appendix at 3.
[98] See note 26 *supra*.
[99] Car #333, used as the basis for the Chrysler prediction, is the outstanding example. See Transcript at 2095-2107; JA 1331, Doc. 143.
[100] Technical Appendix at 10.

their testing. The Administrator admitted that this factor was imprecise.[101] Yet, in the case of General Motors, the use of the assumed value of this factor was critical in allowing the Administrator to make a 50,000 mile emission prediction under the 1975 standards.[102]

The third regulatory assumption relates to the average lead level which will exist in gasoline available for 1975 model year cars. Lead levels in gasoline contribute to the levels of HC and CO both in terms of normal emission control achievable (the 4000 mile emission) and to the deterioration in emissions over time (deterioration factor). Thus, in the case of the Chrysler car used to predict conformity with the 1975 standards, a .03 lead in gasoline produced 4000 mile emissions of .27 grams HC and 1.51 CO, whereas a .05 level of lead resulted in .29 and 1.66 grams respectively. Similarly .03 lead produced a corrected deterioration factor of .67 HC and 1.5 CO, whereas a .05 level produced .73 HC and 1.65 CO.[103]

On December 27, 1972, a regulation was promulgated "designed to assure general availability by July 1, 1974, of suitable gasolines containing no more than .05 grams per gallon of lead. . . ."[104] It was the assumption of the Administrator that the .05 maximum would result in gas containing on the average .03 grams per gallon of lead. The discrepancy between the maximum and average is accounted for by the contamination of lead free gasoline from its point of production to its marketing outlet. Thus EPA will allow a maximum of .05 but anticipates that on the average fuel will be at .03. This assumption is, however, subject to testimony in the record indicating a difference between companies in their ability to achieve gasoline with a low lead level complying with the proposed regulation. Amoco said that its proposal for a .07 maximum "should result in effective lead levels of .02 to .03 grams of lead per gallon."[105] Texaco did not think it could deliver gas to service stations at a lead level below .07.[106] We cannot resolve whether a differential ability really exists, but we also have no refinement and resolution by the EPA (as distinguished from the briefs of its counsel). We do not say this matter is a critical defect; still it leaves a residue of uncertainty that beclouds the EPA assumption of a .03 average, needed in its methodology to predict conformity with the 1975 standards.

2. Engineering and Scientific Assumptions   Engineering or scientific assumptions are made in predicting 4000 mile emissions and deterioration factors, and we shall give separate consideration to each independent variable.

a. The 4000 mile emission factor.   The use of 4000 mile emissions as a starting point is based on certification procedures.[107] No challenge has been made to

---

[101] This statement was made in the context of the application of this assumption to predicting the conformity of General Motors with prescribed standards. Technical Appendix at 47.

[102] Id. at 51.

[103] Id. at 22.

[104] Supplement to Decision at 2.

[105] Letter, B. J. Yarrington, Amoco, to EPA, May 9, 1972, at 2, JA at 1539.

[106] JA at 1704–05.

[107] See note 24 *supra*.

this mileage as a base point, largely because it appears that at this mileage the engine is broken in and emission levels are relatively stabilized.[108] EPA decided to adjust raw data supplied, at least in the case of Ford and Chrysler, of emissions at 4000 miles to take account of a "Lead Adjustment Factor."[109] This was done because in most cases emissions data reflected fuels with a close to zero lead level which had been used by the manufacturers in their testing programs.

Lead adjustment factor.   This Lead Adjustment Factor was calculated using only Ford cars, but the value of the factor was assumed to be the same in adjusting Chrysler 4000 mile emissions with this factor.[110] The cars had been tested with a dynamometer, a type of test equipment used for laboratory testing of an engine. A measurement of the efficiency of the catalytic converter at the 4000 mile mark was the critical value which had to be obtained from the dynamometer since this would indicate what the proper lead adjustment factor would be.[111]

EPA assumed that 200 hours on the dynamometer corresponded to 4000 miles usage, based on a critical and contested EPA assumption that the tests were conducted at 1000 RPM. Petitioners claim that the high temperature readings on the dynamometer reflect a higher RPM, and hence that a testing below 200 hours corresponded to 4000 miles of use. EPA disputes the steps in that chain of reasoning, and argues that a higher temperature may be attributable not to a RPM in excess of 1000, but to a heavy load on the vehicle, and in the alternative contends that even if there was a RPM greater than 1000, the speed may not have increased, due to a shift in gear.

The cause of higher than expected temperature readings cannot be ascertained from the record, and we are left with the alternative contentions of the parties. it is up to EPA, however, to support its methodology as reliable, and this requires more than reliance on the unknown, either by speculation, or mere shifting back of the burden of proof.[112]

b. Deterioration factor.   Methodological problems also existed with the calculation of the deterioration factor, which took account of possible deterioration in emission quality from 4000 miles to 50,000 miles. Different questions arose as to the calculation of this factor for Ford and Chrysler.

[108] Joint Supplement to Briefs of Petitioners General Motors Corporation, Chrysler Corporation and Ford Motor Company at 8.

[109] Technical Appendix at 22 (Chrysler); at 36 (Ford).

[110] Id. at 6.

[111] The parties are apparently agreed that it would be to the advantage of the companies to take fewer hours than 200 on the dynamometer to represent 4000 mile emissions, presumably on the assumption that this will mean that emissions would be higher. This is not readily apparent to the court, given its limited understanding, from the graphs or equations provided in the Technical Appendix, at 5-6, 11-12, 18, 34. If this were a critical issue it might be necessary to arrange further submission on this point, but since it relates to one of many problems with EPA methodology we do not deem it necessary. A lacuna in judicial understanding is to some extent inescapable in matters of such technical difficulty, and here it does not seem critical for the court to refine this particular problem.

[112] A scientific paper was cited by petitioners to establish that RPM was in fact 1750, JA 1616. Apparently this was not in the record made before EPA. In any event, we do not discern how this paper supports the claim made, though we are aware that this statement may merely reflect the court's lack of scientific understanding.

In the case of Ford, the Administrator predicted that emissions would improve from 4000 miles to 50,000 miles, and arrived at a deterioration factor of less than 1.[113] He calculated average deterioration factors for Ford vehicles of .80 HC and .83 CO. This is to be compared with a deterioration factor of 215 used by NAS.[114] The Administrator never explained why there should be no deterioration. Nor does EPA explain how this result can be squared with other data on Ford catalyst efficiencies, which was used in the case of the General Motors prediction, showing 50,000 mile catalyst efficiencies ranging from 21% to 53% for HC and 47% to 72% for CO.[115]

In the case of Chrysler, the deterioration factor was calculated to be less than 1, but this figure was only arrived at after eliminating some data points from the emission measurement on the tested car #333, due to what EPA claimed were unrepresentative points resulting from non-catalyst malfunctions.[116] Although it may be, as EPA argues here, that including the data points would still produce predicted 50,000 emission levels in conformity with the 1975 standard, the fact remains that these data points were removed. Moreover, it is not apparent why one should ignore malfunctions of a car which contribute to high emissions, even if they are not malfunctions of the converter. Malfunctions of cars occur to some degree, and cars operating in 1975 will undoubtedly be subject to them.

Lead adjustment factor. A lead adjustment factor is applied to the deterioration factor, as well as to 4000 mile emissions. EPA estimated on the basis of the questionable Ford dynamometer data, that lead levels had no observable effect, which was contrary to industry testimony on the subject.[117] The Administrator evidently had doubts as to the dependability of these results as well, and therefore assumed a 10% factor for lead adjustment.[118] No explanation is given of the origins of this 10% figure. If the willingness to take some factor evidences distrust in the data, the question then becomes whether 10% is enough.

3. EPA Methodology for General Motors In the case of General Motors an entirely different methodology from that used for Ford and Chrysler was employed. This was adopted due to limited testing by GM of noble metal catalysts.

The methodology was to take the raw emission values produced by a GM car prior to catalyst treatment of any kind multiplied by a factor representing the efficiency of the catalyst, i.e., the percentage of a given pollutant that the catalyst converts to harmless vapor, in order to obtain the projected overall emission performance at 50,000 miles.[119] These methods of calculation were developed by

[113] Technical Appendix at 34.
[114] Interim Standards Report at 8.
[115] JA at 957, Doc. 135.
[116] Technical Appendix at 17.
[117] EPA merely responds to the testimony by stating that it was unaccompanied by data, but offers no expert opinion which indicates that such a relationship does not exist. (2) Brief of Respondent, App. A and B at 24, n. 35.
[118] Technical Appendix at 7.
[119] Id. at 3, 44–55.

the Administrator and were not used by NAS in their evaluation.[120] The catalyst efficiency data were taken from Engelhard converters used principally on Ford cars and applied against the raw emissions of a General Motors engine. This assumed, with no explanation of the validity of such an assumption, that Engelhard catalysts will function as efficiently in General Motors cars as in those of Ford. A prediction was made on the basis of a hypothetical case. One cannot help be troubled by the adoption of this technique for General Motors. It was apparently recognized as at best a second best approach, in terms of the reliability of the prediction, or the same catalyst efficiency procedure would also have been used for Ford and Chrysler.

4. **Statistical Reliability of Assumptions**   In this case the Administrator is necessarily making a prediction. No tests exist on whether this prediction is or is not reliable. It would, therefore, seem incumbent on the Administrator to estimate the possible degree of error in his prediction. The NAS, for example, said that the data of the manufacturers were subject to $\pm 20\text{-}30\%$ margin of error,[121] and this is separate from any margin of error that may be due to the various assumptions made by the Administrator. It is not decisive to say, as EPA argues in its brief, that this is just a matter of quality control in production. The first issue is whether the automobile built with rigid adherence to specifications will perform as predicted. The issue of quality control, whether cars will indeed be built in accordance with specifications, raises a separate and additional problem.

The possibility of error must take into account that only 1 Ford car, 1 Chrysler car, and 1 hypothetical General Motors car form the foundation for predicted conformity with the 1975 standards.[122] The Administrator would say that it is enough to validate the principle of the electric light bulb if only one is seen at work. But we do not yet have one that has worked; instead we have four predictions. Questions like these arise: (1) For how many different types of engines will these predictions be valid? (2) Does it make a difference that the tested cars were experimental and driven under the most controlled conditions? The best car analysis of EPA raises even further doubts when considered alongside the NAS Report which used 55 vehicles in arriving at its recommended interim standard.[123]

V.   CONCLUSION AND DISPOSITION

We may sensibly begin our conclusion with a statement of diffidence.[124] It is not without diffidence that a court undertakes to probe even partly into technical matters of the complexity of those covered in this opinion. It is with even more

[120] No mention of this possible methodology is mentioned in the NAS Interim Report, and the Administrator admits this in Supplement to Decision at 1. See text at note 76.

[121] Interim Standards Report at 7.

[122] Technical Appendix at 41 (Ford 351 C); at 22 (Chrysler car 333); at 51 (General Motors engine 455/full size).

[123] Interim Standards Report at 8. EPA, moreover, offers no explanation as to whether there were "best system" cars besides those included in the Appendix which did not meet the standards, and why one should not be concerned about the fact that the "best system" cars which are in the Technical Appendix, other than those cited in note 103, *supra*, do not meet the standard.

[124] Compare *Blair v. Freeman*, 128 U.S. App. D.C. 207, 210, 370 F.2d 229, 232 (1966).

diffidence that a court concludes that the law, as judicially construed, requires a different approach from that taken by an official or agency with technical expertise. Yet this is an unescapable aspect of the judicial condition, though we stay mindful of the overarching consideration that a court's role on judicial review embraces that of a constructive cooperation with the agency involved in furtherance of the public interest.[125]

> A court does not depart from its proper functions when it undertakes a study of the record, hopefully perceptive, even as to the evidence on technical and specialized matters, for this enables the court to penetrate to the underlying decisions of the agency, to satisfy itself that the agency has exercised a reasoned discretion, with reasons that do not deviate from or ignore the ascertainable legislative intent.[126]

In this case technical issues permeate the "available technology" determination which the Administrator made the focal point of his decision. In approaching our judicial task we conclude that the requirement of a "reasoned decision" by the Environmental Protection Agency means, in present context, a reasoned presentation of the reliability of a prediction and methodology that is relied upon to overcome a conclusion, of lack of available technology, supported prima faciely by the only actual and observed data available, the manufacturers' testing.

The number of unexplained assumptions used by the Administrator, the variance in methodology from that of the Report of the National Academy of Science, and the absence of an indication of the statistical reliability of the prediction, combine to generate grave doubts as to whether technology is available to meet the 1975 statutory standards. We say this, incidentally, without implying or intending any acceptance of petitioners' substitute assumptions. These grave doubts have a legal consequence. This is customarily couched, by legal convention in terms of "burden of proof." We visualize the problem in less structured terms although the underlying considerations, relating to risk of error, are related. As we see it the issue must be viewed as one of legislative intent. And since there is neither express wording or legislative history on the precise issue, the intent must be imputed. The court must seek to discern and reconstruct what the legislature that enacted the statute would have contemplated for the court's action if it could have been able to foresee the precise situation.[127] It is in this perspective that we have not flinched from our discussion of the economic and ecological risks inherent in a "wrong decision" by the Administrator. We think the vehicle manufacturers established by a preponderance of the evidence, in the record before us, that technology was not available, within the meaning of the Act, when they adduced the tests on actual vehicles; that the Administrator's reliance on technological methodology to offset the actual tests raised serious doubts and failed to meet the burden of proof which in our view was properly assignable to him, in the light of accepted legal doctrine and the intent of Congress discerned, in part by taking

---

[125] *Morgan v. United States,* 304 U.S. 1 (1938); *Greater Boston TV v. FCC* (I), *supra.*
[126] *Greater Boston TV v. FCC, supra,* 143 U.S. App. D.C. at 392; 444 F.2d at 850.
[127] *Montana Power Co. v. FPC,* 144 U.S. App. D.C. 263, 270, 445 F.2d 739, 746 (en banc, 1970), cert. denied 400 U.S. 1013 (1971).

into account that the risk of an "erroneous" denial of suspension outweighed the risk of an "erroneous" grant of suspension. We do not use the burden of proof in the conventional sense of civil trials, but the Administrator must sustain the burden of adducing a reasoned presentation supporting the reliability of EPA's methodology.

EPA's diligence in this proceeding, fraught with questions of statutory interpretation, technical difficulties and burdensome time constraints placed on the decision-making process, has been commendable. The agency was presented with a prickly task, but has acted expeditiously to carry out what is perceived to be a drastic mandate from Congress. This statute was, indeed, deliberately designed as "shock treatment" to the industry. Our central difference with the Administrator, simply put, stems from our view concerning the Congressional intent underlying the one year suspension provision. That was a purposeful cushion—with the twin purpose of providing "escape hatch" relief for 1975, and thus establishing a context supportive of the rigor and firmness of the basic standards slated for no later than 1975. In our view the overall legislative firmness does not necessarily require a "hard-nosed" approach to the application for suspension, as the Administrator apparently supposed, and may indeed be furthered by our more moderate view of the suspension issue, particularly in assigning to the Administrator the burden of producing a reasoned presentation of the reliability of his methodology. This is not a matter of clemency, but rather a benign approach that moderates the "shock treatment" so as to obviate excessive and unnecessary risk of harm.

Our decision is also responsive to the differences between the EPA decision and the NAS Report. Although in some instances "the factual findings and technical conclusions"[128] are consistent with those of the Administrator, the NAS conclusion was that technology was not available to meet the standards in 1975. Congress called on NAS, with presumed reliance on the knowledge and objectivity of that prestigious body, to make an independent judgment. The statute makes the NAS conclusion a necessary but not sufficient condition of suspension. While in consideration of the other conditions of suspension, EPA was not necessarily bound by NAS's approach, particularly as to matters interlaced with policy and legal aspects, we do not think that it was contemplated that EPA could alter the conclusion of NAS by revising the NAS assumptions, or injecting new ones, unless it states its reasons for finding reliability—possibly by challenging the NAS approach in terms of later-acquired research and experience.

These factors combine to convince us that, under our view of Congressional intent, we cannot affirm the EPA's denial of suspension as stated. That is not necessarily to assume, as at least some petitioners do, that the EPA's process must be brought to nullity.

The procedures followed in this case, whether or not based on rulings that were "mistaken" when made, have resulted in a record that leaves this court uncertain, at a minimum, whether the essentials of the intention of Congress were achieved. This requires a remand whereby the record as made will be supplemented by further proceedings. In the interest of justice, see 28 U.S.C. § 2106, and

---

[128] Supplement to Decision at 1.

mutual regard for Congressional objective, the parties should have opportunity on remand to address themselves to matters not previously put before them by EPA for comment, including material contained in the Technical Appendix filed by EPA in 1972 subsequent to its Decision.

It is contemplated that, in the interest of providing a reasoned decision, the remand proceeding will involve some opportunity for cross-examination. In the remand proceeding—not governed by the same time congestion as the initial Decision process—we require reasonable cross-examination as to new lines of testimony, and as to submissions previously made to EPA in the hearing on a proffer that critical questions could not be satisfactorily pursued by procedures previously in effect. There is, however, still need for expedition, both by virtue of our order and the "lead time" problem, and the EPA may properly confine cross-examination to the essentials, avoiding discursive or repetitive questioning.

Following our suggestion in *Environmental Defense Fund, Inc. v. EPA*, Slip Opinion No. 71-1365 [4 ERC 1523] (D.C. Cir. May 5, 1972), the Administrator may consider possible use of interim standards short of complete suspension. The statute permits conditioning of suspension on the adoption, by virtue of the information adduced in the suspension proceeding, of interim standards, higher than those set for 1974.[129]

We cannot grant petitioners' request that this court order a suspension since determinations which Congress made necessary conditions of suspension, as to the public interest and good faith, have not been made by the Administrator. The Administrator's decision did not reach these questions and accordingly we must remand for further consideration. The initial requirement that an EPA decision on the suspension, aye or nay, be made within 60 days of the application, obviously does not preclude further consideration following remand by the court. In the interest of justice, 28 U.S.C. § 2106, and the Congressional intention that decisions be made timely in the light of considerations of "lead time" for 1975 model year production, we require the suspension deliberations by EPA to be completed within 60 days. The Administrator's decision on remand must, of course, be consistent with our legal rulings herein—including the need for redefinition of light duty vehicles, and promulgation of an appropriate regulation.

In conformance to the Congressional contemplation of expedition, and our responsibilities as an appellate court, we further require that the Administrator render a decision, on the basis of the best information available, which extends to all the determinations which the statute requires as a condition of suspension.[130]

---

[129] Thus, Section 202(b)(5)(A), 42 U.S.C. § 1857f-1(b)(5)(A), provides, in part:
    If he determines, in accordance with the provisions of this subsection, that such suspension should be granted, he shall simultaneously with such determination prescribe by regulation interim emission standards. . . .
[130] This obviates the possibility of delay if, for example, on remand the Administrator denied the suspension on the basis of only one of the four statutory findings, and this court subsequently reversed.
    Since our disposition on remand requires a public interest determination, it disposes of the claim of petitioner Chrysler that the National Environmental Policy Act, 42 U.S.C. § 4321 et seq., requires that an impact statement be filed by the Administrator pursuant to a suspension decision.
    The purpose of NEPA is to assure presentation to Congress and the public of the environmental impact of executive action. Here Congress has already decided that the environmental dangers require the statutory standards. The only executive decision is of a one year deferral, and the very stuff of such

We do not preclude further consideration of the question of "available technology," especially if developments in the art provide enlightenment. Last but not least, especially in view of Ford's submission and the NAS Report concerning interim standards, we reiterate that the EPA's determination may consist of a conditional suspension that results in higher standards than an outright grant of applications for suspension.

The case is remanded for further proceedings not inconsistent with this opinion.

Bazelon, Chief Judge (concurring in result):

Socrates said that wisdom is the recognition of how much one does not know.[1] I may be wise if that is wisdom, because I recognize that I do not know enough about dynamometer extrapolations, deterioration factor adjustments, and the like to decide whether or not the government's approach to these matters was statistically valid. Therein lies my disagreement with the majority.

The court's opinion today centers on a substantive evaluation of the Administrator's assumptions and methodology. I do not have the technical know-how to agree or disagree with that evaluation—at least on the basis of the present record. My grounds for remanding the case rest upon the Administrator's failure to employ a reasonable decision-making process for so critical and complex a matter. At this time I cannot say to what extent I could undertake an evaluation of the Administrator's findings if they were based on an adequate decisional process.

I cannot believe that Congress intended this court to delve into the substance of the mechanical, statistical, and technological disputes in this case. Senator Cooper, the author of the judicial review provision, stated repeatedly that this court's role would be to "determine the question of due process."[2] Thus the court's proper role is to see to it that the agency provides "a framework for principled decision-making."[3] Such a framework necessarily includes the right of interested parties to confront the agency's decision and the requirement that the agency set forth with clarity the grounds for its rejection of opposing views.

---

a decision, at least with a public interest determination, is to assess, inter alia, the environmental consequences of action and inaction. NEPA's objective will be fully served. As we stated in *National Resources Defense Council, Inc. v. Morton*, 148 U.S. App. D.C. 5, 15, 458 F.2d 827, 837 (1972) [3 ERC 1558], the requirements of NEPA should be subject to a "construction of reasonableness." Although we do not reach the question whether EPA is automatically and completely exempt from NEPA, we see little need in requiring a NEPA statement from an agency whose raison d'être is the protection of the environment and whose decision on suspension is necessarily infused with the environmental considerations so pertinent to Congress in designing the statutory framework. To require a "statement," in addition to a decision setting forth the same considerations, would be a legalism carried to the extreme.

  [1] Plato, Apology of Socrates, § 57B.
  [2] 116 Cong. Rec. 33,086 (1970); cf. 116 Cong. Rec. 33,084 (1970). One Senator referred to the court's "factfinding function"; his remarks make it clear that he could not have been referring to the review function of courts of appeal. 116 Cong. Rec. 33,085 (1970) (Senator Baker).
  [3] *Environmental Defense Fund, Inc. v. Ruckelshaus*, 142 U.S. App. D.C. 74, 88, 439 F.2d 584, 598 (1971).

The majority's interpretation of the present statute and the administrative precedents would give us no right to establish these procedural guidelines. Their opinion maintains that the strict deadlines in the Clean Air Act preclude any right to challenge the Administrator until after the decision has been made. It indicates that, since this hearing was "rule-making" rather than "adjudicatory," cross-examination and confrontation are not required under traditional rules of administrative law.

I understand this viewpoint, but I do not share it. I do not think the authors of the Clean Air Act intended to put such strict limits on our review of the Administrator's decision-making process. Further, the interests at stake in this case are too important to be resolved on the basis of traditional administrative labels. We recognized two years ago that environmental litigation represents a "new era" in administrative law.[4] We are dealing here not with an airline's fares or a broadcaster's wattage, but with all humanity's interest in life, health, and a harmonious relationship with the elements of nature.

This "new era" does not mean that courts will dig deeper into the technical intricacies of an agency's decision. It means instead that courts will go further in requiring the agency to establish a decision-making process adequate to protect the interests of all "consumers" of the natural environment.[5] In some situations, traditional rules of "fairness"—designated only to guard the interests of the specific parties to an agency proceeding—will be adequate to protect these broader interests. This is such a case. Whether or not traditional administrative rules require it, the critical character of this decision requires at least a carefully limited right of cross-examination at the hearing and an opportunity to challenge the assumptions and methodology underlying the decision.

The majority's approach permits the parties to challenge the Administrator's methodology only through the vehicle of judicial review. I do not think this is an adequate substitute for confrontation prior to the decision. I reach this position not only out of concern for fairness to the parties (". . . for if a party first learns of noticed facts through the final report . . . the burden of upsetting a decision announced as final is a heavy one."[6]) but also out of awareness of the limits of our own competence for the task. The petitioners' challenges to the decision force the court to deal with technical intricacies that are beyond our ken.[7] These complex questions should be resolved in the crucible of debate through the clash of informed but opposing scientific and technological viewpoints.

It is true that courts occasionally find themselves in the thick of technological controversies—e.g., in patent cases. But those are different circumstances. We do not review patent disputes until they have been through a full panoply of proce-

---

[4] Id. 142 U.S. App. D.C. at 87, 439 F.2d at 597. To the same effect is Mr. Justice Blackmun's opinion in *Sierra Club v. Morton*, 405 U.S. 727, 755 (1972) (dissenting opinion.)

[5] *Environmental Defense Fund, Inc. v. Hardin*, 138 U.S. App. D.C. 391, 395, 428 F.2d 1093, 1097 (1970).

[6] 2 Davis, ADMINISTRATIVE LAW TREATISE, § 15.14 (1958).

[7] Cf. this court's dictum, in *Constructores Civiles de Centro-Americana v. Hannah*, that "These forebodingly fecund matters were wisely placed beyond the ken of the judiciary." 148 U.S. App. D.C. 159, 168, 459 F.2d 1183, 1192 (1972).

dures involving full rights of confrontation. Further, unlike our decision in a patent case, our decision on the Administrator's action here is sure to be tested by analysis and challenge in Congress, in the scientific community, and among the public.

My brethren and I are reaching for the same end—a "reasoned decision"— through different means. They would have us examine the substance of the decision before us. There are some areas of administrative law—involving issues of liberty and individual rights—where judges are on firm ground in undertaking a substantive review of agency action. But in cases of great technological complexity, the best way for courts to guard against unreasonable or erroneous administrative decisions is not for the judges themselves to scrutinize the technical merits of each decision. Rather, it is to establish a decision-making process which assures a reasoned decision that can be held up to the scrutiny of the scientific community and the public.[8] "[T]he best test of truth is the power of the thought to get itself accepted in the competition of the market."[9] If we were to require procedures in this case that open the Administrator's decision to challenge and force him to respond, we could rely on an informed "market" rather than on our own groping in the dark to test the validity of that decision.

Candor requires the admission that the process of confrontation and challenge might not be possible within the statutory decision period of 60 days. My response would be to permit an extension of the time limit—perhaps 30 days more. This would put less strain on the overall statutory scheme—and on the manufacturer's lead time—than the months that have been expended in litigation, and now a remand, over the decision. Congress did not intend for us to enforce this relatively minor time restriction so strictly as to do major damage to the statute as a whole.

My brethren argue that the 60 day time limit in the statute precluded any opportunity for cross-examination or confrontation at the time of the original decision. But their opinion would apparently permit these procedural rights on the remand. This bit of judicial legerdemain confounds me. I can find nothing in the statute or common sense to support this distinction. If anything, the statute, with its obvious emphasis on reaching a final decision quickly, would dictate procedures at the original decision which were sufficient to produce a reasoned decision without the need for a remand.

Outside the foregoing differences, I agree with much of the majority opinion. I would have preferred to make the "public interest" factor—the considerations set forth in Part III of that opinion—an independent ground for suspension. The court today deals with the public interest indirectly, through the device of burden of proof. I do not fully understand this approach, but I suspect it leads to essentially the same result I favor.

---

[8] Cf. *Citizens' Association of Georgetown v. Zoning Commission,* 477 F.2d 402 (1973).
[9] *Abrams v. United States,* 250 U.S. 616, 630 (1919) (Holmes, Jr., dissenting).

QUESTIONS FOR DISCUSSION

1 Should a court consider the economic importance of an industry in its interpretation of law?

2 If more favorable consideration was given to large industries, would this tend to place the burden of controlling pollution on smaller businesses, which are less financially able to cope with added costs?

3 In its deliberations, should a court consider allegations of conspiracy to retard antipollution progress?

4 Who should fix emission standards?

5 Is it sound policy for Congress to "force the state of the act"?

6 Should a "realistic escape hatch" be provided in environmental legislation? Will such provisions ever remain unused?

7 Is the Administrator in a position to accurately assess "good faith efforts" toward compliance?

8 How might the Administrator determine the "public interest"?

9 Does available technology reasonably include technology not yet in being?

10 Is an adversary proceeding the best way to resolve questions of public interest? Who would speak for the public in such a proceeding?

11 What say regarding test procedures should the industry have been allowed?

12 Is the court's description of itself as "isolated . . . from political pressures" accurate?

13 Should questions concerning "economic roulette" be isolated from political considerations?

14 Is any court competent to judge reports such as that issued by the NAS?

15 Is the economic balancing done in *International Harvester Company v. Ruckelshaus* a proper function of a court of law?

16 Is the court's ruling on "light duty vehicles" consistent with the purpose or language of the Clean Air Act?

17 Can you distinguish between "prediction and prophecy" in environmental or economic matters?

18 Should a court second-guess administrative assumptions or technical expense? Note the dissent of Chief Judge Bazelon.

STATE CONTROL

The Clean Air Act may be said to have "federalized" the law of air-pollution control. *Allway Taxi, Inc., v. City of New York* considers the extent of remaining state authority in the area.

Allway Taxi, Inc., v. City of New York

340 F. Supp. 1120, 3 ERC 2051 (S.D.N.Y. 1972) aff'd, 468 F.2d 624 (1972)

MacMahon, District Judge.

Plaintiffs, fifteen corporations owning and operating licensed taxicabs in New York City, move under Rule 65, Fed. R. Civ. P., for a preliminary injunction against enforcement of a New York City ordinance requiring exhaust emission controls for licensed taxicabs. Defendants cross-move under Rule 12(b)(c), Fed. R. Civ. P., for dismissal of the action for lack of subject matter jurisdiction and for failure to state a claim upon which relief may be granted, or, in the alternative, for judgment on the pleadings.

The action seeks a declaratory judgment that the challenged ordinance[1] is null and void insofar as it sets exhaust emission controls for licensed taxicabs.

The ordinance requires licensed taxicabs to use gasoline containing no more than specified low levels of lead and to use only non-leaded gasoline after January 1, 1974. The ordinance also requires pre-1970 taxicabs to be equipped with emission control devices which comply with 1970 federal standards and later models to be equipped with such emission control devices as may be specified by the New York City Taxi and Limousine Commission.

A preliminary injunction is an extraordinary remedy and should be granted only where the applicant shows a strong likelihood of ultimate success on the merits and irreparable injury unless such relief is granted, or where the applicant makes a limited showing of probable success but raises substantial issues requiring further injury and shows that the harm to him outweighs the injury to others if the relief is denied.[2]

Plaintiffs' claim of ultimate success on the merits depends on the validity of their contention that the ordinance is null and void because the field of motor vehicle emission control has been preempted by the federal Clean Air Act[3] and on

---

[1] Section 2318 of Chapter 65 of the Administrative Code of the City of New York.

[2] *Omega Importing Corp. v. Petri-Kine Camera Co.*, Docket No. 71-1919 (2d Cir., Nov. 8, 1971); *Weiss v. Walsh*, Docket Nos. 71-1398, 71-1852 (2d Cir. Oct. 29, 1971); *Semmes Motors, Inc. v. Ford Motor Co.*, 429 F.2d 1197, 1205-06 (2d Cir. 1970); *Checker Motors Corp. v. Chrysler Corp.*, 405 F.2d 319 (2d Cir.), cert. denied, 394 U.S. 999 (1969).

[3] 42 U.S.C. § 1857. Section 1857f-1 of Title 42 creates federal controls over motor vehicle emissions.

the soundness of their argument that the ordinance is unconstitutional because it denies plaintiffs equal protection of the law.

A local ordinance will be upheld against a claim of preemption unless there is such an actual conflict between the local and federal regulatory schemes that both cannot stand in the same area or unless there is clear evidence of congressional intent to preempt the field. *Florida Lime & Avocado Growers, Inc. v. Paul*, 373 U.S. 132 (1963).

Plaintiffs rely upon two sections of the Clean Air Act, which, they claim, show a clear congressional intent to preempt the regulation of automobile exhaust emissions.

The first preemption section, urged by plaintiffs, prohibits states or their subdivisions from regulating fuel and fuel additives if the federal administrator has found that no control is necessary or has already prescribed standards. 42 U.S.C. § 1857f-6c(c)(4). Since plaintiffs neither show nor contend that either condition has been fulfilled here, we see no conflict at present between the City's regulation of the lead content of gasoline and this preemption section.

The second preemption section, upon which plaintiffs rely, prohibits states or their subdivisions from creating standards for exhaust emission control devices for new motor vehicles and new motor vehicle engines. It also prohibits states from setting standards of approval as conditions precedent to the initial sale or registration of new motor vehicles. 42 U.S.C. § 1857f-6a.

Where exercise of the local police power serves the purpose of a federal Act, the preemptive effect of that Act should be narrowly construed. *Chrysler Corp. v. Tofany*, 419 F.2d 499 (2d Cir. 1969). We think the purpose of the federal Act is served by the challenged ordinance. Surely, New York City has the power at least to try to clean the very air that people breathe. Plainly, that is the purpose of the ordinance, and it is clearly compatible with the goal of the federal Clean Air Act. *Huron Portland Cement Co. v. City of Detroit*, 362 U.S. 440 (1960). Moreover, both the history and text of the Act show that the second preemption section was made not to hamstring localities in their fight against air pollution but to prevent the burden on interstate commerce which would result if, instead of uniform standards, every state and locality were left free to impose different standards for exhaust emission control devices for the manufacture and sale of new cars.[4]

Thus, the second preemption section restricts states and localities from setting their own standards for new motor vehicles, which are defined as motor vehicles "the equitable or legal title to which . . . [have] never been transferred to an ultimate purchaser."[5] The statutory definition reveals a clear congressional intent to preclude states and localities from setting their own exhaust emission control standards only with respect to the manufacture and distribution of new automobiles. That narrow purpose is further suggested by the remainder of the section, which prohibits states and localities from setting standards governing emission control devices before the initial sale or registration of an automobile. Finally,

[4] H.R. Rep. No. 728, 90th Cong., 1st Sess. 1967 U.S. Code Cong. & Admin. News, p. 1956.
[5] 42 U.S.C. § 1857f-7(3).

congress specifically refused to interfere with local regulation of the use or movement of motor vehicles after they have reached their ultimate purchasers.[6]

We do not say that a state or locality is free to impose its own emission
control standards the moment after a new car is bought and registered. That
would be an obvious circumvention of the Clean Air Act and would defeat the
congressional purpose of preventing obstruction to interstate commerce. The preemption sections, however, do not preclude a state or locality from imposing its
own exhaust emission control standards upon the resale or registration of the
automobile. Nor do they preclude a locality from setting its own standards for the
licensing of vehicles for commercial use within that locality. Such regulations
would cause only minimal interference with interstate commerce, since they
would be directed primarily to intrastate activities and the burden of compliance
would be on individual owners and not on manufacturers and distributors.

The challenged ordinance would, at most, require taxicab owners, seeking a
license to operate in the City, to meet at their own expense emission control
standards established by the Taxi and Limousine Commission.[7] Such a requirement is fully supported by the congressional call for local cooperation toward the
prevention and control of air pollution.[8] We conclude that the ordinance is neither
in conflict with, nor precluded by, the second preemption section of the Clean Air
Act.

We next consider plaintiffs' contention that the ordinance denies plaintiffs
equal protection of the law in that it applies only to taxicabs and not to other
motor vehicles.[9]

It is not a requirement of equal protection that "all evils of the same genus be
eradicated or none at all." *Railway Express Agency v. New York*, 336 U.S. 106, 110
(1949). Legislation may approach one phase of a problem at a time as long as it
avoids invidious discrimination. *Williamson v. Lee Optical of Oklahoma, Inc.*, 348
U.S. 483 (1955).

Williamson held that it was not invidious discrimination for the Oklahoma
legislature to regulate the sale of eyeglasses by opticians but not by sellers of
ready-to-wear glasses because the legislature might have felt that the problems of
regulating opticians were greater or different from the problems of regulating
sellers of ready-to-wear glasses.

In the present case, the New York City Council may feel, quite rationally,
that the pollution caused by taxicabs is greater or more acute than that caused by
other vehicles, or it may feel that the problems of regulating taxicabs are distinct

---

[6] 42 U.S.C. § 1857a.

[7] Actually, at present the ordinance does no more than insure the installation and upkeep of the
federally required devices, since New York City has set no standards of its own. Such policing activity
after a car has reached its ultimate purchaser is specifically left to the states and their localities. 42
U.S.C. § 1857-5a(f).

[8] 42 U.S.C. § 1857a.

[9] The section of the statute dealing with low-lead gasoline standards no longer presents an equal
protection problem since those standards have since been made applicable to all automobiles in New
York City.

from the problems of regulating other vehicles. Plaintiffs fail to establish that the distinction created by the ordinance bears no rational relationship to the purpose of the ordinance and, without such a showing, plaintiffs' denial of equal protection argument is without merit.

We turn now to plaintiffs' claim that they will suffer irreparable injury if an injunction is not granted.

Plaintiffs maintain that enforcement of the ordinance will cause them irreparable injury on three grounds. First, they assert that low-lead gasoline is unavailable and that it will cost more than leaded gasoline when it becomes available. Defendants show, however, that Gulf Oil Co. does have qualifying low-lead gasoline available and that it sells for one cent less per gallon than regular leaded gasoline. Defendants further assert that Shell Oil Co. and Mobil Oil Co. also have low-lead gasoline available at substantially the same cost as regular leaded gasoline. Plaintiffs fail to dispute these facts and, thus, fail to show the possibility of irreparable economic injury if required to use low-lead gasoline in their taxicabs.

Plaintiffs' second claim is that the non-leaded gasoline required after January 1, 1974 will be more expensive than leaded fuels and that it will damage the engines of their taxicabs. There is some indication that non-leaded gasoline might cost more than present gasoline, but since its use is not required until 1974, the future requirement poses no likelihood of immediate injury, and the forecast of future injury is too remote and speculative to warrant injunctive relief. Further, defendants show that it is doubtful that non-leaded gasoline will cause damage to taxi engines. All parties agree that by 1973 the major American automobile manufacturers will be producing almost nothing but engines designed specifically for non-leaded gasoline, and since taxis are traded in every 16 to 18 months, most taxis will have such engines by 1974. In light of these facts, plaintiffs' second claim falls short of showing irreparable injury.

Plaintiffs' third argument is that the emission control devices required by the ordinance will be significantly expensive. The requirement of such devices for pre-1970 taxicabs is virtually moot, since taxicabs are traded every 16 to 18 months. As for vehicles manufactured in 1971 and thereafter, the present New York City standards are no stricter than federal standards. Although the ordinance gives the Taxi and Limousine Commission authority to set stricter standards, the commission has not yet done so and, thus, taxicab owners face no present threat of increased cost.

We conclude, therefore, that plaintiffs have failed to establish irreparable injury if a preliminary injunction is denied.

We turn now to defendants' motions. Defendants first seek dismissal of this action for lack of subject matter jurisdiction under 28 U.S.C. § 1331, in that the amount involved is less than $10,000, and for lack of a federal question.

The object of this action is to enjoin the enforcement of an ordinance. The amount in controversy, therefore, is determined by the cost which would be incurred by taxi owners if the ordinance were enforced. *Packard v. Banton,* 264 U.S. 140 (1924). If the ordinance is enforced, plaintiffs might be forced to purchase more expensive gasoline or to install costly emission control devices and, over a period of time, these increased expenses could amount to $10,000, even for a small fleet owner. We, therefore, reject defendants' contention that the necessary jurisdictional amount cannot be established here.

We also reject defendants' contention that no federal question is involved since plaintiffs allege both preemption by a federal statute and denial of their right to equal protection under the Fourteenth Amendment. Thus, we find that this court has jurisdiction over the subject matter of this action, and defendants' motion to dismiss for lack of such jurisdiction is denied.

Defendants' second motion is for dismissal for failure to state a claim upon which relief may be granted. Since we have considered matters outside the pleadings, we shall treat this as a motion for summary judgment and shall consider it on the merits.

This is an action for a declaratory judgment that a New York City ordinance is null and void. There are no disputed issues of fact. We have examined the law involved in our consideration of plaintiffs' motion for a preliminary injunction and have found that the federal Clean Air Act does not preempt New York City from enacting the ordinance in question and that the ordinance does not deprive plaintiffs of equal protection of the law. Consequently, summary judgment in favor of defendants should be granted. . . .

PROBLEMS

1 Suppose a locality is totally undeveloped and free from air pollution. An industry with emissions which reduce air quality seeks to locate there and can show that although the air quality will suffer to a degree, it will still be at a level better than the secondary standards require; that is, it will avoid any adverse effects on any environmental, man-made, or aesthetic factor or process. The industry is of a nature which precludes reduction of emissions. Does the Air Quality Act empower anyone to bar the industry from relocating?

2 A citizens' group seeks to close or force modification of a rendering plant which is emitting noxious but not toxic pollutants into the air. State officials have declined to intervene because of the commercial importance of the plant. Does the Clean Air Act provide the citizens' group with a right of action against the plant? Does the act authorize an action against the state or the federal government for failure to enforce air-quality standards?

3 A factory is required to reduce its emission of air pollutants by 90 percent within two years to meet administratively established standards. The factory operators can produce credible evidence tending to show that: (1) the technology required to achieve a 90 percent reduction is not available; (2) the cost of achieving a 90 percent reduction is twenty times that of a 70 percent reduction and the air quality would not be substantially different; (3) the cost of a 90 percent reduction would force the factory to close. If the administrator's requirements were challenged on the basis that they were arbitrary and capricious to the extent that due process of law is violated, could a court consider any of the three enumerated contentions?

SUGGESTIONS FOR FURTHER READING

Aeischaker, M. L., and M. R. Joelson: *Clean Air Act*, 19 PRAC. LAW. 49, 1973.

Bleicher, S. A.: *Economic and Technical Feasibility in Clean Air Act Enforcement against Stationary Sources*, 89 HARV. L. REV. 316.

Clean Air Act Amendments of 1970: A Congressional Cosmetic, 61 GA. L.J. 153, 1972.

Coordinating the EPA, NEPA, and the Clean Air Act, 52 TEXAS L. REV. 527, 1974.

Currie, D. P.: *Motor Vehicle Air Pollution: State Authority and Federal Preemption*, 68 MICH. L. REV. 1083, 1973.

Guarding the Guardian: The "Citizen Suit" for Clean Air, 3 ENVIRONMENTAL L. 1, 1973.

Guburd, A. E.: *Clean Air Act and Mobile Source Pollution Control*, 4 ECOLOGY L.Q. 523, 1975.

A History of Federal Air Pollution Control, 30 OHIO ST. L.J. 516, 1969.

Muskie, E. S.: *The Role of the Federal Government in Air Pollution Control*, 10 ARIZ. L. REV. 17, 1968.

Nondegradation Controversy: How Clean Will Our "Clean Air" Be? 1974 U. ILL. L.F. 314, 1974.

O'Fallon, J. E.: *Deficiencies in the Air Quality Act of 1967*, 33 LAW & CONTEMP. PROB., 1969.

Schwartz, W. F.: *Mandatory Patent Licensing of Air Pollution Control Technology*, 57 VA. L. REV. 719, 1971.

Taubenfeld, H. J.: *International Environment Law: Air and Outer Space*, 13 NATURAL RESOURCES J. 315, 1973.

United States and Canadian Approaches to Air Pollution Control and the Implications for the Control of Transboundary Pollution, 7 CORNELL INT'L L.J. 148, 1974.

Expert Testimony

An essential element of environmental litigation—indeed, of all litigation—is the orderly presentation of the factual situation on which the dispute is centered. Cardozo was of the opinion that

> More and more we lawyers are awaking to a perception of the truth that what divides and distracts us in the solution of a legal problem is not so much uncertainty about the law as uncertainty about the facts—the facts which generate the law. Let the facts be known as they are, and the law will sprout from the seed and turn its branches toward the light.[a]

Naturally, however, the "facts" are often difficult or impossible to ascertain. In the case of environmental litigation factual disputes may arise over physical, biological, or engineering matters and may concern questions of either what did happen or what would happen. Many of these matters are so beyond the ken of the layman that expert help is needed; as early as 1782 an opinion of an engineer as to the causes of filling in a harbor was accepted as evidence in a civil case.[b]

[a] For a convincing assessment of the role of facts and their determination in the legal context, see Lloyd Paul Stryker, *The Art of Advocacy,* Simon and Schuster, New York, 1954.
[b] *Folkes v. Chadd,* 3 Doug. 157, 340, 99 Eng. Rep. 589, 686 (K.B. 1783).

PRETRIAL ACTIVITIES AND DISCOVERY

Given the need for technical input and keeping in mind the realities of the adversary system,[c] it may be said that the scientist's or engineer's role in environmental litigation is an educational one. Not every complaint taken to a lawyer's office reaches the trial stage. Many situations lack the necessary elements to establish a cause of action, while other situations are satisfactorily settled by means other than litigation. Those instances that do reach the trial level do so only after thorough pretrial procedures.

The elements of drama and surprise so familiar in fictional courtrooms have been largely replaced in reality, at least in civil litigation,[d] with meticulous preparation aided by discovery. "Discovery" is the process by which the factual components of an opponent's case are made known, and discovery was initiated specifically to destroy the element of surprise in a legal action and to enable each side to be as well informed as possible concerning the factual basis of the other's position. Generally, discovery enables one party to examine the other or his witnesses, either orally or by written questions before trial, on any matter relevant to the issues involved in the pending case. These areas include the opposing party's witnesses, experts, and documents, whether or not such material would be admissible in court under the rules of evidence.[e] Also, upon a showing of good cause, the opposing party may be required to produce physical objects for examination. Discovery has an even greater role in environmental litigation because of the confrontations that take place between smaller environmental groups and larger corporations or governmental agencies. As David Sive states in the *Michigan Law Review,*

> This need for discovery is caused primarily by the tremendous inequality of knowledge, between the conservation organization and the governmental agency or other resource user or developer, concerning the project under examination. The mountains of studies, plans, and relevant files usually are all in possession of or controlled by the resource user. The hard evidentiary facts are often buried deep in the platitudinous gobbledygook in which bureaucrats specialize—a process in which the personnel of agencies dealing with resources seem to approach perfection.[f]

Before the commencement of discovery the scientist or engineer may be called upon to educate the attorney as to the general area in dispute, familiarize him with its jargon, and thus aid him in his construction of a legal framework in which to operate. When a reasonable technical foundation is laid, the scientist or engineer may assist in the formulation of questions to be asked of the deponent on discovery. Thereafter, he may aid in interpretation of the responses, the formulation of other questions to be asked at the trial, and, of

---

[c] It should be noted here that not all environmental disputes are settled in court. Many find their way to administrative agency hearings, where the advocacy process is quite different and different rules may apply.

[d] The rules and procedures of discovery to be hereafter discussed are not yet as well developed in criminal litigation, and the element of surprise is, therefore, to some degree retained.

[e] See Federal Rules of Civil Procedure, Depositions and Discovery, Rules 26–37.

[f] D. Sive, *Securing, Examining, and Cross Examining Expert Witnesses in Environmental Cases,* 68 MICH. L. REV. 1175 (1970).

course, in answering the questions posed by the opponent in his discovery process.

Trial preparation does not end with the acquisition and analysis of the factual bases upon which the case rests. Questions to be asked at the trial may be prepared and discussed in advance, not to program the expert's answers, but to ensure agreement on definitions and to further clarify the technical areas. Counsel will also wish to establish for the expert the correct method of answering questions. The answers must be clear and concise, to the layman and scientist alike. The witness must not ramble or soliloquize, nor must the answers be too technical or oversimplified, as the material conveyed will lose its force if it is drab or camouflaged in technical jargon. The lawyer will also preview questions which might be asked by opposing counsel. It is especially important that the scientist be acquainted with the type of nonscientific questions he may encounter. Physical and mental preparation are critical since a witness's visual image in the eyes of the court or jury may rival the substance of the testimony in impact.[9] He may find his qualifications challenged, be ridiculed as an academician without practical experience, or be asked about his fee with the obvious implication of professional prostitution. The expert should be cautioned against returning the hostile remarks. Composed, honest answers are the most effective response to such questions. Persistent badgering by an attorney often does him and his client more damage than it does the opponent.

TRIAL PROCEDURE AND THE EXPERT'S ROLE

An expert's educational role takes on a different cast once the trial begins. He is hired by the attorney who is the client's advocate. In a sense, therefore, the expert witness may take on, albeit unintentionally, the aura of a hired champion. The expert witness in the usual environmental case escapes some of the "paid witness" stigma because he often charges no fee and is rarely a professional witness of the sort one encounters in medical malpractice litigation.

The primary distinction between a lay or observer witness and an expert is that the lay witness may only relate facts as observed by himself, whereas the expert may give his opinion or draw inferences from those facts which a jury would be unable, because of its lack of specialized training, to draw. Thus, while a lay witness may state that a certain body of water containing dead fish was covered with a film of green material, an appropriate expert would be competent to testify to the identification of the floating matter and whether the condition could have caused a major fish kill in that water.

Although the difference between a fact and an opinion may be one of degree of concreteness, expert opinion may materially assist the fact finder, be it judge or jury, in forming a rational conclusion. There are two basic requirements, however, which must be met before the court shall deem an expert's testimony necessary. As McCormick states:

---

[9] Visual or personal impact on the jury is probably less a factor in environmental litigation than it is in other subject areas because most environmental suits involve injunctions, for which no jury is used.

> To warrant the use of expert testimony, then, two elements are required. First, the subject of the inference must be so distinctively related to some science, profession, business or occupation as to be beyond the ken of the average layman, and second, the witness must have such skill, knowledge or experience in that field or calling as to make it appear that his opinion or inference will probably aid the trier of fact in his search for the truth.[h]

Thus, although the subject of the expert testimony must be beyond the ken of the average layman and not be a matter of common understanding, the basic fact-finding function remains with the jury or judge. The true test then, is "not the total dependence of the jury upon such testimony, but their inability to judge for themselves as well as the [expert] witness."[i]

Before offering testimony, the expert must be qualified to the satisfaction of the trial judge, whose ruling is not subject to appellate review except from gross abuse of discretion. The attorney will ask questions of the witness concerning his education, including undergraduate and graduate school, fellowships and foundation research, teaching experience, publications, learned societies, and the totality of experience in the area or areas of specialization. It is most important that the witness state his qualifications fully and truthfully, without exaggeration. If the judge decides that the expert is qualified, his determination is binding on the jury although they may weigh his testimony in light of their assessment of his qualifications.

Precisely what combination of education and experience is required varies greatly with the subject matter and the judge. While great eminence and scholarly attainment may be impressive, any background which is likely to aid the jury appreciably will probably qualify. Thus, while in environmental litigation experts will most often be technically trained, in appropriate circumstances a person of experience and skill but lacking professional training may suffice. In any event, neither a Ph.D. nor a specialty in a particular branch of the discipline in question is required.

After qualification, the first substantive questions will come on direct examination. If the witness has firsthand knowledge of the situation—that is, if he has seen the item in question and examined it—he may describe what he has seen and draw inferences from his observations. Often, however, the expert has no firsthand knowledge and has not made personal observations. In such case, he may be asked hypothetical questions. This procedure requires that the expert assume the truth of prior testimony. Naturally, the hypotheses must be based upon facts in evidence or reasonable inferences from those facts, but they need not include all the material facts or those supportive of the opponent's position. Hypotheses containing other facts may be asked by the opponent on cross-examination. Cross-examination, a cornerstone of the adversary process, has been called "beyond any doubt the greatest legal engine ever invented for the discovery of truth."[j] It is simply the opponent's opportunity to challenge the credibility of the witness, his grasp of the facts, the basis of his opinions, and to inquire whether the opinion would be different if the facts as alleged by the opponent were true.

[h] Charles McCormick, *Law of Evidence*, West Publishing Company, St. Paul, Minn., 1954, sec. 13.
[i] *Lagenfelter v. Thompson*, 179 Md. 502 (1941).
[j] James Wigmore, *Evidence*, 3d ed., Little, Brown and Company, Boston, 1961.

The adversary process has been subject to often repeated criticism as the vehicle for eliciting and making best use of technical information.[k] The use of paid experts and hypothetical questions have both been repeatedly attacked. Both, however, are presently functional parts of the judicial system.[l]

NOTE: PRIVILEGED INFORMATION

Not everything connected with litigation is subject to discovery. Privileged information, such as attorney-client communications, is not available to the opposition.

An extension of this rule was stated in *Hickman v. Taylor,* 329 U.S. 511, 512 (1947), where the Supreme Court said,

> Proper preparation of a client's case demands that he [the lawyer] assemble information, sift what he considers to be the relevant from the irrelevant facts, prepare his legal theories and plan his strategy without undue and needless interference. . . . This work is reflected, of course, in interviews, statements, memoranda, correspondence, briefs, mental impressions, personal briefs, and countless other tangible and intangible ways—aptly though roughly termed by the Circuit Court of Appeals in this case as the "work product of the lawyer." Were such materials open to opposing counsel on mere demand, much of what is now put down in writing would remain unwritten. An attorney's thought, heretofore inviolate, would not be his own. Inefficiency, unfairness and sharp practices would inevitably develop in the giving of legal advice and in the preparation of cases for trial. The effect on the legal profession would be demoralizing. And the interests of the clients and the cause of justice would be poorly served.
>
> We do not mean to say that all written materials obtained or prepared by an adversary's counsel with an eye toward litigation are necessarily free from discovery in all cases. Where relevant and non-privileged facts remain hidden in an attorney's file and where production of those facts is essential to the preparation of one's case, discovery may properly be had. Such written statements and documents might, under certain circumstances, be admissible in evidence or give clues as to the existence or location of relevant facts. Or they might be justified where the witnesses are no longer available or can be reached only with difficulty. . . . But the general policy against invading the privacy of an attorney's course of preparation is so well recognized and so essential to an orderly working of our system of legal procedure that a burden rests on the one who would invade that privacy to establish adequate reasons to justify production through a subpoena or court order. That burden, we believe, is necessarily implicit in the rules as now constituted.

---

[k] This feeling is not new. In 1876 an English judge noted in an often quoted statement that ". . . the mode in which expert evidence is obtained is such as not to give the fair result of scientific opinion to the Court. A man may go, and does sometimes, to half-a-dozen experts. . . . He takes their honest opinions, he finds three in his favor and three against him; he says to the three in his favor, 'will you be kind enough to give evidence?' and he pays the three against him their fees and leaves them alone; the other side does the same. . . . I am sorry to say the result is that the Court does not get that assistance from the experts which, if they were unbiased and fairly chosen, it would have a right to expect." (*Thorn v. Worthington,* L.R. 6 Ch. D. 415, 416 [1876].)

[l] A number of possible improvements are suggested in McCormick, op. cit., sec. 17.

SCOPE OF EXPERT TESTIMONY

Although expert testimony in environmental cases is frequent, appellate decisions on the subject are not. This would seem to stem from the fact that the
rules concerning expert testimony were settled in years past in the context of
medical malpractice cases, and because many of the potential questions are
within the sound discretion of the trial judge and are not reviewable except for
gross abuse. *City of South Portland v. Pine State By-Products, Inc.,* however,
considers the scope of an expert's testimony in an environmental context.

City of South Portland v. Pine State By-Products, Inc.

Supreme Judicial Court of Maine; June 12, 1973, 306 A. 2d 1

Webber, Justice.

On July 25, 1967 defendant corporation, a rendering plant engaged in converting
fish, meat and poultry waste products into commercially salable materials, was
permanently enjoined from causing or allowing offensive odors injurious or dangerous to the health, comfort or property of individuals or of the public to escape
from the defendant's plant to such a degree that they are detectable in any manufacturing or military or other facility or place in the vicinity of its plant by a
person of normal or average sensitivity to odors.

On August 10, 1971 the plaintiff City of South Portland, wherein defendant's
plant is located, filed its complaint charging that on June 2, 1971 and sundry
occasions thereafter the defendant disobeyed said order and was in contempt
thereof. The matter came on to be heard by a single Justice who found for the
defendant. Plaintiff's appeal brings the matter to us for review.

Appellant first contends that reversible error was committed when an expert
witness offered by defendant was permitted to express an opinion and advance a
theory outside the realm of his training and experience. Dr. Amos Turk, admittedly a qualified expert witness with extensive practical and theoretical training
and experience in the field of detection and control of industrial odors and with
particular knowledge of the problems and control system in defendant's plant,
gave a detailed explanation of that control system and reached certain conclusions
with respect to its effectiveness. That his expert opinion was deemed to be persuasive by the Justice below was clearly evidenced by the findings made in this case.
These findings included the following:

> "I was much impressed by the testimony of Dr. Turk who was called as a witness for
> the Defendant. That he is an expert in the field of odor control is established by
> concession. It was his unqualified judgment that the odors complained of could not

have come from the Defendant's plant in the absence of any breakdown of the odor control equipment or the use of material which had putrified to a degree it gave off odor beyond the control of the odor control system.

There was no evidence whatsoever that the odor control equipment had broken down at any time or that the plant had used unsuitable material in its processing. As a matter of fact there was evidence and I do find that on some occasions when the complaints of odor were made the plant was not in operation. * * *

In the present instance I am not satisfied from the evidence that this plant has been the source of any noxious odors on the dates on which complaints were registered."

Since these findings were firmly based on credible evidence, they were determinative of the issue of contempt. The point sought to be raised by appellate can be better understood if the evidentiary background be further elaborated. The plaintiff had presented a number of witnesses, private citizens and South Portland police officers, who described their detection of noxious odors on various dates which they concluded had emanated from defendant's plant. None of these witnesses, however, had entered the defendant's plant to observe whether the plant was operating or whether the control system was functioning. It is apparent that neither the defendant nor the Justice below believed that these witnesses were knowingly and intentionally giving false testimony. It was the theory of the defendant, ultimately accepted by the factfinder, that these witnesses did in fact detect noxious odors but were honestly mistaken as to their source. In this connection the findings state:

"Neither the sincerity nor the truthfulness nor the accuracy of any of the complainants is in doubt in my mind.

I have come to the irresistible conclusion from the evidence that from time to time there were odors so noxious as to produce nausea in the complainants. I have no doubt as to the sincerity or truthfulness of the investigating officers. I do have serious doubts as to the method by which they arrived at their conclusions that the noxious odors emanated from this plant.

*   *   *   *   *   *   *   *   *   *   *   *   *   *   *

I am satisfied, however, that though the officers who investigated and testified were most certainly in good faith when they attributed the specific odors which they detected to this plant, they could well have been in error in attributing the odors to this particular source."

In support of its theory that plaintiff's witnesses, though not untruthful, were honestly mistaken, the defendant elicited from Dr. Turk, over plaintiff's objection, testimony explanatory of the theory of "false alarm." In effect the witness stated that he and other experts engaged in the field of sensory evaluation of materials and detection problems have determined on the basis of their own experience and that of others that one may be predisposed to expect a certain odor from a certain source and as a result sometimes conclude that he detects an odor which does not exist or that an odor he detects emanates from an expected source when in fact it emanates from a different source. The objection to this evidence was grounded on the contention that the "false alarm" theory involved psychiatry and psychology, fields in which the witness had no training and professed no special competence. We discern no error in admitting the testimony. The discretionary ruling of the Justice below as to the qualifications of an expert witness did not depend upon assigning labels to particular learning and experience of the witnesses. The witness demonstrated knowledge and competence in the area of sensory perception of odors which fully qualified him to furnish an opinion as to possibility of human error in detection and the reasons for it. The main issue, whether or not noxious odors emanated from defendant's plant, was decided on the basis of other evidence. The "false alarm" theory related only to whether the plaintiff's witnesses were honestly mistaken. In either event the Justice below was not disposed to accept their testimony as probative. It is understandable that the Justice below should not wish to have the public or the plaintiff's witnesses infer from a finding adverse to plaintiff that he had concluded that these witnesses had been other than truthful. Dr. Turk's theory did no more than to support his conviction that they had made an understandable human error in detection.

Appellant's second contention relates to the factfinder's alleged misuse of a view of defendant's premises. At the request of both parties the Justice below visited the area in the company of opposing counsel. When the hearing was resumed he spread upon the record a detailed report of the observations made at the scene. This included the detection of a number of odors in the area and their apparent sources, as well as a negative observation as to any unpleasant odor emanating from defendant's plant. It is apparent from the ensuing colloquy that the sensory perceptions of counsel at the scene were the same as those recorded by the Court, and indeed counsel for plaintiff stated for the record, "I think you have been very fair in your description." The findings include a fair summation of the report of the view spread upon the record.

Clearly it would have been error for the factfinder to find, for example, that because no offensive odors were emanating from defendant's plant at the time of the view, the same condition obtained on other occasions earlier in the summer. In State v. Slorah (1919) 118 Me. 203, 106 A. 768 we adhered to the rule that a view is not evidence and is taken only to assist the factfinder in better understanding the evidence otherwise produced. It is unnecessary to consider here whether or not the Slorah rule wholly accords with reality or is unnecessarily restrictive. Cf. Chouinard v. Shaw (1954) 99 N.H. 26, 104 A.2d 522. For in our opinion the use made of the view, including the detection of odors by the Justice below, did not violate the Slorah rule. The situation is closely akin to that discussed above in connection with the "false alarm" theory. On the basis of credible evidence the Justice was persuaded that on the dates of the complaints the odors could not and did not originate in defendant's plant. He also had evidence from witnesses as to the presence and sources of other noxious odors in the area, particularly odors emanating from the Stauffer Chemical Co. plant close by the defendant's premises. What he saw and smelled in the course of the view enabled him to better understand the testimony and, above all, to comprehend how it was possible for a number of truthful witnesses to fall into the same error as to the source of the offensive odor they detected. It may be noted, for example, that none of these witnesses was aware that Stauffer Chemical Co. was also at times the source of an industrial odor. We are satisfied that the determinative factual conclusions reached by the factfinder rested upon and were fully supported by credible evidence and were not based upon any misuse of the view as evidence.

*   *   *

Appeal denied.

QUESTIONS FOR DISCUSSION

1 Fact, law, and emotion all are factors in litigation. In what order of importance would you rank them? What other factors go into a decision?
2 Can an educational role be maintained in an adversary system?
3 Do you see anything unfair about the process of discovery? Should the investigative work and testimony of one party be available to the others?
4 Is the "tremendous inequality of knowledge" referred to by Sive really more acute in environmental litigation than other types? Product liability? Criminal law?
5 Does the fact that an expert witness charges no fee add to or detract from his credibility? Does a very high fee signify great competence of purchased testimony?
6 Consider the distinction between fact and opinion. How much is "fact" colored by erroneous or biased perceptions?
7 Might the word "skilled" be substituted for "expert"?
8 Does it seem reasonable that a lay jury should be able to reject an expert's testimony on a technical subject? Should juries be allowed to make technical judgments?
9 Does the very denomination of a witness as an "expert" give undue credence to his testimony?
10 Would a jury probably place more trust in an expert with outstanding academic credentials or in one with superior practical experience?
11 Should specialization in the field at issue be required? A general practice M.D. qualifies as an expert in all cases involving medical problems. Should the title "engineer" or "scientist" qualify a witness as an expert in all branches of those disciplines? Do such considerations rightly concern the weight to be given his testimony rather than his right to offer an opinion?
12 What dangers are apparent in the use of hypothetical questions?
13 Does the process of cross-examination conflict with or depreciate the expert witness's educational role?
14 Should the courts supply expert witnesses at no cost to those litigants who cannot afford to pay for their services? Do you see any dangers inherent in such a proposal?
15 Would you advise the appointment of experts by the court? Could a court employ a scientist or engineer to serve in all cases with scientific components? A panel or team of experts?
16 Does the "false alarm" testimony in *South Portland v. Pine State* seem like pure speculation in this circumstance? Was the witness qualified to speak on the subject?

EFFECT OF EXPERT TESTIMONY

Reserve Mining Company v. EPA illustrates the impact on courts and judges of expert testimony in environmental cases. Note particularly the inferences drawn when testimony identifies risk but cannot predict the outcome with certainty.

Reserve Mining Company v. Environmental Protection Agency

514 F.2d 492 (1975)

Bright, Circuit Judge.

The United States, the States of Michigan, Wisconsin, and Minnesota, and several environmental groups seek an injunction ordering Reserve Mining Company[1] to cease discharging wastes from its iron ore processing plant in Silver Bay, Minnesota, into the ambient air of Silver Bay and the waters of Lake Superior. On April 20, 1974, the district court granted the requested relief and ordered that the discharges immediately cease, thus effectively closing the plant. *United States v. Reserve Mining Co.*, 380 F. Supp. 11 (D. Minn. 1974). Reserve Mining Company appealed that order and we stayed the injunction pending resolution of the merits of the appeal. *Reserve Mining Co. v. United States*, 498 F.2d 1073 (8th Cir. 1974). We affirm the injunction but direct modification of its terms. As to other issues brought before us by appeals during the course of this complex litigation, we affirm in part and reverse in part.

SUMMARY OF DECISION

In this lengthy opinion, we undertake a comprehensive analysis of the relevant scientific and medical testimony and evaluate the claims of the plaintiffs that Reserve's conduct violates express provisions of federal law as well as state laws and regulations and is a public nuisance.

[1] Reserve Mining Company is a jointly owned subsidiary of Armco Steel Corporation and Republic Steel Corporation. The district court joined these parent corporations as parties to this lawsuit at an advanced state of the litigation. The propriety of this joinder is raised on appeal and discussed in part VI of our opinion. Generally we shall make reference only to Reserve, the original defendant.

The following environmental groups intervened as plaintiffs on June 15, 1972, by order of the district court: The Minnesota Environmental Law Institute, the Northern Environmental Council, the Save Lake Superior Association, and the Michigan Student Environmental Confederation. *United States v. Reserve Mining Co.*, 56 F.R.D. 408 (D. Minn. 1972). The Environmental Defense Fund intervened pursuant to the court's order of July 31, 1973, and the Sierra Club has filed an amicus curiae brief on behalf of the plaintiffs.

Numerous parties have intervened as defendants. They include the Northestern Minnesota Development Association, the Duluth Area Chamber of Commerce, the Towns of Silver Bay, Babbitt, and Beaver Bay, and several other civic and governmental units in the area of the Reserve facility. The United Steelworkers of America has submitted an amicus curiae brief on behalf of the defendants.

We summarize our key rulings as follows:

1 The United States and the other plaintiffs have established that Reserve's discharges into the air and water give rise to a potential threat to the public health. The risk to public health is of sufficient gravity to be legally cognizable and calls for an abatement order on reasonable terms.

2 The United States and Minnesota have shown that Reserve's discharges violate federal and state laws and state pollution control regulations, also justifying injunctive relief on equitable terms.

3 No harm to the public health has been shown to have occurred to this date and the danger to health is not imminent. The evidence calls for preventive and precautionary steps. No reason exists which requires that Reserve terminate its operations at once.

4 Reserve, with its parent companies Armco Steel and Republic Steel, is entitled to a reasonable opportunity and a reasonable time period to convert its Minnesota taconite operations to on-land disposal of taconite tailings and to restrict air emissions at its Silver Bay plant, or to close its existing Minnesota taconite-pelletizing operations. The parties are required to expedite consideration and resolution of these alternatives.

5 The evidence suggests that the threat to public health from the air emissions is more significant than that from the water discharge. Consequently, Reserve must take reasonable immediate steps to reduce its air emissions.

I INTRODUCTION

A Summary of Controversy

In 1947, Reserve Mining Company (Reserve), then contemplating a venture in which it would mine low-grade iron ore ("taconite") present in Minnesota's Mesabi Iron Range and process the ore into iron-rich pellets at facilities bordering on Lake Superior, received a permit[2] from the State of Minnesota to discharge the wastes (called "tailings") from its processing operations into the lake.[3]

Reserve commenced the processing of taconite ore in Silver Bay, Minnesota, in 1955, and that operation continues today. Taconite mined near Babbitt, Minnesota, is shipped by rail some 47 miles to the Silver Bay "beneficiating" plant where it is concentrated into pellets containing some 65 percent iron ore. The process involves crushing the taconite into fine granules, separating out the metallic iron with huge magnets, and flushing the residual tailings into Lake Superior. The tailings enter the lake as a slurry of approximately 1.5 percent solids. The slurry acts as a heavy density current bearing the bulk of the suspended particles to the

---

[2] The permit provides in part:

[T]ailings shall not be discharged * * * so as to result in any material adverse effects on fish life of public water supplies or in any other material unlawful pollution of the waters of the lake * * *.

[3] Minnesota granted the permit based on Reserve's theory that the weight and velocity of the tailings as they are discharged from the plant into the lake would ensure deposit of the tailings in the 900 foot depth of the "great trough" area offshore from the proposed facility.

lake bottom. In this manner, approximately 67,000 tons of tailings are discharged daily.[4]

The states and the United States commenced efforts to procure abatement of these discharges as early as mid-1969. These efforts, however, produced only an unsuccessful series of administrative conferences and unsuccessful state court proceedings.[5] The instant litigation commenced on February 2, 1972, when the United States—joined eventually by the States of Minnesota, Wisconsin, and Michigan and by various environmental groups—filed a complaint alleging that Reserve's discharge of tailings into Lake Superior violated § 407 of the Rivers and Harbors Act of 1899 [33 U.S.C. § 401 et seq. (1970)],[6] § 1160 of the pre-1972 Federal Water Pollution Control Act (FWPCA) [33 U.S.C. § 1151 et seq. (1970)][7] and the federal common law of public nuisance.

Until June 8, 1973, the case was essentially a water pollution abatement case, but on that date the focus of the controversy shifted to the public health impact of the tailings discharge and Reserve's emissions into the ambient air. Arguing the health issue in the district court, plaintiffs maintained that the taconite ore mined by Reserve contained an asbestiform variety of the amphibole mineral cummingtonite-grunerite,[8] and that the processing of the ore resulted in the discharge into the air and water of mineral fibers substantially identical and in some instances identical to amosite asbestos.[9] This contention raised an immediate health issue, since inhalation of asbestos at occupational levels of exposure is associated with an increased incidence of various forms of cancer.

Although it is undisputed that Reserve discharges significant amounts of waste tailings into Lake Superior and dust into the Silver Bay air, the parties vigorously contest the precise physical properties of the discharges, their biological effects, and, with respect to the water discharge, the issue of whether a signif-

[4] The Silver Bay processing operation employs about 3,000 workers and is central to the economic livelihood of Silver Bay and surrounding communities.

[5] See *Reserve Mining Co. v. Minnesota Pollution Control Agency*, 294 Minn. 300, 200 N.W. 2d 142 (1972).

[6] Section 407 is also known as the Refuse Act.

[7] Unless otherwise noted, all references to the FWPCA are to the statute as it existed prior to the 1972 amendments. The 1972 amendments, Pub. L. No. 92–500, 86 Stat. 816 (Oct. 18, 1972), amended and reorganized the FWPCA. The current FWPCA is now codified at 33 U.S.C. § 1251 et seq. (Supp. 1974).

The district court found that "[p]ursuant to § 4(a) of P.L. 92–500, the 1972 amendments have no effect on actions pending prior to the effective date of the amendments." 380 F. Supp. at 23 n. 1. The 1972 amendments were passed on October 18, 1972, some eight months subsequent to the initiation of this suit.

[8] Amphibole denotes the mineral family made up by silicates of calcium and magnesium and, usually, one or more other metals (such as iron or manganese). Cummingtonite-grunerite is a general name for a "suite" of amphibole minerals which are essentially identical except for the relative quantities of iron and magnesium in them. The iron-rich members are sometimes referred to as grunerites, although the word cummingtonite is used to refer to the entire suit.

[9] The cummingtonite-grunerite in Reserve's mine was formed when molten igneous rock, now known as the Duluth gabbro, intruded upon and heated a portion of the iron formation of the eastern Mesabi Range, thereby chemically altering it. When this gabbro contacted the iron deposits of the eastern district of the Range it caused the creation of several new minerals and produced a coarsening of grain size of pre-existing minerals such as magnetite and quartz. Among the new minerals formed were several amphiboles, including cummingtonite-grunerite.

icant proportion of the discharge, instead of flowing to the lake bottom with the density current, disperses throughout the lake. Plaintiffs attempted to show that a substantial amount of the fibers discharged by Reserve could be classified as amosite asbestos, and that these fibers could be traced in the ambient air of Silver Bay and surrounding communities and in the drinking water of Duluth and other communities drawing water from the lake. Reserve countered that its cummingtonite-grunerite does not have a fibrous form and is otherwise distinguishable from amosite asbestos. It further maintained that the discharges do not pose any cognizable hazard to health and that, in any event, with respect to the discharge into water, the tailings largely settle to the bottom of the lake in the "great trough" area as initially planned.[10]

The evidence presented on these points was extensive and complex. Hearings on a motion for a preliminary injunction were consolidated with the trial on the merits and during the nine-month period of 139 days of trial, the trial court heard more than 100 witnesses and received over 1,600 exhibits. The parties introduced testimony comparing the mineralogy of Reserve's cummingtonite-grunerite with amosite asbestos, such testimony based on electron microscope analysis of morphology, x-ray and electron diffraction analysis of crystal structure, laboratory analysis of chemical composition, and other identification techniques. As for the possible dispersion of the tailings throughout Lake Superior, witnesses disputed whether Reserve's discharges provided the sole source of cummingtonite-grunerite in the lake and whether the presence of the mineral could thus be used as a "tracer" for Reserve's discharge. In an effort to assess the health hazard, the parties presented extensive expert scientific and medical testimony, and the court itself appointed certain expert witnesses, who assumed the task of assisting the court in the evaluation of scientific testimony and supervising court-sponsored studies to measure the levels of asbestos fibers in the air near Silver Bay, in Lake Superior water, and in the tissues of deceased Duluth residents.

On April 20, 1974, the district court entered an order closing Reserve's Silver Bay facility. In an abbreviated memorandum opinion,[11] the court held that Reserve's water discharge violated federal water pollution laws and that its air emissions violated state air pollution regulations, and that both the air and water discharges constituted common law nuisances. The court's decision, in part, rested on these core findings:

> The discharge into the air substantially endangers the health of the people of Silver Bay and surrounding communities as far away as the eastern shore in Wisconsin.
>
> The discharge into the water substantially endangers the health of people who procure their drinking water from the western arm of Lake Superior including the communities of Beaver Bay, Two Harbors, Cloquet, Duluth [Minnesota], and Superior, Wisconsin. [380 F. Supp. at 16.]

---

[10] See note 3 supra.
[11] *United States v. Reserve Mining Co.,* 380 F. Supp. 11, 15 (D. Minn. 1974).

The district court issued an extensive supplemental memorandum on May 11, 1974,[12] expanding on its earlier findings of fact and conclusions of law. In proceedings detailed in the following section of this opinion, a panel of this court stayed the injunction[13] and subsequently requested the district court to fully dispose of the litigation and enter final judgment. This court, sitting *en banc,* heard the merits of several consolidated appeals at the December 1974 session. We have also taken under consideration other appeals which have been subsequently submitted to us on briefs, but without oral argument. Our disposition follows.

B Discussion of Rulings by the District Court and Previous Proceedings in This Court

In its memorandum opinions of April 20, and May 11, ordering Reserve to cease immediately its discharges into the air and water, the district court predicated its determinations on several counts. On the discharge into water, the court found a violation of several sections of the Minnesota water quality standards. These standards, promulgated pursuant to § 1160(c)(5) of the FWPCA and subsequently approved by the federal government, are denominated as Minnesota Water Pollution Control Regulation 15 (WPC15). The district court found the following parts of WPC 15 violated: WPC 15(a)(4), providing that waters of naturally high quality shall not be degraded; WPC 15(c)(2), a broad provision prohibiting the discharge of wastes which create nuisance conditions or cause "offensive or harmful effects;" WPC 15(c)(6), limiting the allowable suspended solid content of effluent discharges to 30 milligrams per liter; WPC 15(d)(1), controlling the discharge of substances that make certain waters unfit to drink even after chemical treatment; and WPC 26, a general effluent standard for Lake Superior incorporating the standards of WPC 15. Further, the court found that the discharge into Lake Superior endangered the health and welfare of persons in Minnesota, Wisconsin, and Michigan and therefore was subject to abatement pursuant to §§ 1160(c)(5) and (g)(1) of the FWPCA. Finally, the court found that the endangerment to health also constituted both a federal common law nuisance and a nuisance under the applicable laws of Minnesota, Wisconsin, and Michigan. 380 F. Supp. at 55.

As for the air emissions, the court also found liability under both federal and state common law nuisance. Additionally, the court cited Reserve for the violation of several Minnesota air pollution control regulations: APC 1, setting primary and secondary air standards; APC 5 and 6, controlling particulate emissions; and APC 17, setting an emission standard for asbestos. 380 F. Supp. at 55-56.

The trial court based its closure decision on two independent determinations. First, as noted above, the court had concluded that the discharges "substantially endanger" the exposed populations. Second, the court had concluded that, although a method of abatement providing for an alternate means of disposal of wastes with some turn-around time represented a desirable middle course in this

---

[12] *United States v. Reserve Mining Co.,* 380 F. Supp. 11, 21 (D. Minn. 1974).
[13] *Reserve Mining Co. v. United States,* 498 F.2d 1073 (8th Cir. 1974).

litigation,[14] Reserve had demonstrated such intransigence on the issue of abating its water discharge as to render any such middle course impossible. The court thus believed it had no alternative but to immediately enjoin the discharges:

> Defendants have the economic and engineering capability to carry out an on land disposal system that satisfies the health and environmental considerations raised. For reasons unknown to this Court they have chosen not to implement such a plan. In essence they have decided to continue exposing thousands daily to a substantial health risk in order to maintain the current profitability of the present operation and delay the capital outlay (with its concomitant profit) needed to institute modifications. The Court has no other alternative but to order an immediate halt to the discharge which threatens the lives of thousands. In that defendants have no plan to make the necessary modifications, there is no reason to delay any further the issuance of the injunction. [380 F. Supp. at 20.]

Reserve promptly appealed the injunction order of the district court and we issued a temporary stay of that order on April 22, 1974, and scheduled a hearing on Reserve's application for a stay of injunction pending its appeal. That hearing was held on May 15, 1974, before a panel of this court consisting of Judges Bright, Ross, and Webster, and on June 4, 1974, the court issued an opinion granting Reserve a 70-day stay of the injunction. *Reserve Mining Co. v. United States,* 498 F.2d 1073 (8th Cir. 1974). The court conditioned the stay upon Reserve taking prompt steps to abate its air and water discharges, and provided for further proceedings to review whether Reserve had proceeded with the good faith preparation and implementation of an acceptable plan.[15]

[14] The court observed that it:
would like to find a middle ground that would satisfy both considerations. If an [alternative] method of disposal is available that is economically feasible, could be speedily implemented and took into consideration the health questions involved, the Court might be disposed to fashion a remedy that would permit the implementation of such a system. However, if there is no alternative method available, the Court has no other choice but to immediately curtail the discharge and stop the contamination of the water supply of those downstream from the plant. [380 F. Supp. at 17-18.]
[15] We stated:
Accordingly, our stay of the injunction will be conditioned upon Reserve taking prompt steps to abate its discharges into air and water. We invited Reserve to advise this court concerning plans for the on-land disposal of its tailings and the significant control of its air emissions. Reserve's counsel stated that the company envisioned a three and one-half year to five year "turn-around" time, but added that investigation continues in an effort to reduce further the time for achieving abatement.
Our stay of the injunction rests upon the good faith preparation and implementation of an acceptable plan. Therefore, we grant a 70-day stay upon these conditions:
(1) Reserve's plans shall be promptly submitted to plaintiff-states and to the United States for review and recommendations by appropriate agencies concerned with environmental and health protection. Such plan shall be filed with the district court and submitted to all plaintiffs in no event later than 25 days from the filing of this order.
(2) Plaintiffs shall then have an additional 20 days within which to file their comments on such plan.
(3) The district court shall consider Reserve's plan and any recommendations made by the United States and plaintiff-states and make a recommendation, within 15 days following submission of plaintiffs' comments, whether or not a stay of the injunction should be continued pending the appeal.
(4) Based on these plans, comments, and recommendations, this court will then review the status of its stay order within the time remaining. [498 F.2d at 1085-1086 (footnotes omitted).]

The State of Minnesota applied to the Supreme Court to vacate this stay. The Court denied Minnesota this relief in an order entered July 9, 1974. *Minnesota v. Reserve Mining Co.,* 418 U.S. 911, 94 S. Ct. 3203, 41 L. Ed. 2d 1156 (1974). Meanwhile, in accordance with the stay order, the district court evaluated compliance with our order that Reserve proceed in good faith to present a plan of abatement. In a memorandum opinion filed August 3, 1974,[16] the district court, taking cognizance of the opposition of the State of Minnesota to Reserve's proffered plan (the so-called Palisades Plan), rejected Reserve's proposal as unreasonable and recommended against any further stay during the pendency of this litigation. Also, pursuant to our earlier request for advice on the status of unresolved claims, the district court indicated that it had "severed for later resolution the issue of the biological effect of Reserve's discharge on the Lake itself" and that several other issues remained under advisement. 380 F. Supp. at 91 n. 6.

Judges Bright and Ross convened a prehearing conference under Fed. R. App. P. 33 to inquire into consolidation, clarification, and simplification of issues pending an appeal and to advise this court of the time necessary to submit unresolved issues pending before the district court. The cause was then remanded with a request that the district court expedite disposition of the unresolved issues, with this court retaining jurisdiction over the pending appeal of the district court injunction.

Additionally, this court, on its own motion, scheduled a hearing before a panel consisting of Judges Bright, Ross, and Webster to consider the recommendations of the district court against continuing the stay order pending appeal. Following hearings, this court entered an order continuing the stay, concluding that:

> (1) The representations of counsel at the hearing on August 24, 1974, satisfy us that significant progress has been achieved by the parties in seeking agreement for an on-land disposal site and method for abatement of Reserve's discharge into Lake Superior. These negotiations are continuing and will not impede the processing of the pending appeal upon the merits, [and]
>
> (2) No substantial reason has been advanced why the stay order should not be continued pending such appeal other than the argument of imminent health hazard, which this court, for purposes of the stay pending appeal, has already determined adversely to appellees. [*Reserve Mining Co. v. United States,* No. 74-1291 (8th Cir., Aug. 28, 1974.]

Minnesota and the United States applied to the Supreme Court for relief from this further stay order. The Court denied the applications, with Mr. Justice Douglas dissenting. *Minnesota v. Reserve Mining Co.,* 419 U.S. 802, 95 S. Ct. 287, 42 L. Ed. 2d 33 (1974).

On October 18, 1974, the district court issued an unpublished memorandum resolving certain other issues in the case and, noting that there was no just reason

---

[16] *United States v. Reserve Mining Co.,* 380 F. Supp. 11, 71 (D. Minn. 1974).

for delay, directing the entry of final judgment on all claims decided to date. See Fed. R. Civ. P. 54(b).

The district court made the following additional rulings: (1) that Reserve's discharge into the water constitutes a violation of the Refuse Act, 33 U.S.C. § 407; (2) that Reserve's counterclaims, alleging that interference with its present modes of discharge as sanctioned by permits amounts to a deprivation of property and an impairment of contractual rights, should be dismissed; (3) that Reserve's air emissions violate Minnesota air pollution control regulation (APC) 3 Minn. Stat. Ann. § 116.081(1), which require that permits be obtained for the operation of certain emission facilities; (4) that Reserve's discharge of wastes into the Dunka and Partridge Rivers of Minnesota violates Minn. Stat. Ann. § 115.07(1), which requires a permit for the operation of a disposal system; (5) that Minn. Stat. Ann. § 115.07(1) is also violated by Reserve's discharge of wastes from its pilot plant into Lake Superior without a permit; (6) that the evidence is insufficient to justify liability under Minn. Stat. Ann. § 105.41, which makes unlawful the appropriation of state water without a permit; and (7) that the State of Wisconsin could not assert the state's "public trust doctrine" as an affirmative cause of action against Reserve's discharge into Lake Superior. Finally, the court left certain matters undecided, stating:

> The question of fines and penalties, the question of sanctions for failure to make discovery, and the question of liability of defendants for the water filtration systems that may be installed in Duluth, Minnesota, and Superior, Wisconsin, cannot be decided at this time. [Order of Oct. 18, 1974, at 19.]

This final order has produced several additional appeals. We now have under submission the following:

> No. 73-1239: *Reserve Mining Co. v. Environmental Protection Agency,* in which Reserve urges that WPC 15 is arbitrary and unreasonable and challenges the failure of the Administrator of the EPA to require its revision.

> No. 74-1291: *Reserve Mining Co. v. United States,* in which Reserve seeks to vacate the April 20, 1974, order enjoining its discharges into the air and water.

> No. 74-1466: *United States v. Reserve Mining Co.,* in which the United States appeals from the district court's order (April 19, 1974) directing that the Corps of Engineers of the United States provide filtered water at government expense to certain Minnesota communities located on the North Shore of Lake Superior.

> No. 74-1816: *Reserve Mining Co. v. United States,* in which Reserve appeals from the most recent judgment entered October 18, 1974.

> No. 74-1977: *State of Wisconsin v. Reserve Mining Co.,* in which appellant-Wisconsin contests the district court's determination that the Wisconsin public trust doctrine does not provide an affirmative cause of action against Reserve's discharge into Lake Superior.[17]

---

[17] By letter to this court dated December 23, 1974, Wisconsin abandoned this appeal. Accordingly, we dismiss this appeal.

No. 75-1003: *Minnesota Environmental Law Institute v. United States*, in which various environmental plaintiffs contest the district court's decision to "sever" the issue of whether Reserve's discharge constitutes biological pollution of Lake Superior.

No. 75-1005: *State of Michigan v. Reserve Mining Co.*, in which appellant-Michigan contests the district court's decision to "sever" the issue of whether Reserve's discharge constitutes biological pollution of Lake Superior.

During oral arguments and by written submissions, Reserve has advised us that it no longer asks Minnesota to accept its plan to dispose taconite tailings at the Palisades location, see discussion at p. 305 supra. Reserve has now submitted a second proposal to Minnesota for an on-land disposal site in which it proposes to spend approximately $243,000,000 in order to end its discharge of tailings into Lake Superior and curtail its emission of contaminants into the air. This proposed site, which Minnesota has under consideration, is located approximately seven miles inland from the Silver Bay facility, and is referred to as Milepost 7, or Lax Lake site.

II HEALTH ISSUE

The initial, crucial question for our evaluation and resolution focuses upon the alleged hazard to public health attributable to Reserve's discharges into the air and water.

We first considered this issue on Reserve's application for a stay of the district court's injunction pending a determination of the merits of its appeal. We noted the usual formulation of the applicable standards to be met by the party seeking a stay. One of those standards addresses the likelihood of success by the moving party on the merits of the appeal. In applying this standard we made a preliminary assessment of the merits of Reserve's appeal from the trial court's injunction order. We noted that the "rather drastic remedy ordered by the district court * * * was a response to the finding of a substantial danger to the public health," and that our preliminary assessment of whether such a substantial danger was presented "should control our action as to whether to grant or deny a stay." 498 F.2d at 1076-1077.

In this preliminary review, we did not view the evidence as supporting a finding of substantial danger. We noted numerous uncertainties in plaintiffs' theory of harm which controlled our assessment, particularly the uncertainty as to present levels of exposure and the difficulty in attempting to quantify those uncertain levels in terms of a demonstrable health hazard. As we stated then, "* * * it is not known what the level of fiber exposure is, other than that it is relatively low, and it is not known what level of exposure is safe or unsafe." 498 F.2d at 1082. In confirmation of our view, we noted the opinion of Dr. Arnold Brown,[18] the principal court-appointed expert, that no adverse health consequences could be scientifically predicted on the basis of existing medical knowledge. Additionally, we

---

[18] Dr. Arnold Brown is Chairman of the Department of Pathology and Anatomy at the Mayo Clinic of Rochester, Minnesota. He served the court both in the capacity of a technical advisor and that of an impartial witness.

noted the district court's conclusion that there is " '* * * insufficient knowledge upon which to base an opinion as to the magnitude of the risks associated with this exposure.' " 498 F.2d at 1083. We thought one proposition evident:

> [A]lthough Reserve's discharges represent a possible medical danger, they have not in this case been proven to amount to a health hazard. The discharges may or may not result in detrimental health effects, but, for the present, that is simply unknown. [Id.]

On the basis of the foregoing we forecast that Reserve would likely prevail on the merits of the health issue.[19] We limited this forecast to the single issue before us whether Reserve's plant should be closed immediately because of a "substantial danger" to health:

> While not called upon at this stage to reach any final conclusion, our review suggests that this evidence does not support a finding of *substantial danger* and that, indeed, the testimony indicates that such a finding should not be made. *In this regard,* we conclude that Reserve appears likely to succeed on the merits of its appeal on the health issue. 498 F.2d at 1077-1078. (Emphasis added.)

We reached no preliminary decision on whether the facts justified a less stringent abatement order.

As will be evident from the discussion that follows, we adhere to our preliminary assessment that the evidence is insufficient to support the kind of demonstrable danger to the public health that would justify the immediate closing of Reserve's operations. We now address the basic question of whether the discharges pose any risk to public health and, if so, whether the risk is one which is legally cognizable. This inquiry demands separate attention to the discharge into the air of Silver Bay and the discharge into Lake Superior.[20]

---

[19] We also suggested that plaintiffs would prevail in their claim that the discharges, apart from any danger to health, constituted unlawful pollution subject to abatement. In this case we find it necessary to discuss pollution only with respect to its possible adverse health effects.

[20] While we, of course, adhere to the "clearly erroneous" standard in our review of district court findings, we note that many of the issues in this case do not involve "historical" facts subject to the ordinary means of judicial resolution. Indeed, a number of the disputes involve conflicting theories and experimental results, about which it would be judicially presumptuous to offer conclusive findings. In addressing this same type of problem, the District of Columbia Circuit recently observed:

> Where * * * the [EPA] regulations turn on choices of policy, on an assessment of risks, or on predictions dealing with matters on the frontiers of scientific knowledge, we will demand adequate reasons and explanations, but not "findings" of the sort familiar from the world of adjudication. [*Amoco Oil Co. v. Environmental Protection Agency,* 501 F.2d 722, 741 (D.C. Cir. 1974).]

In such circumstances, the finder of fact must accept certain areas of uncertainty, and the findings themselves cannot extend further than attempting to assess or characterize the strengths and weaknesses of the opposing arguments. As Judge Wright observed in dissent in *Ethyl Corporation v. Environmental Protection Agency,* No. 73-2205 (D.C. Cir. filed Jan. 28, 1975) (dissenting opinion n. 74), "* * * the court should [not] view itself as the equivalent of a combined Ph.D. in chemistry, biology, and statistics."

If our review seems unusually detailed, then, it is because we have endeavored to carefully explain the delicate balance of many of the issues in this case. While generally we do not find error in the underlying findings of the district court, we believe that an appreciation of the risk posed by Reserve's discharge demands an understanding of the state of scientific knowledge upon which those findings are based.

A The Discharge into Air

As we noted in our stay opinion, much of the scientific knowledge regarding asbestos disease pathology derives from epidemiological studies of asbestos workers occupationally exposed to and inhaling high levels of asbestos dust. Studies of workers naturally exposed to asbestos dust have shown "excess" cancer deaths[21] and a significant incidence of asbestosis.[22] The principal excess cancers are cancer of the lung, the pleura (mesothelioma) and gastrointestinal tract ("gi" cancer).

Studies conducted by Dr. Irving Selikoff,[23] plaintiffs' principal medical witness, illustrated these disease effects. Dr. Selikoff investigated the disease experience of asbestos insulation workers in the New York–New Jersey area, asbestos insulation workers nationwide, and workers in a New Jersey plant manufacturing amosite asbestos. Generally, all three groups showed excess cancer deaths among the exposed populations, as well as a significant incidence of asbestosis. With respect to cancer generally, three to four times the expected number of deaths occurred; with respect to lung cancer in particular, five to eight times the expected number; and with respect to gastrointestinal cancer, two to three times that expected. Dr. Selikoff described the increase of gastrointestinal cancer as "modest." [A.10:286-287.]

Several principles of asbestos-related disease pathology emerge from these occupational studies. One principle relates to the so-called 20-year rule, meaning that there is a latent period of cancer development of at least 20 years. [A.10:284-285.] Another basic principle is the importance of initial exposure, demonstrated by significant increases in the incidence of cancer even among asbestos manufacturing workers employed for less than three months (although the incidence of disease does increase upon longer exposure). [A.10:279-280] Finally, these studies indicate that threshold values and dose response relationships,[24] although probably operative with respect to asbestos-induced cancer, are not quantifiable on the basis of existing data.[25] [A.10:280, 317-19.]

---

[21] "Excess" cancer deaths refers to an incidence of *observed* cancer deaths among a segment of the population exposed to a certain agent greater than that *expected* from a general population not similarly exposed. The expected incidence of cancer is usually determined by reference to national cancer statistics.

[22] Asbestosis, a respiratory disease, is a diffuse scarring of the lung resulting from the inhalation of asbestos dust.

[23] Dr. Irving Selikoff is Director of the Environmental Sciences Laboratory of Mt. Sinai School of Medicine. He is a nationally recognized authority in asbestos-induced disease and occupational diseases generally.

[24] A threshold value is that level of exposure below which no adverse health effects occur, while the dose response relationship quantifies the association between disease-producing levels of exposure and the incidence of disease.

[25] Reserve presented testimony by several scientists supporting the proposition that the threshold level of asbestos exposure with respect to lung cancer and asbestosis is reasonably well established. Dr. Hans Weill, a Professor of Medicine at Tulane University School of Medicine, testified that his study of asbestos workers exposed for a mean period of 17.3 years indicated that asbestosis does not develop where the concentration of fibers is only five fibers per cc. [A.16:29-30.] Dr. Weill went on to review a series of epidemiological studies also suggesting the existence of a threshold level of exposure for lung cancer. [A.16:33-36.] Moreover, he reasoned that the value of this threshold would not be any lower than that applicable to the development of asbestosis, and thus is at least five fibers per cc. [A.16:43-44.] Dr. Paul Gross, Professor of Pathology at the University of South Carolina Medical

Additionally, some studies implicate asbestos as a possible pathogenic agent in circumstances of exposure less severe than occupational levels. For example, several studies indicate that mesothelioma, a rare but particularly lethal cancer frequently associated with asbestos exposure, has been found in persons experiencing a low level of asbestos exposure.[26] Although Dr. Selikoff acknowledged that these studies of lower-level exposure involve certain methodological difficulties and rest "on much less firm ground" than the occupational studies,[27] he expressed the opinion that they should be considered in the assessment of risks posed by an asbestos discharge.

At issue in the present case is the similarity of the circumstances of Reserve's discharge into the air to those circumstances known to result in asbestos-related disease. This inquiry may be divided into two stages: first, circumstances relating to the nature of the discharge and, second, circumstances relating to the level of the discharge (and resulting level of exposure).

School, likewise viewed these epidemiological studies as establishing a threshold level of exposure for lung cancer. [A.15:33–35.]

On cross-examination, plaintiffs challenged the interpretations of Doctors Weill and Gross, noting various deficiencies in the methodologies of the studies. [A.15:41–44; A.16:37–39.] For example, the testimony indicated that one of the studies had not tracked the workers for a sufficient period of time to determine whether cancer might develop, and that in fact a follow-up study indicated excess cancer deaths after 25 years in even low exposure groups. [A.16:38.] Moreover, plaintiffs' witnesses held firm opinions that although threshold levels probably exist, those levels could not be considered as authoritatively established. [A.10:133–35 (Wagoner); A.10:317–318 (Selikoff); A.13:285–89 (Rankin).]

It is significant that the witnesses generally agreed that no known safe level of exposure exists for mesothelioma. The agreement on this point seems a reflection of the weight given to the studies showing an association between mesothelioma and residence in proximity to an asbestos worker. See note 26 infra.

[26] Dr. Selikoff described some of this research. A study of mesothelioma victims in the northwestern portion of Cape Province, South Africa, in an area where there are many crocidolite asbestos mines and mills, found that in approximately one-half the deaths the only asbestos exposure was that resulting from residence in an area where there was a mine or mill. [A.10:244–245.] A study of mesothelioma victims in Hamburg, Germany, showed rates of mesothelioma of nine per ten thousand and one per ten thousand in two districts which had an asbestos factory, and no occurrence of the disease in the one district without such a factory. A study of 76 cases of mesothelioma drawn from the files of a London hospital showed that, of 45 victims who had not worked with asbestos, nine had simply lived in the household of an asbestos worker, 11 had lived within one-half mile of an asbestos plant. Finally, a study of 42 mesothelioma victims drawn from the files of the Pennsylvania Department of Health revealed that, of 22 victims who had not been occupationally exposed, three had lived in the household of an asbestos worker and eight had lived within one-half mile of an asbestos plant. [A.10:245–47.]

Additionally, Dr. Selikoff reported on several studies of shipyard workers. These studies indicated excess mesothelioma not only among the shipyard insulation workers dealing directly with asbestos, but also among the occupational groups working in proximity with the insulation workers. [A.10:254–62.]

[27] Dr. Selikoff stated:

I would now like to turn to the problem at hand, the question of environmental exposure. And relate what I have just given you from occupational sources to environmental sources. And here we're on much less firm ground.

The cohort studies that were done and are much more readily and easily done among workers, are not readily done in the general population. You cannot identify people who, twenty, thirty, forty years ago breathed asbestos from environmental contamination and compare them with people who you can prove forty years ago didn't breathe asbestos from environmental sources. And, therefore, much of the evidence that I will now place before you is a little unusual. [A.10:243.]

   1   **The Nature of the Discharge**   The comparability of the nature of Reserve's discharge to the nature of the discharge in known disease situations raises two principal questions. The first is whether the discharged fibers are identical or substantially identical to fibers known to cause disease; the second is whether the length of the fibers discharged is a relevant factor in assessing pathogenic effect. The district court found that Reserve's discharge includes known pathogenic fibers and that a lower risk to health could not be assigned to this discharge for reasons of fiber length.

   On the first question—the issue of the identity of the fibers—the argument focuses on whether the ore mined by Reserve contains (and yields wastes during processing consistent with) amosite asbestos. The inquiry is critical because studies demonstrate that amosite, at least in occupational settings, may serve as a carcinogenic (cancer-producing) agent. A principal dispute concerns the precise composition of the mineral cummingtonite-grunerite found in Reserve's taconite ore: Reserve maintains that the cummingtonite-grunerite present in its Peter Mitchell Mine at Babbitt is not asbestiform and is not chemically consistent with amosite asbestos; plaintiffs argue that much of the cummingtonite-grunerite mined by Reserve is substantially identical to amosite asbestos.

   As a general scientific proposition, it is clear that cummingtonite-grunerite embraces a range of chemistries, including the chemistry of amosite asbestos. The mineral also embraces a range of morphologies, from asbestiform, needle-like fibers to block-shaped, crystal aggregates. The crucial factual determination is, thus, whether the particular cummingtonite-grunerite mined by Reserve contains asbestiform fibers consistent with the properties of amosite asbestos.

   The trial court heard extensive evidence as to the chemistry, crystallography and morphology of the cummingtonite-grunerite present in the mined ore. This evidence demonstrated that, at the level of the individual fiber, a portion of Reserve's cummingtonite-grunerite cannot be meaningfully distinguished from amosite asbestos. Reserve attempted to rebut this testimony by showing that the gross morphology of the two minerals differed and that characteristics of the two minerals varied when considered in crystal aggregations. Since, according to the opinions of some experts, the individual fiber probably serves as a carcinogenic agent, the district court viewed the variations in mineralogy as irrelevant and determined that Reserve discharges fibers substantially identical and in some instances identical to fibers of amosite asbestos.

   The second question, that of fiber length, reflects a current dispute among scientists as to whether "short" fibers (i.e., fibers less than five microns in length) have any pathogenic effect. Most of the fibers detected in Reserve's discharges may be termed "short."[28] The evidence adduced at trial included conflicting scientific studies and diverse opinions on this question. Several Reserve witnesses testified concerning animal studies which seem to demonstrate that short fibers are

---

[28] Plaintiffs' witness Dr. William Nicholson, Associate Professor of Community Medicine at the Mt. Sinai School of Medicine, testified that 95 percent of the fibers identified, both in the air and in the water, were less than five microns in length. [A.8:257.]

nontumorigenic.[29] Plaintiffs offered opposing evidence based on contrary studies.[30] Dr. Brown noted his general criticism of the studies on fiber size, stating that the researchers typically did not use electron microscopy to properly "size" the fibers, and thus it cannot be said that the animals are in fact being exposed to only short or only long fibers. [A.23:338-40.]

Presented with this conflicting and uncertain evidence from animal experimentation, and the fact that there are no human epidemiological studies bearing on the issue, the district court concluded that short fibers could not be assigned a lower relative risk than long fibers.[31] This conclusion comports with the uncertain state of scientific knowledge. Furthermore, Dr. Brown and the National Academy of Sciences reached the same conclusion.[32]

2 The Level of Exposure The second major step in the inquiry of the health aspects of Reserve's air emissions is an assessment of the amount of the discharge and the resulting level of exposure. Two principal issues are raised: first, what in fact is the level of exposure; second, does that level present a cognizable risk to health? The district court found the level "significant" and comparable to the levels associated with disease in nonoccupational contexts. 380 F. Supp. at 48.

The first issue was addressed at length in our stay opinion. We noted there the great difficulties in attempted fiber counts and the uncertainties in measurement which necessarily resulted. 498 F.2d at 1079-1080. Commenting on these difficulties, Dr. Brown stated that the fiber counts of the air and water samples could establish only the presence of fibers and not any particular amount, i.e.,

---

[29] Dr. John M. G. Davis, head of the pathology branch of the Institute of Occupational Medicine in Edinburgh, Scotland, described several experiments in which tumor production among laboratory animals was reduced when researchers shortened the fibers to which the animals were exposed. [A.16:141-142.] Dr. George Wright, a former professor at the University of Rochester Medical School, concluded that there was a "cut off" value for fiber length below which mesothelioma could not be induced in experimental animals by intrapleural injection. [A.16:342-343.] Plaintiffs objected to these studies on the ground that generally a "milling process" is used to obtain the needed short fibers, and that through this process the original character of the fibers may be lost. Reserve witness Dr. Davis agreed that the effects of this milling are as yet unresolved. [A.16:207.]

[30] For example, Dr. Selikoff testified to a study in which one group of rats was exposed to chrysotile fibers where only one percent of the fibers were longer than three microns, and a second group was exposed to fibers where five percent of the fibers were longer than five microns. In both groups, 40 percent of the animals eventually developed mesothelioma, although tumors took longer to develop in the group exposed to the shorter fibers. [A.11:19-21.] Reserve generally objected to plaintiffs' studies on the ground that the experimental methodology involved did not sufficiently isolate small fibers. [A.15:98-100.]

[31] The standard set by the Secretary of Labor for permissible occupational exposure to asbestos is drawn in terms of fibers in excess of five microns in length. A dispute surfaced at the trial whether this standard should be read as endorsing the safety of fibers less than five microns. The district court ruled in the negative. Two participants in the formulation of the standard, Dr. Selikoff and Dr. Wagoner, testified that the five micron limit reflected primarily a technological consideration since local laboratories do not possess the equipment to count fibers of a lesser length. [A.10:324-26, 104-105, 171.]

[32] Dr. Brown testified that in his view, "fibers less than five microns are just as dangerous as those over five microns * * *." [A.23:153.] A report by the National Academy of Sciences concluded: "There is, however, no body of knowledge that permits the assigning of relative risk factors to fibers in the electron microscope range compared with fibers in the light microscope range." [A.11:10.]

such a count establishes only a qualitative, and not a quantitative, proposition. The district court recognized these difficulties in counting fibers and observed that "[t]he most that can be gained from the Court [ordered] air study is the very roughest approximation of fiber levels." 380 F. Supp. at 49.

A court-appointed witness, Dr. William F. Taylor,[33] made the most sophisticated attempt to use the fiber counts in a quantitative manner. By taking the average fiber count of five testing sites in Silver Bay, Dr. Taylor concluded that the burden of fibers in the air of Silver Bay exceeded that present in St. Paul, Minnesota (used as a control), by a margin which could not be attributed to chance.[34] [A.23:117.]

The experts indicated that the counting of fibers represents a scientifically perilous undertaking, and that any particular count can only suggest the actual fiber concentration which may be present. Nevertheless, Dr. Taylor's computation indicating some excess of asbestiform fibers in the air of Silver Bay over that of the control city of St. Paul appears statistically significant and cannot be disregarded. Thus, as we indicated in the stay opinion and as the district court concluded,[35] while the actual level of fibers in the air of Silver Bay is essentially unknown, it may be said that fibers are present at levels significantly higher than levels found in another Minnesota community removed from this air contamination.

Given the presence of excess fibers, we must now assess the effects of this exposure on the public. We note first, as we did in the stay opinion, that the exposure here cannot be equated with the factory exposures which have been clearly linked to excess cancers and asbestosis.[36] Our inquiry, however, does not end there. Asbestos-related disease, as noted earlier, has been associated with exposure levels considerably less than normal occupational exposure. The studies indicating that mesothelioma is associated with the lower levels of exposure typi-

---

[33] Dr. Taylor is head of the Medical Research Statistics Section at the Mayo Clinic. He has been a consulting statistician in medical and biological research and a Professor of Biostatistics.

[34] The fiber concentration found was 0.0626 fibers per cc, with a 95 percent confidence interval of from 0.0350 to 0.900 fibers per cc. (Although we indicated in the stay opinion that this count, like the other fiber counts, is subject to a nine-fold margin of error, 498 F.2d at 1078 n. 7. Dr. Taylor's testimony indicates that this particular calculation, embodying as it does the average of several readings, is subject to the lesser margin of error indicated above). It is significant that this concentration, even at its upper range, is far below the legally permissible level for occupational settings, and, thus, obviously below those levels typically associated with occupational exposure to asbestos.

Dr. Taylor warned that his Silver Bay computation, based on only several days of sampling during a particular time of the year, could not be extrapolated to represent the average annual burden of fibers in the air of Silver Bay. [A.23:132–41.]

[35] The district court stated:

* * * It is sufficient if one knows the number ranges between 1,620 fibers per cubic meter and 140,000,000, and that any particular count may be off by a factor of ten. One fact, however, cannot be denied. There is a significant burden of amphibole fibers from Reserve's discharge in the air of Silver Bay. [380 F. Supp. at 49–50.]

[36] In commenting on the possibility of extrapolating the disease experience of occupational workers to the situation presented by Reserve's operations, Dr. Selikoff commented:

Now, does this mean this is going to happen to people who drink or inhale dust from Reserve? Not at all. It doesn't mean this, because this is a *different kind* of exposure. But it does get important, it does show what can happen with amosite in these circumstances. [A.10:279 (emphasis added).]

cal of residence near an asbestos mine or mill or in the household of an asbestos worker are of significance.[37] Although these studies do not possess the methodological strengths of the occupational studies, they must be considered in the medical evaluation of Reserve's discharge into the air.

Of course, it is still not possible to directly equate the exposure in Silver Bay with the exposure patterns in these nonoccupational studies. The studies typically do not attempt to quantify the level of exposure and, as noted above, it is not possible to assess with any precision the exposure level in Silver Bay; thus, exposure levels may be compared only on the most general basis. Furthermore, it is questionable whether Reserve's operations may be equated with those of an asbestos mine or mill; for, while we concur in the trial court's finding that Reserve discharges fibers similar, and in some cases, identical to amosite asbestos, it is true, as testified by plaintiffs' own witnesses, that only a portion of Reserve's discharge may be so characterized.[38] Additionally, it is also true that at least some of the fiber counts reported to the court reflect *all* amphibole fibers present, thereby including fibers inconsistent with amosite asbestos.[39] Even if all the amphibole fibers inconsistent with amosite could still be attributed to Reserve's discharge, it remains uncertain whether the disease effects attributable to amosite may be ex-

[37] See note 26 supra.

[38] For example, Dr. Arthur Langer, Associate Professor of Mineralogy at the Mt. Sinai School of Medicine, testified that 15 of 30 amphibole particles present in an air sample taken at Reserve's facilities in Silver Bay were cummingtonite-grunerite. Of these 15, 14 were consistent with amosite asbestos, and of these 14 "a good number" were identical with amosite. [A. 9:312.]

[39] Plaintiffs' witness Dr. Nicholson reported some sample counts to the court which measured the level of all amphibole fibers present. [A.8:31-32, 121-24, 182-90.] The district court evidenced some concern on this point:

> The Court: I am having a little trouble in figuring out why you are counting amphiboles. It could be actinolite, tremolite, anthophyllite or cummingtonite-grunerite, or some other amphibole that I maybe never heard of. Has he [Dr. Nicholson] conducted further tests to prove that they are cummingtonite-grunerite?
>
> Mr. Hills [attorney for the United States]:
> *   *   *   *   *   *   *   *   *   *   *   *   *   *   *
> With the electron diffraction pattern you determine the crystalline structure which determines amphibole. With the SEM [scanning electron microscope] you can go further and get the exact chemical composition.
>
> The Court: That is right. Have we done that in this instance?
>
> Mr. Hills: I don't believe so in this instance.
>
> The Witness [Dr. Nicholson]: No. These fibers were not subjected to the analysis of the scanning electron microscope.
> *   *   *   *   *   *   *   *   *   *   *   *   *   *   *
> The Court: * * *
> My inquiry was directed to the question—up until this point the emphasis of the Government's case has been on the studies on amosite and the similarity of amosite to grunerite. This is the first time, as I recall, that you have said that other amphiboles are carcinogenic. And you may be able to establish that. But I was wondering what was the significance of putting in other amphiboles without designating them as cummingtonite grunerite? [A.8:124-26.]

tended to these other fibers, or whether the varying forms of asbestos possess differing pathogenic properties.[40]

3 Conclusion Plaintiffs' hypothesis that Reserve's air emissions represent a significant threat to the public health touches numerous scientific disciplines, and an overall evaluation demands broad scientific understanding. We think it significant that Dr. Brown, an impartial witness whose court-appointed task was to address the health issue in its entirety, joined with plaintiffs' witnesses in viewing as reasonable the hypothesis that Reserve's discharges present a threat to public health. Although, as we noted in our stay opinion, Dr. Brown found the evidence insufficient to make a scientific probability statement as to whether adverse health consequences would in fact ensue, he expressed a public health concern over the continued long-term emission of fibers into the air. We quote his testimony at some length.

> [Dr. Brown]. Based on the scientific evidence, I would be unable to predict that the number of fibers in the air of Silver Bay, as seen on four days in October, that I would be unable to predict that cancer would be found in Silver Bay.
>
> Now, going beyond that, it seems to me that speaking now in general terms, where it has been shown that a known human carcinogen, sir, and I make that distinction and I shall make it again, I suspect, a human carcinogen is in the air of any community, and if it could be lowered I would say, as a physician that, yes, it should be lowered. And if it could be taken out of the air completely, I would be even more happy.
>
> But the presence of a known, human carcinogen, sir, is in my view cause for concern, and if there are means of removing that human carcinogen from the environment, that should then be done. [A.23:207-08.]

He explained further:

> As a physician, I take the view that I cannot consider, with equanimity, the fact that a known human carcinogen is in the environment. If I knew more about that human carcinogen, if I knew what a safe level was in the air, if I knew what a safe level was in the water, then I could draw some firm conclusions and advise you in precise terms.

[40] There is some evidence that the various forms of asbestos differ in pathogenicity. Reserve witness Dr. William Smith, Director of the Health, Research Institute at Fairleigh-Dickinson University, testified that tremolite, although implicated as a carcinogen in studies of talc miners, did not induce tumors in experimental animals. [A.15:247.] Reserve witness Dr. Wright testified that the British view crocidolite asbestos as a particularly hazardous agent and the British standard for crocidolite exposure is one-tenth of that established for chrysotile or amosite. [A.16:322.] Dr. Selikoff noted that there are many amphibole minerals, but that few have been studied for their effects upon health. He expressed doubt about the carcinogenicity of tremolite. [A.10:266-267.]

The report of the National Academy of Sciences concludes that such differences are not clearly understood and that no type of asbestos can be regarded as free from hazard. [A.15:134.] This view was endorsed by Reserve witness Dr. Gross. [Id.] We think the district court proceeded correctly in relying on the National Academy report and concluding that no type of asbestos could be deemed safe. However, we note, too, that the discharge of fibers dissimilar from amosite adds further uncertainty to equating the likely health consequences from Reserve's discharge with that found in certain other occupational situations.

That information is not available to me and I submit, sir, it's not available to anyone else. And that until that information is developed in a scientific way, using techniques that would be acceptable to the medical community, until that time has arrived, then I take only the view that I have expressed. [A.23:211.]

But with asbestos, * * * we're dealing with a different situation, we're dealing with a material which is known to cause cancer not only in animals but in humans. [A.23:212.]

Finally, in a post-trial deposition taken December 6, 1974, which the parties have stipulated may be considered by this court, Dr. Brown further testified:

Q. [Mr. Bastow, attorney for the United States]. [I]s there any question in your mind that the people living on the North Shore are being exposed to a human carcinogen in the air and water?

*   *   *   *   *   *   *   *   *   *   *   *   *   *   *

A. [Dr. Brown]. Court studies demonstrated to my satisfaction that similar [asbesti-form] fibers are present in the air of Silver Bay and since I am convinced that asbes-tiform fibers are carcinogenic for humans, my answer to your question would be yes.

He added:

I took some pains to also say that it was my medical opinion that the presence of a human carcinogen in the air and water was not to be taken lightly * * *.

Until I know what the safe level is I therefore could not, as a physician, consider with equanimity the fact that they are being exposed to a human carcinogen. [Brown dep. at 8–12.]

B The Discharge into Water

The claim that Reserve's discharge of tailings into Lake Superior causes a hazard to public health raises many of the same uncertainties present with respect to the discharge into air. Thus, the previous discussion of fiber identity and fiber size is also applicable to the water discharge. In two respects, however, the discharge into water raises added uncertainties: first, whether the ingestion of fibers, as compared with their inhalation, poses any danger whatsoever; and second, should ingestion pose a danger, whether the exposure resulting from Reserve's discharge may be said to present a legally cognizable risk to health.

1 Ingestion of Fibers as a Danger to Health All epidemiological studies which associate asbestos fibers with harm to health are based upon inhalation of these fibers by humans. Thus, although medical opinion agrees that fibers entering the respiratory tract can interact with body tissues and produce disease, it is unknown whether the same can be said of fibers entering the digestive tract. If asbestos fibers do not interact with digestive tissue, they are presumably elimi-nated as waste without harmful effect upon the body.

The evidence bearing upon possible harm from ingestion of fibers falls into three areas: first, the court-sponsored tissue study, designed to measure whether asbestos fibers are present in the tissues of long-time Duluth residents; second, animal experiments designed to measure whether, as a biological phenomenon, fibers can penetrate the gastrointestinal mucosa and thus interact with body tissues; third, the increased incidence of gastrointestinal cancer among workers occupationally exposed to asbestos, and the hypothesis that this increase may be due to the ingestion of fibers initially inhaled.

(a)   The tissue study.   Recognizing the complete lack of any direct evidence (epidemiological or otherwise) on the issue of whether the ingestion of fibers poses a risk, the trial court directed that a tissue study be conducted to determine whether the tissues of long-time Duluth residents contain any residue of asbestos-like fibers.

The study sought to analyze by electron microscope the tissues of recently deceased Duluth residents who had ingested Duluth water for at least 15 years; that is, approximately since the beginning of Reserve's operations. As a "control" check on results, tissue samples were obtained from the deceased residents of Houston, Texas, where the water is free of asbestos fibers. Although this study was necessarily expedited, plaintiffs' principal medical witness, Dr. Selikoff, testified to the sound design of the study and expressed his belief that it would yield significant information.

One of the court-appointed experts, Dr. Frederick Pooley,[41] in explaining the results of the study, stated that he found that the tissues of the Duluth residents were virtually free of any fibers which could be attributed to the Reserve discharge. Dr. Brown said of this study:

> It is my conclusion, from the tissue study that residents of Duluth have not been found to have asbestiform fibers in their tissues when compared with Houston. [A.23:208.]

As we noted in the stay opinion, the parties dispute the significance to be attributed to the results of this study. Dr. Selikoff, prior to the conclusion of the study, expressed this view:

> Now, our feeling was that no matter what air samples show or water samples show or anything else, unless it is found that asbestos is in the tissues of people who have drunk this water * * * if we do not find it in the tissues in appreciable quantities, then I would risk a professional opinion that there is no danger, at least up to this point, to the population no matter what our samples show or water samples. [A.11:95.]

---

[41] Dr. Frederick D. Pooley is a world renowned scientist from Cardiff, Wales, Great Britain, and an expert in the field of identifying physical and chemical properties of asbestos and asbestos-like fibers. Dr. Selikoff, plaintiffs' expert, described Dr. Pooley as the "one man who has competence and knowledge in this matter," i.e., the scientific examination of tissue for the presence of asbestos or asbestos-like fibers.

After negative results had been actually obtained, however, plaintiffs argued, and the district court agreed, that because the specimens of tissue represented only a microscopically minute body area, the actual presence of fibers may have been overlooked.[42]

We note that this limitation had not seemed dispositive prior to the study when Dr. Selikoff commented:

> I would think we should find some fibers there. We're looking for needles in a haystack, but that's all right, we should find needles in the haystack with all the difficulties of the study, the technical difficulties, if we examine sufficiently large numbers of samples in some instances we should find some fibers there. [A.11:77.]

The district court decided, and we agree, that the study cannot be deemed conclusive in exonerating the ingestion of fibers in Lake Superior water as a hazard. The negative results must, however, be given some weight in assessing the probabilities of harm from Reserve's discharge into water. The results also weigh heavily in indicating that no emergency or imminent hazard to health exists.[43] Thus, while this study crucially bears on the determination of whether it is necessary to close Reserve down immediately, the negative results do not dispose of the broader issue of whether the ingestion of fibers poses some danger to public health justifying abatement on less immediate terms.

(b)   Animal studies and penetration of the gastrointestinal mucosa.   At a somewhat more theoretical level, the determination of whether ingested fibers can penetrate the gastrointestinal mucosa bears on the issue of harm through ingestion. If penetration is biologically impossible, then presumably the interaction of the fibers with body tissues will not occur.

This medical issue has been investigated through experiments with animals which, unfortunately, have produced conflicting results. For example, Reserve witness Dr. Davis reported on his experiment in feeding crocidolite and chrysotile asbestos to rats for varying periods of up to six months. He killed the rats at the end of the period and examined their gastrointestinal tissues for evidence of fibers. At the time of trial, light and electron microscopy had so far revealed no evidence of fibers in the tissues. [A.16:143-59.]

Plaintiffs, however, cited contrary studies. Research by George Westlake, in which rats were fed a diet including chrysotile fibers, indicated that fibers had traveled through the colon wall and accumulated in the area of the mesothelium.[44]

---

[42] Dr. Brown did not discount the study because of the limited number of sections that had been obtained:

> * * * I have to go on the data as presented. I think it was a reasonable case. I would have preferred many more sections. I recognize the fact that no such fibers were found to my satisfaction doesn't foreclose the possibility that such fibers exist. I recognize that as a possibility. But for the present I have to assume that fibers aren't there until I see them. [A.23:311-312.]

[43] As Dr. Brown testified:

> It [the tissue study] does tell me that it is not an emergency situation, and that's about as far as I can go. [A.23:209.]

[44] George E. Westlake, Holland J. Spjut, and Marilyn N. Smith, "Penetration of Colonic Mucosa by Asbestos Particles in Rats, Fed Asbestos Dust," 14 *Laboratory Investigation* 2029.

[A.11:23-25.] Pontrefact, who injected chrysotile fibers into the stomachs of rats, found that fibers had dispersed throughout the body tissues.[45] [A.11:37-41.]

On this conflicting scientific evidence, Dr. Brown testified that the Westlake and Pontrefact studies provide some support for the hypothesis that asbestos fibers can penetrate the gastrointestinal mucosa.[46]

(c)   Excess gastrointestinal cancer among the occupationally exposed.   The affirmative evidence supporting the proposition that the ingestion of fibers poses a danger to health focuses on the increased rate of gastrointestinal cancer among workers occupationally exposed to asbestos dust. Plaintiffs' experts attribute this excess incidence of gastrointestinal cancer to a theory that the asbestos workers first inhaled the asbestos dust and thereafter coughed up and swallowed the asbestos particles.

The attribution of health harm from ingestion rests upon a theoretical basis. As Dr. Selikoff explained, there are several possible explanations for the increased evidence of gastrointestinal cancer, some of which do not involve ingestion. [A.11:41-43.] Moreover, as noted previously, the excess rates of gastrointestinal cancer are generally "modest" [A.10:220, 223, 226, 279.], and substantially lower than the excess rates of mesothelioma and lung cancer associated with inhalation of asbestos dust. Also, the experts advised that an analysis of a small exposed population may produce statistically "unstable" results. [A.10:278-80.]

The existence of an excess rate of gastrointestinal cancer among asbestos workers is a matter of concern. The theory that excess cancers may be attributed to the ingestion of asbestos fibers rests on a tenable medical hypothesis. Indeed, Dr. Selikoff testified that ingestion is the "probable" route accounting for the excess in gastrointestinal cancer. [A.11:44.][47] The occupational studies support the proposition that the ingestion of asbestos fibers can result in harm to health.

2   Level of Exposure via Ingestion   The second primary uncertainty with respect to ingestion involves the attempt to assess whether the level of exposure from drinking water is hazardous. Of course, this inquiry is handicapped by the

---

[45] Pontrefact and Cunningham, "Penetration of Asbestos Through the Digestive Tract of Rats," 243 *Nature* 352 (1973).

[46] We note from the record that while attempts to induce tumors in experimental animals through the inhalation of fibers have succeeded, attempts to induce tumors by ingestion have generally failed. [A.15:218-21; A.17:1-21.] Reserve witness Dr. Smith ventured the opinion, based on such studies, that there is no *proof* that the ingestion of fibers causes cancer in man. [A.15:257.] The failure to induce animal tumors by ingestion cannot be dispositive on the issue of whether the ingestion of fibers poses a risk to humans. This is because, as a general matter, animal cancer susceptibility is not directly equivalent to human experience, and, more particularly, because the studies so far undertaken may be criticized for various shortcomings in experimental design. Thus, one of Reserve's own witnesses, Dr. Wright, testified that at least one of the studies may be criticized for using too few animals over too brief an experimental time. [A.17:4.]

[47] When asked his opinion as to whether the ingestion of asbestos can cause cancer, Dr. Brown responded:

> * * * I believe the evidence is probably good enough for me to draw the conclusion that it is likely that one could expect an increased incidence of cancer of the gastrointestinal tract in occupationally exposed people. [A.23:156.]

great variation in fiber counts, and Dr. Brown's admonition that only a qualitative, and not a quantitative, statement can be made about the presence of fibers.[48]

In spite of these difficulties, the district court found that the level of exposure resulting from the drinking of Duluth water was "comparable" to that found to cause gastrointestinal cancer in asbestos workers. 380 F. Supp. at 48. The court drew this finding from an elaborate calculation by Dr. Nicholson in which he attempted to make a statistical comparison between the fibers probably ingested by an asbestos worker subject to an excess risk of gastrointestinal cancer with the probable number of amphibole fibers ingested by a Duluth resident over a period of 18 years. [A.22:228-229.] To make this calculation, Dr. Nicholson computed what he believed to be the level of exposure in a typical occupational environment and multiplied this figure by the total amount of air inhaled by the worker over a four-year period (taken to be the relevant period in which a risk of excess gastrointestinal cancer was posed), thereby obtaining total fibers inhaled. A percentage reduction was then applied to obtain the number of fibers brought up the respiratory tract and swallowed. For Duluth residents, Dr. Nicholson calculated the number of fibers ingested over an 18-year period, assuming a daily intake of two liters of water and a fiber concentration of 25 million fibers/liter. From these assumptions, Dr. Nicholson opined that a Duluth resident over a period of 18 years ingested about two-thirds of the amount of asbestos fibers swallowed by an asbestos worker in four years. As is evident, this calculation is beset by several uncertainties. The assumptions as to fiber concentration in occupational settings and the resulting percentage of fibers ingested involve margins of error. Furthermore, in assuming that the relevant fiber concentration in Duluth water was 25 million fibers/liter, Dr. Nicholson used a figure twice that found by the court as the mean concentration of *all* amphibole fibers.[49] Reserve witness Dr. Gross performed a calculation similar to Dr. Nicholson's, but using somewhat different assumptions, and concluded that Duluth water would have to contain several hundred million fibers/liter and be ingested for 60 years before an exposure comparable with occupational levels would be reached. [A.17:37-51.]

---

[48] Some evidence indicated that the fiber counts in water were approximately one million times higher than those obtained in the air. [A.23:55.] Average fiber counts computed by Dr. Taylor did show that the concentration of amphibole fibers decreased as one moved away from Reserve's Silver Bay facilities, thus supporting plaintiffs' theory of dispersion. [A.23:54-55.] The district court found that Reserve's discharge is largely responsible for the presence of these fibers in the waters along the north shore of the western arm of Lake Superior.

As with the air counts, the water counts apparently include all types of amphiboles, only some of which are consistent with amosite asbestos. Thus, for example, Reserve witness Dr. Champness testified that samples of water taken from Two Harbors, Duluth and Reserve's density current showed that the number of amphibole fibers with roughly the chemistry of amosite ranged from 13 to 34 percent. [A.19:5.] Plaintiffs' witness Dr. Langer testified that 47 percent of the fibers present in Duluth tap water were cummingtonite-grunerite and 8-9 percent of these fibers were in turn consistent with amosite. [A.9:314-315.]

[49] "The Court finds, consistent with the Court's study of amphibole fiber concentrations in the water supplies of Beaver Bay, Two Harbors and Duluth, that on the 28th of August, 1973, in the samples analyzed by seven laboratories that the mean fiber concentrations were: 12.5 million fibers per liter in the public water system at Duluth * * *." 380 F. Supp. at 48.

The comparison has other weaknesses, for without regard to the comparability of the gross exposure levels, the dynamics of the exposure process are markedly different. The vagaries attendant to the use of assumptions rather than facts result in comparisons which are of dubious accuracy. Thus, Dr. Brown testified that, *if* Nicholson's calculations were correct, he would conclude only that the risk was non-negligible. [Brown dep. at 20.]

The Nicholson comparison, although evidentially weak, must be considered with other evidence. The record does show that the ingestion of asbestos fibers poses some risk to health, but to an undetermined degree. Given these circumstances, Dr. Brown testified that the possibility of a future excess incidence of cancer attributable to the discharge cannot be ignored:[50]

---

[50] Since Lake Superior afford water supplies to an estimated 200,000 people of Duluth and other North Shore Minnesota municipalities, as well as Superior, Wisconsin, we think it is essential that the facts regarding the present disease effects of the discharge be accurately stated.

As our review below demonstrates, we conclude that there is no evidence on a scientific or medical basis showing that Duluth residents experience an excess rate of cancer attributable to Reserve's discharge.

The district court in its discussion "Present Effects of Discharge," 380 F. Supp. 53-54, implies that cancer statistics show an initial harm to Duluth residents attributable to the fiber contamination of Lake Superior. While the district court made no explicit findings in this regard, the court observed:

> A great deal of information about the cancer experience of the people of Duluth is available as a result of an ongoing study by the National Cancer Institute. It is too early to attach any real significance to the negative cancer experience of the City of Duluth due to Reserve's discharge. It should be pointed out that Duluth residents do not at this time enjoy a fortunate position with respect to the cancer experience for the entire state of Minnesota. There is at this time a statistically significant excess of rectal cancer with an increasing trend. Dr. Thomas Mason, a statistician for the National Cancer Institute, testified that for the period from 1965 to 1969, being the most recent period available for epidemiological study, Duluth had fifty-two extra deaths from cancer compared to mortality rates from the State of Minnesota. Of these, eleven deaths are attributable to the stomach, large intestine and rectum. [380 F. Supp. at 54.]

Moreover, the district court suggests that Dr. Brown did not consider recent statistical studies in reaching his conclusion that no increase in cancer attributable to Reserve's discharge could be predicted. 380 F. Supp. at 51. n. 34.

We have carefully undertaken a review of the statistical evidence bearing on the question of whether Duluth residents are presently experiencing an excess incidence of cancer. Two studies are of particular relevance. The first, conducted by Dr. Thomas Mason, a staff statistician for the National Cancer Institute, analyzed Duluth cancer rates for the years 1950-69. Duluth rates were compared to rates in Hennepin County (Minneapolis) and the State of Minnesota as a whole for five-year periods beginning in 1950 and ending in 1969. The study attempted to isolate any increase in cancer occurring in both men and women and appearing in the 1960's (preferably the late sixties). The focus on increases during the sixties reflected the assumption that any cancer attributable to Reserve's discharge might demonstrate the "lag" phenomenon evident in occupational exposure to asbestos dust. Only cancer of the rectum showed an increase among both men and women during the period 1965-1969. Although this increase was significant, Dr. Mason concluded that the excess was attributable to chance (or, at the least, not attributable to Reserve's discharge). [Tr. 17,116.] This conclusion was premised on the absence of a theoretical link between the ingestion of asbestos and an isolated increase in rectal cancer; indeed, the occupational studies show that the excess cancers attributable to ingestion occur principally in the upper gastrointestinal tract, with only a slight increase in cancer of the rectum. [Tr. 17,116.] The Duluth statistics reveal no significant excess gastrointestinal cancer apart from the rectal increase.

A second study, conducted by Dr. Barry S. Levy, an epidemiologist assigned to the Minnesota Department of Health by the U. S. Department of Health, Education, and Welfare, covered the years

* * * I would say that it is conceivable that gastrointestinal cancers can develop from the ingestion of asbestos, and what I don't know, Your Honor, is just how low that level of ingestion must be before the likelihood of GI cancer becomes so remote as to be, for all intents and purposes, ignored as a real live possibility. [A.23:157.]

We quote at length Dr. Brown's testimony expressing the medical concern appropriate to the continued discharge of asbestos fibers into Lake Superior:

[Dr. Brown]. After some degree of exposure to the literature and to the testimony given in this trial I would say that the scientific evidence that I have seen is not complete in terms of allowing me to draw a conclusion one way or another concerning the problem of a public health hazard in the water in Lake Superior.

Q. [The court]. Would you define the difference between what you say is scientific proof and medical proof, and then maybe I will give you another kind of proof that I have to live with here and we will see where we are going?

A. Well, science requires a level of proof which is pretty high. That is, we do not accept as truth things that seem to be casually associated with an effect. We have erected certain statistical barriers which force us to come to conclusions based on probability, and Dr. Taylor used those terms. He used .05 per cent, he used things like .01 per cent, criteria which generally are accepted in the scientific community as levels which are consistent with or from which you can conclude that there is some cause and effect relationship.

Q. All right. Now, scientific proof for what purpose? Doesn't the quantum of proof vary with the purpose? Now, I haven't really asked you this before, but wouldn't scientists be satisfied for one purpose and not another, or is that when you stop and put on your medical hat then, after you get a certain quantum of proof?

A. Well, as a scientist, sir, I would say that there are many questions which have been raised in this trial which would provide me with a hypothesis which I would like to see pursued. This is in the abstract scientific sense of an interesting intellectual question for which there is suggestive evidence.

Now, when I turn, however, to the medical side of things, Your Honor, I am faced with the fact that I am convinced that asbestos fibers can cause cancer, I am faced with the fact that I have concluded that the size of the fibers is not particularly helpful in allowing me to decide whether a given fiber is or is not a carcinogenic.

As a medical person, sir, I think that I have to err, if err I do, on the side of what is best for the greatest number. And having concluded or having come to the conclu-

---

1969–1972. Simply stated, it found no excess gastrointestinal cancer among Duluth residents. Dr. Brown stated during the course of the trial:

Scientifically and medically I see no evidence for an increased incidence of cancer in those communities [Duluth, Silver Bay, and the other North Shore communities] that could be attributed to the presence of asbestos fibers in air or water. [A. 23:22 (emphasis added, spelling corrected).]

During his post-trial deposition, Dr. Brown restated his earlier conclusion, making particular reference to the Levy study: "This paper [the Levy study] completely supports that [earlier] view." [Brown dep. at 30.]

sions that I have given you, the carcinogenicity of asbestos, I can come to no conclusion, sir, other than that the fibers should not be present in the drinking water of the people of the North Shore. [A. 23:202-203.]

C   Conclusion

The preceding extensive discussion of the evidence demonstrates that the medical and scientific conclusions here in dispute clearly lie "on the frontiers of scientific knowledge." Industrial Union Department, *AFL-CIO v. Hodgson*, 162 U.S. App. D.C. 331, 499 F.2d 467, 474 (1974). The trial court, not having any proof of actual harm, was faced with a consideration of (1) the probabilities of any health harm and (2) the consequences, if any, should the harm actually occur. See *Carolina Environmental Study Group v. United States*, 510 F.2d 796 at 799 (D.C. Cir., Jan. 21, 1975).

The District of Columbia Circuit was recently confronted with a problem analogous to the one now before us in *Ethyl Corporation v. Environmental Protection Agency*, Civil No. 73-2205 (D.C. Cir., Jan. 28, 1975). The court, faced with a regulation of the Environmental Protection Agency[51] requiring the phased reduction of the lead content in motor vehicle gasoline promulgated pursuant to a statute authorizing a restriction only if the emission product of a fuel or fuel additive "will endanger the public health or welfare," rejected the EPA regulation stating that "the case against auto lead emissions is a speculative and inconclusive one at best." Id. at 6-8. The majority reasoned that in the absence of past harm, no potential consequences can be considered.

> If there can be found potential harm from lead in exhaust emissions, the best (and only convincing) proof of such potential harm is what has occurred in the past, from which the Administrator can logically deduce that the same factors will produce the same harm in the future. [Id. at 14.]

Judge J. Skelly Wright, in dissent, approached the problem of potential harm as encompassed within the statutory term of "will endanger" differently. He discussed this concept of danger to the public health in terms of separate but reciprocal evaluations of both risk and harm:

> While "risk" and "harm" are separate concepts that cannot be compared and ranked * * * there is a reciprocal relationship between them, and they may nòt really be assessed in isolation * * *. The "significance" of the risk * * * can only be ascertained through knowledge of the threatened harm, and it is the total "risk of harm" that must be sufficient to endanger the public health. This relationship does not, however, invalidate the separate analysis * * *, for the parameters of each term must be identified before their interaction can be studied. [Id. at 14 n. 14 of dissenting opinion.]

---

[51] Section 211(c)(1)(A) of the Clean Air Act, 42 U.S.C. § 1857f-6c(c)(1)(A) (1970), authorizes the Administrator of the Environmental Protection Agency to regulate a fuel or fuel additive "if any emission products of such fuel or fuel additive will endanger the public health or welfare * * *."

Judge Wright, believing the EPA regulations valid, concluded that the low probability of harm (greater than a remote possibility) shown by the EPA coupled with the potentially dire consequences which could result from lead emissions justified the EPA regulations. See id. at 10–11 of dissenting opinion.

These concepts of potential harm, whether they be assessed as "probabilities and consequences" or "risk and harm," necessarily must apply in a determination of whether any relief should be given in cases of this kind in which proof with certainty is impossible. The district court, although not following a precise probabilities-consequences analysis, did consider the medical and scientific evidence bearing on both the probability of harm and the consequences should the hypothesis advanced by the plaintiffs prove to be valid.

In assessing probabilities in this case, it cannot be said that the probability of harm is more likely than not. Moreover, the level of probability does not readily convert into a prediction of consequences. On this record it cannot be forecast that the rates of cancer will increase from drinking Lake Superior water or breathing Silver Bay air. The best that can be said is that the existence of this asbestos contaminant in air and water gives rise to a reasonable medical concern for the public health. The public's exposure to asbestos fibers in air and water creates some health risk. Such a contaminant should be removed.

As we demonstrate in the following sections of the opinion, the existence of this risk to the public justifies an injunction decree requiring abatement of the health hazard on reasonable terms as a precautionary and preventive measure to protect the public health.

III DISCHARGE INTO THE AIR

The district court enjoined Reserve's discharge of asbestos fibers into the air of Silver Bay, Minnesota, as a federal common law nuisance, as a public nuisance under state law, as a violation of certain Minnesota air pollution control regulations, APC 1, 5, 6, and 17, 380 F. Supp. 55–56, and as a violation of APC 3(a)(2) and its underlying statute, Minn. Stat. Ann. § 116.081(1) (Supp. 1974), which require a permit for the operation of emission facilities, *United States v. Reserve Mining Co.*, 394 F. Supp. 233 at 242–244 (D. Minn., Oct. 18, 1974).[52]

A Federal Common Law Nuisance

We reject the federal common law of nuisance as a basis for relief. As formulated in *Illinois v. City of Milwaukee*, 406 U.S. 91, 92 S. Ct. 1385, 31 L. Ed. 2d 712 (1972), and *Texas v. Pankey*, 441 F.2d 236 (10th Cir. 1971), federal nuisance law contemplates, at a minimum, interstate pollution of air or water. The United States, while invoking this doctrine, alleges only that Reserve's discharge "significantly endangers the health of all those persons living in the vicinity of the

[52] This order has not been published and will hereafter be referred to as the Order of October 18, 1974.

defendant's taconite ore processing operations." The States of Michigan and Wisconsin do not complain of air pollution and Minnesota alleges that the discharge causes common law public nuisance but does not allege interstate effects. The pleadings indicate that Minnesota's claim rests on Reserve's violation of Minnesota laws by creating an alleged danger to the health of its citizens. We construe Minnesota's complaint as asserting a state nuisance law violation.[53]

Additionally, in our review of the record, we find no evidence of any interstate health hazard, and no testimony from medical witnesses indicating any substantial concern over the health of any citizens exposed to Reserve's air discharge other than those residing in the Silver Bay, Minnesota, area. Although the district court opinion refers to a measurement of cummingtonite-grunerite fibers in snow samples from northern Wisconsin, 380 F. Supp. at 50, and the district court found evidence of these fibers in the air "as far away as Wisconsin * * *,"[54] 380 F. Supp. at 50, the trial court limited to the Silver Bay area any showing of a significant burden of excess fibers. 380 F. Supp. at 48.

---

[53] The complaints of the Environmental Defense Fund and the other private intervening plaintiffs allege that Reserve's discharge into the air creates a public nuisance subject to abatement under federal common law. [A.2:140.] We also reject the nuisance claim raised by these plaintiffs. See note 54 infra.

[54] Only sparse evidence supports this finding. The court's study of air samples encompassed only the level of fibers in Silver Bay as compared with the level of fibers in the control city of St. Paul. Although, as noted previously, testimony established that the average level of all five sites in Silver Bay was significantly greater than the level of fibers in St. Paul, the level at two of the Silver Bay sites, considered individually, was not significantly greater than that of the control city. [A.23:98.] Thus, even as to Silver Bay itself, the immediate area of the discharge, at some sites no statistically significant burden of excess fibers was present.

Plaintiffs have not succeeded in showing any significant excess level of fibers outside of Silver Bay. Plaintiffs' witness Dr. Nicholson took several air samples in Duluth, and concluded:

* * * The sampling periods were fairly short. The density of material on the filters was limited, and in the circumstances it really did not seem profitable to expend that much additional effort to obtain more than these preliminary results. They indicate that amphibole-type fibers can— that is, taking all of them together—that amphibole-type fibers can be found in the air of Duluth, but the amount are in number and mass not what one would term excessively high in comparison with what one can find in other circumstances. [A.8:128.]

Similarly, Dr. Selikoff offered no evidence of any special air pollution problem in Duluth from asbestos fibers.

* * * I don't think we have evidence one way or the other that at this time general community air pollution by asbestos, either chrysotile or amosite, is a problem. * * *
Q. [Mr. Hills, attorney for United States.] Now, is that in Duluth you are talking about, not in Silver Bay?
A. I'm talking about throughout the United States. Let's take chrysotile, general air pollution in the United States has not been shown at this time one way or the other to be or not to be a problem.
      Similarly in Duluth, we have very few pieces of information, we have limited data, we have few counts, there are relatively few fibers and although we have not, in such limited studies, seen amosite fibers in several other U.S. cities that we've looked at, the number that we've seen in Duluth is small at this time and I would not say that we have evidence that this—that general community amosite air pollution in Duluth constitutes a problem. I want that perfectly clear because I don't think we have evidence for this in any way one way or the other. [A.11:80.]

In attempting to show that the air discharge has significant interstate aspects and is not confined to Silver Bay, the trial court made the following observation:

B Violations of Minnesota Law

We turn now to Minnesota's claims that its laws are being violated by Reserve's air discharge.[55] In ordering, on April 20, 1974, an immediate cessation of air discharges containing amosite asbestos, the district court relied upon violations by

---

> Another study was undertaken to try to quantify the fiber load in the area of Reserve's air discharge. This was a study of the snow in the area as a measure of the number of fibers falling on the ground. The measurements were taken in different areas ranging as far away as 46 miles at the National Water Quality Laboratory and 30 miles at Sand Point and Park Point, Wisconsin. Restricting this evidence to an analysis of those areas where the tracer cummingtonite was found, the study shows emissions from Silver Bay being transported in decreasing amounts as you go away from Silver Bay as far as 46 miles. This includes the two sites in Wisconsin. While there were problems with the study insofar as it applied to Michigan the Court will take it as supplementary and corroborative of the other testimony in the case and as evidence of the presence of these fibers in the air as far away as Wisconsin and Duluth. [380 F. Supp. at 50.]

This "snow study," conducted by Dr. Philip Cook, a chemist with the National Water Quality Laboratory, fails to provide an adequate basis for concluding that the air discharge has any significant interstate character. Any attempt to attribute the amphibole material present in the snow to Reserve's discharge is rendered suspect by the fact that taconite tailings are spread on the roads passing through the test areas:

*   *   *   *   *   *   *   *   *   *   *   *   *   *   *

> In each case the sampling was done as far away as possible from the road since we have a problem of tailings being spread on the highways which could confuse the measurement.
>   What we're attempting to measure is the amount of mineral matter which is settling out which would not be coming from the highways, but would be coming from the Reserve Mining Company plant. [A.22:166.]

Moreover, even assuming that the study samples were not unduly contaminated by tailings spread on the local highways, no amphibole levels even remotely comparable to those measured in Silver Bay were found in outlying areas. Thus, in the immediate Silver Bay area, the weight of amphibole per square inch of snow was measured at approximately two milligrams. [A.22:167.] At Two Harbors, some 24 miles to the southwest, the amphibole weight was .01 milligrams, or 0.5 percent of that recorded at Silver Bay. [A.22:172.] At the National Water Quality Laboratory in Duluth, 47 miles to the southwest, the amphibole weight was (somewhat inexplicably) higher than that recorded in Two Harbors, but still only 0.3 milligrams, or 1.5 percent of the Silver Bay level. [A.22:172.] No attempt was made to test the statistical significance of these levels, or to relate the measurements to fiber concentrations in the air. Three Wisconsin sites were studied, located 29 to 41 miles from Silver Bay. Cummingtonite was "detected" at two of the sites, but Dr. Cook had not calculated actual amphibole weights. [A.22:172.]

   At most, the snow study indicates that Reserve's discharge is "detectable" interstate. It offers no support for the view that a significant burden of excess fibers extends beyond Silver Bay; indeed, it supports a contrary inference because the amphibole concentration in Two Harbors, some 24 miles to the southwest, is only a fraction of one percent of that measured at Silver Bay.

   [55] In joining Minnesota as a party plaintiff pursuant to Fed. R. Civ. P. 19(a)(2), the district court assumed that it had jurisdiction over the state claims. There is no independent jurisdictional basis for Minnesota's claims against Reserve, a resident corporation. All claims, however, originate out of a common fact situation. At least with respect to water pollution claims, Minnesota should be considered a necessary party under Rule 19(a)(2). As to Minnesota's claims relating to air emissions, we believe this is an appropriate case in which to invoke pendent jurisdiction. See *Hatridge v. Aetna Cas. & Sur. Co.,* 415 F.2d 809, 816-817 (8th Cir. 1969) (Blackmun, J.); see also *United Mine Workers v. Gibbs,* 383 U.S. 715, 725, 86 S. Ct. 1130, 16 L. Ed. 2d 218 (1966); *Almenares v. Wyman,* 453 F.2d 1075, 1083 (2d Cir. 1971), cert. denied, 405 U.S. 944, 92 S. Ct. 962, 30 L. Ed. 2d 815 (1972); *Leather's Best, Inc. v. S.S. Mormaclynx,* 451 F.2d 800, 809-811 (2d Cir. 1971); *Astor-Honor, Inc. v. Grossett & Dunlap, Inc.,* 441 F.2d 627, 629-630 (2d Cir. 1971); 73 Colum. L. Rev. 153, 165-69 (1973).

Reserve of APC 5, 6, and 17—regulations published by the Minnesota Pollution Control Agency pursuant to Minn. Stat. Ann. § 116.07—and the state's public nuisance law which is formulated at Minn. Stat. Ann. § 609.74(1). 380 F. Supp. at 17. Subsequently, Minnesota amended its complaint[56] under Fed. R. Civ. P. 15(b) to allege violations of APC 1 and 3, and Minn. Stat. Ann. § 116.081(1) relating to air emission permits. Because the district court held that Reserve's discharge also violates these provisions, 380 F. Supp. at 56 and Order of October 18, 1974, at 14, we also examine whether these alleged violations provide alternative or additional grounds for injunctive relief.

1   APC 1   The district court observed that studies of suspended particulate matter in the air over Silver Bay for the months of July through October 1972 disclosed only isolated instances of violation of the primary and secondary air quality standards of APC 1.[57]

> The court noted, however, that the data introduced at trial, * * * reveals that since October 1972 there has been a marked increase in the number of days in which the secondary standard was exceeded and several days in which the primary standard was exceeded. [Order of Oct. 18, 1974, at 14-15.]

On the basis of this evidence, the court properly held that Reserve was in violation of APC 1.

2   APC 5   APC 5 limits the emission of particulate matter from industrial processes.[58] Generally, it prohibits the operation of an existing emission source

[56] To ascertain what wrongs are alleged and the relief requested requires a reading of four different complaints—the second amended joint complaint, the third amended joint complaint, the amended supplemental joint complaint, and the second amended supplemental joint complaint. Rather than filing amended complaint upon amended complaint, the state should have redrafted the entire complaint. If it had done so, we would not now need to struggle with such a disarray of pleadings and allegations.

[57] APC provides in part:

(a) The "primary" air quality standards are levels of air pollutants above which, on the basis of present knowledge, health hazards or impairment may be produced. Health hazards include not only production, aggravation or possible production of disease, but also interference with function. Health impairment includes sensory irritation and impairment of well being by such phenomena as odor. The "secondary" air quality standards are levels which are desirable to protect the public welfare from any known or anticipated adverse effects, such as injury to agricultural crops and livestock, damage to or deterioration of property, annoyance and nuisance of person, sensory impairment and obstruction, or hazards to air and ground transportation.

(b) No person shall emit any pollutant in such an amount or in such a manner as to exceed any ambient air quality standard herein beyond such person's property line, without respect to whether emission regulations stated in other air pollution control regulations of the Agency are also being violated.

[58] APC 5 provides in part:

(a) General Provisions.

(1) This regulation applies to any operation, process, or activity except the burning of fuel for indirect heating where the products of combustion do not directly contact process materials,

unless it has filtration equipment with a collection efficiency of 99 percent by weight. The district court found, and Reserve does not deny, that its present methods of filtration fail to comply with this standard.

3   APC 3 and Minn. Stat. Ann. § 116.081(1)   APC 3(a)(2)(bb) requires that a person "operating an existing installation in which is a source of air contaminants and air pollution shall apply for an operating permit."[59] Minn. Stat. Ann. § 116.081(1) makes unlawful the operation of an "emission facility"[60] without a permit from the Minnesota Pollution Control Agency. The district court properly held that Reserve is in violation of both APC 3 and Minn. Stat. Ann. § 116.081(1) by its failure to obtain a permit for its emissions into the air of Silver Bay.

4   The Stipulation Agreement   Reserve concedes that it does not have a permit as required by APC 3 and Minn. Stat. Ann. § 116.081(1), but contends in its brief that an existing stipulation [A.1:198–210.] with the Minnesota Pollution Control Agency, signed by Reserve in late 1972, "is itself a permit authorizing Reserve's air discharges." That agreement expressly provides that Reserve shall be issued "appropriate installation and operating permits" by the Agency only upon compliance "with applicable laws, regulations and standards of the Agency * * *." [A.1:210.] The agreement does not relieve Reserve of the duty of obtaining the required permits. Reserve also relies upon the stipulation agreement as a defense to Minnesota's claims that it is in violation of APC 1 and 5, standards previously discussed. While the stipulation arguably shields Reserve from criminal liability or

---

except refuse burning and process burning of salvageable material.
    *   *   *   *   *   *   *   *   *   *   *   *   *   *   *

    (5) Any existing emission source which has particulate collection equipment with a collection efficiency of 99 percent by weight or any new emission source which is installed with particulate collection equipment of 99.7 percent efficiency by weight shall be considered as meeting to provisions of this regulation.

[59] APC 3 provides in part:

(a) Installation and Operating Permits for Stationary Sources, Fuel-Burning Equipment, Refuse-Burning Equipment and Control Equipment.
    *   *   *   *   *   *   *   *   *   *   *   *   *   *   *

    (2) Operating Permit
    (aa) No person shall operate any stationary process, fuel-burning equipment, or control equipment therefore without obtaining an operating permit in accordance with the provisions of Minnesota Laws 1971, Chapter 904.
    (bb) A person operating an existing installation which is a source of air contaminants and air pollution shall apply for an operating permit. New operating permits are not required for persons operating emission sources where an operating permit has been issued before January 31, 1972, unless said operating is in violation of Agency air quality rules, regulations and standards.

[60] An emission facility is "any structure, work, equipment * * * or other means whereby an emission is caused to occur." Minn. Stat. Ann. § 116.06(5). An emission is "a release or discharge into the outdoor atmosphere of any air contaminant or combination thereof." Minn. Stat. Ann. § 116.06(4).

civil penalties for its violation of air emission regulations, it cannot shield Reserve from an abatement order based on the existence of a hazard to health from the air emission, for evidence of this hazard had not yet surfaced when Minnesota and Reserve entered into the stipulation.

5 Public Nuisance Because we affirm the district court's findings that Reserve, by its air emission, is violating APC 1, 3, and 5, and Minn. Stat. Ann. § 116.081(1), it follows that Reserve's violations may be enjoined as a public nuisance. Minnesota's pollution control law so provides:

> *Injunctions.* Any violation of the provisions, regulations, standards, orders, stipulation agreements, variances, schedules of compliance, or permits specified in chapters 115 [water pollution control; sanitary districts] and 116 [Pollution Control Agency] *shall constitute a public nuisance* and may be enjoined as provided by law in an action, in the name of the state, brought by the attorney general. [Minn. Stat. Ann. § 115.071(4) (emphasis added).]

In light of this statute, we deem it unnecessary to discuss whether Reserve's air emissions could constitute a public nuisance independently of violations of the state's air pollution control regulations.

6 APC 17 The district court found that Reserve's emission of amosite asbestos fibers into the ambient air violates the asbestos emission regulation, APC 17, of the Pollution Control Agency.[61]
    This regulation designates the use of specific control equipment for emissions within its coverage. The regulation calls for control equipment, referred to in the regulation as a fabric filter and by the parties as a baghouse filter, with a mass collection efficiency of 99.9 percent. See APC 17(e)(2)(bb)(i).[62]

---

[61] APC 17 provides in part:

(a) Definitions.
The following definitions of words and phrases are controlling for the purposes of this regulation:
    *   *   *   *   *   *   *   *   *   *   *   *   *   *   *

    (3) "Asbestos" means any of six naturally occurring, hydrated mineral silicates: Actinolite, amosite, anthophyllite, chrysotile, crocidolite, and tremolite.
    *   *   *   *   *   *   *   *   *   *   *   *   *   *   *

    (8) "Manufacturing operation" means the processing of asbestos or the production of any product containing asbestos, with the exception of any process in which an asbestos material is sprayed.
    *   *   *   *   *   *   *   *   *   *   *   *   *   *   *

    (12) For purposes of this regulation a product shall be deemed to contain asbestos if a detectable amount of asbestos is present in the product or in any material that goes into the product. A detectable amount of asbestos is defined as that amount detectable by the methods of x-ray diffraction, petrographic optical microscopy, or other method approved by the Director.
    [62] This collection efficiency should be contrasted with that required by APC 5, which restricts emission of particulate matter generally. APC 5(b)(5) calls for a collection efficiency of 99 percent by weight for an existing emission source and of 99.7 percent by weight for a new emission source.

APC 17 defines "asbestos" as "any of six naturally occurring, hydrated mineral silicates: Actinolite, amosite, anthophyllite, chrysotile, crocidolite, and tremolite." It defines "manufacturing operation" as the "processing of asbestos if a detectable amount of asbestos is present in the product or in any material that goes into the product."

Minnesota contends that the district court's finding that Reserve's emissions into the air "contain substantial quantities of amosite fibers and fibers similar to amosite," 380 F. Supp. at 89, supports the court's holding that Reserve is in violation of APC 17. Reserve takes the position that compliance with APC 17 is unnecessary for any health reason and necessitates economic waste because baghouse filters cost more to install and maintain than air filtration systems meeting other Minnesota emission control standards.

Reserve urges a restricted application of the phrase "manufacturing operation" as it appears in the regulation and argues that, because taconite is not considered asbestos in the ordinary usage of that term, Minnesota improperly interpreted APC 17 and has unreasonably applied it to Reserve's operation. Reserve further questions the reasonableness of the emission standard defined by the regulation. It argues that even if fabric filters do have a mass collection efficiency of 99.9 percent, the quantity of emissions will vary from plant to plant according to the amount of material processed and without respect to what level of emission is safe to health. We need deal only with Reserve's first objection, that it is not a "manufacturing operation" for purposes of the regulation.

Is Reserve engaged in "the processing of asbestos" or "the production of any product containing asbestos?" On the basis of the record in this case we cannot say that Reserve's taconite should be considered asbestos for the purposes of this regulation or that Reserve's product, iron ore pellets, contains asbestos within the meaning of APC 17(a)(12). The court below made no finding that the pellets contain asbestos. At the most, asbestos occurs as a contaminant in a component, cummingtonite-grunerite, of the taconite that Reserve processes to produce iron ore pellets.

The State of Minnesota adopted APC 17 following the adoption of a national asbestos emission standard, 40 C.F.R. §§ 61.20–.24 (1974), by the Environmental Protection Agency. The Federal Register published this standard on April 6, 1973, 38 Fed. Reg. 8820, and Minnesota adopted its standard on June 11, 1973. We assume that the Minnesota Pollution Control Agency adopted this regulation, in common with APC 1, 3, 4, 11, 15 and 16, pursuant to the state implementation plan requirements of the Clean Air Act of 1955, as amended, 42 U.S.C. § 1857c-5 (Supp. 1974).

In comments accompanying adaption of the national standard the administrator of the EPA identified five major sources of asbestos emissions: (1) mining and milling; (2) manufacturing; (3) fabrication; (4) demolition; and (5) spraying. 38 Fed. Reg. 8820. The administrator made explicit that the EPA regulation, insofar as it relates to mining and milling, applies only to asbestos mines and asbestos mills:

EPA considered the possibility of banning production, processing, and use of asbestos or banning all emissions of asbestos into the atmosphere, but rejected these approaches. The problem of measuring asbestos emissions would make the latter approach impossible to enforce. [Id.]

The administrator made no specific reference to other mining or milling. With respect to manufacturing, the EPA's standard applies to "selected manufacturing operations." Id.[63]

On May 3, 1974, the EPA clarified its asbestos emission standard by stating that it does not apply to asbestos occurring as a contaminant, as distinguished from asbestos as a product. This clarification expressly notes that the release of asbestos as a contaminant in the milling of taconite ore does not constitute milling or manufacturing for purposes of the federal standard. 39 Fed. Reg. 15397 (May 3, 1974). In this revision, the administrator added a definition of "commercial asbestos" to distinguish asbestos which is produced as a product from asbestos which occurs as a contaminant in other materials and to make explicit that materials that contain asbestos as a contaminant do not fall within the standard. The administrator further commented:

> Asbestos is also a contaminant in taconite ore. EPA at this time believes that asbestos releases from the milling of such ores should be covered by the hazardous air pollutant regulations and intends in the near future to propose for comment regulations which would accomplish this. Because the revisions here being promulgated are only *clarifications of the Agency's intentions* at the time the initial hazardous air pollutant regulations for asbestos were published and because they are not being proposed for comment, EPA believes that it is not appropriate to include restrictions on releases of asbestos from taconite milling operations in these revisions. [39 Fed. Reg. 15397 (May 3, 1974) (emphasis added).]

The Administrator then observed that he had not included in the original regulation a definition of "asbestos mill." He clarified the original regulation by defining the phrase and explained the definition in this way:

> The definition excludes the million of ores that contain asbestos minerals only as a contaminant as previously discussed under the definition of "commercial asbestos." As noted earlier, the Agency intends to propose regulations covering taconite milling operations. [Id.]

[63] The selected manufacturing operations include the following:

(1) The manufacture of cloth, cord, wicks, tubing, tape, twine, rope, thread, yarn, roping, lap otherwise textile materials.

(2) The manufacture of cement products.

(3) The manufacture of fireproofing and insulating materials.

(4) The manufacture of friction products.

(5) The manufacture of paper, millboard, and felt.

(6) The manufacture of floor tile.

(7) The manufacture of paints, coatings, caulks, adhesives, sealants.

(8) The manufacture of plastics and rubber materials.

(9) The manufacture of chlorine. [40 C.F.R. § 61.22(c) (1974).]

Minnesota has offered no record of any hearing or other evidence of the purpose of APC 17. We cannot accede to Minnesota's argument that APC 17 should be applied more extensively than the federal regulation after which it is closely patterned in the absence of evidence of an independent background for its adoption. Although Minnesota may adopt more stringent air pollution control standards than the Clean Air Act requires, see 42 U.S.C. § 1857d-1, this record furnishes no implication that it has done so. As bearing on this issue, Dr. John Olin, Deputy Director of the Minnesota Pollution Control Agency, testified only that "I wrote that regulation" [Tr. 18,233.] and that "[w]e would feel that the Reserve operation would fall under [it]." [Tr. 18,240.] On this record, we hold APC 17 as inapplicable to the discharge of asbestos fibers occurring as a contaminant in the processing of iron ore.

In summary, we affirm the district court's holding that Reserve is in violation of APC 1, 3, and 5, and Minn. Stat. Ann. § 116.081(1). As such, Reserve's continuing violations are subject to an abatement order. We disagree with the district court's application of APC 17 to Reserve.[64]

IV FEDERAL WATER POLLUTION CONTROL ACT

The district court found that Reserve's discharge into Lake Superior violated §§ 1160(c)(5) and (g)(1) of the Federal Water Pollution Control Act (FWPCA).[65] 380 F. Supp. at 16. These two provisions authorize an action by the United States

---

[64] The trial court also found Reserve in violation of APC 6. 380 F. Supp. at 17. That regulation provides:

(a) No person shall cause or permit the handling, use, transporting, or storage of any material in a manner which may allow avoidable amounts of particulate matter to become air-borne.

(b) No person shall cause or permit a building or its appurtenances or a road, or a driveway, or an open area to be constructed, used, repaired or demolished without applying all such reasonable measures as may be required to prevent particulate matter from becoming air-borne. The Director may require such reasonable measures as may be necessary to prevent particulate matter from becoming air-borne including, but not limited to, paving or frequent clearing of roads, driveways and parking lots; application of dust-free surfaces; application of water; and the planting and maintenance of vegetative ground cover.

Dr. John Olin, Deputy Director of the Minnesota Pollution Control Agency, testified that "APC 6 * * * deals with fugitive dust, for example, dust from roads, dust in outside activities, dust during car unloading, this type of thing." The court gave no explanation how APC 6 has been violated. The stipulation agreement between Reserve and the Pollution Control Agency, to which we have made previous reference, indicated that Reserve was in compliance with APC 6. [A.1:200.] Neither the opinion of the trial court nor Minnesota's brief contains any discussion of the grounds for finding Reserve in violation of APC 6. In the absence of any substantiation or explanation of its reasoning, we reject the court's conclusion that Reserve is in violation of APC 6.

[65] 33 U.S.C. § 1151 et seq. (1970), as amended, 33 U.S.C. § 1251 et seq. (Supp. 1974). The amendments passed in 1972, are not applicable to this litigation. See note 7 supra.

Section 1160(c)(5) reads:

(5) The discharge of matter into such interstate waters or portions thereof, which reduces the quality of such waters below the water quality standards established under this subsection * * *, is subject to abatement in accordance with the provisions of paragraph (1) or (2) of subsection (g) of this section, except that at least 180 days before any abatement action is initiated under either paragraph (1) or (2) of subsection (g) of this section as authorized by this subsection, the Administrator shall notify the violators and other interested parties of the violation of such standards.

to secure abatement of water discharges in interstate waters[66] where the discharges violate state water quality standards and "endanger * * * the health or welfare of persons." § 1160(g)(1).[67]

Minnesota has adopted water quality standards—Minnesota Water Pollution Control Regulation 15 (WPC 15)—in conformity with the FWPCA.[68] These standards read in relevant part:

> (2) No raw or treated sewage, industrial waste or other wastes shall be discharged into any interstate waters of the state so as to cause any nuisance conditions, such as the presence of significant amounts of floating solids, scum, oil slicks, excessive suspended solids, material discoloration, obnoxious odors, gas ebullition, deleterious sludge deposits, undesirable slimes or fungus growths, or other offensive or *harmful* effects. [WPC 15(c)(2) (emphasis added).]

WPC 15 incorporates selected Minnesota statutory provisions into the water quality standards, including the policy of "protection of the public health" contained in Minn. Stat. Ann. § 115.42 and a definition of "pollution" contained in Minn. Stat. Ann. § 115.01(5) as contamination which renders "impure so as to be actually or *potentially harmful or detrimental or injurious to public health*, safety or welfare * * *." (Emphasis added.)[69]

The evidence shows Reserve's water discharge to be "potentially harmful" to the public health. As such, these discharges pollute the waters of Lake Superior in violation of the Minnesota water quality standards.

---

* * * The court, giving due consideration to the practicability and to the physical and economic feasibility of complying with such standards shall have jurisdiction to enter such judgment and orders enforcing such judgment as the public interest and the equities of the case may require.

By implication, the text of (c)(5) incorporates the substance of (g)(1) into its provisions. Subsection (g)(1) reads:

> (g) If action reasonably calculated to secure abatement of the pollution within the time specified in the notice following the public hearing is not taken, the Administrator—
>
>   (1) in the case of pollution of waters which is endangering the health or welfare of persons in a State other than that in which the discharge or discharges (causing or contributing to such pollution) originate, may request the Attorney General to bring a suit on behalf of the United States to secure abatement of pollution * * *.

[66] Lake Superior, of course, is an interstate body of water.

[67] The only procedural requirement necessary for initiation of a suit under §§ 1160(c)(5) and (g)(1) is a 180-day notice to the alleged polluter. Other enforcement provisions of the FWPCA require lengthy and complex pre-suit administrative proceedings. See §§ 1160(d)(g). We note that the discharges of Reserve have been extensively considered by the Lake Superior Enforcement Conference, which was convened on May 13, 1969, by the Secretary of the Interior pursuant to § 1160(d)(1). The Conference met periodically during the next two years in an effort to procure the abatement of Reserve's discharges. The Conference did not resolve the problem, and on April 28, 1971, the Administrator of the Environmental Protection Agency notified Reserve that it was in violation of the federally approved Minnesota state water quality standards, and this suit was initiated February 2, 1972. For a general discussion of the framework of the FWPCA as it existed prior to the 1972 amendments, see Barry, The Evolution of the Enforcement Provisions of the Federal Water Pollution Control Act: A Study of the Difficulty in Developing Effective Legislation, 68 Mich. L. Rev. 1103 (1970).

[68] As is required by § 1160(c)(5), WPC 15 was approved by the Secretary of the Interior (the predecessor to the Administrator of the Environmental Protection Agency who now must approve standards) on November 26, 1969.

[69] A 1973 amendment altered this section slightly but did not change the portion quoted in the text.

An action under the FWPCA requires proof of an additional element. The United States must establish that the water pollution which is violative of state water quality standards is also "endangering the health or welfare of persons. § 1160(g)(1).

In this review, we must determine whether "endangering" within the meaning of the FWPCA encompasses the potential of harm to public health in the degree shown here.

Provisions of the FWPCA are aimed at the prevention as well as the cure of water pollution. The initial sentence of the FWPCA reads:

> The purpose of this chapter is to enhance the quality and value of our water resources and to establish a national policy for the prevention, control, and abatement of water pollution. [33 U.S.C. § 1151(a).]

The term "endangering," as used by Congress in § 1160(g)(1), connotes a lesser risk of harm than the phrase "imminent and substantial endangerment to the health of persons" as used by Congress in the 1972 amendments to the FWPCA. 33 U.S.C. § 1364 (Supp. 1974).[70]

In the context of this environmental legislation, we believe that Congress used the term "endangering" in a precautionary or preventive sense, and, therefore, evidence of potential harm as well as actual harm comes within the purview of that term. We are fortified in this view by the flexible provisions for injunctive relief which permit a court "to enter such judgment and orders enforcing such judgment as the public interest and the equities of the case may require." 33 U.S.C. § 1160(c)(5).

We deem pertinent the interpretation given to the term "endanger" by Judge Wright of the District of Columbia Circuit in his analysis of the congressional use of the word "endanger" in the context of a provision of the Clean Air Act. 42 U.S.C. § 1857f-6c(c)(1)(A) (1970).

Judge Wright observed:

> The meaning of "endanger" is, I hope, beyond dispute. Case law and dictionary definition agree that endanger means something less than actual harm. When one is endangered, harm is *threatened;* no actual injury need ever occur.
>
> *   *   *   *   *   *   *   *   *   *   *   *   *   *   *
>
> "Endanger," * * * is not a standard prone to factual proof alone. Danger is a risk, and so can only be decided by assessment of risks.
>
> *   *   .   *   *   *   *   *   *   *   *   *   *   *   *   *
>
> [A] risk may be assessed from suspected, but not completely substantiated, relationships between facts, from trends among facts, from theoretical projections from im-

---

[70] The 1972 amendments to the FWPCA grant the Administrator of the Environmental Protection Agency emergency powers to file suit for an immediate injunction where pollution is "presenting an imminent and substantial endangerment to the health of persons." 33 U.S.C. § 1364 (Supp. 1974). Compare 33 U.S.C. § 1161(d) (1970).

perfect data, or from probative preliminary data not yet certifiable as "fact." [*Ethyl Corporation v. Environmental Protection Agency,* No. 73-2205 (D.C. Cir., Jan. 28, 1975) (dissenting op. at 11, 31-33) (emphasis in original) (footnote omitted).]

Although the Supreme Court has not interpreted the concept of "endangering" in the context of an environmental lawsuit, it has emphasized the importance of giving environmental legislation a "common-sense" interpretation. Mr. Justice Douglas, writing for the Court, said:

> This case comes to us at a time in the Nation's history when there is greater concern than ever over pollution—one of the main threats to our free-flowing rivers and to our lakes as well. * * * [W]hatever may be said of the rule of strict construction, it cannot provide a substitute for common sense, precedent, and legislative history. [*United States v. Standard Oil Co.,* 384 U.S. 224, 225, 86 S. Ct. 1427, 1428, 16 L. Ed. 2d 492 (1966).]

See *United States v. Republic Steel Corp.,* 362 U.S. 482, 491, 80 S. Ct. 884, 4 L. Ed. 2d 903 (1960).

The record shows that Reserve is discharging a substance into Lake Superior waters which under an acceptable but unproved medical theory may be considered as carcinogenic. As previously discussed, this discharge gives rise to a reasonable medical concern over the public health. We sustain the district court's determination that Reserve's discharge into Lake Superior constitutes pollution of waters "endangering the health or welfare of persons" within the terms of §§ 1160(c)(5) and (g)(1) of the Federal Water Pollution Control Act and is subject to abatement.[71]

V REFUSE ACT

The United States further asserts as a basis for injunctive relief that Reserve's discharge into the water violates § 13 of the Rivers and Harbors Act of 1899. 33 U.S.C. § 407 (1970). The United States contends that Reserve's discharge is "refuse matter" within the meaning of that section,[72] and that Reserve does not

---

[71] We are not here concerned with standards applied to abatement of a nuisance under non-statutory common law doctrines. In most common law nuisance cases involving alleged harmful health effects some present harm or at least an immediate threat of harm must be established. See *New Jersey v. New York City,* 283 U.S. 473, 51 S. Ct. 519, 75 L. Ed. 1176 (1931); *Arizona Copper Co. v. Gillespie,* 230 U.S. 46, 33 S. Ct. 1004, 57 L. Ed. 1384 (1913); *Georgia v. Tennessee Copper Co.,* 206 U.S. 230, 27 S. Ct. 618, 51 L. Ed. 1038 (1907); *Missouri v. Illinois,* 200 U.S. 496, 26 S. Ct. 268, 50 L. Ed. 572 (1906); *United States v. City of Asbury Park,* 340 F. Supp. 555 (D. N.J. 1972); *City of Louisville v. National Carbide Corp.,* 81 F. Supp. 177 (W.D. Ky. 1948); *DeBlois v. Bowers,* 44 F.2d 621 (D. Mass. 1930). But see *Harris Stanley Coal & Lane Co. v. Chesapeake & O. Ry. Co.,* 154 F.2d 450 (6th Cir.), cert. denied, 329 U.S. 761, 67 S. Ct. 111, 91 L. Ed. 656 (1946); *United States v. Luce,* 141 F. 385, 408 (D. Del. 1905). Cf. *Swift & Co. v. United States,* 276 U.S. 311, 326, 48 S. Ct. 311, 72 L. Ed. 587 (1928). We comment further on common law nuisance, see p. 338 infra.

[72] Section 407 (the Refuse Act) reads in relevant part:

> § 407. Deposit of refuse in navigable waters generally.
>   It shall not be lawful to throw, discharge, or deposit, * * * any refuse matter of any kind or

possess a valid permit sanctioning this discharge. In its Order of October 18, 1974, the district court sustained the position of the United States.

Although the Refuse Act was initially thought to apply to only those discharges which could arguably affect navigation, the cases now make clear that the term "refuse matter of any kind or description" in § 407 includes

> * * * all foreign substances and pollutants apart from those "flowing from streets and sewers and passing therefrom in a liquid state" into the water course. [*United States v. Standard Oil Co.*, 384 U.S. 224, 230, 86 S. Ct. 1427, 1430, 16 L. Ed. 2d 492 (1966).]

See *United States v. Pennsylvania Industrial Chemical Corp.*, 411 U.S. 655, 670–72, 93 S. Ct. 1804, 36 L. Ed. 2d 567 (1973).

The 67,000 tons of taconite tailings Reserve discharges daily into Lake Superior constitutes "refuse matter" within the meaning of § 407. The broad phraseology of § 407, "any refuse matter of any kind or description whatever other than that flowing from streets and sewers * * *," prohibits virtually all deposits of foreign matter into navigable waters except liquids flowing from streets and sewers, absent a valid permit. *United States v. Standard Oil Co.*, 384 U.S. 224, 226, 230, 86 S. Ct. 1427, 16 L. Ed. 2d 492 (1966); *United States v. Ballard Oil Co.*, 195 F.2d 369, 371 (2d Cir. 1952). Cf. *United States v. Pennsylvania Industrial Chemical Corp.*, 411 U.S. 655, 658 & n. 3, 670–72 (1973); *United States v. Rohm & Haas Co.*, 500 F.2d 167, 170 (5th Cir. 1974), cert. denied, 420 U.S. 962, 95 S. Ct. 1352, 43 L. Ed. 439 (1975); *United States v. United States Steel Corp.*, 482 F.2d 439, 442 (7th Cir.), cert. denied, 414 U.S. 909, 94 S. Ct. 229, 38 L. Ed. 2d 147 (1973).

Reserve, however, does have a permit which, it asserts, precludes a finding of a violation of the Refuse Act. The Department of the Army granted this permit in 1948 pursuant to 33 U.S.C. § 403[73] and it authorized Reserve "to construct a steel sheet pile dock * * * and, to deposit tailings from the ore processing mill in [to] Lake Superior * * *." [Reserve Ex. 451, subex. 12.] Reserve received revalidated or modified permits periodically until 1960, when it requested and obtained an amended permit authorizing deposition of tailings "for an indefinite period."

description whatever other than that flowing from streets and sewers and passing therefrom in a liquid state, into any navigable water of the United States, * * * provided * * * that the secretary of the Army, whenever in the judgment of the Chief of Engineers anchorage and navigation will not be injured thereby, may permit the deposit of any material above mentioned in navigable waters, within limits to be defined and under conditions to be prescribed by him, provided application is made to him prior to depositing such material; and whenever any permit is so granted the conditions thereof shall be strictly complied with, and any violation thereof shall be unlawful.

Section 16 of the Rivers and Harbors Act (33 U.S.C. § 411) contains criminal sanctions, but the Supreme Court has held that language in the enforcement section (§ 17) is sufficiently broad to encompass civil suits for injunctive relief. *United States v. Republic Steel Corp.*, 362 U.S. 482, 491–492, 80 S. Ct. 884, 4 L. Ed. 2d 903 (1960); see *Wyandotte Transportation Co. v. United States*, 389 U.S. 191, 201–04, 88 S. Ct. 379, 19 L. Ed. 2d 407 (1967); see also *United States v. Rohm & Haas Co.*, 500 F.2d 167 (5th Cir. 1974), cert. denied, 420 U.S. 962, 95 S. Ct. 1352, 43 L. Ed. 2d 439 (1975); *Connecticut Action Now, Inc. v. Roberts Plating Co.*, 457 F.2d 81, 88–90 (2d Cir. 1972).

[73] Section 403 relates exclusively to impediments to navigation. The district court ruled that "Reserve's permit, although by its terms a Section 10 [§ 403] permit, also met the underlying prerequisites for a Section 13 [§ 407] permit when issued * * *." Order of Oct. 18, 1974, at 3. Thus, according to the district court, when the permit was initially issued in 1948, it was a valid permit under both sections 403 and 407.

The United States contends, and the district court found, that while this permit is valid as it relates to possible impediments to navigation, it does not now sanction the continued dumping of refuse matter into Lake Superior.

Reserve has not received a revalidation of its permit since 1960 and, as noted above, the judicial and administrative interpretation of "refuse matter" has been greatly expanded beyond its initial application solely to navigational matters. Thus, the issue remains whether Reserve's permit sanctions the deposition of refuse matter under the broadened interpretation of the law. On June 29, 1971, at the behest of the Corps of Engineers, Reserve submitted an application for a new permit under the Refuse Act Permit Program.[74] However, before the Corps acted, Congress, in October of 1972, passed the 1972 amendments to the FWPCA which replaced the Refuse Act Permit Program with the National Pollutant Discharge Elimination System (NPDES), 33 U.S.C. § 1342 (Supp. 1974), and converted pending Refuse Act permit applications into NPDES permit applications by § 1342(a)(5). The record shows no action on Reserve's application since the Corps acknowledged receipt in early 1972.

The existence of the pending application, however, does not preclude a determination that Reserve is violating the Refuse Act. Although the 1972 amendments to the FWPCA specifically provide that "in any case where a permit for discharge has been applied for" there can be no violation of the Refuse Act until December 31, 1974, 33 U.S.C. § 1342(k) (Supp. 1974), a savings provision in a footnote to the 1972 amendments preserves a Refuse Act claim such as this one initiated prior to these amendments.[75] See *United States v. Rohm & Haas Co.,* 500 F.2d 167, 170-74 (5th Cir. 1974), cert. denied, 420 U.S. 962, 95 S. Ct. 1352, 43 L. Ed. 2d 439 (1975); *United States v. Ira S. Bushey & Sons,* 363 F. Supp. 110, 119-120 (D. Vt.), aff'd mem., 487 F.2d 1393 (2d Cir. 1973), cert. denied, 417 U.S. 976, 94 S. Ct. 3182, 41 L. Ed. 2d 1146(1974); *United States v. United States Steel Corp.,* 356 F. Supp. 556 (N.D. Ill. 1973). Since Reserve's current application for a new permit cannot be interposed as a defense to a possible Refuse Act violation, Reserve must premise its defense on its current permit issued in 1960.

Clearly, the Corps considered only navigational matters in issuing this permit. The permit reads, in part, as follows:

Note—It is to be understood that this instrument does not give any property rights either in real estate or material, or any exclusive privileges; and that it does not authorize any injury to private property or invasion of private rights, or any infringement of Federal, State, or local laws or regulations, nor does it obviate the necessity of obtaining *State assent* to the work authorized. IT MERELY EXPRESSES THE AS-

---

[74] The Refuse Act Permit Program was established December 25, 1970, pursuant to Executive Order No. 11574, 3 C.F.R. 292 (1974).

[75] That savings provision reads:

No suit, action, or other proceeding lawfully commenced by or against the [EPA] Administrator or any other officer or employee of the United States in his official capacity or in relation to the discharge of his official duties under the Federal Water Pollution Control Act as in effect immediately prior to the date of enactment of this Act [Oct. 18, 1972] shall abate by reason of the taking effect [of these amendments]. [86 Stat. 816, Pub. L. 92-500, § 4.]

SENT OF THE FEDERAL GOVERNMENT SO FAR AS CONCERNS THE PUBLIC RIGHTS OF NAVIGATION. [Reserve Ex. 451, sub-ex 12 (emphasis in original).]

Further, the permit refers almost exclusively to impediments to navigation. A permit which grants government consent to a discharge into waters which does not impede navigation cannot be construed as a consent to continue this discharge upon discovery that the discharged materials may be hazardous to public health. We agree with the district court that Reserve's discharges in the future are subject to abatement under the Refuse Act as we provide in the Remedy Section of this opinion, part VII.[76]

The district court also found that Reserve's discharge into Lake Superior constituted a nuisance under the federal common law of nuisance. 380 F. Supp. at 16, 55. Because relief may appropriately rest on provisions of the FWPCA and on a violation of the Refuse Act, we deem it unnecessary and, indeed, unwise to also rely on federal nuisance law.[77] Compare *Illinois v. City of Milwaukee*, 406 U.S. 91, 107, 92 S. Ct. 1385, 31 L. Ed. 2d 712 (1972). See also 15 B.C. IND. & COMM. L. REV. 795, 811-812 (1974); 14 B.C. IND. & COMM. L. REV. 767, 780-85 (1973); Note, *Federal Common Law and Interstate Pollution*, 85 HARV. L. REV. 1439, 1451-56 (1972). Thus, we rest our resolution of the water issues solely on the FWPCA and the Refuse Act.[78]

---

[76] Reserve argues that a valid Refuse Act permit would be a defense to an alleged violation of the FWPCA. Although this contention is of doubtful validity, see 33 U.S.C. § 1174(1) (1970); *United States v. Pennsylvania Industrial Chemical Corp.*, 411 U.S. 655, 669, 93 S. Ct. 1804, 36 L. Ed. 2d 567 (1973); *Illinois v. City of Milwaukee*, 406 U.S. 91, 104, 92 S. Ct. 1385, 31 L. Ed. 2d 712 (1972); *United States v. United States Steel Corp.*, 482 F.2d 439, 449 (7th Cir.), cert. denied, 414 U.S. 909, 94 S. Ct. 229, 38 L. Ed. 2d 147 (1973), we do not reach this issue under our holding that Reserve's permit does not sanction a continuing discharge of foreign materials into the Lake which are potentially hazardous to health.

[77] We also do not reach the issue of state common law nuisance or whether Minnesota's water quality standards, standing alone, afford adequate grounds for appropriate injunctive relief in this case.

[78] The district court also found Reserve in violation of Minn. Stat. Ann. § 115.07(1), Order of Oct. 18, 1974, at 16, requiring a permit for the disposal of industrial waste into surface waters, by the dumping of waste from its mine pit into the Dunka and Partridge Rivers of Minnesota and waste from its pilot plant into Lake Superior. Minnesota, however, did not request injunctive relief for these alleged violations but only civil fines and penalties. Thus, these are not appealable interlocutory orders under 28 U.S.C. § 1292(a), and can be appealed to this court only if they can be considered as final orders under 28 U.S.C. § 1291.

Pursuant to Fed. R. Civ. P. 54(b), the district court sought to certify the above violations as final orders. Order of Oct. 18, 1974, at 19. This certification, however, is insufficient to give this court jurisdiction over these issues since the district court specifically reserved the assessment of fines and penalties for later resolution. Order of Oct. 18, 1974, at 19.

The assessment of fines and penalties cannot be divorced from liability to produce "more than one claim for relief" under Rule 54(b). See *Keystone Manganese and Iron Co. v. Martin*, 132 U.S. 91, 93-98, 10 S. Ct. 32, 33 L. Ed. 275 (1889); *Barnard v. Gibson*, 48 U.S. (7 How.) 650, 657, 12 L. Ed. 857 (1849); *The Palmyra*, 23 U.S. (10 WHEAT.) 502, 6 L. Ed. 375 (1825); *Smith v. Sherman*, 349 F.2d 547, 552-553 (8th Cir. 1965); *Taylor v. Board of Education*, 288 F.2d 600, 602 (2d Cir. 1961); 9 J. Moore, *Federal Practice* ¶ 110.11 at 137-138 (2d ed. 1974). The partial adjudication of a single claim is not appealable even though the district court has issued a Rule 54(b) certificate. See *Aetna Cas. & Sur. Co. v. Giesow*, 412 F.2d 468, 470 (2d Cir. 1969); *United States v. Burnett*, 262 F.2d 55, 58-59 (9th Cir. 1958). Compare *Sears, Roebuck & Co. v. Mackey*, 351 U.S. 427, 437, 76 S. Ct. 895, 100 L. Ed. 1297 (1956); 6

VI MISCELLANEOUS ISSUES

Before discussing the appropriateness of the remedy imposed by the district court, we resolve a number of issues subsidiary to the parties' main contentions.

A Reserve Mining Co. v. Environmental Protection Agency

In No. 73-1239, *Reserve Mining Co. v. Environmental Protection Agency,* Reserve has filed an original petition with this court based on 33 U.S.C. § 1369(b)(1) (Supp. 1974), seeking to annul the Minnesota state water quality standards—WPC 15—as arbitrary and unreasonable, and asking that we order the Administrator of the Environmental Protection Agency, pursuant to 33 U.S.C. § 1313(a) (Supp. 1974), to direct that Minnesota modify WPC 15 to bring it into conformity with the standards of the FWPCA. Reserve filed this petition on April 13, 1973, but it has not further briefed this question nor has the EPA submitted a brief. Since Reserve has not pressed this issue before us by its briefs or in oral argument, we consider the issue abandoned and we dismiss this petition.

B Separate Appeals of Environmental Plaintiffs and State of Michigan

In Nos. 75-1003 and 1005, the environmental plaintiffs of Michigan seek to perfect an appeal from a portion of the district court's Order of October 18, 1974. The part appealed from reads:

> Evidence that Reserve's discharge harms the ecology of Lake Superior is unnecessary to the entry of final judgment terminating litigation on the merits, and the Court will not allow the introduction of any such evidence by any party.[79]

If we were to reverse the district court on the health issue, then, presumably further hearings would be required on the ecological issues. However, since we affirm the existence of a health hazard and direct its abandonment, no additional trial is required on the remaining ecological questions relating to Lake Superior. We dismiss these appeals.

C Wisconsin's Claims

Wisconsin, as a plaintiff-intervenor, argues that Reserve's water discharge violates various Wisconsin statutes and causes a public nuisance subject to abatement

---

J. Moore, Federal Practice ¶ 54.34[1] at 526–527 (2d ed. 1974). See generally Frank, *Requiem for the Final Judgment Rule,* 45 TEX. L. REV. 292 (1966). Thus, there has been no final adjudication of the issues which would give this court jurisdiction under 28 U.S.C. § 1291, and Reserve may not at this time appeal from the district court's declaration of liability.

[79] This language was incorporated into the Order of October 18, 1974, *nunc pro tunc* by action of the district court on November 4, 1974.

under Wisconsin common law. Since we order abatement pursuant to other statutes, a determination of these issues is unnecessary to a resolution of this case.[80]

D Joinder of Armco and Republic Steel Corporations

Armco Steel Corporation and Republic Steel Corporation—the two parent corporations of Reserve—appeal from their joinder as defendants pursuant to Red. R.
Civ. P. 19(a)(1). The district court first joined Armco and Republic as defendants
on January 2, 1974. On January 22, 1974, this court set aside the joinder order.
Armco Steel Corp. v. United States, 490 F.2d 688 (8th Cir. 1974). In that order we
stated:

> We make it clear, however, that our direction to the district court to set aside the
> joinder order is without prejudice to the rights of the plaintiffs to subsequently move
> that Armco and Republic be joined as parties following completion of the evidence
> relating to health hazards and liability. At that time, the record may show some basis
> for joining Armco and Republic in order to provide appropriate relief. Our ruling will
> not necessarily preclude subsequent joinder of Armco and Republic if the plaintiffs
> make a proper showing of adequate need for these parties in the litigation. [Id. at 691.]

On March 29, 1974, the district court, finding that the evidence relating to
public health had been substantially completed, rejoined Armco and Republic.
The two corporations claim that they have been denied due process by this joinder
at a late stage of the trial and that in any event this joinder under Fed. R. Civ. P.
19 was invalid since they are not necessary or indispensable parties.

We examine these arguments. Armco and Republic allege that their late
entrance into the litigation prevented them from adequately protecting their interests. They contend that Reserve is an entity separate and distinct from Armco and
Republic and Reserve has not been representative of these newly-joined parties-
defendant. On this contention, the district court observed:

> It is the finding of this Court that the independent corporate identity of Reserve
> Mining Company must be and is disregarded since this Court cannot allow the inter-
> position of corporate entity to frustrate the implementation of a judgment that is
> required by justice * * *. The Court finds that this subsidiary (Reserve) is so domi-
> nated by its parents (Armco Steel Corp.) that it is a mere agency or instrumentality of
> the parents. [380 F. Supp. at 27.]

The district court concluded:

> Reserve is the personification of Armco and Republic in the State of Minnesota.
> *   *   *   *   *   *   *   *   *   *   *   *   *   *   *

[80] Wisconsin has moved to strike certain documents filed with this court by Reserve relating to
the Milepost 7 site. See p. 307 supra. We deny this motion. However, our reference to these documents
is solely for the purpose of supplementing the information presented to us at oral argument by Reserve
and Minnesota.

In addition, the privity between Republic, Armco and Reserve is sufficient to give *res judicata* effect to the decision of this Court against Armco and Republic. Therefore they are not prejudiced by joinder. [Id. at 29.]

We believe the evidence amply demonstrates that Armco and Republic, as the sole stockholders of Reserve, have interests substantially identical with those of Reserve and that the district court did not abuse its direction under Rule 19(a) in ruling "that complete relief [could] not be accorded plaintiffs" unless Armco and Republic were joined. 380 F. Supp. at 27. Moreover, Armco and Republic show no prejudice from this late joinder. We affirm on this appeal.

E   Filtered Drinking Water Supplies

The United States appeals from an order of the district court issued April 19, 1974, requiring the Army Corps of Engineers to provide filtered drinking water to localities along Lake Superior "without [permitting the Corps to obtain] any agreement from the affected cities at this time as to reimbursement." The United States claims that the district court invaded the discretionary powers granted by Congress solely to the Chief of Engineers to "provide emergency supplies of clean drinking water, on such terms as he determines to be advisable * * *."[81]

On April 5, 1974, the Chief of Engineers determined that certain cities on Lake Superior required emergency supplies of clean drinking water and he directed the North Central Engineers to provide the water.

Although the United States seeks to appeal the district court's ruling on this issue, at oral argument counsel for the United States informed the court that the Corps of Engineers was complying with the district court's order and would "continue to do so regardless of the outcome of this appeal * * *." We construe the district court's order as applying only to the existing allocation of federal funds for this purpose. Thus, in light of the Government's statement at oral argument, we dismiss the appeal as moot.[82]

F   Reserve's Defense of Res Judicata

Reserve argues that the Minnesota state district court decision of December 15, 1970 (reproduced in the Supplement to Reserve's brief at 107), and the Minnesota Supreme Court decision reviewing that case, Reserve Mining Co. v. Minnesota

---

[81] Section 82 of Pub. L. 93-251, 88 Stat. 12 (Mar. 7, 1974). The full text of § 82 reads:

The Chief of Engineers, in the exercise of his discretion, is further authorized to provide emergency supplies of clean drinking water, on such terms as he determines to be advisable, to any locality which he finds is confronted with a source of contaminated drinking water causing or likely to cause a substantial threat to the public health and welfare of the inhabitants of the locality.

[82] The United States informs us that very little use is being made of the filtered drinking water supplies provided by the Corps of Engineers:

[O]nly one of the six communities * * * is proceeding to filter its water supply, even under the terms ordered by the Court. The other communities are relying on the stop-gap of filtering tap water at public eating places and a few designated fire halls. As a result, no home taps in these communities are receiving filtered water. [Br. for U.S. at 53 n. 6.]

Pollution Control Agency, 294 Minn. 300, 200 N.W.2d 142 (1972), operate to bar Minnesota from litigating here those issues decided in the Minnesota courts.

Reserve initiated the Minnesota state litigation in an attempt to determine the validity and applicability to it of the state water quality standards, WPC 15. Minnesota counterclaimed for an injunction, asserting that Reserve's discharges were polluting the lake and constituted a public nuisance. The state district court found certain provisions of WPC 15 either not applicable to Reserve or else "unreasonable, arbitrary, and invalid as applied to * * * Reserve." The state district court came to no conclusion as to pollution but directed an alteration in the method of discharge in order to confine the distribution of tailings within the great trough area. See note 3 supra. The question of a possible health hazard in Reserve's discharges did not come before that court. The appeal to the Minnesota Supreme Court raised only narrow procedural grounds and the court did not consider the merits. 200 N.W.2d at 143. The Minnesota Supreme Court remanded the case to the Minnesota Pollution Control Agency for further proceedings. Id. at 148.

The doctrine of *res judicata* serves to bar an action where the prior proceedings have produced a final decision on the merits. *G. & C. Merriam Co. v. Saalfield*, 241 U.S. 22, 28, 36 S. Ct. 477, 60 L. Ed. 868 (1916); *McDonnell v. United States*, 455 F.2d 91, 96-97 (8th Cir. 1972); *1B J. Moore, Federal Practice* ¶ 0.409[1] at 1003-1004 (2d ed. 1974). The inconclusive and nonfinal decision in the ecological pollution case in the Minnesota courts does not warrant applying the doctrine of *res judicata* in the instant case.

G   Amendments under Fed. R. Civ. P. 15(b)

Reserve contends that the trial court abused its discretion in allowing Minnesota to amend its complaint April 22, 1974, in order to allege violations by Reserve of a number of statutes and regulations relating to air emissions.

Rule 15(a) specifically provides that permission to amend "shall be freely given [by the court] when justice so requires." See *Foman v. Davis*, 371 U.S. 178, 182, 83 S. Ct. 227, 230, 9 L. Ed. 2d 222 (1962). Where the trial court has authorized amendment, the standard of review by the court of appeals is abuse of discretion. E.g. *Zatina v. Greyhound Lines, Inc.*, 442 F.2d 238, 242 (8th Cir. 1971); *Strauss v. Douglas Aircraft Co.*, 404 F.2d 1152, 1155-58 (2d Cir. 1968). In our review of the record, we find no abuse of discretion by the district court in permitting the amendments.

H   Reserve's Counterclaims

Reserve pleaded various counterclaims seeking compensation for the possible closing of its plant. The district court dismissed all counterclaims and Reserve appeals that dismissal arguing that the counterclaims were not fully litigated. The district court did not allow Reserve to present evidence supporting these claims but dismissed them as without merit in light of its findings in the main action.

The counterclaims were not fully litigated. We cannot say at this time that Reserve cannot sustain any counterclaims on any state of the record as it may develop in the future. Reserve still operates its plant. It seeks the cooperation of the state and federal governments in obtaining a new on-land tailings disposal site. Its assertion of counterclaims is premature until the state or federal government takes improper action which forces Reserve to close. On remand, the judgment shall show the dismissals as without prejudice.

VII REMEDY

As we have demonstrated, Reserve's air and water discharge pose a danger to the public health and justify judicial action of a preventive nature.

In fashioning relief in a case such as this involving a possibility of future harm, a court should strike a proper balance between the benefits conferred and the hazards created by Reserve's facility. In its pleadings Reserve directs our attention to the benefits arising from its operations, as found by a Minnesota state district court, as follows:

> In reliance upon the State and Federal permits as contemplated by [Reserve] and the agencies issuing the permits prior to such issuance [Reserve] constructed its plant at Silver Bay, Minnesota. [Reserve] also developed the Villages of Babbitt and Silver Bay and their schools and other necessary facilities where many of [Reserve's] employees live with their families, as do the merchants, doctors, teachers and so forth who serve them. [Reserve's] capital investment exceeds $350,000,000. As of June 30, 1970 [Reserve] had 3,367 employees. During the calendar year 1969, its total payroll was approximately $31,700,000; and it expended the sum of $27,400,000 for the purchase of supplies and paid state and local taxes amounting to $4,250,000. [Reserve's] annual production of 10,000,000 tons of taconite pellets represents approximately two-thirds of the required pellets used by Armco and Republic Steel, the sole owners of Reserve, 15% of the production of the Great Lakes [ore] and about 12% of the total production of the United States. Between four and six people are supported by each job in the mining industry, including those directly involved in the industry and those employed in directly and indirectly related fields. [Reserve Mining Co. v. Minnesota Pollution Control Agency (Dist. Ct., Lake County, Dec. 1970), reproduced at A.1:261 and Supplement to Reserve's Br. at 114.]

We understand that plaintiffs do not deny these allegations.

The district court justified its immediate closure of Reserve's facility by characterizing Reserve's discharges as "substantially" endangering the health of persons breathing air and drinking water containing the asbestos-like fibers contained in Reserve's discharges. 380 F. Supp. at 16. The term "substantially" in no way measures the danger in terms of either probabilities or consequences. Yet such an assessment seems essential in fashioning a judicial remedy.

Concededly, the tail court considered many appropriate factors in arriving at a remedy, such as (a) the nature of the anticipated harm, (b) the burden on Reserve and its employees from the issuance of the injunction, (c) the financial ability of Reserve to convert to other methods of waste disposal, and (d) a margin of safety for the public.[83]

---

[83] See Note, *Imminent Irreparable Injury: A Need for Reform,* 45 S. CAL. L. REV. 1025 (1972).

An additional crucial element necessary for a proper assessment of the health hazard rests upon a proper analysis of the probabilities of harm. See *Ethyl Corporation v. Environmental Protection Agency,* No. 73-2205 (D.C. Cir., Jan. 28, 1975) (dissenting op. at 10–19); *Carolina Environmental Study Group v. United States,* 510 F.2d 796, at 799 (D.C. Cir., Jan. 21, 1975). Cf. *Society of Plastics Industry, Inc. v. Occupational Safety & Health Administration,* 509 F.2d 1301 (2d Cir., Jan. 31, 1975), cert. denied, 421 U.S. 992 (1975), 95 S. Ct. 1998, 44 L. Ed. 2d 482; Gelpe & Tarlock, *The Uses of Scientific Information in Environmental Decisionmaking,* 48 S. CAL. L. REV. 371, 412–427 (1974).

With respect to the water, these probabilities must be deemed low for they do not rest on a history of past health harm attributable to ingestion but on a medical theory implicating the ingestion of asbestos fibers as a causative factor in increasing the rates of gastrointestinal cancer among asbestos workers. With respect to air, the assessment of the risk of harm rests on a higher degree of proof, a correlation between inhalation of asbestos dust and subsequent illness. But here, too, the hazard cannot be measured in terms of predictability, but the assessment must be made without direct proof. But, the hazard in both the air and water can be measured in only the most general terms as a concern for the public health resting upon a reasonable medical theory. Serious consequences could result if the hypothesis on which it is based should ultimately prove true.

A court is not powerless to act in these circumstances. But an immediate injunction cannot be justified in striking a balance between unpredictable health effects and the clearly predictable social and economic consequences that would follow the plant closing.

In addition to the health risk posed by Reserve's discharges, the district court premised its immediate termination of the discharges upon Reserve's persistent refusal to implement a reasonable alternative plan for on-land disposal of tailings. See discussion pp. 304–305 & note 14 supra.

During these appeal proceedings, Reserve has indicated its willingness to deposit its tailings on land and to properly filter its air emissions. At oral argument, Reserve advised us of a willingness to spend 243 million dollars in plant alterations and construction to halt its pollution of air and water.[84] Reserve's offer to continue operations and proceed to construction of land disposal facilities for its tailings, if permitted to do so by the State of Minnesota, when viewed in conjunction with the uncertain quality of the health risk created by Reserve's discharges, weighs heavily against a ruling which closes Reserve's plant immediately.

Indeed, the intervening union argues, with some persuasiveness, that ill health effects resulting from the prolonged unemployment of the head of the family on a closing of the Reserve facility may be more certain than the harm from drinking Lake Superior water or breathing Silver Bay air.

Furthermore, Congress has generally geared its national environmental policy to allowing polluting industries a reasonable period of time to make adjust-

---

[84] See p. 307 supra. This commitment exceeds by 40 to 60 million dollars the amount found by the district court that Reserve could afford to spend to abate the hazards. See 380 F. Supp. at 19.

ments in their efforts to conform to federal standards. See, e.g., Federal Water Pollution Control Act, 33 U.S.C. § 1160 (1970); Clean Air Act, 42 U.S.C. §§ 1857c-5 to -8 (1970); National Environmental Policy Act, 42 U.S.C. § 4331 (1970). In the absence of an imminent hazard to health or welfare, any other program for abatement of pollution would be inherently unreasonable and invite great economic and social disruption. Some pollution and ensuing environmental damage are, unfortunately, an inevitable concomitant of a heavily industrialized economy. In the absence of proof of a reasonable risk of imminent or actual harm, a legal standard requiring immediate cessation of industrial operations will cause unnecessary economic loss, including unemployment, and, in a case such as this, jeopardize a continuing domestic source of critical metals without conferring adequate countervailing benefits.

We believe that on this record the district court abused its discretion by immediately closing this major industrial plant. In this case, the risk of harm to the public is potential, not imminent or certain, and Reserve says it earnestly seeks a practical way to abate the pollution. A remedy should be fashioned which will serve the ultimate public weal by insuring clean air, clean water, and continued jobs in an industry vital to the nation's welfare.

The admonition of Chief Justice Burger, sitting as a circuit justice, in refusing a stay order in *Aberdeen & Rockfish R.R. v. SCRAP,* 409 U.S. 1207, 93 S. Ct. 1, 34 L. Ed. 2d 21 (1972), is pertinent here:

> Our society and its governmental instrumentalities, having been less than alert to the needs of our environment for generations, have now taken protective steps. These developments, however praiseworthy, should not lead courts to exercise equitable powers loosely or casually whenever a claim of "environmental damage" is asserted. * * * The decisional process for judges is one of balancing and it is often a most difficult task. [Id. at 1217–1218, 93 S. Ct. at 7.]

Reserve must be given a reasonable opportunity and a reasonable time to construct facilities to accomplish an abatement of its pollution of air and water and the health risk created thereby. In this way, hardship to employees and great economic loss incident to an immediate plant closing may be avoided. See *Georgia v. Tennessee Copper Co.,* 206 U.S. 230, 239, 27 S. Ct. 618, 51 L. Ed. 1038 (1907); *United States v. City and County of San Francisco,* 23 F. Supp. 40, 53 (N.D. Cal. 1938), rev'd. 106 F.2d 569 (9th Cir. 1939), rev'd (aff'g district court), 310 U.S. 16, 60 S. Ct. 749, 84 L. Ed. 1050 (1940); see also *Transcontinental Gas Pipe Line Corp. v. Gault,* 198 F.2d 196, 198 (4th Cir. 1952).

We cannot ignore, however, the potential for harm in Reserve's discharges. This potential imparts a degree of urgency to this case that would otherwise be absent from an environmental suit in which ecological pollution alone were proved. Thus, any authorization of Reserve to continue operations during conversion of its facilities to abate the pollution must be circumscribed by realistic time limitations. Accordingly, we direct that the injunction order be modified as follows.

A The Discharge into Water

Reserve shall be given a reasonable time to stop discharging its wastes into Lake Superior. A reasonable time includes the time necessary for Minnesota to act on Reserve's present application to dispose of its tailings at Milepost 7 (Lax Lake site), see p. 307 supra, or to come to agreement on some other site acceptable to both Reserve and the state. Assuming agreement and designation of an appropriate land disposal site, Reserve is entitled to a reasonable turn-around time to construct the necessary facilities and accomplish a changeover in the means of disposing of its taconite wastes.

We cannot now precisely measure this time. Minnesota must assume the obligation of acting with great expedition in ruling on Reserve's pending application or otherwise determining that it shall, or that it shall not, afford a site acceptable to Reserve. We suggest, but do not determine, that with expedited procedures a final administrative decision should be reached within one year after a final appellate decision in this case.

Upon receiving a permit from the State of Minnesota, Reserve must utilize every reasonable effort to expedite the construction of new facilities. If the parties cannot agree on the duration of a reasonable turn-around time, either party may apply to the district court for a time-table which can be incorporated in the injunction decree, subject to our review.

Should Minnesota and Reserve be unable to agree on an on-land disposal site within this reasonable time period, Reserve, Armco and Republic Steel must be given a reasonable period of time thereafter to phase out the Silver Bay facility. In the interests of delineating the rights of the parties to the fullest extent possible, this additional period of time is set at one year after Minnesota's final administrative determination that it will offer Reserve no site acceptable to Reserve for on-land disposal of tailings.

If at any time during negotiations between Reserve and Minnesota for a disposal site, the United States reasonably believes that Minnesota or Reserve is not proceeding with expedition to facilitate Reserve's termination of its water discharge, it may apply to the district court for any additional relief necessary to protect its interests. Nothing in this opinion shall be construed as prohibiting the United States from offering advice and suggestions to both Reserve and the State of Minnesota concerning the location of the site or the construction of the on-land disposal facilities.

B Air Emissions

Pending final action by Minnesota on the present permit application, Reserve must promptly take all steps necessary to comply with Minnesota law applicable to its air emissions, as outlined in this opinion.

Reserve, at a minimum, must comply with APC 1 and 5. Furthermore, Reserve must use such available technology as will reduce the asbestos fiber count in the ambient air at Silver Bay below a medically significant level. According to the record in this case, controls may be deemed adequate which will reduce the fiber count to the level ordinarily found in the ambient air of a control city such as St. Paul.[85]

We wish to make it clear that we view the air emission as presenting a hazard of greater significance than the water discharge. Accordingly, pending a determination of whether Reserve will be allowed to construct an on-land disposal site or will close its operations, Reserve must immediately proceed with the planning and implementation of such emission controls as may be reasonably and practically effectuated under the circumstances. We direct that the injunction decree incorporate ¶ B2 of the stipulation between Reserve and Minnesota relating to air emissions, reading as follows:

> However, if following final court or administrative agency action relating to the existing discharge to Lake Superior, Reserve decides to substantially suspend or reduce, or to discontinue, its pelletizing operations at Silver Bay then Reserve, upon giving reasonable notice, shall be relieved from further implementation of the compliance program scheduled in this Stipulation, provided that the Agency may reasonably retain such conditions of this Stipulation, or reasonably impose such other or modified conditions as may be appropriate in connection with such suspension, reduction or discontinuance of operations. [A.1:203.]

Assuming that Reserve is granted the necessary permits to build an on-land disposal site, the existing stipulation between Minnesota and Reserve relating to air emissions, subject to modification because of litigation delay to this date, shall serve as a general guideline for time requirements on air controls.[86] If the parties are unable to come to an accord for a time-table for installation of emission controls based upon the stipulation agreement, either Minnesota or Reserve may apply to the district court for an appropriate order to supplement the injunction decree in conformity with the views expressed here. We reserve jurisdiction to review any such supplemental order.

C Additional Directions

We believe some additional directions will be helpful to the district court in fashioning its decree in conformity with this opinion. The matters of furnishing Reserve with an on-land disposal site and issuing necessary permits relevant to the

---

[85] We here order Reserve to meet a court-fashioned standard which may exceed the standards of existing air pollution control regulations, excepting APC 17. The Minnesota Pollution Control Agency may condition issuance of a permit for the emission of air contaminants or the operation of an emission facility, such as the Reserve plant, upon the prevention of air pollution. Minn. Stat. Ann. § 116.07(4a). Minnesota defines air pollution as

> * * * the presence in the outdoor atmosphere of any air contaminant or combination thereof in such quantity, of such nature and duration, and other such conditions as *would be injurious to human health or welfare* * * *. [Minn. Stat. Ann. § 116.06(3) (emphasis added).]

By this injunction we impose upon Reserve the duty not only to comply with APC 1 and 5 but also to take additional steps, if any are necessary, to abate its air pollution within the meaning of Minn. Stat. Ann. § 116.06(3). The broad remedial policy behind Minnesota's pollution control laws authorizes injunctive relief of this scope. See Minn. Stat. Ann. § 115.071(4).

[86] That stipulation may be found at A.1:198-210.

air and water discharges are governed by provisions of Minnesota state law. See Minn. Stat. Ann. §§ 116.07(4a) and 115.05 (Supp. 1974). The resolution of the controversy over an on-land disposal site does not fall within the jurisdiction of the federal courts.[87] Moreover, it follows that neither Michigan, Wisconsin, nor the environmental groups have any right of participation in that decision-making process except as may be otherwise provided by Minnesota law.[88]

Although we requested the district court to resolve all issues before it, the court reserved the question of possible fines and penalties against Reserve, stating that

> the Court has some discretion in the matter and it is this Court's view that it is not in a position to evaluate the equities until it is apprised of the course of action defendants must take in order to come into compliance with applicable law. [Order of Oct. 18 at 19.]

Unfortunately, it is possible that some parties may read this statement as a veiled threat that, if Reserve closes its plant rather than acquiesces to Minnesota's proposals for an on-land site for tailings disposal which Reserve deems unsuitable, the district court will levy substantial fines and penalties against it. While we are quite sure the district court intended no such implication and would not use its judicial power for such an improper purpose, we believe it is proper to comment that Reserve is free to close its operation if it cannot practically meet Minnesota's requirements for an on-land disposal site without the fear of substantial fines and penalties being levied against it because of this election.

Upon remand, we suggest that the district court request Dr. Brown to advise the court concerning new scientific or medical studies which may require a re-evaluation of the health hazard (either as more or less serious than as apprehended during this lawsuit) attributable to Reserve's discharges. A similar request should also be posed to Dr. Selikoff and his group of researchers. Either party may apply for a modification of the time requirements specified herein should significant new scientific information justify a reassessment of the hazard to public health.

Additionally, the district court should take proper steps to ensure that filtered water remains available in affected communities to the same extent as is now provided by the Corps of Engineers, although not necessarily at the expense of the Corps.

---

[87] We note that both the district court and this court have sought to encourage a settlement among the parties on an on-land disposal site. While these efforts were judicially proper during the course of the litigation, upon entry of a judgment in this case the federal courts must permit the State of Minnesota and Reserve to resolve the question of an on-land disposal site under the appropriate state procedures.

[88] Minnesota, of course, in ruling upon any proposed on-land disposal site must abide by the basic principles of due process of law. Should Minnesota, acting in an arbitrary and capricious manner, deny Reserve a permit for an on-land disposal site, thus forcing Reserve to close, Reserve's claims, if any, against Minnesota resting on provisions of the state or federal constitutions are preserved by reason of our direction that Reserve's counterclaims shall be dismissed without prejudice.

Finally, this court deems it appropriate to suggest that the national interest now calls upon Minnesota and Reserve to exercise a zeal equivalent to that displayed in this litigation to arrive at an appropriate location for an on-land disposal site for Reserve's tailings and thus permit an important segment of the national steel industry, employing several thousand people, to continue in production. As we have already noted, we believe this controversy can be resolved in a manner that will purify the air and water without destroying jobs.

The existing injunction is modified in the respects stated herein. This case is remanded to the district court for the entry of a decree in accordance with our directions and for such further proceedings consistent with this opinion as may be just and equitable.

ORDER ON REMAND

For reasons stated below, we find it necessary to issue this special order on remand to protect the integrity of the processes of this court.

We filed our detailed and carefully drawn, unanimous *en banc* opinion in these cases on March 14, 1975. Although these cases remained exclusively in our jurisdiction subject to any request for reconsideration by any of the parties, see Fed. R. App. P. 40, and before issuance of any mandate, the district court called the parties and other persons together for a hearing the very next day, March 15, 1975. After learning of this hearing through news dispatches published in the daily press, we requested that the clerk of the district court furnish each member of the *en banc* court with a transcript of the hearing.

We have reviewed this transcript. We can only characterize the district court proceedings of March 15 as irregular. Indeed, since no mandate had yet been issued from this court to the district court, the various orders, directions to parties, suggestions to the Governor of Minnesota, members of Congress, and the Minnesota State Legislature, and all other actions taken by the trial judge at these proceedings are a complete nullity. Until we issue our mandate, the district court lacks jurisdiction over these cases. See, e.g., *G & M Inc. v. Newbern,* 488 F.2d 742, 746-47 (9th Cir. 1973); see also *Bailey v. Henslee,* 309 F.2d 840, 844 (8th Cir. 1962).

We have an additional concern over the actions of the district court judge at that hearing. The judge initiated steps which appear to be in conflict with the express language of this court's opinion of March 14, 1975. Moreover, the district court judge and counsel for certain of the plaintiffs suggested in that hearing that Reserve Mining Company will be able to continue its present discharges for seven to ten years as a consequence of our modification of the district court's injunction. We made no such prediction nor authorized any unnecessary delay in abatement of air and water discharges.[1]

[1] See our opinion of March 14, 1975, at 347-349. In light of the comments which surfaced at this March 15 hearing, we think it appropriate to note that during oral argument before us on December 9, 1974, Reserve stated that following approval by the State of the tailings disposal site now proposed,

We recognize that by March 15 insufficient time had elapsed from the issuance of our opinion for the district court judge and counsel to study and reflect on all matters covered in it. This lack of time may explain but it does not excuse conduct, statements, or requests for and the issuance of orders contrary to this court's opinion.

Because of the nature of the March 15 proceedings, we deem it necessary to advise the trial judge and counsel for all parties, including intervenors, that they must respect the letter and spirit of our opinion as incorporated in the mandate of this court. See *In re Potts,* 166 U.S. 263, 267-68, 17 S. Ct. 520, 41 L. Ed. 994 (1897); *Thornton v. Carter,* 109 F.2d 316, 320 (8th Cir. 1940); *Goldwyn Pictures Corp. v. Howells Sales Co.,* 287 F. 100, 102-03 (2d Cir. 1927); see also *Sibbald v. United States,* 37 U.S. (12 Pet.) 487, 492-95, 9 L. Ed. 1167 (1838). Neither the district court nor any party is free to ignore our determinations, including the determination that "[t]he resolution of the controversy over an on-land disposal site does not fall within the jurisdiction of the federal courts[,]" opinion of March 14, 1975, at 539. We think it inappropriate to characterize such a determination as "advisory" or dictum. [Mar. 15 Tr. at 43.] Until modified by us or reversed or modified by the Supreme Court, our opinion governs the rights and obligations of the parties and all intervenors.

We expect and insist that our mandate be carried out promptly, fairly, efficiently, and without deviation from its letter and spirit. See *Cascade Natural Gas Corp. v. El Paso Natural Gas Co.,* 386 U.S. 129, 136, 142-43, 87 S. Ct. 932, 17 L. Ed. 2d 814 (1967). Furthermore, the district court judge should not interfere in matters concerning the parties which lie outside his jurisdiction in these cases.

Finally, we believe it is appropriate to caution counsel that although each may be an adversary with regard to opposing parties, all serve as officers of the court and all are bound to respect and follow the law as laid down by a final appellate judgment in this case.

We direct that a copy of this order be incorporated into and made a part of the judgment on remand.

PROBLEMS

1 Suppose a recent M.S. graduate in remote sensing is continuing his studies for the Ph.D. He is retained by an attorney as an expert witness in a case dealing with a wetlands boundary dispute. He is asked, and allowed to answer over objection, whether in his opinion wetlands can be accurately mapped from a satellite photo, whether the site in question is ecologically or commercially valuable, and how much he is being paid to

---

it could complete construction of new facilities in three years or less. [Dec. 9 Tr. at 26.] We also understand that partial abatement of discharges into Lake Superior would take place in advance of such construction completion date. Reserve also represented during this oral argument that it could begin installing air pollution control equipment on existing facilities immediately. [Dec. 9 Tr. at 178.] The initiation of this timetable in part now depends upon action yet to be taken by the State of Minnesota on Reserve's application for a disposal site.

testify. An appeal is based upon the judge's ruling allowing expert testimony on the subject in general, the three questions in particular, and on the witness's qualifications. How should the appeal be resolved?

2 In a case concerned with the cause and rate of erosion of coastal property since the construction of a jetty, the plaintiff called as a witness a respected professor of civil and soil engineering who, although he had not visited the area in question, had undertaken extensive calculations based upon data collected by others. The defendant, not having the financial resources to hire a professional, called as his witness a local resident of long standing with normal perception and intelligence. Both witnesses were allowed to testify and offered conflicting opinions on the rate at which the area has eroded and the effect of the construction of the jetty. The jury's decision indicated that the opinion of the defendant's expert had been accepted. Would the plaintiff have any ground for appeal?

SUGGESTIONS FOR FURTHER READING

Kornblum, G. O.: *Expert as Witness and Consultant,* 20 PRAC. LAW. 13, 1974.

Leventhal, H.: *Environmental Decisionmaking and the Role of the Courts,* 122 U. PA. L. REV. 509, 1974.

Lind, E., J. Thibant, and L. Walker: *Discovery and Presentation of Evidence in Adversary and Non-Adversary Proceedings,* 71 MICH. L. REV. 1129, 1973.

Schulman, R. E.: *To Be or Not to Be an Expert,* 57 WASHINGTON U.L.Q. 1973, 1973.

Sive, D.: *Securing, Examining, and Cross Examining Expert Witnesses in Environmental Cases,* 68 MICH. L. REV. 1175, 1970.

Glossary

Ab orco usque ad coelum   Latin for "from the underworld to the heavens."

Amicus curiae   Latin for "a friend of the court." One who is allowed to introduce argument to protect his interest or view although he has no right to appear in a suit.

Answer   The defendant's reply to the complaint; this may consist of a general denial or an affirmative defense.

Appellant   The person who brings an appeal, usually the loser at the trial.

Appellee   The person against whom an appeal is brought, usually the victor at the trial.

Bill in equity   A complaint or petition addressed to a court of equity, usually one seeking an injunction.

Burden of proof   The necessity of affirmatively proving facts in dispute; this generally rests on the plaintiff.

Certiorari   *See* writ of certiorari.

Complaint   The initial step on the part of the plaintiff in a civil action; the document in which the plaintiff states the facts constituting his cause of action and the relief sought.

Condemnation   The process by which private property is taken for public use, without the owner's consent, but upon payment of just compensation.

Declaratory judgment   A judgment which declares the rights of the parties or expresses an opinion on a point of view without ordering that anything be done.

Defendant   The person against whom a lawsuit is brought.

Demurrer   An allegation by a defendant which contends that, even if the facts alleged by the plaintiff are true, they are insufficient to require the defendant to answer.

Deposition   A written declaration under oath, or made orally and reduced to writing, made before trial for use at the trial.

Eminent domain   The power under which private property is taken for public use without the owner's consent, but upon payment of just compensation.

Enjoin   To prohibit by means of an injunction.

Indictment   An accusation of criminal behavior made by a grand jury.

Injunction   A prohibitive court order forbidding a defendant to act. *See also* mandatory injunction.

In rem   An action against a thing rather than a person. Used most often in admiralty to allow proceedings directly against a vessel.

Interrogatories   Written questions propounded to a witness who is making a deposition.

Judicial notice   A court's action recognizing the truth of certain facts without the production of evidence; usually utilized where the facts are established by common notoriety such as historical events or major geographical features.

Jurisdiction   The authority or right of a court to take cognizance of a case; includes jurisdiction of persons and subject matter.

Legislative history   The compendium of hearing records, speeches, and the like which precedes the enactment of a statute.

Litigation   A contest or suit in court.

Mandamus   *See* writ of mandamus.

Mandatory injunction   An injunction which commands one to perform an act or prohibits refusal to so do.

Negligence   The failure to act as a reasonably prudent person would in the same or similar circumstances.

Nuisance   That which disturbs one in possession of property; often the result of an unreasonable use of property by its owner.

Ordinance   A rule established by the legislative body of a municipal corporation.

Original jurisdiction   Jurisdiction of an appellate court to take cognizance of a case at its inception, rather than awaiting a trial or action by a lower court.

Petition   A term synonymous with "complaint" in some states.

Petitioner   The person who initiates legal proceedings begun by petition.

Plaintiff   The person who initiates a lawsuit.

Pleadings   The allegations of the plaintiff and the proffered defenses, disclosing to the court the matters in dispute.

Remand   To send back to a lower court for further action.

Respondent   The person against whom an action begun by petition is brought, or who opposes the petition.

Restraining order   An order which may be issued on an application for an injunction which prohibits the conduct complained of until a hearing on the application can be had.

Riparian   Relating to the banks of a river; descriptive of the rights of persons who own lands on the banks of watercourses.

Scienter   Evil knowledge or intent.

Sic utere tuo ut alienum non laedas   Latin for "use your own property in such a manner as not to injure that of another."

Statute   A law enacted by a legislature; the term applies only to written law as distinguished from unwritten or case law.

Stipulation   An agreement between parties to facts or procedures, thus removing them as issues at trial.

Strict liability   A theory of liability in which fault is not a factor.

Summary judgment   A judgment made by a court without a jury where no questions of fact are present.

Tort   A private or civil wrong independent of contract.

Trespass   The unlawful physical invasion of the property of another.

Vacate   To set aside or annul a decision by a lower court.

Venue   The place or location in which a court with jurisdiction may hear a case.

Writ of certiorari   A writ of review; certiorari is the appellate process for reviewing the action of an inferior court.

Writ of mandamus   Latin for "we command"; an order of a court to a private or public official commanding the performance of his duties.

Bibliographical Notes

The remarkable volume of legal publication results in a complicated and often duplicative bibliography. The materials used or referred to in this book, however, may be placed in one of the following classes.

REPORTERS

When an appellate court, and occasionally a trial court, reaches a decision, the opinion is usually published in a reporter. Reporters are not ordinarily separated by subject but rather print the opinions in the order they are written. The number preceding the reporter's name refers to the volume; that which comes thereafter refers to the page. Thus 125 U.S. 262 is the citation of the case in volume 125 of the *United States Supreme Court Reports* beginning at page 262.

U.S. Reports; Supreme Court Reporter; Lawyers' Edition   These three publications reproduce the decisions of the Supreme Court of the United States. The reports are identical but the pagination is different. Thus, 389 U.S. 290, 88 Sup. Ct. 438, and 19 L. Ed. 2d 530, all report the same case.

Federal Reporter (F.2d)   The *Federal Reporter*, now in its second series, contains the opinions of the United States Courts of Appeals.

Federal Supplement (F. Supp)   The *Federal Supplement* contains, on a selective basis, opinions of the United States district courts.

State Reporters   State appellate court opinions are given in reporters divided geographically. State court decisions from the West Coast, for example, are in the *Pacific Reporter* (P.2d); Wisconsin is in the *North Western Reporter* (N.W.), and the like. Some states also print opinions in state reporters such as the California Reports, New York Reports, and so on.

Environment Reporter Cases (ERC)   This private publication is a specialized reporter for selected environmental cases from both state and federal courts. The cases it reports are almost always reported elsewhere as well. Thus, 465 F.2d 492 and 4 ERC 1945 present the same case.

LAW REVIEWS

Law reviews, law school journals edited by senior students under faculty supervision, are a cornerstone of scholarly legal comment. Virtually all law schools publish them, and they are referred to by volume and page in the same manner as reporters. Thus, 65 Harvard Law Review 1131 refers to an article in volume 65 beginning at page 1131. Such references are usually abbreviated, thus: 65 HARV. L. REV. 1131. Some articles in law reviews, often referred to as "notes," are written by students on the staff. When such articles are cited, the author's name is usually omitted.

Most law reviews are general; but a few, such as *Environmental Law* (Lewis and Clark School of Law), are specialized.

The *Index to Legal Periodicals* indexes all major law reviews.

TEXTS

Legal texts are available on virtually all subjects; among the classics are Prosser on torts and Wigmore on evidence.

Black's Law Dictionary, 4th ed., West Publishing Company, St. Paul, Minn., 1951.
Blackstone, William: *Commentaries*, J. B. Lippincott Company, Philadelphia, 1888.
Bosselman, Fred, David Callies, and John Banta: *The Taking Issue*, Council on Environmental Quality, Washington, D.C., 1973.
Cardozo, Benjamin: *The Nature of the Judicial Process*, Yale University Press, New Haven, Conn., 1921.
Cooley, Richard A., and Geoffrey Wandesford-Smith: *Congress and the Environment*, University of Washington Press, Seattle, 1970.
Dietze, Gottfried: *The Federalist*, Johns Hopkins Press, Baltimore, 1966.
E. L. Dolgin and T. G. Gailbert (eds.): *Federal Environmental Law*, West Publishing Company, St. Paul, Minn., 1974.
Holmes, Oliver Wendell: *The Common Law*, Belknap Press of Harvard University Press, Cambridge, Mass., 1963.
Kimbrough, Robert: *Summary of American Law*, Lawyers Cooperative Publishing Company, Rochester, N.Y., 1974.
McCormick, Charles: *Law of Evidence*, West Publishing Company, St. Paul, Minn., 1954.

Miller, William Galbraith: *Data on Jurisprudence*, Green, London, 1903.
Powell, Richard, and Patrick Rohan: *Real Property*, Matthew Bender & Company, Inc., New York, 1968.
Prosser, William: *Torts*, 3d ed., West Publishing Company, St. Paul, Minn., 1964.
Restatement of Torts, 2d ed., American Law Institute at Washington, D.C., 1934.
Saleilles, Raymond: *De la personnalité juridique*, Rosisseau, Paris, 1910.
Stryker, Lloyd Paul: *The Art of Advocacy*, Simon and Schuster, New York, 1954.
Wigmore, James: *Evidence*, 3d ed., Little, Brown and Company, Boston, 1961.
Wright, Charles: *Federal Courts*, 2d ed., West Publishing Company, St. Paul, Minn., 1963.

CODES

Statutory law is ordinarily found in codes. The statutory law of the United States is found in the *United States Code* (abbreviated U.S.C.). Citation to codes is by title and section rather than by volume and page. Thus, 43 U.S.C. 1152 refers to Title 43, Section 1152.

Most states have codified their statutory law, and the system of citation is similar.